ISLAND BIOLOGY

ISLAND BIOLOGY

SHERWIN John CARLQUIST

with illustrations
by Sherwin Carlquist
and Michael J. Cole

COLUMBIA UNIVERSITY PRESS
New York and London
1974

Sherwin Carlquist is Horton Professor of Botany at Claremont Graduate School and Research Associate at the Rancho Santa Ana Botanic Garden in Claremont, California.

Library of Congress Cataloging in Publication Data

Carlquist, Sherwin John, 1930–
  Island biology.

  Includes bibliographies.
  1. Island ecology. I. Title.
QH541.5.I8C37   574.5'26   73–4643
ISBN 0–231–03562–4

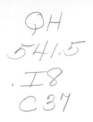
To Evelyn Hooker
and Lois Langland

PREFACE

At a time when insular biotas are, in many respects, little known beyond the floristic and faunistic level, yet when a number of these same biotas are endangered, apology is not necessary for presentation of materials that could be called "natural history." The material in this book will reveal not how much is known but how very many interesting questions remain to be asked and answered, largely by field studies.

Past literature is covered, directly and indirectly, but the emphasis is on recent findings. There is little value in republishing or attempting to summarize fine works such as David Lack's *Darwin's finches*—such books and papers speak for themselves. I have attempted to present new material and new syntheses, or stimulating comparisons, that have not to any great degree appeared previously in book form. At the time I wrote *Island life,** I had made observations on islands but, aside from anatomical studies, had not published data relevant to concepts of evolution on islands. I attempted to supply supporting data for some ideas in a series of five papers, published under the somewhat cumbersome series title, "The Biota of Long-distance Dispersal."

Interest in those five papers suggested to me that, instead of continuing the series, I should present the material in book form, augmented by new materials. The content of the papers is represented—in revised, expanded, updated, and, I hope, improved form—in chapters 1, 2, 11, and 13. Chapter 1 serves as an introduction or précis of my concepts of the

* New York, Natural History Press, 1965.

natural history of islands. Aside from those four chapters, the content of this book represents original material. I have deliberately attempted as far as possible to avoid, both in content and in illustration, duplication of material presented in *Island life; Hawaii, a natural history;* * or various papers I have written dealing with anatomical aspects of insular plants. Exhaustive citation of literature is not attempted; rather, key papers with good citations are mentioned. Sources of literature on insular plants and animals are extraordinarily diverse, and readers will, I hope, forgive me if certain quite worthy papers have been overlooked.

This book obviously has a bias somewhat more in favor of botany than zoology; this reflects my training but is also capable of rationalization on the basis that zoologists have studied insular patterns in a more conspicuous way than botanists.

For help during my field work and for other assistance, acknowledgment is due a great number of individuals. I have listed them in my earlier books and papers, and rather than reprint a long list of names, I wish to thank again those whom I have previously acknowledged. Those who have made contributions to this book, and whom I have not previously mentioned, include José Cuatrecasas, from whose negatives I printed the photographs of paramo plants in chapter 14. The bird, plant, and insect drawings in chapters 4, 8, 12, and 14 are the work of Michael J. Cole. Photographs have also been contributed by Mrs. Evelyn Humphreys and Alex George, as credit lines indicate, in chapter 8. The remaining drawings and photographs are my work. Identification of New Guinean alpine plants was provided by Pieter van Royen. Specimens documenting my photographs presented here are located at the Rancho Santa Ana Botanic Garden, Claremont, California. I am responsible if there are misidentifications or errors in nomenclature. I have deliberately omitted author citations on binomials because these are available in the taxonomic works I cite.

* New York, Natural History Press, 1970.

CONTENTS

ISLAND BIOLOGY

CHAPTER ONE

PRINCIPLES OF DISPERSAL
AND EVOLUTION

The faunas and floras of oceanic islands possess many distinctive characteristics that have long attracted attention. Interest in these lands as "evolutionary laboratories" crystallized during the Darwin-Wallace era and has not yet diminished. Floristic and faunistic studies of islands have been frequent (see Blake and Atwood, 1942; Darlington, 1957; Thorne, 1963), although more are needed and will undoubtedly be produced. Discussions of the possibility of dispersal to oceanic islands, and of whether particular islands are oceanic or continental, have occupied an inordinate number of pages and created considerable controversy. Within this outpouring there have been a few outstanding contributions dealing with the problems of dispersal and patterns of insular evolution. Those commendable for their comprehensiveness and rational outlook include Gulick (1932), Zimmerman (1948), Darlington (1957), and Thorne (1963). To a suprising degree, the assessments which most appeal to me are those that confirm and extend the concepts of Darwin (1859) and Wallace (1880). Adherents of alternative proposals may still be found, but there appears to be a growing consensus among biologists regarding many of the ideas that I shall discuss.

Although it seems a departure from the Darwin-Wallace line of natural history, the book by MacArthur and Wilson (1967), *The Theory of Insular Biogeography*, is a natural product of these lines of inquiry.

NOTE: This chapter is a revision of a paper (Carlquist, 1966). For permission to present materials from this paper, acknowledgment is gratefully extended to the *Quarterly Review of Biology*.

Wallace, for example, noted faunistic and floristic richness or impoverishment on islands, and offered explanations. That such factors as distance from source area, ecological richness, and "saturation" should be expressed as a series of mathematical models (as offered by MacArthur and Wilson) is a natural culmination of ideas advanced by Darwin and Wallace and extended by such workers as Ernst Mayr and P. J. Darlington, Jr. Recent papers that incorporate such considerations in analyzing insular patterns, of various areas and of groups of organisms, are those of Soulé (1966), Wilson and Taylor (1967), Greenslade (1968a, 1968b), Simberloff (1969), Simberloff and Wilson (1969) and Wilson and Simberloff (1969). Similar papers, applying to situations other than true islands, are cited in chapter 15. Some workers have noted discrepancies between their results and particular mathematical models (Sauer, 1969; Soulé and Stewart, 1970; Lack, 1971). Model construction is derived from actual situations viewed (usually) collectively, and cannot be expected to predict the fauna or flora of any given island. Although the interest and intrinsic clarity of mathematical models of insular situations are great, the appropriate ways for biologists of various types to use them are open to question. While the pathway from natural situations to mathematical models is clear, application of a model to a particular region or taxonomic group is not always justifiable, because any real situation is replete with complicating factors that a model obviously cannot predict.

Reasons for presentation of this material at this time are several. Interest has shifted recently from a primarily floristic-faunistic outlook to a concern for evolutionary processes on islands. Principles that have emerged clearly, as well as those that can only be tentatively enunciated, are reviewed here because a foundation for further research seems needed and because a critical sifting of past hypotheses and a summary of recent work may prove helpful. An earlier generation of biologists stressed the amazing speciation that has occurred on oceanic islands. Today's biologists are inquiring into the background of this speciation: its origin, direction, and underlying mechanisms. The basic mechanisms of evolution on oceanic islands are the same as those on continental islands, and no new "laws" are needed; yet the direction that evolution takes on islands, and the products that result, are often quite distinctive, at least modally. Understanding of these evolutionary concepts must be based on sound principles of dispersal and biogeography. Therefore these topics as they apply to the waif biotas (establishments via long-distance dispersal) must be reviewed, however briefly. For example, the peculiar rosette trees of the Juan Fernandez Islands (see chapter 10) must be interpreted as relicts by those who see long-distance dispersal as an inadequate explanation for the Juan Fernandez flora, and such individuals invoke short-distance dispersal across land bridges, or cite continental drift. Those who can envisage these islands as being recent and as populated by means of long-distance dispersal can, on the contrary, regard the rosette trees as innovations—the products of recent evolution.

Literature on the evolution of island biotas is widely scattered among zoological, botanical, evolutionary, ecological, and other journals and books. Too often, consideration is limited to patterns of only one group, or only animals, or only plants. There is a definite need for integrating the data from various disciplines. Information from one field not only often proves valuable to studies in other fields, but also must eventually be coordinated into larger patterns.

The biota that is characteristic of oceanic islands is, ironically, not always found on such islands and may occur in other situations as well. Oceanic islands near continents may show an essentially continental pattern. A completely glaciated island will bear a biota that is entirely oceanic in character (Fleming, 1963). Older freshwater lakes exhibit a full range of insular features (see chapter 9), and equatorial highlands (chapter 14) are definitely worth consideration as "nearly insular" situations. A remote oceanic island may be too new or ecologically too poor to have shown the evolutionary patterns that will be described. Despite incongruities such as these, the concept that there are oceanic and continental islands, with differences reflecting their geological histories, still seems useful and is generally accepted (Fosberg, 1963). No scheme for classification of islands, can hope, however, to reflect unexceptionably both the geological history and the nature of the biota.

Most oceanic islands are volcanic, and volcanic islands are, on a geological scale, relatively short-lived structures. Therefore, true oceanic islands display clearly the early and middle stages in the phylesis of a waif biota, but such islands may vanish before evolutionary products are well advanced (for example, before they are differentiated to the level of distinct families). Later stages in the evolution of biotas established subsequent to long-distance dispersal are often shown instead on old continental islands. For example, New Caledonia and New Zealand have been isolated for a very long time—since the Cretaceous, if not much longer. Waif arrivals on these islands have had a much longer time in which to evolve than have arrivals to the Hawaiian Islands, which are probably no older than the Miocene. The discerning biologist can, in most instances, detect which elements in the New Zealand biota are waif immigrants, and he can follow their evolutionary patterns separately from those that probably are relicts of an era of continental interconnection or near-interconnection. Among the relicts are conifers and primitive flowering plants, as well as the reptile *Sphenodon* and the frog *Leiopelma*. With an extended period of isolation and with a sizable land mass available for occupancy, the waif biota of New Zealand has been able to evolve extensively, to show waif evolutionary patterns better than such biotas on most oceanic islands.

It is ironic that the evolutionary products of waif biotas are perhaps best studied on old continental or continental-like islands; nevertheless it is possible to cite oceanic islands on which insular patterns are well fulfilled. Among these, the Hawaiian Islands surely deserve first place, although part of the evolutionary history of Hawaiian organisms may have taken place on adjacent islands that are now atolls (the Leeward Islands of the Hawaiian chain) or now-vanished adjacent islands. The Hawaiian Islands are favored by ecological richness, extreme remoteness, and (for oceanic islands) relative oldness. The Galápagos Islands, although famed for their insular biota, are relatively young, relatively poor ecologically, and relatively close to continental areas. With the exception of the Darwin's finches, the Galápagos biota best serves to show earlier stages in the evolution of insular groups (see chapter 6). Completing this spectrum from old to young waif biotas, the earliest stages in evolution are perhaps best studied in animals and plants that have been introduced to islands by man. Mice have proved good examples (Berry, 1964).

Some persons will note that waif biotas are represented in noninsular situations as well: mountaintops, especially those of equatorial highlands (see chapter 14), lakes (see chapter 9), caves (see chapter 15) and the like. This is true. Islands differ in some degree from all of these situations by offering, at least in some cases, a wider gamut of habitats (shore to alpine, aquatic to xeric) instead of a single extreme habitat (caves) or one that grades off into continental patterns (the lower limits of equatorial highlands). Some noninsular waif biotas can be very informative, however, and are among the examples cited in this book. I cannot emphasize too strongly that aspects of insular patterns permeate continental situations. Thus a waif biota can occur wherever arrival is by means of long-distance dispersal and where isolation is high for a prolonged period of time. The assumption made here that waif arrivals on continental islands can be distinguished from preinsular arrivals will no doubt be challenged. Means of separating the two groups are inferential but should improve as our knowledge of waif-biota characteristics becomes surer. I believe that most groups on an old continental island can be thus discriminated and that we should aim for such discrimination. The basis for the distinction is now, and will continue to be, largely a comparison with oceanic islands. For example, if conifers and flowering plants with numerous primitive characteristics are subtracted from the New Zealand flora, and if differences in climate are taken into account, the composition of that flora is remarkably similar in families and even in many genera to the Hawaiian flora.

Hypotheses regarding the dispersal and evolution of waif biotas are presented here as a series of principles, or, if one prefers, topic sentences. The number of such principles could be enlarged or reduced, and ideas placed under some headings could just as well have been entered under others. Many of the ideas are closely related and lead me to conclude that there is an "insular syndrome" which derives from (1) difficulties of long-distance dispersal; (2) isolation after establishment; (3) ecological opportunities—"vacant niches"; and (4) to a much lesser extent, the moderation of a maritime climate. The consequences of these factors are, however, manifold. Some of the principles stated in this chapter will appear to be restatements of the obvious, but others will represent views that have not hitherto been discussed to any appreciable extent in the literature on waif biotas. For definitions to classify islands as continental or oceanic, the reader can consult Darlington (1957), Carlquist (1965), or Hubbell (1968).

Principles

1. *Disharmony in composition of an insular biota is considered a prime source of evidence for the occurrence of long-distance dispersal.*

The distinction between harmonic and disharmonic biotas is a simple one: a harmonic flora or fauna contains a spread of forms with poor to excellent dispersal ability, whereas waif biotas will result from only the more easily dispersed end of the spectrum. An excellent criterion for dispersibility is the maximum gap of salt water that may have been crossed by natural means by particular groups of plants and animals. A distance measured from a continental area to an oceanic island is the most reliable. Admittedly, the gap crossed may have been greater, because the continental source population may have been inland, or narrower if a strait has widened since dispersal occurred. A rating of dispersibility was developed by Darlington (1957) for animals, and has been extended to plants by Carlquist (1965). Within taxonomic groups, dispersibility is related to size of disseminule, desiccation resistance, cold resistance, and other features that can vary widely within a group and that depend, of course, on the nature of the vector. The idea that particular groups have differential thresholds, or hurdle-values (approximate maximum limits of dispersibility), is basic, however, to the concept of disharmony.

A demonstration of disharmony is rendered more difficult by the fact that some regions, insular and otherwise, have biotic depauperation for ecological reasons. However, poorer faunas or floras are usually deprived of species with good dispersibility as well as of those with poor dispersibility. By coincidence, some poorly dispersing groups also happen to be restricted to ecologically "good" situations (e.g., some conifers).

Good dispersibility is often correlated with ability to occupy pioneer habitats—a reasonable correlation because pioneer habitats are widely scattered (e.g., beaches) and often open for occupancy suddenly, whereas stable habitats, such as rain forests, are limited in extent and do not change rapidly. The possibility of confusion between biotic depauperation owing to distance and that due to ecological factors is great, and has caused some workers, who are unwilling to make a distinction, to reject the concept of disharmony and thus also that of long-distance dispersal. The

6

alternatives they must therefore select (hypothetical land bridges or continental drift) are far more unlikely in the case of oceanic islands—and
even in situations other than oceanic islands (see chapter 2). Strong support for the concept of disharmony comes from the fact that it occurs not
once, but in as many replications as there are oceanic islands. The limit of
dispersal ability of snakes is shown by their absence not only from Samoa,
but also from Hawaii and the Society Islands. *Metrosideros* (Myrtaceae)
is a tree that has reached all the major high islands of the Pacific, starting
from an Indo-Malesian * source or sources. Likewise, lizards (once thought
not to reach Samoa [Darlington, 1957]) may be native on Hawaii and
Easter Island.

A continental island can harbor both harmonic and disharmonic
elements. New Zealand, Fiji, and New Caledonia are floristically notable
for old harmonic elements of poor dispersibility (e.g., Araucariaceae), presumably derived from times when this island arc was connected or nearly
connected with an Antarctic route, perhaps in Cretaceous times (Thorne,
1963). Since that time, waif elements have also populated these islands.
They bulk larger, presumably both by virtue of continual immigration
(with the excellent "invasiveness" which that implies) and by the diversification of these arrivals.

An oceanic island, by definition, will have only a waif biota. Some
biologists tend to overemphasize the difficulties of dispersal for groups with
which they are most familiar. For oceanic islands, however, there can be
no exceptions to overwater (including oceanic drift) dispersal. Not generally appreciated is the tendency for loss of dispersibility after arrival (see
principles 16 and 17, and the detailed accounts in chapters 11 and 12).
Consequently, the present dispersibility of any given insular species cannot
always be used as a basis for estimates of dispersibility. The pivotal controversy, as to which islands are continental and which are oceanic, seems
to be dwindling. Only a few islands are still difficult to interpret, and the
growing consensus regarding the interpretation of most islands suggests

---

* "Malesia" is used in this book to connote the Malay Peninsula and all islands
north of Australia eastward to the easternmost Solomon Islands. "Indo-Malesia"
includes Malesia plus Southeast Asia as far west as India. The terms Indo-Malaysia
and Malaysia as used in older works must be abandoned because of formation of the
nation of Malaysia.

that there is likewise increasing agreement on some of the principles discussed here. For a few islands that seem to have been previously connected to or closer to the source areas, the time of connection may remain problematic, as may the degree of separation if always separated and the possibility of formerly larger or smaller area.

2. *Positive adaptations for long-distance dispersal and for establishment are the key to disharmony, and disharmony is thus not a negative concept. All elements in disharmonic biotas such as those of oceanic islands are capable of long-distance dispersal or are derived from ancestors that were capable of it.*

Organisms that are clearly adapted to dispersal across very long or unlimited distances include spore-bearing plants, strand plants, and some birds and insects (see chapter 2). Species with virtually unlimited dispersibility (e.g., strand plants) are a constant element on islands; they provide no problems in interpretation, nor do they usually develop evolutionary patterns of interest. The strand flora usually remains a strand flora, and rarely evolves into montane species. Exceptions include *Erythrina* and *Acacia* (Rock, 1919b) on the Hawaiian Islands. For further information on strand plants that have evolved into inland sites, and the reasons why this has occurred in a limited number of instances, see chapter 11 (also certain halophytic elements in the Australian flora, chapter 9). Although dispersal by seawater flotation has contributed little to montane floras of islands, one must remember that some plants for which seawater dispersal may seem doubtful are, in fact, capable of it (e.g., *Gossypium* [Stephens, 1958a, 1958b, 1963, 1964], and *Lagenaria* [Whitaker and Carter, 1954, 1961]). In the case of *Gossypium*, the Tahitian and Hawaiian cottons are endemics, and there is no evidence of derivation from cultigens; in any event, the same principles apply to other, noneconomic Malvaceae.

Positive adaptations for dispersal by virtue of habits, habitats, and resistance to salt water occur in lizards. One widespread gecko, *Hemidactylus garnoti*, is a uniparental species (i.e., its eggs hatch without fertilization). This characteristic makes possible the dispersal to Hawaii and elsewhere, because any single individual can start a new population. Two species of skinks have crossed the Pacific from Asia to islands off the South American coast, very likely without the aid of man. One of these, *Ablepharus boutoni*, lives on sea beaches; it nests in epiphytes on nearby

8

trees that might often be washed out to sea. One New World gecko, of wide distribution, lays its eggs communally under bark or in tunnels of trees, and lizard eggs are notably resistant to seawater. For further information on the role of oceanic drift, see chapter 2.

Rafting is probably most effective over relatively short distances but is doubtless responsible for cases of land-animal (mammal and reptile) transport (for reviews and observed examples, see Darlington, 1938; McCann, 1953; Wheeler, 1916; Zimmerman, 1948).

For the remaining species, birds or winds must be the vectors. Gressitt and his co-workers are to be congratulated for extensive aerial trapping experiments which demonstrate clearly not only that aerial transport of insects and spiders is likely, but also that the species caught represent groups in the same proportions as they occur in insect faunas of oceanic islands (Clagg, 1966; Gressitt, 1956, 1961a; Gressitt, Leech, and O'Brien, 1960; Gressitt, Leech et al., 1961; Gressitt and Nakata, 1958; Gressitt, Sedlacek, Wise, and Yoshimoto, 1961; Gressitt and Yoshimoto, 1963; Harrell and Holzapfel, 1966; Thornton and Harrell, 1965; Yoshimoto and Gressitt, 1959, 1960, 1961, 1963, 1964; Yoshimoto, Gressitt, and Mitchell, 1962; see also the earlier literature cited in these papers and in Richter, 1970). Actual dispersal events can be witnessed with such rarity that these experiments are as close to definitive proof as can be expected. The contention of such workers as Visher (1925), Ridley (1930), Setchell (1926, 1928, 1935), Andrews (1940), Zimmerman (1948), Myers (1953), and Fosberg (1963) that aerial dispersal is a reality over extended distances for very small or air-floatable disseminules seems to be justified.

Dispersal of birds with migratory habits is easily explained. Land birds, however, are notably sedentary (Mayr, 1940). As Mayr notes, however, involuntary flight owing to storms can be invoked to explain distribution of land birds in Polynesia. Birds that migrate moderate distances in a seasonal pattern as different food sources become available might be better candidates for long-distance dispersal than extremely sedentary species. Some workers have a tendency to believe that long-distance dispersal of land birds is such a rare occurrence that it simply never happens. Rare occurrences do suffice to explain dispersal, however (see principle 4). The successful colonization of the Hawaiian Islands by only a few groups of land birds is witness to their sedentary nature but also to the likelihood that very infrequent exceptions have sufficed for establishment. Lack (1971) stresses that the absence of land-bird groups on islands may not result so much from difficulty of dispersal as from lack of suitable ecological sites; he contends that islands that appear by MacArthur and Wilson's (1967) predictions to be "unsaturated" may, in fact, have no open ecological niches. For a further discussion of dispersal of land birds to islands, see chapter 2.

Transport of fruits, seeds, and eggs externally or of fruits and seeds internally by birds must be regarded as the dispersal mechanism of many species (Ridley, 1930; Gulick, 1932; Zimmerman, 1948; Falla, 1960; Holdgate, 1960; Wace, 1960). Observational and experimental evidence for these modes of transport is increasing. Barbed or viscid fruits or seeds have been observed attached to feathers. The experimental work of Proctor and others (see chapter 2) shows that internal transport of seeds by shorebirds over long distances is entirely within the realm of possibility. In fact, dispersal of fruits and seeds by migratory birds is probably the method by which most groups of angiosperms arrived on the high islands of the Pacific (fig. 2.7). We can see this by analyzing dispersal mechanisms of native floras of islands, as Skottsberg (1928) and Lems (1960b) have done. Continental disjunctions, such as the famed central Chile–western North America pattern (Constance et al., 1963) should be regarded as opportunities for discovering modes of long-distance dispersal, not as mysteries.

Ability for long-distance dispersal is shown in the Pacific by the points at which genera terminate, in relation to source areas. Smith (1955) has shown that 101 genera of flowering plants have their eastern terminus on Fiji, the most easterly major island within the line delimiting andesite rocks (which suggest the former presence of larger land areas). Of the genera that do continue beyond Fiji—to Samoa, for example—many (or endemic genera derived from them) extend all the way to the Society Islands or Hawaii, a fact that suggests that the flora of Polynesia is indeed the flora of long-distance dispersal.

Present dispersal configurations of island plants and animals may be less favorable than those of their ancestors (see principles 16 and 17) a possibility neglected by some authors (e.g., Remington, 1971). In some cases, one would do better to investigate the present dispersal mechanisms of mainland relatives of island plants and animals rather than those of the insular representatives themselves. As Williams (1969) and Tryon (1971) note, only a few of the "available" species in a source area are preadapted for successful dispersal and colonization. Brown and Alcala (1970) have presented ingenious demonstrations of these phenomena for Philippine reptiles.

3. *Long-distance dispersal is probably not achieved invariably by only a single individual or disseminule, but may in some instances be expected to result from simultaneous (or nearly simultaneous) introduction of more than one individual or disseminule. This could still be said to constitute a single "dispersal event."*

There is a tendency to believe that introduction of a single seed can and will suffice to establish a new plant species. This possibility cannot be denied, but several circumstances point to additional possibilities. The requirement of more than one seed holds true for dioecious plants (see principle 20 and chapter 13). A single individual of a plant also seems less likely to yield progeny destined for long-term success, owing to its limited content of genetic variability (see principle 10). Animals require at least a breeding pair or a gravid female. A single gravid female would introduce some heterozygosity, but a flock of adults would introduce more and would be expected to be a better source of genetic variation.

In addition to these relatively demonstrable reasons, one can suggest other cogent ones. The frequent observation of stragglers among migratory birds (Munro, 1960; Lack, 1971) suggests repeated introduction, although repeated introductions are not indicated in the West Indian anoline lizards (Williams, 1969). Repeated stragglers succeeded recently in establishing a breeding colony of purple gallinules on Tristan da Cunha (Rand, 1955). Repeated arrival of straggling monarch butterflies on Canton Island was observed by Zwaluwenberg (1942). Shifts in ocean currents may throw onto beaches unprecedented deposits of seeds of a previously absent species. Such populations of *Mucuna* seeds were observed on New Zealand beaches in 1956 (Mason, 1961). *Mucuna* seedlings that do not survive can be observed from time to time on the Leeward Islands in the Hawaiian chain (fig. 2.6, bottom right). Rafting would tend to bring a small population rather than one individual, as with the ants observed by Wheeler (1916). The distribution pattern of some genera that occur on virtually all the high Pacific islands, such as *Metrosideros*, suggests that one and only one introduction of a single establishable seed to each of these islands is, viewed as a statistical matter, rather unlikely.

The rapid colonization of the Krakatau islets by animals (Dammermann, 1948) and plants (Docters van Leeuwen, 1936) after the volcanic devastation of Krakatau suggests introduction of many disseminules of a species. This is also the case on Surtsey, the newly emerged island near Iceland (Einarsson, 1967) and on the defaunated islets in the Florida Keys (Simberloff, 1969; Simberloff and Wilson, 1969; Wilson and Simberloff, 1969). The equilibrium theory of MacArthur and Wilson (1963), which seems well justified, depends on a continuous rate of immigration rather than a few random accidents.

Arrival of a gravid female of an animal species, or of a single seed of a self-fertile and self-pollinating plant may seem a favorable condition for establishment on islands—but are these *absolute* requirements? That *all* angiosperm immigrants to islands self-pollinate seems unlikely (see chapter 13). Introductions are probably not on a yearly or continual basis except for oceanic drift or other unusually efficient dispersal means. Introduction may well result from violent occurrences such as storms that might deposit quantities of alien jetsam on an island.

4. *Among organisms for which long-distance dispersal is possible, eventual introduction to an island is more probable than nonintroduction.*

This principle, together with appropriate calculations, was clearly enunciated by Simpson (1952). Calculations demonstrating probabilities of this sort had been offered earlier by Matthew (1915) and Darlington (1938). The calculations of Fosberg (1948) on the origins of the Hawaiian flora suggested the inevitability of the outcome. Attention is called to Fosberg's estimate that the Hawaiian species of no fewer than 23 genera of flowering plants have resulted from two independent introductions, whereas three or more introductions are hypothesized for Hawaiian species of 11 other genera (and the reader must keep in mind that Fosberg deliberately calculated only the absolute minimum number of required introductions). Similar calculations probably could be made of hypothetical immigrants in other groups of organisms and in other waif biotas.

Odd chance distributions do, of course, occur. *Lepinia* (Apocynaceae), which occurs on Tahiti and Ponape, is probably an example (Fosberg, 1963). Peculiar distributions of this sort are discussed by Falla (1960),

12

who suggests that habits of birds which are possible vectors may be respon-sible. The distribution of *Bidens* in the Pacific suggests the operation of chance (Carlquist, 1965). Other disjunct distributions on a worldwide basis that seem to suggest chance include *Pilostyles* (Rafflesiaceae) and *Coriaria* (Coriariaceae). Drastic disjunctions sometimes prove to be the result of incorrect taxonomic interpretation. The supposed occurrence of *Lipochaeta* (Asteraceae) on the Hawaiian Islands, Galápagos Islands, and New Caledonia now proves to be a case of three different genera that had not been distinguished because of insufficient study (Harling, 1962).

5. *Elements are present in proportion to not only dissemination ability but also to establishment ability. Establishment ability is a charac-teristic of every species and group but cannot be viewed except in relation to the ecological conditions provided by the recipient island.*

Difficulties of establishment seem much greater than those of trans-port. One can safely say that among successful introductions of dissemi-nules in good condition, only a fraction manage to survive and establish a continuing colony. Animals with wide food preferences and plants of pioneer habitats and easily satisfied pollination requirements appear espe-cially favored. In many cases, greater tolerance for aridity seems an advan-tage—but not universally. Carnivores are less favored than herbivores, since elements in a food chain must become established on an island before secondary ones can be. Perhaps this explains why the insect fauna of Tris-tan de Cunha contains an exceptionally high proportion of phytophagous species (Brinck, 1948). According to Gressitt (1961b), insects that inhabit plant debris or are leaf miners or wood borers are especially successful on oceanic islands. "Weedy" or "versatile" species seem to make more suc-cessful colonists (Williams, 1969; Baker and Stebbins, 1965).

Many forest trees or other forest plants can become established only when soils suitable for them are present. An exception is the chief forest tree of the Hawaiian Islands, *Metrosideros*, which can grow and eventually form a forest on new lava flows (Robyns and Lamb, 1939; Skottsberg, 1941; see also fig. 2.1). Lava pioneers are especially likely to succeed on oceanic islands and, by no coincidence, many plants of oceanic islands fall into this category. Rangitoto, a recent volcanic island in Auckland harbor, New Zealand, is vegetated by plants of the New Zealand flora that can grow on bare lava. Most genera found on Rangitoto are also found on Hawaii and

Tahiti (Carlquist, 1965), or are very much alike (e.g., the araliads *Notho-panax* in New Zealand and *Cheirodendron* in the Hawaiian Islands).

Ecological requirements for establishment are numerous, and unsuitable conditions must screen out many potentially successful colonists. Examples on Canton Island, described by Zwaluwenberg (1942), show this phenomenon clearly. Wilson (1959) has shown that, in the Pacific, ants of open and marginal habitats have been the migrants to new island areas. After arrival on islands, they evolve into more specialized interior sites. Establishment may fail because an apparently suitable niche is preempted (Lack, 1969, 1971; Williams, 1969). What seems to be an "unsaturated" condition on an island may not be: as we understand better the ecology of island species, we often discover that available resources are being fully utilized. Another reason for failure, actually observed in the field, is that animals suited ecologically for a particular island may not find there an adequate food supply to maintain a breeding population (lack of predation may also be instrumental here). Examples of otherwise successful animal immigrants "overeating" their resources are given in chapter 13. Problems of island colonization have recently been summarized by MacArthur (1972).

Animals have the advantage of being able to seek suitable environments upon arrival, whereas plants, to survive, must be deposited upon locations suitable for their growth and reproduction. Moreover, suitable pollinating agents must be present, or else self-pollination must be possible. The claim that hermaphroditism or self-pollination is advantageous at the time of establishment (Baker, 1955) seems readily understandable, but species with long-term tenure on islands seem to show the value of outcrossing (see chapter 13).

Perennial plants have been alleged to possess an advantage over annuals because their longevity increases the likelihood of securing sufficient pollination to produce seeds to establish and maintain a species (Wallace, 1895), but alternative explanations for the lack of annuals on islands may take precedence (see principle 14 and chapter 10).

6. *Migration to islands is governed by probability, and ordinary concepts of migratory routes and biological provinces do not apply well to many islands.*

The statement above is a criticism of the division of islands (chiefly in the Pacific Ocean) into provinces, subprovinces, and the like. Plants of equatorial highlands, such as the Afroalpine flora, are also anomalous in this respect (see chapter 14). The concepts of biological provinces and migratory routes are primarily derived from, and therefore best applied to, continental situations. The best systems of biological provinces for islands, such as those of Thorne (1963) and the workers he has cited, still remain unsatisfying to me for the following reasons:

1. Groups of plants and animals on a particular island (or equatorial highland "island") are present roughly in proportion to the distance from suitable source areas. Many islands have acquired their biota from several sources. Can the Hawaiian Islands logically be put into an Oriental province when appreciable portions of their flora and fauna are American in origin (Fosberg, 1948)? The diverse sources of the New Zealand flora and fauna defy categorization into anything but multiple provinces and multiple routes (Dawson, 1958, 1963; McDowall, 1964). Darlington (1957) has shown that animals have reached the West Indies from many sources and have used many ports of entry. These and other examples provide difficulties that, in my opinion, override whatever merits the province and route devices may have.

2. Although there is value in emphasizing major faunal regions, such as those delimited by Wallace's Line and Weber's Lines, these concepts apply to large land areas, not to oceanic islands. For example, the marsupials, which are a chief criterion of the Australo-Papuan region, do not reach oceanic islands or New Zealand.

3. Criteria for one province differ from those for another. Placental mammals characterize the Malayan area, whereas biotic depauperation is the best criterion for Micronesia. In this connection, the Tuamotus must fall into Micronesia floristically, although geographically they are Polynesian.

4. Each biologist will erect provinces and routes differently from others because, inevitably, each person will stress some groups not stressed by others, or will give different weight to historical, climatic, ecological, or geographic factors. No two biologists appear to agree about the designation of provinces or routes, nor would agreement necessarily be desirable.

5. The concepts of provinces and migration routes result from analyses of data but in their final expression do not themselves yield infor-

mation. They are a shorthand that cannot be translated. Because there is no substitute for knowledge of original data, the construction of hypothetical routes and provinces serves only their authors' ideas. Other persons would be well advised to acquire the original data if they want to comprehend distribution patterns on islands.

7. *Guyots and other now-vanished high islands or lands more extensive formerly than now may have aided dispersal to oceanic islands as subsidiary source areas or "stepping-stones" but not as dry land bridges. Continental drift does not explain oceanic island patterns, and even intercontinental disjunctions are more easily explained by long-distance dispersal, in many cases.*

One can agree tentatively with Zimmerman (1948) that disseminules are abundant near a source and become progressively fewer with distance. If so, the presence of an island chain would improve the dispersal possibilities of a species. That this arrangement is indeed effective is shown by the Hawaiian Islands. Although the nearest area with any appreciable land surface is the North American continent, the Hawaiian biota is predominantly Indo-Malesian. However, the prevailing winds do not seem to favor immigration from Indo-Malesia, at least at lower levels in the atmosphere (jet-stream winds at higher levels do seem more favorable). The many small islands and atolls that lie west and south of the Hawaiian chain very likely aided, when they were larger high islands, in transmitting plants and animals to the Hawaiian Islands. Realizing the potential importance of these vanished lands, Zimmerman (1948) called for the development of paleontological information about the Pacific basin. Such data are now rapidly accumulating (Cloud, 1956; Cloud, Schmidt, and Burke, 1956; Durham, 1963; Hamilton, 1953, 1956; Ladd, 1958; Ladd et al., 1953; Menard, 1956; Menard and Hamilton, 1963; Stark and Schlanger, 1956). The authors cited have contributed to a picture of large former archipelagos, some as early as the Eocene, lying in the mid-Pacific. The maps by Menard and Hamilton (1963) strongly suggest a dispersal potential for previously existing islands and should serve to reduce greatly the skepticism concerning long-distance dispersal as a means for populating the Hawaiian Islands and other Pacific islands.

Stepping-stone islands are potentially less effective as a source for dispersal than large land masses, because dispersal may be expected to be proportionate to the number of individuals in a source area (Johnson, 1960a, 1960b). Moreover, autochthonous loss of dispersal mechanisms may lower the dispersal function of stepping-stone islands. That such islands function as staging areas in dispersal cannot be denied, however.

Within archipelagos, redispersal occurs, often with interesting consequences as a result of successive events of isolation and reinvasion (Hamilton and Rubinoff, 1963; Greenslade, 1968a, 1968b; see also examples from the Drosophilidae and Drepanididae in chapter 4). Many theoretical possibilities of how archipelagos may affect dispersal have been summarized by Carlquist (1965) and MacArthur and Wilson (1967). One can say that any species with enough dispersal ability to bring it to an archipelago can be expected to succeed in dispersing (but not, perhaps, in establishing) itself throughout the archipelago (Tryon, 1971). A species may lose its pioneering ecological characteristics, however (Wilson, 1959).

The implications of long-distance dispersal for continental drift theories are discussed in chapter 2. Briefly, one can say that biotic distribution patterns must be examined in the light of long-distance dispersal possibilities; work that fails to do so cannot be accepted. Although relictual patterns can and do occur on continents, data now at hand show how long-distance dispersal has very likely operated in intercontinental disjunctions.

8. *The size and systematic composition of insular biotas are determined by many factors that differ in relative importance from island to island.*

The factors that affect biotic composition are discussed with considerable mathematical sophistication by MacArthur and Wilson (1967). However, to say which factors are of prime importance is difficult. Even for particular islands, factors are not easily ranked, although attempts have been made (Hamilton and Rubinoff, 1963; for a critique, see Carlquist, 1965). Among the factors claimed to be important are island area and altitude (Darlington, 1957; Tryon, 1971); size, nearness, and richness of source (Zimmerman, 1948); latitude, climate, island age, and geological events. Archipelago effects (size of island, size of neighboring island, nearness to neighboring island, altitude, altitude of neighboring island) are manifold (Hamilton and Rubinoff, 1963).

Factors influential in an island's biotic richness are measures of ecological opportunity, the degree to which barriers to dispersal to an island can be overcome, the number of barriers within an island that can serve for isolation and therefore promote speciation, and the requirement for a certain minimal area for maintenance and evolution of a population (see principle 10).

9. *Relicts in the strictest sense are few or absent on oceanic islands, although every immigrant group has a history, and one can designate older island autochthones as "recent relicts."*

Good dispersal ability is not entirely restricted to phylogenetically "advanced" groups. If "primitive" forms have migrated to oceanic islands but the mainland remnants have become extinguished recently, the insular representatives appear as relicts. This is probably the case with the primitive flowering plant *Lactoris* (Carlquist, 1964) and the fern *Thyrsopteris* on the Juan Fernandez Islands. These islands do not appear to be ancient, and the remainder of their flora and fauna contains no relicts. In the West Indies, the cycad *Microcycas* and the insectivore *Solenodon* (together with its fossil relative *Nesophontes*) may be considered relicts (McDowell, 1958; Darlington, 1957). Other than the examples cited, no spectacular relicts can be found on oceanic islands.

If one wishes to think in terms of a "Pliocene relict," a few might occur on oceanic islands—perhaps *Hesperomannia* (Asteraceae) on the Hawaiian Islands, for example. That genus is mentioned because its closest relatives are now withdrawn to areas not likely to be source areas, but mutisioids similar to *Hesperomannia* might have been more widespread in western North America (Mexico?) during the Pliocene. With few exceptions, however, we should look first at the probability that groups on volcanic oceanic islands have close counterparts in likely source areas and are therefore not relictual.

Insular groups may tend to have a rapid cycle of speciation and extinction, and the latter stages may be said to contain, in a sense, relict species (see principle 18).

Why are there so few real relicts among the waif biotas, whereas continental islands, such as Tasmania, are notable for relictism? One answer may lie in the fact that the most successful groups in the waif biotas are those that appear to be evolutionarily upgrade or weedy and that have a greater degree of genetic momentum. Most antique groups make relatively poor immigrants, both because of their generally poorer adaptability and because they often have poorer dispersal mechanisms.

10. *Immigrant species must overcome the restriction of genetic material related to the very small size of the initial population if effects such as inbreeding are to be countered; in any case, the portion of the genetic content of a species that the insular establishment represents will influence the nature of the resulting insular population.*

This is, in effect, a restatement of Mayr's "founder principle." The small size with which waif groups begin is one of the unique features of insular existence. With a few exceptions, such as the strand flora, an immigrant population will receive no new genetic material from the parent population. If such infusions occurred with any frequency, endemism on islands would be much lower than it is. Because infusions do occur relatively often among the strand species, endemism among them is in fact quite low (Fosberg, 1963).

Genetic variability can be increased by mutation after migration. The degree to which mutations are retained depends not only on the mutability of a species but also on the ecological opportunity. Removal of introduced animals from the Channel Islands of California has permitted greater expression of genetic diversity in the dwarf island fox (*Urocyon littoralis*) and the island moth *Estigmene* (Remington, 1971). Chromosomal polymorphism in West Indian populations of *Drosophila willistoni* is greater on islands that are ecologically diverse (Dobzhansky, 1957). *Metrosideros polymorpha*, the chief forest tree of the Hawaiian Islands, is extraordinarily diverse and has proved difficult for taxonomists. This multiform tree ranges from bare lowlands to high bogs, where it is a small subshrub (Rock, 1917), and it may be, according to the area, in an almost continual cycle of hybridization. Polymorphism characterizes many island species; there may be a potential value to lack of interspecific barriers on islands (see chapter 13). Notable examples of variable island species in stages of expansion occur in the land shell *Partula* (Crampton, 1916, 1925, 1932; Schwabl and Murray, 1970). There is every reason to believe that physiological and ecological opportunities play controlling roles. A small area and ecological poverty are cited by MacArthur and Wilson (1963, 1967) as reasons why extinction is high on some oceanic islands. A population's requirement for a land area large enough to maintain genetic variability and thus to maintain the species itself is cited by various authors. Darlington (1957)

19

believes that this requirement explains the extinction of large mammals on Ceylon; it may also explain why the pygmy mammoth, whose reduced stature may reflect excessive inbreeding, became extinct on the California offshore islands. Similar size reduction has occurred to a marked degree in an American bison herd introduced to Santa Catalina Island (R. F. Thorne, personal communication, 1972).

Weedy immigrants would be expected to have the advantage of high mutability. Moreover, the broader ecological tolerances of weedy plants and animals would permit occupancy by more individuals in a given island, thus increasing potential genetic variability. Smaller body size would also favor development of larger populations, which similarly could be genetically more viable.

Berry (1964) has demonstrated in island mice that only a fraction of the species' gene pool is present in island immigrants, thus influencing the nature of the insular population.

11. *Rapid evolution of island immigrants is not only possible but frequent. Change after arrival is inevitable.*

"Explosive" evolution is demonstrated by various groups that have had good ecological opportunities. Among outstanding examples may be cited the Hawaiian Drosophilidae (about 400 species according to C. Elmo Hardy [personal communication, 1966]) or the Hawaiian species of *Cyrtandra* (Gesneriaceae); about 130 species of *Cyrtandra* on Oahu alone are claimed by St. John (1966).

Actual times have been estimated for some cases of rapid insular evolution. Five species of endemic banana-constant moths have evolved in the approximately 1000 years since human introduction of the banana to Hawaii (Zimmerman, 1960). In Lake Lanao in the Philippines, four endemic genera of cyprinid fish have evolved in 10,000 years or less (Myers, 1960). Endemism has reached the level of families in the fishes of Lake Baikal (Comcphoridac [Kozhov, 1963]) and two Burmese lakes (see chapter 3).

Biologists are increasingly aware that geological time is short on volcanic islands. Evolution must proceed within this span, although to this length of time can be added that available on an archipelago as a whole, as well as that on stepping-stone islands, if any.

Factors assisting rapid evolution on oceanic islands include lack of competitors and predators, presence of a wide spectrum of ecological opportunities, and presence of isolating mechanisms (ridges, etc.) that favor small, rapidly changing populations. Prominent geographical relief may have been partly responsible for the remarkable speciation of *Partula* (Crampton, 1916, 1925, 1932). Lava flows can subdivide populations and provide isolation (Zimmerman, 1948), and catastrophic episodes of volcanism may well spur evolution. The barriers among islands of an archipelago seem important in promoting speciation of insular groups (Darlington, 1957). Other forms of reproductive isolation among insular species are possible, however, and should not be overlooked (Bailey, 1956).

When distinct endemic species and genera evolve, one should expect changes in any part of a plant or animal. For example, it is illogical to expect that the dispersal mechanism in the extraordinary Hawaiian silversword, *Argyroxiphium* (Asteraceae), is the same as that of the ancestors of this endemic genus. Possibilities that genes may have pleiotropic effects should not be overlooked.

12. *Situations new to immigrants will dictate their courses of evolution on islands—if they can cross ecotones into them. Adaptive radiation is the inevitable result on an island or archipelago where a small number of immigrants meets a broad spread of ecological opportunities.*

The "genus-and-family-poor but species-rich" condition is one reflection of adaptive radiation on oceanic islands. What is not reflected in taxonomic terms is the tendency for island species to evolve into ecological niches that would be occupied by a member of an entirely different group on a comparable mainland area. The absence of mammals on most oceanic islands has led to the assumption of mammalian roles by birds and reptiles. For example, the dodo of Mauritius, a large terrestrial herbivore, represented a sort of avian rabbit or sheep. Phases of adaptive radiation are related to topics discussed under principles 14 through 17 below, in which diversification of habits within groups is cited.

Because only a few groups such as the Darwin's finches (Lack, 1945, 1947; Bowman, 1961) or the Hawaiian honeycreepers (Amadon, 1950) have been discussed as examples of adaptive radiation, I have attempted to broaden the picture of this phenomenon by discussing numerous groups and geographical regions, in chapters 3 through 9. Understanding of adaptive radiation may benefit from field knowledge, but in some groups where distinctive forms suggest adaptations we have no field knowledge with which to implement suggestions concerning potential adaptive radiation.

Time is a requisite for completion of a cycle of adaptive radiation. On some islands, time (as well as other conditions) has been sufficient for achievement of spectacular radiation. In some cases, not merely one but several cycles of adaptive radiation may occur within a group, as in the Hawaiian honeycreepers (chapter 4).

13. *An immigrant group that is not faced with, or cannot enter, because of inherent limitations, a broad spectrum of ecological opportunities on an island may evolve into one or a few niches.*

In addition to "definitive" adaptive radiation, islands may bear portions of a gamut of adaptive radiation. Examples of incomplete or lopsided adaptive radiation are abundant on islands. These examples usually demonstrate entry into a few new habits or mechanisms—often unusual ones for the groups to which the particular organisms belong. The Hawaiian species of *Viola* and *Bidens* are remarkable in being herbaceous to woody shrubs, but they do not form large shrubs or trees (see chapter 10).

Islands may play a role in fostering peculiar adaptations, such as that of the seaweed-eating marine iguana of the Galápagos Islands, *Amblyrhynchus* (chapter 15.) New dispersal mechanisms (chapter 11) or pollination mechanisms (chapter 13) may develop in plants. The tool-using Galápagos finch *Cactospiza* is part of a program of adaptive radiation, but it is in addition a unique development. Developments in categories such as these occur on mainland areas, of course, as well as on islands. One can speculate that examples such as those given represent responses to unusual conditions on islands and may well have been preserved in the less competitive island situation.

14. *New growth forms evolve among plants on oceanic islands. Most conspicuously, there is a tendency toward increased stature.*

The chief changes that seem to occur are from herb to rosette tree or rosette shrub, herb to shrub, shrub to rosette shrub, and shrub to true tree. Because these tendencies have not been explored and analyzed to any appreciable extent since the essay of Hemsley (1885), I have attempted to document them in chapter 10. The reasons that "insular woodiness" has occurred on particular island groups and the factors that seem of paramount importance in particular localities are discussed at length there.

In addition to viewing insular woodiness from the standpoint of ecological and biogeographical factors, one can view this phenomenon from
the standpoint of taxonomic groups. This, like many other insular phenomena, occurs most abundantly in relatively plastic, evolutionarily upgrade groups. For example, unusual woodiness of Asteraceae is demonstrated on the Hawaiian Islands (Rock, 1913), the Juan Fernandez Islands
(Skottsberg, 1953), St. Helena (Melliss, 1875), the Canary Islands
(Schenck, 1907; Børgesen, 1924) and many others. The numerous taxonomic groups (even to the tribes of Asteraceae, independently of each
other) that follow these trends on islands, and the numerous ecologically
suitable islands that demonstrate insular woodiness, are useful in the same
way that replications and control groups are in experimental areas of science, and offer equivalent security of interpretation.

Insular woodiness is characteristic of certain continental areas as well
as oceanic islands. Most conspicuous are the alpine zones of equatorial
South America and equatorial Africa. The plants of these areas are discussed in chapter 14.

Although a few workers have interpreted insular rosette trees as relicts
(Skottsberg, 1956; Lems, 1960a, 1961), this interpretation seems to be a
minority view. Reasons that point to a nonrelict interpretation of insular
and equatorial highland rosette trees seem compelling and are detailed in
chapter 10. One new line of evidence that would not have been expected
comes from wood anatomy, particularly the concept of paedomorphosis
or neoteny (Carlquist, 1962). The strong tendency for change of habit in
insular plants has confused some workers, for certain insular plants may
superficially look more like each other than like their respective mainland
relatives. For example, Keck (1936) thought that the Hawaiian silverswords (*Argyroxiphium*) might be related to a Juan Fernandez genus with
similarity in habit, *Robinsonia*. In reality, *Argyroxiphium* is a member of
the tribe Heliantheae, subtribe Madiinae (Carlquist, 1959) of Asteraceae,
whereas *Robinsonia* belongs to the tribe Senecioneae.

15. *Changes in form, size, and color of animals often occur on islands:
gigantism, dwarfism, changes in body proportions, and melanism are
among the changes represented.*

The animals that show the trends well are, as one might expect, evolutionarily plastic groups. Insects, birds, reptiles, and land molluscs are

among them. Birds and insects, being mostly volant, often have alterations in shape, size, and proportions related to transitions from flight to flightlessness, and are considered under principle 17. The topic of flightlessness is reviewed in detail in chapter 12 because much evidence, particularly in insects, has now accumulated.

Gigantism is common among insular animals as compared with their mainland relatives (Berland, 1924; Mertens, 1934; Steven, 1953; Hill, 1959; Cook, 1961; Berry, 1964; Darlington, 1971). Because recent studies seem to permit more secure interpretations of this phenomenon, it is reviewed in detail in chapter 15.

Dwarfism, however, is also notable on islands. The following reasons are offered:

1. Smaller forms on islands may reflect the small size of immigrant species, a fact related to their greater ease of dispersal.

2. Smaller size may be an adaptation to pressures of predators, if the pressure is greater on a particular island (Hecht, 1952), although this pressure has also been claimed to be effective in promoting gigantism (see chapter 15).

3. Smaller size may be an adaptation to smaller food articles or food supplies on an island. A small animal could maintain a population of viable size in a situation where food is scarce.

Changes in proportion that are evident on islands include fatter bodies, fatter tails, and thicker limbs in reptiles (Mertens, 1934). These changes, shown well by lizards, may be forms of gigantism, and to that extent they are explained in relation to this topic (chapter 15). Lack of need for locomotion may underlie these trends, as may need for water storage during dry seasons. Shorter limbs and tails are also characteristic of many island reptiles. A good instance is reported in a well-designed study of lizards (Kramer, 1951). Stubby legs and clumsy habits are claimed for some island insects, as in Hawaii (Perkins, 1913). Adaptation to a terrestrial way of life where food supplies are secured by crawling may be responsible. Kramer interpreted the shorter limbs and tails in the lizards he studied as responses to the lack of predator pressure and to the short-distance nature of locomotion on small islets.

Increase in bill size of birds on islands has been noted repeatedly and is discussed in chapter 15. Change in plumage color of birds on islands (chapters 6 and 15) and melanism (chapter 15) have been subjects of recent investigations.

16. *Dispersal mechanisms and dispersal ability may be lost during the evolution of plants on oceanic islands.*

Plants owe their presence on oceanic islands to excellence of dispersal mechanisms. In many cases, these mechanisms are still intact and demonstrable. In other groups, they have been lost. In a comparison with representatives that retain good dispersibility, any morphological changes that tend to decrease dispersibility will be readily visible. After noticing numerous examples of these trends on the Hawaiian Islands and other Pacific islands, I decided to investigate the phenomenon in detail. The results are presented in chapter 11. Although "loss of dispersibility" is a convenient heading to use when discussing various changes that lead to deterioration in dispersal mechanisms of seeds and fruits, this phenomenon is not a single trend. What may result in lessening of dispersibility in propagules of one group may not produce the same result in another group. Only particular insular areas demonstrate these phenomena. However, because numerous taxonomic groups and insular areas do show parallel changes, one can offer some likely interpretations.

A subtle concept related to loss of dispersibility in propagules—but extremely important nonetheless—is the probability of shift in ecological preferences by groups on islands. Very likely, most groups become adapted to ecological conditions on islands (or islandlike areas). To the extent that these conditions differ from those of source areas, and adaptation occurs, these plants (and animals) will have lost the ability to disperse successfully to new sites. This concept seems potentially much more important than is the relatively small surface area of islands in explaining why successful dispersal from islands to mainland areas does not, apparently, occur.

A reasonable corollary, however, is that an insular species can disperse to, and establish itself on, an ecologically similar island without difficulty. This seems to be borne out in certain instances. It may, for example, explain the surprising number of angiosperm species endemic to more than one of the California Channel Islands. They include *Crossosoma californicum, Jepsonia malvifolia,* and *Haplopappus canus* (see Raven, 1967, for a listing). The distances between some of the islands occupied by these species are greater than distances to the mainland. The only explanation

25

for this distribution is that species such as *Galvezia speciosa* are adapted to a particular range of insular climates and can disperse long distances from one of the Channel Islands to another yet cannot obtain a foothold on the nearby mainland coast. A maritime species with broader tolerances could occur both on islands and on a few coastal mainland areas; *Coreopsis gigantea*, in fact, has such a distribution.

17. *Flightlessness may evolve in volant groups of animals in response to insular conditions. Ecological shift may produce equivalent restriction to insular areas.*

The number of flightless birds and insects among waif biotas on islands is quite startling. Early noted by Darwin (1855), it has received comment and interpretation from various authors, such as Perkins (1913), Darlington (1943), Brinck (1948), Zimmerman (1948, 1957), Hagen (1952), Gressitt, Leech, and Wise (1963), Holloway (1963), and Gressitt (1964). A list of flightless birds has been assembled (Carlquist, 1965).

Darlington's (1943) study of flightlessness in carabids of the West Indies and the New Hampshire mountains was notable for the systematic way in which it attempted to isolate and formulate decisive interpretations for factors that lead to flightlessness. The Carabidae are a good group for study, because they are widespread and are apparently sensitive to factors that tend to promote flightlessness. More recent literature supports many of Darlington's interpretations. However, flightlessness in islands and islandlike areas appears to involve additional factors, and thus a more complicated picture appears. Darlington's stress on a stable habitat of limited geographical extent obviously does apply to certain instances of flightlessness. But does it apply to the extreme conditions of the subantarctic islands and equatorial alpine regions? In an attempt to analyze this picture, I have devoted chapter 12 to a discussion of flightlessness, and a terminal section of chapter 14 to a commentary on flightlessness in the equatorial alpine region. Flightlessness also characterizes many cave insects (May, 1963; see also chapter 15) and some groups of parasitic insects, such as the flies that parasitize bats (Streblidae, Nycteribiidae). The latter circumstance suggests that a host-parasite relationship may constitute, in some respects, an insular situation.

If, as Darlington stresses, adaptation to stable habitats of limited geographical extent is strongly related to flightlessness, does ecological shift by animal species at large on islands result in a loss of dispersibility? Apparently it does. The Tornatellinidae (Cooke and Kondo, 1960) form an interesting example. Although some genera of this family, such as *Tornatellinides*, range literally from one side of the Pacific to the other, they seem unable to establish on mainland areas. Apparently they are adapted to insular conditions, and some factors in mainland areas must be inimical to them—either climatic factors to which they are not adapted, or the superiority there of continental genera of land shells. As with plants (see principle 16), ecological shift on islands may be irreversible, and increasing specialization leads to what can be termed loss of dispersibility, although it might also be placed under other headings.

18. *Competitive ability is often decreased slightly to markedly among endemics of oceanic islands.*

The statement above has an intentional vagueness that hinges on the inexactness of the concept of competition. The phenomenon seems real enough, although difficult to demonstrate precisely or to quantify, and aspects have been noticed by many biologists. One indication is the rapidity with which indigenous island species yield to continental species (see Elton, 1958; innumerable examples could, of course, be cited). Competitive ability would appear to depend upon constant selective pressure, and is thus abundantly represented on continents, where numerous aggressive groups are evolving simultaneously. This pressure is lowered or vanishes when a species migrates to an island where there are fewer species and where ecological opportunities not severely contested. Each immigrant group would, in this view, lose competitive ability after arrival, so that at any time the total flora or fauna would be less competitive than on a continent. However, one might prefer to cite more precise factors. Certainly some groups on mainland areas become "less competitive," and the reasons are presumably similar to the less competitive characteristics of insular groups. Even within the native floras and faunas of islands, there are weedier endemics. The question why insular biotas as a whole seem to have a lower level of competitiveness is not easy to answer, although some of the observations that follow may appeal as factors. The nature of competition, with reference to geographical areas at large, has been scrutinized and mathematically formulated by MacArthur (1972).

In the Hawaiian Islands, almost any introduced continental species of plant seems capable of replacing autochthonous species of comparable ecological requirements. Of course, soils have been disturbed by man and his domesticates, yet native island species (with some exceptions) show poorer self-replacement after disturbance than do native species of a comparably disturbed continental area. The rain forests of Kauai now host a remarkable variety of weeds, including many garden flowers, few of which would be noxious—if they were weedy at all—in continental areas. Even high bogs are not exempt from weeds (*Rubus* is now covering the bogs of Mt. Kaala, Oahu). This situation augurs poorly for attempts at conservation of island endemics. Not only are weeds well-entrenched in many areas of the Hawaiian Islands, but efforts to remove them would very likely only renew and widen the areas of disturbance and encourage more weedy growth than before. Many plants that are now weeds in the Hawaiian Islands can hardly be kept out of many areas because of their good dispersal mechanisms (e.g., *Schinus* and *Psidium* are spread by frugivorous birds). Among the Hawaiian endemics that seem capable of occupying disturbed sites are species of *Scaevola*, *Pipturus*, and *Acacia*. Even with these, one could name more aggressive continental species of comparable ecological requirements.

Loss of competitive ability may in part be due to genetic depauperation, a fate that seems common to most island autochthones. One would expect that even in prehuman times some genera had lost momentum. There do seem to be such genera in the Hawaiian biota. These include two genera of land shells, *Carelia* (Cooke, 1931) and, to a lesser extent, *Achatinella* (Cooke and Kondo, 1960). Among plant genera, the lobelioid *Delissea* has been labeled "decadent" by Rock (1962). Other Hawaiian plant genera that could be described in this way include *Hesperomannia*, *Hibiscadelphus*, *Kokia*, *Pteralyxia*, *Remya*, *Rollandia*, and some species of many other genera, such as *Cyanea* and *Clermontia*.

Irreversible adaptation to highly specialized locations or food sources may be a key to these vanishing genera. Specializations are presumably irreversible if loss of variability occurs. An insular phylad would be expected to be either in a process of expansion and speciation as it draws on genetic variability (retained or acquired), or in a state of decadence, as adaptability to new situations dwindles. The upgrade groups would be expected to replace the downgrade ones, so that taxa in both categories could be found at any given time. Paucity of individuals would seem to play a key role in loss of genetic variability. Adaptation to an ecological zone of limited extent (and on oceanic islands, any zone would be limited in extent) would result in a smaller number of individuals per species. Excessive specialization is exemplified among Hawaiian animals by the land shell *Achatinella,* which is capable of eating only epiphytic algae and fungi, not foliage. The Hawaiian drosophilids subsist on a very limited number of food sources, including leaves of the endemic arborescent Araliaceae and rotting portions of lobelioids—foods unusual for these genera (Carson et al., 1970). Some Hawaiian insect species apparently are so restricted that they occur only on a single tree (Zimmerman, 1948).

Most oceanic islands lack herbivores; large mammalian herbivores are especially conspicuous in the list of absentees. The effect of a large mammalian herbivore is drastic and is related to a wholly different ecosystem than that found on oceanic islands. Not only do herbivores consume large quantities of plant material, but they also create considerable disturbance by trampling and by creating and maintaining trails. Insular autochthones that evolve in the absence of large herbivores do not have any resistance to them, with few exceptions. For example, Hawaiian plants are notably nonpoisonous, free from armament, and free from many characteristics thought to be deterrents to herbivores (oils, resins, stinging hairs, coarse texture) (Carlquist, 1970). Herbivores have been introduced to virtually all major oceanic islands and archipelagos, with predictable effects. A review of these topics, island by island, is hardly necessary for field biologists who know islands. Because so many oceanic islands have been afflicted by man-introduced herbivores, and because oceanic island floras (and indirectly, faunas) are affected by them, insular biotas can be said to be vulnerable compared to continental biotas.

The same situation holds for animal predators, which are absent to a large degree on oceanic islands, and for parasites. When these organisms are introduced to islands, the native animals—which have, in the course of evolution, lost resistance to parasites—will be more vulnerable than continental relatives that have evolved in coexistence with predators and parasites.

A minor aspect that could be termed a form of vulnerability is the fearlessness that characterizes insular animals (see principle 22 for citation of literature).

Problems of endangered species and extinction are acute on most islands, and a discussion of these questions forms the last section of chapter 15.

19. *Means for outcrossing tend to be highly developed in at least the long-term autochthonous biotas of oceanic islands. Species without potential for outcrossing are probably doomed to shorter tenures.*

Baker (1955) hypothesized that self-compatibility is advantageous for establishment of plant immigrants on islands. This concept seems operative, although it does not altogether rule out establishments of non-self-fertile plants (see chapter 13). In any case, there is apparently a selective advantage among island autochthones for mechanisms that tend to promote or ensure outcrossing. Where population size is limited, as it necessarily is on islands, and where inflow of new genetic material is cut off by the sea barrier, maximization of outcrossing seems a necessity.

Flowers may be wholly outcrossing, as in the case of dioecious, self-sterile, or heterostyled species. Self-sterility and heterostyly are rare on islands, but dioecism is exceptionally common in certain insular floras. Other floral conditions that tend to promote outcrossing include gynodioecism, monoecism, protandry, protogyny, and wind pollination. Such conditions tend to bulk larger in the floras of oceanic islands than in comparable mainland areas. Briefly, one can cite high outcrossing potential, by virtue of the abundance of the floral types listed above, in the Juan Fernandez Islands (Skottsberg, 1928, 1938), the Desventuradas Islands (Skottsberg, 1963), New Zealand (Godley, 1955; Franklin, 1962; Rattenbury, 1962; Dawson, 1964), and the Hawaiian Islands (Skottsberg, 1936a, 1936b, 1944a, 1944b, 1945; Fosberg, 1956; see also chapter 13).

Because floral conditions and other factors tending to promote outcrossing are diverse and complex, I have devoted chapter 13 to this topic, which requires detailed analysis.

20. *Natural hybridization acquires a positive value in evolution of the waif flora and, in some cases, fauna.*

In a sense, this is merely an extension of principle 19, because exchange and circulation of genetic material, a desideratum in a finite population cut off from new genetic material, is achieved.

Taxonomic literature on insular floras (and sometimes faunas) often mentions that some species are unusually "variable," "unstable," or "polymorphic." These conditions would suggest that hybridization, or some aspect related to it, is operative. Yet taxonomists who have written floras or monographs of insular genera have not often reported hybridization, probably because until recently students in taxonomy were not trained to detect and report hybrids. Nevertheless, there have been reports of hybridization in waif floras: by Dawson (1960) in *Acaena*, Fosberg (1956) in *Gouldia*, Franklin (1962, 1964) in *Gaultheria* and *Pernettya*, Gillett and Lim (1970) in *Bidens*, Lems (1958) in *Adenocarpus*, Nicharat and Gillett (1970) in *Pipturus*, Rock (1919a) in *Clermontia*, Sherff (1935) in *Dubautia*, and Skottsberg (1939) in *Viola*. "Cyclic hybridization" is reported in the New Zealand flora by Rattenbury (1962), and numerous reports of hybrids in the New Zealand flora can be gleaned from Cockayne and Allan (1934) and Allan (1961). Hybridization in the land shell *Partula* is clearly indicated by Schwabl and Murray (1970).

Hybrids might be said to occur between races (although some botanists will argue that this violates the meaning of the term hybrid) as well as between species on islands. A successful condition (at least in plants) would seem to be that of a population that takes advantage of reproductive isolation in speciating into new ecological territory, but that retains fertility with other populations. As conditions change, gene flow among a series of semiseparate populations (and by "populations" one can include different taxonomic species) could maintain a high level of adaptability. Instances, modes, and extent of natural hybridization remain rewarding avenues for investigation by students of insular botany. These investigations are particularly urgent, because they can be pursued only while insular floras are relatively intact. I applaud the studies of Gillett (1966) on *Scaevola* and Gillett and Lim (1970) on Hawaiian species of *Bidens*. Further commentary on the role of hybridization in insular floras will be found in chapter 13.

21. *Pollination relationships correspond to and change with respect to availability of insects and other pollinating agents on islands.*

Wallace (1895) noted the paucity of conspicuous flowers in the floras of the Galápagos Islands and New Zealand, a fact he correlated with poverty of insects on those islands. This insect poverty is best described,

31

however, in terms of the absence or scarcity of particular groups, such as butterflies in the Galápagos (Wallace, 1895) or long-tongued bees in New Zealand (Rattenbury, 1962). The Hawaiian forest flora also is abundant in small green or whitish flowers that are poor in scent. Smaller flowers have probably established preferentially or evolved in these habits to suit the smaller sizes, and the habits and preferences, of available pollinators. As will be noted, the waif insect fauna consists of immigrants belonging to smaller size classes, and this situation may have promoted the evolution of smaller floral sizes. That island conditions do influence pollination mechanisms is suggested by Hagerup (1950a, 1950b, 1951). Flowers on oceanic islands often have simple, open forms, suitable to entry by a wide variety of potential pollinators.

Massing of flowers might serve to attract pollinators, and is theoretically advantageous if pollinators are scarce. This factor might help to explain the occurrence of insular rosette trees with large inflorescences, such as *Wilkesia* and *Trematolobelia* (Hawaiian Is.) or *Centaurodendron, Yunquea,* and *Dendroseris* sect. *Phoenicoseris* (Juan Fernandez Is.). On these islands other plants with massive inflorescences could also be cited.

Wallace (1895) has claimed that the perennial habit aids in securing pollinators. That interpretation of this habit seems questionable, because a few additional flowering seasons will probably not serve to secure pollination if suitable pollinators are not present in adequate numbers in any given year. Probability seems to favor either the continual presence of a suitable insect in sufficient numbers or else its complete absence from an island. The high proportion of perennials on oceanic islands probably is related primarily to climatic factors (see principle 14 as well as the detailed account in chapter 10).

The attractiveness of Asteraceae to a variety of insects is alleged by Wallace (1895) to be a reason for the abundance of this family on islands. If operative, this reason is probably subsidiary to the good dispersibility, weediness, and adaptability that are characteristic of this family.

Change from insect pollination to wind pollination (partly or wholly) solves the problem of scarcity of suitable insect pollinators. Autochthonous evolution into anemophily may have occurred on a few islands (e.g., with *Rhetinodendron* on the Juan Fernandez Islands [Skottsberg, 1928]). Anemophily might help to explain the success of some genera on oceanic islands (e.g., *Plantago, Coprosma*).

22. *Some mutations that would be lethal or disadvantageous in continental environments have a more nearly neutral value in the less competitive environment of an oceanic island.*

The less disadvantageous nature of many mutations (see the closely allied principle 18) is easy to state but difficult to demonstrate, although many of the changes described under previous headings might qualify as examples. One feature that clearly does qualify is the fearlessness that typifies many insular animals. Many descriptions of fearlessness in insular animals, particularly birds, have been offered (Lönnberg, 1920; Beebe, 1924; Rand, 1938; Greenway, 1958; Rice, 1964; Carlquist, 1965). Where predators are absent, evasive action would seem to be an unnecessary behavioral characteristic, perhaps wasteful, because excessive wariness could interfere with other activities such as feeding.

Development of conspicuous color patterns may be a visual equivalent of fearlessness, reflecting as it does fearless behavior and the absence of predators. This characteristic occurs prominently among certain lizards (Mertens, 1934; Carlquist, 1965).

Various forms of apparent reproductive inefficiency might characterize some animals and plants on islands, although this subject is difficult to explore. Changes in fertility may not be so much inefficiency as alterations to the lowered rates of reproduction required to maintain a small insular population, or adaptation to a limited food supply. Further commentary on these topics is offered in chapter 13.

On the Brazilian island of Queimada Grande, an unusually high percentage of individuals of the viper *Bothrops insularis* are hermaphrodites (sterile), and the percentage seems increasingly large. For an account, see Mertens (1960), who summarizes, for example, the work of A. R. Hoge et al. (published in the *Memoirs of the Institute of Butantan*, vol. 29, 1959). This situation would probably be disadvantageous in a mainland environment. Slow maturation or delayed adulthood of island birds (Hagen, 1952) may represent adjustment to the altered nature of reproduction on a small land area. Greater longevity of island animals has been observed in several cases (see chapter 13); although longevity would itself be of no advantage on islands, it may represent release from predator pressure. Reptiles and amphibians are usually killed before reaching full size. If enemies and hazards are reduced on islands, more individuals would reach full size than on mainland areas.

In the case of seeds and fruits that lose dispersibility, there appear to be malformations that have no selective advantage, as in *Yunquea*, *Dendroseris*, and perhaps some species of *Bidens*. For whatever reasons such malformations occur, they seem quite unusual for the family to which these genera belong, Asteraceae, and do not seem to have occurred on mainland areas (see chapter 11).

23. *Endemism, although high on oceanic islands, is not itself a criterion for identification of an island as oceanic. There are various reasons for high and low endemism. The nature of endemism may prove informative as a way to illustrate certain features concerning insular biotas.*

Oceanic islands tend to have endemics that are restricted to lower categories, particularly species, and to a lesser extent, genera. Old continental islands may possess endemic families, even orders, as relicts from continents. Setchell (1928) hints at this.

Endemism is a constant byproduct of evolutionary change, and the percentage of endemics is more a measure of degree of isolation in time and space than of mode of origin of islands. Ecological opportunity is also involved, for shift into new ecological sites usually is accompanied by changes that promote endemism. Atolls have a low rate of endemism not only because they are not isolated (dispersal is easy via migratory birds and oceanic drift) but because they are ecologically relatively uniform.

If an island biota contains phylogenetically primitive forms with poor dispersal ability, a continental origin for the island may be suspected, or it might be continentlike (an island composed of sedimentary rocks, but not previously connected to a land mass; whether such islands exist is problematic, and differences between them and continental islands separated from land masses for very long periods would be difficult to detect). For example, the presence of Araucariaceae strongly suggests that New Caledonia is an old continental island.

An interesting commentary on endemism of marine shore faunas of islands is offered by McDowall (1968). He shows that endemism of marine fishes is high where ocean currents do not provide an island with a supply of species from other areas (e.g., 33 percent endemism for Easter Island, 50 percent for the Juan Fernandez Islands) or when islands are extremely isolated (e.g., Kerguélen). Presumably, if currents came from islands of different marine environment than recipient islands, endemism would still be high. Islands in the paths of suitable currents, however, have very low rates of marine fish endemism (5 percent for Bermuda). McDowall also shows that high endemism in marine faunas in general on islands is related to lack of pelagic stages in particular taxonomic groups.

Comments on endemism and its relation to speciation in various insular areas will be found in chapter 3.

24. *Evolutionarily plastic groups are sensitive indicators of directions of evolution in the biota that results from colonization by means of long-distance dispersal.*

Groups such as insects or composites (Asteraceae) may be expected to fit themselves rapidly and closely to the templates provided by the island environment. As an example of the usefulness of this concept, one can discount Skottsberg's (1956) claim that peculiar growth forms on the Juan Fernandez Islands are relicts. One would expect such growth forms, if they were relicts, to be members of relatively primitive or slowly evolving groups. Instead, the Juan Fernandez rosette trees and rosette shrubs occur in upgrade, predominantly herbaceous groups, characterized by weediness and rapid evolution; for example, the Plantaginaceae, the Apiaceae, and three tribes of the Asteraceae.

One can hardly doubt that *Chenopodium* is a weedy genus of flowering plants. Not surprisingly, it has reached the Hawaiian Islands and the Juan Fernandez Islands and has formed arborescent endemic species there. One might expect that those families that contain agricultural weeds in abundance in Europe might be represented on oceanic islands; they are. In some cases (*Sonchus, Lepidium, Rumex,* and *Artemisia*) the same genera are involved.

Some groups that do not appear to be weedy are nonetheless evidently excellent at colonization of pioneer areas—for example, the lobelioids (especially *Lobelia* and *Clermontia*) of the Hawaiian Islands. Several species of those two genera often occur there on road cuts and new lava.

35

References

Allan, A. H. 1961. *Flora of New Zealand*, vol. 1. Wellington, R. E. Owen, Government Printer.

Amadon, D. 1950. The Hawaiian honeycreepers (Aves, Drepaniidae). *Bull. Amer. Mus. Natur. Hist.* 95:151–262.

Andrews, E. C. 1940. Origin of the Pacific insular floras. *Proc. Sixth Pacific Sci. Congr.* 4:613–20.

Bailey, D. W. 1956. Re-examination of the diversity in *Partula taeniata*. *Evolution* 10:360–66.

Baker, H. G. 1955. Self-compatibility and establishment after "long-distance" dispersal. *Evolution* 9:347–49.

Baker, H. G., and G. L. Stebbins, Jr., eds. 1965. *The genetics of colonizing species.* New York, Academic Press.

Beebe, W. 1924. *Galapagos: World's end.* New York, G. P. Putnam's Sons.

Berland, L. 1924. Araignées de l'île de Pâques et des îles Juan Fernandez. *Natur. Hist. Juan Fernandez Easter I.* 3:419–37.

Berry, R. J. 1964. The evolution of an island population of the house mouse. *Evolution* 18:468–83.

Blake, S. F., and A. C. Atwood. 1942. *Geographical guide to floras of the world*, pt. 1. U.S. Dept. Agr. Misc. Publ. 401. Washington, D.C.

Børgesen, F. 1924. Contributions to the knowledge of the vegetation of the Canary Islands. *Mém. Acad. Roy. Sci. Danemark, Sect. Sci.*, ser. 8, 6:285–395.

Bowman, R. I. 1961. Morphological differentiation and adaptation in the Galápagos finches. *Univ. Calif. Publ. Zool.* 58:1–302.

Brinck, P. 1948. Coleoptera of Tristan da Cunha. *Results Norwegian Sci. Exped. Tristan da Cunha* 17:1–121.

Brown, W. C., and A. C. Alcala. 1970. The zoogeography of the herpetofauna of the Philippine Islands, a fringing archipelago. *Proc. Calif. Acad. Sci.*, 4th ser., 38(6):105–30.

Carlquist, S. 1959. Studies on Madiinae: Anatomy, cytology, and evolutionary relationships. *Aliso* 4:171–236.

Carlquist, S. 1962. A theory of paedomorphosis in dicotyledonous woods. *Phytomorphology* 12:30–45.

Carlquist, S. 1964. Morphology and relationships of Lactoridaceae. *Aliso* 5:421–35.

Carlquist, S. 1965. *Island life.* New York, Natural History Press.

Carlquist, S. 1966. The biota of long-distance dispersal. I. Principles of dispersal and evolution. *Quart. Rev. Biol.* 41:247–70.

Carlquist, S. 1970. *Hawaii, a natural history.* New York, Natural History Press.

Carson, H. L., D. E. Hardy, H. T. Spieth, and W. S. Stone. 1970. The evolutionary biology of the Hawaiian Drosophilidae. In *Essays in evolution and genetics in honor of Theodosius Dobzhansky*, ed. M. K. Hecht and W. C. Steere, pp. 437–543. New York, Appleton-Century-Crofts.

Clagg, H. B. 1966. Trapping of air-borne insects in the Atlantic-Antarctic area. *Pacific Insects* 8:455–66.

Cloud, P. E., Jr. 1956. Provisional correlation of selected Cenozoic sequences in the western and central Pacific. *Proc. Eighth Pacific Sci. Congr.* 2:555–73.

Cloud, P. E., Jr., R. G. Schmidt, and H. W. Burke. 1956. Geology of Saipan, Marianas Islands. Part I. General Geology. *U.S. Geol. Survey Prof. Papers* 208A:1–126.

Cockayne, L., and H. H. Allan. 1934. An annotated list of groups of wild hybrids in the New Zealand flora. *Ann Bot.* 48:1–55.

Constance, L., L. Heckard, K. L. Chambers, R. Ornduff, and P. R. Raven. 1963. Amphitropical relations in the herbaceous floras of the Pacific coast of North and South America: A symposium. *Quart. Rev. Biol.* 38:109–77.

Cook, L. M. 1961. The edge effect in population genetics. *Amer. Natur.* 95:295–307.

Cooke, C. M., Jr., 1931. The land snail genus *Carelia*. *Bishop Mus. Bull.* 85:1–97.

Cooke, C. M., Jr., and Y. Kondo. 1960. Revision of Tornatellinidae and Achatinellidae (Gastropoda, Pulmonata). *Bishop Mus. Bull.* 221:1–303.

Crampton, H. E. 1916. Studies on the variation, distribution and evolution of the genus *Partula*. *Carnegie Inst. Wash. Publ.* 228:1–311.

Crampton, H. E. 1925. Contemporaneous differentiation in the species of *Partula* living on Moorea, Society Islands. *Amer. Natur.* 59:5–35.

Crampton, H. E. 1932. Studies on the variation, distribution and evolution of the genus *Partula*. The species inhabiting Moorea. *Carnegie Inst. Wash. Publ.* 410:1–335.

Dammermann, K. W. 1948. The fauna of Krakatau 1883–1933. *Verh. kon. Ned Akad. Wetensch. Afd. Natuurk.*, ser. 2, 44:1–594.

Darlington, P. J., Jr. 1938. The origin of the fauna of the Greater Antilles, with discussion of dispersal of animals over water and through the air. *Quart. Rev. Biol.* 13:274–300.

Darlington, P. J., Jr. 1943. Carabidae of mountains and islands: Data on the evolution of isolated faunas and on atrophy of wings. *Ecol. Monogr.* 13:37–61.

Darlington, P. J., Jr. 1957. *Zoogeography.* New York, John Wiley & Sons.

Darlington, P. J., Jr. 1971. Carabidae on tropical islands, especially the West Indies. In *Adaptive aspects of insular evolution*, ed. W. L. Stern, pp. 7–15. Pullman, Wash., Washington State University Press.

Darwin, C. 1855. Letter to J. D. Hooker, March 7, 1855. In *Life and letters of Charles Darwin*, ed. F. Darwin, New York, Basic Books.

Darwin, C. 1859. *On the origin of species by means of natural selection.* Reprint of first edition, 1950. London, Watts & Co.

Dawson, J. W. 1958. Interrelationships of the Australasian and South American floras. *Tuatara* 7:1–6.

Dawson, J. W. 1960. Natural *Acaena* hybrids growing in the vicinity of Wellington. *Trans. Roy. Soc. New Zealand* 88:13–27.

Dawson, J. W. 1963. Origins of the New Zealand alpine flora. *Proc. New Zealand Ecol. Soc.* 10:1–4.

Dawson, J. W. 1964. Unisexuality in the New Zealand Umbelliferae. *Tuatara* 12:67–68.

Dobzhansky, T. 1957. Genetics of natural populations. XXVI. Chromosomal variability in island and continental populations of *Drosophila willistoni* from Central America and the West Indies. *Evolution* 11:280–93.

Docters van Leeuwen, W. M. 1936. Krakatau, 1883–1933. *Ann. Jard. Bot. Buitenzorg*, 46–47:xii + 506.

Durham, J. W. 1963. Paleogeographic conclusions in light of biological data. In *Pacific basin biogeography*, ed. J. L. Gressitt, pp. 355–65. Honolulu, Bishop Museum Press.

Einarsson, E. 1967. The colonization of Surtsey, the new volcanic island, by vascular plants. *Aquilo, ser. Bot.* 6:172–82.

Elton, C. S. 1958. *The ecology of invasions by animals and plants*. New York, John Wiley & Sons.

Falla, R. A. 1960. Oceanic birds as dispersal agents. *Proc. Roy. Soc. London*, ser. B, 152:655–59.

Fleming, C. A. 1963. Paleontology and southern biogeography. In *Pacific basin biogeography*, ed. J. L. Gressitt, pp. 369–82. Honolulu, Bishop Museum Press.

Fosberg, F. R. 1948. Derivation of the flora of the Hawaiian Islands. In *Insects of Hawaii: Introduction*, E. C. Zimmerman, pp. 107–19. Honolulu, University of Hawaii Press.

Fosberg, F. R. 1956. Studies in Pacific Rubiaceae: I–IV. *Brittonia* 8:165–178.

Fosberg, F. R. 1963. Plant dispersal in the Pacific. In *Pacific basin biogeography*, ed. J. L. Gressitt, pp. 273–81. Honolulu, Bishop Museum Press.

Franklin, D. A. 1962. The Ericaceae in New Zealand (*Gaultheria* and *Pernettya*). *Trans. Roy. Soc. New Zealand, Bot.* 1:155–73.

Franklin, D. A. 1964. *Gaultheria* hybrids on Rainbow 'Mountain. *New Zealand Jour. Bot.* 2:34–43.

Gillett, G. W. 1966. Hybridization and its taxonomic interpretation in the *Scaevola gaudichaudiana* complex of the Hawaiian Islands. *Evolution* 20:506–16.

Gillett, G. W., and E. K. S. Lim. 1970. An experimental study of the genus *Bidens* in the Hawaiian Islands. *Univ. Calif. Publ. Bot.* 56:1–62.

Godley, E. J. 1955. Breeding systems in New Zealand plants. I. *Fuchsia. Ann. Bot.* 19:549–59.

Greenslade, P. J. M. 1968a. Island patterns in the Solomon Islands. Bird fauna. *Evolution* 22:751–61.

Greenslade, P. J. M. 1968b. The distribution of some insects in the Solomon Islands. *Proc. Linnaean Soc. London* 179:189–96.

Greenway, J. C., Jr. 1958. *Extinct and vanishing birds of the world*. New York, American Committee for International Wild Life Protection.

Gressitt, J. L. 1956. Some distribution patterns of Pacific island faunas. *Syst. Zool.* 5:11–32.

Gressitt, J. L. 1961a. Problems in the zoogeography of Pacific and Antarctic insects. *Pacific Insects Monogr.* 2:1–94.

Gressitt, J. L. 1961b. Zoogeography of Pacific Coleoptera. *Verh. XI Internat. Kongr. Entomol.* 1:463–65.

Gressitt, J. L. 1964. Insects of Campbell Island. Summary. *Pacific Insects Monogr.* 7:531–600.

Gressitt, J. L., R. E. Leech, and C. W. O'Brien. 1960. Trapping of air-borne insects in the Antarctic area. *Pacific Insects* 2:245–50.

Gressitt, J. L., R. E. Leech, and K. A. Wise. 1963. Entomological investigations in Antarctica. *Pacific Insects* 5:287–304.

Gressitt, J. L., R. E. Leech, et. al. 1961. Trapping of air-borne insects in the Antarctic area. Part 2. *Pacific Insects* 3:559–62.

Gressitt, J. L., and S. Nakata. 1958. Trapping of air-borne insects on ships on the Pacific. *Proc. Hawaiian Entomol. Soc.* 16:363–65.

Gressitt, J. L., J. Sedlacek, K. A. Wise, and C. M. Yoshimoto. 1961. A high-speed airplane trap for air-borne organisms. *Pacific Insects* 5:549–55.

Gressitt, J. L., and C. M. Yoshimoto. 1963. Dispersal of animals in the Pacific. In *Pacific basin biogeography*, ed. J. L. Gressitt, pp. 283–92. Honolulu, Bishop Museum Press.

Gulick, A. 1932. Biological peculiarities of oceanic islands. *Quart. Rev. Biol.* 7:405–27.

Hagen, Y. 1952. Birds of Tristan da Cunha. *Results Norwegian Exped. Tristan da Cunha* 20:1–248.

Hagerup, O. 1950a. Thrips pollination in *Calluna. Kong. Danske Vidensk. Selsk. Biol. Medd.* 18(4):1–16.

Hagerup, O. 1950b. Rain pollination. *Kong. Danske Vidensk. Selsk. Biol. Medd.* 18(5):1–19.

Hagerup, O. 1951. Pollination in the Faroes—in spite of rain and poverty of insects. *Kong. Danske Vidensk. Selsk. Biol. Medd.* 18(15):1–48.

Hamilton, E. L. 1953. Upper Cretaceous, Tertiary, and Recent planktonic Foraminifera from mid-Pacific flat-topped seamounts. *Jour. Paleontol.* 27:204–37.

Hamilton, E. L. 1956. Sunken islands of the mid-Pacific mountains. *Geol. Soc. Amer. Mem.* 64:1–97.

Hamilton, T., and I. Rubinoff. 1963. Isolation, endemism and multiplication of species in the Darwin finches. *Evolution* 17:388–403.

Harling, G. 1962. On some Compositae endemic to the Galápagos Islands. *Acta Horti Bergiani* 20:63–120.

Harrell, J. C., and E. Holzapfel. 1966. Trapping air-borne insects on ships in the Pacific. Part 6. *Pacific Insects* 8:33–42.

Hecht, M. K. 1962. Natural selection in the lizard genus *Aristelliger. Evolution* 6:122–24.

Hemsley, W. B. 1885. Endemic and arborescent Compositae in oceanic islands. *Rep. Sci. Results Voyage H.M.S. Challenger, Bot.,* 1:19–24.

Hill, J. E. 1959. Rats and mice from the islands of Tristan da Cunha and Gough, South Atlantic Ocean. *Results Norwegian Sci. Exped. Tristan da Cunha* 46:1–5.

Holdgate, M. W. 1960. The fauna of the mid-Atlantic islands. *Proc. Roy. Soc. London,* ser. B, 152:550–67.

Holloway, B. A. 1963. Wing development and evolution of New Zealand Lucanidae (Insecta: Coleoptera). *Trans. Roy. Soc. New Zealand, Zool.* 3:99–116.

Hubbell, T. H. 1968. The biology of islands. *Proc. Nat. Acad. Sci. U.S.A.* 60:22–32.

Johnson, C. G. 1960a. A basis for a general system of insect migration and dispersal by flight. *Nature* 186:348–50.

Johnson, C. G. 1960b. Present position in the study of insect dispersal and migration. *Rep. Seventh Commonwealth Entomol. Conf., London:* 140–45.

Keck, D. D. 1936. The Hawaiian silverswords: Systematics, affinities and phytogeographic problems of the genus *Argyroxiphium.* *Occas. Papers Bishop Mus.* 11(19):1–38.

Kozhov, M. 1963. *Lake Baikal and its life.* The Hague, Dr. W. Junk, Publishers.

Kramer, G. 1951. Body proportions in mainland and island lizards. *Evolution* 5:193–206.

Lack, D. 1945. The Galápagos finches (Geospizinae). *Occas. Papers Calif. Acad Sci.* 21:1–151.

Lack, D. 1947. *Darwin's finches.* Cambridge, Cambridge University Press.

Lack, D. 1969. The numbers of bird species on islands. *Bird Study* 16:193–209.

Lack, D. 1971. Island birds. In *Adaptive aspects of insular evolution,* ed. W. L. Stern, pp. 29–31. Pullman, Wash., Washington State University Press.

Ladd, H. S. 1958. Fossil land shells from western Pacific atolls. *Jour Paleontol.* 32:183–98.

Ladd, H. S., E. Ingerson, R. C. Townsend, M. Russell, and H. K. Stephenson. 1953. Drilling on Eniwetok Atoll, Marshall Islands. *Bull. Amer. Assoc. Petrol. Geol.* 37:2257–80.

Lems, K. 1958. Botanical notes on the Canary Islands. I. Introgression among the species of *Adenocarpus,* and their role in the vegetation of the islands. *Biol. Inst. Nac. Invest. Agron. (Madrid)* 39:351–60.

Lems, K. 1960a. Botanical notes on the Canary Islands. II. The evolution of plant forms in the islands: *Aeonium.* *Ecology* 41:1–17.

Lems, K. 1960b. Floristic botany of the Canary Islands. *Sarracenia* 5:1–94.

Lems, K. 1961. Botanical notes on the Canary Islands. III. The life form spectrum and its interpretation. *Ecology* 42:569–72.

Lönnberg, E. 1920. The birds of the Juan Fernandez Islands. *Natur. Hist. Juan Fernandez Easter I.* 3:1–17.

MacArthur, R. H. 1972. *Geographic ecology.* New York, Harper and Row, Publishers.

MacArthur, R. H., and E. O. Wilson. 1963. An equilibrium theory of insular zoogeography. *Evolution* 17:373–87.

MacArthur, R. H., and E. O. Wilson. 1967. *The theory of island biogeography.* Princeton, N.J., Princeton University Press.

McCann, C. 1953. Distribution of the Gekkonidae in the Pacific area. *Proc. Seventh Pacific Sci. Congr.* 4:27–32.

McDowall, R. M. 1964. The affinities and derivation of the New Zealand fresh-water fish fauna. *Tuatara* 12:59–67.

McDowall, R. M. 1968. Oceanic islands and endemism. *Syst. Zool.* 17:346–50.

McDowell, S. B., Jr. 1958. The Greater Antillean insectivores. *Bull. Amer. Mus. Natur. Hist.* 115:113–214.

Mason, R. 1961. Dispersal of tropical seeds by ocean currents. *Nature* 191:408–9.

Matthew, W. D. 1915. Climate and evolution. *Ann. N.Y. Acad. Sci.* 24:171–318.

May, B. M. 1963. New Zealand cave fauna. II. The limestone caves between Port Waikato and Piopio Districts. *Trans. Roy. Soc. New Zealand, Zool.* 3:181–204.

Mayr, E. 1940. The origin and the history of the bird fauna of Polynesia. *Proc. Sixth Pacific Sci. Congr.* 4:197–216.

Melliss, J. C. 1875. *St. Helena.* London, L. Reeve & Co.

Menard, H. W. 1956. Recent discoveries bearing on linear tectonics and seamounts in the Pacific basin. *Proc. Eighth Pacific Sci. Congr.* 2a:809.

Menard, H. W., and E. L. Hamilton. 1963. Paleogeography of the tropical Pacific. In *Pacific basin biogeography,* ed. J. L. Gressitt, pp. 193–217. Honolulu, Bishop Museum Press.

Mertens, R. 1934. Die Insel-Reptilien, ihre Ausbreitung, Variation, und Artbilding. *Zoologica* 32:1–209.

Mertens, R. 1960. *The world of amphibians and reptiles.* New York, McGraw-Hill Book Co.

Munro, G. C. 1960. *Birds of Hawaii.* 2d ed. Rutland, Vt., Ridgeway Press.

Myers, G. S. 1953. Ability of amphibians to cross sea barriers, with especial reference to Pacific zoogeography. *Proc. Seventh Pacific Sci. Congr.* 4:19–26.

Myers, G. S. 1960. The endemic fish fauna of Lake Lanao, and the evolution of higher taxonomic categories. *Evolution* 14:232–333.

Nicharat, S., and G. W. Gillett. 1970. A review of the taxonomy of Hawaiian *Pipturus* (Urticaceae) by anatomical and cytological evidence. *Brittonia* 22:191–206.

Perkins, R. C. L. 1913. *Fauna Hawaiiensis: Introduction.* Cambridge, Cambridge University Press.

Rand, A. L. 1938. Results of the Archbold Expedition. No. 22. On the breeding habits of some birds of paradise in the wild. *Amer. Mus. Novitates* 993:1–8.

Rand, A. L. 1955. The origin of the land birds of Tristan da Cunha. *Fieldiana, Zool.* 37:139–63.

Rattenbury, J. A. 1962. Cyclic hybridization as a survival mechanism in the New Zealand forest flora. *Evolution* 16:348–63.

Raven, P. H. 1967. The floristics of the California Islands. In *Proceedings of the symposium on the biology of the California Islands,* ed. R. N. Philbrick, pp. 57–71. Santa Barbara, Calif., Santa Barbara Botanic Garden.

Remington, D. C. 1971. Natural history and evolutionary genetics of the California Channel Islands. *Discovery* (Yale Univ.) 7(1):3–18.

Rice, D. W. 1964. The Hawaiian monk seal. *Natur. Hist.* 73(2):48–55.

Richter, C. J. J. 1970. Aerial dispersal in relation to habitat in eight wolf spider species (*Pardosa,* Araneae, Lycosidae). *Oecologia* 5:200–14.

Ridley, H. N. 1930. *The dispersal of plants throughout the world.* Ashford, England, L. Reeve & Co.

Robyns, W., and S. H. Lamb. 1939. Preliminary ecological survey of the Island of Hawaii. *Bull. Jard. Bot. Bruxelles* 15:241–93.

Rock, J. F. 1913. *The indigenous trees of the Hawaiian Islands.* Honolulu, privately published.

Rock, J. F. 1917. The ohia lehua trees of Hawaii. *Terr. Hawaii Board Agr. Forest. Bull.* 4:1–76.

Rock, J. F. 1919a. A monographic study of the Hawaiian species of the tribe Lobelioideae, family Campanulaceae. *Mem. Bishop Mus.* 7(2):1–394.

Rock, J. F. 1919b. The arborescent indigenous legumes of Hawaii. *Terr. Hawaii Board Agr. Forest. Bull.* 5:1–153.

Rock, J. F. 1962. Hawaiian lobelioids. *Occas. Papers Bishop Mus.* 23:65–75.

St. John, H. 1966. Monograph of *Cyrtandra* (Gesneriaceae) on Oahu, Hawaiian Islands. *Bishop Mus. Bull.* 229:1–466.

Sauer, J. D. 1969. Oceanic islands and biogeographical theory: A review. *Geogr. Rev.* 59:582–93.

Schenck, H. 1907. Beiträge zur Kenntniss der Vegetation der Kananrischen Inseln. *Wiss. Ergebn. Deutsch. Tiefsee-Exped. Dampfer "Valdivia"* 2(1:2):225–406.

Schwabl, G., and J. Murray. 1970. Electrophoresis of proteins in natural populations of *Partula* (Gastropoda). *Evolution* 24:424–30.

Setchell, W. A. 1926. Les migrations des oiseaux et la dissémination des plantes. *Compt. Rend. Soc. Biogéogr.* 3:54–57.

Setchell, W. A. 1928. Migration and endemism with reference to Pacific insular floras. *Proc. Third Pan-Pacific Sci. Congr.* 1:869–75.

Setchell, W. A. 1935. Pacific insular floras and Pacific paleogeography. *Amer. Natur.* 69:289–310.

Sherff, E. E. 1935. Revision of *Tetramolopium, Lipochaeta, Dubautia* and *Railliardia. Bishop Mus. Bull.* 135:1–136.

Simberloff, D. S. 1969. Experimental zoogeography of islands. A model for insular colonization. *Ecology* 50:296–314.

Simberloff, D. S., and E. O. Wilson. 1969. Experimental zoogeography of empty islands. *Ecology* 50:278–95.

Simpson, G. G. 1952. Probabilities of dispersal in geologic time. *Bull. Amer. Mus. Natur. Hist.* 99:163–76.

Skottsberg, C. 1928. Pollinationsbiologie und Samenverbreitung auf den Juan Fernandez Inseln. *Natur. Hist. Juan Fernandez Easter I.* 2:503–47.

Skottsberg, C. 1936a. The arboreous Nyctaginaceae of Hawaii. *Svensk Bot. Tidskr.* 30:722–43.

Skottsberg, C. 1936b. Vascular plants from the Hawaiian Islands. II. *Medd. Göteborgs Bot. Trädgard* 10:97–193.

Skottsberg, C. 1938. On Mr. C. Bock's collection of plants from Masatierra (Juan Fernandez), with remarks on the flowers of *Centaurodendron. Medd. Göteborgs Bot. Trädgard* 12:361–73.

Skottsberg, C. 1939. A hybrid violet from the Hawaiian Islands. *Bot. Notis.* (1939): 805–12.

Skottsberg, C. 1941. Plant succession on recent lava flows in the Island of Hawaii. *Göteborgs Kungl. Vetens. Vitterhets-Samhäll Handl.,* ser. b, 1(8):1–32.

Skottsberg, C. 1944a. On the flower dimorphism in Hawaiian Rubiaceae. *Ark. Bot.* 31a(4):1–28.

Skottsberg, C. 1944b. Vascular plants from the Hawaiian Islands. *Medd. Göteborgs Bot. Trädgard* 15:275–531.

Skottsberg, C. 1945. The flower of *Canthium. Ark. Bot.* 32a(5):1–12.

Skottsberg, C. 1953. The vegetation of the Juan Fernandez Islands. *Natur. Hist. Juan Fernandez Easter I.* 2:793–960.

Skottsberg, C. 1956. Derivation of the flora and fauna of Juan Fernandez and Easter Island. *Natur. Hist. Juan Fernandez Easter I.* 1:193–438.

Skottsberg, C. 1963. Zur Naturgeschichte der Insel San Ambrosio (Islas Desventuradas, Chile). 2. Blütenpflanzen. *Ark. Bot.*, ser. 2, 4:465–88.

Smith, A. C. 1955. Phanerogam genera with distributions terminating in Fiji. *Jour. Arnold Arboretum* 36:273–92.

Soulé, M. 1966. Trends in the insular radiation of a lizard. *Amer. Natur.* 100:47–64.

Soulé, M., and B. R. Stewart. 1970. The "niche-variation" hypothesis: A test and alternatives. *Amer. Natur.* 104:85–97.

Stark, J. T., and S. O. Schlanger. 1956. Stratigraphic succession on Guam. *Proc. Eighth Pacific Sci. Congr.* 2:262–66.

Stephens, S. G. 1958a. Factors affecting seed dispersal in *Gossypium*. *N.C. Agr. Exp. Sta. Tech. Bull.* 131:1–32.

Stephens, S. G. 1958b. Salt water tolerance of seeds of *Gossypium* species as a possible factor in seed dispersal. *Amer. Natur.* 92:83–92.

Stephens, S. G. 1963. Polynesian cottons. *Ann. Missouri Bot. Gard.* 50:1–22.

Stephens, S. G. 1964. Native Hawaiian cotton (*Gossypium tomentosum* Nutt.). *Pacific Sci.* 18:385–98.

Steven, D. M. 1953. Recent evolution in the genus *Clethrionomys*. *Symp. Soc. Exp. Biol.* 7:310–19.

Thorne, R. F. 1963. Biotic distribution patterns in the tropical Pacific. In *Pacific basin biogeography*, ed. J. L. Gressitt, pp. 311–54. Honolulu, Bishop Museum Press.

Thornton, I. W. B., and J. C. Harrell. 1965. Air-borne Psocoptera trapped on ships and aircraft, 2—Pacific ship trappings, 1963–64. *Pacific Insects* 7:700–702.

Tryon, R. 1971. Development and evolution of fern floras of oceanic islands. In *Adaptive aspects of insular evolution*, ed. W. L. Stern, pp. 54–62. Pullman, Wash., Washington State University Press.

Visher, S. S. 1925. Tropical cyclones and the dispersal of life from island to island in the Pacific. *Amer. Natur.* 59:70–78.

Wace, N. M. 1960. The botany of the southern oceanic islands. *Proc. Roy. Soc. London*, ser. B, 152:475–90.

Wallace, A. R. 1880. *Island life*. London, Macmillan & Co.

Wallace, A. R. 1895. *Natural selection and tropical nature*. London, Macmillan & Co.

Wheeler, W. N. 1916. Ants carried in a floating log from the Brazilian coast to San Sebastian Island. *Psyche* 28:180.

Whitaker, T. W., and G. F. Carter. 1954. Oceanic drift of gourds—experimental observations. *Amer. Jour. Bot.* 41:697–700.

Whitaker, T. W., and G. F. Carter. 1961. A note on the longevity of seed of *Lagenaria siceraria* (Mol.) Standl. after floating in sea water. *Bull. Torrey Bot. Club* 88:104–6.

Williams, E. 1969. The ecology of colonization as seen in the zoogeography of anoline lizards on small islands. *Quart. Rev. Biol.* 44:345–89.

Wilson, E. O. 1959. Adaptive shift and dispersal in a tropical ant fauna. *Evolution* 13:122–44.

Wilson, E. O., and D. S. Simberloff. 1969. Experimental zoogeography of islands. Defaunation and monitoring techniques. *Ecology* 50:276–77.

Wilson, E. O., and R. W. Taylor. 1967. An estimate of the potential evolutionary increase in species density in the Polynesian ant fauna. *Evolution* 21:1–10.

Yoshimoto, C. M., and J. L. Gressitt. 1959. Trapping of air-borne insects on ships on the Pacific. II. *Proc. Hawaiian Entomol. Soc.* 17:150–55.

Yoshimoto, C. M., and J. L. Gressitt. 1960. Trapping of air-borne insects on ships on the Pacific. III. *Pacific Insects* 2:239–43.

Yoshimoto, C. M., and J. L. Gressitt. 1961. Trapping of air-borne insects on ships on the Pacific. IV. *Pacific Insects* 3:556–58.

Yoshimoto, C. M., and J. L. Gressitt. 1963. Trapping of air-borne insects in the Pacific-Antarctic area, 2. *Pacific Insects* 5:873–83.

Yoshimoto, C. M., and J. L. Gressitt. 1964. Dispersal studies in Aphididae, Agromyzidae and Cynipoidea. *Pacific Insects* 6:525–31.

Yoshimoto, C. M., J. L. Gressitt, and C. J. Mitchell. 1962. Trapping of air-borne insects in the Pacific-Antarctic area. 1. *Pacific Insects* 4:847–58.

Zimmerman, E. C. 1948. *Insects of Hawaii*, vol. 1: *Introduction*. Honolulu, University of Hawaii Press.

Zimmerman, E. C. 1957. *Insects of Hawaii*, vol. 6: *Ephemeroptera-Neuroptera-Trichoptera*. Honolulu, University of Hawaii Press.

Zimmerman, E. C. 1960. Possible evidence of rapid evolution in Hawaiian moths. *Evolution* 14:137–38.

Zwaluwenberg, R. H. van. 1942. Notes on the temporary establishment of insect and plant species on Canton Island. *Hawaiian Planter's Rec.* 46:49–52.

CHAPTER TWO

LONG-DISTANCE DISPERSAL:
EVIDENCE AND IMPLICATIONS

The majority of biologists hold that oceanic islands have acquired their floras and faunas by means of long-distance dispersal, and agree that these islands include the volcanic islands of the Pacific (i.e., those north and east of the so-called andesite line) as well as those of the Atlantic (the Macaronesian islands—from the Azores to the Cape Verde Islands, and including Madeira and the Canary Islands—and such islands as St. Helena and Tristan da Cunha) and Indian Ocean (e.g., the Mascarene islands). In addition, once-glaciated islands (the so-called subantarctic islands, for example) are recipients of waif immigrants in the same way. Older islands known to have been strongly isolated for very long periods of time (New Zealand, New Caledonia) have received at least an appreciable portion and probably the vast majority of their immigrants by long-distance dispersal. The equatorial mountaintops, discussed in chapter 14, also have been populated in this manner, as have areas of other distinctive habitats that are separated from each other by marked disjunctions.

Reasons for belief in the operation of long-distance dispersal to oceanic islands lie in floristics and faunistics (lines of evidence reviewed by Thorne [1963] and others) and knowledge of the biology of the organisms. Geological research provides no rational evidence for hypothetical land links between the volcanic islands cited above and mainland areas. Geological studies also show how short-lived volcanic islands are. A review of the

NOTE: This chapter is a revision of a paper (Carlquist, 1967). For permission to present materials from this paper, acknowledgment is gratefully extended to the *Bulletin of the Torrey Botanical Club*.

literature is unnecessary here; the reader can consult chapter 1 and the literature cited by Thorne (1963) and Carlquist (1970).

Other lines of evidence or inference are related to fruit and seed morphology, or to various adaptations for dispersibility in animals. Contributions on plant dispersal by Guppy (1906) and Ridley (1930) are especially noteworthy; Zimmerman (1948) reviews some persuasive observations concerning animal distribution. In recent years, the reality of aerial dispersal of insects and spiders has been established with remarkable clarity by Gressitt, Yoshimoto, and their co-workers (see chapter 1 for full citation). Attention should also be called to a thoughtful and ingenious paper by Hurst (1969). Other papers are cited under appropriate categories below. Although I feel that the reality of long-distance dispersal is overwhelming, obviously much more remains to be learned about the mechanisms by which it takes place. Many advances have been made in recent years, however, and certain aspects seem worthy of examination at this time, both to demonstrate what is at hand and to indicate what new types of evidence might be most meaningful.

Land-Animal Dispersal

Dispersal of insects and spiders over long distances by air has been well established. There seems to be skepticism by a few biologists, however, concerning dispersal of land birds. This may surprise some amateurs, who probably regard the flying ability of land birds as an obvious mechanism of dispersal. Yet Deignan (1963) is so pessimistic about dispersal of land birds to islands that he claims that contemporary patterns of distribution of land birds on islands will predict what geologists must inevitably find concerning former land connections. To those familiar with observational data on land birds, this is simply not true. For example, species of Darwin's finches do reach some of the islands in the Galápagos where they never are able to form breeding colonies (Lack, 1969). These examples and others (see Lack, 1971) show that land birds, although they are indeed "sedentary," as Mayr (1940) claimed them to be, are not as sedentary as the more conservative zoologists would have us believe. A compelling instance—illustrating how careful observation pays large dividends—is offered by Bannerman and Bannerman (1965). They report that Madeira has only

46

27 resident species of land birds, compared with about 200 in Morocco. Of the 200 species in Morocco, however, the Bannermans have observed no fewer than 69 of those not resident on Madeira to appear as occasional visitors on the island. The distance between Madeira and Morocco is great enough that we can extrapolate to islands at large, and conclude that occasional visits by land birds are easily sufficient to explain establishment of insular breeding colonies. We must remember that there have been relatively few islands on which ornithologists have attempted to record occasional visitors or stragglers, so skepticism is completely unjustified.

The difficulty in establishment of land birds on islands seems much greater than that of dispersal to islands. One establishing species may shut out subsequent potential residents. An interesting possible example is cited by Lack (1971). Of the two European species of kinglets, the goldcrest (*Regulus regulus*) has colonized the Azores, whereas the firecrest (*R. ignicapillus*) has colonized the Canary Islands and Madeira. Very likely, the goldcrest was the first to reach the Azores, whereas the firecrest reached the Canaries and Madeira first. Each colonization forestalled establishment of the other species within an archipelago. Alternatively, one could speculate that some subtle ecological distinction has favored the goldcrest on the Azores and the firecrest on the Canaries and Madeira.

Important new data on problems of dispersal and establishment of animals on islands are offered in the work of Williams (1969) on anoline lizards in the West Indies. Williams emphasizes that vagility is linked to habitat versatility. In other words, lizards of lowland dry forest and marginal areas will be able to travel and withstand desiccation better than will upland lizards; the lowland lizards also, of course, are likely to arrive upon terrain more nearly like that of their source area. Wilson (1959) has emphasized a similar situation for ants, and the same is apparent to me in the case of insular plants: most of the wet-forest species seem to be derivatives (although one could cite exceptions, such as *Cyrtandra* in the Hawaiian Islands). Williams (1969) describes evolution into more stable or mesic habitats as "decay of versatility." One might also mention that not only are dry lowland areas larger than wet-forest areas (if any) on most islands, but they are also nearer the site of origin for a dispersal event (presumably by rafting in the case of lizards, and often by shorebirds or even marine birds for plants).

47

Williams gives considerable attention to problems of coexistence and competition. He, like Lack, finds that some anoline species are denied success in colonization of a particular island because their ecological requirements are too similar to those of an already established occupant. Noting the critical difficulty in the first phases of establishment because of small population size, Williams feels that a potential colonist is highly disadvantaged unless a competing species is completely absent, or a previously established resident (anoline species) occupies a wholly different ecological niche. Even a potentially superior invader, he feels, might not succeed against an already established colonist species with a "safe" population level. Coexistence is possible if several colonizing species have been preadapted in sympatry on complex source islands and then migrate simultaneously to a new island. "Ecological release" can occur on small islands: where two species of anoles cannot be supported, the one successful colonist will tend to broaden its ecological range. This evolutionary tendency might seem to be beyond the scope of the present discussion, but a species that has undergone ecological release might well forestall establishment by newer immigrants—perhaps even on the larger islands.

Williams notes that although we can easily see cases in which several species have established, we cannot readily visualize exclusion of other species by a successful colonist. He stresses that we have been too concerned with the possibility of competition as a source of "character displacement" between competing species during autochthonous development on a single island. While character displacement may occur among large continental populations (Brown and Wilson, 1965), congeners on an island may have developed their mutually exclusive ecological requirements prior to one or both invasions of that island.

Williams is to be congratulated for his method, which was "to derive all statements from an empirical basis"—the study of actual *Anolis* populations. I do object, however, to his erroneous interpretation of my (1966a) paper, implying that I believe in lizard colonization of islands by means of "multiple rafting." I did not use that term, nor did I suggest any such possibility for lizards, which I did not mention in that context at all. I was merely attempting to suggest that, for animals suited to dispersal, a *single individual* on a raft is not necessarily sufficient, nor is a *single seed* brought by a flock of birds invariably the founder of a plant colony. A colonizing species may well invade by means of a single dispersal event, but this may not necessarily involve only one individual. There is nothing in Williams's data to preclude the possibility that two gravid *Anolis* females of a given species, rather than a single individual, successfully rode a raft to a particular island. The results would be identical, although several individuals brought by a single dispersal event would, potentially, bring the presumptive advantage of greater heterozygosity. We would probably not be able to measure whether a contemporary population stemmed from one gravid female or three. If rafting is indeed a chance event—as it must be, like other types of long-distance dispersal—what are the chances that every "raft" contains only a single gravid female? It is much more likely that some rafts contain one individual, but other rafts several individuals that establish (see chapter 1, principle 3).

Another problem in establishment of land animals on islands is that their ecological requirements may be met but they may gradually overeat their food supply and then vanish. Such instances have been reported in recent time in the case of the Australian duck, *Aythya australis*, a natural immigrant to New Zealand, which died out within 30 years after first being observed (Fleming, 1962); and for the reindeer, introduced by man to St. Matthew Island, Bering Sea (Klein, 1968). This also apparently happened in the "rabbit plagues" of Laysan and Lisianski (Hawaiian Leeward Is.); self-extinction and near self-extinction had occurred when the Tanager Expedition visited these islands in 1922. Thus, for reasons such as those cited here, Lack (1971) finds that some islands regarded as "unsaturated" may, in fact, be "saturated" with suitable species.

With regard to land molluscs, there seems to be relatively little objection to possibilities of long-distance dispersal. Examples of attachment to birds have been cited (see Zimmerman, 1948). The work of Malone (1965b) is pertinent here. Gastropod eggs may be more resistant to seawater or desiccation than suspected; adults can, of course, resist desiccation to varying degrees. The relatively large size of certain insular gastropods may deter some biologists from believing in their dispersibility, but alteration in size of land molluscs has undoubtedly taken place on islands, and we have every reason to believe that gigantism has occurred during evolution of some of them (see chapter 15). A highly interesting exercise in this regard would be a study of size distributions of continental land molluscs, insular land molluscs, and—most importantly—size of types likely to have been ancestral to contemporary insular land molluscs. Results of such a study might well show what the work of Gressitt and co-workers has shown in insects: that insular populations show establishment of smaller representatives predominantly.

Experimental work on colonization of animals has been done by Wilson and Simberloff (1969) and Simberloff and Wilson (1969). Their papers show the rapidity with which colonization can take place on nearby islets, and are admirable examples of how experimental techniques can be used in dispersal studies. These studies on islets of the Florida Keys have been used as the basis of theoretical models by Simberloff (1969).

Plant Dispersal

In this chapter, information and speculation on long-distance dispersal of plants have been selected and placed in a context somewhat different from those employed by other authors. The modes of dispersal likely to have resulted in the present native floras of Pacific islands are the primary object of analysis here. The correlations that result are informative and somewhat surprising, with many implications concerning dispersal to areas other than those detailed, and dispersal of groups other than vascular plants.

By calculating the proportions of a specific flora that have presumably arrived by air flotation, internal transportation in birds, etc., and by comparing the percentages with those of the same categories in floras of other islands, we can see that the ecology of the recipient island is tremendously important. Distance from source area is to some extent secondary in determining which modes of dispersal are effective in populating a particular island. Such problems as so-called succession on lava flows prove to be related to differential dispersal ability (fig. 2.1, top left, right). Dispersibility is the key to the surprising floristic and faunistic affinities between Polynesian and Mascarene islands. With the precedent of evidence on dispersal to oceanic islands, many supposed difficulties in explanation of inter- and intra-continental disjunctions seem much more easily soluble.

Data on dispersal methods have been drawn from various sources, such as Guppy (1906), Ridley (1930), Fosberg (1963) and my own observations. In using fruit and seed morphology as an indicator of probable dispersal method, one can hypothesize a certain degree of loss of dispersibility during autochthonous evolution on islands, but only in particular taxonomic groups and in particular islands, such as the Hawaiian Islands (see chapter 11 for a discussion of loss of dispersibility in plants). Direct observations of plant dispersal to islands (other than via oceanic drift) are virtually impossible, so indirect lines of evidence must be used. One might have expected that aerial trapping experiments, such as those used by Gressitt, Yoshimoto, and co-workers in studying insect dispersal might be useful to botanists. This is not true for flowering plants, because, according to the data below, aerial flotation of seeds appears to be insignificant except rather close to source areas. There are, to be sure, a number of papers dealing with aeroplankton (Bold, Brown, and Larson, 1964; Brown, 1971; Chang, 1967; Fulton, 1966a, 1966b, 1966c; Fulton and Mitchell, 1966; Gregory and Monteith, 1967; Heise and Heise, 1948; Hirst, Stedman, and Hogg, 1966; Hirst, Stedman, and Hurst, 1967; Kohlmeyer, 1966; Kramer and Pady, 1968; McDonald, 1962; Maynard, 1968; Moar, 1969; Overeem, 1937; Schlichting, 1964). Although these papers do not deal with seeds, many of their considerations may well apply to small airborne seeds, so they cannot be disregarded in this connection. With respect to spore-bearing plants, the papers just cited form overwhelming evidence that long-distance dispersal is a reality.

Observations by ornithologists give useful hints about dispersal of plants by birds. For example, the bibliography of McAtee (1947) is interesting, because data in the papers he cites were not collected with the intention of stressing or "proving" long-distance dispersal of plant disseminules by birds. Such observations are indicative of how dispersal via birds might usefully be investigated further. The importance of dispersal via birds suggests to me that botanists interested in dispersal problems must turn intensively to observational and experimental work with birds if methods of long-distance dispersal are ever to be "demonstrated." We must be realistic in such investigations, however. Obviously, many kinds of birds probably have no function in long-distance dispersal. The papers cited by McAtee (1947) all deal with land birds, for example. On the other hand, waterfowl and especially shorebirds seem likely vectors. The experimental evidence (Proctor, 1968; Vlaming and Proctor, 1968) on the potential effectiveness of shorebirds is outstanding in showing that potential transport is far greater than many workers would have suspected. Other interesting papers in relation to bird dispersal of seeds include those of Guppy (1897), Low (1937), McAtee (1918), and Roessler (1936). Contributions allied to this topic include those of Sauer (1957) and Wagner (1965).

Ironically, information on dispersal of small disseminules by birds is relatively abundant. Among recent papers on dispersal of algae by birds are those by Malone (1965a), Proctor (1961, 1962, 1966), Proctor and Malone (1965), and Proctor, Malone, and Vlaming (1967). Likewise, we are not lacking in observations on dispersal of fungi by birds, thanks to studies by Pugh (1964a, 1964b, 1965a, 1965b, 1966a, 1966b) and the workers he cited. The irony in these observations is that algae and fungi are easily dispersed by wind (see aeroplankton papers cited earlier), so that bird vectors are not as significant for study as they would be in the case of seed transport. Of course, algae and fungi on and in birds can be relatively easily studied, whereas occurrence of seeds in birds suited to long-distance transport of flowering plants is difficult to study in the wild, or in collected birds.

Processes of long-distance dispersal in plants are thoroughly credible, but only if unsupportable hypotheses can be eliminated. We can no longer accept Guppy's idea that different taxonomic groups dispersed at different times (e.g., "age of ferns," "age of Compositae"). Nor can we agree with the full implications of Guppy's claim that "agencies of dispersal . . . have ceased to be active" in the Pacific. High islands may well have existed where only atolls or seamounts now stand, and such former high islands may once have served as subsidiary source areas or stepping-stones for populating more remote islands. Nevertheless, the birds that function now in dispersal are probably much the same as those that have done so in previous eras of the relatively recent geological past, and Guppy's suggestion that now-vanished, and presumably migratory, fruit-eating pigeons were vectors in dispersal of plants must be largely dismissed as visionary.

Although noting the improbability of some of Guppy's ideas, one must concede that his work provides most of the information we have on dispersal of Pacific plants, and the contributions since his are relatively few. Guppy's survey of the Hawaiian flora with respect to methods of dispersal is understandably incomplete. If the Hawaiian flora arrived entirely via long-distance dispersal, however, we must ultimately be able to account for each and every arrival with respect to dispersal. We must similarly be able to account for other Pacific floras. The geographic sources of insular floras are reasonably well understood, thanks to the work of Fosberg (1948), Balgooy (1960), and Thorne (1963). We need comparable information (which must, again, be speculative) on the probable means of arrival of the plant immigrants to oceanic islands.

The tabulations and computations presented here for the Hawaiian flora were influenced by Fosberg's (1948) tabular summary of Hawaiian angiosperms. Fosberg's list presents geographical sources, numbers of immigrants, and numbers of contemporary species. Using his immigrant-number estimates (with certain alterations), I computed percentages for seven methods of arrival. Only clearly native taxa were included. Lists similar to Fosberg's were then prepared for other Pacific floras, and percentages of the methods of arrival were estimated for each of those floras. Admittedly, some floras are better known than others, and my speculations on modes of arrival may be incorrect in particular cases. Errors may or may not tend to balance out within a flora, but I doubt that markedly different figures for particular modes of arrival would be obtained by other workers.

The following floras were used as sources for making the estimates: San Clemente I., Calif.: Raven (1963a); Revillagigedo Is.: Johnston (1931); Cocos I.: Stewart (1912); Galápagos Is.: Stewart (1911); Desventuradas Is.: Skottsberg (1937, 1963); Juan Fernandez Is.: Skottsberg (1922b, 1928, 1951); Easter I.: Skottsberg (1922a, 1927, 1951); Oeno I.: St. John and Philipson (1960); Rapa I.: Brown (1931, 1935); Society Is.: Drake del Castillo (1893), Moore (1933, 1963); Rarotonga: Cheeseman (1902); Tonga: Yuncker (1959); Samoa: Reinecke (1898), Christophersen (1935, 1938); Marquesas Is.: Brown (1931, 1935); Equatorial Is.: Christophersen (1927); Laysan I.: Christophersen and Caum (1931), Lamoureux

(1963); Hawaiian Is.: Hillebrand (1888), Christophersen and Caum (1931), Fosberg (1948). Certain floras were not used if too few species occurred for an accurate picture of modes of arrival (e.g., Clipperton I.).

Analysis of the Hawaiian Flora

Concepts of means of arrival are presented in the tabular summary that follows. It is offered so that my decisions on probable arrival method for each introduction to the Hawaiian flora can be examined. Only native seed plants are considered. Vascular cryptogams may be assumed to have arrived via air flotation of spores, with a few exceptions, such as *Marsilea* (Malone and Proctor, 1965), although spores can travel via birds as well.

The desirability of using the Hawaiian biota as a source for study of biological phenomena related to oceanic islands has been stressed previously. In the present study, the fact that the Hawaiian Islands are exceptionally remote yet have ecological diversity broad enough to support a wide variety of immigrants is significant. That the Hawaiian Islands have acquired their native flora by means of long-distance dispersal has not been seriously challenged. Whereas now-vanished archipelagos may have aided dispersal from Indo-Malesian source areas, no such former islands have been hypothesized between the Hawaiian Islands and North America. American sources must be claimed for no fewer than 50 successful arrivals in the Hawaiian angiosperm flora. If long-distance dispersal can explain these 50 (which represent, in fact, all seven modes of transport described below), then dispersal over shorter distances can surely be explained as well.

For each genus, interpretations are given in parentheses. In each case the first figure indicates the number of successful introductions needed to account for the native species now resident. This may be considered as the minimum number of introductions necessary, and a somewhat larger number is conceivable in some instances. Next is an abbreviation indicating presumed mode of arrival. The abbreviations are:

    A = Air flotation
  BB = Birds—seeds or fruits attached to feathers mechanically by
          barbs, bristles, awns, trichomes, etc.

BI = Birds—seeds or fruits eaten and carried internally

BM = Birds—seeds or fruits embedded in mud on feet

BV = Birds—seeds or fruits attached to feathers by viscid substances, or viscid quality of fruit parenchyma surrounding seeds

DF = Oceanic drift—frequent or repetitive, as suggested by demonstrable ability of fruits or seeds to float for prolonged period

DR = Oceanic drift—rare, on one or only a few occasions; seeds or fruits probably resistant to seawater but unable to float for prolonged periods and thus likely to have arrived via rafting; or, alternatively, plants suited to oceanic drift, but rare arrivals because of unsuitable patterns of ocean currents

The last item within each set of parentheses is the estimated number of contemporary species plus subspecies and varieties, both endemic ones (e) and wide-ranging ones (w) that are native to one or more areas in addition to the Hawaiian Islands.

In some cases, more than one type of dispersal occurs within a genus. For example (contrary to Fosberg, 1948), I hold that at least three introductions rather than one are necessary to account for the Hawaiian species of *Scaevola* (Goodeniaceae). Oceanic drift has brought the common beach species, *Scaevola S. taccada* (fig. 2.6, top left, right). *Scaevola glabra* (including *S. kauaiensis*) represents an early and rather distinctive immigrant (regarded as a segregate genus, *Camphusia*, by some) in which fruit and seed gigantism has occurred autochthonously (Carlquist, 1966c; see chapter 11), as have other morphological changes. The remainder (e.g., *S. gaudichaudiana*, fig. 2.3, top right, and *S. coriacea*, fig. 2.6, top right) of the Hawaiian species stem from a third stock.

If a clear decision as to mode of arrival could not be reached, a preference is expressed by indicating one method in upper case letters, the alternative in lower case. If two arrivals in a genus are claimed to have come by different means, both choices are given in upper case.

Mode of arrival was computed not only for ancestors of the entire angiosperm flora of the Hawaiian Islands, but also for those segments that

55

came from each of the source areas suggested by Fosberg. By this means I hoped, for example, to see if immigrants from America and from Indo-Malesia came predominantly by different methods. In fact, no such differences emerged, and the methods of long-distance dispersal seem relatively alike in different geographical areas. Among the few figures that appear to show significant deviation are the relatively high number of arrivals in mud on birds' feet (6 of them) and the low number internally in birds (1) from boreal regions. Among the pantropical species, repetitive oceanic drift rates notably high (11 introductions out of 27), which merely shows that many of the pantropical species have achieved their wide distribution by virtue of the great efficiency for wide dispersal that is characteristic of oceanic drift.

Another type of computation proved somewhat more significant, and these results are given at the end of the compilation of genera. For each of the seven modes of arrival recognized, the number of contemporary Hawaiian species was divided by the number of immigrants hypothetically necessary to account for those species. Thus, a ratio denoting degree of speciation in relation to each mode of arrival could be obtained. This figure is discussed below under various dispersal headings.

MONOCOTYLEDONS. Pandanaceae: *Freycinetia* (1, BI, 1 e); *Pandanus* (1, DF, 1w). Potamogetonaceae: *Potamogeton* (2, BI, 2w). Ruppiaceae: *Ruppia* (1, BM, 1w). Naiadaceae: *Naias* (1, BM, 1w). Hydrocharitaceae: *Halophila* (1, DF, 1w). Poaceae: *Agrostis* (2, BB, 2e, 1w); *Andropogon* (1, BB, 1w); *Calamagrostis* (2, BB, 2e); *Cenchrus* (1, BB, 3e); *Deschampsia* (1, BB, 3e); *Digitaria* (1, BB, 1w); *Dissochondrus* (1, BB, 1e); *Eragrostis* (1, BI or bb, 12e); *Festuca* (1, BB, 1e); *Garnotia* (1, BB, 1e); *Heteropogon* (1, BB, 1w); *Isachne* (2, BB, 1e, 1w); *Ischaemum* (1, BB, 1w); *Lepturus* (1, DF, 1w); *Microlaena* (1, BB, 1w); *Oplismenus* (1, BB, 1w); *Panicum* (3, BI, BB, BM, 23e;) *Paspalum* (2, BB, 2w); *Poa* (1, BB, 4e); *Sporobolus* (1, BV, 1w); *Trisetum* (1, BB, 2e). Cyperaceae: *Carex* (6, BM, BI, 6e, 3w); *Cladium* (and derivatives *Baumea* and *Vincentia*) (3, BI, 2e, 1w); *Cyperus* (8, BI, BM, 16e, 7w); *Eleocharis* (1, BM, 1w); *Fimbristylis* (1, BM or bi, 1e, 1w); *Gahnia* (2, BI, BM, 6e); *Oreobolus* (1, BB, 1e); *Rhynchospora* (2, BI or bb, 1e, 2w); *Scirpus* (5, BM or BI, 1e, 4w); *Scleria* (1, BM, 1e); *Uncinia* (1, BB, 1w). Arecaceae: *Pritchardia* (1, BI, or dr, 2–30e). Flagellariaceae: *Joinvillea* (1, BI, 1e). Juncaceae: *Luzula* (1, BM, 3a). Liliaceae: *Astelia* (1, BI or bv, 12e); *Dianella* (1, BI, 3e); *Dracaena* (*Pleomele*) (1, BI, 2e); *Smilax* (1, BI, 2e). Iridaceae: *Sisyrinchium* (1, BM, 1e). Orchidaceae: *Anoectochilus* (1, A, 2e); *Habenaria* (1, A, 1e); *Liparis* (1, A, 1e).

DICOTYLEDONS. Piperaceae: *Peperomia* (3, BV, 48e, 2w). Ulmaceae: *Pseudomorus* (1, BI, 1w); *Trema* (1, BI, 1w). Urticaceae: *Neraudia* (1, BI, 9e); *Pilea* (1, BM, 1w); *Pipturus* (1, BV, 13e); *Touchardia* (1, BI, 1e); *Urera* (2, BI, 3e). Santalaceae: *Exocarpus* (1, BI, 3e); *Santalum* (2, BI, 6e). Loranthaceae (Viscaceae): *Korthalsella* (2, BV or BI, 6e, 2w). Polygonaceae: *Polygonum* (1, BI, 1w); *Rumex* (1, DR or bi, 2e). Chenopodiaceae: *Chenopodium* (1, BM, 1e). Amaranthaceae: *Achyranthes* (1, BB, 2e); *Aerva* (1, BB, 1e); *Charpentiera* (1, BI or bm, 3e); *Nototrichium* (1, BB, 5e). Nyctaginaceae: *Boerhavia* (3, BV, 3w); *Pisonia* (3, BV, 3e). Phytolaccaceae: *Phytolacca* (1, BI, 1e). Aizoaceae: *Sesuvium* (1, DF, 1w). Portulacaceae: *Portulaca* (3, DF, 4e, 2w). Caryophyllaceae: *Sagina* (1, BM, 1e); *Schiedea* (and *Alsinodendron*) (1, BM, 32e); *Silene* (1, BI or BM, 5e). Ranunculaceae: *Ranunculus* (1, BM or bb, 2e). Menispermaceae: *Cocculus* (1, BI, 2e). Lauraceae: *Cassytha* (1, DF, 1w); *Cryptocarya* (1, BI, 1e). Capparaceae: *Capparis* (1, DR or dr, 1w). Brassicaceae: *Lepidium* (2, BV, 4e). Droseraceae: *Drosera* (1, BM, 1w). Saxifragaceae: *Broussaisia* (1, BI, 2e). Pittosporaceae: *Pittosporum* (1, BV, 30e). Rosaceae: *Acaena* (1, BB, 2e); *Fragaria* (1, BI, 1w); *Osteomeles* (1, BI, 1w); *Rubus* (1, BI, 2e). Fabaceae: *Acacia* (1, DR, 3e); *Caesalpinia* (2, DF, 2w); *Canavalia* (1, DF or DR, 2e); *Sophora* (1, DR, 4e); *Sesbania* (1, DR, 1e); *Strongylodon* (1, DF, 1w); *Vicia* (1, BI, 1e); *Vigna* (2, DF, 2e, 1w). Geraniaceae: *Geranium* (1, BB, 6e). Zygophyllaceae: *Tribulus* (1, BB, 1w). Rutaceae: *Zanthoxylum* (*Fagara*) (1, BI, 14e); *Pelea* (1, BI, 40e); *Platydesma* (1, BI, 5e). Euphorbiaceae: *Antidesma* (1, BI, 4e); *Claoxylon* (1, BI, 2e); *Drypetes* (1, BI, 1e); *Euphorbia* (1, BI, 30e); *Phyllanthus* (1, BI, 2e). Aquifoliaceae: *Ilex* (1, BI, 1e). Celastraceae: *Perrottetia* (1, BI, 1e). Anacardiaceae: *Rhus* (1, BI, 1e). Sapindaceae: *Alectryon* (1, BI, 2e); *Dodonaea* (1, DF or DR, 3e, 1w); *Sapindus* (1, BI, 1e). Rhamnaceae: *Alphitonia* (1, BI, 1e); *Colubrina* (2, DF, 1e, 1w); *Gouania* (1, DR, 3e). Elaeocarpaceae: *Elaeocarpus* (1, BI, 1e). Malvaceae: *Abutilon* (2, DF, 2e, 1w); *Gossypium* (1, DR, 1e); *Hibiscadelphus* (1, DR, 4e); *Hibiscus* (4, DR, 10e); *Kokia* (1, DR, 4e); *Sida* (2, DF, 2w). Sterculiaceae: *Waltheria* (1, DR, 1w). Theaceae: *Eurya* (1, BI, 2e).

Thymeleaceae: *Wikstroemia* (1, BI, 20e). Flacourtiaceae: *Xylosma* (1, BI, 2e). Cucurbitaceae: *Sicyos* (1, BB or dr, 10c). Myrtaceae: *Syzygium* (*Eugenia*) (2, BI, 4e); *Metrosideros* (1 or 2, A, 5e). Begoniaceae: *Hillebrandia* (1, BM, 1e). Haloragaceae: *Gunnera* (1, BI, 7e). Araliaceae: *Cheirodendron* (1, BI, 5e); *Reynoldsia* (1, BI, 1e); *Tetraplasandra* (1, BI, 10e). Apiaceae: *Peucedanum* (1, DR, 3e); *Sanicula* (1, BB, 4e). Ericaceae: *Vaccinium* (1, BI, 8e). Epacridaceae: *Styphelia* (1, BI, 2e). Primulaceae: *Lysimachia* (2, DF, BM, 12e, 1w). Myrsinaceae: *Embelia* (1, BI, 1e); *Myrsine* (1, BI, 25e). Sapotaceae: *Nesoluma* (1, DR or bi, 1w); *Planchonella* (1, BI, 6e). Ebenaceae: *Diospyros* (*Maba*) (1, BI, 7e). Plumbaginaceae: *Plumbago* (1, BV, 1w). Loganiaceae: *Labordia* (2, BI, 40e). Oleaceae: *Osmanthus* (*Olea, Negrestis*) (1, BI, 1e). Apocynaceae: *Alyxia* (1, BI, 1e); *Ochrosia* (1, DR, 1e); *Pteralyxia* (1, DR, 2e); *Rauwolfia* (1, BI, 7e). Convolvulaceae: *Breweria* (1, BV or dr, 2e); *Cressa* (1, DF, 1w); *Cuscuta* (1, DF or BI, 2e); *Ipomoea* (7, DF, 4e, 5w); *Jacquemontia* (1, DR, 1e). Hydrophyllaceae: *Nama* (1, BB, 1e). Verbenaceae: *Heliotropium* (2, DF, 1e, 1w). Lamiaceae: *Lepechinia* (1, BV, 1w); *Phyllostegia* (1, BI, 40e); *Stenogyne* (1, BI, 40e); *Haplostachys* (1, DR, 3e); *Plectranthus* (1, BB, 1w). Solanaceae: *Lycium* (1, DF, 1w); *Nothocestrum* (1, BI, 6e); *Solanum* (1, BI, 7e). Scrophulariaceae: *Bacopa* (1, BM, 1w). Myoporaceae: *Myoporum* (1, BI, 1e). Gesneriaceae: *Cyrtandra* (1 or 2; BI, 130e). Plantaginaceae: *Plantago* (2, BV, 19e). Rubiaceae: *Bobea* (1, BI, 4e); *Canthium* (1, BI, 1w); *Coprosma* (3, BI or bv, 27e); *Gardenia* (2, BI, 2e); *Hedyotis* (and *Gouldia*) (1, BM or BI, 50e); *Morinda* (1, DR, 1e, 1w); *Nertera* (1, BI, 1w); *Psychotria* (1, BI, 1w); *Straussia* (1, BI, 10e). Campanulaceae: *Brighamia* (1, BI, 1e); *Clermontia* (1, BI or BV, 30e); *Cyanea, Delissea,* and *Rollandia* (1, BI or BV, 48e); *Lobelia* (1, BM, 15e); *Trematolobelia* (1, BM, 3e). Goodeniaceae: *Scaevola* (3, BI and DR, 9e, 1w). Asteraceae: *Adenostemma* (1, BV, 1w); *Argyroxiphium, Dubautia* (incl. *Railliardia*), and *Wilkesia* (1, BV or BB, 37e); *Artemisia* (1, BV, 3e); *Bidens* (1, BB, 30e); *Hesperomannia* (1, BB, 5e); *Lagenophora* (1, BV, 3e); *Lipochaeta* (1, BB, 35e); *Remya* (1, BB, 2e); *Tetramolopium* (1, BB, 10e).

Ratios of numbers of contemporary species in the Hawaiian flora to the numbers of postulated immigrant antecedents for the various dispersal types are as follows:

A: 2.3   BV: 7.4

BB: 4.7   Birds (all means): 5.7

BI: 6.0   DF: 1.4

BM: 4.9   DR: 2.5

Ratio for angiosperm flora as a whole: 4.8

By way of footnotes, the following comments can be offered. A number of species included in Fosberg's list have been omitted because I feel they are dubiously native (perhaps this was unwise: *Argemone* may be native and the species endemic). The *Dubautia-Argyroxiphium-Wilkesia* complex can now be regarded as American in affinities. *Lipochaeta* is also clearly American rather than Indo-Pacific in origin. *Bidens* is probably better regarded as American than Austral, despite its occurrence in the South Pacific. *Trematolobelia* probably does not stem from the same event of introduction as do the Hawaiian species of *Lobelia*.

Comments on Modes of Dispersal in the Hawaiian Flora

AIR FLOTATION

In the Hawaiian angiosperm flora, air flotation appears to have been of minimal importance. The only seed plants that probably arrived by this means are *Metrosideros* (fig. 2.1, top right, bottom left) and the three genera of orchids. Even these could conceivably have arrived in mud on birds' feet. The complexity of *Metrosideros* in the Hawaiian Islands might be more readily explained if there has been more than a single introduction. Hybridization between earlier and later immigrants could account for the existing patterns. Of course this complexity could equally well have resulted from differentiation of *Metrosideros* stocks at different sites within the Hawaiian Islands, followed by redispersal so that distinctive products were juxtaposed and hybridized. The likelihood that *Metrosideros* seeds (fig. 2.1, bottom left) reached the Hawaiian and other Pacific islands by means of wind dispersal is heightened by the experimental work of Corn (1970). Her experiments showed that wind velocities of only 3 to 12 mph are required for *M. polymorpha* seeds to be carried aloft, and that the seeds can survive temperatures of -30 C for at least 6 hr. However, she also found that *Metrosideros* seeds could germinate after soaking in seawater for 39 days plus an additional 7 days during which seeds were dry.

59

FIG. 2.1. Examples suggesting dispersal by wind or by mud on birds' feet. TOP LEFT, *Nephrolepis exaltata* (Davalliaceae); 1955 Puna lava flow, Hawaii. TOP RIGHT, *Metrosideros polymorpha* (Myrtaceae) seedling; 1955 Puna lava flow (photographed 1965). BOTTOM LEFT, *Metrosideros polymorpha* seeds compared to typewriter letters. BOTTOM RIGHT, *Lobelia cardinalis* (Campanulaceae) seeds compared to typewriter letters.

Of the three genera of orchids, *Liparis* and *Habenaria* have reached many islands of the world. Among the reasons these two have attained a wide distribution may be their simple pollination requirements. The Hawaiian climate seems suited to orchids (several species have naturalized), but perhaps the small number of native species may be explained by lack of suitable pollinators. Another possible factor that should be investigated is whether orchid seeds are capable of resisting desiccation and cold temperatures, such as would prevail in the upper atmosphere.

Composites (Asteraceae) are often thought to be well adapted for wind dispersal, but the Hawaiian composites do not seem to have arrived in this manner. Those best fitted for wind dispersal (Cichorieae, Senecioneae, Cynareae) are the groups notably absent. Those three tribes are, however, present in the Juan Fernandez Islands, which are much nearer to mainland source areas. Wind dispersal may be possible for composites with plumose pappus, but the limit for such types is probably much less than the distance between a source area and the Hawaiian Islands. Even species with plumose pappus can be envisaged as capable of transport while enmeshed in bird feathers. Travel of fruits of Asteraceae in bird feathers has, in fact, been observed under ordinary circumstances (Ridley, 1930). Fruits of *Layia platyglossa* (fig. 2.2, bottom left) seem to have this capability, and it is noteworthy that *Layia* belongs to the subtribe Madiinae of Heliantheae, a subtribe represented in the Hawaiian Islands by the endemic genera *Dubautia*, *Argyroxiphium*, and *Wilkesia*.

Ferns in the Hawaiian flora seem suited for air flotation of spores, except for *Marsilea* and possibly, in another group of pteridophytes, *Selaginella*, which has relatively large megaspores. *Marsilea* has been mentioned as a bird-dispersed plant (Proctor and Malone, 1965). One feature of the Hawaiian fern flora that seems exceptional is the very high rate of endemism (70.8 percent). Fosberg (1948) gives it as 64.9 percent, but division of his total for endemic species plus varieties by his total for all native fern species plus varieties yields 70.8 percent. Although this percentage is lower than for Hawaiian angiosperms (94.4 percent according to Fosberg), it is high by comparison with rates of endemism for ferns in other areas, insular or not. Evidently transport to the Hawaiian Islands by air flotation is not as easy or as frequent for fern spores as has generally been supposed. That so few seed plants appear to have arrived by this means in Hawaii indicates the difficulty involved. Possibly spores of wet-forest ferns are more easily killed by desiccation than those of other ferns, and the long route to the Hawaiian Islands would prove fatal for many forest species (see, for example, Lloyd's studies cited in chapter 11). If arrival events of Hawaiian ferns have in fact been infrequent and nonrepetitive (only a single introduction of a species), then isolation leading to endemism could occur.

The significance of air flotation within the present-day Hawaiian flora is probably different from the relatively small role it played in bringing angiosperms to the islands. A clear demonstration is the pattern of vegetation that appears on new lava flows. Despite suggestions by various workers that "succession" in the sense of Clements is involved, the entire matter appears to relate primarily to dispersal ability. The supposed sequence from lichens to trees does not exist. Lichens, many ferns (fig. 2.1, top left), and a scattering of angiosperms appear almost simultaneously. Among the earlier angiosperms visible on lava flows are *Metrosideros* (fig. 2.1, top right), *Dubautia* (*Railliardia*) *ciliolata* or other *Dubautia* species, *Rumex giganteus*, and *Dodonaea viscosa* (or segregate species). The pappus of *Dubautia* permits it to cross relatively short distances by wind, and *Rumex* and *Dodonaea* have winged fruits. These colonists probably arrive on new flows by air flotation and tumbling, despite the likelihood that they arrived ancestrally in the Hawaiian Islands in other ways, except for ferns and *Metrosideros*.

Hawaiian genera with fleshy, attractive fruits, such as *Styphelia*, *Coprosma*, and *Vaccinium* also appear soon on Hawaiian lava flows. These three genera are typically dispersed by frugivorous birds. That both native and introduced birds are quite active in dispersal of seeds is shown by the exceptionally rapid spread of such weeds as *Psidium* and *Schinus*. Consequently, species with fleshy fruits may reach new lava flows only a short time after the wind-dispersed species. A wide variety of species can grow on new lava flows, and succession related to development of soil profiles is not present. Indeed, the Kona forest on Hawaii is among the most magnificent in the Hawaiian Islands, yet it grows on minimal soil of relatively undecomposed lava flows.

The Hawaiian genus *Trematolobelia* is evidently an autochthonous derivative of *Lobelia*. Fruit and seed morphology appear to have altered in the direction of greater efficiency for wind dispersal, at least over relatively short distances (Carlquist, 1962). Circumstances suggest, however, that *Lobelia* arrived in the Hawaiian Islands in mud on birds' feet. *Lobelia* seeds (fig. 2.1, bottom right) are relatively small, and many species of *Lobelia* favor muddy habitats.

AVIAN TRANSPORT OF SEEDS AND FRUITS

Adherence of seeds and fruits to feathers by means of hairs, barbs, bristles, or similar appendages is one of four methods suggested for transport by birds. Indeed, it is the most distinctive of the four, and instances can be recognized with the least probable error. In the Hawaiian flora, most grasses appear to have arrived in this fashion. Other very likely candidates include *Uncinia* (Cyperaceae: fig. 2.2, bottom right), *Sanicula* (Apiaceae), *Acaena* (Rosaceae), and *Bidens* (Asteraceae, fig. 2.2, top left, right). Endemism is notably high in groups dispersed in this manner (see table, p. 58). Of the genera just listed, the species native to the Hawaiian Islands are also apparently endemic. This fact suggests that transport of dry fruits by appendages caught in bird feathers occurs on an infrequent or nonrepetitive basis (see Carlquist [1966a] for a discussion of "single dispersal events"; also chapter 1, principle 3).

In the cases of supposed internal transport of seeds and fruits by birds, alternative interpretations are possible. When seeds are small and fruit parenchyma is even moderately sticky, the possibility definitely exists that seeds could be attached to head feathers when a bird eats portions of a fruit. Such a small-seeded fruit occurs in *Clermontia* (fig. 2.3, top left), in which the baccate fruit breaks open at maturity. Concomitantly with this rupture, latex is released and provides an additional means of adhesion. Also in this category are the other baccate Hawaiian lobelioids (*Cyanea*, *Rollandia*, *Delissea*, and possibly *Brighamia*). Other groups in the Hawaiian flora in which seeds are very small, and thus possibly transported externally as well as internally, include *Vaccinium* (characteristically a food of the Hawaiian goose, according to Guppy [1906]), *Labordia* (and its South Pacific relative, *Geniostoma*), *Cyrtandra*, and *Pipturus*. In addition, some groups with relatively large seeds have fruit parenchyma that is notably viscid; *Korthalsella* and *Peperomia*, for example.

Large-seeded fruits in the Hawaiian flora that are likely to be eaten by

FIG. 2.2. Examples suggesting dispersal in bird feathers by means of barbs or bristles. TOP LEFT, RIGHT, *Bidens pilosa* (Asteraceae). TOP RIGHT shows close-up of barbed awns and hairs on fruit; fruits are 15 mm long. BOTTOM LEFT, fruits of *Layia platyglossa* (Asteraceae); fruits are 10 mm long. BOTTOM RIGHT, *Uncinia tenella* (Cyperaceae), hooked appendages on fruits; portion shown is 3 mm long.

64

birds are either relatively small fruits, if single-seeded, or large because of probable gigantism that is presumably related to loss of dispersibility (Carlquist, 1966b, 1966c; see chapter 11). No single-seeded fruit longer than 1 cm need be postulated as ancestral for any angiosperm in the native, bird-dispersed flora. Most are much smaller; those of *Gunnera* (fig. 2.3, bottom right), for example. Fruits that are virtually black, as in *Scaevola* (fig. 2.3, top right), fruits that are greenish and seemingly inconspicuous (fig. 2.3, bottom left), and fruits in which accessory structures form fleshy attractive organs (fig. 2.4, top right) are among the many types that are adapted for effective dispersal by frugivorous birds. The contrast between a black seed and a fleshy red aril makes *Alectryon* (fig. 2.4, top left) an obvious candidate for dispersal by frugivorous birds, and even shiny, non-fleshy, black seeds in dry capsules, such as those of *Zanthoxylum* (fig. 2.4, bottom left) are often sought. Acquaintance with the Hawaiian flora convinces one that adaptation to dispersal by frugivorous birds is abundantly present. Even if some small-seeded fruits have been transported externally on birds (and that is assumed here), the number of immigrants brought internally in birds still remains the largest single category of dispersal in the Hawaiian flora (38.9 percent, representing at least 101 establishments). This percentage may seem high, but it is lower than the percentage of internally transported immigrants needed to account for other Polynesian floras (fig. 2.7). The fact that internal transport by birds is the only way one can account for two Juan Fernandez natives, *Coprosma* and *Santalum*, demonstrates the tremendous capability of this dispersal method. *Drimys* of the Winteraceae is often thought to be an old, relict genus of angiosperms, but it has fruits ideally suited for birds to eat (fig. 2.4, bottom right). It has probably reached the Juan Fernandez Islands from the South American mainland in this way.

That events of internal transport of seeds by birds are infrequent seems indisputable, but one need not believe that they are therefore nonexistent. Nor should one or need one depend on highly improbable means of transport via birds. Visits by typical frugivorous land birds to the Hawaiian chain are undoubtedly rare; among the stragglers listed by Munro (1960) there are no birds like pigeons. The stragglers include mostly marine birds, waterbirds, and birds of prey. Many ducks and teals are in Munro's list and have been sighted with great regularity, according to

FIG. 2.3. Fruits probably dispersed by frugivorous birds. TOP LEFT, *Clermontia arborescens* (Campanulaceae), fruit 3 cm in diam., seeds visible; Lanai. TOP RIGHT, *Scaevola gaudichaudiana* (Goodeniaceae), fruits 10 cm long; Kohahuanui, Oahu. BOTTOM LEFT, *Phyllostegia racemosa* (Lamiaceae), fleshy seeds (each 8 mm wide) in groups of four; Saddle Road, Hawaii. BOTTOM RIGHT, *Gunnera chilensis* (Haloragaceae), fruits on inflorescence; each fruit 3 mm in diam.; cultivated, Strybing Arboretum, Calif.

ornithologists who have worked in the Hawaiian Islands (Eugene Kridler, personal communication, 1966). Ducks could presumably carry a wide variety of fruits or seeds—particularly from boreal source areas. Ducks would be less likely to transport plants from Indo-Pacific regions, however.

How have the 53 hypothetical Hawaiian immigrants by internal transport in birds arrived from Indo-Malesia? On the answer to this question literally hinges the credibility of long-distance dispersal as a whole, for if these introductions can be satisfactorily explained, others certainly can also. We can, to be sure, imagine atolls that were once high islands and that therefore enhance dispersal possibilities from Indo-Malesia to the Hawaiian Islands. However, such islands are meaningless as stepping-stones in dispersal unless suitable bird vectors exist. As a hint of possible birds, we may consider Peale's observation (reported by Guppy [1906]) that the principal food of the bristle-thighed curlew (*Numenius tahitensis*) is, at least at certain times and in certain localities, fruits of *Canthium odoratum* (Rubiaceae). Many fruits in the Hawaiian flora are comparable to those of *Canthium* in size and morphology. No single-seeded fruit larger than that of *Canthium* need be postulated as ancestral to the Hawaiian flora.

Many botanists probably would not expect shorebirds such as the curlew to eat fruits and seeds to any appreciable extent. Such birds can be omnivores, however, and Peale's report is not an isolated one. One may cite, for example, Munro's (1960) report of consumption of seeds by such shorebirds as the sanderling, the ruddy turnstone, and the stilt. Shorebirds generally are wide ranging; the bristle-thighed curlew, for example, migrates between Alaska and Tahiti; other shorebirds exceed that range.

Some will recall pessimistic estimates (e.g., by Ridley [1930]) on the brief length of time that elapses between ingestion and excretion of fruits by birds. On more than one occasion, however, workers have emphasized mitigating circumstances: the contents of a bird's digestive tract may not be completely emptied, and a few seeds may remain for longer periods; birds may not always fly on empty stomachs, as some workers claim they do; storms may alter habits of digestion, excretion, and preening from what they are normally; and a few seeds may by chance adhere to anal regions. Those who are dubious about the potential of internal transport

FIG. 2.4. Fruits probably adapted to dispersal by frugivorous birds. TOP LEFT, *Alectryon subcinereum* (Sapindaceae), native of Australia, black seeds 7 mm in diam. surrounded by red arils; cultivated, Los Angeles Arboretum. TOP RIGHT, *Exocarpus gaudichaudii* (Santalaceae), fruits 7 mm long, each surrounded by white fleshy cup; Hualalai, Hawaii. BOTTOM LEFT, *Zanthoxylum (Fagara)* (Rutaceae), fruits showing black seeds; Z. *oahuensis*, seeds 8 mm long, above (Oahu), Z. *kauaiensis* below. BOTTOM RIGHT, *Drimys winteri* (Winteraceae), fruiting carpel (12 mm long) and abortive carpel; cultivated, University of California Botanic Garden, Berkeley.

68

of seeds by birds stress the rarity of its occurrence, not realizing that they are thereby supporting an argument for its existence and effectiveness. If this—or any other—kind of dispersal were frequent, isolation leading to speciation and endemism would be impossible. A means of transport does not need to be frequent to be operative.

The potential effectiveness of shorebirds in seed transport is remarkably demonstrated in the experimental work of Proctor (1968) and Vlaming and Proctor (1968). They show that shorebirds have exceptionally long retention of seeds—many seeds were retained more than 100 hr in their experiments, some more than 300 hr. Shorebirds tend to retain larger hard seeds (2–6 mm long) better than do other kinds of birds, according to these authors. Shorebirds do not regurgitate pellets, a characteristic that makes them excellent candidates for seed dispersal, and seeds are excreted in a viable form (only viable seeds were reported in the paper by Vlaming and Proctor [1968]). If one combines experimental data like these (which ought to be extended, however), with known flight speeds of birds (e.g., from Cottam, Scooter, and Williams, 1942), long-distance dispersal of seeds to islands by shorebirds can be said to progress from possibility to the category of reality.

Where dispersal by birds is concerned, one must not dismiss possibilities out of hand. Preest (1963) discounts any possibility for long-distance transport of *Nothofagus* and podocarp seeds, but most of the species he illustrates have small seeds capable of potential dispersal by birds, and only *Podocarpus ferrugineus* has seeds too large for probable long-distance transport. Seeds of *P. ferrugineus* may represent loss of dispersibility by means of autochthonous seed gigantism of the sort described in chapter 11. We have no evidence that all *Nothofagus* and podocarp seeds fail to withstand digestion by birds, or that they always have failed. Indeed, we have evidence to the contrary: *Podocarpus* has reached Tonga, an archipelago of oceanic islands.

The most elusive category of dispersal by birds is inclusion of seeds in mud on birds' feet (or some similar type of external adherence). Main lines of inference leading me to claim this method of dispersal for a particular species include small seed size and the tendency for plants to grow in marshes, mud flats, or along streams. Seeds that could become embedded in mud might, to be sure, easily be eaten by birds and distributed as described in preceding paragraphs. For this and other reasons, arrival in mud on birds' feet is difficult to predicate with any certainty. This method has nonetheless served for an estimated 12.8 percent of the establishments in the Hawaiian angiosperm flora. This percentage is higher than that claimed on most other Polynesian islands, however (fig. 2.7). The importance of this means of transport to the Hawaiian Islands may be related to the likelihood that ducks and other waterbirds assume a greater role, if only by default, in long-distance dispersal here than they do elsewhere. As a corollary, one might infer that transport internally in birds is somewhat more difficult because of remoteness of the Hawaiian Islands.

With respect to avian transport of seeds and fruits that have viscid surfaces, one can cite such clear examples as *Boerhavia* (fig. 2.5, top left, top and center right) and *Pisonia* (fig. 2.5, bottom left, right). Other examples are more subtle or perhaps show a lesser degree of efficiency for this means of travel. The fact that *Boerhavia diffusa* or *Pisonia umbellifera* ranges over wide stretches of the Pacific without even subspecific differentiation among distant islands testifies to the excellence of this dispersal device. Repetitive reintroduction that swamps distinctive characteristics in incipient speciation evidently occurs (apparently the principles offered by Williams [1967] with regard to difficulty in establishment by successive invaders owing to small population size do not apply to strand plants, although they do seem to apply in lizards; see chapter 1). Indeed, *Boerhavia* could probably not persist on some remote atolls where it grows if reintroductions did not provide new genetic material. According to the considerations of MacArthur and Wilson (1963), small remote islands foster a high rate of extinction. A species must therefore be restocked frequently. One may contend that a particular beach species is not "reinforced genetically" by establishment of new arrivals on an island, but rather disappears and then is restocked by a new arrival. However, that does not explain lack of speciation or variation in pantropical strand species, and we must therefore assume that new arrivals of a species can establish and interbreed with individuals of an earlier establishment. One can witness dispersal events in a plant such as *Boerhavia* (see fig. 2.5, top right). Similar evidence could be cited concerning *Pisonia*. A relationship between sooty terns and *Pisonia* on Rose Atoll, near Samoa, is mentioned by Munro

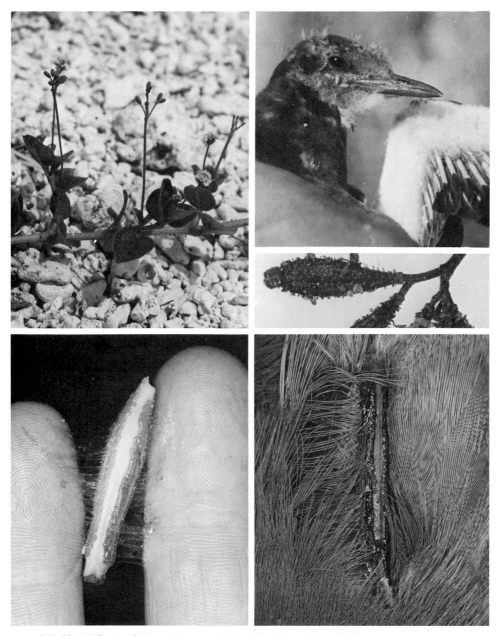

FIG. 2.5. Viscid fruits of Nyctaginaceae adapted for dispersal on feathers. TOP LEFT, TOP AND CENTER RIGHT, *Boerhavia diffusa*; fruits 3 mm long. TOP LEFT, plant growing on East I., French Frigate Shoals, Hawaiian Is. TOP RIGHT, juvenile sooty tern with fruits stuck to feathers (several below eye), East I., French Frigate Shoals. CENTER RIGHT, fruits enlarged; grains of sand adhering to fruits. BOTTOM LEFT, RIGHT, *Pisonia umbellifera*; fruits 5 cm long. BOTTOM LEFT, fruits held between fingers to show viscid material on surfaces; BOTTOM RIGHT, fruit embedded in feathers.

(1960). On Heron Island, Queensland, marine birds become so thickly covered by *Pisonia* fruits that they are immobilized and become prey for rats (R. F. Thorne, personal communication, 1965).

Another plant that seems to owe a wide distribution in the Pacific to viscidity of seeds is *Lepidium*. Viscidity accounts for the occurrence of *Lepidium owaihense* on small and remote islands such as the islets of Pearl and Hermes Reef. On this atoll, I observed it as one of the first colonists on an islet, "South North Island" that was formed recently by shifting of sand within the lagoon and had acquired, as of 1966, only four species of angiosperms. *Lepidium owaihense* is also present in the Line Islands (Christophersen, 1927). Mature seeds of this species become gelatinous when wetted. This characteristic also occurs in other Hawaiian genera, such as *Plantago* (see Hyde, 1970) and *Euphorbia*. *Plantago* is not as wide ranging within the Islands as *Euphorbia*, probably because *Plantago* has narrower ecological requirements rather than because of poorer dispersibility.

Pittosporum has seeds covered with a viscid, almost oily substance. The distribution of this genus in the Pacific includes some rather remote islands and is probably attributable to this seed characteristic. However, *Pittosporum* seeds are black or orange and may therefore be attractive to seed-eating birds. *Pittosporum* rarely grows close to where marine birds nest—although a relationship cannot be ruled out, because marine birds can nest on wet-forest cliffs. In any case, dispersal events would be expected to be relatively infrequent compared to those of *Boerhavia*, so the higher endemism in *Pittosporum* species in the Pacific is understandable.

Shore- and waterbirds do migrate and do eat plant material and are otherwise suitable as vectors, but the question of efficacy of marine birds remains. Do marine birds ever characteristically undertake interisland travel or do they, as is often averred, invariably return to a home island? Recent work shows that considerable interisland travel does occur. For example, on Laysan Island, 69,900 sooty terns were banded. Of these, 611 returns were discovered on Laysan, 7 on Johnston, 4 on Lisianski, and 2 on Kure. Similarly, of the red-footed boobies banded on French Frigate Shoals, 225 returns were noted, but 18 birds traveled to Johnston, 8 to Laysan, 3 to Midway, 2 to Oahu, 2 to Kauai, 1 to Pearl and Hermes Reef, and 1 to Wake Island (Richard Crossin, unpublished data). Interestingly, some of the individuals on Sand Islet of Johnston were later recorded back on French Frigate Shoals. That in a single year so much interisland movement (of which these figures surely represent a modest sampling) occurs in marine birds means that these birds are entirely adequate as potential vectors. The white-tailed tropic bird must travel widely, judging from the observations offered by Munro (1960). Moreover, it nests in cliff faces, such as those of northern Kauai, where it could come into contact with a variety of plants. Because these are windward, north-facing cliffs, wet-forest species (the *Metrosideros* forest) range much closer to sea level than one would expect. Thus it is quite likely that a seabird, the white-tailed tropic bird, might be a vector for upland plants. The sooty-rumped petrel, a Hawaiian endemic, can nest far inland and at altitudes from 500 m to above 2000 m, as in Haleakala (Carlquist, 1970). Suggestions that marine birds can nest inland and that this habit may explain some peculiar distribution patterns in New Zealand are offered by Falla (1960).

Although marine birds would not be expected to eat much vegetable matter, they sometimes do. According to Ridley (1930), gulls eat "all sorts of berries, and especially those of *Empetrum nigrum.*" Interestingly, *Empetrum* is one of the plants that shows the well-known amphitropical distribution in temperate North and South America (Constance, 1963). The Hawaiian species of *Bidens* that show the least loss of dispersibility, and that therefore suggest mode of arrival best, are those that live on bluffs where marine birds nest (see chapter 11). Various instances in which marine birds have been observed to carry seeds and fruits are given by Ridley (1930). Albatrosses (*Diomedea*) and petrels may well have brought disseminules to Macquarie Island and other subantarctic islands, according to Taylor (1954). Turbott (1951) reports the red-billed gull feeding on fruits of *Meryta sinclairii* (Araliaceae); *Meryta* is definitely a tree of forest habitats, not a strand plant.

Despite the cited possibilities for marine birds, most of the arrivals alleged to be bird-dispersed (fig. 2.7) on high oceanic islands are due to shorebirds and, to a lesser extent, waterbirds. The work of Vlaming and Proctor (1968) shows us how experimental evidence can aid in dissipating skepticism about this matter. No doubt, further evidence will reinforce their findings. Thus one already can view the fruition of Ridley's opinion: "There is at first the endeavor in the absence of precise knowledge to disregard the bird and to look for a land-connection. With the increase in our acquaintance with the efficacy of bird-agency in seed distribution there is abandonment of such a view."

OCEANIC DRIFT

Oceanic drift is considered here to include two phenomena—frequent or repetitive drift, and rare or infrequent drift (rafting, for example). The distinction was suggested by the fact that some plants, such as *Ipomoea pes-caprae*, are pantropical and show virtually no variation from one island to another, whereas in the Hawaiian Islands there are littoral or lowland plants that one would say should belong to the drift flora on general considerations but that are higher in endemism and poor at flotation, for example, many Fabaceae (see chapter 11). Experimental proof that some species poor in buoyancy have seeds that nevertheless germinate after soaking in seawater has been given in a number of instances (e.g., Stephens, 1958, 1966; Whitaker and Carter, 1961; Wilson, 1970; Corn, 1973). Further commentary on such species is considered in explanations of the phenomenon of loss of dispersibility (chapter 11).

In cases of repetitive drift, lack of endemism would be expected. Plant species that are obviously adapted to flotation are, of course, familiar. So much literature has been devoted to this topic that at this time a bibliography seems unnecessary to demonstrate the operativeness of this dispersal mechanism. Papers by Stephens (1966) and Gunn (1968) deserve mention, however, for demonstrating the basis of flotation mechanisms. Drift species illustrated here include *Scaevola taccada* (fig. 2.6, top left, right) and *Mucuna* (fig. 2.6, bottom left, right). The first plants on Surtsey, a volcanic islet that emerged from the sea near Iceland, were typical oceanic drift species, such as *Cakile edentula* (Einarsson, 1967).

Less obvious in their dispersal mechanism are certain species of the littoral flora that range widely in the Pacific but that do not show variability or have buoyant fruits and seeds. This is the case in *Portulaca lutea* (fig. 2.6, center left) and *Sesuvium portulacastrum*; vegetative plants prove to be buoyant, however, and one can suspect that this faculty is responsible for introduction of these species to remote islands. Vegetative fragments of these plants can root in the manner of cuttings and are not damaged by seawater, in my observations. Wide-ranging littoral species that may

74

FIG. 2.6. Capability for seawater dispersal of plants. TOP LEFT, *Scaevola taccada* (Goode-niaceae), fruits 14 mm long on branch; Kalapana, Hawaii. TOP RIGHT, fruits (exocarp removed) of *Scaevola taccada* (pale) and *S. plumieri* (dark) float, while seeds of *S. coriacea* sink. CENTER LEFT, *Portulaca lutea* (Portulacaceae); branchlet floating in white enamel tray of water; from

(*continued*)

spread by flotation of vegetative portions include *Lycium sandwichense* (Rapa, Easter I., Tonga, Hawaii) and *Capparis sandwichiana* (Hawaii, Pitcairn I., Tuamotus, Rarotonga, Cook Is.). Vegetative portions of *Lycium* can float. Guppy (1906) reports that fresh fruits and seeds of *Capparis sandwichiana* do not float; my experiments showed, however, that dried fruits can float indefinitely.

An interesting phenomenon apparently not yet appreciated is that seeds in the drift flora are not forced to grow only on the spots where the surf deposits them. On Necker Island, I repeatedly observed seeds of *Mucuna* and *Aleurites* (the former viable, the latter dead) in and around nests of boobies, far above the surf. Apparently boobies habitually pick up these objects and deposit them at nesting sites, a behavior for which I know no explanation. A similar phenomenon was observed among Laysan albatrosses on Pearl and Hermes Reef and other islands of the Hawaiian Leeward chain visited by the *Ironwood* scientific party (of which I was a member) in 1966. Numerous carcasses of Laysan albatrosses were examined in which floating objects—plastic articles, pumice, charcoal—remained within the body cavity. These objects were evidently picked up at sea by adult albatrosses, then fed to albatross chicks that died as a result (Kenyon and Kridler, 1969). This finding suggests that albatrosses might act conjunctively with oceanic drift to abet arrival of floating objects, including seeds.

Rafting or similar infrequent dispersal via oceanic drift is difficult to assess. Guppy (1906) found in Hawaii a few instances of ecological shift of littoral elements into inland sites. I offer the following list of Hawaiian genera in which this shift has happened: *Ochrosia, Dodonaea, Mezoneurum, Canavalia, Erythrina, Sophora,* and *Colubrina*. Endemic species are thereby produced. The ecological shift suggests arrival on the Hawaiian Islands on a very infrequent basis—one can easily hypothesize a single successful Hawaiian establishment for the genera listed above. An allied phenomenon is the notable absence in the native Hawaiian flora of so many mangrove or littoral genera common in the South Pacific—*Barring-*

FIG. 2.6 (*continued*)
Gardner Pinnacles, Hawaiian Is. BOTTOM LEFT, RIGHT, *Mucuna* spp. (Fabaceae), seeds 3–4.5 cm in diam., Pearl and Hermes Reef, Hawaiian Is. BOTTOM LEFT, assortment of seeds washed ashore. BOTTOM RIGHT, seedling on beach: germination successful but plant dying at tip, will not survive.

tonia, Rhizophora, Bruguiera, Avicennia, Suriana, Calophyllum, Terminalia, and *Batis,* to name only a few. Suitable ecological sites are present—at least half of the genera named have been introduced to the Hawaiian Islands by man and have naturalized themselves. The conclusion suggested by both the littoral elements dispersed by single events and now endemic, and the littoral genera expected but not found in the Hawaiian Islands is that these islands are strongly isolated from the South Pacific. The drift flora of the Pacific is primarily a South Pacific flora, which exchanges easily among South Pacific islands and archipelagos, but apparently does not frequently cross the transverse equatorial currents. The westward-running North and South Equatorial Currents, separated by the eastward-running Equatorial Countercurrent, would form a triple barrier to south-to-north flotation of the drift flora.

Factors of Ecology and Distance

To place in relief certain factors that are operative in long-distance dispersal, I have prepared figure 2.7 and the summary in table 2.1. The numbers for the Hawaiian Islands represent a situation in which ecology is richly diversified, area is relatively great, but remoteness also is very great. Samoa differs only in degree of remoteness: it is much closer to source areas of Indo-Malesia. The other two columns list the highest and lowest percentage in the Pacific for each dispersal type, and indicate on what island or archipelago those extremes occur.

One must interpret percentages in a skeptical fashion if the flora is

TABLE 2.1.

Comparisons of Pacific islands with respect to dispersal types

Dispersal type	Hawaiian Islands	Samoa	Lowest Percentage	Highest Percentage
A	1.4	15.1	0 (Eq. atolls)	18.0 (San Clemente I.)
BB	12.8	4.0	0 (Eq. atolls)	29.0 (J. Fernandez Is.)
BI	38.9	50.8	0 (Oeno I.)	50.8 (Samoa, Tonga)
BM	12.8	5.5	2.8 (Rarotonga)	21.0 (J. Fernandez Is.)
BV	10.3	4.3	2.1 (Cocos Is.)	15.4 (Oeno I.)
DF	14.3	17.8	3.0 (J. Fernandez Is.)	63.6 (Eq. atolls)
DR	8.5	3.5	0 (Cocos Is.)	8.5 (Hawaii)

based on a small number of original immigrants. Still correlations are remarkably clear. In the case of air flotation, a low percentage is expected on atolls simply because atoll plants are chiefly drift plants. Oceanic drift

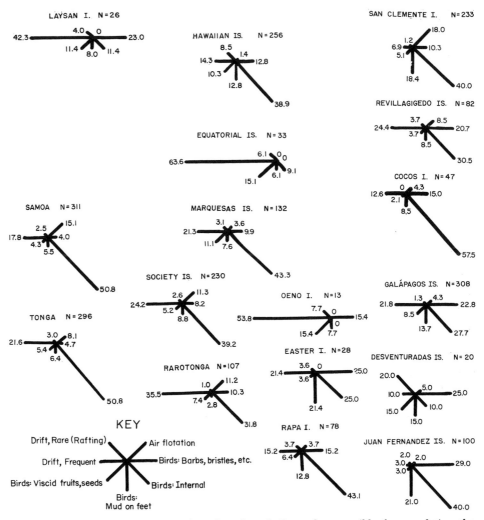

FIG. 2.7. Diagrammatic representation of modes of dispersal responsible for populating the islands of the eastern Pacific and Polynesia with seed plants. Diagrams are arranged geographically, although distances are distorted. For each flora, the number of immigrants presumed necessary to account for the contemporary native species has been calculated (N). Of these, the percentage thought to have arrived according to each of the seven methods shown in the key has been calculated and presented graphically. Only native species are included. The figures for the Hawaiian Islands include the Leeward chain; figures for Laysan alone are also presented.

is ecologically linked in plant species to preference for the beach habitat—
and atolls are, of course, nothing but mid-ocean beaches. Aerial flotation
would be a poor method for populating atolls and remote islands with
flowering plants because it operates so poorly across long oceanic distances.
Thus we can anticipate the very low percentages on the Hawaiian Islands
and on Rapa. The high percentage on San Clemente reflects its nearness
to a continent. Relative nearness to a source area aids in air flotation of
seeds to Samoa (the high figure is based chiefly on orchids). The figure
for the Revillagigedos (8.5 percent) is moderately high, indicating a threshold value for dispersal by air flotation: islands farther from the mainland
or other source areas than the Revillagigedos may be expected to have
minimal percentages for air flotation—perhaps 2 percent.

Bristly or barbed fruits seem best suited for dispersal to islands where
birds are by far the most important vectors, and the high figure for the
Juan Fernandez Islands is understandable. High figures also occur on
islands near sources—the Revillagigedos, the Desventuradas, and the
Galápagos, for example. These are dry islands, however, and the dispersal
of bristly or barbed fruits may represent successful dispersal of dry-forest
elements, as opposed to the fleshy fruit types found in wet forests. The
efficacy of transport of barbed or bristly fruits lessens with distance,
although not nearly as sharply as that of air flotation. The low figure for
atolls reflects this trend, but perhaps more importantly reflects the overwhelming importance of oceanic drift for atolls and the necessarily lesser
significance of other means of transport.

The ecological correlation of oceanic drift with atoll habitat certainly
explains the low figure for internal transport of fruits and seeds in birds to
atolls. Fleshy-fruited species are most characteristic of wet or moderately
dry forest, so that the high percentage for Samoa is almost predictable. The
high figure for Tonga may be unexpected in view of Tonga's less favorable
ecology (although there are forested uplands on some islands, such as Eua),
but nearness to source area undoubtedly favors this mode of transport for
Tonga, which is close to the rich flora of Fiji. That the Hawaiian Islands
show only relatively slight diminution in internal transport by birds means
that this mode of transport is entirely effective over long distances, provided the habitat for fleshy-fruited species—the wet forest, chiefly—is
present on the recipient island, as is true in Hawaii. In this connection,

one cannot help noticing that the Galápagos Islands are low in arrivals by means of internal transport in birds and also have no true rain forest. A rather high figure might not be expected for San Clemente Island, but this dry island is so near to mainland areas that, according to my interpretations, small-seeded plants with dry capsules (e.g., *Brodiaea*) may have arrived there by means of seed-eating birds. There are also, however, fleshy-fruited species in the San Clemente flora: among them, *Rhus*, *Heteromeles*, and *Ribes*. There are even a few fleshy-fruited species on atolls— *Solanum nelsoni* and *Santalum ellipticum* on islands of the Leeward Hawaiian chain, for example.

Not much discrimination among islands can be claimed for the figures on arrival in mud on birds' feet; the figures are all relatively low and thus deviations are not strongly significant. The low figure for Rarotonga may reflect the limited uplands of that island, with fewer "muddy" habitats. The Juan Fernandez Islands, on the contrary, have a proportionately high area of wet, scrubby uplands suited for plants of muddy regions. The low figure for Samoa could merely indicate that arrival of fleshy-fruited trees is so successful that other forms of travel are inevitably of lesser significance. The high percentage on San Clemente may reflect closeness to a continental area, occasional visits by passerine birds, and a nonforest ecology (which does have a moist winter, however). The high percentage on Easter Island (21.4) would be unexpected unless one had noted a distinctive habitat on that island: the muddy margins of a crater lake.

Viscid-fruited and viscid-seeded species are not a homogeneous group, ecologically, and discerning significance is less easy. Some are beach plants, like *Boerhavia* and *Pisonia*, so that the high figure on Oeno, a raised atoll, is understandable, and low percentages on higher wet islands are to be expected. Such forest trees as *Pittosporum* have this method of dispersal, as do perhaps *Korthalsella*, *Vaccinium*, and the baccate Hawaiian lobelioids. This fact may explain the relatively high figure for the Hawaiian Islands; where distance is a problem, sticky seeds—presumably capable of almost indefinite transoceanic travel on birds—would be more successful immigrants by default. This latter aspect, as well as wet-forest ecology, may explain low figures for Samoa and Cocos, where distance is not a great problem. In angiosperms generally, dispersal by means of viscid seeds is fairly infrequent, and thus we would not expect it to bulk large at all in

insular floras; it probably is greater in insular than in mainland floras because of its efficiency across great distances.

The highest percentage of arrival by means of repetitive drift is found,
predictably, on the atolls, most of which are "all beach." There is very
little beach area on the Juan Fernandez Islands, so the low percentage
there is no surprise. A similar situation exists on Rapa. Extensiveness of
the available beach habitat on particular Pacific islands appears to be
almost perfectly correlated with their percentages of drift plants. The high
figure for the Galápagos may be an example; also, the xeric lowlands of
the Galápagos, beach or otherwise, might be said to favor strand plants,
which are basically halophytic in ecology.

Infrequent or single-event drift (perhaps rafting in some cases) is
high in the Hawaiian Islands because these islands are so well cut off by
the transverse equatorial currents, as mentioned earlier, from entrance of
South Pacific elements. The data of Stephens (1966) are pertinent here,
because the cottons evidently do not face this problem. Dispersal of the
cottons is from North and South American coasts, via westward-running
currents: South Pacific islands are populated via the South Equatorial Current, North Pacific islands via the North Equatorial Current. Nonetheless,
Hawaii is not truly in the range of even the North Equatorial Current, and
the endemism of its *Gossypium* is understandable.

The consequences of rare events of oceanic drift in permitting or
promoting ecological shift and endemism in the Hawaiian Islands and a
few other islands are discussed in chapter 11. One must also note that not
all plants of the drift flora are suited to areas where they arive. *Mucuna*
and *Entada*, although frequently found on Hawaiian beaches, do not form
mature plants if they germinate (fig. 2.6, bottom left, right). These plants
do occur in Hawaii near the ocean, but in shady forests where vines may
overhang the water and release seeds into the sea, or into streams.

In short, the overriding role that ecology of the recipient island plays
in dispersal cannot be strongly enough stressed. This aspect of my (1967)
paper has been confirmed by the study of Whitehead and Jones (1969) on
Kapingamarangi. Odd disjunct distributions may be the result of chance
in some cases, but far more frequently they result from disjunctions in
suitable ecological conditions. We should first suspect this latter explanation, since long-distance dispersal is not, apparently, at all difficult for

many groups of plants. Ecological specificity may, in turn, be based on geology and the geological history of an area; examples are cited, for example, by Burrows (1964, 1965) in the New Zealand flora.

Long-Distance Dispersal to Regions Other Than Polynesia

MASCARENE ISLANDS

If, as I have stated earlier (1966a), disharmony is an indication that certain plants and animals are positively adapted to long-distance dispersal, these species ought to be more conspicuous on oceanic islands. A phenomenon that might not have been predicted, however, is the tendency of the Mascarene flora and fauna to be somewhat "Polynesian" in character. Computations demonstrate this tendency. Despite the fact that the Seychelles, Réunion, Mauritius, and Rodriguez are close to Madagascar and Africa, their floras contain many of the genera characteristic of Polynesia. The islands named are included in Baker's (1877) flora. Of the 408 genera of indigenous flowering plants in this flora, 158 occur also in Polynesia (Samoa to Easter I. on the east, Hawaii on the north, Rapa on the south). When one compares smaller floristic units, this similarity becomes even more striking. If one regards 210–216 genera of flowering plants as ancestors of the Hawaiian angiosperm flora, 115, or 53–56 percent, of these also occur in the Mascarene flora. To be sure, a number of these genera are elements of the drift flora that might be expected to be widespread on islands. But many genera common to the two areas are not drift plants at all; for example, *Dianella, Dracaena, Astelia, Pipturus, Peperomia, Diospyros* (including *Maba*), *Myrsine, Psychotria, Canthium, Pittosporum, Elaeocarpus,* and *Zanthoxylum* (*Fagara*). One would certainly not expect to find American and boreal elements on the Mascarene Islands, owing to the enormous distance involved. Likewise, one would not expect African elements in the Hawaiian flora. If one deducts these elements, respectively, the degree of similarity between the Mascarenes and Polynesia is really quite high, and is an expression of the portion of the Indo-Malesian flora that is adapted for long-distance dispersal. Interestingly, there is a marked zoological counterpart to the floristic phenomenon. Gressitt (1956) shows a Pacific-Mascarene distribution for several insect groups, such as Chrysomelidae-Hispinae and Cerambycidae. Mascarene-Polynesian affinity can even be shown in land shells. *Elasmias* (Tornatellinidae) is an insular Pacific genus that has an extension on the Mascarene islands (Cooke and Kondo, 1960). The family Tornatellinidae seems strongly adapted for long-distance dispersal, judging from the distribution maps these authors offer.

INTERCONTINENTAL DISPERSAL

Intercontinental dispersal is potentially very important; the degree and nature of possible intercontinental long-distance dispersal bears a direct relationship to the evidence on which rests the probability of continental drift, or the geological epochs at which it occurred. Also in question are theories of dispersal between mountains on the same or different continents. One area that has been of critical significance is the disjunction between two pockets of mediterranean climate: western North America and central Chile (and adjacent regions). This area has been the subject of a review and individual papers by Chambers (1963), Constance (1963), Heckard (1963), Ornduff (1963) and Raven (1963b). Difficulties in interpreting the disjunction as the product of dispersal by bird agencies have been hinted by Constance (1963) and stated rather more strongly by Cruden (1966). Although Cruden claims not to be motivated by disbelief in birds as potential vectors, he evidently wishes us to consider an alternative hypothesis—a series of mountaintops as stepping-stones across the tropics, bridging the two temperate regions. Although the amphitropical disjunction needs a more thorough examination to determine whether seeds or fruits of those particular genera and species are adapted to long-distance dispersal (as I believe they are), the following comments can be offered to support the concept of birds as dispersal agents. The background of studies in Polynesia and in the Mascarenes is an essential ingredient, for distant oceanic islands provide compelling evidence of the realities of long-distance dispersal.

1. The distances of the North America–South America disjunction are of the same level of magnitude as those of the America-Polynesia disjunction. If 20 percent (at least 52 immigrants) of the establishments arrived in Hawaii from American sources, mostly via birds, then the amphitropical American disjunction does not seem highly improbable on the

basis of long-distance dispersal. Moreover, the North America–Hawaii or North America–Polynesia disjunction is the result of one-way dispersal, whereas both western North America and Chile have mutually been able to serve as potential source areas for the amphitropical disjuncts, doubling the chance of successful long-distance dispersal.

2. The list of plants showing amphitropical disjunction is very similar to the list of migrants from American or boreal regions to Hawaii: *Artemisia*, *Aster*, *Caesalpinia*, *Carex*, *Fragaria*, *Geranium*, *Lepidium*, *Luzula*, *Poa*, *Ranunculus*, *Rubus*, *Sanicula*, *Scirpus*, *Stipa*, *Vaccinium*, and *Viola* (not to mention "close" groups, such as *Madia* in the Americas, and *Dubautia* in Hawaii). Moreover, fruit morphology is very similar to that of the America-Hawaii disjuncts. The list of genera showing both disjunctions indicates clearly an exceptional ability for long-distance dispersal. A few genera in either disjunct pattern could be said to have "no obvious dispersal mechanism," but this would be a mistake. Anything that has been able to cross 2000 or more miles of ocean to Hawaii must have an effective dispersal mechanism (but not necessarily, of course, so efficient that more than a single successful establishment would occur). We must remember that birds may eat, and carry internally, fruits other than those which are fleshy and brilliantly colored. For example, ducks eat and transport a wide variety of fruits and seeds that are inconspicuous and often greenish or brownish and woody in texture (Ridley, 1930). There is, of course, the possibility that in a few cases the lack of a dispersal mechanism might indicate a loss of dispersibility (Carlquist, 1966b, 1966c; see chapter 11).

3. No "mountaintop stepping-stones" have been proposed for the North America–Hawaiian Islands disjunction, nor are they necessary to explain the dispersal that has occurred. The proposal of intervening mountaintops to serve as way stations in the amphitropical disjunction also seems unnecessary. At best, it merely cuts long-distance dispersal into a series of shorter segments, and thus demands successive events of long-distance dispersal while at the same time making the process less probable, for reasons given in comment 4.

4. Mountaintops in the tropics are not equivalent to temperate climates, montane or otherwise (see chapter 14). They differ particularly with regard to seasonal changes in temperature and day-length, but also

in rainfall patterns, soils, etc. To accept a mountaintop hypothesis, we must expect temperate-zone plants to make numerous adaptations to tropical mountains. This is not unreasonable, for some have done that, but to explain the amphitropical disjunction by the mountaintop hypothesis we must invoke something more preposterous: after the plants have adapted to tropical mountains, we must imagine that they can readapt to temperate-zone conditions in the opposite hemisphere—and these adaptations and retrograde changes are numerous. They must then disappear in the tropics yet appear as closely related species (congeners) only in the two mediterranean pockets. If the roster of amphitropical disjuncts did adapt to the tropical mountaintops, why did they disappear so completely there? The data from Polynesia show just the reverse of the mountaintop hypothesis. They show that intervening way stations (e.g., Samoa as a point between Fiji and Tahiti) have retained more immigrants than the end points. Moreover, relatively little ecological change has occurred in most angiosperm stocks on islands (the Hawaiian Islands are exceptional in this regard). The various authors of the papers cited on the amphitropical herbaceous disjuncts emphasize the genetic closeness of Chilean to California plants, or vice versa, evidencing remarkably little evolutionary change since the time of disjunction. However, if we accept mountaintops as way stations, at the very least we must imagine considerable physiological change, first progressive then retrograde, no evidence of which is now visible. The morphology of the amphitropical disjuncts hints at no period of residence on tropical mountaintops. The amphitropical pattern, according to the data of the authors cited, suggests great recentness compared with Polynesian patterns, which themselves must be fairly recent.

5. The islands of Polynesia have received a relatively large quantity of waif disseminules; what has been severely limiting seems not lack of transport, but ecological conditions and sufficient land area suitable for establishment and then survival over a number of generations. The patterns of figure 2.7 that were discussed earlier show that Pacific islands have "selected out" from a flow of immigrants those that are exactly suited ecologically to recipient islands. The disjunction between mediterranean pockets in North and South America occurs precisely because ecological conditions are so nearly identical in the two regions, yet are unlike in intervening areas. If plants had to adapt to equatorial alpine peaks, some

relicts of this supposedly recent migration ought to be there still. Instead, the floras of the equatorial Andean highlands are quite different (chapter 14).

6. Cruden (1966) has assessed his evidence concerning bird groups in a very conservative fashion. There certainly are, as his paper indicates, some species that could serve as vectors, by virtue of their migratory patterns. The point is not how many species do, in fact, have this route, but how many individuals travel it. If one migratory bird species followed the Cordilleran route annually in sufficient numbers, we would have the vectors needed. Another question, evidently not investigated, is whether the birds known to follow this migratory route come into contact with seeds and fruits of any of the species of plants concerned. Unless this question can be answered negatively, we cannot dismiss the probability that birds utilizing the Cordilleran flyway have served as vectors.

The tropical South America–western Africa (or even eastern Africa) disjuncts among flowering plants are often cited as corroborative evidence —together with geology (although rarely by one who knows both fields well)—as evidence of continental drift (e.g., Corro, 1964; Aubréville, 1969). Do the angiosperm elements in common between South America and Africa suggest that these continents did drift apart? Thorne (1972) has reviewed these angiosperm patterns in a comprehensive and detailed fashion that supersedes all prior essays on this topic. Thorne has demonstrated that:

1. We can disregard the 110 species common to tropical West Africa and tropical America; they are almost certainly the result of human introductions or recent long-distance dispersal by good vectors, because (if not weeds) they grow in aquatic, maritime, riparian, or other habitats likely to be visited by migratory birds on a regular basis. One species with a wide range on both continents is *Rhipsalis baccifera*, the only cactus known to occur in a supposedly native state in the Old World. This is not conceivably a relict distribution, because *Rhipsalis* is a highly specialized cactus, well-suited to long-distance dispersal (it may even have been introduced to Africa within historical time, possibly by man), and because it has a wide distribution in both Africa and the New World, without any hint of subspeciation between the continents. That only one species of

this family with perhaps 2000 species in 100 genera has crossed the Atlantic is typical of many patterns we find at the generic level.

2. There are 12 angiosperm families restricted primarily to Africa plus South America. This number is suspiciously small, yet these families must be the ones to provide the bulk of evidence if continental drift had acted to produce floristic disjunctions between the two continents. Eight of the families (Bromeliaceae, Cactaceae, Caricaceae, Humiriaceae, Loasaceae, Mayacaceae, Rapateaceae, and Vochysiaceae) are essentially American: they include at least 3500 species, of which no more than 10 occur in Africa. If continental drift separated portions of these families, shouldn't the development on both continents be more nearly balanced? Evidently these patterns are not the result of continental drift; the barrier to migration across the Atlantic is great and explains the patterns. One of the eight primarily American families (Cactaceae) has been discussed above. All 12 families seem well-suited to long-distance dispersal, so the finding that a few species have crossed the Atlantic is not surprising. A typical case is Rapateaceae: the sole African representative, *Maschalocephalus dinklagei* (the genus is monotypic), a plant of Liberian marshes, is (for this family) a highly specialized plant very close to the genera geographically nearest it in South America—*Windsorina* and *Potarophytum* (Maguire et al., 1958; Carlquist, 1961, 1966d). If continental drift were involved, one would expect not only better balance on both sides of the Atlantic, but also more primitive portions of these families in both continents, not just one specialized genus. Rapateaceae are usually marsh plants, so dispersal mechanisms are easy to envisage. Other families also have clear means of dispersal: Humiriaceae and Vochysiaceae have buoyant fruits, for example; Mayacaceae are aquatic plants likely to be distributed by waterbirds.

The four families that are about equally divided between South America and Africa (Hydnoraceae, Canellaceae, Turneraceae, and Velloziaceae) are not difficult to explain. There is one genus of Hydnoraceae (*Hydnora*) in Africa, and one in South America (*Prosopanche*). Small-seeded parasitic plants often have very wide distributions with large disjunctions—*Pilostyles* in the Rafflesiaceae, for example, has much greater disjunctions than does Hydnoraceae.

3. Not only is there strong imbalance in representation between African and American portions of families and genera on both continents, and not only are the elements that the continents have in common notably good at long-distance dispersal (the mangrove genera *Lacuncularia* and *Combretum,* for example), but they also are all representatives of what are commonly termed "specialized" families (i.e., families with numerous characteristics considered specialized for angiosperms). "Relict" genera and families certainly do not link Africa and South America. Among conifers, Araucariaceae links all continents equally, for it is present or known in fossil form on all of them. The remaining conifers, especially genera with primitive characteristics, are notably absent in Africa. Among angiosperms, Australasia–South America patterns are seen in the "primitive" families Winteraceae, Chloranthaceae, and Monimiaceae. Those three families can be envisioned as achieving their Australasian–South American distribution by long-distance dispersal: *Drimys* (fig. 2.4, bottom right) is also suited for this. The "annonalean" or "ranalian" families present in South America have, it seems, not come via Africa, and Africa is notable for lack of these families.

4. Although there is definite affinity between South America and one or more regions of Africa (including Madagascar) in terms of angiosperm genera (111 are limited to this distribution pattern), stronger affinities link these continents with other regions than each other. As Thorne (1972) states, "African floristic relationships thus are also much stronger with Asia than with America," and he notes that the genera in common between Africa and South America are far outweighed by those that have failed to cross the Atlantic.

5. On the basis of size and ecology, one would expect a much larger affinity between South America and Africa on the basis of long-distance dispersal alone. Both Africa and South America have broad expanses of similar ecological zones, and both have enormous land areas that can serve as source and target (recipient) areas for disseminules. The presence of such a small degree of affinity between Africa and South America despite their similarities may be due to the fact that both of these continents have harmonic flora, and invasion of one by disseminules from the other is not as easy as invasion of a relatively "open" oceanic island.

If the floras of the Hawaiian and other Pacific islands can be explained by long-distance dispersal, intercontinental disjunctions surely can be. It is somewhat mysterious that those who study intercontinental disjunctions do not appear to compare their questions and data to situations on insular areas. The Hawaiian Islands are much more remote, have a smaller target area for disseminules, and have existed for a much shorter period of time than have the North America–South America or the South America–Africa land areas on which disjunctions are cited. As a footnote, instances of long-distance dispersal *within* continents often escape notice but are equally significant (Wilson, 1970). Gillett (1965) has cited a single species (*Trigonella laciniata*) that has made a dramatic leap within Africa. The African equatorial peaks and the Ethiopian highlands are pertinent. Not only have they acquired elements from the temperate floras of Europe and South Africa by long-distance dispersal, but also dispersal among these peaks (which are by no means close) has occurred within relatively recent time (see chapter 14).

The concept of continental drift is supported by an increasing number of workers. However, most estimates of its time scale place its occurrence at rather ancient dates compared to the development of modern angiosperm floristic assemblages. I wish to underline strongly that those who compile evidence pointing toward continental drift are doing themselves a disservice when they cite angiosperm floras as evidence. If intercontinental affinities can be explained by long-distance dispersal, the fabric of evidence for continental drift is only weakened by using angiosperms as examples. If continental drift has occurred, the reliable evidence for it will surely come primarily from geology and geophysics, not from biology.

Concluding Remarks

Although one could become overenthusiastic about the occurrence of long-distance dispersal, this phenomenon obviously plays a supreme role for oceanic islands, and at least a significant role in the case of "continental" islands and continental masses. Most biologists appear to have little difficulty in accepting concepts of long-distance dispersal, but a few (mostly botanists) have been reluctant. Thorne (1972) notes with delightful irony how some botanists find the transport of a tiny seed on a bird—

a seemingly casual event—preposterous, yet plunge headlong into hypotheses that require incredibly drastic geological upheavals over exceptionally short periods of time. Oceanic islands are, to me, archives of the fact of long-distance dispersal and the way in which it works and has worked in the past. Matched ecology of donor and recipient areas appears to be a requirement of prime importance, far more than efficiency of vectors. The vectors are omnipresent. Some, to be sure, do not operate over indefinite distances, and some plant and animal groups are poorly adapted for long-distance dispersal. Still, when assessing floristic and faunistic composition of islands and other areas, should we not begin by considering the positive hypothesis that dispersal over distances can occur, rather than beginning with a null hypothesis? Biologists seem occasionally piqued that, in dealing with long-distance dispersal, we are dealing with a phenomenon that involves chance and is not subject to precise and orderly principles in the same way that embryo development of vertebrates is. That should not detract, however, from the reality of the phenomenon. We must also remember that all plant and animal groups are capable of evolving with respect to dispersal mechanisms. Too often, I note the tendency to imply, if only by default, that a given plant or animal group can change in innumerable ways but its dispersal mechanism and dispersibility remain precisely the same. The data of chapters 11 and 12 are offered as one corrective to this implication, and should be considered, in fact, as a further source of evidence that long-distance dispersal is operative.

References

Aubréville, A. 1969. Essais sur la distribution et l'histoire des angiospermes tropicales dans le monde. *Adansonia* 9:189–247.

Baker, J. C. 1877. *Flora of Mauritius and the Seychelles*. London, L. Reeve & Co.

Balgooy, M. M. J. van. 1960. Preliminary plant-geographical analysis of the Pacific. *Blumea* 10:385–430.

Bannerman, D. A., and W. M. Bannerman. 1965. *A history of the birds of Madeira, the Desertas, and the Porto Santo Islands*. Edinburgh and London, Oliver & Boyd.

Bold, H. C., M. R. Brown, and D. A. Larson. 1964. Airborne algae: Their abundance and heterogeneity. *Science* 143:583–85.

Brown, F. B. H. 1931. Flora of southeastern Polynesia. I. Monocotyledons. *Bishop Mus. Bull.* 84:1–194.

Brown, F. B. H. 1935. Flora of southeastern Polynesia. III. Dicotyledons. *Bishop Mus. Bull.* 130:1–386.

Brown, R. M., Jr. 1971. Studies of Hawaiian fresh water and soil algae. I. The atmospheric dispersal of algae and fern spores across the island of Oahu, Hawaii. In *Contributions to phycology*, ed. B. C. Parker and R. M. Brown, Jr. Houston, Tex., Allen Press.

Brown, W. L., Jr., and E. O. Wilson. 1965. Character displacement. *Syst. Zool.* 5:49–64.

Burrows, C. J. 1964. Some discontinuous distributions of plants within New Zealand and their ecological significance. Part I. *Tuatara* 12:125–33.

Burrows, C. J. 1965. Some discontinuous distributions of plants within New Zealand and their ecological significance. Part II. *Tuatara* 13:9–29.

Carlquist, S. 1961. Pollen morphology of Rapateaceae. *Aliso* 5:39–66.

Carlquist, S. 1962. *Trematolobelia:* Seed dispersal; anatomy of fruits and seeds. *Pacific Sci.* 16:126–34.

Carlquist, S. 1966a. The biota of long-distance dispersal. I. Principles of dispersal and evolution. *Quart. Rev. Biol.* 41:247–70.

Carlquist, S. 1966b. The biota of long-distance dispersal. II. Loss of dispersibility in Pacific Compositae. *Evolution* 20:30–48.

Carlquist, S. 1966c. The biota of long-distance dispersal. III. Loss of dispersibility in the Hawaiian flora. *Brittonia* 18:310–35.

Carlquist, S. 1966d. Anatomy of Rapateaceae—roots and stems. *Phytomorphology* 16:17–38.

Carlquist, S. 1967. The biota of long-distance dispersal. V. Plant dispersal to Pacific islands. *Bull. Torrey Bot. Club* 94:129–62.

Carlquist, S. 1970. *Hawaii, a natural history.* New York, Natural History Press.

Chambers, K. L. 1963. Amphitropical species pairs in *Microseris* and *Agoseris* (Compositae: Cichorieae). *Quart. Rev. Biol.* 38:124–40.

Chang, T. 1967. A preliminary survey of airborne algae in the Taipei atmosphere. *Taiwania* 13:1–9.

Cheeseman, T. F. 1902. The flora of Rarotonga, the chief island of the Cook group. *Trans. Linnaean Soc.,* ser. 2, Bot., 6:261–313.

Christophersen, E. 1927. Vegetation of Pacific equatorial islands. *Bishop Mus. Bull.* 44:1–79.

Christophersen, E. 1935. Flowering plants of Samoa. *Bishop Mus. Bull.* 128:1–221.

Christophersen, E. 1938. Flowering plants of Samoa. II. *Bishop Mus. Bull.* 154:1–77.

Christophersen, E., and E. L. Caum. 1931. Vascular plants of the Leeward Islands, Hawaii. *Bishop Mus. Bull.* 81:1–41.

Constance, L. 1963. Amphitropical relationships in the herbaceous flora of the Pacific coast of North and South America: A symposium. Introduction and historical review. *Quart. Rev. Biol.* 38:109–16.

Cooke, C. M., Jr., and Y. Kondo. 1960. Revision of Tornatellinidae and Achatinellidae (Gastropoda, Pulmonata). *Bishop Mus. Bull.* 221:1–303.

Corn, C. 1973. Seed dispersal methods in Hawaiian *Metrosideros*. American Institute of Biological Sciences, 25th anniversary volume, in press.

Corro, G. del. 1964. La gondwania: el antigue contienente australe. *Mus. Argentina Cienç. Natur. "Bernardino Rivadavia" Publ.* 12:1–90.

Cottam, C., C. Scooter, and C. S. Williams. 1942. Flight and running speeds of birds. *Wilson Bull.* 54:121–31.

Cruden, R. W. 1966. Birds as agents of long-distance dispersal for disjunct plant groups of the temperate western hemisphere. *Evolution* 20:517–32.

Deignan, H. G. 1963. Birds in the tropical Pacific. In *Pacific basin biogeography*, ed. J. L. Gressitt, pp. 263–69. Honolulu, Bishop Museum Press.

Drake del Castillo, E. 1893. *Flore de la Polynésie française*. Paris, G. Masson.

Einarsson, E. 1967. The colonization of Surtsey, the new volcanic island, by vascular plants. *Aquilo, ser. Bot.* 6:172–82.

Falla, R. A. 1960. Oceanic birds as dispersal agents. *Proc. Roy. Soc. London,* ser. B, 152:655–59.

Fleming, C. A. 1962. History of the New Zealand land bird fauna. *Notornis* 9:270–74.

Fosberg, F. R. 1948. Derivation of the flora of the Hawaiian Islands. In *Insects of Hawaii*, vol. 1: *Introduction*, E. C. Zimmerman, pp. 107–19. Honolulu, University of Hawaii Press.

Fosberg, F. R. 1963. Plant dispersal in the Pacific. In *Pacific basin biogeography*, ed. J. L. Gressitt, pp. 273–82. Honolulu, University of Hawaii Press.

Fulton, J. D. 1966a. Microorganisms of the upper atmosphere. III. Relationship between altitude and micropopulation. *Appl. Microbiol.* 14:237–40.

Fulton, J. D. 1966b. Microorganisms of the upper atmosphere. IV. Microorganisms of a land air mass as it traverses an ocean. *Appl. Microbiol.* 14:241–44.

Fulton, J. D. 1966c. Microorganisms of the upper atmosphere. V. Relationship between frontal activity and the micropopulation at altitude. *Appl. Microbiol.* 14:245–50.

Fulton, J. D., and R. B. Mitchell. 1966. Microorganisms of the upper atmosphere. II. Microorganisms in two types of air masses at 690 meters over a city. *Appl. Microbiol.* 14:232–36.

Gillett, J. B. 1965. *Trigonella laciniata* L. in Zambia—a probable instance of long-distance transport of seeds by birds. *Kew Bull.* 19:387–88.

Gregory, P. H., and J. L. Monteith, eds. 1967. *Airborne microbes*. Cambridge, Cambridge University Press.

Gressitt, J. L. 1956. Some distribution patterns of Pacific island faunac. *Syst. Zool.* 5:11–47.

Gunn, C. R. 1968. Stranded seeds and fruits from the southeastern shore of Florida. *Gard. Jour.* (N.Y. Bot. Gard.) Mar./Apr. 1968:43–54.

Guppy, H. B. 1897. On the postponement of the germination of seeds of aquatic plants. *Proc. Roy. Soc. Phys. Sci.* 13:344–59.

Guppy, H. B. 1906. *Observations of a naturalist in the Pacific between 1896 and 1899*, vol. II: *Plant dispersal*. London, Macmillan & Co.

Heckard, L. R. 1963. The Hydrophyllaceae. *Quart. Rev. Biol.* 38:117–23.

Heise, H. A., and E. R. Heise. 1948. The distribution of ragweed pollen and *Alternaria* spores in the upper atmosphere. *Jour. Allergy* 19:403–427.

Hillebrand, W. 1888. *Flora of the Hawaiian Islands*. London, Williams & Norgate.

Hirst, J. M., O. J. Stedman, and W. H. Hogg. 1967. Long-distance spore transport: Methods of measurement, vertical spore profiles and detection of immigrant spores. *Jour. Gen. Microbiol.* 48:329–55.

Hirst, J. M., O. J. Stedman, and G. W. Hurst. 1967. Long-distance spore transport: Vertical section of spore clouds over the sea. *Jour. Gen. Microbiol.* 48:357–77.

Hurst, G. W. 1969. Meteorological aspects of insect migrations. *Endeavour* 27 (104):77–81.

Hyde, B. B. 1970. Mucilage-producing cells in the seed coat of *Plantago ovata*: Developmental fine structure. *Amer. Jour. Bot.* 57:1197–1206.

Johnston, I. M. 1931. The flora of the Revillagigedo Islands. *Proc. Calif. Acad. Sci.* 4th ser., 20:8–104.

Kenyon, K. W., and E. Kridler. 1969. Laysan albatrosses swallow indigestible matter. *Auk* 86:339–43.

Klein, D. R. 1968. The introduction, increase and crash of reindeer on St. Matthew Island. *Jour. Wildlife Manage.* 32:350–67.

Kohlmeyer, J. 1966. Ecological observations on arenicolous marine fungi. *Z. Allg. Mikrobiol.* 6:95–106.

Kramer, C. L., and S. M. Pady. 1968. Viability of airborne spores. *Mycologia* 60:448–49.

Lack, D. 1969. Subspecies and sympatry in Darwin's finches. *Evolution* 23:252–63.

Lack, D. 1971. Island birds. In *Adaptive aspects of insular evolution*, ed. W. L. Stern, pp. 29–31. Pullman, Wash., Washington State University Press.

Lamoureux, C. H. 1963. The flora and vegetation of Laysan Island. *Atoll Res. Bull.* 97:1–14.

Low, J. 1937. Germination tests of some aquatic plants important as duck foods. B.S. Thesis, Utah State University, Logan, Utah. 27 pp.

MacArthur, R. H., and E. O. Wilson. 1963. An equilibrium theory of insular zoogeography. *Evolution* 17:373–87.

McAtee, W. L. 1918. Food habits of the mallard ducks of the United States. *U.S. Dept. Agr. Publ.* 720, pp. 1–25.

McAtee, W. L. 1947. Distribution of seeds by birds. *Amer. Midland Naturalist* 38:214–23.

McDonald, J. E. 1962. Collection and washout of airborne pollens and spores by raindrops. *Science* 135:435–36.

Maguire, B., and contributors. 1958. The botany of the Guayana Highland. Part III. *Mem. N.Y. Bot. Gard.* 10:1–156.

Malone, C. R. 1965a. Dispersal of plankton: Rate of food passage in mallard ducks. *Jour. Wildlife Manage.* 29:529–33.

Malone, C. R. 1965b. Killdeer (*Charadrius vociferus* Linnaeus) as means of dispersal for aquatic gastropods. *Ecology* 46:551–52.

Malone, C. R., and V. W. Proctor. 1965. Dispersal of *Marsilea mucronata* by water birds. *Amer. Fern Jour.* 55:167–70.

Maynard, N. G. 1968. Significance of air-borne algae. *Z. Allg. Mikrobiol.* 8:225–26.

Mayr, E. 1940. The origin and history of the bird fauna of Polynesia. *Proc. Sixth Pacific Sci. Congr.* 4:197–216.

Moar, N. T. 1969. Possible long-distance transport of pollen to New Zealand. *New Zealand Jour. Bot.* 7:424–26.

Moore, J. W. 1933. New and critical plants from Raiatea. *Bishop Mus. Bull.* 102:1–53.

Moore, J. W. 1963. Notes on Raiatean flowering plants. *Bishop Mus. Bull.* 226:1–36.

Munro, G. C. 1960. *Birds of Hawaii.* 2d ed. Rutland, Vt., Ridgeway Press.

Ornduff, R. 1963. Experimental studies in two genera of Helenieae (Compositae): *Blennosperma* and *Lasthenia*. *Quart. Rev. Biol.* 38:141–50.

Overeem, M. A. van. 1937. On green organisms occurring in the lower troposphere. *Rec. Trav. Bot. Neerl.* 34:389–439.

Preest, D. S. 1963. A note on the dispersal characteristics of the seed of the New Zealand podocarps and beeches and their biogeographical significance. In *Pacific basin biogeography*, ed. J. L. Gressitt, pp. 415–24. Honolulu, Bishop Museum Press.

Proctor, V. W. 1961. Dispersal of *Riella* spores by waterfowl. *Bryologist* 64:58–61.

Proctor, V. W. 1962. Viability of *Chara* oospores taken from migratory water birds. *Ecology* 43:528–29.

Proctor, V. W. 1966. Dispersal of desmids by waterbirds. *Phycologia* 5:227–32.

Proctor, V. W. 1968. Long-distance dispersal of seeds by retention in digestive tract of birds. *Science* 160:321–22.

Proctor, V. W., and C. R. Malone. 1965. Further evidence of the passive dispersal of aquatic organisms via the intestinal tract of birds. *Ecology* 46:728–29.

Proctor, V. W., C. R. Malone, and V. L. de Vlaming. 1967. Dispersal of disseminules recovered from the intestinal tract of captive killdeer. *Ecology* 48:672–76.

Pugh, G. J. F. 1964a. Fungal contamination of autumn migrants. *Bardsey Observ. Rep.* 12:1–3.

Pugh, G. J. F. 1964b. Dispersal of *Arthroderma curreyi* by birds, its role in the soil. *Sabouraudia* 3:275–78.

Pugh, G. J. F. 1965a. Fungi recorded on birds from Skokholm. *Skokholm Bird Observ. Rep.* 1965: 21–24.

Pugh, G. J. F. 1965b. Cellulolytic and keratinophilic fungi recorded on birds. *Sabouraudia* 4:85–91.

Pugh, G. J. F. 1966a. Associations between birds' nests, their pH, and keratinophilic fungi. *Sabouraudia* 5:49–53.

Pugh, G. J. F. 1966b. Fungi on birds in India. *Jour. Indian Bot. Soc.* 45:296–303.

Raven, P. H. 1963a. A flora of San Clemente Island, California. *Aliso* 5:289–347.

Raven, P. H. 1963b. Amphitropical relationships in the floras of North and South America. *Quart. Rev. Biol.* 38:151–77.

Reinecke, F. 1898. Die Flora der Samoa-Inseln. II. *Bot. Jahrb.* 25:578–708.

Ridley, H. N. 1930. *The dispersal of plants throughout the world.* Ashford, England, L. Reeve & Co.

Roessler, E. S. 1936. Viability of weed seeds after ingestion by California linnets. *Condor* 38:62–65.

St. John, H., and W. R. Philipson. 1960. List of the flora of Oeno Atoll, Tuamotu Archipelago, south-central Pacific Ocean. *Trans. Roy. Soc. New Zealand* 88:401–3.

Sauer, J. 1957. Recent migration and evolution of the dioecious amaranths. *Evolution* 11:11–31.

Schlichting, H. E., Jr. 1964. Meteorological conditions affecting the dispersal of airborne algae and protozoa. *Lloydia* 27:64–78.

Simberloff, D. S. 1969. Experimental zoogeography of islands. A model for insular colonization. *Ecology* 50:296–314.

Simberloff, D. S., and E. O. Wilson. 1969. Experimental zoogeography of islands. The colonization of empty islands. *Ecology* 50:278–95.

Skottsberg, C. 1922a. Catalogue of Easter Island phanerogams. *Natur. Hist. Juan Fernandez Easter I.* 2:63–84.

Skottsberg, C. 1922b. The phanerogams of the Juan Fernandez Islands. *Natur. Hist. Juan Fernandez Easter I.* 2:95–240.

Skottsberg, C. 1927. The vegetation of Easter I. *Natur. Hist. Juan Fernandez Easter I.* 2:487–502.

Skottsberg, C. 1928. Pollinationsbiologie und Samenverbreitung auf den Juan Fernandez-Inseln. *Natur. Hist. Juan Fernandez Easter I.* 2:503–547.

Skottsberg, C. 1937. Die Flora der Desventuradas-Inseln. *Acta Horti Gotoburg.* 5(6):1–88.

Skottsberg, C. 1951. A supplement to the pteridophytes and phanerogams of Juan Fernandez and Easter I. *Natur. Hist. Juan Fernandez Easter I.* 2:763–92.

Skottsberg, C. 1963. Zur Naturgeschichte der Insel San Ambrosio (Islas Desventuradas, Chile). *Ark. Bot.,* ser. 2, 4:465–88.

Stephens, S. G. 1958. Factors affecting seed dispersal in *Gossypium* and their possible evolutionary significance. *N.C. Agr. Exp. Sta. Tech. Bull.* 131:1–32.

Stephens, S. G. 1966. The potentiality for long-range oceanic dispersal of cotton seeds. *Amer. Natur.* 100:199–210.

Stewart, A. 1911. A botanical survey of the Galápagos Islands. *Proc. Calif. Acad. Sci.,* 4th ser., 1:7–288.

Stewart, A. 1912. Notes on the botany of Cocos Island. *Proc. Calif. Acad. Sci.,* 4th ser., 1:375–404.

Taylor, B. W. 1954. An example of long distance dispersal. *Ecology* 35:569–72.

Thorne, R. F. 1963. Biotic distribution patterns in the tropical Pacific. In *Pacific basin biogeography,* ed. J. L. Gressitt, pp. 311–50. Honolulu, Bishop Museum Press.

Thorne, R. F. 1972. Floristic relationships between Tropical Africa and Tropical America. In *Tropical forest ecosystems in Africa and South America: A comparative review,* ed. B. J. Meggars and E. S. Ayensu, pp. 27–47. Washington, D.C., Smithsonian Institution.

Turbott, E. G. 1951. Notes on the birds of the Three Kings Islands. *Rec. Auckland Inst. Mus.* 4:141–43.

Vlaming, V. L. de, and V. W. Proctor. 1968. Dispersal of aquatic organisms: Viability of seeds recovered from the droppings of captive killdeer and mallard ducks. *Amer. Jour. Bot.* 55:20–26.

Wagner, R. H. 1965. The annual seed rain of adventive herbs in a radiation-damaged forest. *Ecology* 46:517–20.

Whitaker, T. W., and G. F. Carter. 1961. A note on the longevity of seed of *Lagenaria siceraria* (Mol.) Standl. after floating in sea water. *Bull. Torrey Bot. Club* 88:104–6.

Whitehead, D. R., and C. E. Jones. 1969. Small islands and the equilibrium theory of insular biogeography. *Evolution* 23:171–79.

Williams, E. 1969. The ecology of colonization as seen in the zoogeography of anoline lizards on small islands. *Quart. Rev. Biol.* 44:345–89.

Wilson, E. O. 1959. Adaptive shift and dispersal in a tropical ant fauna. *Evolution* 13:122–44.

Wilson, E. O., and D. S. Simberloff. 1969. Experimental zoogeography of islands. Defaunation and monitoring techniques. *Ecology* 50:276–77.

Wilson, R. C. 1970. Anthocarp dispersal and its ecological implications. Ph.D. Thesis. Claremont Graduate School, Claremont, Calif.

Yuncker, T. G. 1959. Plants of Tonga. *Bishop Mus. Bull.* 220:1–283.

Zimmerman, E. C. 1948. *Insects of Hawaii*, vol. 1: *Introduction*. Honolulu, University of Hawaii Press.

CHAPTER THREE

ADAPTIVE RADIATION IN ISLANDS:
DEFINITIONS AND COMMENTS

The nature of adaptation is often discussed in books on evolution and may, in fact, be said to constitute the major concern of some books, such as Grant's *The Origin of Adaptations* (1963). Simultaneously we see the term "adaptive radiation" often used, sometimes briefly defined. Adaptive radiation is one of the more intriguing concepts in evolution, because it has manifold overtones. The concept is usually not explicitly defined—rather, it is applied to examples, such as the Darwin's finches of the Galápagos Islands, and example thereby becomes definition. To see the limits of this idea, and how it impinges on other modes of speciation and diversification, I have decided to present what I consider a series of implications evident in usages of this term with reference to insular and island-like situations.

1. Adaptive radiation connotes entry of a group into a variety of habitats. This in turn implies that in a reasonably discrete geographical region, usually an island but more particularly an archipelago, there is a diversity of habitats available. In terms of vegetation, one often thinks of a range such as dry coastal plain, dry inland scrub, dry upland forest, wet montane forest, bogs, subalpine scrub, and alpine subscrub. Such a range would be represented well, for example, on the Hawaiian Islands. A fresh-water lake may also offer many habitats (see examples in chapter 9).

2. A plant group showing adaptive radiation would be expected to be represented by species in many, although not necessarily all, of these habitats. The diversity of habitats occupied is more often implied than is

adaptation to the totality of an ecological range. Many areas, of course, do not offer a broad range of ecological amplitude. In any case, diversification among available habitats is considered a basic criterion of adaptive radiation. A single habitat might be used differently by derivatives of the same group. For example, *Dubautia menziesii* is an alpine shrub, *Argyroxiphium sandwichense* a rosette plant; both are members of the same complex and are sympatric on Haleakala, Maui.

3. A particular animal group not only may show occupation of varied climatic zones, but also may enter varied behavioral and dietary modes. Lack (1944) showed that, among birds, closely related species tend to occupy separate habitats, or, if they do coexist, they take different foods— which can be called "resource partitioning" in a single area. Examples of resource partitioning occur in unexpected ways in lizards studied by Schoener (1968). For example, perch diameter, perch height, and perch nature (leaves as well as bark) separate *Anolis* species in the Bahamas. The length and volume of prey items and preference for particular taxonomic groups of insects are criteria for resource-partitioning among the Bimini anole species (Schoener, 1968), just as they are among the Darwin's finches (Bowman, 1961, pl. 6). Among the Indefatigable Island geospizids, Bowman illustrated visible differences in prey sizes and volumes and types for *Camarhynchus psittacula*, *C. parvulus*, *Certhidea olivacea*, and *Cactospiza pallida*.

In the Bimini *Anolis* species, Schoener (1968) describes not merely differences, but specifically which species have more generalized requirements or tolerances in a given area, which have the narrowest. The effect of sexual dimorphism in size of *Anolis* in relation to size of prey and volume of prey was earlier expressed for a single *Anolis* species (Schoener, 1967).

Similar resource partitioning occurs on other West Indian islands, such as Grenada and Martinique (Schoener and Gorman, 1968). In addition to factors such as those cited above, Schoener finds that sympatric *Anolis* species differ modally in head length and body temperature. Schoener and Gorman (1968) liken differences in snout length in lizards to bill differences in birds.

We are now familiar with the phenomenon whereby two sympatric species of a given genus on an island will differ, for example, in the case of a bird, in bill size and shape—differences indicating divergence in feeding habits. If a single species of a given genus is present on an island, intermediate bill size and shape (and presumably prey) occur—and the range in bill dimensions will perhaps be as great as the combined ranges for the two sympatric species on another island. Graphic illustrations of this phenomenon have been offered by Lack (1947, chapter 8) in the geospizids and Bock (1970) in the Hawaiian honeycreepers (see also fig. 4.5 in this book). We can easily understand that if a single species of a genus exists on an island, it may widen its range in diet and morphology, a phenomenon termed "character release" (see Grant, 1966; Williams, 1969). The phenomenon whereby congeners on an island develop mutually exclusive ecological ranges has been termed "character displacement" (Brown and Wilson, 1956). Character displacement can involve features other than ecological requirements. For example, two congeneric species of frogs may have the greatest voice difference in the area of sympatry, in which case this should be regarded as an isolating mechanism.

What is not certain, to judge from the literature, is how character displacement occurs. The idea that two species diverge ecologically so that selection favors individuals which do not compete with those of a congeneric species on an island is tempting. Certainly the presence of congeneric species would prevent character release by either species; the competition would tend to enforce differences. There is the possibility that the differences would be enforced most strongly at geographical interfaces between two species. Once "character displacement" had been secured, they could become sympatric. However, for such a situation to exist, there must already be at least some degree of differentiation between two species that occupy different parts of an island. Williams (1969) has rightly stressed that an invading species, unless different in ecological requirements from a species already resident, will be potentially unsuccessful in establishment. Where, then, can the new invader acquire characteristics different from those of the previously established resident on a given island?

Of course, mainland source areas can provide congeneric species different enough so that both can establish on an offshore island. This may be the case for the Tres Marías Islands congeners cited by Grant (1966).

Alternately, how can species with requirements different enough to be sympatric evolve on an island? One possibility lies in the archipelago effect. If a single bird (or plant) species establishes on an island, it will, with ecological opportunity, undergo character release. This will mean a greater range in its ecological capabilities. Character release can quite conceivably take the form of race formation within a single island. As in the ecotype concept, a single variable species (like *Metrosideros polymorpha* in the Hawaiian Islands) may range from relatively dry forest to quite wet forest, into bogs (as a subshrub instead of a tree), and into specialized habits on windswept ridges. Presumably a similar ecotype formation could occur on a moderately large island in the case of a bird, where a certain forest area would provide one sort of prey, yet a different forest area would be rich in another. If opposite ends of this spectrum were dispersed to a second island in an archipelago, they would be able to coexist in a single forest if both types of prey were available there.

4. Although the reasoning just given suggests the beginnings of adaptive radiation, most examples feature not a pair of divergent species, but many of them, often on a single island, such as the variety of geospizid species on Indefatigable Island (fig. 6.1). How are such broader programs of adaptive radiation realized? Bock (1970) rightly points to "cumulative change" as a way of expressing this process. Another way of describing it might be "successive ecological shifts." If a group has sufficient time and ecological opportunity, and if it is sufficiently plastic, ecological shifts (perhaps like those cited in the preceding section) can occur. In the case of the Hawaiian honeycreepers, character release that involved a spectrum including more nectar–few insects at one end and less nectar–more insects at the other would represent an ecological shift. The more nectarivorous line could radiate into various niches, each niche a secondary ecological shift, while the insect-feeding line could radiate into other new niches (small insects vs. large, in borings vs. on surface). Adaptive radiation is thus a series of ecological shifts, and there is no group that exemplifies the "perfect" stage in adaptive radiation. "Secondary cycles" of adaptive radiation may be present, as in Amadon's (1950) interpretation of differences within the genus *Psittarostra* of the Hawaiian honeycreepers, or we may see a group with incipient adaptive radiation, like the shrubby insular Hemizonias of California (Carlquist, 1965).

There is, additionally, the possibility that in any group cited as an example of adaptive radiation, the maximal differentiation has already been reached. There is every reason to believe that such processes can occur very rapidly (see, e.g., Myers, 1960), and that, in a finite area, niche occupation and ecological shift have proceeded to a maximal extent. Consequently, what looks like "incipient adaptive radiation" may, in fact, be the farthest penetrations of which a group is capable in a given area.

5. Disharmony in a relatively discrete geographical region is the implied condition predisposing to adaptive radiation, at least in most of the examples cited. If a variety of niches available to a group are not already efficiently occupied (e.g., saturated with species adapted to each niche), they are invadable and speciation will take the form of diversification into different habitats or into other biological gamuts. Oceanic islands offer obvious examples of disharmony, but continental situations provide many examples as well. Australia was disharmonic with respect to mammals when the marsupials entered, so their radiation there is an obvious result. One may argue that Australia (or the Australian-Papuan region, since New Guinea, Australia, and Tasmania were connected with each other until recently) is an insular situation. Some examples of adaptive radiation in continental areas are cited briefly in chapter 9 as a way of placing in relief the insular examples.

However, the major continents themselves can be disharmonic with respect to particular groups at various times in their geological history. To cite radiation of, say, cacti or bromeliads (both are large families restricted to North and South America, with only the most token representation elsewhere) may seem to inflate the concept beyond logical bounds, but it is an obvious extension of the disharmonic concept.

Keast (1961, 1968, 1971) has shown that in some areas of Australia, open niches have been colonized—on Tasmania, for example, mostly by species from adjacent feeding zones. Because of excessive cold in Pleistocene Tasmania, that island became disharmonic and has been ecologically "refilled" in post-Pleistocene time. Southwestern Australia as a floristic province is a superb example of an insular area and, for this reason, is discussed in detail in chapter 8. Likewise, the alpine and subalpine zones of equatorial Africa, South America, and Malesia seemed to me to be inevitable components in an examination of insular adaptive radiation

101

(chapter 14). Disharmony in these cases may not seem obvious, for one may have the preconception of a single ecological zone. However, in both cases there are a variety of niches, and disharmony has been strong, for reasons stated in chapters 8 and 14.

. 6. Autochthonous development within a given area is virtually assumed in the usage of the term adaptive radiation. If Darwin's finches represented a collection of mainland finches, independently dispersed to and established upon the Galápagos, we would not cite them as examples of adaptive radiation (unless in the broadest possible context, saying that finches as a whole represented a case of adaptive radiation). Another way of saying this is that the species of a genus in *an area* are monophyletic, the products of a single invasion rather than several invasions (and therefore, *for that area,* polyphyletic). This may seem so obvious as to be superfluous, but the differences may be subtle where the possibilities exist that products of several invasions may look like products of a single continuum. Lemurs are now restricted to Madagascar, but they were once much more widely distributed. How much of the diversity of Madagascar lemurs is the result of evolution on Madagascar, how much is relictual preservation of evolution that took place elsewhere?

7. A particular taxonomic group is basic to the concept of adaptive radiation. It need not be endemic to the region in question; many cited are endemic, however, like the Hawaiian honeycreepers. Adaptive radiation is most often not cited at higher taxonomic levels, e.g., family and above. However, Stebbins (1967) has used the concept of adaptive radiation with respect to flowering plants at large. Although this extension is a useful way of stressing problems of evolution in angiosperms, its usage in this context is somewhat by way of analogy with the insular and islandlike instances that provide the bulk of examples cited. The taxonomic levels most often cited are subfamily (Geospizinae of Fringillidae), groups of related genera (the *Dubautia-Argyroxiphium-Wilkesia* complex), genus (*Rollandia* or *Cyanea*: chapter 4), or subgenus (*Senecio* subg. *Dendrosenecio*: chapter 14). Diversification within a single species is not often considered adaptive radiation—usually only an incipient form of it. The concept of ecotype formation is more applicable within a species. It is possible to regard all evolution as successions of adaptive radiation, as is done by Mayr (1963), in a sense. However, in this instance, we need the

insular examples of adaptive radiation as modules to which other cases can be compared.

8. Disharmony leading to adaptive radiation is a product of difficulty of dispersal to an (insular) area (if we discount depauperation of a biota for reasons of poor ecology, of course). MacArthur and Wilson (1967, p. 175) stress an aspect of this by saying that a group established on an island at the limit of the group's dispersal possibility (which they term the "radiation zone") will be likely to undergo adaptive radiation. An obvious example would be land birds on the Hawaiian Islands. As Lack notes, only five passerine bird establishments by natural means have occurred on the Hawaiian Islands. Faced with the ecological richness of this archipelago, they inevitably underwent radiation. However, we might ask why the honeycreepers radiated so spectacularly and the other four passerine establishments did not. Were the honeycreepers older immigrants, or just more capable of ecological shift?

The idea of a group at its dispersal limits is very appealing, but we must keep in mind that different groups have different dispersal abilities. If we compare the Hawaiian Islands to the Canary Islands, where many more passerine bird establishments—and virtually no adaptive radiation in the avifauna—have occurred, this is easy to understand. However, about 250 angiosperm establishments occurred in the Hawaiian Islands, and adaptive radiation in Hawaiian angiosperms has been spectacular. Obviously, the opportunity for plant radiation in the Islands is much greater than that for birds. There are several reasons why this should be true. A breeding population of a bird species may require a much larger territory than would a plant species. Isolation within an island may be much greater for a plant species than an animal species. For example, *Cyrtandra* grows in deep ravines, of which there are many on Oahu, and the intervening ridges can serve as isolating barriers that have permitted extraordinary speciation in that genus (126 species on Oahu, according to St. John [1966]). Thus, we have to consider not only dispersal limits of a group, but also differential dispersibility for various groups, and the ecological requirements, ecological plasticity, and population characteristics of each. We also have to consider ecological opportunity on recipient islands—what appears to be uniform for one group of organisms may be a series of ecological niches for another. Furthermore, recentness of colonization may be a factor in explaining lack of radiation. This is hypothesized (with reservation) by MacArthur and Wilson (1967), and they cite the possibility that recentness may explain lack of radiation of New Zealand frogs, Antillean insectivores, Solomon Islands mammals, Fijian snakes, and Samoan lizards. However, when we consider the rapid radiation and speciation of groups such as the Hawaiian drosophilids or the Galápagos geospizids, the earlier examples do not seem easily explained by lack of time. The New Zealand frog *Leiopelma*, related to frogs in northwestern America, is undoubtedly not recent in New Zealand. Leiopelmid frogs are known from Upper Jurassic (Sharell, 1966). That this frog is prevented from radiation in New Zealand by ecological restrictions is suggested by the following passage (Sharell, 1966):

> The native frogs of New Zealand have adapted themselves most won-
> derfully to life and their mode of breeding to the rigorous conditions
> of their environment. Life is precarious enough on these mountain
> tops, and as there is no water for tadpoles to live in and to develop
> into frogs [in], their eggs are enclosed in gelatinous capsules, filled
> with a watery fluid, and inside this capsule, the embryo develops, miss-
> ing out the long tadpole stage, and developing directly into tailed
> froglets.

Dispersal difficulty is not, of course, a matter of distance alone; we tend to forget other factors because we cannot visualize them easily. Lack (1947) has noted that passerine bird dispersal to the Galápagos may have been more difficult because these islands are in a region of calm, whereas Macaronesian islands are favored by prevailing winds.

9. Recentness of diversification is an implication partly involved in the concept of adaptive radiation, although rarely made explicit. Recent-ness is suggested by persistence of various types, whereas greater age would dictate progressive extinction of at least some of them. Persistence among recent species chiefly would be expected on oceanic islands, where popu-lation size for each product of adaptive radiation in a group would be expected to be finite. We would not cite a group as exemplary of adaptive radiation unless a series of modifications were still extant.

Products of adaptive radiation may persist well on islands because of lowered predation and competition. However, equal relictualism for all or even many products of an adaptive radiation seems unlikely, and only recentness seems of overriding importance in explaining the excellent gamut of niche occupation we see in the "good" examples of adaptive radiation. There are a few exceptions such as the New Caledonian conifers (chapter 7) or the marsupials of Australia, but even in those groups, and ones like them, we see gaps, almost certainly due to extinctions (known as fossils in the case of the Australian marsupials). Even in the Hawaiian honeycreepers we see a difference between the subfamily Drepanididae (probably more extinctions, fewer adaptive modes) and the subfamily Psittarostrinae (fewer extinctions, more numerous adaptive modes).

10. One way often utilized for defining adaptive radiation is comparing the products of adaptive radiation on an island or islandlike area to mainland counterparts that would belong to a series of disparate families. For example, a parrot would be considered the counterpart of *Psittarostra* in the Hawaiian honeycreepers, a meliphagid the counterpart of *Hemignathus procerus* or *Drepanis*, etc.

11. Despite the fact that a gamut of adaptations is basic to adaptive radiation, discontinuities in the range of forms within a taxonomic group are also implied in this concept. The Hawaiian species of *Metrosideros* (Myrtaceae) can be said to represent a wide range of adaptations, ranging from one of the tallest island trees in wet forests, to miniature shrubs in bogs, to scrubby trees on windy ridges, spanning edaphic conditions from new lava to mature soils. However, Hawaiian *Metrosideros* represents an almost continuous series of forms, very probably the result of constant hybridization. One could designate the entire complex as a single species, *M. polymorpha*, or single out as many subspecies or segregate species as one wished. In any case, the intercontinuity among infraspecific variants evidently disqualifies *Metrosideros* from consideration as an example of "adaptive radiation" in the typical sense; "good" taxonomic species throughout most if not all of a group seem a requisite for its designation as an example of this process.

12. Speciation (or diversification to the level of genera) progresses by means of continual shifts into new habitats and habits, and thus a contrast is made with vicarious species. The largest genus of angiosperms in the Hawaiian flora is *Cyrtandra*. Although this genus is not lacking in diversity

in certain characteristics, many of the species are alike in habit, and the differences that separate them appear to be nonadaptive in many cases, the result of drift permitted by geographic isolation. *Cyrtandra* is especially characteristic of deep wet gulches; where these are numerous, isolation and thereby drift would tend to occur. This may account for the phenomenal number of species on Oahu (St. John, 1966). At least the species within each section of the genus (e.g., sect. *Chaetocalyx*) would be regarded as vicarious species and would be contrasted with the products of adaptive radiation. Strid (1970) regards *Nigella* (Ranunculaceae) on the Aegean Islands as an example of "nonadaptive radiation." These *Nigella* species show morphological differences in relatively minor ways, and Strid claims that they all have roughly the same ecological preferences. Differences in this group appear to have resulted from the "founder principle" (namely, the limitations of genetic content of the founding immigrants predetermine the composition of the resultant population), with subsequent action of genetic drift. We could call the *Nigella* species vicarious species rather than products of "nonadaptive radiation." The equatorial alpine species of *Senecio* and *Lobelia* and the paramo species of *Espeletia* (chapter 14) contain many examples of vicarious species, but adaptive radiation has also occurred in these groups. Although the contrast is made to vicarious species, the concept of adaptive radiation does not exclude instances of vicarious species within a group as well: it is a matter of the preponderance of "adaptive" instances over "nonadaptive" instances in a group.

13. There is a strong implication in the concept of adaptive radiation that products are strikingly different, often exceptional. The diverse growth forms of the *Dubautia-Argyroxiphium-Wilkesia* complex on the Hawaiian Islands, and the fact that these genera represent growth forms and habitat preferences different from, and beyond, those of mainland tarweeds makes them a good example of insular adaptive radiation. A group in which species look much alike but occupy diverse niches might not at first be cited as an example, but could, with suitable ecological studies, be cited thus. There is often the implication that the nature of the adaptation be readily apparent in terms of morphology (bill size and shape in birds as an indicator of diet; plant size, leaf size and shape, indument, and degree of succulence as indicators of xeromorphy or mesomorphy).

Myers (1960) stresses exceptional developments, "supralimital specializations," as components of adaptive radiation. Among the instances he cites in fishes are the exceptional developments of the cyprinids of Lake Lanao and the cichlids of Lake Tanganyika (see chapter 9). Other examples he cites include a scaleless genus of cyprinids, *Sawbwa*, in Lake Inlé, Burma (Annandale, 1918), and the strikingly altered species of *Orestias* in Lake Titicaca. If autochthonous products of evolution in lake fish are supralimital and types connecting them to other fish are extinguished, we would have no choice but to recognize them as families. Considering the supralimital developments in other lakes, this explanation may apply to two monotypic genera that are sole representatives of their families: *Chaudhuria caudata* (Chaudhuriidae) in Lake Inlé, Burma (Annandale, 1918) and *Indostomus paradoxus* (Indostomiidae) in Lake Indawygi, Burma (Prashad and Mukerji, 1929). Authors such as Myers (1960) and Zimmerman (1948) have stressed that exceptional products of adaptive radiation on islands or in islandlike situations demonstrate to us better than examples on continents how new families and orders have arisen evolutionarily.

14. With a few notable exceptions, adaptive radiation seems to occur mostly in groups that could be called weedy, evolutionarily upgrade, or plastic. That composites (Asteraceae) and insects furnish many examples of adaptive radiation on islands is no accident. Composites, often characteristic of weedy or disturbed situations on mainland areas, plainly have a number of features that tend to promote rapid speciation and ecological shift. This is certainly true of the family on continental areas, so its adaptive radiation on islands is not surprising. Chapter 4 contains examples of adaptive radiation in both Asteraceae and insects in the Hawaiian Islands. We should observe, however, that taxonomic groups not often considered weeds do have excellent pioneering and character-release capabilities, and have exhibited adaptive radiation in islands (see chapter 1). There is a link between good dispersal and pioneer qualities.

15. As stressed by Baldwin (1953, p. 382), there is a tendency to read as adaptive all differing or distinctive characteristics within a group cited as an example of adaptive radiation. In an insular area, nonadaptive characteristics may be established and preserved coincidentally with adaptive ones. The Hawaiian honeycreepers are a superb example of adaptive radiation, but color and pattern of plumage, as well as a few other characteris-

tics, appear to have no adaptive significance (Amadon, 1950; Baldwin, 1953). Plumage color in the birds of the Tres Marías Islands has changed, but apparently through decrease in selection for distinctive plumage recognition patterns (see chapter 15).

16. Species involved in cases of true adaptive radiation on islands show just as "perfect" or "complete" adaptation to environment as do comparable continental species to their respective environments. Speaking of the Australian marsupials, Darwin (1859) thought of them as "divided into groups differing but little from each other, and feebly representing carnivorous, ruminant, and rodent mammals." I have offered a refutation of Darwin's judgment of the Australian marsupials (1965). Similarly, Bock (1970) says, with respect to the Hawaiian honeycreepers, "I know of no reason to assume that any species of drepanidid has a bill morphology poorly adapted for its feeding methods." The fact that products of adaptive radiation on islands are more readily subject to extinction, or seem less competitive than continental types introduced by man, has been equated by some authors with imperfect adaptation, as Darwin evidently did. Extinction of marsupials or honeycreepers results not from imperfect adaptation, but from other causes. These causes may include introduction of predators, parasites, and competitors, and seems invariably to involve destruction of natural areas by man. Groups that have evolved in the absence of such influences are more readily vulnerable to them (see chapter 1, principle 18).

17. If one group invades and radiates within an archipelago or similar area, it may preclude not establishment of other immigrants, but adaptive radiation in those later arrivals. This may explain why the drepanidids are the only group of Hawaiian birds to exhibit adaptive radiation, and may apply to the Darwin's finches as well. Earliness of invasion may not be advantageous if a group is unable to diversify into new ecological niches. Thus, a genus such as *Cryptocarya* (Lauraceae) could well be an earlier immigrant to Hawaii than the ancestors of the *Dubautia-Argyroxiphium-Wilkesia* complex but, if so, has not been able to radiate (there is only one species, *C. mannii*). Because Lauraceae (other than the parasitic *Cassytha*) are so consistently elements of stable moist forest, one would expect this limitation. That *Cryptocarya* is indeed an older immigrant in the Hawaiian flora is suggested by its occurrence only on the oldest island where moist forest is present, Kauai.

Examples have been cited of instances in which successful earlier establishments on islands may forestall later establishments (chapter 2). Forestalling not a second establishment but the adaptive radiation of that second establishment seems a logical extension of this concept. On the other hand, Lack (1947) submits the possibility that if dispersal from a source area is good, new immigrants (more efficient, presumably, than relatively less competitive insular species) may displace products of earlier adaptive radiation. In such a way, groups of flowering plants may have displaced conifers on New Caledonia (chapter 7). Continual displacement is basic to the MacArthur-Wilson equilibrium theory (MacArthur and Wilson, 1967), although one could express this in terms not of displacement but of replacement.

18. A group with moderately poor dispersibility may conceivably undergo adaptive radiation better than one with good dispersibility within an archipelago. Excellence of dispersal would tend to result in lack of speciation or diversification, for continual reinvasion of a site from various sources might tend to "swamp out" ecological shift—as it almost certainly does in the strand flora. Excellent dispersibility may account for the fact that the only species of lobelioid present on all major islands of the Hawaiian chain, *Trematolobelia macrostachys*, is the sole species of its genus. *Trematolobelia* has an unusually efficient dispersal mechanism (Carlquist, 1962). Isolation of a population within an archipelago long enough for it to undergo ecological shift is easy to imagine. Once ecological shift has occurred, however, the population has "lost dispersibility" by being unable to reinvade its original habitat.

19. Adaptive radiation is the product of invasion of an "invadable" situation. Given areas are invadable by particular groups at particular times —often for geological and climatic reasons. Although hypothetical curricula could be designed here, these basic evolutionary programs are well known. In particular, I refer the reader to the accounts of Mayr (1963, especially pp. 481–585) and Grant (1963, especially pp. 392–423, 519–68).

"Diversity" and Adaptive Radiation

In recent years, much attention has been paid to the number of species (genera, families) present on insular areas, and the relationship of species numbers to factors such as area and isolation. These topics have been so extensively and excellently discussed by MacArthur and Wilson (1967) that there is no need to repeat that readily available material here. Two subsequent contributions may be mentioned: Balgooy's "A study on the diversity of island floras" (1969), and Simberloff's "Taxonomic diversity of island biotas" (1970). For all of these authors, diversity is a synonym or near-synonym for richness in number of species. Although adaptive radiation clearly impinges on the "richness" concept of floras and faunas, the two concepts differ markedly, as we shall see, and thus the material to be offered here is not an elaboration of diversity concepts in the sense of these authors. Rather, I am viewing diversification from the natural-history standpoint, in order to see what ecological shifts occur, what morphological changes occur, and in which islands or archipelagos. Simberloff's study is almost entirely alien to my present discussion, for he deals nearly exclusively with continental islands or fringing archipelagos, whereas I have, in effect, used "definitive" oceanic islands as a source of characteristics, and have extended these concepts to other islands and to islandlike areas to the extent to which they apply there in order to note changes as one shifts to "less definitive" islands. Simberloff's conclusions may well be correct for his material, but because his data were derived from "near" islands, his conclusions may or may not apply to other situations (they clearly do not apply to the Hawaiian Islands, for example). Balgooy offers data from seed plants which, in essence, confirm the various conclusions of MacArthur and Wilson. Balgooy's measure of diversity is the genera-per-family ratio, whereas Simberloff deals with the species-per-genus ratio. What relationship, if any, do these ratios bear to instances of adaptive radiation? For the purposes of this discussion, I have presented a table based on angiosperm floras of various regions (table 3.1), introduced species excluded. These floras or compilations are, of course, not equally complete in coverage of their respective areas or comparable in taxonomic concepts of their authors, but these flaws alter statistical values little except where noted in the discussion. The reader should be aware that, among these areas, our knowledge of southwestern Australia is particularly inadequate, and we may expect the number of species known there to increase by as much as 10 percent.

From the data on numbers of families, genera, and species, a genera-per-family (G/F) ratio has been computed, much as done by Balgooy (1969). Balgooy's preference for this ratio seems to lie chiefly in his contention that there is less disagreement among taxonomists on the limits of genera and families than there is on species. This may or may not be true, but, in any case, I have also calculated the species-per-genus (S/G) ratio, as used in a number of examples by MacArthur and Wilson (1967) and throughout the paper by Simberloff (1970). In addition, I have computed a species-per-family (S/F) ratio, for which there is little precedent. The S/F ratio seemed an interesting indication of speciation, and one in which the difference among floras might be stressed in a more highly pronounced form.

Infraspecific categories have been omitted with the exception of the Hawaiian flora. Here, Fosberg's estimate includes species plus varieties, and is the only recent accurate estimate; Fosberg's figure is probably not far from the figure for species alone that would be recognized by more "liberal" taxonomists working in that flora. However, I believe that monographers dealing with the Hawaiian flora since the time of Hillebrand (1888) have tended to recognize species in excess of what current concepts might indicate. Consequently, I have included, in parentheses, what I would consider a conservative estimate for the number of Hawaiian angiosperm species (1200), *excluding* subspecies or varieties. Even with a conservative estimate, however, the position of the Hawaiian flora in the ratios remains the same, and it still shows appreciably greater S/G or S/F ratios than do any other insular floras.

The ratios obtained seem entirely as one would expect on the basis of similar work by the authors cited. However, I feel that the results show that *one ratio alone does not express diversity adequately.* For example, the Hawaiian Islands have a relatively low G/F ratio (2.6), but a high S/G or S/F ratio (at least 14.5), rating much higher than a large continental island area like the British Isles.

The conclusions, as seen from the perspective of native angiosperms, seem obvious. Islands support a fraction of the diversity of large continental areas, with the exception of the very few islands or islandlike areas that tend to foster speciation to a high extent: the Hawaiian Islands and southwestern Australia. These areas would probably show similar figures in the case of insect faunas, but not land-bird faunas, where speciation on

TABLE 3.1.
Angiosperm floras and "diversity"

	Families	Genera	Species	Genera per family	Species per genus	Species per family	Endemism %
Continental areas							
California	145	1030	5529	7.1	5.4	38.1	38.0
West Virginia	131	660	2040	5.0	3.1	14.8	0
Continental island							
British Isles	133	611	1666	4.6	2.7	12.5	0
Islandlike areas							
Afroalpine flora	35	112	279	3.2	2.5	8.0	?
Southwestern Australia	99	543	3886	5.5	7.2	39.2	(90+?)
Old continental island							
New Caledonia	141	662	2600	4.7	3.9	18.4	(90.0?)
Oceanic islands							
Annobon	38	100	115	2.6	1.2	3.0	14.8
Canary Is.	78	397	826	5.1	2.1	10.6	53.3
Fernando Po	100	468	826	4.7	1.8	8.3	12.0
Galápagos Is.	67	189	386	2.8	2.0	5.8	40.9
Hawaiian Is.	83	216	1729	2.6	8.0	20.8	94.4
			(1200)		(5.6)	(14.5)	
Juan Fernandez Is.	43	90	146	2.1	1.6	3.4	66.7
Marquesas Is.	58	111	151	1.9	1.4	2.6	52.3
Mauritius	102	299	705	2.9	2.4	6.8	?
Príncipe	64	206	276	3.2	1.3	4.2	12.7
St. Helena	18	34	45	1.9	1.3	2.5	88.9
Saõ Tomé	94	353	556	3.8	1.6	5.9	19.4

Sources of data: California (Smith and Noldeke, 1960); West Virginia (Strabaugh and Core, 1964); British Isles (Clapham, Tutin, and Warburg, 1962); Afroalpine flora as defined by Hedberg (Hedberg, 1957); southwestern Australia, as defined by McComb (McComb, 1966); Canary Is. (Lems, 1960); Galápagos Is. (Stewart, 1911); Hawaiian Is. (Frosberg's data, from Zimmerman [1948]); Juan Fernandez Is. (Skottsberg, 1956); New Caledonia (Thorne, 1965); Marquesas (Balgooy, 1969; Skottsberg, 1956); Mauritius (Baker, 1887); Gulf of Guinea islands (Excell, 1944); and St. Helena (Melliss, 1875).

insular areas is less than for angiosperms or insects. Land-snail faunas would appear similar to angiosperm floras except that drier areas, such as Western Australia, are less favorable for land snails than for angiosperms. Mammals and reptiles are so poor, or even absent, on many islands that they could not be used in a table comparable to table 3.1.

The factors for "depauperation" vary from one island group to another. There is no doubt that size is the most important, but not exclusively, by any means. One can note that the Canary Islands and Fernando Po are identical (or virtually so) in number of species. The degree of isolation does not seem drastically different: Fernando Po is 35 km from the nearest point on the African mainland, the Canary Islands 100 km at the least. The area of the Canary Islands (7500 sq. km) is 3.25 times that of Fernando Po (2000 sq. km), and the altitudinal range of the Canaries (3700 m) a little greater than that of Fernando Po (3000 m). However, the nearest source area for the Canaries is very dry, and many floristic elements of the Canaries have been acquired from areas much farther away. Thus, isolation for the Canaries is greater than appears at first glance. Also, the Canarian climate is much drier than that of Fernando Po, which supports a true rain forest. The Canary Islands have appreciably fewer families (78) than Fernando Po (100). The equity in species numbers has been evolved by autochthonous speciation on the Canaries, and endemic genera (12) have developed there as well. Endemism does not correlate reliably with diversity however. The California flora has an exceptionally high rate of speciation (38.1 per family) but its endemism (38.1 percent), although notably high (especially considering that the area is defined politically rather than phytogeographically) is not nearly as high as that of the Hawaiian Islands, New Caledonia, St. Helena, Juan Fernandez, the Canary Islands, or the Marquesas.

Endemism is also very high in southwestern Australia, as defined by McComb (1966). Southwestern Australia is much richer in speciation than Western Australia as a whole; the remainder of that state is floristically poor; the figure of 39.2 species per family, although the highest in the table, will probably turn out to be too low as southwestern Australia becomes better known. If one extracts figures from Beard (1967), the S/F ratio for southwestern Australia becomes 40.5, and that surely does not include a number of recently discovered species. No reliable estimates of endemism in southwestern Australia are available, because the precise limits of southwestern Australia as a province and ranges of species within and beyond it are problematical. About 40 percent of the genera of southwestern Australia are endemic.

Endemism, like diversity, is controlled by various factors, chiefly area, ecological breadth, and isolation. I very much doubt that any mathematical formula could predict endemism well, both because islands with high—or low—rates of endemism fall into those categories for different reasons, and because some factors, such as age, geology, and edaphic conditions are very important but difficult or impossible to measure. MacArthur and Wilson (1967, p. 74) present, in fact, not a formula but a graph comparing area to percentage of endemic species of birds for three kinds of islands: solitary, well-isolated islands, such as New Caledonia; single islands near mainland areas, such as Tasmania; and islands in the Gulf of Guinea. If one had graphed angiosperms instead, quite different results would have been obtained. MacArthur and Wilson state that

> the accumulation on islands of species generated within the archipelago provides the best measure of what is loosely referred to in the literature as adaptive radiation. Specifically, adaptive radiation takes place as species, when generated within archipelagos, disperse between islands and, most importantly, accumulate on individual islands to form diversified associations of sympatric species. In equilibrial biotas, then, the following prediction is possible: adaptive radiation will increase with distance from the major source region and, after corrections for area and climate, reach a maximum on archipelagos and large islands located in a circular zone close to the outermost dispersal range of the taxon.

Their definition of the conditions under which adaptive radiation occurs seems among the better ones. However, where vascular plants are concerned, sympatry seems the reverse of what has happened: in plants, radiation into different ecological niches has been accompanied by an almost inescapable allopatry. Sympatry would be difficult to find in any of the Hawaiian species of *Euphorbia*, a fine example of adaptive radiation, and it is infrequent in the *Dubautia-Argyroxiphium-Wilkesia* complex, provided that by "sympatry" we mean (as logically should be the case) par-

114

ticular geographical ranges on an island or islands rather than the total island as the unit on which sympatry is based. The stress MacArthur and Wilson place on remoteness of a large island or an archipelago is well taken.

Endemism does appear to be a better reflection of these factors and what I would term adaptive radiation than do most other measures. Programs of adaptive radiation (as I would apply the term) are fulfilled in remarkably different ways in various localities. Southwestern Australia has been included in this book because the conditions under which adaptive radiation has occurred there are highly unusual, yet exemplary of the concept. I would say that endemism of at least 50 percent on the specific level is a threshold for adaptive radiation in flowering plants on oceanic islands, old continental islands, and perhaps even some islandlike situations. If we could better define phytogeographically areas like California, the endemism level might be 50 percent on certain continental areas (adaptive radiation is certainly present in typically California genera, but the geographic range of the products often extends beyond California or is much restricted within it). If we consider a threshold level of 50 percent endemism as an indicator of likely adaptive radiation, however, we must subtract small islands (like St. Helena) and archipelagos with relatively small total area (the Marquesas). The Hawaiian Islands are spectacular in adaptive radiation not only of angiosperms, but also of insects, land birds, and even ferns. However, adaptive radiation may be present in New Caledonia (see chapter 7), but certainly not in the same way or degree as in the Hawaiian Islands—and New Caledonia cannot be said to show adaptive radiation well in birds.

The S/F figure (table 3.1) proves very interesting with regard to adaptive radiation. If we take as a threshold value about 8.5 species per family for oceanic islands and old continental islands, and perhaps 30 species per family for continental areas and islandlike areas, we have above those levels all the islands and areas where adaptive radiation can be said to be represented well. This corresponds to the "species-rich-but-family-poor" concept cited earlier. A different threshold value on continental areas would be justified because, with larger areas, more numerous instances of vicarious species could be expected, and, more importantly, several invasions of genera are probable, rather than just a few, because dispersal within a continent is less difficult. The S/G ratio and the G/F ratio are very poor at predicting where we will find adaptive radiation as defined by the instances cited in the chapters that follow. Obviously, in dealing with a flexible concept and with many distinctive types of island areas, precision is virtually impossible, but the descriptive materials are intended to highlight modes of speciation and evolution on insular areas and to call attention to pertinent factors and results, not quantify them.

References

Amadon, D. 1950. The Hawaiian honeycreepers (Aves, Drepaniidae). *Bull. Amer. Mus. Natur. Hist.* 95(4):1–262.

Annandale, N. 1918. Fauna of the Inlé Lake. *Rec. Indian Mus.* 14:1–214.

Baker, J. G. 1887. *Flora of Mauritius and the Seychelles*. London, L. Reeve & Co.

Baldwin, P. H. 1953. Annual cycle, environment, and evolution in the Hawaiian honeycreepers (Aves: Drepaniidae). *Univ. Calif. Publ. Zool.* 52:285–398.

Balgooy, M. M. J. van. 1969. A study on the diversity of island floras. *Blumea* 17:139–78.

Beard, J. S., ed. 1967. *Descriptive catalogue of Western Australian plants*. Perth, W.A., King's Park Board.

Bock, W. J. 1970. Microevolutionary sequences as a fundamental concept in macroevolutionary modes. *Evolution* 24:704–22.

Bowman, R. I. 1961. Morphological differentiation and adaptation in the Galápagos finchs. *Univ. Calif. Publ. Zool.* 58:1–302.

Brown, W. L., Jr., and E. O. Wilson. 1956. Character displacement. *Syst. Zool.* 5:49–64.

Carlquist, S., 1962. *Trematolobelia*: Seed dispersal; anatomy of seeds and fruits. *Pacific Sci.* 16:126–34.

Carlquist, S. 1965. *Island life*. New York, Natural History Press.

Clapham, A. R., T. G. Tutin, and E. F. Warburg. 1962. *Flora of the British Isles*. Cambridge, Cambridge University Press.

Darwin, C. 1859. *On the origin of species by means of natural selection*. Reprint of first edition, 1950. London, Watts & Co.

Exell, A. W. 1944. *Catalogue of the vascular plants of S. Tomé (with Príncipe and Annobon)*. London, British Museum (Natural History).

Grant, P. R. 1966. Ecological compatibility of bird species on islands. *Amer. Natur.* 100:451–62.

Grant, V. 1963. *The origin of adaptations*. New York and London, Columbia University Press.

Hedberg, O. 1957. Afroalpine vascular plants. *Symb. Bot. Upsal.* 15(1):1–411.

Hillebrand, W. 1888. *Flora of the Hawaiian Islands*. London, Williams & Norgate.

Keast, A. 1961. Bird speciation on the Australian Continent. *Bull. Mus. Comp. Zool.* (*Harvard*) 123:305–495.

Keast, A. 1968. Competitive interaction and the evolution of ecological niches as illustrated by the Australian honeyeater genus *Melithreptus* (Meliphagidae). *Evolution* 22:762–84.

Keast, A. 1971. Adaptive evolution and shifts in niche occupation in island birds. In *Adaptive aspects of insular evolution*, ed. W. L. Stern, pp. 39–53. Pullman, Wash., Washington State University Press.

Lack, D. 1944. Ecological aspects of species formation in some passerine birds. *Ibis* 86:260–86.

Lack, D. 1947. *Darwin's finches.* Cambridge, Cambridge University Press.

Lems, C. 1960. Floristic botany of the Canary Islands. *Sarracenia* 5:1–94.

MacArthur, R. H., and E. O. Wilson. 1967. *The theory of island biogeography.* Princeton, N.J., Princeton University Press.

McComb, J. A. 1966. The sex forms of species in the flora of the south-west of Western Australia. *Austral. Jour. Bot.* 14:303–16.

Mayr, E. 1963. *Animal species and evolution.* Cambridge, Mass., Harvard University Press.

Melliss, J. C. 1875. *St. Helena.* London, L. Reeve & Co.

Myers, G. S. 1960. The endemic fish fauna of Lake Lanao, and the evolution of higher taxonomic categories. *Evolution* 14:323–33.

Prashad, B., and D. D. Mukerji. 1929. The fish of the Indawygi Lake and the streams of the Myitkina District (Upper Burma). *Rec. Indian Mus.* 31:161–223.

St. John, H. 1966. Monograph of the genus *Cyrtandra* (*Gesneriaceae*) on Oahu. *Bishop Mus. Bull.* 229:1–465.

Schoener, T. W. 1967. The ecological significance of sexual dimorphism in size in the lizard *Anolis conspersus. Science* 155:474–77.

Schoener, T. W. 1968. The *Anolis* lizards of Bimini: Resource partitioning in a complex fauna. *Ecology* 49:704–26.

Schoener, T. W., and G. C. Gorman. 1968. Some niche differences in three Lesser Antillean lizards of the genus *Anolis. Ecology* 49:819–30.

Sharell, R. 1966. *The tuatara, lizards and frogs of New Zealand.* London, Collins.

Simberloff, D. S. 1970. Taxonomic diversity of island biotas. *Evolution* 24:23–47.

Skottsberg, C. 1956. Derivation of the flora and fauna of Juan Fernandez and Easter Island. *Natur. Hist. Juan Fernandez Easter I.* 1:193–438.

Smith, G. L., and A. M. Noldeke. 1960. A statistical report on A *California Flora. Leafl. West. Bot.* 9:117–27.

Stebbins, G. L., Jr. 1967. Adaptive radiation and trends of evolution in higher plants. In *Evolutionary biology*, ed. T. Dobzhansky, M. K. Hecht, and W. C. Steere, vol. I, pp. 101–42. New York, Appleton-Century-Crofts.

Stewart, A. 1911. A botanical survey of the Galápagos Islands. *Proc. Calif. Acad. Sci.*, 4th ser., 1:7–288.

Strasbaugh, P. P., and E. L. Core. 1964. Flora of West Virginia. Introduction. *West Virginia Bull.*, ser. 65, 3(1):i–xxxi.

Strid, A. 1970. Studies in the Aegean flora. XVI. Biosystematics of the *Nigella arvensis* complex with special reference to the problem of non-adaptive radiation. *Opera Bot.* 28:1–168.

Thorne, R. F. 1965. Floristic relationships of New Caledonia. *Univ. Iowa Stud. Natur. Hist.* 20(7):1–14.

Williams, E. E. 1969. The ecology of colonization as seen in the zoogeography of anoline lizards on small islands. *Quart. Rev. Biol.* 44:345–89.

Zimmerman, E. C. 1948. *Insects of Hawaii*, vol. 1: *Introduction*. Honolulu, University of Hawaii Press.

CHAPTER FOUR

ADAPTIVE RADIATION:
HAWAIIAN ISLANDS

Numerical and Geographical Aspects of Adaptive Radiation

The ecological diversity of the Hawaiian Islands has been described and illustrated by a number of authors (e.g., Zimmerman, 1948a; Carson et al., 1970; Carlquist, 1970a). Also, these and other authors have cited the remarkably clear geological progression in age of the islands from west to east (oldest, Kure and Midway Islands; youngest, Hawaii). There is little need for a summary of these factors, which the reader can readily obtain elsewhere. The discussion below will refer to them in a self-explanatory manner. Assuming these factors, how have they acted on various groups of organisms? What are the types of speciation we find, what are the ecological adaptations, and what morphological diversification has occurred?

FLOWERING PLANTS

Table 4.1 lists, by island, the numbers of native (but not necessarily endemic) species for several of the larger genera of flowering plants in the Hawaiian Islands. These include the nine largest genera of flowering plants in the Hawaiian flora, with the exception of *Cyrtandra* (Gesneriaceae). In the baccate lobelioids, two smaller genera, *Delissea* and *Rollandia*, have been included because they are very close to the larger genera *Cyanea* and *Clermontia*. I consider *Dubautia* to be a single genus, but species referred to *Dubautia* (*sensu stricto*) and to *Railliardia* are also listed separately for convenience. Distribution data are for the species level, and distribution

119

TABLE 4.1.

Distribution of species of Hawaiian angiosperms

Family and genus	Niihau	Kauai	Oahu	Molokai	Maui	Lanai	Hawaii	Other islands
Asteraceae								
Bidens	2	7	20	9	9	4	8	
Dubautia (s. lato)	0	10	6	3	14	3	9	
Dubautia (s. stricto)	0	(9)	(3)	(1)	(2)	(1)	(1)	
Railliardia	0	(1)	(3)	(2)	(12)	(2)	(8)	
Lipochaeta	4	8	7	9	10	3	6	3 (Kahoolawe)
Campanulaceae-								
Lobelioideae (total)	1	21	28	14	31	6	40	
Clermontia	0	1	4	6	10	3	17	
Cyanea	0	17	10	8	20	2	20	
Delissea	1	2	3	0	1	1	3	
Rollandia	0	1	11	0	0	0	0	
Lamiaceae								
Phyllostegia	0	6	7	5	10	3	6	
Stenogyne	0	2	1	3	11	1	9	
Piperaceae								
Peperomia	1	10	12	20	21	14	16	
Rutaceae								
Pelea	0	27	22	6	18	4	10	
Totals	8	91	103	59	124	38	100	
Island area (sq. mi)	72	555	604	260	728	141	4030	
Rainfall (median, in.)	?	99	58	42	75	21	75	

Sources of data: Bidens (Sherff, 1937); Dubautia and Lipochaeta (Sherff, 1935b); baccate lobelioids (Rock, 1919, 1957, 1962; Wimmer, 1956); Phyllostegia and Stenogyne (Sherff, 1935a); Peperomia (Yuncker, 1933); and Pelea (Stone, 1969).

of subspecies and varieties is included within species. The taxonomic judgments of the authors cited have been accepted except in the lobelioids, where names likely to be synonyms (see Carlquist, 1970a) have been subtracted.

Viewed simply in numerical terms, the table shows several interesting features. First, the island of Hawaii is numerically much too species-poor (see total of species for all genera); this island would not correspond with species-prediction equations as discussed by MacArthur and Wilson (1967). All ecological factors on Hawaii favor speciation, and the "impoverished" flora seems due to the island's newness. The geological evidence now available shows that very little of this island is pre-Pleistocene. The appreciable speciation that has occurred on Hawaii in a relatively short period of time reveals the effect of the rich ecology and probably also the effect of other factors. Perhaps the isolating effect of several high mountains and the innumerable successive lava flows has been effective. Ecological factors such as altitude and rainfall relate closely to area in the Hawaiian Islands, so a relatively high rate of speciation is not unexpected. One might not have predicted that Maui would be species-rich if newness is a factor, but West Maui is much older geologically than East Maui, and the combination of two large mountains of differing age on a single island, together with great ecological diversity, obviously provides a variety of niches; Maui could, with justification, be regarded and computed as two islands rather than one. As the most ancient of the five larger islands, Kauai might be expected to have a greater number of species than formulae based on all of the islands would predict. However, remoteness is an operative factor: the other four large islands, plus Lanai and Kahoolawe, form a fairly tight group, whereas the relative isolation of Kauai renders it a poor recipient or target for events of interisland dispersal. There seems little doubt that Kauai has been a major "source area" because of its age, as appears clear in the case of the Hawaiian drosophilids (Carson et al., 1970; see also fig. 4.1). With respect to angiosperms, Kauai is slightly richer in genera compared with other islands in the chain. However, we would expect newer islands to be centers of speciation. Larger genera in the Hawaiian Islands probably have experienced recent speciation, and owe their size to lack of extinction.

If the island of Hawaii is too new for angiosperm speciation in proportion to its size, the other islands are not. However, we find some interesting patterns if we look at individual genera. The largest angiosperm genus in the Islands is *Cyrtandra*. St. John (1966), in his monograph on the Oahu species, recognizes 118 that are endemic to that island and claims 169 for the Hawaiian chain as a whole. This would indicate that 41 occur exclusively on islands other than Oahu. Perhaps the number of non-Oahu species might be higher if St. John had studied all Hawaiian Cyrtandras. In any case, the preponderance of species obviously occurs on Oahu, despite the fact that it is the third largest island and only slightly larger than Kauai. Moreover, most of the Oahu species are restricted to the Koolau Mts. The basis for this pattern is to be sought in the ecological preferences of *Cyrtandra* and the nature of the Koolau Mts. *Cyrtandra* is characteristic of deep, wet gulches, although some species grow in other areas

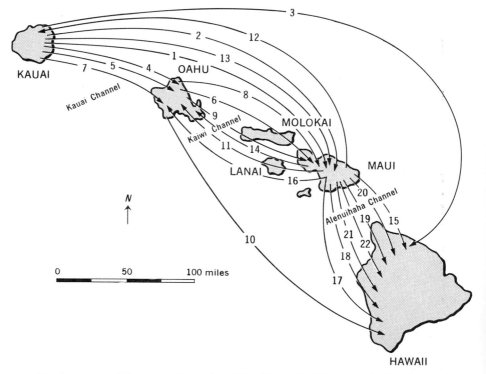

FIG. 4.1. Summary of the proposed number (22) of interisland founders in the picture-winged Drosophilas of Hawaii. From Carson et al. (1970), in *Essays in evolution and genetics in honor of Theodosius Dobzhansky*, ed. M. K. Hecht and W. C. Steere, © Meredith Corp. Reproduced by permission of Appleton-Century-Crofts, Educational Div., Meredith Corp.

of wet rain forest. The Koolau Mts. form a series of such gulches, which not only offer numerous localities suitable for *Cyrtandra* but also are isolated from each other by barriers of relatively dry, sunny ridges, so that an isolating mechanism favorable to speciation in this genus is replicated many times. The explosive speciation of the land shell *Achatinella* in the Koolau Mts. is a significantly parallel example.

If we look at the genera in table 4.1, we find that *Bidens* also has speciated predominantly on Oahu. *Bidens* shows very nearly the inverse of the ecological requirements of *Cyrtandra*, for it tends to grow on ridges. Thus, for *Bidens*, the gulches are barriers that provide an isolating mechanism.

Pelea seems clearly species-rich on the two older major islands, Kauai and Oahu. I suspect that this woody genus speciates at a rate relatively slower than those of the other genera shown in Table 4.1, which are either herbs (*Peperomia, Phyllostegia, Stenogyne*) or shrubby (occasionally arborescent) representatives of predominantly herbaceous families. One generally expects more rapid speciation in herbaceous groups than in woody ones; the number of herbaceous individuals that can occupy a given area is greater and the life cycle is briefer. None of the truly arboreal genera in the Hawaiian flora has speciated to anything like the extent of the herb or woody-herb groups listed in the table. That size of individuals is related to speciation seems clear, and the limited size of island areas also may well be related to it. Certainly species richness is directly related to area and to body size of individuals. For example, Necker Island supports 37 species of insects, 5 species of flowering plants (2 small shrubs, 3 herbs), 1 species of land snail, and no land birds. This example illustrates survival rather than speciation, to be sure, but is indicative of the factors involved. If speciation is slower in woody groups, the older islands would indeed be expected to bear more species of *Pelea*. I am making the assumption that *Pelea* reached the Hawaiian Islands—perhaps arriving on Kauai—early: its greatest diversity, as well as the greatest number of species, is on Kauai. The other genus with a high representation of species on Kauai is *Dubautia*—especially *Dubautia* in the narrow sense. The paleate heads of *Dubautia s.s.* are more primitive than those of *Railliardia*, which have bare receptacles. *Dubautia s.s.* not only has more species on Kauai, but the species also are more diversified there. Maui appears to be the center of diversification for the *Railliardia* species, and the species on Hawaii are either the same as those on Maui or vicarious species close to those on Maui.

Maui is the center of species richness for several of the genera in table 4.1. There is an interesting concentration of *Peperomia* species on Molokai, Maui, and Lanai. The number of species on Molokai and Maui is higher than one would expect. Kauai is relatively poor in *Peperomia* species, despite a high median rainfall that ought to favor *Peperomia*. This situation suggests the possibility that *Peperomia* arrivals and establishments occurred first on the eastern islands, in which case Kauai would have served as a recipient island.

Kauai and Oahu are the only islands on which all four genera of baccate lobelioids occur. However, *Clermontia* and *Cyanea* are much more numerous in species on the eastern islands. *Delissea*, the only baccate genus represented on the westernmost and probably oldest major island, Niihau, may retain the most numerous primitive characteristics in the baccate lobelioids. *Cyanea*, close to *Delissea*, is well represented on Kauai. *Cyanea* most likely is underrepresented on Oahu because *Rollandia*, probably a close derivative of *Cyanea*-like ancestors, has radiated on Oahu and may have forestalled radiation of *Cyanea* and perhaps also *Clermontia* there. *Cyanea*-like ancestors probably are the source of *Clermontia*, which differs chiefly in its growth form and its few-flowered (usually 2-flowered) inflorescences. The *Clermontia* species most like *Cyanea* are *C. haleakalensis* (Maui), *C. multiflora* (Maui, Oahu), *C. samuelii* (Maui), and *C. wailauensis* (Molokai)—all with several-flowered inflorescences. The transition from *Cyanea* to *Clermontia* may well have occurred on Maui, or possibly Oahu. If this is true, it might explain the large number of *Clermontia* species on the island of Hawaii. *Cyanea* and *Clermontia* are wet-forest genera, and the abundance of *Clermontia* species in the broad areas of wet forest on the island of Hawaii is understandable. Kauai is poor in *Clermontia* species (only one, *C. clermontioides*, occurs there), which suggests that it has been a recipient island: *C. clermontioides* is close to *C. kakeana* and *C. oblongifolia* of Oahu, from which stock it may have originated.

Morphological aspects of radiation in the lobelioids are discussed later.

INSECTS

Interestingly, the geographical distribution of species of major insect groups parallels that of angiosperms (table 4.2). Data are from Zimmerman (1948b) and Hardy (1964, 1965). The chief differences can be seen in the greater degree of speciation on the newer (eastern) islands. In view of the angiosperm data, one might not have expected this finding: in angiosperm species tabulated, Oahu and Maui exceed Hawaii, whereas in insect species, Hawaii exceeds all other islands. Why have insect species been formed more readily on the island of Hawaii? (Some of the species are not endemic to that island, but of course most are endemic to the island.) The most likely answer seems to be that insects speciate more rapidly than angiosperms. In view of their much shorter life cycles and the fact that insect populations can be small (in area) and localized geographically, this is understandable. One might claim that insects disperse within an archipelago more readily than angiosperms, but this is probably not a factor in the present examples: otherwise, we would find fewer instances of one-island endemism, whereas the proportion is, in fact, much the same for insects and angiosperms. Moreover, although virtually all the genera of angiosperms listed in table 4.1 have *reached* the island of Hawaii, they

TABLE 4.2.

Distribution of certain Hawaiian insect species, by island

Family and genus	Niihau	Kauai	Oahu	Molo-kai	Maui	Lanai	Hawaii	Other islands
Drosophilidae (all native species)	0	62	92	81	128	13	125	0
Dolichopodidae (total)	0	(20)	(55)	(31)	(37)	(6)	(42)	0
Campsicnemus	0	7	36	25	30	5	35	0
Eurynogaster	0	13	19	8	7	1	7	0
Lygaeidae								
Neseis	0	2	6	7	10	3	11	0
Nysius	0	7	8	7	8		12	11[a]
(both genera)	0	(9)	(14)	(14)	(18)	(7)	(22)	(11)
Totals	0	101	161	126	183	26	189	11
Island area (sq. mi)	72	555	604	260	728	141	4030	
Rainfall (median, in.)	?	99	58	42	75	21	75	

[a] Species of *Nysius* on smaller islands are as follows: Kahoolawe, 2; Nihoa, 2; Necker, 2; French Frigate Shoals, 2; Lisianski, 1; Pearl and Hermes Reef, 2.

evidently have not speciated there in proportion to the land area. Even with insects, although the total of species by islands in table 4.2 is highest on Hawaii, the number (189) is by no means commensurate with the much greater area of that island.

More rapid speciation of insects seems favored by conditions that do not serve as good isolating mechanisms for angiosperms. A kipuka (forest area surrounded by new lava flows, like an island), for example, might be too small to harbor a genetically viable population of an angiosperm species, but it might contain literally thousands of individuals of an insect species.

The insect examples listed in table 4.2 are of interest because the dipterous families (Drosophilidae, Dolichopodidae) are primarily adapted to wet forest, whereas the heteropterous family (Lygaeidae) is characteristic of dry localities. The ability of *Nysius* to colonize low, dry islands in the Leeward chain is illustrative in this regard. Both dipterous and heteropterous groups in table 4.2 show similar distribution of species with respect to islands, however: all three families are well represented on Hawaii, although the totals for Maui are very similar. Recentness of the island of Hawaii must be the reason why, as with angiosperms, species number is not proportional to area. This gives us a dramatic example of how current mathematical formulae, which must of necessity omit factors of geology and climate, cannot be used in particular instances. Admittedly, the island of Hawaii is unusual in being both very large and very recent, compared with volcanic islands at large. Its ecological diversity, however, is entirely commensurate to its size, so we cannot cite lack of available habitats as a reason for lack of species—although possibly its broad, relatively noneroded surfaces do not yet offer as many isolating mechanisms as would ridges and valleys on older islands.

In Drosophilidae, we have accumulating evidence that Kauai has served as the staging area for invasions of the newer islands. The map presented by Carson et al. (1970) and reproduced here as figure 4.1, together with the supporting data of those authors, provides abundant evidence in support of this view. Systematists who have considered problems of inter-island distribution might have hypothesized this result and brought certain morphological lines of evidence to bear (e.g., the *Dubautia-Railliardia* example cited above), but the evidence from cytology of the drosophilids is conclusive. One notes from the map that there is by no means a perfect west-to-east linear sequence, however: Kauai to Maui, followed by subsequent invasion of the intervening island, Oahu, is the case for some of the species groups.

Dispersal events of the larger, expanding groups of insects in the Hawaiian Islands are probably relatively recent. The occurrence of *Nysius* very likely represents recent colonization, rather than relictualism from a period when these islands were large, high islands. There is a parallel in angiosperms and birds. The occurrence on Laysan of the recently (ca. 1923) extinguished honeyeater *Himatione saguinea freethii* and the extant honeycreeper ("Laysan finch") *Psittarostra cantans*, together with the now-extinct sandalwood and *Pritchardia* palm, represent relatively recent dispersal to Laysan from the high islands.

LAND SNAILS

The two major groups showing interesting speciation patterns on the Hawaiian Islands are the achatinellids (Tornatellinidae, subfamily Achatinellinae; also considered a family, Achatinellidae) and amastrids (Cochlicopidae, subfamily Amastrinae; also considered a family, Amastridae).

The achatinellids are absent from Kauai, and the Molokai-Maui complex of islands is considered a likely place of origin, according to Zimmerman (1948a, based on information from C. M. Cooke and Y. Kondo). According to this hypothesis, a *Partulina*-like ancestor, perhaps an *Achatinella*, colonized that island group, then Oahu. On Oahu it radiated spectacularly into numerous species (for a visual summary, see Carlquist, 1970a). As mentioned earlier, *Achatinella* is probably parallel to the angiosperm genus *Cyrtandra* in its speciation, and for much the same reasons. Perkins (1913) lays stress on the tendency of *Achatinella*, according to his observations, to form colonies on particular trees or groups of trees and to stray little from characteristic host plants. With this low mobility, one would expect that the ridges and valleys (habitats different in their host plants) would indeed serve as effective isolating mechanisms.

Partulina has radiated on Maui and Molokai, and a *Partulina* complex is also found on Oahu, indicating a second invasion of Oahu (the first is

127

considered to have given rise to *Achatinella*, which, in its strict sense, is endemic to Oahu). Other achatinellid genera include *Perdicella* (Maui and Molokai: eight species) and *Newcombia* (Molokai and Maui: nine species).

The amastrids, on the other hand, are centered on the older islands. The genus *Carelia* (20 species), now extinct on Niihau and found in sub-fossil form there, is restricted in the living state to Kauai, and even there the genus is decadent, with some species extinct or known only from sub-fossil shells. *Amastra* has radiated to all the major islands. The distribution of described (but not necessarily valid) species, according to Thwing (1907) is as follows: Kauai, 10; Oahu, 52; Molokai, 14; Maui, 17; Lanai, 12; Hawaii, 6. The Kauai species show a notable diversity, including the gigantic *A. knudsenii*, which, by virtue of its striate columellar plait, is said to show affinity to *Carelia* (Thwing, 1907). The genera with remarkably flat shells, *Pterodiscus* and *Planamastra*, are also centered on the older islands. *Laminella* (described species, not necessarily all valid) is distributed as follows: Oahu, 6; Molokai, 4; Maui, 4; Lanai, 3.

LAND BIRDS

Because the Hawaiian honeycreepers provide such superior examples of adaptive radiation, one might expect this excellence to be reflected in geographical distribution of species and genera. There is, to be sure, a character-displacement effect: congeners on a single island tend to differ in bill morphology (this will be discussed later). However, geographical sequences in genera and species of honeycreepers, showing progressively greater specialization, do not seem to occur. The representation of *Psittarostra*, whose morphology suggests an end product of evolution, is heavy on the island of Hawaii (*P. bailleui, P. palmeri, P. flaviceps, P. kona*); *P. psittacea* is present on the six major islands, while *P. cantans* has reached small western islands, Laysan and Nihoa, probably in recent time. Perhaps the new adaptive mode of *Psittarostra* permitted it to invade both eastern and western islands successfully. *Loxops* and *Himatione*, the most "primitive" genera in their respective subfamilies, occur on all major islands of the chain. *Ciridops* is known only from the island of Hawaii. These and other patterns (data from Amadon, 1950) suggest no geographical se-

128

quences except at the infrageneric level. Perhaps, then, the honeycreepers have dispersed easily from island to island into all suitable niches. The recentness of adaptive radiation in this group is difficult to estimate. Bock (1970) concludes that radiation may have required as little as one million years, although he concedes that ten million years have been available for it. Although dispersal of land birds to the Hawaiian Islands has been difficult, redispersal within the chain has evidently been comparatively easily accomplished. The pattern of drepanidid distribution parallels that of Lygaeidae among insects. To be sure, the rarity and early extinction of some of the Hawaiian honeycreepers may have left gaps in our geographical distribution; *Ciridops* might have occurred on islands other than the island of Hawaii, for example. However, there is no reason to assume that any of the honeycreepers ranged much more widely than our records of them indicate (see Amadon, 1950). More difficult to explain are some of the other bird distributions within the Islands. The occurrence of the Hawaiian crow (*Corvus tropicus*) only in one area on the island of Hawaii might be the result of a relatively recent establishment.

Morphological and Ecological Aspects of Hawaiian Adaptive Radiation

Each major group of plants or animals has undergone different patterns of adaptive radiation in the Hawaiian Islands, although there are a few striking parallels. Some of these patterns have been studied with relative thoroughness, as in the Hawaiian honeycreepers, for which, however, field observations have been relatively few until recently. For such groups, I can only offer syntheses of what has already been offered by various authors. Other groups, such as the lobelioids, are known to taxonomists, but the data have been expressed very little in evolutionary terms. For these, literature and original field observations can be synthesized. In still other groups, such as certain of the land shells and insects, more thorough examinations of ecology and other factors relating to evolution are needed or are under way at present. For some rare, endangered, and extinct groups, definitive data may never be available, and we will only be able to speculate about modes and ranges of adaptation.

FLOWERING PLANTS

Lobelioids

The Hawaiian lobelioids form an interesting series of examples of adaptive radiation, because each genus demonstrates distinctive modes of speciation.

Delissea. This genus, suggested by Rock (1919) and Wimmer (1956) to be ancient and "decadent" (as Hawaiian plants go), may be similar to the ancestral stock of the baccate lobelioids. It is distinctively a genus of lower elevations or drier upland localities. The extreme is probably represented by the Niihau population, named *D. niihauensis* by St. John (1959). *Delissea niihauensis*, now extinct, was evidently a stem succulent. One would guess that when Niihau's eastern ridge was populated by native dry forest and scrub plants, such as *Reynoldsia, Lipochaeta,* and *Erythrina,* that *D. niihauensis* grew in somewhat protected places and resembled to a moderate degree the endemic stem-succulent lobelioid *Brighamia.* The native locality for *D. niihauensis* could not have been more than several hundred feet in altitude, for Niihau reaches a maximum altitude of 1281 ft; it may have occupied the lowest elevation of any lobelioid except *Brighamia.* Another altitudinal extreme is represented by *D. undulata,* whose only known current locality is Puu Lehua, approximately 5000 ft elevation, between Hualalai and Mauna Loa, on Hawaii. This may be the last extant population of this *Delissea* (Carlquist, 1970a). The Puu Lehua locality, characterized by small cinder cones, is definitely dry forest: *D. undulata* has unbranched stems 18–90 cm tall, and grows among *Acacia koa* trees under which a few native shrubby genera, such as *Lipochaeta,* persist. In 1966 I found plants broken by cattle, yet still alive, indicating that this species of *Delissea* also has qualities of a stem succulent.

Other species of *Delissea* apparently occurred in localities at low elevations but probably less xeric than those of the two preceding species. *Delissea subcordata* is distinctive in being a branched shrub, but its broad leaves and known localities suggest a more mesic adaptation. It apparently is an understory element (it may still be extant) in low but moist gulches on Oahu. We do know *D. rhytidosperma* from elevations between 2000 and 3000 ft in the Waimea Canyon on Kauai, which would place it in relatively dry *Acacia koa* forest or *Styphelia-Dodonaea* scrub. Its narrow leaves certainly suggest a more xeromorphic adaptation than do the broad ones of

D. subcordata. Delissea rhytidosperma can be called a branched shrub or small tree.

Cyanea. As mentioned earlier, *Cyanea*, which has lateral inflorescences indefinite in flower number, may represent a stock close to ancestral stocks of the baccate Hawaiian lobelioids. If ecological shift into wet forest represents a divergence from original adaptation, as it seems to in many Hawaiian genera (e.g., *Bidens*), *Cyanea* could be considered a wet-forest derivative of *Delissea*-like ancestors. Virtually all species of *Cyanea* occupy wet forest; the range is probably between as little as 50 in. annual rainfall in leeward koa forests for species such as *C. angustifolia* (Mt. Tantalus, Manoa Trail) or *C. leptostegia*, in tall koa forest of the Kokee region of Kauai. Even these koa forests are transitional to *Metrosideros* forests and are usually a mixture of the two trees. In the most mesic localities for *Cyanea*, rainfall may be as high as 400 in. annually, as on the northern slopes of East Maui (Olinda Trail: *C. aculeatiflora, C. hamatiflora,* etc.) or on the upper slopes of Puu Kukui, West Maui (*C. atra*). Some species of *Cyanea* occupy deep shady gulches where rainfall may be less, but available moisture is great and evaporation low (e.g., *C. solenocalyx* on upper Molokai). Although this range of moisture is broad, all the environments could be described as mesic. The nature of adaptation in *Cyanea* that is visible in terms of morphology is not so much to rainfall belts but to different modes of vegetative structure that represent alternative ways of occupying wet-forest areas.

The range in growth forms in *Cyanea* can be characterized according to the scheme of figure 4.2. The smallest and simplest are exemplified by *C. pilosa* and closely related species (*C. bishopi, C. longipedunculata, C. acuminata*). These species, mostly placed in sect. *Pilosae* of *Cyanea*, typically are unbranched rosette plants with upright stems of limited length, not much more than 1 m in height, with most individuals lower. They grow as forest-floor elements in wet *Metrosideros* forest; leaves are broad and thin, but hairy. In that respect, as well as in their small white flowers and habitat preference, they mimic, in a generalized way, some of the Hawaiian species of *Cyrtandra*. The Cyaneas of sect. *Pilosae* may well be reductions not only in plant size but also in flower size. In any case, some unbranched or sparsely branched plants of moderate stature probably were basic to the taller rosette trees of *Cyanea*.

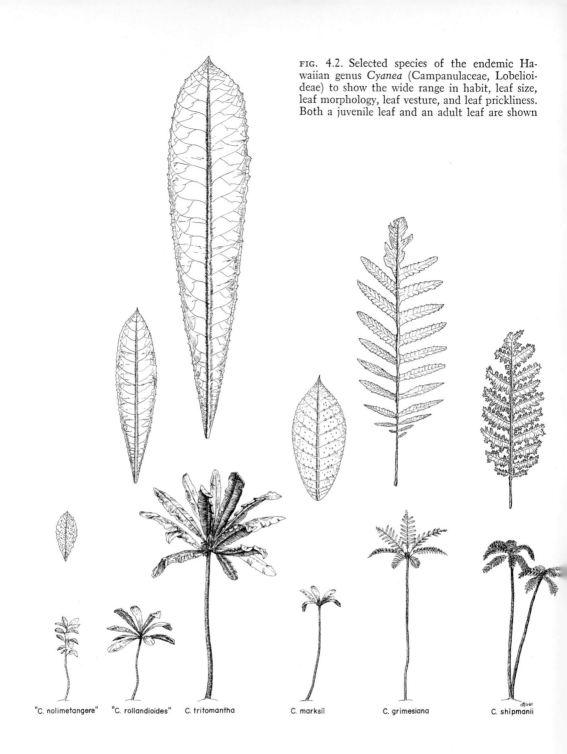

FIG. 4.2. Selected species of the endemic Hawaiian genus *Cyanea* (Campanulaceae, Lobelioideae) to show the wide range in habit, leaf size, leaf morphology, leaf vesture, and leaf prickliness. Both a juvenile leaf and an adult leaf are shown

"C. nolimetangere"   "C. rollandioides"   C. tritomantha   C. marksii   C. grimesiana   C. shipmanii

for *C. leptostegia*. One typical leaf is shown for all other plants. The alleged species "*C. nolime-tangere*" and "*C. rollandioides*" are considered to be juvenile stages of *C. tritomantha*. Separate scales are given for habit and for leaves.

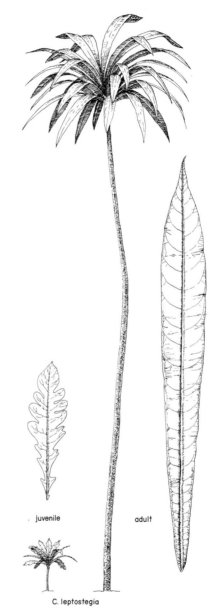

C. pilosa   C. gayana   C. angustifolia   juvenile   adult

C. leptostegia

133

A *Cyanea* of intermediate stature would resemble a *Delissea*. Species from Kauai, such as *C. gayana* (fig. 4.2), *C. recta, C. fissa,* and *C. hirtella,* would fill this description. These are rosette herbs, somewhat woody at their bases, with larger leaves. While always understory elements in wet forest, they grow to 2 m or more. The leaves are thin and broad, suggesting shaded conditions. Inflorescences are short and congested. Visiting birds would probably perch on main stems while feeding on the flowers; ornithophily is suggested by size of flowers (over 2 cm long) and color (white with purplish guidelines).

Cyanea angustifolia (fig. 4.2) and segregate or related species (*C. fauriei, C. sylvestris*) remind me both of the preceding species of *Cyanea* and of *Delissea.* The *C. angustifolia* group, however, typically grows in somewhat drier situations, such as relatively low elevations of the leeward Koolau Mts. behind Honolulu, where *C. angustifolia* can readily be seen. Degree of branching varies with age of plant, type of forest, and perhaps injury to the main stem. Most individuals eventually branch in a fountainlike fashion, however. An unbranched plant of *C. angustifolia,* with pendant clusters of flowers of moderate size, certainly recalls species of *Delissea,* especially when one considers that *C. angustifolia* favors somewhat drier habitats than those of other *Cyanea* species. The koa-ohia forest where *C. angustifolia* grows is dry only by comparison to other *Cyanea* habitats. The branching habit seems related to the sunnier, almost scrublike conditions where *C. angustifolia* grows. It occurs at or near the summits of ridges where koa and ohia (*Metrosideros*) trees are smaller, and where more sunlight would penetrate than in lower valleys.

Although all of the abovementioned species of *Cyanea* share some aspects of a *Delissea*-like ancestry, those described below seem to me to represent departures from that ancestry clearly beyond anything in *Delissea,* and peculiar to the genus *Cyanea.* The most striking of these tendencies is formation of giant rosette trees, represented most conspicuously by *Cyanea leptostegia* (fig. 4.2) of Kauai. Similar species include *C. carlsoni* (Hawaii), *C. regina* (Oahu), *C. superba* (Oahu), *C. gibsoni* (Hawaii), and *C. arborea* (Maui). These species tend to be unbranched (with few exceptions), to grow in moderately wet forest, and to reach heights of 14 m. The leaves are long, strap-shaped, and sessile. The height of these plants seems related to height of surrounding forest. *Cyanea leptostegia,* for example, grows in the relatively tall koa forest of Kokee, Kauai. The single rosette tends, therefore, to reach better-illuminated levels of the forest. Leaves of these species are leathery, have strong midribs, and seem better adapted to wind action and desiccation than do those of the preceding groups of *Cyanea* species. The large size of the leaves may be related to the fact that these tall plants bear only a single cluster of leaves. A juvenile plant of *C. leptostegia* has a relatively narrow stem and lobate, thin leaves, a foliar dimorphism indicating adaptation of juvenile leaves to lower illumination near the forest floor. Young plants have long internodes and narrow stems, eventually widened by production of a broader woody cylinder. An adult plant of *C. leptostegia* has very short internodes at the level of the leaf rosette. At the same time, the pith is very wide near the rosette, so that the total width of the stem is nearly as great as that of the base of the plant, which has a wider woody cylinder but a narrow pith. The upper stem has a xylem-cylinder configuration maximizing strength, and because of its circumference is suited to bearing more numerous leaves. If pith (and therefore stem) diameter did not increase upwardly, too few leaves to support a large plant might be produced, and the stem might fracture more easily above. The secondary xylem of the upper stem (Carlquist, 1969b) does show greater mechanical strength, by virtue of thicker-walled libriform fibers, than does the wood at the base of the plant. Inflorescences are not long and pendant, but borne on short peduncles, among leaves. This suggests that birds visting the flowers would perch not on the stems but on the strong, sessile leaves, which could withstand such usage by virtue of their stout midribs, whereas in *C. angustifolia*, visiting birds would perch on the stem just below the long, pendant flower clusters and probe upward into the inflorescences.

A series of *Cyanea* species that bear spiny or highly prickly leaves and stems in the juvenile condition, and moderately prickly or merely hirsute leaves in the adult condition has been typically grouped with the *C. leptostegia* group. These prickly species—represented on Oahu and, to a much greater extent, on the islands to the east—represent unique innovations among Hawaiian lobelioids. They seem to be basically unbranched rosette herbs or rosette trees of intermediate height, characteristic of very wet forest, and may not have been derived at all from the notably glabrous *C. leptostegia* group. A typical and critical example of the prickly rosette-tree Cyaneas is represented by *C. tritomantha* (fig. 4.2), from wet ohia forests inland from Hilo. Although a rosette tree to 5 m, it is undoubtedly an understory element, for it grows in tall ohia forests with *Cibotium* tree ferns. The leaves of adult plants of *C. tritomantha* are exceptionally long and broad, and are borne on thick, succulent petioles that may serve as perch sites for birds visiting the flowers, which are large, and white or slightly purplish. Leaves are only moderately prickly or slightly hirsute; internodes are very short, and if one saw only an adult plant, one could perhaps group this species with the *C. leptostegia* group. However, this would be a mistake, as I have suggested earlier (1970a). The juvenile stages of *C. tritomantha* were apparently undescribed or disregarded until my field studies in 1966. At that time, I attempted to find a series of *Cyanea* species reported from the same area as *C. tritomantha: C. nolimetangere, C. rollandioides,* and *C. bryanii,* for example. When I did locate them, I discovered them to be, in all likelihood, merely various stages in the development of *C. tritomantha.* That they could have been named as species results only from the fact that these juvenile stages can bear flowers. Seedlings of *C. tritomantha* bear broad, highly prickly, thin leaves and have long internodes. Shoots corresponding to these seedlings were also observed as sucker shoots, or shoots in response to injury, on adult *C. tritomantha* plants. These prickly seedlings were the basis for *C. nolimetangere* Rock. Very possibly they may stay in this juvenile stage for a long period of time (they do bear flowers in this condition), and perhaps in some cases never are able to mature into adult plants. In clearings near the virgin *Metrosideros* forest where I saw *C. tritomantha,* I noticed plants with longer, less prickly leaves. These plants bore flowers and tended to branch somewhat, in this sunnier habitat. Such individuals correspond well to what has been named *C. rollandioides* and perhaps to other species, such as *C. fernaldii.* Minor differences in calyx morphology may account for naming of several species that essentially represent an intermediate stage in the development of *C. tritomantha.* In the same general area, *Cyanea* plants to 3 m, still with relatively long internodes, and with leaves intermediate in size and vesture between those of "*C. rollandioides*" and those of *C. tritomantha,* were seen. These plants have been named *C. bryanii* by Rock. The flowers of "*C. bryanii*" are within the range of variability of *C. tritomantha.* If one only had herbarium sheets of these stages available for study, one could, understandably, name several species, but field studies dictate otherwise. To my knowledge, there are no studies that follow the development of *Cyanea* species from seedling to adult plant.

The situation described opens possibilities that other named prickly-leaved Cyaneas may represent juvenile stages, but unraveling this complex situation to its fullest extent will not prove easy for several reasons. (1) Some of the named prickly Cyaneas are very scarce and may even be extinct, and field studies will be difficult or impossible; although we can suspect that some are juvenile stages of others, we cannot be positive. (2) There is variability in floral morphology within *Cyanea* species, and a juvenile stage with flowers slightly different from those of an adult plant may cause some to support segregation. If only slight floral differences separate them, however, one should be suspicious: calyx-lobe length and morphology are notoriously variable in *Cyanea*, and might even vary with degree of adulthood of the plant. (3) There probably are prickly species that are *permanently juvenile*. One clear example seems to be *Cyanea marksii* (fig. 4.2). This plant grows in the Honaunau forests of Kona, island of Hawaii, well removed from any tree-Cyaneas that could conceivably be related to it. It takes the form of a miniature rosette tree to 2 m, very prickly on stems and leaves. To be sure, it grows near (but not in) forest openings, but no "versions" of this plant corresponding to an adult form have ever been found in the Honaunau forests (although *C. stictophylla*, in this region, should be reexamined to be sure there is no relationship to *C. marksii*). *Cyanea marksii* may well be a permanently juvenile species.

The prickly species of *Cyanea* on Maui are poorly known, and similar considerations may apply to them. *Cyanea ferox* may be a permanently juvenile species. However, taxonomic designation of plants with differing degrees of prickliness as varieties (*Cyanea ferox* var. *horrida*) without field study seems inadvisable—these are probably different degrees of juvenilism. Broad-leaved Cyaneas with sinuate leaves may well be juvenile stages (just as sinuate leaves are juvenile in *C. leptostegia*). One notes in this regard plants named *Cyanea atra* var. *lobata*—very likely juvenile stages of *C. atra*, a species similar in habit, when adult, to *C. tritomantha*. I am suspicious of certain taxa, collected very infrequently, that are named on the basis of sinuate leaves, such as *C. quercifolia* or *C. solanacea*. They should be

137

compared with *C. holophylla* to see if they are developmental stages or perhaps permanently juvenile species. Other prickly species from Maui, such as *C. aculeatiflora* (with distinctive prickly flowers and fruits) and *C. hamatiflora* are undoubtedly valid species based on adult plants, but we do not know what the younger stages look like. The possibility remains that juvenile stages capable of flowering might have been named as distinct species.

The interesting feature of the prickly Cyaneas is not the taxonomic confusion but the apparent adaptations to various conditions they seem to represent, by virtue of marked or slight polymorphism from juvenile to adult. A seedling of a palmiform *Cyanea* grows under conditions quite different from those of an adult plant. Greater prickliness on seedlings may represent protection from phytophagous insects—or even molluscs (Carlquist, 1962), although this is as yet entirely speculative. Prickliness that disappears as a plant becomes adult suggests this possibility (as in the giant *Euphorbia, E. candelabrum*), but the paucity of herbivores in the native Hawaiian fauna complicates this speculation—especially since prickliness occurs only in some of the species of *Cyanea* (and some Rollandias), not in other lobelioids of the world.

Permanent juvenilism of a sort (but other factors as well) may be involved in a trio of interesting species: *C. asplenifolia, C. grimesiana,* and *C. shipmanii* (fig. 4.2). Of these, *C. asplenifolia* (Maui) and *C. grimesiana* (Maui, Molokai, Oahu, Lanai, Hawaii) agree in having pinnate leaves, not unlike those of *C. ferox*. Juvenile leaves of *C. grimesiana*, as I have observed in the field, are pinnatifid but also markedly prickly, showing that this group of species is probably related to the palmiform group. The same is true of *C. shipmanii*, known only from *Metrosideros* forests at 6000 ft on Mauna Kea. This species is more striking, however, in that the leaves are not merely pinnate but bipinnatifid, nearly bipinnate. The ecological adaptation of these three species is perhaps not what one might expect. Pinnate leaves suggest a shady forest-floor habitat. However, the pinnate-leaved Cyaneas occupy an even more apppropriate niche: deep shady gulches, which receive less light than would an equivalent area of flat rain forest. The stems of these species do become elongate, up to about 2.5 m in height, which places them in better-lit portions of ravines, but still in deep shade.

Thus, *Cyanea* has undergone an amazing degree of adaptive radiation with respect to habit. Because *Cyanea*, like *Delissea*, *Rollandia*, and *Clermontia*, is an endemic genus, we can be certain that this radiation is autochthonous. Flower colors vary in *Cyanea* (white, white streaked with purple, purple, rose, pink). In some species (*C. atra*, *C. marksii*, and *C. aculeatiflora*), corollas are deep purple outside, white within. Corolla and calyx-lobe shapes differ among the species. Corollas and calyces of *C. aculeatiflora* are densely covered with prickles (Carlquist, 1962). These floral variations alone constitute an unexpected diversity. Different pollination agents may be involved in these floral types; certainly different positioning of pollinating birds must be involved during their feeding activities on the various Cyaneas. Even supposing most species to be ornithophilous, we are faced with the question, discussed later in the case of *Clermontia*, why there should be diversity in floral morphology and color.

Rollandia. *Rollandia* is a genus endemic to Oahu, with the single exception of *R. parvifolia* Forbes, an apparently valid *Rollandia* collected only once at its type locality on Kauai. *Rollandia* on Oahu has shown a surprising range in habit and habitat (fig. 4.3). Although all Rollandias, like all Cyaneas, could be called rosette herbs (or rosette trees), this brief description covers a diversity of expressions and ecological correlations. Some wet-forest species, such as *R. crispa*, have broad leaves, tomentose to various degrees. *Rollandia crispa* is branched or unbranched, to 1.3 m in height; *R. calycina*, which has longer racemes, is similar but taller, to 2 m. While most Rollandias can be called understory species, *R. crispa* and *R. calycina* are forest-floor species with rose flowers. They remind me of Cyrtandras in their habit. This is even more striking in *R. humboldtiana*, a species 1–2 m tall, often unbranched, with long, drooping racemes of white flowers. *Rollandia humboldtiana* tends to grow in very muddy, wet, shady localities. Another arborescent species, to 3 m, is *R. lanceolata*. This species occurs in moderately moist situations (*Acacia koa* forests) and forms chiefly unbranched rosette "trees." The corolla color of *R. lanceolata* varies from pale green with purplish stripes to pale red or deep purple. The relatively hairy leaves of *R. lanceolata* seem adapted to its drier habitat; their broad shape, however, suggests shadiness, as do leaves of *R. crispa*, *R. humboldtiana*, and *R. calycina*. Hairy leaves

139

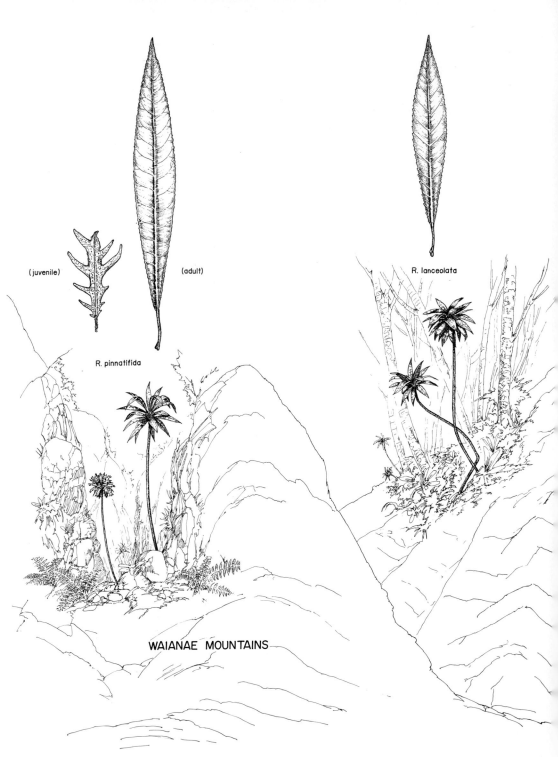

(juvenile)   (adult)

R. lanceolata

R. pinnatifida

WAIANAE MOUNTAINS

140

FIG. 4.3. Selected species of the endemic Hawaiian genus *Rollandia* (Campanulaceae, Lobe-lioideae). This genus on Oahu (only one non-Oahu species is known) shows a great range in habit, habitat, leaf size, and leaf vesture. *Rollandia pinnatifida* is from the Waianae Mts.; the remaining species are from the Koolau Mts. Drawings are placed approximately in relation to characteristic altitudes for these species, and background for each species illustrates the typical associated vegetation. Scales same as those in fig. 4.2.

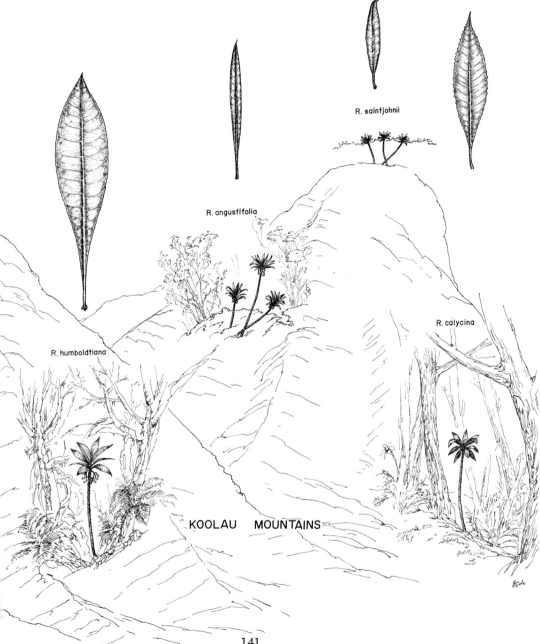

141

occur in a population that was named R. *waianeensis* by St. John. This plant may be conspecific with R. *lanceolata* var. *tomentella,* as Wimmer (1956) suggests, but not, as Wimmer alternatively suggests, a hybrid between R. *lanceolata* and R. *calycina.*

Two species recognized on the basis of glabrous leaves and calyx characters, R. *purpurellifolia* and R. *longifolia,* reach 5 m and 3.3 m, respectively. Thus R. *purpurellifolia* is comparable in habit to R. *crispa,* R. *longifolia* to R. *lanceolata.*

An interesting tree-*Rollandia* that evidently has been long misunderstood is one called R. *kaalae* by Wawra, although the probable earliest name for it is R. *pinnatifida* G. Don.; its synonymy includes *Cyanea selachicauda* Degener. This plant grows deep in moist gulches of the otherwise moderately dry Waianae Mts. (fig. 4.3). Juvenile foliage, markedly sinuate, is produced for many years, and the plant can flower during this juvenile period. Adult leaves ultimately are lanceolate, like those of R. *lanceolata* or R. *crispa.* Lobate juvenile leaves also occur in R. *longiflora* (Rock, 1919). Their significance seems the same as that of sinuate leaves cited in the discussion of *Cyanea.* Occurrence of juvenile leaves of this description in *Cyanea* and *Rollandia* makes uncertain the taxonomic status of *Delissea sinuata* Hbd. and *D. laciniata* Hbd.; both species are known from type specimens only. However, the occurrence of lobate leaves in these three genera is more importantly regarded as three independent adaptations to conditions of low light intensity.

Narrow, glabrous leaves characterize R. *angustifolia* (fig. 4.3). Although this species is not very tall, it grows in scrubby ridge forest and is likely to occur there as an emergent rosette plant of nearly the same height as the shrubby species of *Coprosma, Syzygium,* and others with which it grows. The shiny, thickish, but narrow leaves of R. *angustifolia* are probably suited to the higher light intensity the crown of this plant receives, on cloudy ridges of the leeward Koolau Mts. *Rollandia angustifolia* has purple or purplish-veined flowers.

An extreme in adaptation, perhaps not related to R. *angustifolia* but reminiscent of it in reduction of leaf surface, is R. *saintjohnii.* This species occurs in the low, scrubby, krummholz-like vegetation at the summit ridges of the Koolau range. Constant pressure from trade winds that sweep with tremendous force up the steep windward cliffs (pali) of the Koolau range result in a low, scrubby vegetation that consists mainly of species which would attain greater stature in more sheltered localities. However, *R. saintjohnii* (fig. 4.3) is adapted to and grows only in such windswept localities. Its leaves are the thickest in the genus (about three times as thick as those of *R. calycina* [Carlquist, 1962]), suggesting condensation of form related to wind. A hypodermis can be said to be present in leaves of R. *saintjohnii* (but absent in those of *R. calycina*), and it has a much thicker palisade. Prickles are conspicuous on leaves and stems of *R. saintjohnii*, a fact which suggests a phase of juvenilism (Carlquist, 1962). As one might expect, prickles of this prominence occur elsewhere in the genus *Rollandia* only on the juvenile leaves of *R. pinnatifida*. Both the prickles and the lobate nature of juvenile leaves underline affinity between *Rollandia* and *Cyanea*, separated on the basis of whether the staminal tube is united to the corolla (*Rollandia*) or not.

Clermontia. As mentioned earlier, *Clermontia* seems to be a derivative of *Cyanea* or *Delissea* in which number of flowers is reduced. *Clermontia* is easily recognized, however, by its shrubby, much-branched habit. This habit (present in all except *Clermontia haleakalensis*, which looks like a *Cyanea* vegetatively) is unlike that of other Hawaiian lobelioids. There is a certain range in *Clermontia* with respect to size. At margins of open bog areas on Puu Kukui, *Clermontia micrantha* forms only a small shrub. *Clermontia arborescens* and *C. hawaiiensis* can be treelike and attain heights of more than 6 m. Most species grade imperceptibly between these extremes.

Epiphytism characterizes a few species. *Clermontia peleana* is exclusively epiphytic; *C. clermontioides* and *C. parviflora* are often seen as epiphytes, although by no means invariably so. Other species of *Clermontia* occur only occasionally as epiphytes. In range of habit, *Clermontia* is not exceptional. Moreover, the size and shape of leaves are relatively unvaried throughout the genus.

Clermontia is remarkable, however, in the diversity of floral morphology, color, and size. This variation has been illustrated elsewhere (Rock, 1919; Carlquist, 1970a) and does not need repetition here. I am puzzled by the reasons for this diversity (as well as the floral diversity in *Rollandia* and *Cyanea*). The nature of pollination biology would be the possibility most readily sought by the evolutionary biologist. These apparently ornithophilous flowers are known to be visited by the nectar-feeding honeycreepers (Amadon, 1950; Spieth, 1966). The three species of meliphagids (all but *Moho braccatus* of Kauai are apparently now extinct [Richardson and Bowles, 1964]) may have visited lobelioid flowers. Among the honeycreepers, *Vestiaria* (one species, widespread in the islands, still extant) and some of the species of *Hemignathus* (e.g., *H. procerus*, fig. 4.11) might be or have been effective in lobelioid pollination. The two species of *Drepanis* were definitely nectar-feeders, and might have been very effective in lobelioid pollination. However, the number of species of bird pollinators does not exceed 10 at the most, and perhaps is as few as seven, of which most are known only from a single island each, and perhaps only a limited area on each island. However, there are a large number of endemic lobelioid species. Among the baccate genera Wimmer (1956) recognizes *Delissea*, 8; *Cyanea*, 58; *Rollandia*, 12; and *Clermontia*, 27. Additionally, among nonbaccate Hawaiian lobelioids there are *Trematolobelia* (one species with three subspecies), *Brighamia* (one species, possibly with several geographical races), and the nonendemic genus *Lobelia*, which has 10 endemic Hawaiian species. I regard Wimmer's species concept as too narrow and would recognize about 10 percent fewer species. However, supposing that there are about 105 valid lobelioid species in the Hawaiian Islands, all of them endemic, how are we to explain the diversity in the floral patterns they show? The number of species of bird pollinators obviously does not at all match the number of types of lobelioid flowers.

There are several possibilities. Do (or did) honeycreepers and meliphagid individuals show flower-constancy for particular lobelioid species? As many as three or four species of lobelioids can be found in a single area; for example, *Clermontia arborescens*, *C. grandiflora*, and *C. kakeana* all occur at Haelaau, Puu Kukui, Maui. Among observations to date, only one, that of Perkins (1903) gives us any indication that flower-constancy might be operative. Writing of the feeding habits of *Hemignathus*, he says, "The two common species [*H. lucidus* and *H. procerus*] are both partial to the nectar of some kinds of arborescent Lobeliaceae . . . especially to those with large corollas, whereas to some kinds they pay no attention at all, however profusely they may be in flower." On this slim evidence one might make a case for flower-constancy, but only as a starting point for further observations. Although flower-constancy is not expected in birds as much as in certain groups of insects, it certainly remains a possibility.

There is relatively little separation among species of the lobelioid genera with respect to flowering time, so temporal isolation cannot be invoked as a speciation mechanism. Almost all the *Clermontia* species, for example, can be found in flower in July and August, and some species flower over a period of perhaps 6 months. Some of the most abundant species have greenish flowers (e.g., *C. kakeana*), which would seem least attractive to potential pollinators. One could cite a tendency for lobelioid species of deep shade to have white, more conspicuous flowers, species of better-lit situations to have colored flowers, but there are too many exceptions to credit such a suggestion seriously. Even if the correlation were perfect, it would only explain one dimension of the diversity in floral color, size, and morphology in these genera.

Other factors one might cite include ecological shift, genetic drift, redispersal of variants, and multiplicity of appeal to potential pollinators. Although some of the baccate lobelioids are sympatric, small differences in slope exposure, moisture, and shade tolerance separate the habitats of "sympatric" species. Unfortunately, ecological data are not readily available in monographs of the lobelioids, owing to paucity of information on herbarium labels. However, field botanists familiar with lobelioids do know characteristic preferences for the various species. Ecological shift is basic to adaptive radiation in all major Hawaiian angiosperm genera, and the lobelioids are no exception, as some of the distinctions listed suggest. During ecological shift, one can easily envision changes in growth form and size, but changes in floral morphology and color may have accompanied them. One could invoke genetic drift as an explanation for minor changes, such as color differences. If variants are dispersed to new sites within the islands, geographical isolation would provide a mechanism permitting genetic drift to operate. Certainly the Hawaiian Islands are rich in such isolating mechanisms.

Lobelioids can hybridize, and natural hybrids are known especially in *Clermontia* (Carlquist, 1970a). Probably hybrids were more frequent when pollinating birds were more abundant. That hybrids can be found at all, in view of paucity of pollinating birds, is rather surprising. Lobelioids can

145

self-pollinate and probably owe their continued presence in the Hawaiian flora to this mechanism, although one can imagine that a high degree of selfing might eventually be deleterious. If, however, hybrids were once frequent, one can imagine that a source of variability to supply distinctive new populations has existed. However, one must still explain development of the extremes which can yield hybrids; the cited factors collectively do not seem sufficient. One must not underestimate the possibility that color and shape of lobelioid flowers, within certain limits, may not be adaptive, just as Amadon (1950) and Baldwin (1953) have claimed that plumage colors in the honeycreepers have no apparent adaptive significance.

One may, as a last resort, hypothesize diversity in floral size and morphology as a way of presenting a "diversified appeal" to particular pollinators, just as on a given mainland area of California there are hummingbird flowers in a number of different families and genera. Development of diversity of ornithophilous flowers among Hawaiian lobelioids would then depend on two factors. First, one must assume a "disharmony" in the Hawaiian ornithophilous floras—in other words, not all the potential appeals to birds were originally present, because some groups (e.g., Bignoniaceae) are absent. This would explain why *Hibiscadelphus* and *Kokia*, endemic genera of Malvaceae, evolved curved tubular flowers autochthonously in the Islands. This is true also in *Geranium arboreum*, which I have seen visited by *Himatione sanguinea* (Polipoli Rd, Haleakala). One can imagine even that there might be character displacement, so that species of *Clermontia* in a given area differ in appeal by virtue of size and color—and that if a second species enters the range of a *Clermontia* or *Cyanea*, it must, as discussed in chapter 3, exploit a different range of appeals to pollinators. It is also possible that minor differences in curvature, size, and display of flowers within the lobelioids might offer precise and different pollinating mechanisms, providing isolating factors. At any rate, it seems evident that the lobelioids now represent several stocks, each of which, by sheer probability, is capable of a different range of possibilities, rather than all stocks trending in the same direction.

Lobelia. Although *Trematolobelia* shows only subspecific differentiation related to geography, the Hawaiian species of *Lobelia* show radiation into diversified situations. They could all be described as characteristic of openings in wet forest. However, these "openings" are quite varied. For

L. gaudichaudii (*sensu lato*), the openings are open bogs. For *L. tortuosa*, which has purple flowers, unlike the white (or pinkish) flowers of *L. gaudichaudii*, the habitat is dripping cliffs near waterfalls on Kauai. Blue-flowered species (*L. hillebrandii, L. hypocleuca, L. oahuensis, L. yuccoides*) favor scrub in very moist, cloud-swept localities, often on steep slopes on various islands. *Lobelia oahuensis* can be observed on road cuts on Mt. Kaala.

Dubautia-Argyroxiphium-Wilkesia complex

These three genera (four, to authors who recognize *Railliardia*) probably arose from a single ancestral stock. They form undoubtedly the most outstanding example of adaptive radiation among Hawaiian angiosperms. The habits and habitats of species in this complex have been illustrated rather extensively elsewhere (Carlquist, 1970a). Leaf anatomy of *Argyroxiphium, Dubautia,* and *Wilkesia* has been explored (Carlquist, 1957, 1959a), as has wood anatomy (Carlquist, 1958) and anatomy of the heads (Carlquist, 1959b). Although some references are made to ecology in these papers, a more explicit series of correlations can be presented.

There is little doubt that the primary adaptation of this complex, like that of its mainland madiinean relatives, is rather xeric. There seems a likelihood that the tarweeds (Asteraceae: Heliantheae, subtribe Madiinae) were more widespread in late Tertiary times in California and Mexico. They probably included shrubby forms, like *Adenothamnus validus* (northern Baja California) and the fruticose species of *Hemizonia* on the offshore Californian islands, or *Raillardella scabrida* (Lake Co., northern California). These appear truly like relicts, although the annual tarweeds are now abundant and widespread in central western California.

The Hawaiian immigrants probably diverged early into the rosette plants *Argyroxiphium-Wilkesia* and the shrubby *Dubautia*, although hybrids between the two groups are evidently still possible, for *A. sandwichense* × *D. menziesii* hybrids have been reported and others may occur (see chapter 13).

Argyroxiphium-Wilkesia. The silvery-leaved species of *Argyroxiphium* are probably specialized in leaf anatomy. Even with regard to the indument alone, they are exceptional in the subtribe, and only such mainland species as *Raillardella argentea,* itself an alpine specialization, offer parallels. The

147

green-leaved species (*A. grayanum, A. virescens, Wilkesia gymnoxiphium*) resemble ancestral types more closely. *Wilkesia* has less complicated leaves (the three superposed series of bundles in *Argyroxiphium* leaves are undoubtedly a specialization [Carlquist, 1957]), but has some seemingly specialized characteristics, such as the verticillate leaves (which may be a permanent juvenilism of sorts: production of verticillate leaves can be seen in seedling stages of all Argyroxiphiums, and occasionally in entire shoots of *A. grayanum*). *Wilkesia* is an upland plant but favors dry, open sites at about 2000 ft and above, on Kauai. *Argyroxiphium* is clearly alpine, and probably does not occur below 4000 ft. *Argyroxiphium virescens*, in high, dry to somewhat moist, but cloudswept sites on Haleakala, East Maui, perhaps represents an early adaptation from dry lowland conditions to dry alpine conditions—or dry mid-elevation conditions. *Argyroxiphium virescens* is monocarpic. Evidently the *A. virescens* stock has given rise to *A. grayanum*, a non-monocarpic shrub species from the bogs of Puu Kukui, West Maui, and certain boggy areas on northwestern Haleakala. It represents a rather rapid entry into highly mesic (but still montane) conditions. The silvery-leaved species of *Argyroxiphium*, however, seem basically adapted to dry conditions (although in alpine localities where rising cloud masses may sweep through), and their leaves suggest definite adaptation to brilliant sunshine and desiccating air. *Argyroxiphium sandwichense* occurs on Haleakala and once occurred on all three peaks of the island of Hawaii. *Argyroxiphium kauense* occurs in a peculair "dry cloud forest" at 6000 ft on the southwestern rift zone of Mauna Loa. Although this open forest locality on relatively new lava seems dry, the misty clouds that sweep upwards daily permit such bog species as *Oreobolus furcatus* to occur at this locality, although most associated species are typically alpine or subalpine. The fact that *A. kauense* has rosettes raised on woody stems rather than acaulescent ones, as in *A. sandwichense*, suggests release from the acaulescent habit of *A. sandwichense*, which experiences frost to which a ground-level rosette would be a form of resistance.

An entry into an even more extremely wet locality is represented by *A. caliginii*, a silversword growing in open bog areas of West Maui. *Argyroxiphium caliginii* is almost as "silvery leaved" as *A. sandwichense* but has adopted an almost apomictic habit in the bogs. It is not monocarpic; instead, the rosettes branch at the base, and these prostrate shoots root in the bog. Very few plants flower, in my experience. Perhaps the lack of suitable pollination conditions in the bog has induced this characteristic. Interestingly, heads are pendant in this species, and thus apparently escape wetting by mist and rains. Flowers are dull yellow brown, unlike the brightly colored flowers (yellow or purple) of the other Argyroxiphiums. Hydathodes, to permit jettisoning of excess water, have been developed in leaves of *A. caliginii* (Carlquist, 1957). That the direction of ecological shift in *Argyroxiphium* has been from drier to wetter localities seems clear. Wood anatomy alone would dictate this conclusion: all species of *Argyroxiphium* have the short vessel elements that are characteristic of xeromorphic plants; the bog species have only slightly longer vessel elements, suggesting a recent shift into the bogs (Carlquist, 1958). Thick leaves, rich in water-storing pectic accumulations in intercellular spaces, occur in the bog species, although this pronounced xeromorphic adaptation has no significance in the bog habitat (Carlquist, 1957); it simply is not disadvantageous, and has not been lost. Asteraceae evidently have a capability for rapid ecological shift, and *Argyroxiphium* demonstrates this dramatically. How can such a seemingly abrupt shift take place so readily? The answer probably lies in the fact that despite differences in moisture availability, the high-elevation bogs are subject to intermittent bright sunshine and nocturnal cold, features of dry alpine sites. Moreover, the Hawaiian bogs are probably rather strongly disharmonic (the total bog area in the Islands is not great, and similar bogs in source areas are remote), so that invasion of bogs by montane Hawaiian genera is not difficult.

The ancestors of *Argyroxiphium* and *Wilkesia* may well not have been dry lowland species, and elevations no lower than 2000 ft should be hypothesized for ancestors of the *Dubautia-Argyroxiphium-Wilkesia* complex. These ecological preferences are likely for all temperate elements in the Hawaiian flora, especially those probably from North America, for upland Hawaiian climates simulate (except in day length) lowland maritime California climates, for example. Interestingly, the *Dubautia* complex does not seem to occur below 1000 ft anywhere in the Islands.

Dubautia. As noted in table 4.1, the species of *Dubautia, sensu stricto,* are on the older western islands chiefly, while "*Railliardia*" tends to be on the eastern islands. The sect. *Dubautia* species may be considered more primitive, as stated earlier, because of presence of receptacular bracts.

However, species of sect. *Dubautia* are mostly in quite mesic situations. If the Hawaiian tarweeds originally established in drier sites, the various extant species of *Dubautia s.s.* must be hypothesized to have undergone shift into moister sites, and, with few exceptions (e.g., perhaps *D. plantaginea*), the ancestral stock in drier areas has now vanished. Thus, divergence from the original ancestors into *Dubautia s.s.* and *Railliardia* on the one hand and *Argyroxiphium* and *Wilkesia* on the other probably occurred prior to invasion of wet forest. To be sure, there are hybrids between species of sect. *Dubautia* and sect. *Railliardia* of *Dubautia* (Sherff, 1935b). If divergence of *Argyroxiphium-Wilkesia* from *Dubautia* (including *Railliardia*) took place in drier localities, *Argyroxiphium* must have retained a primitive feature in its ray flowers (lacking in *Dubautia* and *Railliardia*, as well as in *Wilkesia*). The heads of *Argyroxiphium* and *Wilkesia* suggest gigantism, perhaps related to the monocarpic habit, but an expression that involves loss of dispersibility (see chapter 11). Loss of ray flowers can take place easily in Asteraceae. Conspicuousness of rays in the silverswords may relate to alpine pollinators. In any case, *Argyroxiphium* seems a Maui-centered complex (four species there) at present.

If *Dubautia, sensu stricto*, entered the rain forest early, we ought to have some stages in this shift. *Dubautia plantaginea*, a representative from moderately wet forest, has leaves with venation like that of vernal leaves of mainland tarweeds (Carlquist, 1959a, p. 198). Leaf anatomy shows similar features in species of *Dubautia s.s.* that probably represent recent shifts into the wet forest of the summit plateau of Kauai (*D. paleata, D. railliardioides*). Lack of alteration in leaf anatomy of these species compared with that of *D. plantaginea* may be explained by the fact that although they grow in zones of higher rainfall, they characterize forest margins rather than the wet forest itself. *Dubautia laxa, D. knudsenii, D. molokaiensis*, and *D. reticulata* show reduction in number of palisade layers, thinner leaves, and absence of bundle-sheath extensions, all of which may be related to lower light intensity in dense forests or misty ridges where these species typically grow. The broad, glabrous, relatively thin leaves of *D. knudsenii* typify adaptation to uniformly mesic rain forest. *Dubautia knudsenii* is a true tree.

Leaves of *D. latifolia* are unique among tarweeds: they have reticulate venation, whereas longitudinally oriented veins predominate in all others (most notably in *Wilkesia*). In addition, coriaceous leaf texture in this species is the result of fibrous bundle-sheath extensions. This odd and nearly extinct species is unique in the group in its vining habit. It typically grows in lower, drier areas of the upper Waimea Canyon on Kauai and forms inflorescences when it reaches the canopy of the forest. Its leaves can only be called those of a sclerophyllous plant. However, herbarium specimens, as would be expected, have only leaves adjacent to the inflorescence. Such leaves would be expected to be less mesic in construction. Leaves lower on these vining plants may have been quite different, but unless this species is studied in the field, we may never know.

Dubautia waialealae is notable for representing an adaptation to the wettest locale in the Hawaiian Islands, the summit area proper of Kauai. This species has more fibers on bundles in leaves than one might expect, but this characteristic might be explained by the value of shorter, tougher leaves in a bog area often buffeted by strong misty winds. Lack of a well-defined palisade in leaves of *D. waialealae* is related to the almost perpetually cloudy conditions of the Waialeale bog.

The *Railliardia* species of *Dubautia* are mostly alpine and may represent an advance to upland dry sites. One may not think of Kilauea, 4000 ft elevation, as an alpine locality. However, many Hawaiian alpine elements occur there (*Vaccinium, Silene*). The Kilauea species *Dubautia* (*Railliardia*) *ciliolata* can also be found at high elevations on the island of Hawaii, as can another species that occurs at Kilauea, *D. (R.) scabra*. *Dubautia menziesii*, a Haleakala alpine, is characteristic for this site in its leaf adaptations. Leaves are short and stiff, and especially thick—a condensation in form reminiscent of the condensed leaf form in the Haleakala silversword. Leaves of *D. menziesii* tend to be isolateral. The large fibrous bundle caps in leaves are correlated with stout texture. Chloroplasts are abundant throughout the leaf, indicating adaptation to high light intensity. Cuticle is exceptionally thick, indicating minimal water loss in the dry alpine situation. Air spaces are smaller in this leaf than in leaves of forest species, and secretory canals are smaller or absent. Of these features, only the diminished secretory canals do not have an obvious correlation, as compared with angiosperms at large, to the alpine habitat.

Invasion of the alpine areas by both *Argyroxiphium* and the Railliardias is interesting, because the shrubby habit of the latter (perhaps rather like the ancestral habit of the complex) is quite unlike the rosette habit of the former. One cannot say which entered the alpine zone first; they may have shifted into different alpine zones within the chain, then redispersed so as to be sympatric. The alpine Railliardias and *Argyroxiphium* point up the fact that most of the Hawaiian alpine flora is derived from species of dry lowlands; the same genera, often the same species, tend to appear both at low dry localities and high dry sites: *Styphelia, Dodonaea, Artemisia, Wikstroemia*. There are a few primarily or exclusively alpine genera: *Silene, Geranium, Sisyrinchium,* and *Vaccinium,* for example. However, the Hawaiian alpine flora seems even more disharmonic than the flora as a whole, so radiation of lower-elevation and even wet-forest elements (*Sadleria, Coprosma*) into the alpine zones seems to have occurred. This has occurred in the Canary Islands also (chapter 5).

Since leaf size and leaf shape are sensitive indicators of mesomorphy or xeromorphy in *Dubautia*, it is interesting to find that xylem shows these trends as well (fig. 4.4). Xylem evolution, in general, tends to lag behind external morphology as an indicator of xeromorphy or mesomorphy, but in many Asteraceae it has adapted very sensitively to habitat. The average dimensions of vessel elements, given in figure 4.4, show a most amazing degree of correlation. The cell diameters probably give a better indication of available moisture in the habitat of any given species than would even a very good rainfall map. Areas subject to frequent cloud cover tend to receive more rain, but they also provide increased moisture availability because of retarded evaporation. Areas with less cloud cover naturally tend to bear less vegetation, and the bare soil dries out rapidly, a fact also related to the porosity of Hawaiian soils. Thus, there are factors which, for a plant, make a wet Hawaiian forest "wetter" than rainfall figures would suggest, and dry areas, in effect, "drier." Ecological gradients are therefore sharper than one might expect. This may help explain why vessels are so well correlated. Short, narrow vessels indicate xeromorphy. Vessel grouping and density, as seen in transections of woods, are also greater in xeric species of *Dubautia*, as one would expect from studies of angiosperm woods at large (Carlquist, 1958).

152

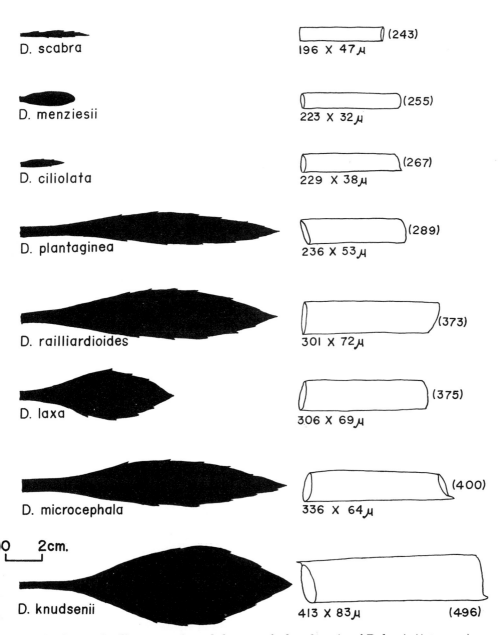

D. scabra
196 X 47μ (243)

D. menziesii
223 X 32μ (255)

D. ciliolata
229 X 38μ (267)

D. plantaginea
236 X 53μ (289)

D. railliardioides
301 X 72μ (373)

D. laxa
306 X 69μ (375)

D. microcephala
336 X 64μ (400)

0   2cm.

D. knudsenii
413 X 83μ (496)

FIG. 4.4. Leaves, in silhouette, and vessel elements of selected species of *Dubautia* (Asteraceae). Average adult leaves are shown (scale indicated). Vessel elements are drawn to represent the average length and width (figures below vessel element in each species). Species are arranged in order of the figure obtained by adding the average vessel width and vessel-element length (in parentheses at right for each). Data original and from Carlquist (1958).

153

Pelea

Pelea (Rutaceae) is a genus nearly endemic to the Hawaiian Islands. Two species occur in the Marquesas. In turn, the genus is close to *Melicope, Evodia (Euodia)*, and *Acronychia* of the South Pacific. Independently, Stone (1969) prepared a monograph of the genus and I devoted a section of a book (1970a) to diversity in *Pelea.* In habit, *Pelea* ranges from small shrubs (*P. waialealae*) to species 16 m tall (*P. zahlbruckneri, P. pallida, P. hawaiensis.* Although most Peleas are shrubs of intermediate height, three species are scandent and could almost be called vines (*P. ovata, P. adscendens, P. anisata*). *Pelea* and its relatives seem basically adapted to moderately wet forest. If so, a few species (*P. pallida, P. sandwicensis, P. hawaiensis, P. radiata,* and *P. grandifolia*) may have adapted to habitats of a slightly drier nature; these species are from the rather dry koa-sandalwood forest of low (below 2000 ft) elevations. Bog species include *P. waialealae, P. recurvata, P. cruciata, P. parvifolia* var. *sessilis,* and *P. orbiculata.* Leaf size tends to be largest in less mesic species, smallest in the bog species, intermediate in wet-forest species. *Pelea* provides a good example of adaptive radiation, although the entire genus is basically woody, and leaf texture does not vary greatly (however, I would guess that interesting differences in leaf anatomy with relation to ecology could be found). Some species have developed cauliflory in the Hawaiian Islands, whereas others have large open panicles. The adaptive significance of this variation is unclear.

That the range in habit and habitat of *Pelea* seems a divergence to arborescence and to smaller shrubs from shrubs of intermediate size is interesting, for shrubs tend to show less adaptive radiation than genera in the Hawaiian flora that represent predominantly herbaceous families. Moreover, the Hawaiian Peleas are far more diverse than *Melicope, Evodia,* and *Acronychia* together. This diversity may have developed autochthonously more than once in the Hawaiian Islands; Stone (1969) recognizes four sections (two are recognized in earlier treatments), none of which has a stereotyped habit or habitat range. The Marquesan species do not belong to sect. *Apocarpa,* which is presumed to be primitive in having separated carpels. If this interpretation is accurate, the Marquesan Peleas may be immigrants from Hawaii rather than intermediates of a group that termi-

154

nates in the Hawaiian Islands, as is considered to be the case in most genera of plants and animals.

Coprosma

Another shrubby genus that has shown appreciable radiation is *Coprosma* (Rubiaceae). This Pacific genus is represented by about 27 species in the Hawaiian Islands. As Oliver's (1935) monograph suggests, the black-fruited *C. ernodeoides* may have been an establishment independent of the one that led to the remaining Hawaiian species, all of which are orange-fruited. Among the orange-fruited species, there are distinctive adaptations. By far the majority of Coprosmas are broad-leaved, rain-forest species. However, *C. ochracea* is a distinctive, miniature bog shrub with coriaceous leaves (Carlquist, 1970a, p. 355). *Coprosma montana* is a microphyllous species of dry alpine localities, such as the cinder cones of Haleakala, where the silversword grows, and at high elevations on the island of Hawaii.

Cyrtandra

Gesneriaceae seems basically an herbaceous family, as does the gesneriad genus *Cyrtandra*. The family does have, however, the capacity for increased woodiness. Very likely, the Hawaiian species represent a single stock. One would suspect this from the chromosome number, $n = 17$, which is otherwise unusual in the genus. *Cyrtandra* can be cited, as it was earlier in this chapter, as a large genus that shows much vicarious speciation in the Hawaiian Islands. However, there is a notable range in habit among the Hawaiian species. Some can become small trees, to 6 m (for example, *C. gayana*, *C. kalihii*, *C. waiolanii*). Most are little-branched, upright herbs, but some (*C. oenobarba*) are decumbent. There is some cauliflory in Hawaiian species (*C. lysiosepala* [Carlquist, 1970a, p. 127]). However, the most curious adaptation is the production of flowers on shoots at ground level, so that inflorescences invariably trail along the ground surface. This habit, which suggests a distinctive (but unknown) pollination system, occurs in *C. stupantha* and *C. kaulantha* (St. John, 1966). This habit has probably developed in the two Hawaiian species independently of the same adaptation in a Borneo species, *C. basiflora*. Some distinctive features in Hawaiian Cyrtandras are of unknown adaptive value, if any. Most Cyrtandras have ellipsoid or fusiform fruits, but *C. brevicornuta*, *C.*

155

calpidicarpa, and *C. cornuta* have elongate fruits to 12.5 cm in length (St. John, 1966). Other features of questionable adaptive significance include ovaries glabrous in anthesis but hairy at maturity (*C. laxiflora,* etc.), densely hairy versus glabrous leaves (species with each type can be found sympatrically), and the various calyx types. *Cyrtandra* flowers, in the Hawaiian Islands and elsewhere, may be actinomorphic or zygomorphic. The difference is not great, and zygomorphy is undoubtedly reversible, according to Burtt's data for Gesneriaceae.

Pritchardia

This palm genus probably represents an eastern-Pacific extension of *Livistona.* At any rate, there are some low-elevation species in areas of less than 25 in. annual rainfall, as *P. remota* on Nihoa (perhaps formerly also on Laysan), but Pritchardias can occur in areas where rainfall exceeds 250 in. per year. The population termed *P. beccariana* behind Hilo is a tall tree, reaching forest canopy levels in the unusually tall ohia forest there. Populations in the rather more scrubby forest of the Koolau Mts., Oahu, tend to mimic surrounding woody plants in their short trunks; such populations have been called *P. martii, P. macdanielsii,* etc. *Pritchardia* was probably a widespread lowland genus, as shown by fossils (Carlquist, 1970a, p. 61), but the lowland climate may have been much wetter in former times, as during the Pleistocene, when climatic belts were presumably lower. The range in fruit size in *Pritchardia* is phenomenal, and is discussed in chapter 11.

Euphorbia

An excellent example of adaptive radiation, *Euphorbia* (Euphorbiaceae) shows increased stature with ecological shift into successively moister sites. As such, it is an example of "insular woodiness," and is discussed in that connection in chapter 10. Illustrations of the various species and their habits have been offered earlier (Carlquist, 1970a), and need no repetition here. However, in the time since that account, a new species, *E. haeleeleana,* has been described (Herbst, 1971). This novelty appears to represent the tallest *Euphorbia* (14 m) in the Hawaiian Islands, but cannot be cited as an end-product of increased woodiness in the same line as the other species because, according to Herbst, it is not a chamaesycoid *Euphorbia,* as

the others all are. The aspects of adaptive radiation in the Hawaiian chamaesycoid Euphorbias that relate to wood anatomy have been described
(Carlquist, 1970b), and are notable in that, as with *Dubautia*, ecologically
interpretable features of wood anatomy in these species parallel degree of
mesomorphy or xeromorphy. Leaf anatomy of the Hawaiian chamaesycoid
Euphorbias, a project currently under investigation, appears strongly related also; leaves range in texture from succulent in coastal species to
papery, of short duration, in dry forest, to leathery in rain-forest species.

Scaevola

Like Euphorbia, *Scaevola* (Goodeniaceae) in the Hawaiian Islands
shows a series in increased woodiness. Therefore, comments on this genus
are offered in chapter 10. Illustrations have been given in Carlquist (1970a),
and ecological correlations in wood anatomy have also been offered (Carlquist, 1969a). The lowland species, *S. coriacea*, has succulent leaves—reminiscent of the lowland chamaesycoid Euphorbias, although more conspicuous—and a sprawling habit. Coriaceous leaves characterize most species;
the leaves of the dry-upland *S. gaudichaudii* are more restricted in size,
however, than those of rain-forest species such as *S. gaudichaudiana* and
S. chamissoniana. Truly coriaceous leaves occur in the species of wet forest
on older islands, *S. glabra*, which offers a parallel to the wet-forest Euphorbias such as *E. rockii*.

FERNS

Two fern genera have shown shift into various distinctive localities.
The endemic genus *Sadleria* (Blechnaceae) might be called a typical rain-
forest fern, but *S. cyatheoides* pioneers on new lava and can also be found
in alpine sites where it is subject to occasional mists, above 7500 ft in elevation, as on Haleakala. *Sadleria squarrosa* is a peculiar species found only
on dripping cliffs or other wet, steep surfaces in deep shade.

Amphoradenium (an endemic Hawaiian genus of Polypodiaceae) is
always a fern of wet forest or bog. However, it exploits these habitats in a
variety of ways. The terrestrial species may be small or large, with bipinnate or tripinnate leaves. The epiphytes include tiny thin-leaved species,
such as *A. hymenophylloides*, as well as species with long, drooping leaves,
such as *A. pinnatifidum* (Carlquist, 1970a).

157

BIRDS: THE HAWAIIAN HONEYCREEPERS

The Drepanididae are the most frequently cited example of adaptive radiation in the Hawaiian Islands. To be sure, their fame in this regard is by no means as great as that of the Darwin's finches in the Galápagos Islands. The range in adaptations and its extensiveness are far greater than those of the Darwin's finches, and a more spectacular example of adaptive radiation on oceanic islands would be difficult to find among avifauna. The lesser publicity of the honeycreepers is related to two main facts. First, extinction among them has been high, and even of the extant species only a few are at all common. Therefore, we know little about their habits. A second problem is that the honeycreepers are, with a few exceptions, birds of dense, wet forest, and study of them in the wild is difficult. If we knew about their habits in depth, we would undoubtedly have a heightened appreciation of various aspects of their adaptive radiation. Such studies are in progress, as shown by the results of Berger (1972), and soon we may be able to add some important dimensions to the story we already have about these birds.

Students of the Hawaiian biota have available for inspection a number of well-illustrated studies of the drepanidids. These have explored and graphically expressed in various ways the information we have at present. The monograph of Amadon (1950) summarizes all previous information, and offers a classification and nomenclature that have been followed by subsequent workers. Baldwin (1953), Richardson and Bowles (1964), and Spieth (1966) have contributed field studies, and Bock (1970) has expressed the theoretical framework of evolution of this family. Those who seek illustrations will find the early lithographs the best. Those of Wilson and Evans (1890–1899) have the merit of representing all species of honeycreepers. The plates of Rothschild (1893–1900) are elegant and accurately represent both birds and their associated plants, but they do not include all honeycreeper species. Acceptable illustrations are offered by Munro (1960) and Carlquist (1965, 1970a).

Rather than repeat the many details related to this adaptation, I prefer to present the factors on which the radiation is based—what is of prime importance, what is secondary, and what is not relevant to the main story.

1. All authors stress bill morphology and associated feeding apparatus (bill musculature, tongue morphology) as visible indicators. The narrow,

short, straight bill is considered primitive, although which of the present genera best exemplifies this is not certain. Bock (1970) chooses *Ciridops* (presumably a fruit eater) of the subfamily Drepanidinae as representing more numerous primitive characteristics, whereas Amadon (1950) stresses *Loxops,* but also *Himatione.*

These latter two species differ in diet: *Loxops* (figs. 4.6–4.9) is primarily an insect feeder, whereas *Himatione* feeds on nectar plus insects. The ancestry of the family is uncertain. Tanager-like ancestry has been suggested (Amadon, 1950), but the fact that the honeycreeper tapeworm parasite (*Anonchotaenia brasiliense*) is known otherwise only from a South American icterid, *Cacicus* (Voge and Davis, 1953), seems compelling evidence. Both thraupids (tanagers) and icterids are nine-primaried passerines.

The two subfamilies of honeycreepers are the yellow-plumaged Psittarostrinae (figs. 4.6–4.15) and the "red-and-black" plumaged Drepanidinae (*Ciridops, Palmeria, Himatione, Vestiaria, Drepanis*). The former are basically insectivores; the latter are basically nectarivores, but also eat insects. Which subfamily exhibits more features that would have been seen in the ancestral stock is open to question, but Baldwin (1953) and Bock (1970) appear to favor Drepanidinae. Changes in plumage color in Drepanidinae are considered the result of nonadaptive genetic drift (Bock, 1970).

2. Bock (1970) has emphasized that if a single species is present on an island, it may be variable, as most species are, and natural selection can maintain and widen products of this variability (character release—see chapter 3). As long such a population is not pressed by the environment to subdivide, it will remain a single, highly varied unit. If two congeners invade a particular island and coexist successfully, these two residents, rather than being intermediate, will tend to diverge, or at least the differences between them will be enforced (character displacement—see chapter 3). This has been shown graphically for *Loxops* by Bock (1970): see figure 4.5. On Kauai, double invasions have produced the divergent pair *Loxops parva* (fig. 4.6), with a short, delicate, nearly straight bill, and *L. virens stejnegeri* (fig. 4.9), which has a stouter, longer, decurved bill. A similar phenomenon has happened on Hawaii, where *L. virens virens* has a short, curved, delicate bill but *L. sagittirostris* (fig. 4.8) has a nearly

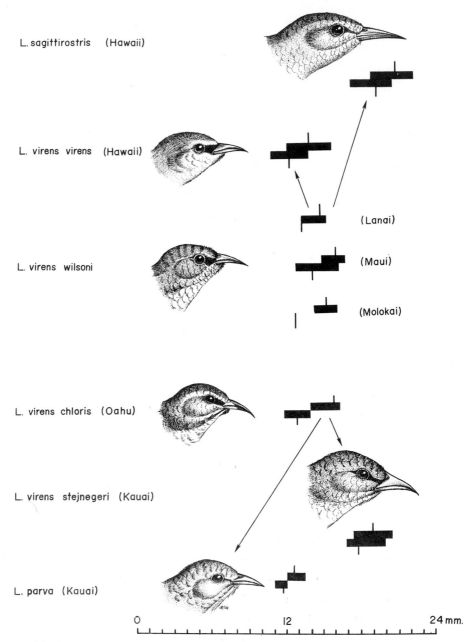

FIG. 4.5. Comparative bill sizes of the *Loxops virens* group of species (Drepaniidae). Graph represents range of culmen length for females (horizontal bar above in each) and males (bar below in each); vertical lines represent means. Ranges and means are not known for all. Arrangement from top to bottom corresponds to geographical sequence of the islands. Divergence in bill shapes is shown on Hawaii and on Kauai, where pairs of species of this group are sympatric; divergence is interpreted as representing nonoverlap of ecological requirements. Redrawn from a graph presented by Bock (1970), constructed from data of Amadon (1950).

FIG. 4.6. Bill and feeding habits of *Loxops parva* (Drepanididae). In this and succeeding drawings (to 4.15, inclusive) of Drepanididae, subfamily Psittarostrinae, bill in profile is shown at left, portion of bird in feeding situation at right. All are drawn to the scale shown here. *Loxops parva* feeds on insects available on leaf surfaces; it also takes insects from shallow flowers.

straight, long, stouter bill. As shown in the figures, even these small differences result in ecological separation (resource partitioning), for food is thereby obtained from different sites.

This example is used by Bock to indicate how more extreme products in honeycreepers may have originated. Cumulations of divergences by variability, isolation, double invasions, character divergence, and further ecological shifts have produced, according to Bock, such divergent types as the parrot-billed *Psittarostra* (figs. 4.14, 4.15) and the sickle-billed *Hemignathus procerus* (fig. 4.11). Sympatry of these various types can be expected to occur, because they will exploit different portions of available resources. Sympatry implies reproductive isolation, and one can hypothesize a positive value for reproductive isolation as a mechanism than would prevent merging of these types and would enforce character displacement.

3. In Psittarostrinae, a variety of diets and methods of feeding have evolved. These are summarized in figures 4.6 to 4.15 and are self-explanatory. However, the reason that divergences can become cumulative is that any particular type is a preadaptation for more extreme types, which it may reach by a sort of character release if new niches remain available. This process might be expected to occur rapidly. For example, the curved bills of *Loxops*, suited for extracting insects from relatively shallow localities, can be considered as preadapted to, by extension, the longer curved bills of *Hemignathus*, which aid in extraction of insects from deeper locations (figs. 4.10–4.12).

161

FIG. 4.7. Bill and feeding habits of *Loxops coccinea*. This bird takes caterpillars and larvae on leaf surfaces and in buds. It is able to open buds, such as the ones shown, by means of its "crossbill" beak tip, which is also illustrated as seen from above, to the right of the bill seen in profile.

4. In Drepanidinae, there has been a divergence in diet among the five genera, but not nearly as strong as that in Psittarostrinae, nor are intermediates or variable species present. However, even Drepanidinae shows remarkable differentiation among the genera. *Ciridops* (monotypic) apparently was frugivorous (fruits of the palm *Pritchardia* are claimed to be its food source; if so, one of the smaller-fruited species of *Pritchardia* is to be suspected). *Himatione* (monotypic) feeds on nectar in open, shallow flowers (*Metrosideros*) and eats insects. *Palmeria* (monotypic) also had a mixed diet, although the decurved beak suggests more of a tendency toward nectar-feeding and away from a primarily insectivorous diet. *Vestiaria* (monotypic) is alleged to be a nectar-feeder primarily, on tubular, curved flowers. However, it is known to have taken small insects,

FIG. 4.8. Bill and feeding habits of *Loxops sagittirostris*, which takes insects found in moderately deep crevices, which it can probe by virtue of its relatively long, stout beak, as in shaggy bark.

162

such as *Drosophila*, which breed in lobelioid flowers (Spieth, 1966). One must remember that even nectarivorous birds are likely to eat insects (which in turn feed on pollen or nectar) present in flowers in the process of feeding on nectar. *Drepanis* (two species) is alleged to have been completely nectarivorous, for example, although one can imagine it might ingest occasional insects in the process of feeding in large, nectar-rich flowers likely to contain insects.

Baldwin (1953) explains evolution of the honeycreepers by saying that Drepanidinae represents an early burst of basically nectarivorous birds.

FIG. 4.9. Bill and feeding habits of *Loxops virens stejnegeri*. This species secures caterpillars and insects from bark, among *Freycinetia* stems, and in the sheathing bases of *Freycinetia* leaves. It also feeds on nectar from ohia (*Metrosideros*) flowers, and has a tongue adapted for this.

This could explain the relictlike condition (almost all genera monotypic). The Psittarostrinae would be, to Baldwin, as well as Amadon, a "second burst," its recentness denoted by the "survival of poorly adapted intermediate forms." To Baldwin, this explains why the Psittarostrinae have not occupied the nectarivorous habit so completely as Drepanidinae—this niche was preempted by the older subfamily.

Psittarostrinae, in my opinion, could represent an active burst of evolution explainable not so much by persistence of "poorly adapted intermediate forms" but by the opportunities of insectivory. Assuming that a breakthrough to insectivory was made, *this resource can be exploited in a much greater variety of ways, because of the many sizes and types of insects, and sites in which they are to be found*, many of which are

FIG. 4.10. Bill and feeding habits of *Hemignathus lucidus*. It is reported to hammer with its bill on wood, dislodging or driving out insects (especially the weevil *Oödemas*). It also on rare occasions has been seen to take nectar from ohia (*Metrosideros*) flowers.

illustrated in figures 4.6 to 4.15. On the other hand, nectar-feeding is a relatively stereotyped activity, varying only in the type of flower sought and in the inclusion of varying degrees of insect food along with nectar. In addition, the nectarivorous opportunities in the Hawaiian Islands are more limited: not only is there competition from the meliphagids (now extinct), but nectar availability is much less during the winter months, whereas insects and their developmental stages are available throughout the year. To be sure, *Psittarostra* (figs. 4.14, 4.15) represents evolution "beyond" insectivory (although it does eat some large insects and caterpillars), but its seed-eating and foliage-eating habits may be considered a natural consequence of the preadaptation of the stout bill of *Pseudonestor* (fig. 4.13), which is adapted to crushing stout twigs in search of insects and larvae.

5. Differentiation among drepanidids with respect to feeding apparatus and food sources almost inevitably leads to differentiation in habitat or type of forest or levels within forest which particular species frequent. For example, if *Pseudonestor* (fig. 4.13) characteristically ate larvae and insects obtained by crushing *Acacia koa* twigs, it would not occur in wet-forest areas where nectar-rich ornithophilous flowers (*Metrosideros*, lobelioids) are present, but would remain in the dry koa forest. The larger-seeded forest trees are chiefly those of dry lowland forest (*Diospyros*, *Colubrina*, *Santalum*) or subalpine forest (*Myoporum*, *Sophora*), so *Psit-*

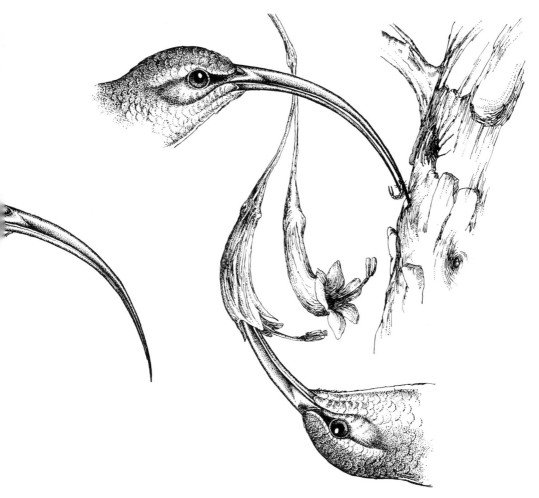

Fig. 4.11. Bill and feeding habits of *Hemignathus procerus*. This species is reported to have fed on nectar in large-flowered lobelioids, such as the *Clermontia* shown here. Because these flowers are pendant, feeding is from below. *Hemignathus procerus* is also reported to have sought insects in leaf bases of *Freycinetia arborea*, or in crevices or borings. It, like *H. lucidus*, had a tapping habit in coaxing insect prey from crevices.

tarostra, if it sought the larger seeds, probably occurred primarily in such zones rather than in deep, wet forest. *Psittarostra bailleui* apparently favored subalpine forest on Hawaii, whereas the other species sought seeds in lowland forest—except for *P. psittacea*, whose fondness of *Freycinetia* fruits (fig. 4.14) and lobelioid fruits would place it in the moist *Metrosideros* forests where those plants grow. *Loxops parva* on Kauai (fig. 4.6)

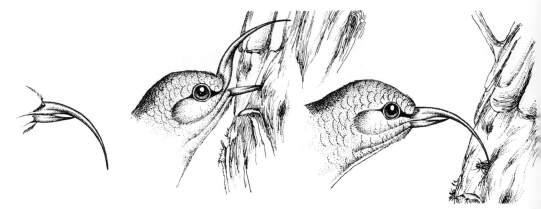

FIG. 4.12. Bill and feeding habit of *Hemignathus wilsoni.* The markedly unequal upper and lower mandibles have different functions. The lower is driven forcibly and repeatedly into wood or bark in order to dislodge insects. Bits and pieces of wood loosened in this manner are grasped with both mandibles and torn or tossed away. The lower mandible is stout and serves not merely as a chisel but as a lever as well. The upper could serve as a probe. This bird has never been reported to feed on nectar.

would be expected to operate in the forest canopy, by taking insects from leaves and stems, whereas *L. virens stejnegeri,* also of Kauai, would be expected to occur at lower levels within the forest, if it exploited leaf bases of the liana *Freycinetia* and extracted insects from bark of tree trunks. Baldwin (1953) notes that

> *Loxops virens* frequents the middle and lower layers of forest trees, whereas *Himatione* and *Vestiaria* occupy the upper story. *Loxops* ventures into shrubby formations to a far greater degree than do the other two birds. . . . *Loxops* seeks food among leaves and bark more than do the other birds, whereas *Himatione* captures flying insects more readily. *Loxops* tends to remain in more restricted feeding areas than do *Himatione* and *Vestiaria* at any given time of the year. The development and maintenance of such dissimilarities as these must prevent serious competition among the three species.

Evolution of nectar-feeding drepanidids in the Hawaiian avifauna is permitted by the almost indefinite flowering season of ornithophilous plants, although they flower more abundantly during summer. Without sources of nectar throughout the year, nectarivory would have been impossible. At least some individuals of *Metrosideros,* the chief tree of Hawaiian wet forests, can be found in flower at any time in the year.

Climatic moderation is undoubtedly basic to such prolonged flowering seasons.

Short-distance migrations by honeycreepers within a habitat, related to flowering patterns of particular trees, have been noted by Baldwin (1953).

6. Although drepanidid bills are undoubtedly adaptive in nature, they are nevertheless not specific with respect to diet, and drastic changes can occur. For example, the powerful beak of *Psittarostra* suggests crushing of large seeds. However, the Laysan species, *P. cantans*, feeds chiefly on seeds of a grass, *Eragrostis variabilis*, the most abundant plant on Laysan, because large-seeded plants (except *Tribulus*, whose seeds *P. cantans* also eats) are infrequent or absent on Laysan. Likewise, the treeless atoll habitat of Laysan is rather different, at first glance, from forests on the high islands. Although there are typical small differences in leg size and other characteristics of *P. cantans* in comparison with Psittarostras of the high islands, these are not really as sharp as in the difference in habitat (*P. cantans* spends most of its time on the ground, and even perches during only part of its feeding time). Morphology may well lag behind relatively sudden ecological shifts. This lag was stressed in the instance of the bog silversword, *Argyroxiphium caliginii*, in which only a few morphological features have

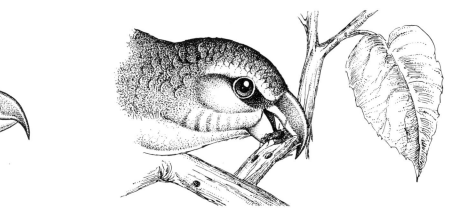

FIG. 4.13. Bill and feeding habits of *Pseudonestor xanthophrys*. This species is reported to have crushed and broken twigs in order to obtain larvae, pupae, and immature cerambycid beetles, but more notably *Clytarlus pennatus* and *C. modestus*, in koa trees. On trees of *Pelea*, it sought larvae of *Plagithmysus*. In addition to crushing and breaking, it employed a ripping and wrenching technique on bark and wood (always healthy wood, never rotten).

shown a shift to bogs from the dry-alpine habitat of the closely related A. *sandwichense.*

7. The two subfamilies of drepanidids differ in song type (Baldwin, 1953) and such other features as skull development and postjuvenile molt. These differences are difficult to explain.

Likewise, I am unable to explain why so many species of *Psittarostra* (five) should occur on the island of Hawaii, whereas the other islands have a single species each, or none. Possibly the vast tracts of lowland, large-seeded forest and dry, upland, large-seeded forest provided greater scope for survival of the various species on Hawaii, and each species may have had distinctive ecological preferences, as hinted earlier. Perhaps only on such a relatively large island could such preferences be satisfied, for dry-forest areas are (or were) more limited on the other islands, so that populations of a "favored plant" for a *Psittarostra* species would not be large enough on smaller islands to support a viable population. Alternatively, the five species on Hawaii may represent survivals of intergrades, survivals possible because competition is less keen where very large areas are involved or is likely to lead to extinction less quickly. *Psittarostra bailleui* appears geographically isolated from other species by its high-altitude preference.

Lessened competition on larger land areas might explain why *Drepanis*

FIG. 4.14. Bill and feeding habits of *Psittarostra psittacea*. According to several reports, P. *psittacea* fed on fruits of *Freycinetia arborea*, shown here. These fruits are formed in long, conelike aggregations, and each individual fruit has a relatively small seed. Berries of lobelioids were also sought, as well as leafy matter, which it chewed finely. It has been reported to catch caterpillars and feed them to its young.

168

FIG. 4.15. Bill and feeding habits of *Psittarostra kona*. The fruits of *Myoporum*, shown here, formed a mainstay of its diet. It cracked these large hard seeds with its stout beak. Fresh leaves and caterpillars were also eaten.

pacifica and *Ciridops anna* are both endemic to Hawaii; alternatively, more abundant food supplies may have permitted their survival there. If these are "relict" representatives of the "older subfamily" Drepanidinae, their survival on a newer island might be explainable. However, an alternative explanation is possible: *Ciridops* and *Drepanis* are not relictual but are relatively recent end products, produced autochthonously on the newer islands. There does not appear to be detailed evidence for regarding Drepanidinae as older than Psittarostrinae, and I feel that we must still be open-minded on phylogeny within drepanidids. For example, there is no reason to believe that any of the living genera is highly similar to, or nearly identical with, the original stock of the drepanidids, yet one reads statements that a particular genus may be primitive. What is meant is presumably that its bill features and feeding habits are like those of the early honeycreepers—but we do not know for sure what the drepanidid ancestors were, nor is there reason to believe that any of the contemporary genera represents survival of the ancestral stock without change.

INSECTS

There is no question that, as the most numerous group of species on the Hawaiian Islands, insects have diversified to an exceptional extent. According to Zimmerman (1948a), between 233 and 254 original insect immigrants can account for the 3722 species of endemic insects (perhaps the figure for species would be much higher today because discoveries have been made since 1948). This compares with the very similar number of probable immigrants (272) for angiosperms, which have yielded 1633 endemic species (perhaps 1200, according to a more conservative view). The logical question, in view of these figures, is how much adaptive radiation, as defined earlier, has accompanied this explosive speciation. This question is considerably more difficult to answer than in the case of plants, because the habits of insects, revealed only by painstaking field studies, are more difficult to study than are angiosperm adaptations; and because adaptive morphological changes by insects are fewer and more subtle than those of other groups of organisms. Nevertheless, thanks to the work of several enterprising entomologists, we can cite at least a number of instances of adaptive radiation. These can be described under three headings, as listed below.

Shift in Vegetation Zone and Host Specificity. The basic contribution in this regard is the compilation by Swezey (1954). His work is organized in terms of flowering-plant hosts, listed alphabetically. However, by using the index, one can easily see the range in host plants to which any insect group is adapted. Swezey's compilation is of particular value because many of the observations recorded then could no longer be made, since a number of insect species have become extinct. One must always be careful in using host-plant lists, for there can be a difference between plants on which particular insects have merely been seen and those which bear a definite nutritional relationship to the insects. With this caution, however, we may cite some examples.

The Hawaiian Lygaeidae (Heteroptera) offer good instances. This family has been investigated by Usinger (1942), whose study was basic to one of Zimmerman's (1948b) monographs in *Insects of Hawaii*. The three large genera of Lygaeidae are *Oceanides*, *Neseis*, and *Nysius*. There is no question that these genera show host specificity by species to particular angiosperm species, and that the range of angiosperms utilized and therefore habitats occupied is exceptionally large. *Oceanides* ranges from coastline to alpine localities, and different species are adapted to different plants, in areas of markedly divergent climate and rainfall. If Lygaeidae are a group of insects basically characteristic of moderately dry localities, *Oceanides* has, during its evolution in the Hawaiian Islands, made every degree of transition into the wet forest. The host plants represent most of the common plant genera within each zone. Unfortunately, we do not know the plant species, although we can guess at some of them from the plant genera cited, because of endemism of plant species in particular areas. However, particular species of *Oceanides* have been recorded from several unrelated plant genera in many cases, so that knowledge of these plant species is unimportant. There appears to be considerable overlap among *Oceanides* species in host-plant genera utilized, so that geographical speciation must have been important, and isolating barriers other than those involving plant chemistry are obviously operative.

The same patterns occur in *Nysius* and *Neseis*. *Nysius* appears to favor low-elevation dry localities to a greater degree, for species occur on most of the Hawaiian Leeward Islands where host plants include the grass *Eragrostis* and the native *Chenopodium* (*C. oahuense*). However, other *Nysius* species have adapted to situations of much greater moisture. *Nysius communis*, for example, occurs in the Puu Kukui bogs of Maui, where the host plants include *Argyroxiphium grayanum* and *Lobelia gaudichaudii* var. *gloria-montis*. *Nysius communis* is equally well adapted to alpine localities, such as Haleakala, where its host plants are *Argyroxiphium sandwichense*, *A. virescens*, and *Artemisia*. *Neseis* species show a range from rain forest to dry alpine localities, with correlative host plants. The three species of the subgenus *Icteronysius* are entirely alpine.

Other groups of insects, however, show more precise specificity, where the plant species evidently serves as the primary isolating mechanism. Zimmerman (1948a) says, for example, "We find such great host-specificity among the plagithmysine longhorn beetles that if we find borings in a species of tree unrecorded as harboring a species of the group we conclude that the borings are those of a new species. Thus, some new species of these beetles have been discovered, and others are known only from borings and may be captured sooner or later." Perkins (1913) gives an example, "Thus, even within a few square yards, the three species of longhorn beetles, *Plagithmysus darwinianus*, *P. lamarckianus*, and *P. varians* occur. It is hardly conceivable that species can be more closely allied than these and remain distinct. Each keeps to its own food-plant, and though occurring on adjoining trees, do not mix or interbreed. *Plagithmysus darwinianus* has been found chiefly on *Sophora*, *P. lamarcki-*

171

anus on *Pipturus, P. varians* on *Acacia.*" The feature of interest stressed by Perkins and Zimmerman is that of an isolating mechanism. However, I can cite this example in connection with adaptive radiation because these three beetle species have adapted to three quite different host plants. One may suspect that adaptation to the three host plants was aided in previous time by geographical isolation, and, following development of specificity, the three beetle species have become distinct. This idea would seem to be supported by a comment of Muir (1917), "I believe that one of the first steps in species formation among Hawaiian Delphacidae is a change of food-plant."

Although other features may be of greater interest in speciation of Hawaiian drosophilids, host plants (and animals) have played a significant role. Although most drosophilids feed in decaying bark or leaves, one genus, *Titanochaeta*, has a totally different food source, the eggs of spiders (Carson et al., 1970). The number of plant genera which Hawaiian drosophilids feed upon and breed in is relatively small, but diversified: fermenting leaves and bark of *Cheirodendron* (Araliaceae); leaves, flowers, fruits, and bark of lobelioids (*Clermontia* especially); leaves of *Pisonia* (Nyctaginaceae); some fungi (particularly *Polyporus*, a bracket fungus); and exudates from cut stumps of tree ferns (*Cibotium*). The nature of the chemistry of these diverse substrates may be less important than some of their physical characteristics; for example, rate of decay, retention of moisture, and presence of suitable yeasts and molds. Even so, the list of food plants (32 genera) is diverse in one or more of these respects.

With respect to Hawaiian drosophilids, Carson et al. (1970) state that

> if only one immigrant was introduced, this stock early split into the scaptomyzids and the drosophiloids. If there were separate introductions for each of these major groups, then they were constrained by the poverty of food sources to partially overlap in their use of substrates. Both groups radiated into various ecological niches, the scaptomyzids evolving as physically small species, able to tolerate exposure to higher light intensities, and thus able to use substrates such as the flowers of morning-glories [*Ipomoea*] and certain non-rotting vegetation as well as the same fermenting materials that the drosophiloids use. The drosophiloid stock evolved species that are in

172

general larger than the scaptomyzids and more restricted to the areas of low light intensity in the dense forest.

Adaptive Radiation with Regard to Morphology. With respect to morphology, the most obvious contrasts occur in coloring. Because there are a number of independent instances of diversification with respect to color in the Hawaiian insect fauna, one would tend to assume that predation must be an important factor. The scarcity of observations on actual predation of Hawaiian insects and the value of color that stimulates substrate does not rule out this possibility. Field observations and laboratory experiments would be of great value.

Zimmerman (1948a, pp. 142–43) cites a number of examples of apparent protective coloration, and they need not all be repeated here. One of his striking examples, however, is the following:

> Near the summit of Haleakala on Maui, I found specimens of the pale, silvery-colored *Geranium tridens* growing with their branches intermixed with those of the dark-leaved *Coprosma montana*. On the pale *Geranium* were colonies of a very pale *Nesosydne* leafhopper. On the dark foliage of the *Coprosma* was a black species of the same genus! Although the branches of the two shrubs intermixed, the two leafhoppers kept to their own hostplants.

One may mention that the dark color of the *Coprosma* is striking, because of the tendency of the branches to be covered by black lichens or fungi.

The example, also in *Nesosydne*, of divergence of two species with respect to juvenile versus adult foliage of *Acacia koa* (Zimmerman, 1948a) is particularly striking. On the pale-colored (glaucescent) bipinnate juvenile leaves, one finds only *Nesosydne koae*. On the phyllodes (adult leaves with flattened petiole, lacking leaf blade) of older plants one can find *N. rubescens*, whose color matches the bright green or yellowish shade of the *Acacia* phyllodes. Not only do adults in these two *Nesosydne* species simulate colors in these respective parts of the plant, but the nymphs do also. *Nesosydne koae* deposits eggs in young shoots bearing juvenile foliage. *Nesosydne rubescens*, with a different ovipositor structure, lays eggs in the edges of the leaves and in phyllodes.

Zimmerman (1948a) also stresses insect coloration by comparing the "faunulas" found on distinctive adjacent trees. *Pipturus* (Urticaceae) looks pale because of grayish bark and densely woolly leaves. *Metrosideros* (Myrtaceae) has dark gray bark and deep green, glabrous leaves. Insect assemblages of adjacent trees of *Pipturus* and *Metrosideros* reveal differences in color: all the *Pipturus*-inhabiting species of insects tend to be light in color, whereas the *Metrosideros* insect species are dark.

Such color differences extend to habitats other than host plants. Williams (1939, p. 297) states that among dolichopodid flies of the genus *Eurynogaster*, species "that occur along streams, waterfalls, wet banks bordering rapids, at springs and dripping wet banks are largely blue, green, or coppery, while those frequenting the forest floor or trails and often the leaves of plants, are of duller hues." Zimmerman (1948a) expands this example, stating that forest-floor species are brownish, foliage-inhabiting species are greenish, and species of wet banks or pools tend to have a metallic glitter like that of watery surfaces. Moreover, he notes that "the species which frequent permanent streams are excellent and agile water skaters; those found on still ponds are fair to good skaters; but the species which hunt about areas where standing water exists only as temporary puddles, and the flies which frequent wet ground in the absence of standing water are poor skaters." That these distinctions have occurred is interesting, for all of the dolichopodid flies can be called wet-forest inhabitants, as stressed by Hardy (1964); the radiation, then, is related to exploitation of distinctive sites within the wet forest.

Adaptive Radiation with Respect to Behavior. The examples from Dolichopodidae suggest different modes of behavior of species with respect to water, and one genus of that family, *Campsicnemus*, has flightless Hawaiian species in which the wings only aid in hopping. Flightlessness is discussed in chapter 11 (see also Zimmerman, 1948a). The most striking examples of adaptive radiation in behavior in Hawaiian insects occur, however, in the drosophilids. Hawaiian drosophilids are characterized by "lek" behavior. That is, like the birds of paradise, they have well-defined mating sites that are different from the localities at which feeding takes place. In continental drosophilids, mating occurs at feeding sites. The only exceptions to lek behavior in Hawaiian drosophilids occur in the *anomalipes* and *quasianomalipes* groups. Lek behavior by itself could not be cited as an example of adaptive radiation. Rather, the different types of lek behavior are of interest here.

The remarkable patterns and diversifications in Hawaiian drosophilids are summarized by Spieth (1968). Exemplifying these behavioral patterns is the following passage:

> Each male defends a limited area, such as a single leaf, a fern pinna, a section of a fern frond stem [= petiole], or a portion of a tree trunk. Concurrently he advertises his presence visually or otherwise. Thus males of some species (e.g., *D. crucigera*, *D. grimshawi*, and *D. engyochracea*) repeatedly drag the tip of their abdomens over the substrate and in doing so deposit a thin film of liquid. . . . Others assume a ritualized posture and extrude and retract a bubble of fluid from their anal papillae. . . . Defense of territory against intruders, typically other males but occasionally nonreceptive females, usually involves physical contact between the individuals, and many of the species exhibit ritualized postures such as curling and slashing which involves wing, leg, and body movements. . . . The most vigorous fly, usually the largest, appears to be the victor in such contests, the original possessor of the area often being displaced by the intruder. The mere assumption of the aggressive posture, without physical contact, frequently is sufficient to determine the outcome of the contest. If the two individuals are of disparate size, the assumption of the aggressive posture usually causes the smaller to flee. Under field conditions, the contestants apparently do not physically injure each other.

Morphological adaptations related to various of these ritualized behavior patterns occur, of course. Moreover, radiation has occurred with respect to sites of courtship behavior. As noted by Spieth,

> these sites are not randomly distributed in the rain forest where the flies live, but each species has special preferences, apparently determined by factors such as light, humidity, temperature, and spatial conditions. Invariably they are in close proximity to where the individuals feed and the females oviposit. . . . Each leaf on a single branch of a given shrub may have a male on its under surface, or the frond stems [= petioles] of a particular tree fern may have a male patrolling and defending a two to four foot section of each [petiole].

For a more detailed account of these behavioral characteristics and the morphological features of the flies associated with these performances, one should consult Spieth (1968). Obviously, many more details remain to be discovered, considering the large number of *Drosophila* species in the Hawaiian Islands. While one cannot hope for comparable data on mating behavior and sites in all of these, increased knowledge will surely result in a more complete picture of this phenomenal instance of adaptive radiation.

MOLLUSCA

Two groups of land molluscs have speciated in a remarkable way on the Hawaiian Islands: the amastrids and the achatinellids (see discussion earlier in this chapter). The amastrids are largely terrestrial, whereas the achatinellids are arboreal. This divergent preference in habitats may explain why each has undergone adaptive radiation and speciation; if both occupied similar ecological niches, speciation of one group would likely have been suppressed by the other.

The speciation of the achatinellids has been due, as stated earlier, to the great degree of dissection of habitats suitable to them, and to the tendency for colonies to migrate very little and very slowly. Although many of the distinctive species patterns may merely be the product of genetic drift, Perkins (1913) claimed that distinctive colors of achatinellids might serve a protective function. In my experience, achatinellid snails are by no means camouflaged, although they may be less conspicuous merely by their typical position on lower surfaces of leaves. For example, the brown-and-white striped *Achatinella mustelina* always occurs on green leaves; in the genus at large, green species are infrequent, but would be expected to be the ones best suited for protective coloration. Perkins questions what could be a predator; he finds no really plausible bird, and only birds would be likely to serve as predators for land snails of this size. The concept of genetic drift was not really developed in Perkins's time, so his search for an adaptive significance is understandable.

There is a noticeable degree of host-plant fidelity in achatinellids. They are absent on some tree species, present on others, in any given area; they avoid, with few exceptions, species of plants introduced by man. *Achatinella* grazes on fungi and algae on leaves, not on the leaves themselves. Some features of leaf texture or leaf chemistry may, however, tend to favor *Achatinella* species, or be preferred by them. There may be some radiation with respect to host plants in this genus. If so, this matter needs careful investigation and assessment.

In the genus *Amastra,* and in the closely related genera *Carelia, Pterodiscus,* and *Planamastra,* there is remarkable differentiation in shell size and shape (see Zimmerman, 1948a; Carlquist, 1970a). Such distinctive forms seem to suggest an explanation in terms of adaptive radiation. So far, however, we do not have enough field data to present distinctions in habit and habitat that might suggest explanations. This remains an interesting problem for investigation.

References

Amadon, D. 1950. The Hawaiian honeycreepers (Aves, Drepaniidae). *Bull. Amer. Mus. Natur. Hist.* 95(4):153–262.

Baldwin, P. H. 1953. Annual cycle, environment and evolution in the Hawaiian honeycreepers (Aves: Drepaniidae). *Univ. Calif. Publ. Zool.* 52:285–398.

Berger, A. J. 1972. *Hawaiian bird-life.* Honolulu, University of Hawaii Press.

Bock, W. J. 1970. Microevolutionary sequences as a fundamental concept in macro-evolutionary models. *Evolution* 24:704–22.

Carlquist, S. 1957. Leaf anatomy and ontogeny in *Argyroxiphium* and *Wilkesia* (Compositae). *Amer. Jour. Bot.* 44:696–705.

Carlquist, S. 1958. Wood anatomy of Heliantheae (Compositae). *Trop. Woods* 108:1–30.

Carlquist, S. 1959a. Vegetative anatomy of *Dubautia, Argyroxiphium,* and *Wilkesia* (Compositae). *Pacific Sci.* 13:195–210.

Carlquist, S. 1959b. Studies on Madiinae: Anatomy, cytology, and evolutionary relationships. *Aliso* 4:171–236.

Carlquist, S. 1962. Ontogeny and comparative anatomy of thorns of Hawaiian Lobeliaceae. *Amer. Jour. Bot.* 49:413–19.

Carlquist, S. 1965. *Island life.* New York, Natural History Press.

Carlquist, S. 1969a. Wood anatomy of Goodeniaceae and the problem of insular woodiness. *Ann. Missouri Bot. Gard.* 56:358–90.

Carlquist, S. 1969b. Wood anatomy of Lobelioideae (Campanulaceae). *Biotropica* 1(2):47–72.

Carlquist, S. 1970a. *Hawaii, a natural history.* New York, Natural History Press.

Carlquist, S. 1970b. Wood anatomy of Hawaiian, Macaronesian, and other species of *Euphorbia. Bot. Jour. Linnaean Soc.* 63, suppl. 1:181–93. (Also as *New Research in plant anatomy,* ed. D. Cutler. London, Academic Press.)

Carson, H. L., D. E. Hardy, H. T. Spieth, and W. S. Stone. 1970. The evolutionary biology of the Hawaiian Drosophilidae. In *Essays in evolutionary biology in honor of Theodosius Dobzhansky,* ed. M. K. Hecht and W. C. Steere, pp. 437–543. New York, Appleton-Century-Crofts.

Hardy, D. E. 1964. *Insects of Hawaii*, vol. 11: *Diptera: Brachycera II–Cyclorhapha.* Honolulu, University of Hawaii Press.

Hardy, D. E. 1965. *Insects of Hawaii*, vol. 12: *Diptera: Cyclorhapha.* Honolulu, University of Hawaii Press.

Herbst, D. 1971. A new *Euphorbia* (Euphorbiaceae) from Hawaii. *Pacific Sci.* 25: 489–90.

MacArthur, R. H., and E. O. Wilson. 1967. *The theory of island biogeography.* Princeton, N.J., Princeton University Press.

Muir, F. 1917. New Hawaiian Delphacidae. *Proc. Hawaiian Entomol. Soc.* 3:168–221.

Munro, G. C. 1960. *Birds of Hawaii.* 2d ed. Rutland, Vt., Ridgeway Press.

Oliver, W. R. B. 1935. The genus *Coprosma. Bishop Mus. Bull.* 132:1–207.

Perkins, R. C. L. 1903. *Fauna Hawaiiensis: Vertebrata*, vol. 1, pt. 4, pp. 365–466. Cambridge, Cambridge University Press.

Perkins, R. C. L. 1913. *Fauna Hawaiiensis: Introduction*, vol. 1, pt. 6, xv–ccxxviii. Cambridge, Cambridge University Press.

Richardson, F., and J. Bowles. 1964. A survey of the birds of Kauai, Hawaii. *Bishop Mus. Bull.* 227:1–49.

Rock, J. F. 1919. A monographic study of the Hawaiian species of the tribe Lobelioideae, family Campanulaceae. *Mem. Bishop Mus.* 7(2):1–394.

Rock, J. F. 1957. Some new Hawaiian lobelioids. *Occas. Papers Bishop Mus.* 22(5): 35–66.

Rock, J. F. 1962. Hawaiian lobelioids. *Occas. Papers Bishop Mus.* 23(5):65–75.

Rothschild, W. 1893–1900. *The avifauna of Laysan and the Hawaiian possessions.* London, R. H. Porter.

St. John, H. 1959. Botanical novelties on the island of Niihau, Hawaiian Islands. Hawaiian plant studies 25. *Pacific Sci.* 13:156–90.

St. John, H. 1966. Monograph of *Cyrtandra* (Gesneriaceae) on Oahu, Hawaiian Islands. *Bishop Mus. Bull.* 229:1–465.

Sherff, E. E. 1935a. Revision of *Haplostachys, Phyllostegia*, and *Stenogyne. Bishop Mus. Bull.* 136:1–101.

Sherff, E. E. 1935b. Revision of *Tetramolopium, Lipochaeta, Dubautia* and *Railliardia. Bishop Mus. Bull.* 135:1–136.

Sherff, E. E. 1937. The genus *Bidens.* Part I. *Field Mus. Natur. Hist. Publ.*, Bot. ser. 16:1–346.

Spieth, H. T. 1966. Hawaiian honeycreeper, *Vestiaria coccinea* (Forster) feeding on lobeliad flowers, *Clermontia arborescens* (Mann) Hillebrand. *Amer. Natur.* 100: 470–73.

Spieth, H. T. 1968. Evolutionary implications of sexual behavior in *Drosophila.* In *Evolutionary biology*, ed. T. Dobzhansky, M. K. Hecht, and W. C. Steere, vol. 2, pp. 157–93. New York, Appleton-Century-Crofts.

Stone, B. C. 1969. The genus *Pelea* A. Gray. *Phanerogamarum Monogr.* 3:1–180.

Swezey, O. 1954. Forest entomology in Hawaii. *Bishop Mus. Spec. Publ.* 44:1–266.

Thwing, E. W. 1907. Reprint of original descriptions of *Achatinella*, with additional notes. *Occas. Papers Bishop Mus.* 3(1):1–196.

Usinger, R. L. 1942. The genus *Nysius* and its allies in the Hawaiian Islands. *Bishop Mus. Bull.* 173:1–167.

Voge, M., and B. S. Davis. 1953. Studies on the cestode genus *Anonchotaenia* (Dilepididae, Paruterininae) and related forms. *Univ. Calif. Publ. Zool.* 59:1–30.

Williams, F. X. 1939. Biological studies in Hawaiian water-loving insects. Part IIIB, Diptera. *Proc. Hawaiian Entomol. Soc.* 10:281–315.

Wilson, S. B., and A. H. Evans. 1890–1899. *Aves Hawaiienses: The birds of the Sandwich Islands.* London, R. H. Porter.

Wimmer, F. E. 1956. Campanulaceae—Lobelioideae. *Das Pflanzenreich* IV 267b (106):1–260.

Yuncker, G. T. 1933. Revision of the Hawaiian species of *Peperomia. Bishop Mus. Bull.* 112:1–131.

Zimmerman, E. C. 1948a. *Insects of Hawaii*, vol. 1: *Introduction.* Honolulu, University of Hawaii Press.

Zimmerman, E. C. 1948b. *Insects of Hawaii*, vol. 3: *Heteroptera.* Honolulu, University of Hawaii Press.

CHAPTER
FIVE

ADAPTIVE RADIATION:
CANARY ISLANDS AND OTHER
MACARONESIAN ISLANDS

Although the term Macaronesia is not as generally used as it should be, and is not yet recognized officially, it is of value for referring to a biogeographically related group of volcanic archipelagos: the Azores, Madeira, the Canary Islands, the Cape Verde Islands, and a few minor islets near or between these major groups. Of these, the Canary Islands are of predominant interest because their larger area and greater elevation make them the prime archipelago of Macaronesia for biological diversity. Madeira is biologically rich, considering its remoteness; it represents a mesic outlier of the Canary Islands, in effect. It can be bracketed with the Canaries biologically, but it is separated from them by a distance much greater than the gaps among the Canaries, so that it does not participate in archipelago effects except in somewhat peripheral ways. However, some groups of plants on Madeira must be considered part of Canarian patterns of adaptive radiation. The relatively depauperate floras of the Azores and the Cape Verde Islands are decidedly peripheral to Madeira-Canary patterns, although some of the same genera do occur. The reason for this is not merely the remoteness of the Azores and the Cape Verde Islands, but also their small area and low elevation.

Area and altitude are important factors in species abundance on an island, and can play a part—if other suitable factors are present—in promoting adaptive radiation. Table 5.1 has been prepared to offer a view of these factors. Introduced as well as native vascular plants are included

TABLE 5.1

Areas, altitude, and vascular plant species of the Canary Islands

	Lanza-rote	Fuerte-ventura	Gran Canaria	Tene-rife	Go-mera	La Palma	Hierro	All islands
Area (sq km), total	873	1725	1534	2060	378	728	277	7575
below cloud belt	873	1725	1030	1170	208	363	194	5563
in cloud belt			470	445	170	260	82	1427
above 1500 m			34	445		105	1	585
Highest point, m	670	807	1950	3711	1484	2423	1520	3711
No. of species, vascular plants	366	348	763	1079	539	575	391	1531

Source: Data from Lems, 1960.

in the table. Inclusion of introduced plants seems valid for demonstrating species richness of the various islands. Table 5.1 shows that habitat diversity, rather than any of the individual measures, is the prime key to biological diversity. Thus, Fuerteventura has a larger area than Gran Canaria but less than half the number of plants, because it is essentially a flat island compared with Gran Canaria, and has only a lowland vegetation. In fact it has only a fraction of the lowland flora because it lacks the barrancos and other topographic diversity that would be present in the lowlands of a high island. Gran Canaria and Tenerife are roughly comparable in areas of lowland and cloud belt, but Tenerife has a much greater alpine zone (above 1500 m), and this provides another key to species diversity: *it is not as important that each zone be present on an island as that these zones be of sufficient size to maintain variable and viable populations of species.* This explains why La Palma, which has appreciable areas in each of the zones, does not have exceptional species richness: area within each zone is too small to permit much species diversity or diversification. In this regard, one should note that Tenerife is divided by a pass into the high, recent El Teide caldera, and the older Anaga range, which reaches into the cloud-forest zone. Presence of all zones on La Palma does permit it to bear a greater number of species than Lanzarote or Fuerteventura, although the latter islands have greater areas. The geological recentness of La Palma, compared with others of the Canaries, may also be a reason why it has fewer species than does Tenerife.

Angiosperms

Although zoologists may find the Canary Islands and Madeira poor in adaptive radiation, the botanist can find numerous good examples. *Sonchus* (Asteraceae), *Euphorbia* (*Euphorbiaceae*), and *Limonium* are excellent examples of adaptive radiation on these islands. They would be considered here except that in each of these examples there is a series in increased woodiness, and I have chosen to include them in chapter 10, which should be considered in part an annex of this chapter. Also, these groups show changes in wood anatomy concomitant with radiation into more mesic areas from drier ones (chapter 10). Increased woodiness is certainly involved in adaptive radiation of *Echium* (Boraginaceae), but other aspects of adaptive radiation are presented by this genus as well.

Echium. Continental species of *Echium* are small, herbaceous plants, generally annuals. This growth form is easily seen on the Canary Islands because the weedy European *E. plantagineum* (fig. 5.1, top left) is a common plant, introduced by man to the Canaries as it has been to other areas where it has also become a weed (e.g., Australia). There are native annual Echiums in the Canary Islands, such as the endemic *E. triste*. However, a number of short-lived perennial Echiums should also be cited among Canarian endemics. These include *E. bonnettii*, *E. hierrense* (fig. 5.1, top right), and *E. strictum* (fig. 5.2, top left). A moderated climate permits these species to persist for more than a single season. For example, *E. strictum*, which grows in open areas in the cloud forest, receives enough moisture so that neither protracted drought nor freezing winter temperatures terminate its life-span. The largest species of *Echium*, *E. candicans* (fig. 5.2, top right) is reminiscent of a gigantic *E. strictum*. *Echium candicans* grows in the wet laurel forests of Madeira—probably the most mesic habitat in Macaronesia—and thereby attains greater size and has leaves larger than those of other shrubby species. *Echium candicans* reflects a pioneering quality common to *Echium* species by growing in openings in the laurel forests, but these openings are small in area and not really drier than the surrounding laurel forest. Therefore, not surprisingly, *E. candicans* is almost indefinite in life-span, although it never becomes a true tree.

FIG. 5.1. Species of *Echium* (Boraginaceae) from the Canary Islands. TOP LEFT, *E. planta-gineum* habit; this plant is an introduced weed in the Canaries, grows during the wet season. TOP RIGHT, *E. hierrense*, inflorescence with leaves, showing the dense covering of upwardly appressed hairs on leaves. BOTTOM LEFT, *E. onosmaefolium*, specimen about 2 m tall; note central trunk and shaggy bark; Barranco de Arguineguin, Gran Canaria. BOTTOM RIGHT, *E. leucophaeum* var. *angustissimum*, shrub about 1 m tall; Barranco de San Andres, Tenerife.

Perhaps if a true rain forest were present in Macaronesia, *Echium* could be represented by real trees, as is *Dubautia* in the Hawaiian Islands. *Echium candicans* represents the farthest advance toward mesomorphy that the Macaronesian climate permits (except perhaps for *E. pininana*). *Echium candicans* has been cultivated in southern and northern California (usually as "*E. fastuosum*"), and there plants live for 10 years or more near the coast, but at sites about 40 mi inland the plants survive for fewer years because low humidity and higher summer temperatures cause excessive transpiration.

Most shrubby Macaronesian Echiums are not, however, laurel-forest species. For example, *E. onosmaefolium* (fig. 5.1, bottom left) and *E. leucophaeum* (fig. 5.1, bottom right) are lowland or dry-montane species. *Echium onosmaefolium* is perhaps the largest shrubby *Echium* in the Canary Islands. Among the mechanisms that seem related to its longevity are its shaggy, corky bark, whose layers would reduce transpiration, and reduction of leaves, both in number and in size. During the dry season, a plant can be relatively leafless. *Echium leucophaeum* may also produce smaller and fewer leaves during the dry season. Significant in this species are the very hairy, silvery leaves, which may reduce transpiration by forming a "windbreak" on leaf surfaces or by reflecting incident illumination, or both. Leaves of *E. hierrense* (fig. 5.1, top right) are similarly silvery or felty, and represent potential reduction in transpiration sufficient for survival in the dry season. On Tenerife, *E. giganteum* represents the closest approach in the Canarian flora to *E. candicans* of Madeira, and, like it, has relatively broad leaves.

Echium pininana (figs. 5.2, bottom left, center; 5.4, bottom right) is a striking endemic of La Palma. It is taller than other Echiums, but achieves this height by virtue of being unbranched. *Echium pininana* grows in dense laurel forests, and when young has long internodes. As it reaches better-illuminated levels, internodes become shorter, leaves become larger, and the plant flowers. *Echium pininana* is monocarpic, whereas most other perennial species of *Echium* do not die after flowering. There seems little doubt that *E. pininana* is an adaptation to laurel-forest areas; unlike *E. candicans*, it can grow in dense areas and does not require openings in the forest. The parallel between *E. pininana* and *Wilkesia* of the Hawaiian Islands (see Carlquist, 1970a, for illustrations) is

FIG. 5.2. Species of *Echium* from relatively mesic localities in the Canary Islands and Madeira. TOP LEFT, *E. strictum*, plant about 0.5 m tall; at head of Barranco de San Andres, Tenerife. TOP RIGHT, *E. candicans*, shrub 2.5 m tall; in opening of laurel forest, Ribeiro Frio, Madeira. BOTTOM LEFT, CENTER, *E. pininana*. BOTTOM LEFT shows specimens from the wild, with inflorescences; Los Roques y Los Silos, La Palma; BOTTOM CENTER shows a specimen grown from seeds of the wild plants; cultivated, in Santa Barbara, Calif. BOTTOM RIGHT, *E. simplex*, plants ca. 2 m tall (inflorescence included); cultivated in Jardin Canario, Gran Canaria.

185

remarkable. If grown in cultivation (fig. 5.2, bottom center), *E. pininana* does not form a tall stem, and internodes are all of intermediate length. Apparently, under natural conditions, flowering occurs only when the leaf crown reaches upper, better-lit levels of the forest, and presumably accumulates sufficient photosynthates to flower. The same is true of *Wilkesia*, which also flowers "prematurely" in cultivation.

Echium simplex (fig. 5.2, bottom right) is a species of relatively low elevations on Tenerife, but in relatively mesic sites on the Anaga Peninsula. Like *E. pininana*, it is monocarpic, but acaulescent. Because sufficient illumination is present near the ground level in its habitat, the lack of an elongate stem in *E. simplex* is understandable. A thin felt of silvery hairs is present on leaves of *E. simplex*, whereas leaves of *E. pininana* are hispid but not covered by "shading" or "reflecting" hairs. The large leaf size in both *E. simplex* and *E. pininana* seems correlated with the fact that the production of a single massive inflorescence requires a broad area of photosynthetic surface that is provided, in each case, by means of a rosette of large leaves.

Similar in form to *E. simplex* is the alpine species of Tenerife, *E. bourgeauanum* (fig. 5.3, top left), which has bright crimson flowers rather than whitish ones, as in *E. simplex*. The conspicuous color may relate to the factors that tend to produce conspicuous, brightly colored flowers in alpine angiosperms in various parts of the world. Rosettes of *E. bourgeauanum* are narrow, rather silvery (but with some hispid hairs), and probably resist low alpine humidity and high levels of illumination; they are sufficient, however, in the brilliant illumination of the Teide caldera, for enough photosynthesis to produce, after several seasons, the single massive inflorescence that terminates the life of an individual. In virtually all respects *E. bourgeauanum* forms a striking parallel to the dry alpine species of *Argyroxiphium* (chapter 4) on the Hawaiian Islands. Thus we see how similar selective factors, acting on two unrelated genera, have operated to produce similar results.

There is no Hawaiian parallel, however, to a second alpine species of Tenerife, *E. auberianum* (fig. 5.3, top right, bottom left). This species occurs on cinder cones within the caldera of El Teide. It is an acaulescent rosette plant, but it does not form a massive rosette of leaves, then flower and die. Each flowering shoot does die after flowering and fruiting, but

FIG. 5.3. Species of *Echium* from areas of recent volcanism in the Canary Islands. TOP LEFT, *E. bourgeauanum,* plants about 2 m tall; caldera of El Teide, Tenerife. TOP RIGHT, *E. auberianum,* plant 1 m tall; Arenas Negras cinder cones, El Teide, Tenerife. BOTTOM LEFT, same, base of plant to show perennial rootstock, from the top of which stems arise. BOTTOM RIGHT, *E. leucophaeum* growing as a reduced shrub on cinders; Volcán San Antonio, La Palma.

FIG. 5.4. *Echium* species as cultivated in the Rancho Santa Ana Botanic Garden, Claremont, Calif. (plantings by Kornelius Lems), photographed after a freeze (ca. − 3 C) in December 1967, to show differential damage. TOP LEFT, *E. nervosum* (Madeira), leaf tips killed, stems intact. TOP RIGHT, *E. webbii* (La Palma), little or no damage; plants still surviving well as of 1972. BOTTOM LEFT, *E. faramae* (Lanzarote), all plants killed. BOTTOM RIGHT, *E. pininana* (La Palma), little or no damage.

new innovations are formed on the perennial, succulent caudex (fig. 5.3, bottom left). This habit, which recalls other genera of Boraginaceae, such as *Cynoglossum*, seems well adapted to the alpine cinder-cone habitat. Flowering shoots are limited in duration, so that, as snow melts and the soil dries, shoots are not exposed during the dry summer and autumn months. Moreover, the caudex seems adapted to cinder cones; if it becomes buried more deeply as cinders slide downslope, it can still innovate shoots in successive years and the shoots will reach the surface. Significantly, both *E. auberianum* and *E. bourgeauanum* are resistant to the cold temperatures of the high caldera. *Echium bourgeauanum* (like *Argyroxiphium sandwichense*) has the apical bud protected by a dense series of leaves, and the sessile nature of the rosette prevents damage to the stem, which is extremely short. *Echium auberianum* survives freezing temperatures by means of its underground caudex, which innovates shoots only during the growing season.

Echium leucophaeum (figs. 5.1, bottom right; 5.3, bottom right) can be found on new cinder cones, as on Volcán San Antonio (fig. 5.3, bottom right). In these plants, leaves are extremely narrow and silvery with dense hairs, the plants being nearly prostrate. These characteristics suggest an ecotype successful on cinder cones, which are relatively dry and brilliantly illuminated, with much heat radiated from the cinders during daylight hours. Plants of *E. leucophaeum* in dry lowlands (fig. 5.1, bottom right) are taller, but reduction of leaf surface corresponds to lower moisture availability.

Although this account does not include mention of all Macaronesian *Echium* species, those not specified can be grouped with the adaptational modes described. One dimension of adaptive radiation that is not visible, however, is climatic tolerance. These factors were demonstrated by an experimental planting of various *Echium* species at the Rancho Santa Ana Botanic Garden, in Claremont, California. This planting was undertaken in summer, 1965, by the late Kornelius Lems. In late December, 1967, an unusually severe freeze (about 25 F) occurred at the Botanic Garden. This freeze was highly informative, because differential cold tolerances were illustrated graphically (fig. 5.4). Observations made in February, 1968, when damage could be clearly assessed, revealed the following:

E. aculeatum (a species close to *E. leucophaeum*), from middle
elevations on Tenerife: half of the plants killed.

E. aculeatum, from low elevations on Hierro: all plants killed.

E. bourgeauanum, from El Teide, Tenerife: all plants killed.

E. faramae, from lowlands, Lanzarote: all plants killed (fig. 5.4,
bottom left).

E. giganteum, middle elevations, Tenerife: all plants killed.

E. leucophaeum, from lowlands, La Palma: almost killed; some
plants survived but died soon after February, 1968.

E. nervosum, from lowlands of Madeira: leaves damaged, but
plants survived, new leaves produced (fig. 5.4, top left).

E. onosmaefolium, middle elevations, Gran Canaria: leaves and
younger stems damaged, but new shoots formed and plants
surviving well.

E. pininana, from laurel forests, La Palma uplands: tips of leaves
damaged, but plants otherwise intact (fig. 5.4, bottom right).

E. strictum, Tenerife upper lowlands: all plants killed.

E. webbii, caldera of La Palma: all plants intact (fig. 5.4, top
right).

Lowland plants, and plants of frost-free (or relatively frost-free) areas
not far above the coast on Macaronesian islands, were subject to the
greatest damage or killing. Of these, larger, woodier plants (*E. nervosum,
E. leucophaeum, E. onosmaefolium*) survived better, possibly because not
all parts of the plant were reached by freezing, or possibly because the
chances of survival of some stems on a larger plant are greater. *Echium
faramae* and *E. strictum* were clearly vulnerable, and reminded me of how
a large ornamental annual could be killed by frost in a garden. The best
survival was for higher-elevation (but not alpine) species: *E. webbii*, for
example. In fact, at the date of writing, these plants are still growing successfully; they also survive hot, dry summers in Claremont, whereas the
horticulturally popular *E. candicans* survives Claremont summers poorly.
Obviously upland Echiums have evolved frost-resistance not present in
the lowland species. Partial frost resistance in the lowland Madeira species,
E. nervosum, may be explained by the fact that on that more northerly
island, frosts can occur nearer the coast. One might have expected *E. bour-*

geauanum to survive, but evidently this plant was dying in the Botanic Garden prior to the freeze. One might speculate that heavy soil, warm temperatures on autumn and winter days, or artificial watering—combined with pathogenic fungi—contributed to its decline.

Descriptions of growth forms in *Echium* have been offered (Lems, 1961). Readers should be warned that Lems changed his ideas on phylogeny of growth forms subsequent to that paper but did not have an opportunity to revise his concepts. The same applies to the account of trichomes in the genus (Lems and Holzapfel, 1968). Trichomes, as well as wood anatomy (Carlquist, 1970b), correlate closely with ecology in *Echium*. There seems little doubt that there has been evolution toward increased woodiness in *Echium* on Macaronesian islands, conforming to that of many groups on islands (chapter 10). The diversification within Echiums on Macaronesia is, however, of great interest, and one cannot help drawing a parallel with the *Dubautia-Argyroxiphium-Wilkesia* complex on the Hawaiian Islands. Because there are no true rain forests in Macaronesia, equivalent climatically to those of the Hawaiian Islands, the adaptive radiation in *Echium* seems "foreshortened" compared with the Hawaiian complex.

Aeonium. A large number of species of this genus, which is nearly endemic to Macaronesia, occur in the Canary Islands. Two species are restricted to the Cape Verde Islands, two to Madeira, one is endemic to Morocco (*A. arboreum*), and one (*A. leucoblepharum*) to Abyssinia and Somaliland (Praeger, 1932). Even if one were to regard the mainland African species as relics, it seems obvious that radiation has occurred abundantly on the Canary Islands. If one regards the mainland African species as relics, one is taking a difficult interpretation, for each of them is similar to a Canarian species, whereas they are not similar to each other. They could possibly be, in one or both cases, results of dispersal from islands to mainland. At any rate, the Canarian Aeoniums offer a good example of radiation in growth form on the Islands.* There is, indeed, a

* My plate of four species of *Aeonium* (Carlquist, 1965, fig. 8.5) misidentifies a plant as *A. glutinosum*; it probably is *A. holochrysum*, although excessive hybridization in cultivated Aeoniums makes any plant in cultivation suspect where indentification is concerned. *Aeonium arboreum* is, by its presence in that plate, implied to be a Canarian species; it was, in fact, thought to be from the Canaries for many

range from the acaulescent species such as A. *tabulaeforme* (Tenerife) and A. *glandulosum* (Madeira) to the shrubby species such as A. *manriqueorum* and A. *haworthii*. Some (A. *glandulosum*) can be annual or biennial, whereas the shrubs are of indefinite duration. A contrast can be drawn between the monocarpic species (some of which are acaulescent, some tall) and the non-monocarpic, shrubbier species. However, even the shrubby species are relatively determinate in growth, as shown by their tendency to form abundant aerial roots on upper stems, which tend to fall off and root, or root when the main stem falls over onto the ground. The accumulation of secondary xylem is limited because of this tendency. However, the habitats occupied by *Aeonium* species show a remarkable range; one might expect this genus to be characteristic only of dry situations because of its succulence, which is not really markedly different from one species to another. To be sure, there are lowland species, but even these tend to grow in barrancos (A. *holochrysum*, A. *manriqueorum*, A. *sedifolium*, A. *viscatum*), just as A. *arboreum* grows in similar barrancos on the nearby Moroccan coast (Praeger, 1932). Other species of xeric localities below the forest belt include A. *nobile*, A. *percarneum*, A. *saundersii*, and A. *tabulaeforme* (Lems, 1960). In the cloud forest, one can find A. *goochiae* (laurel forest) and A. *cuneatum*. *Aeonium* also enters subalpine conditions (A. *caespitosum*, A. *spathulatum*), but apparently never is a true alpine plant. Although its succulence would seem to qualify it for such habitats, none of the Canarian Aeoniums are resistant to heavy frost. In diameter, *Aeonium* rosettes differ widely, from 80 cm (A. *canariense*) to about 3 cm (A. *sedifolium*).

Lamiaceae. Lamiaceae have radiated into a variety of Canarian habitats. *Leucophae*, a Canarian genus dubiously segregated from *Sideritis*, is endemic. It ranges from near sea level to the subalpine zone. *Leucophae massoniana* occurs in lowland barrancos, although in moister parts of them. Cliffs are the habitat of L. *gomerae*, with pendulous stems. The large-leaved L. *macrostachys* grows in laurel forests, while L. *eriocephala* is a sub-

years; it is apparently restricted to Morocco (Praeger, 1932). In my (1965) text, it is called "A. *arborescens*" by mistake, although it is correctly labeled on the figure. There are Canarian species, such as A. *manriqueorum*, which form shrubs as large as those of A. *arboreum*, and could be cited as Canarian representatives of this growth form that have evolved there autochthonously.

alpine cliff plant (Lems, 1960). The genus *Micromeria* can range from dry lowland barrancos (*M. densiflora, M. linkii*) to pine forests (*M. lanata*), to openings in laurel forests (*M. lepida*), to rocky subalpine localities (*M. benthamii, M. teydensis, M. tragothymus*).

Dipsacaceae. The three endemic Canarian species of *Pterocephalus* occupy diverse localities. *Pterocephalus dumetorum* (fig. 10.9, bottom left, right) is a shrub of subalpine scrub, whereas *P. lasiosperma* grows in "subalpine desert" (Lems, 1960), and *P. virens* is a lowland species.

Ecotype Formation in Various Families. There are instances in the Canarian flora of highly variable species that cover a broad altitudinal span and may form distinctive ecotypes in various zones. These include *Andryala pinnatifida* (Asteraceae) and *Cheiranthus virescens* (Brassicaceae). The latter may be considered conspecific both with the alpine *C. scoparius* and the Madeiran species *C. mutabilis*, which can be found on banks of waterfalls as well as in subalpine grassland. These species may represent incipient adaptive radiation. However, their adaptation to any localities other than dry ones seems superficial and recent. Where they do occur in more mesic localities, they seem to be chance pioneers in openings, as with *C. mutabilis* along waterfalls in laurel forest on Madeira. However, entry into more mesic localities as an opening phase in adaptive radiation may occur in just such a way, so we should not neglect examples of this sort as irrelevant to consideration of adaptive radiation.

Animals

The Canary Islands, as well as the Azores and other Macaronesian islands, have relatively "harmonic" passerine bird faunas. This, as Lack (1947) notes, may be the reason why these islands show no cases of adaptive radiation in their avifauna. Although the avifauna of Macaronesian islands is depauperate in land birds in comparison with mainland areas (e.g., Bannerman and Bannerman, 1963), this reflects the fact that there are fewer niches available on the islands—that is to say, fewer niches of sufficient extent to support breeding populations. As Bannerman and Bannerman (1963) also note, many straggling land birds from Morocco visit Madeira; access is obviously easy, which tends to make an island fauna less strongly disharmonic, so that adaptive radiation is forestalled. Lack (1947) has noted the possibility that successively newer immigrants, more aggressive than the insular species already there, will tend to wipe out groups that have undergone adaptive radiation. In Macaronesia, it would seem that on account of easy access, adaptive radiation in birds never had a chance. MacArthur and Wilson (1967), as noted earlier (chapter 3), hypothesize that on remote large islands and archipelagos, adaptive radiation is likely to occur if the distance from a source area is at a maximum range of dispersal for a particular group of animals. Lack finds the Galápagos Islands more remote from the mainland than they would seem geographically, because those islands lie in a region of calms, whereas winds favor immigration to Macaronesia from source areas. Lack of adaptive radiation in Macaronesian avifauna does not seem due to lack of time: the angiosperm radiation has become pronounced. Apparently, what constitutes "opportunity" for one group does not for another.

In the Canarian avifauna, there are cases of incipient speciation in birds. For example, there are four geographic races in the titmice (*Parus teneriffae*) according to Bannerman and Bannerman (1963). In the case of chaffinches on the Canary Islands, Lack, agreeing with Mayr (1942), finds the two species of *Fringilla* to be the result of two successive introductions, not radiation. The endemic species, *F. teydea*, is hypothesized to be the older. It breeds only in pine forests on Gran Canaria and on Tenerife. Its adaptations are discussed in chapter 15. On those two islands, *F. coelebs*, hypothesized as a more recent introduction and native also in Europe, "avoids" pine forest and lives in laurel forest and chestnut woodland. However, on La Palma, *F. teydea* is absent, and *F. coelebs* occurs in all forest types, as it does in Europe. These examples suggest that, with respect to avifauna, resource availability is tight and unsuited to diversification of a group: a given bird species either meets the needs of a niche (and possibly changes somewhat to achieve a more precise adaptation to that niche) or is excluded by the many other competitors resident on the islands.

Radiation has undoubtedly occurred in Macaronesian insect groups, but data on this point are very difficult to secure in a clear fashion. Wollaston's data for Madeiran Coleoptera do give a number of hints in this direction, but his information is of greater interest in underlining the occurrence of flightlessness in Macaronesian insects, and is discussed in that connection (chapter 12). There does not appear to be any striking radiation among Macaronesian reptiles, although interesting size differences can occur in a single species represented on various of the islands, probably for reasons discussed in similar instances in chapter 15.

Comment on Macaronesian Patterns

As mentioned above, Macaronesian islands do not seem remote enough that strong disharmony can foster adaptive radiation in birds—whereas the five passerine establishments on the ecologically rich Hawaiian Islands have had opportunity for adaptive radiation.

There have, however, been situations of opportunity for angiosperms on Macaronesian islands, especially on the Canary Islands. Unfilled niches in the Canarian and Madeiran floras have been occupied largely by members of herbaceous, "weedy," evolutionarily upgrade groups, not woody ones. All of the examples cited (*Echium, Sonchus, Euphorbia* sect. *Tithymalus, Limonium, Aeonium, Leucophae, Micromeria,* and *Pterocephalus*) are herbaceous or, at most, "woody herbs." These have radiated into all zones. Interestingly, the laurel forest contains products of radiation in several of these groups, so it obviously is not a "closed" community. However, lowland scrub and heather scrub do seem to contain most products of radiation. Differences in topography (e.g., barrancos) and moisture availability have provided more ecological opportunity in the lowlands and, of course, the total area of lowlands is greater than that of the higher zones. Alpine zones are relatively poor in products of adaptive radiation, but not only is this a much more severe environment, the total land area of this habitat in Macaronesia also is limited.

Ecological opportunity for angiosperms is considerable in Macaronesia. Herbaceous groups seem favored for establishment in the lowlands, as one might expect: this zone is where virtually all man-introduced weeds have established. Lowland groups seem favored for rapid adaptation to alpine conditions, as on the Hawaiian Islands. For example, the lowland Macaronesian species *Plantago arborescens* (fig. 10.10, top left, right) has a close species, *P. webbii* (fig. 10.10, bottom left), in the alpine zone, but

Plantago is not represented in the moister forest areas. Crucifers show this condition clearly in Macaronesia. Ecological shift of Brassicaceae into wet-forest areas has occurred to a minimal extent. The Hawaiian Islands exceed Macaronesia both in disharmony and in ecological richness, so that greater radiation would be expected in Hawaii. Compared with the Hawaiian flora, the Macaronesian flora shows a somewhat truncated (on the mesic end of the spectrum) adaptive radiation. Nevertheless, the Macaronesian, and especially the Canarian, flora is second only to the Hawaiian flora among plant assemblages illustrative of adaptive radiation. The Galápagos flora is far more truncated in mesic opportunities than is the Macaronesian flora (chapter 6). In Macaronesian floras, there does not seem to be much displacement of "older" groups by newer groups. The laurels and perhaps the pine are "relictual" preservations, but they have neither radiated nor been displaced (except as a result of human activities). The laurels are "recent relics," for these volcanic islands are not truly ancient at all. The conifers of New Caledonia (chapter 7) and New Zealand are much older, and show both more pronounced relictism and also radiation into a variety of ecological habitats.

References

Bannerman, D. A., and W. M. Bannerman. 1963. *Birds of the Atlantic Islands*, vol. I: *A history of the birds of the Canary Islands and of the Salvages*. Edinburgh and London, Oliver and Boyd.

Carlquist, S. 1965. *Island life*. New York, Natural History Press.

Carlquist, S. 1970a. *Hawaii, a natural history*. New York, Natural History Press.

Carlquist, S. 1970b. Wood anatomy of *Echium* (Boraginaceae). *Aliso* 7:183–99.

Lack, D. 1947. *Darwin's finches*. Cambridge, Cambridge University Press.

Lems, K. 1960. Floristic botany of the Canary Islands. *Sarracenia* 5:1–94.

Lems, K. 1961. Botanical notes on the Canary Islands. III. The life form spectrum and its interpretation. *Ecology* 42:569–72.

Lems, K., and C. M. Holzapfel. 1968. Evolution in the Canary Islands. I. Phylogenetic relations in the genus *Echium* (Boraginaceae) as shown by trichome development. *Bot. Gaz.* 129:95–107.

MacArthur, R. H., and E. O. Wilson. 1967. *The theory of island biogeography*. Princeton, N.J., Princeton University Press.

Mayr, E. 1942. *Systematics and the origin of species*. New York, Columbia University Press.

Praeger, L. 1932. *An account of the Sempervivum group*. London, Royal Horticultural Society.

CHAPTER SIX

ADAPTIVE RADIATION: GALÁPAGOS, JUAN FERNANDEZ, AND SMALLER PACIFIC ISLANDS

The Galápagos Islands

The Galápagos Islands do indeed represent many interesting biological phenomena and have the advantage of relatively good preservation of many elements in the biota, with a few notable exceptions. However, we must remember that the Galápagos biota is not a rich one at all. In fact, its impoverishment and simplicity permit insular patterns to be seen. The Hawaiian Islands are probably richer in all insular phenomena. Their very complexity might have proved confusing for Darwin, although I like to think that if the itinerary of H.M.S. *Beagle* had included the Hawaiian Islands rather than the Galápagos and allowed Darwin sufficient time to study that biota, he might have emerged with a clearer picture of adaptive radiation and other insular phenomena. However, the very clarity and simplicity of the Galápagos biota rendered patterns clearly visible, and perhaps we owe to this simplicity the fact that Darwin was able to make effective observations there. Yet, as Lack (1947) reminds us, Darwin himself was slow in realizing the significance of the Darwin's finches.

To be sure, the Darwin's finches (Fringillidae, subfamily Geospizinae) are a good example of adaptive radiation, for reasons to be discussed. They fulfill almost all of the definitions suggested in chapter 3. The only Galápagos plant group that partially fulfills the criteria of adaptive radiation is *Scalesia* (Asteraceae, tribe Heliantheae). Other plant and animal groups suggest phases of adaptive radiation, but these phases are greatly "foreshortened" by the nature of the Galápagos environment and by other factors. In analyzing why only one Galápagos example shows "classic" adaptive radiation and others only a few partial phases of this concept, most none at all, we can learn considerably not only about the Galápagos environment but about the nature of adaptive radiation as well.

Darwin's Finches. We could imagine a greater diversification in adaptive radiation of a group of birds than the geospizids show. For example, the nectarivory of the Hawaiian honeycreepers is missing—and for a very good reason. Flowering seasons are short in the Galápagos, and the few flowers available during this season are not good nectar flowers (nor would we expect them to be, if establishment of ornithophilous plants is related to presence of bird pollinators).

However, one of the primary points of interest in the geospizids is their presentation of a nearly unbroken series of intermediates between extremes (fig. 6.1). This is, in a way, more instructive than the adaptive radiation of the honeycreepers, where we see (especially in the subfamily Drepanidinae) some obvious gaps, probably due to extinctions. Geospizid adaptive radiation features the following characteristics:

1. There has been occupation of a variety of ecological niches, not just a few. In terms of diet, we see a range (fig. 6.1), from 100 percent insectivory to mainly plant feeding.

2. The morphology of bills and the ways in which they work form external evidences not only of diet but also of the various mechanisms (probing, grasping, biting, crushing), by which this diet is obtained. Bowman (1963) constructed appealing analogies to tools like pliers of various types (see also Carlquist, 1965), but he has analyzed form and musculature (1961) of the bill apparatus in a sophisticated fashion.

3. Likewise, color indicates ground-feeding (blacker tones of plumage), which is also related to herbivory. Tawnier colors are related to feeding in branches of shrubs and trees, which in turn connotes insectivory. This is clearly shown in the scheme of Bowman (1963), reproduced here as fig. 6.2.

4. Theoretically the Darwin's finches might achieve diversity yet be able to occupy only a single vegetational zone, taking advantage of dif-

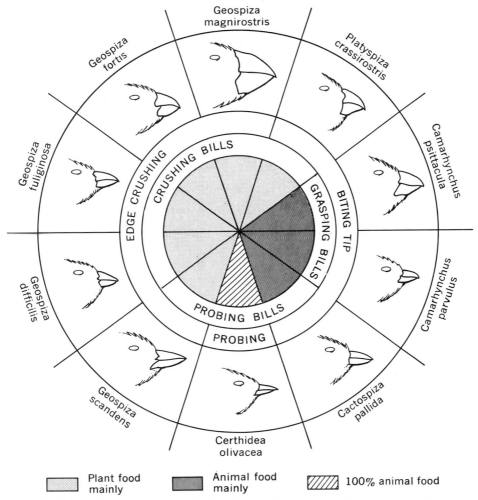

FIG. 6.1. Schematic representation of the relationships between bill structure and feeding habits in ten species of Geospizinae from Indefatigable I., Galápagos Is. Redrawn from Bowman (1961); reproduced by permission of the University of California Press.

ferent resources within this zone. In fact, the Darwin's finches occupy all conceivable zones (Lack, 1947). *Geospiza* tends to occupy the arid and transitional zones. *Cactospiza*, *Platyspiza*, and *Camarhynchus* tend to be more inland and upland in preferences, ranging from transitional into the humid *Scalesia* forest. *Certhidea* ranges among all zones. *Pinaroloxias*, which occurs on Cocos Island and is thus a Galápagos outlier, occurs in the coconut forests of that wet tropical island. Even in a single species,

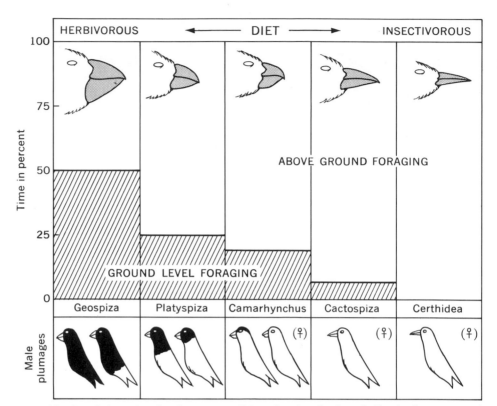

FIG. 6.2. Correlation of male plumage condition, foraging level, and diet in five genera of Geospizinae. Redrawn from Bowman (1963); reproduced by permission of the California Academy of Sciences.

Geospiza difficilis, some subspecies are lowland, some are upland in their adaptations (Lack, 1947, p. 27).

5. The various genera of geospizids are not merely several relictual types, but represent a more or less continuous spread of types. There are, in addition, "unexpected" or "supralimital" adaptations, such as the tool-using finch, *Cactospiza pallida*.

6. The various taxa of Darwin's finches are equivalent to different families on mainland areas. Bowman (1963) has offered the following "equivalents" or comparisons:

> *Geospiza* spp.: like mainland Fringillidae
> *Geospiza scandens:* like Icteridae
> *Cactospiza pallida:* like Thraupidae

> *Certhidea olivacea:* like Parulidae
> *Pinaroloxias inornata:* like Coerebidae
> *Camarhynchus psittacula:* like Paradoxornithidae
> *Camarhynchus parvulus:* like Paridae

If, instead of the single invasion of the geospizids, invasions by stocks representing all of the families listed had taken place, radiation by the geospizids would undoubtedly have been forestalled. However, land birds do not disperse easily to oceanic islands more than several hundred miles from the mainland (and as Lack notes, the Galápagos are in a region of calms, where winds are not likely to bring birds), so the Galápagos landbird fauna is undoubtedly quite disharmonic. This has permitted radiation of ancestral types of the Darwin's finches.

7. Geospizids show secondary indications of diversification. These are perhaps much like the opening stages of adaptive radiation, in which character release occurs (see chapter 3). For example, *Geospiza fortis* is the sole *Geospiza* on Daphne Major Island. It has a smaller beak than does *G. fortis* on Charles and Chatham Islands, where *G. fortis* competes with the characteristically small-beaked *G. fuliginosa* (Lack, 1947, p. 832). *Geospiza fuliginosa*, in turn, has smaller beak size on Charles and Chatham that it has on an island where *G. fortis* is absent. On Crossman Island, for example, the beak of *G. fortis* has a broader range in size, for it is the sole *Geospiza* there, and is not subject to the character displacement effect of congeners on a single island.

8. Although the Galápagos Islands are "habitat poor" for many groups, they do represent a variety of habitats for a bird group such as the finches, which show plasticity and versatility in diet capabilities. Most other bird—or vertebrate—groups, if we could see habitat diversity "through their eyes," would not have a broad range of opportunities available to them.

Other Animal Groups. The other Galápagos groups do not show good instances of what could be called adaptive radiation. The giant tortoises exemplify race formation, but these races or subspecies do not appear to differ in ecology, habitat, or diet (although obviously food sources are more abundant, and different in species content, on the various islands, there is no evidence that any of the tortoises has developed specific preferences for the plant assemblages of any particular island). The distinctively shaped shells of the tortoise subspecies could be thought to represent the product of genetic drift, or the result of the "founder principle." However, shell differences in tortoises at large can have selective value. In the case of the Galápagos tortoises, rarity of most of the subspecies makes selective advantage of the various shell shapes difficult to demonstrate, but this possibility cannot be ruled out.

This subspeciation owing to genetic drift seems true of the various island populations of the lizard genus *Tropidurus*, although further studies may reveal differences among the various island populations of more than a "strictly taxonomic" nature.

There is no doubt that several insect genera have speciated appreciably in the Galápagos environment. There may be aspects of adaptive radiation among these, but, if so, the available literature is weak in ecological data; one cannot find the basis for ecological distinctions that might underlie adaptive radiation. The reasons for this lack are clear: most Galápagos entomological studies are based on museum specimens rather than on collection of extensive data in the field. Because of the peculiarities of the Galápagos environment, field studies of entomology remain one of the more promising avenues open for investigation.

Scalesia (Asteraceae). Adaptive radiation on oceanic islands often, although by no means invariably, seems to proceed by ecological shift from dry or relatively dry into more mesic sites. This seems true in *Scalesia*. The reasons why this should have occurred are clear. Establishment of a plant group in the Galápagos depends, with few exceptions, upon tolerance of the dry conditions that occupy such a large area compared with the area of humid places suitable for trees. Ecological shift in flowering plants on islands from wet to dry is relatively infrequent, and if it were true in *Scalesia,* one would expect diversity among the humid-forest species, combined with penetration of arid areas by only a few species. In reality, the reverse is true: numerous dry lowland species, with decrease in number of *Scalesia* species with increasing altitude. The arborescent species, *S. pedunculata* (3–20 m tall) and *S. microcephala* (at most, 3.5 m tall), are exceptional for height in their tribe, Heliantheae. Although shrubs are not infrequent in Heliantheae, true trees are. Let us assume that arborescence is secondary in *Scalesia,* as it probably is throughout the family Asteraceae.

The altitudinal distribution of *Scalesia* species is as follows (data from Arthur Cronquist, in Wiggins and Porter, 1971):

LOWLAND SPECIES

S. aspera: "near the shore but in less barren, more mesic sites than *S. affinis.*"

S. atractyloides: "pioneer on and around recent lava flows."

S. crockeri: "on bluffs and in lava crevices near the shore" (*S. crockeri* is very close to *S. aspera*).

S. helleri: "pioneer on cliffs and raw lava, especially near the shore."

S. stewartii: "in barren lava beds and cinders, from near the coast to above 200 m" (*S. stewartii* is very close to *S. atractyloides*).

S. villosa: "a pioneer on barren cinder slopes on lava beds."

LOW-TO-MIDDLE-ELEVATION SPECIES

S. affinis: "a pioneer on lava beds and cinder slopes and ridges, from sea level to about 600 m."

S. incisa: "a pioneer of cliffs and raw lava to at least 520 m."

MIDDLE-ELEVATION SPECIES

S. cordata: "relatively mesic sites (and apparently not on raw lava) from about 50 m upward to about 400 m or higher."

MIDDLE-TO-UPPER-ELEVATION SPECIES

S. microcephala: "at middle and upper altitudes, from about 350 m upward, in less barren habitats than *S. affinis.*"

S. pedunculata: "in relatively mesic or wet sites, not on raw lava, from about 60 m upward, often forming considerable forests, pure or mixed with other kinds of trees and shrubs."

In addition to its greater stature and moist upland habitat, *S. pedunculata* shows adaptation to an arboreal and more nearly mesic role in its relatively large leaves (3–30 cm long, 12 cm wide). Most other *Scalesia* species have leaves that rarely exceed 10 cm in length. For photographs of leaves of the various *Scalesia* species, see Carlquist (1965).

Opuntia (Cactaceae). In their account of this genus in the Wiggins and Porter (1971) flora, Anderson and Walkington described *Opuntia* as a "highly variable genus in the Galápagos, exhibiting rapid radiation that has resulted in marked morphological differences and establishment of several specific and infraspecific taxa within the archipelago." Undoubtedly the youth of the archipelago means that these species and subspecies (as they should probably be called, although this Flora unfortunately utilizes "variety" as the only infraspecific category) are relatively new. However, do these taxa exemplify adaptive radiation? In some ways, yes. Among the populations recognized as *Opuntia echios,* some are trees (to 12 m in "var. *gigantea*"), some low and prostrate ("var. *zacana*"). The typical populations ("var. *echios*") extend from sea level to 380 m or higher, whereas some ("var. *zacana*") occur only near sea level. In O. *megasperma,* the typical population ("var. *megasperma*") occurs to only 50 m on Charles Island and nearby Champion Island, whereas the Chatham Island population ("var. *mesophytica*") occurs in the upper transition zone and *Scalesia* zone at about 250 m.

These examples and others, however, suggest in part vicarious species and in part populations that have, during the process of isolation in different islands, adapted to different zones (although these zones, admittedly different, are not comparable to the much broader ecological range presented by vegetational zones in the Hawaiian Islands). The fact that there are no truly mesophytic sites in the Galápagos would predispose this moderate ecological shift. One could question whether *Opuntia* would be able to enter true rain forest if it were present on the Galápagos Islands. The Galápagos Opuntias show diversity, but do not qualify as good examples of adaptive radiation (compared, for example, to Hawaiian angiosperm genera; see chapter 4), unless we wish to define adaptive radiation in terms of the ecological diversity of the habitat, no matter how limited that diversity. We clearly do not have to alter our concepts of adaptive radiation where the Darwin's finches are concerned.

Acalypha (Euphorbiaceae). Acalypha is represented in the Galápagos Islands by endemic species in ecologically different sites (Wiggins and Porter, 1971). We do not know if the species represent products of a single introduction, which would be useful to know if we were to assess the nature of adaptive radiation in this genus.

Other Genera of Angiosperms. In *Chamaesyce* (or *Euphorbia* sect. *Chamaesyce*) of the Euphorbiaceae, the Galápagos species range from herbs to subshrubs—but C. (*E.*) *viminea* is apparently introduced by man

(Svenson, 1963). This problem is repeated by a genus of another family, *Alternanthera* (Amaranthaceae). *Alternanthera rugulosa*, a small tree (3–4 m), would be notably arborescent compared to shrubby or prostrate Galápagos species, and might have been cited as an end-product of radiation in *Alternanthera*. However, *A. rugulosa* is not an autochthone; it has recently been collected in Peru (Eliasson, in Wiggins and Porter, 1971). The Galápagos Alternantheras must represent two (or possibly more) introductions.

Many Galápagos species in various families (e.g., *Piscidia carthaginensis, Cordia* spp.) show a full altitudinal range from coast to uplands. Thus all altitudes, despite differences in vegetation, may be considered basically similar in being more or less xeric. Ecological shift by Galápagos groups may occur, but the climatic range available for shifting may well be within the tolerances of a single species.

Commentary. The synopses given show only two examples of adaptive radiation, in the best sense, in the Galápagos Islands: the geospizids and (to a lesser extent) *Scalesia*. My discussion of the Darwin's finches is only illustrative and is not to be considered a substitute for the works of Lack (1947) and Bowman (1961, 1963), which should be read by any serious student. The key to lack of adaptive radiation is the limited or "foreshortened" ecological span of the Galápagos environment. The amount of rainfall in the "cloud forest" and the effect of the protracted cloud cover, which may enhance the effect of available moisture, are not known. However, even the "cloud forest" is relatively dry. If this were not true, species corresponding to those of mainland wet forest would be expected, but they are notable by their absence (whereas wet-forest elements are present in the Hawaiian flora, both as immigrants from wet-forest source areas and as adaptations from drier to wetter areas). The Galápagos environment must be considered, in comparison with climates at large, to be variously xeric, with mere modifications of xeric environments. The geospizids are not affected by the dryness because they can exploit this environment in various ways: insect and plant foods are relatively varied for them, both within a given altitudinal level and certainly within the gamut of altitudinal levels. Although the Galápagos flora is disharmonic, it is apparently far less disharmonic than the land-bird fauna. The Galápagos flora contains an assortment of drier Middle American plant groups, yet these are presented with relatively limited habitat diversity within the Galápagos.

205

In literature on the Galápagos Islands biota, one notes the implication that recentness of the archipelago may be a limitation to the development of patterns of adaptive radiation, so that one might expect additional radiation given more time. This is, to me, unlikely. The time elapsed on the Galápagos seems sufficient for radiation into the available environments; it has certainly been sufficient for the geospizids to occupy what are probably all the niches available to that group. Thus the factors suppressing adaptive radiation in the Galápagos as compared with other insular areas seem to be, in probable order of importance: lack of strong ecological diversity; closeness to mainland areas; and geological recentness.

The Juan Fernandez Islands

An inherent interest of the Juan Fernandez Islands is that on these relatively small islands there has been any adaptive radiation at all. The small size of the two islands (Masafuera and Masatierra) and outlying islets (e.g., Santa Clara) seems too limited to promote adaptive radiation. Nevertheless, two groups of composites (Asteraceae) show what could be called adaptive radiation. One group is from the tribe Senecioneae: *Robinsonia* and genera close to it (*Rhetinodendron* and *Symphyochaeta*); by a wider definition, all three genera could perhaps be considered a single genus. The other example is *Dendroseris*, a genus of Lactuceae (Cichorieae). As recognized here, *Dendroseris* includes the segregate genera (which certainly merit subgeneric status) *Phoenicoseris*, *Hesperoseris*, and *Rea*. For habit illustrations of these, the reader can consult Skottsberg (1922, 1953) and Carlquist (1965).

Although all species of *Robinsonia*, *Rhetinodendron*, and *Symphyochaeta* could be considered shrubs, they vary considerably in habit, ranging from a subshrub 1–2 m tall to a true tree, 5–6 m or more. The gamut in growth form is not overwhelming, for all could be called rosette trees. However, the habitats do vary from obligate epiphytism on tree ferns (*R. evenia*) in very moist forest to growth on montane scrubland and open cliff faces (*R. gayana*). I have liquid-preserved material of all the species of *Robinsonia* and of the two genera closely allied to it. This material, collected on more than one occasion by Carl Skottsberg, was kindly given to me by him in 1956. Upon compiling habit and habitat data for the species and then comparing these to transections of leaves (figs. 6.3, 6.4), I noticed a remarkable degree of correlation. Therefore I have decided to present data on leaf anatomy here rather than wait until a more extensive account of comparative data from other portions of the plant could be presented. Descriptions of habits and habitats are from Skottsberg (1953). The species are arranged here from most to least mesomorphic, based chiefly on anatomical considerations, but the correlation with habitat appears so close that either basis could have been used.

Robinsonia evenia (fig. 6.3, top left). Masatierra: upper montane region, seldom below 500 m; epiphytic on *Blechnum cycadifolium* and *Dicksonia* tree ferns; 2–3, or even 4, m tall. Leaves very thick; 1 hypodermis layer; 2–3 layers of elongate palisade cells; thin-walled, spongy, chlorophyllous tissue with large air spaces; fibers few or none on bundles; 1 abaxial secretory canal per vein, on average.

Symphyochaeta macrocephala (fig. 6.3, center right). Masatierra: Puerto Frances to Pangal, 300 to 350 m; same habit as *Robinsonia*, but more straggling; 2 m or less. Leaves very thin; 1 layer of hypodermis (2 near large veins); 2 layers of elongate palisade cells; thin-walled, compact, chlorophyllous, spongy tissue; no fibers adjacent to veins; 1 abaxial and 1 adaxial secretory canal per bundle, on average; all cells of the leaf rather small.

Robinsonia masafuerae (fig. 6.3, top right). Masafuera: 650–1370 m, preferring fern-rich gullies; hardly surpassing 2 m; closely related to *R. evenia*, and sometimes epiphytic. Leaves medium thin; 1 hypodermis layer; 2 layers of elongate palisade cells; thin-walled, chlorophyllous, spongy tissue; some fibers adjacent to larger bundles; few or no abaxial secretory canals adjacent to bundles.

Robinsonia gracilis (fig. 6.3, bottom left). Masatierra: ridge between Piedra Agujemada and Laura Valleys to Cordón Salsipuedes, never below 500 m; not often epiphytic, although seedlings may start as epiphytes on *Blechnum* and *Dicksonia*; 1–2 m tall. Leaves thin, 1 layer of hypodermis; 2 layers of rather cuboidal palisade; spongy tissue chlorophyllous, but with some

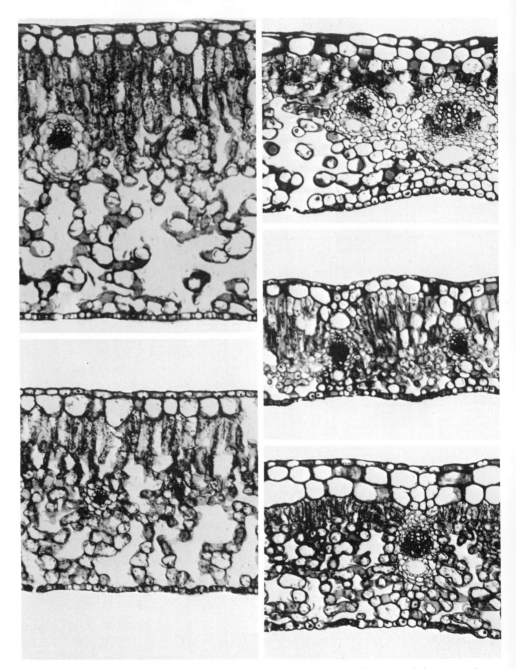

FIG. 6.3. Leaves of the Juan Fernandez rosette-shrub Senecioneae (Asteraceae) in transection, adaxial face above. TOP LEFT, *Robinsonia evenia*. BOTTOM LEFT, *R. masafuerae*. TOP RIGHT, *R. gracilis*. CENTER RIGHT, *Symphyochaeta macrocephala*. BOTTOM RIGHT, *Rhetinodendron berteri*. Leaf of *R. evenia* is 0.8 mm thick, and all leaves are photographed at the same scale of magnification. Materials furnished by Carl Skottsberg.

resemblance to hypodermis; fibers at phloem poles of bundles absent or nearly so; 1 abaxial secretory canal per bundle.

Rhetinodendron berteri (fig. 6.3, bottom right). Masatierra: open brushwood and forest along the ridge, rarely below 500 m, of the elevated central part of the island; shrubs 2–4 m, trees of 5 m occasional, one tree 8 m observed. Leaves medium thin; 2 layers of hypodermis; 1 layer of palisade; thin-walled, spongy tissue on abaxial side resembling hypodermis cells; fibers on bundles few or none.

Robinsonia gayana (fig. 6.4, left). Masatierra: montane scrub, descending to about 200 m, often in crevices of cliffs; shrub to 3, rarely 4, m tall. Leaves medium thin; 1 layer of hypodermis; 2 (–3) layers compact palisade; spongy tissue on abaxial side thick-walled and very much like hypodermis cells; fibers present at phloem poles (abaxial side of leaf) of veins; 1 abaxial and 1 adaxial secretory canal per bundle, on average.

Robinsonia thurifera (fig. 6.4, right). Masatierra: slope of Cordón Chifladores above Puerto Frances, 350–450 m; Portezuelo

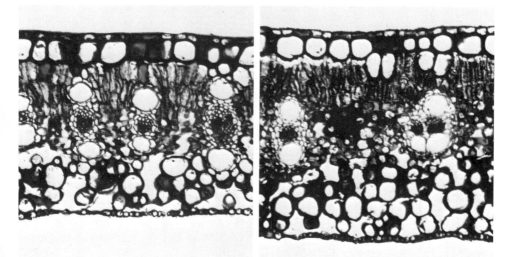

FIG. 6.4. Leaves of "less mesic" species of Juan Fernandez rosette-shrub Senecioneae (Asteraceae) in transection, adaxial face above. LEFT, *Robinsonia gayana.* RIGHT, *R. thurifera.* Scale of magnification as in fig. 6.3.

de Villagra, 550–600 m; to 5 or 6 m tall, consistently the largest species of the genus; flowers later than any other tree or shrub in the islands. Leaves medium thick; 1–2 layers of hypodermis; 2 layers of compact palisade; abaxial spongy tissue wide, notably thick-walled and hypodermis-like; a few fibers adjacent to phloem poles of veins; 1 adaxial and 1 abaxial secretory canal per vein.

To those not acquainted with concepts of mesomorphy and xeromorphy in leaf anatomy, the following can be offered. Hypodermis, a characteristic of brightly illuminated situations, tends to increase with exposed situations, but there is also, in the *Robinsonia* group, a curious conversion of spongy tissue to a sort of second hypodermis in the less mesomorphic species. In effect, this makes the leaves much like isolateral leaves, which often characterize brightly illuminated localities (often also correlated with positioning of the leaf in manners other than horizontal, as in some of the Eucalypts). Increased presence of secretory canals with greater illumination and "xeromorphy," although not uniform, seems evident. Secretory canals and cavities are most abundant in composites of dry localities, such as those of the southwestern United States. While thinness would be expected to be a mesomorphic characteristic—as it is in *Symphyochaeta macrocephala*, the thick leaves of *Robinsonia evenia* are decidedly mesomorphic, for the thickness is not the result of compaction of cells but of a very large air-space system. There is a tendency, with decreasing mesomorphy, for increase in presence of fibers near bundles. Fibers tend to be associated with a more leathery leaf texture and characterized leaves of greater duration in sunnier localities.

The habitat can be called less mesomorphic if the species grows in scrub rather than rain forest. Large size (*R. thurifera*) and growth on cliff faces (*R. gayana*) would connote less mesomorphy, for there is greater exposure to illumination under these circumstances. Epiphytism on tree ferns (*R. evenia*, *R. gracilis*), the straggling habit (*Symphyochaeta*) and association with ferns (*R. masafuerae*), all within cloud forest, are maximally mesic habitats and mesomorphic habits.

In the other group to be considered, *Dendroseris* (*sensu lato*), very thick leaves with large hypodermis cells, 2–3 cells thick, can be said to characterize less mesomorphic species. Such features (Carlquist, 1967) occur in *D. litoralis* and *D. (Rea) pruinata. Dendroseris litoralis* grows only on lowland cliffs of Morro Viñillo (an islet near Masatierra), on a rather low islet, Santa Clara Island, and on Morro del Spartán, also a low islet near Masatierra. *Dendroseris (Rea) pruinata* is a near-maritime species, scattered in dry ravines of Masatierra and Santa Clara (Skottsberg, 1953). The rain-forest species of *Dendroseris* have much more meso-morphic types of leaf construction, and the reader can consult Carlquist (1967) for further information. Because *Dendroseris* occupies a wider range of ecological situations than does *Robinsonia* and allies, it can better be cited as an example of adaptive radiation—especially when one takes into account the greater range of growth forms in *Dendroseris (sensu lato)*. However, the *Robinsonia* group clearly shows a range of diversification that can be considered early or middle stages in adaptive radiation (or perhaps better, adaptive radiation within limits).

Other Fernandezian genera certainly show alteration in growth form and ecological shift, and one would cite them in connection with adaptive radiation if only they represented a series of species instead of merely one or two, and thereby could occupy several distinctive ranges of habitats. It is conceivable that some of the genera may once have had more numerous species, but diversification seems relatively recent in the Juan Fernandez Islands, and it is, I feel, no accident that adaptive radiation is represented in the most "active" family evolutionarily, the Asteraceae.

Other Pacific Islands

We do not yet know enough, to judge from the literature, about adaptive radiation in the biotas of certain islands, such as in the ants of Fiji, or (as a similar example) the frogs of the Seychelles. Where several distinctive species occur on a small island, such as the three species of *Zosterops* on Lord Howe Island, we may suspect, in agreement with Lack (1947), that these represent independent colonizations, not autochthonous speciation. To be sure, coexistence on a single island does tend to force minimal overlap in habits (and, in the case of *Zosterops*, bill morphology) so that a situation simulating adaptive radiation has been achieved.

We might have expected that the various Polynesian high islands—the

Marquesas, the Society Islands, and Samoa—would bear examples of adaptive radiation. For the most part, they do not. Perhaps there are only two good examples among flowering plants. One of these is *Fitchia* (Asteraceae). It includes a tree in wet forests of Rarotonga, *F. speciosa* (Carlquist, 1957), but can also be a small shrub, as in *F. cordata* on the scrubby ridges of Bora Bora (Carlquist, 1965; Carlquist and Grant, 1963). The species of Tahiti are intermediate. One can cite *Oparanthus* (Asteraceae) as an example of adaptive radiation in southeastern Polynesia, but its range is not as great as that of *Fitchia*, although there are interesting divergences in leaf anatomy (Carlquist, 1957). On Samoa, the endemic genus *Sarcopygme* (Rubiaceae) has several species, but they do not appear to show distinctive ecological modes.

The land snail *Partula*, made famous by Crampton as a case of speciation on insular areas, does not really illustrate adaptive radiation. The habits of the various species seem quite similar, with geographic isolation the main feature of speciation. The archipelagos of southern Polynesia evidently consist of islands too small or too recent to have good "archipelago effects" which seem so often to lead to programs of adaptive radiation. These islands appear to have received that portion of the Indo-Malesian (and, in the case of *Fitchia* and *Oparanthus*, American) flora that excels at long-distance dispersal, and to have provided isolation sufficient for formation of endemic species but not space enough (particularly with respect to sufficient areas in various ecological zones, especially wet forest) for adaptive radiation to have occurred. To be sure, there are interesting endemic genera of flowering plants (e.g., *Apetahia*, *Sclerotheca*) or land snails in southern Polynesia, but if these represent products of adaptive radiation, the related or ancestral forms are now extinct, and they stand isolated. We do not know how much the older Leeward Islands, now atolls, of the Hawaiian chain may have contributed to adaptive radiation now visible on the major Hawaiian islands, but the presence of a sequence (and we should note that the Leeward Islands form a rather *continuous* sequence geologically, leading into the newest and highest eastern islands) in the Hawaiian chain may well have been one of the factors leading to the remarkable adaptive radiation in the Hawaiian biota. Such sequences are not present in southern Polynesia, although older groups of islands, now atolls (the Tuamotus, for example), are present there. Consequently, the lack of examples of adaptive radiation in southern Polynesian islands seems directly related to lack of extensive land areas in appropriate ecological zones. In the case of Fiji, there is relatively little adaptive radiation mentioned; perhaps authors have not discussed the Fijian flora in this respect, or the relatively harmonic nature of the Fijian biota (compared with those of more remote islands) may have forestalled adaptive radiation there.

References

Bowman, R. I. 1961. Morphological differentiation and adaptation in the Galápagos finches. *Univ. Calif. Publ. Zool.* 58:1–302.

Bowman, R. I. 1963. Evolutionary patterns in Darwin's finches. *Occas. Papers Calif. Acad. Sci.* 44:107–40.

Carlquist, S. 1957. The genus *Fitchia* (Compositae). *Univ. Calif. Publ. Bot.* 29: 1–144.

Carlquist, S. 1965. *Island life*. New York, Natural History Press.

Carlquist, S. 1967. Anatomy and systematics of *Dendroseris* (sensu lato). *Brittonia* 19:99–121.

Carlquist, S., and M. L. Grant. 1963. Studies in *Fitchia* (Compositae). Novelties from the Society Islands, anatomical studies. *Pacific Sci.* 17:282–98.

Lack, D. 1947. *Darwin's finches*. Cambridge, Cambridge University Press.

Skottsberg, C. 1922. The phanerogams of the Juan Fernandez Islands. *Natur. Hist. Juan Fernandez Easter I.* 2:95–240.

Skottsberg, C. 1953. The vegetation of the Juan Fernandez Islands. *Natur. Hist. Juan Fernandez Easter I.* 2:793–960.

Svenson, H. K. 1963. Opportunities for botanical study on the Galápagos Islands. *Occas. Papers Calif. Acad. Sci.* 44:53–58.

Wiggins, I. L., and D. M. Porter. 1971. *Flora of the Galápagos Islands*. Stanford, Calif., Stanford University Press.

CHAPTER SEVEN

ADAPTIVE RADIATION:
NEW CALEDONIA AND NEW ZEALAND

New Caledonia and New Zealand share certain biogeographic character-istics: both are islands that have been in existence for longer periods of time than the volcanic islands of the Pacific; they contain various ancient elements, some of such poor dispersibility (Araucariaceae) that very early contact or near-contact with other land masses is suggested. However, both have acquired most of their biotas via long-distance dispersal. This conclusion is suggested not only by the disharmony in their biotas, like that of the larger volcanic islands of the Pacific, but by the "non-primitiveness" of many of their families and genera (e.g., the birds on New Caledonia, with the exception of the kagu). The insular phenomena they exhibit are so much like those on, say, the Hawaiian Islands, that similar processes of waif-biota evolution must have been operative, albeit for longer periods of time. However, some elements in the biotas of New Zealand and New Caledonia may be very recent—there is nothing to suggest that over-water dispersal to them has ceased. In any case, both New Caledonia and New Zealand have an admixture of old and new elements, and we can see adaptive radiation in both categories.

New Caledonia

The flora of New Caledonia appears fairly harmonic (especially considering its curious rock and soil types and moderately dry climate) but the fauna is devoid of mammals and is essentially oceanic (see Thorne, 1965, and references cited by him). The reason for this ironic situation has mystified some, but the explanation seems, in fact, rather simple. The fauna probably did reach the island over oceanic distance. That New Caledonia was once a larger island and probably was, at a remote time, separated by shorter distances from other land masses southwest of the andesite line seems likely. If this is true, ancient floristic elements—the Araucariaceae in particular—may have arrived at that time, whereas marsupials and certainly placentals were not present then in the land mass contributing immigrants to New Caledonia. Although Australia, including New Guinea, did receive marsupials and monotremes, New Caledonia was not connected with (or was farther from) the Malesian "mainland" at that time. Because the animal groups present no particular problems (although there are some interesting features in the reptiles), the nature of diversification and radiation in the New Caledonian flora has been chosen for examination here.

Only the Araucariaceae (*Araucaria* and *Agathis*) appear to have such poor dispersibility that they would require short over-water distances or land connections for arrival in New Caledonia. Araucarias such as A. *cookii* obviously do disperse within New Caledonia from one suitable site to another, so there is no reason to assume that they are incapable of short-range dispersal. The New Caledonian genus of Taxaceae, *Austrotaxus*, is far removed geographically from other Taxaceae, which may have receded since this stock reached the present land mass of New Caledonia. The Podocarpaceae, like the preceding gymnosperms, would appear primitive and not easily dispersible. *Acmopyle*, with large seeds (fig. 7.6, top left), is extant only on New Caledonia and Fiji. *Dacrydium*, with relatively small seeds, would seem more readily dispersible. However, *Dacrydium* seeds lack the fleshy cone, attractive to birds, that *Podocarpus* seeds have, and are probably more poorly dispersed, as the narrower range of *Dacrydium* compared with that of *Podocarpus* seems to confirm. *Dacrydium* does not extend farther eastward into the Pacific than Fiji. Interestingly, D. *lycopodioides* (fig. 7.4, bottom right) occurs on both New Caledonia and Fiji. *Dacrydium* once had a wider extent, for fossils indicate that it occurred in India (Jurassic), Argentina (Eocene) and Antarctica (Oligocene), according to Florin (1963). Not only do *Agathis*, *Acmopyle*, and *Dacrydium* among gymnosperms reach their current easternmost Pacific station on Fiji, but also many genera of angiosperms stop there (Smith, 1955).

I see no reason why New Caledonian flowering plants cannot be hypothesized to have arrived via long-distance dispersal or, in a few cases, shorter-distance dispersal. To be sure, there are relatively "primitive" angiosperm groups, such as the Winteraceae and a monogeneric family, Amborellaceae (fig. 7.6, top right). However, *Amborella* has small, red, fleshy fruits that seem capable of bird dispersal, and fruits of *Drimys* of the Winteraceae (fig. 2.4, bottom right) seem eminently dispersible—although these groups now may well be relatively specialized in habitat requirements and no longer able to succeed readily at establishing. One endemic New Caledonian genus of Winteraceae, *Zygogynum*, is probably an example of autochthonous loss of dispersibility (Carlquist, 1965). There are other families well represented in the New Caledonian flora that could be called primitive, such as Cunoniaceae (fig. 7.6, bottom left, right). However, the fact that genera of Cunoniaceae have a number of primitive features does not mean that they are poor at long-distance dispersal. The contrary is true: *Weinmannia* occurs on oceanic islands such as Tahiti. With the exception of some of the conifers, then, the New Caledonian flora may well have resulted from long-distance dispersal. However, the various establishments probably occurred over a relatively long period of time. To say that there are "old arrivals" and "new arrivals" might be misleading, but we can make some reasonable guesses. For example, one can cite those taxonomic groups in the New Caledonian flora that also occur on volcanic islands such as Tahiti, Samoa, or the Hawaiian Islands. The roster of such families in the New Caledonian flora, gymnosperms excepted, is not extraordinarily different from families present on more remote volcanic oceanic islands.

"OLD" ADAPTIVE RADIATION

For the reasons cited in the preceding section, we can assume that the conifers represent early immigrants to New Caledonia. The Araucariaceae are rather interesting in this respect. *Agathis* occurs on New Caledonia, Fiji, New Zealand, Queensland, the Malesian islands, and Malaya, but does not show what could be called adaptive radiation within any of these localities or even in all localities considered as a whole. *Araucaria* on New Caledonia is quite different: there perhaps eight species occur. Although some of these are close, the gamut of New Caledonian species represents almost as broad a range as the entire remainder of the genus. New Caledonian Araucarias tend to occupy distinctive localities. *Araucaria cookii* (fig. 7.1, top left) occurs near the coast, often in valleys where seepage of fresh water occurs. In this way, it can even occur just behind the beach and actually can come into contact with strand plants such as *Pandanus* and *Cerbera*. The leaves of *A. cookii* are small (5×4 mm); the habit of the tree is slender and conical. *Araucaria bernieri* (fig. 7.1, top right) is very narrow, but not conical; mature trees tend to have a terminal crown of horizontal branches. The habitat of *A. bernieri* is the Montagne des Sources and low adjacent valleys on the Plaine des Lacs. A close species, *A. balansae*, grows on higher ground; its leaves are extremely narrow (4×2 mm). *Araucaria muelleri* (figs. 7.1, bottom right; 7.2, top left) occupies much the same sites as *A. bernieri* (although it tends to grow more on mountains around the Plaine des Lacs). The leaves of *A. muelleri* (fig. 7.2, top left) are exceptional in size (30×20 mm), much like those of the Chilean species *A. araucana*, but markedly incurved. Trees of *A. muelleri* are distinctive because of their paucity of branches. *Araucaria rulei* (fig. 7.1, bottom left) occupies cloud forest of higher mountains, such as Mt. Mou. Other New Caledonian species include *A. humboldtensis*, which has the habit of *Dacrydium araucarioides*, and grows only on Mt. Humboldt. *Araucaria biramulata*, distinctive in its bifurcate branches (Sarlin, 1954), grows only at the Mois de Mai mine on the Plaine des Lacs. *Araucaria montana* occurs on mountaintops in northern New Caledonia. It has rounded leaves (12×8 mm). The habit of mature trees of *A. montana* is very narrow, like that of *A. bernieri*; when younger, trees look like those of *A. rulei*.

Supposing that all of these species are, in fact, valid and distinctive, one is faced with the question, Could all of these species have originated on an island the size of present-day New Caledonia (6360 sq. mi or 17,000 sq. km, one-seventh the size of Cuba)? The size of populations of most *Araucaria* species seems far below the breeding size of all but a few conifer species—and those could be called declining or relictual species. This suggests that diversification of the neocaledonian Araucarias probably

FIG. 7.1. *Araucaria* (Araucariaceae) species from New Caledonia, showing distinctive habits and habitats. TOP LEFT, A. *cookii*; small valley at coast, near Plum. TOP RIGHT, A. *bernieri*; upper Rivière de Madeleine, Plaine des Lacs. BOTTOM LEFT, A. *rulei*; summit of Mt. Mou. BOTTOM RIGHT, A. *muelleri*, lower Rivière de Madeleine, Plaine des Lacs.

FIG. 7.2. Conifers from New Caledonia. TOP LEFT, *Araucaria muelleri*, foliage and young female cone. TOP RIGHT, BOTTOM LEFT, RIGHT, *Neocallitropsis comptonii* (Cupressaceae); banks of Rivière de Madeleine. TOP RIGHT, habit, tree about 4 m tall. BOTTOM LEFT, foliage and female cones. BOTTOM RIGHT, seed, showing capability of flotation.

took place on a larger land mass—not a continent, but a "larger New Caledonia."

If three species of *Agathis* (Araucariaceae) and three of *Libocedrus* (Cupressaceae) can be recognized as endemic to New Caledonia, as claimed by Sarlin (1954), these other conifer genera reinforce the situation just cited for *Araucaria*. Likewise, the New Caledonian species of *Dacrydium* are interesting because one of them, *D. lycopodioides* (fig. 7.4, bottom right), also occurs on Fiji. Dispersal of *D. lycopodioides* across the present distance between New Caledonia and Fiji is not impossible, and lack of differentiation between the New Caledonian and Fijian populations suggests this has occurred, for a long period of separation would be expected to result in at least some differentiation. The genus *Dacrydium* (Podocarpaceae) may have radiated on New Caledonia, but this radiation again seems to have taken place early. My reason for this conclusion is not merely that gymnosperms are an ancient group. Rather, I would guess that if *Dacrydium* shares, as it seems to, the slow-evolving characteristics of most contemporary conifers, radiation would not have occurred if numerous stocks of angiosperms had been present, competing for the niches *Dacrydium* now occupies on New Caledonia.

The diversity of the New Caledonian Dacrydiums is exceptional— a range in form exceeding that of *Dacrydium* elsewhere. *Dacrydium araucarioides* (fig. 7.3, top left, right) appears to be a xeromorph. It grows on purple-brown, highly mineralized soils as an element of a semi-open scrubby woodland. Leaves are narrow, incurved, and imbricate; branches are thick (fig. 7.3, top right). At an opposite extreme is *D. taxoides* (fig. 7.3, bottom left). Its leaves, although basically arranged in a spiral, are positioned so as to form flattened sprays; both surfaces appear identical, and the leaves are broad, looking quite unlike the needlelike leaves of most *Dacrydium* species. *Dacrydium taxoides* is a small tree, shaped irregularly by the other understory elements in the cloud-forest areas where it characteristically grows. The sprays of broad, flat leaves seem related to shaded conditions and to greater availability of moisture. Also in a cloud-forest area is *D. lycopodioides* (fig. 7.4, bottom right). Judging from juvenile foliage of other Dacrydiums, *D. lycopodioides* appears almost like a permanently juvenile form. This would not be unexpected, for it grows in shady levels of the Mt. Mou cloud forest. The leaves are narrow,

FIG. 7.3. *Dacrydium* (Podocarpaceae) species from New Caledonia. TOP LEFT, RIGHT, *D. araucarioides*. TOP LEFT, habit of tree, about 5 m tall; western Plaine des Lacs. TOP RIGHT, foliage and female cones, inconspicuous, 2-seeded, at tips of branchlets. BOTTOM LEFT, *D. taxoides*, foliage bearing a female cone with one seed; leaves 2–3 cm long; summit of Mt. Mou. BOTTOM RIGHT, *D. balansae*, branches showing male strobili and female cones; near Thio.

221

FIG. 7.4. *Dacrydium* (Podocarpaceae) species from New Caledonia. TOP LEFT, RIGHT, BOTTOM LEFT, *D. guillauminii*; Rivière de Madeleine, Plaine des Lacs. TOP LEFT, habit, trees at edge of river, about 2 m tall. TOP RIGHT, foliage, including female cone, 2-seeded, at tip of branchlet. BOTTOM LEFT, seeds, showing capability of flotation. BOTTOM RIGHT, *D. lycopodioides*, foliage; Montagne des Sources.

densely imbricate, borne on slender twigs. *Dacrydium balansae* (fig. 7.3, bottom right) has foliage not unlike that of D. *araucarioides*, but D. *balansae* is densely branched and is characteristic of more mesic locations than is D. *araucarioides*.

An expected adaptation is represented by D. *guillauminii* (fig. 7.4, top left, right, bottom left). This plant forms small trees—some only 2 m tall at maturity—along the banks of rivers on the Plaine des Lacs. The branches are few and thick, the foliage needlelike, appropriate to the sunny climate of the Plaine des Lacs. *Dacrydium guillauminii* shows obvious adaptations to the riparian habitat. The trunk is wide below, tapering upwards, a form characteristic of some woody plants that withstand occasional flooding. Wood of the broad base is exceptionally light in texture and weight (tracheids are very thin-walled; intercellular spaces are present), although wood of upper portions of the tree is denser. Not unexpectedly, seeds of D. *guillauminii* float (fig. 7.4, bottom left), either fresh or dried.

An obvious question—which might seem to vitiate at least part of the preceding account—is how much radiation of *Dacrydium* has taken place autochthonously on New Caledonia. Some seems clearly to have done so, although we must remember that in addition to the present distribution of the genus (Tasmania, Fiji, New Caledonia, New Zealand, Malesia, southeast Asia, Chile) *Dacrydium* is known from fossils in Australia, India, and possibly Antarctica (Florin, 1963). However, the great diversity of the New Caledonian Dacrydiums and their apparent adaptations to unusual and highly specialized environments suggests that virtually all the peculiar features of the New Caledonian Dacrydiums are autochthonously evolved.

The riparian syndrome shown in D. *guillauminii* is also represented in the genus *Podocarpus* in New Caledonia by P. *minor* (= P. *palustris*). *Podocarpus minor* (fig. 7.5, top left, right, bottom left) and D. *guillauminii* are the only conifers that show these marked adaptations. *Podocarpus minor* becomes a little larger than D. *guillauminii*, is more richly branched, and has oval leaves, which are, however, very thick, almost succulent. The exceptionally large seeds do float (fig. 7.5, bottom left). Although nine species of *Podocarpus* occur on New Caledonia, they do not represent radiations from a single stock. As shown by Florin (1963), *Podocarpus*

FIG. 7.5. *Podocarpus* (Podocarpaceae) species from New Caledonia. TOP LEFT, RIGHT, BOTTOM LEFT, *P. minor* (= *P. palustris*). TOP LEFT, habit, tree 3 m tall; floodplain of Rivière de Madeleine, Plaine des Lacs. TOP RIGHT, foliage, showing seeds 3 cm long. BOTTOM LEFT, seeds, showing capability of flotation. BOTTOM RIGHT, *P. ustus*, close-up of mounted herbarium specimen, showing cones with immature seeds; foliage would be red in living plants of this parasitic species.

224

on New Caledonia is represented by the following subgenera and sections: *Stachycarpus*, *Microcarpus*, *Polypodiopsis*, and *Podocarpus* sections B, D, and F. This representation on such a small area suggests a remarkable degree of relictism. However, some autochthonous radiation in *Podocarpus* is probable. In addition to the riparian *P. minor*, the genus is represented on New Caledonia by the world's only parasitic gymnosperm, *P. ustus* (fig. 7.5, bottom right). These two extreme modifications appear autochthonous. There are moderate streams and lakes for *P. minor*, certainly, and the abundance of Podocarpaceae as host plants for *P. ustus* would have favored origin of a parasitic species on this island.

On New Caledonia there are two monotypic endemic conifer genera, *Neocallitropsis* (fig. 7.2, top right, bottom left, right) and *Austrotaxus*. *Neocallitropsis* seems related to *Callitris* and *Actinostrobus* of Australia but, if so, retains characters primitive for the group. *Neocallitropsis* seems to grow near streams (but not on the immediate margins), and floatability of its seeds (fig. 7.2, bottom right) suggests adaptation. *Austrotaxus* is not closely related to other genera of Taxaceae and is the sole southern-hemisphere representative of the family, except for *Taxus* in Sulawesi (Celebes). The large leaves of *Austrotaxus*, similar to those of *Podocarpus macrophylla*, seem adapted to cloud forest. *Neocallitropsis* and *Austrotaxus* underline the harmonic quality of the conifer flora of New Caledonia. In fact, a more harmonic conifer flora—considering the small size of New Caledonia—would be hard to imagine. The conclusion seems inescapable that conifers were present on New Caledonia at an early time. The peculiar soil types of New Caledonia would not even seem suited for conifers, but the New Caledonian conifers obviously have adapted, and in the case of *Araucaria*, *Dacrydium* (and, to some extent, the other genera) are not only adapted to the unique climatic and edaphic regimes of New Caledonia, but have speciated as well. The speciation and adaptation probably occurred at a time when conifers and taxads were genetically a more plastic and rapidly evolving group, and niche occupation by conifers and taxads was relatively unopposed by angiosperms. The lesson of the northern hemisphere is that angiosperms have gradually displaced gymnosperms, and that gymnosperms retain dominance mostly at higher latitudes and higher elevations. In the southwestern Pacific we see some replication of this phenomenon. Consulting the distribution maps of fossil and living conifers by Florin (1963), we see that mainland Australia retains some living conifers: *Araucaria, Agathis,* numerous Cupressaceae (*Callitris* and *Actinostrobus*), and a few Podocarpaceae (*Podocarpus* and *Microstrobus*). However, genera one would expect to find are absent. *Phyllocladus* (Podocarpaceae) ought to be on mainland Australia today, for it is on islands recently connected to Australia: Tasmania and New Guinea. The same applies to three genera confined to Tasmania: *Diselma* (Cupressaceae), *Athrotaxis* (Taxodiaceae), and *Microcachrys* (Podocarpaceae). Likewise, *Papuacedrus* (Cupressaceae) is confined to New Guinea. Groups absent from Australia but present on New Guinea and nearby islands include *Podocarpus* sections *Nageia, Polypodiopsis,* and *Dacrycarpus,* as well as *Dacrydium.* The most obvious explanation seems to be that Australia has been a large land area that has served as a "target" for angiosperm groups that have dispersed across oceanic distances. Moreover, this area has functioned to increase genetic diversification, and aggressive angiosperm groups (especially those adapted to dry areas, which most conifers are not) have been so successful that many gymnosperm groups have been unable to retain their niches.

"NEW" ADAPTIVE RADIATION

There seems to have been abundant time for transoceanic dispersal of angiosperm groups to New Caledonia. All of the "successful" groups in the New Caledonian flora seem suited to long-distance dispersal. Among those with small seeds capable of wind dispersal are *Hibbertia* (Dilleniaceae), *Nepenthes* (Nepenthaceae), *Casuarina* (Casuarinaceae), all Epacridaceae, all Cunoniaceae, and capsular Myrtaceae. Araliaceae, Goodeniaceae (fig. 7.7, top left, right, bottom left), and many other New Caledonian elements are clearly suited to dispersal by frugivorous birds. Although some families in New Caledonia have large-seeded, fleshy fruits, such as Sapotaceae and Clusiaceae, this is not as great an obstacle as it might seem. Sapotaceae have reached, by natural means, such remote islands as those of Hawaii (where *Planchonella* fruits exhibit various degrees of gigantism; see chapter 11). For the reasons stated in chapter 11, increase in fruit and seed size does not seem unlikely in New Caledonia, where other examples of loss of dispersibility can be found (e.g., *Zygogynum* of the Winteraceae).

226

Radiation of over-water immigrants depends on the range of available habitats. New Caledonia would not seem as ecologically diversified as, say, the Hawaiian Islands. Edaphic diversity is great. New Caledonia has, as the rather intense mining indicates, areas rich in chromium, nickel, and other heavy metals. Uplifts of limestone are not uncommon. There are distinctive pockets of serpentine. The broad lowlands seem parched most of the year, but in cloud-forest areas and valleys there are quite mesic habitats. The cloud forests, however, are subject to prolonged periods of sunshine, so that canopy shrubs and trees must be able to withstand desiccation. The soils, so unlike those typical of Indo-Malesian source areas that potentially could contribute to the New Caledonian flora, undoubtedly have prevented establishment of numerous groups of plants (and perhaps, directly and indirectly, of some animal groups as well). These conditions theoretically offer varied niches to each successful group; thus more abundant adaptive radiation might be expected. However, even with the peculiar conditions of New Caledonia that have undoubtedly deterred establishments, the many years available for establishments have overcome this bottleneck, and the New Caledonian flora is less disharmonic (and therefore poorer in adaptive radiation) than one might expect, compared with Southeast Asian angiosperms.

The amazing habital similarity of New Caledonian angiosperm taxa probably relates to the relatively foreshortened ecological diversity. There is a modal tendency for smaller, rather sparsely branched shrubs, 2–8 m tall, with very leathery elliptical leaves 5–20 cm long. Numerous examples of these can be seen in the angiosperms illustrated in figures 7.6, 7.7, and 7.8. Anatomical studies would probably reveal parallel construction of leaves among various groups, and are worth the effort. Because of the "adaptive mode" of these angiosperms, one should keep open the possibility that ancestral habits in these groups were not the same as the present-day sclerophyll species.

Despite this mode, there is a range apparent in larger genera. In *Hibbertia*, for example, there are New Caledonian species with smaller, sclerophyllous leaves. However, *H. badouinii* (fig. 7.7, bottom right) is not a shrub but a rosette tree to 10 m, with clusters of long, membranous leaves at tips of branches. It is much like rosette trees in rain forests of oceanic islands, such as *Cyanea* (Campanulaceae) on Hawaii or *Robinsonia* or *Den-*

FIG. 7.6. Plants from New Caledonia. TOP LEFT, *Acmopyle pancheri* (Podocarpaceae), foliage and cone bearing a seed 2 cm in diam.; summit of Mt. Mou. TOP RIGHT, *Amborella tricho-poda* (Amborellaceae), twig bearing fruits, each ca. 1 cm long; Plateau de Dogny. BOTTOM LEFT, *Pancheria insignis* (Cunoniaceae), tip of stem showing compound woolly leaves, inflorescences; summit of Mt. Mou. BOTTOM RIGHT, *P. communis*, branch with inflorescence; leaves about 3 cm long; Plaine des Lacs.

FIG. 7.7. Plants from New Caledonia. TOP LEFT, RIGHT, *Scaevola beckii* (Goodeniaceae); base of Mt. Doré. TOP LEFT, habit; plant is 1 m tall. TOP RIGHT, leaves and portion of inflorescence. BOTTOM LEFT, *S. montana*, branch showing flowers and fruits; leaves are ca. 5 cm long; lower Mt. Koghi. BOTTOM RIGHT, *Hibbertia badouinii*, rosette of leaves from a large rosette shrub about 6 m tall; leaves are ca. 20 cm long, flowers 7 cm in diam.; summit of Mt. Mou.

229

FIG. 7.8. *Myodocarpus* (Apiaceae) from New Caledonia. TOP LEFT, RIGHT, BOTTOM LEFT, *M. fraxinifolius*. TOP LEFT, habit of tree, 6 m tall; pass between Nouméa and Plaine des Lacs. TOP RIGHT, branch, showing pinnate habit of leaves. BOTTOM LEFT, inflorescence, showing the flattened dry fruit. BOTTOM RIGHT, *M. involucratus*; leaves are entire, ca. 20 cm long; summit of Mt. Mou.

droseris (Asteraceae) on the Juan Fernandez Islands. The New Caledonian species of *Scaevola* (fig. 7.7, top left, right, bottom left) mostly occur in upland cloud forest and, like other Pacific species, have relatively thin, broad leaves (e.g., *S. montana*). However, the lowland *S. beckii* (fig. 7.7, top left, right) shows modifications typical of drier lowland sites—branches and leaves are few, leaves are thick and purple brown.

Pancheria of the Cunoniaceae (fig. 7.6, bottom left, right) is an endemic genus with perhaps as many as 30 species (Guillaumin, 1948). These species are highly diversified in leaf type, and only two of many are shown here. Of these, *P. insignis* (fig. 7.6, bottom left) has densely hairy, compound leaves. This species occurs in the Mt. Mou cloud forest. A contrast is formed by *P. communis* (fig. 7.6, bottom right) from the Plaine des Lacs. It has small, simple leaves that are thickish, sclerophyllous, and perhaps isolateral, in contrast to the clearly bifacial condition found elsewhere in the genus.

Some foliar distinctions in New Caledonian angiosperms do not at first glance seem to bear close relationships to habitat features. In *Myodocarpus* of the Araliaceae (fig. 7.8), for example, *M. involucratus* (fig. 7.8, bottom right), a species of cloud forest and intermediate scrub, has simple leaves. In *M. fraxinifolius* (fig. 7.8, top left, right, bottom left), a taller rosette tree of scrubby areas adjacent to the Plaine des Lacs, pinnately compound leaves occur. However, the leaflets prove to be thicker than those of *M. involucratus*, suggesting semi-succulence. Compound leaves in *M. fraxinifolius* may represent a relationship, perhaps not strong now, to growth of a rosette tree in areas shaded by trees and shrubs. Where foliar dimorphism occurs, more dissected leaves are characteristic of lower levels in a forest. This may not obtain in *Myodocarpus*, or, if dissected leaves are a juvenile form, they seem to have advantages in the adult plant as well, in the case of *M. fraxinifolius*.

Myodocarpus exemplifies another problem typical of evolution in certain New Caledonian plants. In its habit, *Myodocarpus* could not be more typical of Araliaceae (*sensu stricto*). Its dry fruit (fig. 7.8, bottom left), however, would place it in a nearby family, Apiaceae (Umbelliferae). Is *Myodocarpus* a vestige of the stock from which these two families (united by some authors) were diverging? Or is *Myodocarpus* an apiad that has become woodier on an insular area, as has *Bupleurum* in the Mediterranean region? If the latter hypothesis is true, it can be true only to the extent that *Myodocarpus* probably never had any truly herbaceous ancestors—as did, by contrast, such genera as *Melanoselinum* on Madeira (fig. 10.2, top right). New Caledonia, without doubt, has an unusual assemblage of plants rich in primitive characteristics—particularly the conifers, Winteraceae, and Amborellaceae. But we may well be in error if we are thereby influenced to regard a given New Caledonian genus as more "primitive" in its family than genera elsewhere. Even assuming this is true for a particular genus, this does not prove that the New Caledonian flora (with the exception of conifers other than Podocarpaceae) could have arrived only across a dry-land zone or small water gap from a source area. If New Caledonian angiosperm genera have more numerous primitive characteristics than relatives elsewhere, this probably is due to the fact that they arrived early by means of long-distance dispersal.

ANIMALS

With the exception of the flightless kagu (*Rhynochaetos jubatus*), the New Caledonian avifauna is just about what we would expect for a not-too-old volcanic island in this geographical region, and the roster of birds (Delacour, 1966) suggests recentness and no examples of adaptive radiation, probably because New Caledonia is not at the limit of dispersibility for land birds. The gekkonid lizards of New Caledonia have been regarded as representing adaptive radiation (MacArthur and Wilson, 1967). Two endemic genera of Gekkonidae (*Rhacodactylus* and *Eurydactylus*) and one nonendemic genus (*Bavayia*) contribute to this pattern. Among skinks, New Caledonia is notable for a giant form, *Riopa bocourti* (Mertens, 1934).

Assuming that among insects the phasmatid *Clitarchus* (Nakata, 1961) and the longicorn Enicodini (Gressitt, 1961) may be relatively primitive, other insect groups in New Caledonia have few relictual aspects. New Caledonian ants are cited as an example of adaptive radiation by MacArthur and Wilson (1967).

Changes in size and form—some perhaps recent—apply to land snails as well (Solem, 1961). We may be astonished at the large size of *Placostylus*, and deem it incapable of long-distance dispersal—and in its present form perhaps it does lack dispersibility. However, *Placostylus* may be a

232

gigantism, perhaps old in origin, of a once smaller and more vagile land shell. Gigantism is common among the land shells of the Hawaiian Islands, and certainly among New Caledonian land shells as well (see chapter 15). Gigantism in these groups can be regarded as part of a program of adaptive radiation into new habitats.

New Zealand

In view of its exceptional ecological richness and long isolation, New Zealand would be expected to exhibit remarkable speciation and adaptive radiation. New Zealand has probably been separated by wide water gaps since the time when it acquired conifers. Few or no water barriers at an early date might be hypothesized for the arrival of some conifers. Araucariaceae seem poorly dispersible, yet *Agathis* reached New Zealand, as did *Araucaria* (known there as a fossil: Florin, 1963). The southern beech, *Nothofagus*, may have reached New Zealand at a similar time. It is present in Patagonia, New Caledonia, Tasmania, and Australia, a distribution somewhat like that of the Araucariaceae. An Antarctic arc of greater land areas may once have existed and permitted these ranges. However, marsupial and placental mammals (other than bats) never reached New Zealand, which, like New Caledonia, has a strongly disharmonic fauna: birds, insects, land shells, a few reptiles (including the primitive *Sphenodon*), a few amphibians (including the primitive *Leiopelma*), and freshwater fishes (although no primary-division freshwater fishes). The success of introduced marsupials and placentals certainly demonstrates that potential niches for these have existed.

Favorable to adaptive radiation on New Zealand are the great range in altitude (to 12,349 ft) and in rainfall: as low as 20 in. on the eastern coast of South and North Islands to above 200 in. in the western coastal and montane areas of South Island. Volcanics augment a diversified series of metamorphic and sedimentary rocks (Hochstetter, 1959). Vegetational formations, consequently, present a broad spectrum—too broad to summarize here; Cockayne (1958) has offered a highly detailed study. Cockayne (1927) has also presented an appealing semipopular account of the vegetation.

Several features detract, however, from the potential ecological diversity of New Zealand. First, New Zealand is decidedly temperate, and even the northernmost part of North Island cannot be considered really subtropical. The wet coastal forests, however, are comparable to higher elevations in the Hawaiian rain forests. Second, the Pleistocene glaciation of New Zealand (Hochstetter, 1959) in essence reduced the available land area severely and thus had the net effect of reducing the biota to a much more cold-hardy flora than New Zealand would support under current conditions. The time since glaciation has undoubtedly featured speciation and radiation of at least some of the surviving groups, but postglaciation time has not, in all likelihood, been sufficient for over-water immigration of many of the less cold-hardy groups, much less been sufficient for their speciation.

CONIFERS

Compared with New Caledonia, New Zealand is notably poor in radiation of Araucariaceae. *Araucaria* became extinct in prehuman time, and only *Agathis australis* represents the family there today. Perhaps New Zealand is more nearly marginal for Araucariaceae, but certainly it must have been more so in the Pleistocene, and the rather slowly evolving *Agathis* has not speciated since that time.

Dacrydium and *Podocarpus* are another matter: these two genera (which can even be regarded as a single genus) show not merely an array of species in New Zealand, but a spectrum of growth form and habitat preference. Probably this radiation occurred prior to glaciation, with few if any exceptions. Most distinctive of New Zealand Dacrydiums is *D. laxifolium*, the "pygmy pine," a sprawling or almost vinelike shrub with branches to only 2.5 mm in diameter. This subshrubby alpine species is perhaps the least woody conifer in the world, other than the parasitic *Podocarpus ustus* of New Caledonia. *Dacrydium biforme* and *D. bidwillii* (the "bog pine") also grow in alpine New Zealand but are shrubs, about 1–2 m tall. These stand in contrast to such arboreal species of lowland or montane forest as *D. cupressinum* (the common "rimu" or "red pine"), *D. intermedium,* and *D. colensoi.*

In *Podocarpus, P. dacrydioides,* to 50 m or more, can be a huge tree of "lowland swamp forest." One can contrast it with the prostrate alpine shrub, *P. nivalis*. However, such extremes may represent more than one introduction of *Podocarpus* to New Zealand rather than autochthonous radiation on the islands. *Podocarpus nivalis* appears very close to *P. alpina* of Australia. *Podocarpus totara*, *P. spicatus*, *P. ferrugineus*, and *P. hallii* are medium-sized trees most frequently found in lowlands; some individuals of these species are rounded in shape, and look more oaklike than coniferlike at a distance. Small size of leaves in these species suggests adaptation to a forest that is only moderately moist. *Podocarpus spicatus* may be related to the South American *P. andinus*, according to Florin (1951), who apparently regards cone types in these species as primitive.

ANGIOSPERMS

In discussing angiosperms of New Zealand, one can present growth forms and habitats and enumerate examples, or one can see the range of niches occupied by particular genera. The former point of view is very tempting, because growth forms and habitats are so distinctive for New Zealand plants.

A number of these forms are illustrated by species of *Hebe* (Scrophulariaceae), as shown in figure 7.9 (regrettably, only a small range can be illustrated). The majority of the approximately 100 species of this genus are native to New Zealand, the remainder to other austral areas (Allan, 1961). *Hebe* can be a true tree, as in *H. parviflora* var. *arborea*, to 7.5 m tall. This variety occurs in mesic localities in the relatively warm North Island and its offshore islands, and moderation of the maritime climate is probably related to arborescence. *Hebe salicifolia* (fig. 7.9, bottom right) is a shrub to 5 m, from South Island. Lowland and mid-elevation localities in New Zealand host a number of somewhat smaller broad-leaved shrubs (1–2 m). At increasingly higher elevations, one tends to find progressively smaller shrubs with smaller leaves. Whereas mid-elevation shrubby species tend to be branched from above the base, the alpine and subalpine species are branched from the base or at ground level. Because New Zealand mountains are rich in scree areas, most of the high-elevation species branch from below the rocks and rubble which perpetually fall on them, and thus renewal buds are potentially removed from killing cold. This is true of the three species illustrated as figure 7.9, top left and right, and bottom left. Prostrate stems characterize some alpine species, such as *H. ramosissima*,

FIG. 7.9. Species of *Hebe* (Scrophulariaceae) from New Zealand. TOP LEFT, *H. hectori* var. *demissa*, leaves about 3 mm long; Arthur's Pass. TOP RIGHT, *H. tetrasticha*, leaves about 5 mm long; Porter's Pass. BOTTOM LEFT, *H. epacridea*, leaves 10–12 mm long; Arthur's Pass. BOTTOM RIGHT, *H. salicifolia*, leaves 90–100 mm long; cultivated in Garberville, Calif.

H. petriei, and *H. haastii* (Allan, 1961). *Hebe macrantha* is exceptional in its very large flowers, borne on prostrate stems; the large flowers remind me of the tendency toward large flowers in other alpine genera.

Decrease in leaf size can be shown well by alpine Hebes; this change would be expected in these physiologically dry habitats. Water is available as snow melts, but not as the (often porous) soils dry out in warm weather or freeze during winter; humidity is low in alpine localities, and greater wind action aggravates the effect of desiccation, so microphylly is an almost inevitable adaptation. *Hebe epacridea* (fig. 7.9, bottom left) shows an early step in xeromorphy, *H. tetrasticha* (fig. 7.9, top right) and *H. hectori* var. *demissa* (fig. 7.9, top left) show progressively further expressions. Species like the latter, known as "whiplash" Hebes, are notable for their coniferlike foliage. Because *Hebe* often has decussate phyllotaxy, these species resemble various genera of Cupressaceae. The factors that favor conifers such as *Juniperus* in comparable alpine localities on mainland areas are plainly operative in evolution of *Hebe* as well. One may ask why, with a relatively great number of conifers in New Zealand, coniferlike *Hebe* species should evolve in New Zealand. One reason is that particularly appropriate conifer-equivalents, such as Cupressaceae, are absent in New Zealand. Another explanation is the ability of *Hebe* to occupy a greater variety of niches. However, alpine conifers have been evolved (or relictually preserved) in alpine New Zealand (*Dacrydium laxifolium, D. biforme, D. bidwillii*, and *Podocarpus nivalis*). This suggests that a selective pressure for these growth forms definitely does exist. The endemic scrophulariaceous genus of cushion plants *Pygmaea* probably represents a *Hebe* that has evolved fully into the cushion-plant habit.

In addition to distinction in habit, preferences in edaphic situations occur in *Hebe*. If one reviews the data in Allan (1961), one finds that rocky places, even disturbed places, form a predominant habitat for *Hebe* species. This habitat suggests that *Hebe* is a pioneering group. Some species are described as favoring "forest margins," "grasslands," or "scrub." Habitats like these also suggest characteristics of a pioneering group. However, among species for which rocky habitats are specified, there is a diversity of preferences, suggesting adaptive radiation: "sea-cliffs" (*H. speciosa, H. obtusata*); "under falls" (*H. acutiflora*); "maritime cliffs where there is a maximum of spray" (*H. chathamica*); "on serpentine" (*H. urvilleana*);

"rock platforms on river banks" (*H. recurva*); "on rocks in tussock grass-land" (*H. amplexicaulis*); "limestone rocks" (*H. raoulii* var. *maccaskillii*); and some seem to favor volcanic rocks. There are many alpine species, in-evitably in rocky places, but even these are varied in preferences; some grow on shingle on steep slopes, some in fell fields, and one entire section (*Buxifoliatae*) of the genus occurs in swampy alpine places. At least one species (*H. diosmifolia*) grows in "dense woods" and thus appears to have entered the most stable habitats. The genus *Parahebe* can be regarded as a more herbaceous (subshrub) phase of *Hebe*, and thus represents an adap-tation to situations suited for herbs. The great degree of hybridism in *Hebe* (see Allan, 1961) is also an indication of the rapid evolution that has occurred (perhaps following glaciation) without concomitant forma-tion of genetic barriers. Geographical isolation and shift into various edaphic preferences have evidently operated to promote speciation (and the predominantly rocky habitats favored by Hebes are, by their particular geographic nature, isolated—stream beds, for example).

Coprosma (fig. 7.10) has 45 species in New Zealand, and 45 on other Pacific islands (Allan, 1961), so that New Zealand is obviously a primary area of speciation of the genus. In its growth forms, it constitutes a prime example of adaptive radiation. These include broad-leaved arboreal spe-cies. Interestingly, as in *Hebe*, these tend to occupy mesic sites in northern, warmer New Zealand (data from Allan, 1961): *C. tenuifolia* (to 5 m; North I.; alluvial soils); *C. acutifolia* (to 10 m; Kermadec Is.); *C. australis* (to 6 m; Three Kings Is., North I. to 42° S; marginal forest); *C. robusta* (to 6 m; Three Kings Is., North I., South I., Chatham Is.; forest and shrubland on alluvial soils); *C. macrocarpa* (to 5 or even 10 m; Three Kings Is., North I., and adjacent islets); *C. chathamica* (15 m; Chatham Is.; forest); *C. peti-olata* (to 6 m; Kermadec Is.); *C. repens* (to 8 m; Kermadec Is., Three Kings Is., North I., South I. to 41°30'S); *C. lucida* (to 6 m; North I., South I., Stewart I.).

Such trees probably represent secondary entrants into the truly arbo-real category and are really large shrubs that can, under favorable condi-tions, form trees One species not listed above, but which corresponds to this description, is *C. foetidissima* (fig. 7.10, bottom right), a rain-forest species that can attain 6 m. The shrubby species that do not attain tree-hood tend to be much smaller leaved, and they occupy drier or colder locali-

FIG. 7.10. Species of *Coprosma* (Rubiaceae) from New Zealand. TOP LEFT, *C. pseudocuneata*, leaves 18–20 mm long; Arthur's Pass. TOP RIGHT, *C. brunnea*, leaves 20–25 mm long; river-bed, Franz Josef Glacier. BOTTOM LEFT, *C. crassifolia*, leaves 12–15 mm in diam.; between Westport and Greymouth. BOTTOM RIGHT, *C. foetidissima*, branch with male and female flowers; leaves 90–100 mm long; between Arthur's Pass and Hokitika.

ties. Examples of the many species in this category are *C. pseudocuneata* (fig. 7.10, top left), *C. brunnea* (fig. 7.10, top right), and *C. crassifolia* (fig. 7.10, bottom left). Of these, *C. brunnea* is a prostrate mat-plant of montane river beds and cold lowlands. *Coprosma pseudocuneata* is an alpine shrub of herb fields; its branches appear stunted and stiff, condensed, with almost succulent leaves. *Coprosma crassifolia* is not an alpine plant but grows in shrubland. It has orbicular leaves, spaced well apart on stout branches. This species could qualify as a "divaricating shrub" because of the branching pattern (see below). The opposite to arborescence is illustrated by *C. petriei* (fig. 7.11, top left). This species is very small-leaved, and forms exclusively prostrate stems. If the stems were crowded, short, and upright, we could call it a true cushion plant; it does grow with cushion plants such as *Scleranthus* and *Raoulia*. Flowers are borne virtually at ground level, so that on female plants the large red or purple berries appear to be lying on the ground. Like cushion plants, *C. petriei* grows in montane regions in grassland, on margins of streams, and in rocky habitats.

Cushion Plants. Cushion plants are highly characteristic of the New Zealand flora because this growth form is so well adapted to montane regions (see also chapter 14). Cushion plants are microphyllous and thus transpire minimally in dry summer months or during winds. The compaction of stems, side by side, further reduces transpiration. Old stems and leaves can serve as wicks, and roots from younger portions grow down through the cushion. The cushion, as a sort of ground cover, aids in reducing water evaporation from the soil beneath it. The cushion habit is also a form of resistance to cold. The many renewal buds are below the surface of the cushion and are not damaged by freezes. However, the numerous stems can produce inflorescences rapidly during the summer, and produce large numbers of flowers and fruits at cushion surfaces. Because flowers and fruits are borne at surfaces of cushions, they emerge rapidly during the growing season, and protection against occasional summer frost is also afforded. *Raoulia* (Asteraceae) is an ideal example of autochthonous evolution of cushion plants in New Zealand. The genus is almost exclusively native to New Zealand; a few outlier species have reached alpine New Guinea. Some species are merely prostrate and matlike, others form leafy upright stems, short but separate, and with moderately small leaves. The true cushion Raoulias such as *R. australis*, shown in figure 7.11, bottom left

FIG. 7.11. Prostrate and cushion plants from New Zealand. TOP LEFT, *Coprosma petrei*, male plant in flower; Porter's Pass. TOP RIGHT, *Dracophyllum prostratum* in flower, growing in a cushion of *Scleranthus* (Caryophyllaceae); Arthur's Pass. BOTTOM LEFT, RIGHT, *Raoulia australis*. BOTTOM LEFT, habit of cushion; near Wanaka. BOTTOM RIGHT, view of surface of cushion in flower; leaves 4–5 mm long.

and right, and the famous *R. eximia* have developed in New Zealand, probably from ancestors with prostrate stems. Within the single genus *Raoulia*, a variety of growth forms and habits is represented. However, *Raoulia* is, in turn, only one phase of radiation in helichrysoid composites, a radiation which includes shrubs as well. *Raoulia* leaves are not only very small, but also woolly, which aids in frost resistance or desiccation resistance, or both. For illustrations of *Raoulia* and allied genera that can form cushions, the reader can consult Philipson and Hearn (1962).

Cushion plants, particularly those that are more matlike and prostrate, can form "seed beds" in which other species can germinate. Thus, cushions of *Scleranthus* may host seedlings of *Dracophyllum*, which can in turn become cushions. Thus, in alpine regions suited for them, cushion plants are "contaminated" with other cushion species. A stage in this process is illustrated in figure 7.11, top right. Species like *Dracophyllum muscoides, D. prostratum, D. pronum, Pernettya nana, Gaultheria depressa, Coprosma pumila, C. petriei, Pimelea prostrata,* and *Myrsine nummularia* are unusual in their reduced stature, probably evolved autochthonously in New Zealand. Some cushion plants extend well beyond New Zealand (e.g., *Oreobolus, Scleranthus, Gaimardia, Donatia, Phyllachne*) and although they may not represent evolution of this growth form on New Zealand itself, they do demonstrate existence of selective factors that have led to autochthonous evolution of this form in *Raoulia, Pygmaea,* and others. *Cotula* is unusual in New Zealand in that it is an herb group that forms mats, whereas it is often only an annual elsewhere. These examples point up the tendency of adaptive radiation in evolutionarily plastic groups such as Asteraceae, Scrophulariaceae, and Rubiaceae.

Divaricating Shrubs. Although not unique to New Zealand, the so-called divaricating shrubs, mentioned above, are remarkably abundant in the New Zealand flora. Went (1971) claims 51 species in 23 families as representing this habit in the New Zealand flora. Some (Dawson, 1963; Went, 1971) have implied that divaricating shrubs are unique to New Zealand, but they are not. A number are evident to me in the California flora: *Cercocarpus intricatus* and *C. ledifolius* (Rosaceae), to name only two at random. A divaricating shrub may be defined as a woody shrub in which branches tend to be at right angles and in which apical dominance is lessened, although not totally absent. Divaricating shrubs tend to have stout stems and small leaves.

Many genera also represented by "ordinary" broad-leaved shrubs or other growth forms have evolved divaricating shrubs that are characteristic of New Zealand's shrublands. *Coprosma crassifolia* (fig. 7.10, bottom left) was cited earlier. In the small genus *Corokia* (Saxifragaceae? Cornaceae?) with three New Zealand species, *C. buddleoides* (fig. 7.12, bottom right) and *C. macrocarpa* contrast with the divaricating shrub *C. cotoneaster* (fig. 7.12, bottom left). An almost identical situation is represented by *Melicytus* (Violaceae), with three broad-leaved New Zealand species, such as *M. ramiflorus* (fig. 7.13, bottom right), and one other New Zealand species, *M. micranthus* (fig. 7.13, bottom left), that is a divaricating shrub, or a close approach to that habit.

Many other genera have entered the divaricating-shrub habit. Shown here are *Pittosporum crassicaule* (fig. 7.14, top left) and *Aristotelia fruticosa* (fig. 7.14, top right). Other divaricating species of *Pittosporum* include *P. rigidum*, *P. anomalum*, *P. divaricatum*, and *P. lineare*. Further good examples include *Muhlenbeckia astonii* (Polygonaceae), *Myrtus pedunculata* (Myrtaceae), *Plagianthus divaricatus* (Malvaceae), *Paratrophis microphylla* (Moraceae), *Pennantia corymbosa* (Icacinaceae), *Neopanax anomalum* (Araliaceae), *Myrsine divaricata* (Myrsinaceae), many species of *Coprosma* (Rubiaceae), several of *Olearia* (Asteraceae: *O. odorata*, *O. virgata*), and *Helichrysum glomeratum* (Asteraceae). Divaricating shrubs represent tendencies, not a unitary growth form; in any case, ordinary evolutionary principles can explain their development, and Went's (1971) "floating gene" hypothesis should be rejected.

Microphylly. Numerous New Zealand plants, including divaricating shrubs, cushion plants, and mat plants, could be cited as examples of microphylly. However, some small-leaved plants, such as *Hymenanthera alpina* (fig. 7.13, top right) of the Violaceae and a thorn-shrub, *Discaria toumatou* (fig. 7.14, bottom left), of the Rhamnaceae could come under this heading. Virtually all of the New Zealand Epacridaceae could be called microphyllous. The microphyllous habit suits alpine and montane regions for reasons cited earlier for the whiplash *Hebe* species.

Broom Shrubs and Cladode Shrubs. Xeromorphy in dry montane regions is found in a number of New Zealand genera that have other

FIG. 7.12. Plants from New Zealand. TOP LEFT, RIGHT, *Metrosideros perforata* (Myrtaceae). TOP LEFT, habit, plant climbing on a tree; near Paeroa. TOP RIGHT, note wiry stems, leaves about 15 mm in diam. BOTTOM LEFT, *Corokia cotoneaster* (Cornaceae), stems have rather small leaves 10–12 mm; from plant in cultivation, Claremont, Calif. BOTTOM RIGHT, *C. buddleioides*, tip of shoot, showing leaves 70–80 mm long; cultivated on University of Auckland campus.

244

FIG. 7.13. Plants from New Zealand. TOP LEFT, *Muhlenbeckia ephedrioides* (Polygonaceae), a broom plant; cultivated at the Dominion Scientific Industrial and Research Organization, Botany Division, Lincoln, N.Z. TOP RIGHT, *Hymenanthera alpina* (Violaceae), leaves about 20 mm long; near Queenstown. BOTTOM LEFT, *Melicytus micranthus* (Violaceae), leaves about 12 mm long; cultivated, University of Auckland campus. BOTTOM RIGHT, *M. ramiflorus*, branch with leaves ca. 70 mm long; between Greymouth and Westport.

growth forms as well; for example, *Muhlenbeckia ephedroides* (fig. 7.13, top left). Other examples include species of *Carmichaelia* (Fabaceae) such as *C. uniflora*, *C. kirkii*, and *C. curta*. Other New Zealand legume broom-shrub genera include *Notospartium*, *Chordospartium*, and *Huttonella*. Most species of *Carmichaelia* and the monotypic *Corallospartium* (Faba-ceae) are close to the broom habit, but they have flattened leafless branches and should be called cladode shrubs.

Pronounced and Persistent Juvenilism. Surprisingly, the phenomenon of juvenile leaves quite different from adult leaves is present in about 200 species of New Zealand seed plants, of which 165 remain juvenile for a year or more (Cockayne, 1958). According to him, the 165 species belong to 50 genera in 30 families, so here we are dealing with a phenomenon for which selective factors must be operative. Cockayne claims that in 106 cases the juvenile appears to be more mesophytic than the mature form, and in 97 cases more xeromorphic, while in 39 cases there is little differ-ence: thus degree of dryness is apparently not involved here as a selective factor in juvenilism. One possible explanation is that the New Zealand forest is unusually dense—at least denser than the characteristic habitat for some of the genera that compose it; for example, *Hoheria* (Malvaceae) or the numerous Araliaceae, such as *Pseudopanax*. In other instances, "adaptive modes" of adult plants (such as the divaricating shrubs) are so distinctive that juvenile leaves resembling less specialized members of par-ticular genera are almost inevitable. Cockayne (1958) notes that in the whiplash *Hebe* species and the cupressoid Podocarpaceae, shoots with ju-venile (mesomorphic) leaves may be found close to the ground on plants growing in exceptionally moist conditions. Cockayne provides an extensive listing of species known characteristically to flower on juvenile shoots—a situation confusing to the inexperienced botanist. The parallels to the juvenile stages of the Hawaiian lobelioids are striking (see chapter 4), and the reasons are probably similar in many of the New Zealand instances. Juvenile leaves in Hawaiian lobelioids and in most New Zealand plants with juvenilism are broader (at least in proportion to length) and more lobed than are adult leaves.

Climbing plants in particular seem to exhibit pronounced juvenilism in New Zealand. One of these, *Metrosideros perforata*, is illustrated in fig-ure 7.12, top left and right. The juvenile shoots form in profusion as this

FIG. 7.14. Divaricating shrubs (TOP LEFT, RIGHT) and plants with armature (BOTTOM LEFT, RIGHT) from New Zealand. TOP LEFT, *Pittosporum crassicaule* (Pittosporaceae), leaves about 10 mm long; Arthur's Pass. TOP RIGHT, *Aristotelia fruticosa* (Elaeocarpaceae), stems in flower; leaves 12–14 mm long; Arthur's Pass. BOTTOM LEFT, *Discaria toumatou* (Rhamnaceae), *(continued)*

247

epiphytic liana climbs a tree. The adult leaves are larger (even if they still are smaller than those of most other species of *Metrosideros*), and internode length is reduced as adult shoots form. Adult shoots form only when *M. perforata* attains the forest canopy, and one would not easily guess the identity of the plant from juvenile shoots alone.

Rubus shows juvenilism in narrowing of laminae on leaflets in some species. In *R. squarrosus* laminae are almost absent; the bare prickly midrib of leaflets serves as an efficient climbing-attachment organ that is sufficient, however, for photosynthesis. Presumably Cockayne would have listed this condition as being more xeromorphic than presence of a lamina, but xeromorphy is not really applicable here. Shade leaves in seed plants at large tend to have fewer photosynthetic cells than do adult leaves, so absence of a lamina in *R. squarrosus* may be interpretable in this way.

Thorniness. Absence of armature in the Hawaiian flora is striking. One might expect a similar absence in New Zealand, equally as free from native mammalian herbivores as the Hawaiian Islands. However, a number of New Zealand plants (like the *Rubus* species just mentioned) have spines, thorns, or prickles. Two are shown here: *Aciphylla* sp. (fig. 7.14, bottom right) and *Discaria toumatou* (fig. 7.14, bottom left). The entire genus *Aciphylla* (Apiaceae) could be cited. Other examples include *Hymenanthera angustifolia* (Violaceae), *Carmichaelia angustata* (Fabaceae), *Urtica ferox* (Urticaceae), juvenile leaves of *Pseudopanax* (Araliaceae), and *Olearia ilicifolia* (Asteraceae). However, the tough, tangled, microphyllous branches of many of the divaricating shrubs seem to have virtually the same effect as thorny branches. If these various "armor" devices have a selective value in deterring herbivores, as one would expect, we would have to cite herbivores likely to have provided such pressure. Avian herbivores, such as the giant extinct moas and other extant herbivorous birds, might be one factor. Apiaceae is a notably unarmed family; the strong development of armature in the many species of *Aciphylla* seems difficult to explain on other grounds, although a component of xeromorphy might be invoked in this and other cases.

FIG. 7.14 *(continued)*
branches, showing thorniness, in flower; below Porter's Pass. BOTTOM RIGHT, *Aciphylla* sp. (Apiaceae), showing needlelike leaves, about 30 cm long, and inflorescence bracts; cultivated at the Dominion Scientific Industrial and Research Organization, Botany Division, Lincoln, N.Z.

Scree Plants. In habit and color, New Zealand scree plants are unusually interesting. There is nothing unique about them, for scree slopes elsewhere in the world bear autochthones equally striking in adaptation. The features of interest are the large roster of species in New Zealand (see Philipson and Hearn, 1962) and the groups to which they belong—like *Cotula* and *Crasspedia* (Asteraceae) and *Ranunculus*—genera one might not expect to have scree adaptations, but which have radiated into this habitat under the disharmonic conditions of the New Zealand flora. Color mimicry is striking in New Zealand scree plants, and they truly are often difficult to discern in their natural habitat. Certain instances of scree plants were cited earlier in *Hebe.*

Arborescence. For discussions of arborescence in the New Zealand flora, see chapter 10.

INSECTS

The best examples of adaptive radiation in the New Zealand fauna are perhaps the wetas, considered as belonging to two families of Orthoptera, Henicidae (ground wetas and straight-bodied wetas) and Rhaphidophoridae (the arched-bodied wetas—often called cave wetas but found on trees as well—with long legs and antennae). The henicids can be very large. *Deinacrida* and *Hemideina* consume rotting wood, and their large mouth parts and movements (running, never springing) correspond to this habit. *Hemideina* burrows in rotten wood and is often found among foliage. *Deinacrida* occurs among leaves and stones in montane regions. *Hemiandrus* lives in small burrows in soft logs and riverbanks. *Zealandrosardus* occurs under stones on montane slopes and under logs.

The Rhaphidophoridae are smaller and much more delicate wetas, capable of rapid jumping movements. *Pharmacus montana,* for example, springs from rock cavities in mountain areas of the Southern Alps. Other rhaphidophorids live in tunnels, caves, holes in logs, and under rocks. For illustrations and further references, see Natusch (1967).

FRESHWATER FISHES

The Galaxiidae is the largest family of freshwater fishes in the New Zealand icthyofauna, and may represent an older element (McDowall,

1970). Although McDowall speaks of the "limited extent of the radiation of the New Zealand Galaxiidae" as evidence that they are a conservative group, their adaptive radiation in New Zealand is quite evident. To be sure, none are herbivores, none are piscivorous, and none live in streams that lack forest cover (except for alpine streams). Within their diet of stream invertebrates, however, many adaptations are evident. Those species that feed in rapid water tend to be more slender in form. Some (*Galaxias brevipinnis, G. postvectis*) have receding lower jaws, an adaptation to feeding from the stream bottom. *Galaxias prognathus*, however, has a notably protruding lower jaw, related to feeding from the undersides of rocks. The solitary and secretive nature of most species exposes them to damage from close contact with rocks and logs, and this is evidently counteracted by the greatly thickened fins and truncated caudal fins of those species. In those species, pectoral fins also are in a low latero-ventral position, correlated with resting on the bottom. In *G. brevipinnis*, corrugations are present on lower surfaces of pectoral fins, permitting grasping of the stream bottom despite rapid flow of water. The few species that live in open pools and shoal have much more membranous fins, placed in a higher lateral position. Shoaling species such as *G. maculatus* (like shoaling fishes in general) have silvery coloration on the abdomen. Some *Galaxias* species in New Zealand have superior climbing ability (*G. brevipinnis, G. fasciatus, G. postvectis*), and show this in that pelvic fins are nearly flush with the ventral trunk and have the laminae facing downwards. Two lacustrine species (*G. usitatus* and *G. gracilis*) are notable for their long gill rakers. Gill-raker reduction occurs in the alpine species *G. divergens* and *G. prognathus*. The most striking adaptation evident in New Zealand galaxiads, and very possibly an autochthonous development following immigration of the original galaxiad stock from Australia, according to McDowall, is the ability to live in situations subject to drying: the genus *Neochanna*. *Neochanna* (three species) lives in swamps, swampy creeks, and springs, and can acstivate during droughts. The semi-burrowing habit appears in such morphological features as lost or reduced pelvic fins, reduced eyes, long nostrils, low median fins approximately confluent with the caudal fin, and a rounded caudal fin. Even with the limitations that McDowall (1970) suggests, his fine monograph clearly indicates interesting parameters of adaptive radiation in galaxiads of New Zealand.

COMMENTS ON NEW ZEALAND PATTERNS

The avifauna of New Zealand, although quite interesting on other grounds, shows relatively little adaptive radiation. Such genera as *Acanthisitta, Xenicus, Cyanorhamphus,* and *Anthornis* have formed what should be called vicarious species, judging from the data of Oliver (1955). These vicarious species must be recent, for differences within such genera among species of North Island, South Island, and the Chatham Islands are small. There may have been adaptive radiation among the moas, judging from differences in size among the fossils, but we will perhaps never have sufficient information for a definitive statement. Vertebrates other than birds are either relictual (*Leiopelma, Sphenodon*), or little-speciated immigrants of more recent epochs, such as the geckos.

Even if New Zealand had escaped glaciation, it still might not bear as broad spectrum of adaptive radiation as do the Hawaiian Islands. New Caledonia agrees with New Zealand in this respect. In both cases, we are dealing with older islands. However, neither of these old islands has the Hawaiian advantage of being a true archipelago, nor is climate as favorable as that in Hawaii. There is no doubt that events of dispersal throughout an archipelago, followed by speciation and adaptive shift on various islands, then redispersal to island of origin can lead to diversification.

How, then, have the cases of adaptive radiation cited for New Zealand and New Caledonia occurred? First, there is the possibility that for antique groups, such as conifers, an archipelago—or larger island with internal barriers—may have existed where only one island (e.g., New Caledonia) now is present. Adaptive radiation in this case would have occurred long ago, and its presumptive products have not yet been extinguished. Second, there is the possibility that, in recent time, evolutionarily plastic groups have speciated adaptively. If they have, it could be explained if suitable habitats for a given genus occur in discontinuous fashion. For example, pockets of scrubland, alpine regions, and areas of particular soil types could, in effect, provide archipelagos, or even a series of archipelagos—and adaptive radiation could occur (possibly following glaciation). This may explain radiation in New Zealand species of *Hebe*, the wetas, or the galaxiad fishes.

References

Allan, H. H. 1961. *Flora of New Zealand*, vol. I. Wellington, R. E. Owens, Government Printer.

Carlquist, S. 1965. *Island life*. New York, Natural History Press.

Cockayne, L. 1927. *New Zealand plants and their story*. Wellington, W. A. G. Skinner, Government Printer.

Cockayne, L. 1958. *The vegetation of New Zealand*. 3d ed. Weinheim, Germany, H. R. Engelmann (J. Cramer).

Dawson, J. W. 1963. A comment on divaricating shrubs. *Tuatara* 11:193–94.

Delacour, J. 1966. *Guide des oiseaux de la Nouvelle-Calédonie et de ses dépendances*. Neuchâtel, Switzerland, Editions Delachaux & Niestlé.

Florin, R. 1951. Evolution in cordaites and conifers. *Acta Horti Bergiani* 15(11): 285–388.

Florin, R. 1963. The distribution of conifer and taxad genera in time and space. *Acta Horti Bergiani* 20(4):121–312.

Gressitt, J. L. 1961. Problems in the zoogeography of Pacific and Antarctic insects. *Pacific Insects Monogr.* 2:1–94.

Guillaumin, A. 1948. *Flore analytique et synoptique de la Nouvelle-Calédonie: Phanerogames*. Paris, Office de la Recherche Scientifique Coloniale.

Hochstetter, F. von. 1959. *Geology of New Zealand*. Transl. and ed. C. A. Fleming. Wellington, R. E. Owen, Government Printer.

MacArthur, R. H., and E. O. Wilson. 1967. *The theory of island biogeography*. Princeton, N.J., Princeton University Press.

McDowall, R. M. 1970. The galaxiid fishes of New Zealand. *Bull. Mus. Comp. Zool.* 139(7):341–432.

Mertens, R. 1934. Die Insel-Reptilien, ihre Ausbreitung, Variation, und Artbildung. *Zoologica* 32(6):1–209.

Nakata, S. 1961. Some notes on the occurrence of Phasmatodea in Oceania. *Pacific Insects Monogr.* 2:107–21.

Natusch, S. 1967. *Animals of New Zealand*. Christchurch, Whitcombe and Tombs.

Oliver, W. R. B. 1955. *New Zealand birds*. 2d ed. Wellington, A. H. and A. W. Reed.

Philipson, W. R., and D. Hearn. 1962. *Rock garden plants of the southern alps*. Christchurch, Caxton Press.

Sarlin, P. 1954. *Bois et forêts de la Nouvelle Calédonie*. Nogent-sur-Marne, France, Centre de Technique Forestier Tropical.

Smith, A. C. 1955. Phanerogam genera with distributions terminating in Fiji. *Jour. Arnold Arboretum* 36:273–92.

Solem, A. 1961. New Caledonian land and fresh-water snails. An annotated check list. *Fieldiana, Zool.* 41:415–501.

Thorne, R. F. 1965. Floristic relationships of New Caledonia. *Univ. Iowa Stud. Natur. Hist.* 20(7):1–14.

Went, F. W. 1971. Parallel evolution. *Taxon* 20:197–226.

CHAPTER EIGHT

ADAPTIVE RADIATION: THE FLORA
OF SOUTHWESTERN AUSTRALIA

Selection of a single portion of Australia as a site for discussion of adaptive radiation may seem a dubious exercise at first glance. Conceding that Australia can be considered insular, can patterns of southwestern Australia be examined independently of the remainder of the continent? Many genera of angiosperms occur in both temperate western and eastern Australia. The significance of the southwestern flora lies primarily in the extent to which it is disharmonic, and in the genera that have radiated in a spectacular fashion in that region. There are a number of aspects in which southwestern Australian plants show insular characteristics in heightened form. Western Australia was indeed an island in the Cretaceous (Noakes, 1966), but in the Tertiary, outlines of the continent were not drastically different from their present extents. However, Western Australia proves to be insular with respect to angiosperms in many ways.

To be sure, Australian vertebrates do not show sharply insular patterns. Some genera are confined to the West (see Keast, 1961). Some other vertebrates, such as the marsupial *Thylacinus*, once occurred in Western Australia, as fossil records indicate, so significance should not be attached to absence of these genera. Among angiosperms, however, there is an appreciable generic endemism and an extremely high species endemism (see chapter 3), even if we cannot define southwestern Australia precisely as a province. Also, this region is still poorly known. For example, during three months of intensive field work in southwestern Australia in 1967, I was able to augment the family Stylidiaceae by approximately 10 percent: 10 new species of *Stylidium*, 1 new species of *Levenhookia*, and 7 new subspecies of *Stylidium* (Carlquist, 1969). Very likely, new species could be added to many of the larger genera in southwestern Australia.

Southwestern Australia, rather than Western Australia as a whole, is a natural biogeographic region to consider. To the east and northeast of the southwestern province, rainfall tapers to extremely low levels, providing barriers and isolation virtually as effective as seawater in demarcating the more mesic southwestern flora. The northern portions of Western Australia are also very dry and have a subtropical rather than temperate regime, but also have a summer rainfall pattern, rather than a winter pattern as in the southwest. The frost-free coastal zone extends as far south as Shark Bay (these data and other facts on temperature, rainfall, and geology cited below are from the *Atlas of Australian resources*, 1952–1966). The northern limit of the southwestern province could conveniently be placed at Shark Bay, where the 10-in. rainfall isohyet runs, or, somewhat further south, at the mouth of the Murchison River, which coincides with an isohyet of 15 in. per year. Along the southern coast of Western Australia, rainfall decreases eastwardly toward the Nullarbor Plain. The 15-in. isohyet at Cape Arid would be a convenient boundary for the southwestern Province. Not far to the east of Cape Arid there is also a sharp change in geology: a boundary between the granitics of the west and the Nullarbor limestones, which represent a giant Tertiary embayment. If one follows the 10-in. isohyet from Shark Bay toward the southeast, one finds that it includes such localities as Southern Cross and, very nearly, Kalgoorlie. Localities interior to Kalgoorlie show a sharp reduction in number of plant species. The subdesert areas from Kalgoorlie and Norseman westward should be included in the southwestern province.

If defined roughly as above, the southwestern province is an island of mediterranean climate, well separated from similar climates in eastern Australia by the long stretches of desert. Rainfall forms an almost evenly increasing gradient toward the southwestern tip of the continent at Point D'Entrecasteaux, where rainfall exceeds 60 in. per year. Clearly, rainfall is not distributed in such a way that any marked moisture microclimates occur along the increasing gradient to the southwest; however, microclimates do result from the variation in moisture availability owing to different soil types and drainage.

Topography forms few isolating barriers within southwestern Australia, for the province is remarkably flat. The Darling Scarp behind Perth is a minor feature, and the Stirling Range, although the most notable series of elevations in the southwest, would hardly qualify as mountains (the highest point, Bluff Knoll, is 3640 ft). Basic rock types, as shown on geological maps, are remarkably unvaried in the southwestern province. Most of the area consists of a pre-Cambrian (Archaean) granitic shield. The only exceptions to this are the Jurassic sandstone and shales, near the coast from Geraldton south nearly to Perth, and the pre-Cambrian shales (Proterozoic) of the Stirling Range and a few nearby areas. A strip of the western coast consists of sand, but this is granitic sand derived from the ubiquitous granites. The combination of topography and restricted rock types probably accounts for the remarkable endemism of *Darwinia* species on the Stirling Range (fig. 8.23), but Darwinias occur on other topography and soil types as well in southwestern Australia.

Soils across broad stretches of southwestern Australia are not as uniform as underlying rock types would suggest, however. Lateralization is widespread. Laterized soils are reddish, and often contain red-brown pebbles of laterite. Laterized soils tend to be moderately or strongly alkaline. On the other hand, granitic sands, varying from bright white to yellow (at Southern Cross), tend to be acidic. Sand areas, if not well drained, form "bogs" or "swamps" during the winter, but ironically take on a desertlike aspect during the summer months. Granitic sands are not, as previously thought, derived directly from decomposition domes or other facies, but represent wind-carried accumulations, presumably derived from former beaches. Areas of granitic sands—known as "sand heaths" to botanists—are peculiar in their lack of micronutrients, which spared them from farming until recent discovery of this lack.

The contrast between laterite and granite sand areas is a striking one, because the species composition of the respective soil types is so different. One can literally find an assemblage of perhaps a hundred species on an area of white sand, then cross to a laterite area a few yards away and find a totally different assemblage of species. Although there are some extensive laterite areas, often these two sand types occur as a series of islands. In some places, granite sand will be the continuous phase, in others, the discontinuous phase. Thus southwestern Australia is edaphically a "two-phased archipelago," and this, together with superimposed rainfall and topographic features, accounts for the rather fantastic speciation that has occurred. Rapid evolution in a mosaic-type soil distribution is stressed by Snaydon (1970). The relation between edaphic endemism and "catastrophic selection" was described by Lewis (1962) and further emphasized by Raven (1964). Beadle (1966) notes the poor nutrient content of certain soils in Australia. Although Beadle does not, in my opinion, prove his contention that phosphate impoverishment leads to xeromorphy and sclerophylly, the existence of nutrient-poor soils is itself significant.

Southwestern Australia contains areas difficult for establishment of many angiosperm groups because of relatively low rainfall, high soil porosity, temperature extremes, and peculiar soil types, some of which are poor in nutrients. The net consequence is that only a limited number of establishments have succeeded in the isolated southwestern province. We have, therefore, a disharmonic condition. For those groups preadapted to establishment, however, there has been enormous opportunity for radiation.

Beadle (1966) assumes that we must rely on land connection with Asia during the Cretaceous for entry of 180 angiospem families to Australia. This is surely false. Many of these angiosperm families are capable of long-distance dispersal, which explains why a few have strongly disjunct distributions (e.g., Restionaceae, Rafflesiaceae) that include Australia. There is no reason whatever to believe that Australia has been less effective than oceanic islands as a recipient of immigrants via long-distance dispersal. Australia presents a much larger target area than a volcanic island, and has had greater longevity as a land surface. In addition, long-distance dispersal has undoubtedly operated within Australia itself. It has been operative between the two mesic and sub-mesic temperate areas, southwestern and southeastern Australia. One certainly need not hypothesize plants growing at ecologically unsuitable mid-stations. Wind-carried seeds can be picked up, once fallen to a land surface, and carried farther by successive gusts, an advantage not shared by seeds carried across oceanic distances. The difficulty of dispersal to, and establishment in, southwestern Australia is great enough, however, that we can justifiably regard the southwestern flora as a "flora of long-distance dispersal" (that is, a flora produced by evolution of ancestors that arrived via long-distance dispersal).

For example, *Dodonaea viscosa*, a common lowland plant of Pacific islands, may have arrived on maritime sites, such as limestone bluffs just south of Geraldton. Localities with alkaline and xeric qualities like those of the immediate coast occur in inland areas as "islands": pockets of alkaline laterite, margins of former salt lakes, etc. Rapid evolution in one of these edaphic islands, followed by dispersal to others and further change there, may explain the varied and variable species of *Dodonaea* in the southwest. Likewise, it would explain the formation of numerous inland species of *Frankenia*, typically a beach genus, in this province. Similar considerations undoubtedly apply to other halophyte genera that have speciated markedly in southwestern Australia: *Bassia, Chenopodium,* and *Atriplex* of the Chenopodiaceae; and *Kochia* and *Ptilotus* (*Trichinium*) of the Amaranthaceae. Those groups characteristic of the white sand "winter bogs," such as *Drosera* (fig. 8.29, bottom left, right), would likewise react to the insular distribution of white sand. Numerous small populations, interconnected by events of dispersal, form a scheme ideal for rapid evolution, according to many evolutionists. In this case, the distribution of white sand pockets in southwestern Australia would be perfect.

Once a species has diverged from parent stocks and been separated by formation of sterility barriers from similar species, it can redisperse to areas occupied by ancestral species and become sympatric. During my field work in the southwest, I frequently found several species of *Stylidium* growing together and often flowering at the same time, but interspecific hybrids were extremely rare. I attribute this lack mainly to sterility of hybrids. There are other means of barrier formation among species, however. In *Stylidium*, for example, sympatric species can have different flowering times. Also, distinctive flower patterns with respect to flower size, corolla-lobe shape, color, and display position, and length and position of the column may make cross-pollination impossible in this genus (Carlquist, 1969). Some species of *Stylidium* have developed selfing mechanisms (Carlquist, 1969); flower-constancy in pollinating insects for this genus is apparently also a reality (Erickson, 1958). There has been an evolutionary shift to new insect pollinators in some species, such as *S. insensitivum* (Carlquist, 1969).

Even viewing southwestern Australia in an oversimplified scheme of archipelagic patterns of granitic sand and laterite, one can see other mechanisms by which soil patterns could promote rapid evolution. If white granitic sand occurs in pockets within a laterite area, the fringes of the sand pockets could offer intermediate soil types. Ecotypes tolerant to sand-laterite mixtures could develop in a sand-inhabiting species, and from the intermediates a laterite species could develop. In *Drosera*, this may have happened; although most species are characteristic of sand heaths, some occur on laterite soils or, like *D. macrophylla*, are tolerant of both or of various soil mixtures (Erickson, 1968). In *Stylidium*, the peculiar *S. preissii* is a sand species, although the only closely related species, *S. imbricatum*, occurs on laterite gravels, but only where sand has infiltrated the gravels. If some species of a genus are sand species, others laterite species (as is true in *Stylidium*), both phases of the soil mosaic can serve as "islands" stimulating evolution.

Even if climatic factors such as temperature and rainfall form a gradual gradient from the southwest coast inland, these gradients can still be entirely operative as selective factors. One can envision numerous genera of flowering plants evolving into drier habitats, or, on the other hand, more mesic habitats, by forming successively more xeromorphic or mesomorphic ecotypes across distances of hundreds of miles. In some places, these gradients can be very sharp. For example, Esperance is a coastal locality that is relatively mesic compared with desertlike areas only a short distance inland.

Evolutionary trends in the southwestern flora are surely not unidirectional. There is no reason to suppose that mesomorphy is always more primitive, xeromorphy secondary, even within a single genus. In fact, some plants of higher rainfall areas seem to be recent invasions. One might expect this because, in area alone, the broader zones of dry country would offer larger bases for establishment than the relatively wet southwestern corner. Dry areas, with less or no soil profile development, would also be expected to be "open communities," suitable for pioneers, as compared with the well-developed podzolized soils of the wet karri forests of southwesternmost Australia. Shorter dispersal distances would be required for migration of a subdesert species from east to west (or the reverse) in temperate Australia, because more mesic areas are localized in extreme southwest and southeast.

Radiation in Taxonomic Groups

One can view adaptive radiation in southwestern Australia in terms of what growth forms and other modes of structure have been produced in particular genera, or one can view these phenomena one by one. I am taking both viewpoints. The first illustrates most clearly that any given genus covers a range of phenomena but not all of them. The latter, presentation of morphological modes, suggests what significance these may have in terms of adaptations, and how these form a remarkable array of parallelisms. Information on plants of southwestern Australia has been derived from my fieldwork there in 1962 and 1967, and also from the valuable books of Blackall and Grieve (1956, 1959, 1965) and Beard (1965). Beard offers rough data on ranges and very brief descriptions, whereas the pictorial keys of Blackall and Grieve contain condensed visual information.

DAVIESIA (FABACEAE)

Daviesia, a genus of small shrubs, is represented by a few species in eastern Australia. The southwestern species, however, are more numerous and remarkably diverse (figs. 8.1–8.3). Virtually all of them represent various types of reduction or condensation of photosynthetic surfaces—the diversity within this general phenomenon is amazing. Few of the southwestern species have true leaves, but those that do show restriction in form. *Daviesia obtusifolia* (fig. 8.1, top left) has oblanceolate leaves with both surfaces identical (isolateral), like those of many eucalypt species. The wedge-shaped leaves of *D. dielsii* (fig. 8.1, top right) are also isolateral, rather thick, each tipped by a spine. Leaves of *D. teretifolia* (fig. 8.1, bottom left) are needlelike and tend to point upwards (they are thus minimally exposed to sunlight), and each is tipped by a spine. *Daviesia pachyphylla* (fig. 8.1, bottom right) is a sparsely branched shrub with branches densely covered by leaves not unlike rose thorns, but with a more inflated appearance. The interior of the leaves is spongy, but the leaves are very stiff, not succulent, thus making the spine at the tip effectively pungent. Narrower and sparser—but clearly spine-tipped and stout—are leaves of *D. polyphylla* (fig. 8.2, top left). Leaves of *D. polyphylla* do not

259

FIG. 8.1. Species of *Daviesia* (Fabaceae) from Western Australia. TOP LEFT, *D. obtusifolia*, leaves 6 cm long (from a color photograph by Fred W. Humphreys, courtesy of Mrs. Evelyn Humphreys). TOP RIGHT, *D. dielsii*, wedge-shaped leaves 15 mm long; between Eneabba and Gingin. BOTTOM LEFT, *D. teretifolia*, needlelike leaves 60 mm long; between Gibson and Scaddan. BOTTOM RIGHT, *D. pachyphylla*, conical leaves 15 mm long; between Ravensthorpe and Hopetoun.

260

FIG. 8.2. Species of *Daviesia* (Fabaceae) from Western Australia. TOP LEFT, *D. polyphylla*, spinelike leaves 20 mm long; Cape Le Grand. TOP RIGHT, *D. retroflexa*, spinclike leaves 25 mm long; between Ravensthorpe and Esperance. BOTTOM LEFT, *D. divaricata*; near Mullewa. BOTTOM RIGHT, *D. aphylla*, broom shrub in flower; near Melville.

261

FIG. 8.3. Fabaceae from Western Australia. TOP LEFT, *Daviesia euphorbioides*, stems 1 cm in diam.; Wongan Hills. TOP RIGHT, *D. trigonophylla*, stems angled because of decurrent leaf bases; Chester Pass. BOTTOM LEFT, *D. epiphylla*, flattened stems 2–5 cm wide (from a color photograph by Fred W. Humphreys, courtesy of Mrs. Evelyn Humphreys). BOTTOM RIGHT, *Brachysema aphyllum*, flattened branch 15 mm wide, bearing a flower 60 mm long; near Northampton.

appear demarcated from the stem by any external juncture. This is also true of *D. retroflexa* (fig. 8.2, top right), the leaves of which point downwards. The angle of the leaves suggests that they might be effective as climbing hooks, although *D. retroflexa* does not often appear to be a climbing shrub. *Daviesia aphylla* (fig. 8.2, bottom right) and *D. divaricata* (fig. 8.2, bottom left) could be called broom shrubs. Stems of *D. aphylla* are leafless, as the name suggests. Stems of *D. divaricata* are more branched, producing a tangle of stems, and terminate in thornlike fashion. *Daviesia divaricata* should probably be termed a thorn shrub rather than a broom shrub.

Daviesia euphorbioides (fig. 8.3, top left) is nearly leafless: the leaf vestiges are spinelike. Stems of *D. euphorbioides* are expanded, chiefly by means of a broadened pith, and the plant is thus rather like an "inflated" broom shrub. This species cannot be called a true succulent. *Daviesia trigonophylla* (fig. 8.3, top right) reminds one of *D. polyphylla*, but leaf bases are decurrent and fused into three longitudinal ridges on each stem, so that the stems are cladode-like. More definitively a cladode plant is *D. epiphylla* (fig. 8.3, bottom left), with glaucous flattened branches, capable of photosynthesis on all surfaces. These branches can be considered cladodes, but the spine-tipped lobes probably represent leaf portions, whereas in a true cladode plant a flattened stem lacking leaves is ordinarily implied.

The various forms illustrated in *Daviesia* do not seem related to habitat differentially. One might expect leafy species such as *D. obtusifolia* to be from a more mesic habitat, *D. polyphylla* to occur in xeric localities. Although perhaps the range in climate is not great, *D. obtusifolia* extends from the Stirling area inland to the Coolgardie subdeserts. *Daviesia polyphylla* occurs at the margins of swamps, as at Cape Le Grand, but also in shade of jarrah (*Eucalyptus marginata* or *E. rostrata*) forest elsewhere. However, all the species of *Daviesia* are presumably subject to about equal herbivore pressure, and all of those illustrated seem to lack tender leaves yet have spines and thorns. The species illustrated can be interpreted as various responses to herbivore pressure, as well as expressions of xeromorphy. Perhaps all the habitats of these species can be considered xeric at least during the warmest months of the year.

BRACHYSEMA (FABACEAE)

Brachysema (figs. 8.3, bottom right; 8.4; 8.5) is characteristic of southwestern Australia, although it also occurs in northeastern Australia. Thus, as in *Daviesia,* most although perhaps not all of the morphological features of *Brachysema* may be autochthonous developments in the southwest. *Brachysema* in southwestern Australia is notable for having the most disparate types of habit. For example, *B. aphyllum* (fig. 8.3, bottom right) represents true cladode formation; vestigial leaves can be seen on margins of the long cladodes, which tend to sprawl, forming a prostrate shrub. However, there are species of *Brachysema* with true leaves. *Brachysema sericea* (fig. 8.4, top left) grows in seasonally wet sand heath, so its broad-leaved habit does correlate with mesic habitat. This is also true of other leafy species: *B. lanceolatum* (fig. 8.4, top right) tends to be scandent in other shrubs in eucalypt woodland; *B. bracteolosum* (fig. 8.4, bottom left), a shrub to 2 m in the Stirlings, also occurs with mesomorphic species. *Brachysema praemorsum* (fig. 8.4, bottom left) is a subshrub, an understory element in shady woodland. *Brachysema daviesioides* (fig. 8.5, top left, right) and *B. tomentosum* (fig. 8.5, bottom left, right) are both peculiar, however, in being subshrubs with very large flowers borne on inflorescences that represent specialized shoots formed a little below ground level. *Brachysema daviesioides* is a leafless thorn shrub, with scarlet flowers forming a circle as they emerge from the ground at the base of the plant. *Brachysema tomentosum* has flattened stems, and is thereby a cladode shrub or subshrub. Flowers are pale yellow green. Both of these species occur in relatively dry, open areas, so reduction in vegetative surface is understandable. *Brachysema daviesioides* would seem more adapted to herbivore deterrence. Why large curved flowers, seemingly ornithophilous, should occur at ground level is rather mysterious, and is one of many unsolved questions about this plant that observational work might be able to clarify.

BANKSIA (PROTEACEAE)

Whereas species of *Banksia* are shrubs of various sizes in other parts of Australia and southernmost New Guinea, the southwestern species show a maximal divergence in habit (fig. 8.6). *Banksia grandis* (fig. 8.6, top left) is a true tree, to 50 ft. Typical of shrubby species are *B. sphaerocarpa* (fig. 8.6, top right), which may be under 1 ft high at maturity in some

FIG. 8.4. Species of *Brachysema* (Fabaceae) from Western Australia. TOP LEFT, *B. sericea*, leaves about 4 cm long; near Cranbrook. TOP RIGHT, *B. lanceolatum*, leaves white on reverse, cm long; Toolbrunup. BOTTOM RIGHT, *B. praemorsum*, leaves about 22 mm long (from a color about 5 cm long; cultivated, Los Angeles Arboretum. BOTTOM LEFT, *B. bracteolosum*, leaves 8 photograph by Fred W. Humphreys, courtesy of Mrs. Evelyn Humphreys).

265

FIG. 8.5. Species of *Brachysema* (Fabaceae) from Western Australia. TOP LEFT, RIGHT, *B. daviesioides*. TOP LEFT, habit of plant, about 0.5 m tall; near Perenjori. TOP RIGHT, bright red flower, 60 mm long, at base of plant. BOTTOM LEFT, RIGHT, *B. tomentosum*. BOTTOM LEFT, habit, showing flattened stems, about 0.5 m tall; near Southern Cross. BOTTOM RIGHT, base of plant, showing pale yellow brown flowers 70 mm long.

FIG. 8.6. Species of *Banksia* (Proteaceae) from Western Australia. TOP LEFT, *B. grandis*, habit of tree, 7 m tall; near Yanchep. TOP RIGHT, *B. sphaerocarpa*, shrub in flower, 1.5 m tall; near Dandaragan. BOTTOM LEFT, *B. nutans*, branches showing pendant inflorescences; cultivated, King's Park, Perth. BOTTOM RIGHT, *B. prostrata*, habit of plant (for size of leaves, see fig. 8.13), showing head of flowers and head of fruits at ground level; near Scaddan.

267

populations, to 2 ft in others; and B. *nutans* (fig. 8.6, bottom left), a shrub about 1 m high in which inflorescences are nodding and tend to be borne near the ground. At the opposite extreme from B. *grandis* is B. *prostrata* (fig. 8.6, bottom right), a plant that can only be called an "underground shrub." Its stems are stout and woody but always grow as stolons below the soil surface, with only the large leaves exposed—a habit reminiscent of the bracken fern, *Pteridium*. Inflorescences terminate shoots, and are borne at ground level, thus providing another example of a seemingly ornithophilous flower borne at the soil surface. The ecological significance of the various growth forms seems clear enough. *Banksia grandis* occupies relatively mesic sites along the western coast to the north and south of Perth. Other tree species of *Banksia* in the southwest include B. *menziesii* (fig. 8.32, top), B. *prionotes*, B. *speciosa*, and B. *ilicifolia*. Although these all are plants of white granitic sands, none occurs very far from the coast, whereas shrubby species can occur farther inland. *Banksia prostrata* may represent a fire adaptation, for all renewal buds are below the ground surface.

OTHERS

Perhaps the most outstanding example of diversity in growth form and tendencies in other vegetative morphological details is *Acacia*, but this genus is pan-Australian. The reader can obtain a picture of its scope (which is greatest in Western Australia) by consulting Blackall and Grieve (1959). Many other good examples of adaptive radiation in habit are discussed below in terms of particular tendencies; such genera include *Scaevola* and *Dampiera* (Goodeniaceae), *Drosera* (Droseraceae), *Comesperma* (Polygalaceae), *Hakea* and *Grevillea* (Broteaceae), *Tetratheca* (Tremandraceae), and *Stylidium* (Stylidiaceae). This list is by no means complete, and virtually any angiosperm genus in southwestern Australia tends to contain a range in growth form.

Modes of Adaptation

BROOM SHRUBS

As noted by Diels (1906), broom shrubs are common in the southwestern province. Four are illustrated here (fig. 8.7). *Scaevola restiacea*

FIG. 8.7. Broom plants from Western Australia. TOP LEFT, *Scaevola restiacea* (Goodeniaceae), flowers about 18 mm long; near Merredin. TOP RIGHT, *Dampiera juncea* (Goodeniaceae), flowers about 15 mm long; near Moora. BOTTOM LEFT, *Comesperma scoparium* (Polygalaceae), flowers about 12 mm long; near Merredin. BOTTOM RIGHT, *Tetratheca efoliata* (Tremandraceae), flowers 15 mm in diam.; south of Southern Cross.

269

FIG. 8.8. Cladode plants from Western Australia. TOP LEFT, RIGHT, *Dampiera alata* (Goodeniaceae). TOP LEFT, habit of plant, branched from near ground, ca. 0.6 m tall; Wongan Hills. TOP RIGHT, close view of stems, about 15 mm at widest. BOTTOM LEFT, *Tetratheca affinis* (Tremandraceae), flowers are pendant; north of Mt. Barker. BOTTOM RIGHT, *Platysace compressa* (Apiaceae), cladodes are thickish, about 15 mm at widest; Cape Le Grand.

(fig. 8.7, top left) and *Dampiera juncea* (fig. 8.7, top right) illustrate that this habit has been evolved independently in two genera of Goodeniaceae; a third instance is *Leschenaultia juncea. Scaevola tortuosa* is a broom shrub probably close to S. *restiacea. Comesperma scoparius* (fig. 8.7, bottom left) is interesting, because the remainder of this polygalaceous genus does not have this habit. This is also true of *Tetratheca efoliata* (fig. 8.7, bottom right), the sole broom shrub of the Tremandraceae. Other broom shrubs in the southwestern flora include *Leptomeria spinosa* and *L. pauciflora* (Santalaceae); *Exocarpus spartea* and *E. aphylla* (Santalaceae); *Choretrum* (four spp.; Santalaceae); *Psammomoya choretroides* (Celastraceae); *Boronia juncea* and *B. defoliata* (Rutaceae); *Logania nuda* (Loganiaceae); *Sphaerolobium vimineum, Jacksonia capitata,* and *Daviesia aphyllum* (fig. 8.2, bottom right) of the Fabaceae; *Stylidium junceum* and S. *squamosotuberosum* (Stylidiaceae [Carlquist, 1969]). Although monocotyledons cannot be considered shrubs, many Restiaceae and Cyperaceae could be considered to represent this adaptive mode. Other angiosperms could easily be added to the list. Although it is difficult to generalize, most often the broom shrubs in southwestern Australia tend to occupy more inland, hotter habitats than do their leafy congeners. For example, *Tetratheca efoliata* occurs inland near Southern Cross, whereas other species occur closer to the coast. Another potential value of the adaptation is that the habit permits plants to limit transpiration greatly, so that flowering can occur later in the season. Another possibility is that the plant does not die to ground level as soon. Renewal buds of most of the broom shrubs mentioned occur at or below ground level. In addition to reduction of transpirational surface, broom shrubs tend to be very fibrous in structure and thereby may excel at herbivore resistance; lack of leaves would definitely seem to contribute to lack of visible appeal for herbivores. The proportion of plants with broom-type construction seems higher in southwestern Australia than elsewhere in the world, although comparable figures are not available.

CLADODE SHRUBS

Certainly southwestern Australia exceeds other areas in the proportion or total number of angiosperms in which flattened stems, usually with vestigial leaves, form the vegetative system of the plant. These occur, for example, in *Dampiera alata* (fig. 8.8, top left, right). Interestingly, three other *Dampiera* species may have acquired this habit independently: *D. trigona* var. *latealata*, *D. lindleyi*, and *D. epiphylloidea*. *Tetratheca affinis* (fig. 8.8, bottom left) is the sole species of its family (Tremandraceae) to have acquired the cladode habit. One would not expect a member of Apiaceae to form cladodes, but *Platysace compressa* (fig. 8.8, bottom right) clearly does. Although one might not term this perennial a shrub because it is not woody, it has all the appearances of a shrub, forming tangled mounds, as on the granitic domes of Cape Le Grand. The cladodes of *P. compressa* are quite succulent and resist drying. Legumes (Fabaceae) seem particularly subject to cladode formation, as shown by figures 8.3, bottom left and right, and 8.9. Different modes of cladode formation can be seen. *Sphaerolobium alatum* (fig. 8.9, top left) has thick, woody, glaucous cladodes, broadly elliptical in transection. *Bossiaea walkeri* (fig. 8.9, top right) has thin wings, especially in internodal regions, along the length of the upright stems. Cladodes of *Acacia glaucoptera* (fig. 8.9, bottom left) are very broad and leaflike; the marginal teeth may represent participation of phyllode vestiges in the cladode. Cladodes of *Jacksonia eremodendron* (fig. 8.9, bottom right) resemble prickly leaves very closely and could easily be mistaken for leaves, except for their position axillary to leaf vestiges and the fact that flowers are borne along margins of the cladodes. Other legumes from southwestern Australia that form cladodes include additional species of *Jacksonia* (*J. alata*, *J. compressa*, *J. pteroclada*, *J. carduacea*, *J. decumbens*, *J. floribunda*), two species of *Templetonia* (*T. sulcata*, *T. egena*), and several legumes illustrated earlier: *Brachysema aphyllum* (fig. 8.3, bottom right), *B. tomentosum* (fig. 8.5, bottom left, right), and *Daviesia epiphylla* (fig. 8.3, bottom left). *Acacia* is the legume genus of southwestern Australia with the largest number of cladode-forming species, however—*Acacia alata*, *A. diptera*, *A. ataxiphylla*, *A. trigonophylla*, and *A. stenoptera*, for example. A monocotyledon, *Anarthria scabra* (Restiaceae), can qualify as a cladode-former because it has flattened inflorescence axes.

The significance of cladode species is not easy to assess, for they are by no means sympatric. However, if we compare the ranges of cladode species to those of, say, broom shrubs or thorn shrubs, we find cladode species more nearly coastal or mesic in habitat preference. This is clear in *Acacia glaucoptera*, *Tetratheca affinis*, *Sphaerolobium alatum*, *Daviesia epiphylla*, and *Platysace compressa*. More nearly coastal preference seems

FIG. 8.9. Cladode-forming species of Fabaceae from Western Australia. TOP LEFT, *Sphaerolo-bium alatum*, stems about 1 cm wide; Mt. Barker. TOP RIGHT, *Bossiaea walkeri*, glaucous flat-tish branches about 1 cm wide; north of Norseman. BOTTOM LEFT, *Acacia glaucoptera*, flat-tened stems incorporating leaf bases, typically 5 cm at widest; west of Esperance. BOTTOM RIGHT, *Jacksonia eremodendron*, prickly leaflike cladodes about 4 cm wide; Badgingarra.

FIG. 8.10. Thorn shrubs from Western Australia. TOP LEFT, RIGHT, *Comesperma spinosum* (Polygalaceae). TOP LEFT, habit, about 0.5 m tall; Ghooli. TOP RIGHT, view of twigs and flowers, which are 7 mm long. BOTTOM LEFT, *Scaevola oxyclona* (Goodeniaceae), showing tanged twigs; bud of flower is 8 mm long; Spargoville. BOTTOM RIGHT, *S. spinescens*, twigs, showing succulent leaves; twigs terminate in spines, not abundantly shown here; leaves about 1.5 cm long; north of Morawa.

evident in the cladode-forming species of *Dampiera*. There are exceptions: *Bossiaea walkeri* is an inland species, but its thick, glaucous cladodes make it resemble a woody succulent. In general, I am tempted to say that clad- odes can only be expansions of stems from ancestors with broomlike or microphyllous habits. Cladode species might represent invasions of more mesic areas, therefore. Comparisons with closely related species in respec- tive genera would be very informative. Cladodes appear to have greater duration—even for more than a single year, as in *Acacia glaucoptera*— and thus represent less fugacious structures than leaves. Functionally, cladodes are rather like phyllodes in isolateral structure, although presum- ably with greater longevity. Cladode formation may represent moderate increase in surface area in plants that have lost the capability of forming normal leaves or laminae. Cladodes would seem well adapted to a medi- terranean climate, where limited surface area can exist in conditions of warm temperature and low humidity, and such plants would not be killed by frosts. Virtually all of the southwestern cladode plants occur in the region noted as having fewer than 5 days of frost per year.

THORN SHRUBS

The only obvious common denominator of thorn shrubs is that branch tips are converted into thorns. There is an obvious alliance with plants in which leaves are converted into spines, or even plants with prickly leaves: the purpose of all these devices seems to be herbivore deterrence. Thorn shrubs do have reduced leaves, and are often aphyllous. If aphyllous, they differ little, physiologically, from broom shrubs; they differ in appearance in that their branches form a tangle. *Comesperma spinosum* (fig. 8.10, top left, right) is a good example of this growth form, as compared with *C. sco-parium* (fig. 8.7, bottom left). The same is true of *Scaevola oxyclona* (fig. 8.10, bottom left) as compared to *S. restiacea* (fig. 8.7, top left) or *S. tor-tuosa*. In other cases, like *S. spinescens* (fig. 8.10, bottom left), leaves are present—semisucculent, rather fugacious. Thorn shrubs in the southwest- ern Australian flora are almost too numerous to mention, but the list would include *Leptomeria exocarpoides* (Santalaceae); *Hybanthus epacroides* (Violaceae); *Grevillea inconspicua* (Proteaceae); *Prostanthera tysoni* (La-miaceae); *Plagianthus incanus* and *P. microphylla* (Malvaceae); *Blackallia connata* (Rhamnaceae); virtually all species of *Cryptandra* (Rhamnaceae);

275

Psammomoya ephedroides (Celastraceae); *Eriostemon deserti* (Rutaceae); *Leptospermum spinescens, Melaleuca thymoides* and many other Myrtaceae; and a large number of legumes, including *Acacia exocarpoides, A. nodiflora, A. congesta, A. cuneata, Bossiaea preissii, B. concinna, B. peduncularis, B. leptacantha, B. rufa, Jacksonia foliosa* (and other *Jacksonia* species), *Mirbelia spinosa* and other *Mirbelia* species. Thorn shrubs in southwestern Australia do connote xeromorphy, not only because of aphylly or microphylly, but also because they suggest greater herbivore retardation, as would be expected in drier localities where herbivore pressure on limited available vegetation would be expected to be greatest. In fact, the thorn shrubs listed above do, as a whole, tend to occupy sites farther inland than do their equivalents in broad-leaved and cladode-forming habits.

TWINING PLANTS

Twining or scandent plants in southwestern Australia are surprising because they belong to genera and even families in which the twining habit is unknown in representatives outside of this area. To be sure, vining representatives are to be expected in many groups; *Kennedya* and *Hardenbergia* of the Fabaceae, for example. Likewise, *Cassytha* (Lauraceae) is a genus of twining parasites; the presence of a large number of species (eight) in the southwest is noteworthy, however. A genus such as *Comesperma* (Polygalaceae), already cited as containing a thorn shrub and a broom shrub, might not be expected to include a vining species, but it does, *C. volubile* (fig. 8.11, top left). Pittosporaceae is certainly not a family of scandent plants, but twining representatives include *Marianthus erubescens* (fig. 8.11, top right) and most other species of *Marianthus; Sollya fusiformis; Cheiranthera filifolia* and *C. parviflora; Pronaya elegans;* and several species of *Billardiera. Drosera* would not be expected to be a scandent genus from its behavior elsewhere in the world, but the vining species (approximately 10 of them) are, in fact, the most conspicuous Droseras (fig. 8.11, bottom left) in southwestern Australia. One would not expect vining species in a genus commonly regarded as consisting of trees and shrubs, *Acacia*, but two such species occur in the southwest (*A. volubilis, A. inops*). *Stylidium laciniatum*, a narrow endemic of the Frankland River area, is habitally unique in its family. In *S. laciniatum*, inflorescence axes are markedly elongate, as in the closely related *S. junceum*; however, they twine

FIG. 8.11. Twining plants from Western Australia. TOP LEFT, *Comesperma volubile* (Polygalaceae), twining stems; tip portion with inflorescence shown, flowers about 1 cm long; Denbarker Rd., between Denmark and Mt. Barker. TOP RIGHT, *Marianthus erubescens* (Pitto-

(*continued*)

upward on restiads or shrubs, and flower upon reaching the top of the forest understory. *Utricularia volubilis*, from wet flats near the coast from Perth to Albany, is also unique in its family (Lentibulariaceae) in its twining inflorescences, which reach 90 cm in length and climb on stems of aquatic monocotyledons (Erickson, 1968). It grows in deep water and has polymorphism in its insect traps, depending on how deeply they are immersed beneath the water surface.

   Thysanotus (Liliaceae) has various habits; most species are typical tufted plants, with bulbs or fibrous roots and upright scapes. In *T. patersonii* (fig. 8.11, bottom right), however, the stems are twining, leafy, and of almost indefinite extent, often forming masses on shrubs. Several restiads have spiral or twining stems; *Calorhaphus gracillima*, *Leptocarpus tenax*, and *Loxocarya flexuosa*, for example. These may not be true climbing plants, but may rather exhibit "three-dimensionalization" of the vegetative form for other reasons discussed below under Leaf Morphology. Among orchids, *Thelymitra flexuosa* has twisted stems, and *T. spiralis* has leaves with a helical form.

LEAF MORPHOLOGY

   That plants of the southwest should exhibit a variety of leaf types is not surprising. The features of interest are that (1) such widely divergent leaf types occur within single genera, and evidently most of them represent autochthonous developments; (2) some of these leaf types are unique, not found elsewhere; (3) with all genera compared, there is such a high degree of parallelism in types, or "convergent evolution"; and (4) there is apparently easy reversibility in morphology, and leaf morphology, a rapidly evolving feature, can exhibit sensitive adaptation for a particular habitat, although it may in some cases lag behind physiological adaptation, and various leaf types are equally successful in a given locality. Some bizarre types may have a generalized adaptive value, but their form in detail cannot be explained in adaptive terms of a single factor or a few factors, and probably must involve the nature of the leaf type ancestral to that of a

FIG. 8.11 (*continued*)
sporaceae), twining stems and flowers, which are about 5 cm long; Miling–Pithara road. BOTTOM LEFT, *Drosera heteromera* (Droseraceae), tip of twining stem with flower 2 cm in diam.; near Toodyay. BOTTOM RIGHT, *Thysanotus patersonii* (Liliaceae), flowers 2 cm in diam. and twining stems; near Perenjori.

FIG. 8.12. Plants illustrating evolution of particular leaf types in Western Australia. TOP LEFT, *Chorilaena quercifolia* (Rutaceae), head of flowers and lobate leaves 5 cm long, covered by stellate hairs. TOP RIGHT, *Dampiera hederacea* (Goodeniaceae), showing lobate leaves 4 cm long, covered by stellate hairs; near Pemberton. BOTTOM LEFT, *Scaevola crassifolia* (Goodeniaceae), broad leaves with glutinous surfaces, typically 5–6 cm long; beach at Mandurah. BOTTOM RIGHT, *Dampiera teres* (Goodeniaceae), leaves terete or slightly flattened, 2 cm long; Dandaragan.

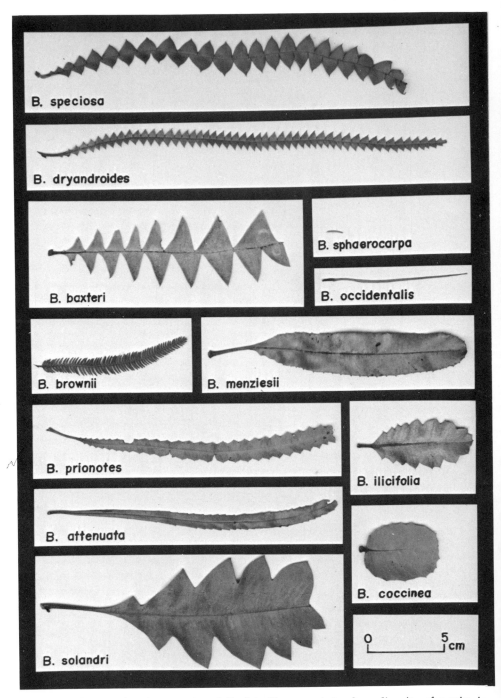

B. speciosa

B. dryandroides

B. baxteri

B. sphaerocarpa

B. occidentalis

B. brownii

B. menziesii

B. prionotes

B. ilicifolia

B. attenuata

B. coccinea

B. solandri

0   5
|___|___| cm

FIG. 8.13. Leaves of various species of *Banksia* (Proteaceae) to show diversity of species in southwestern Australia. Further explanation, describing ecological correlations of these species, is in the text.

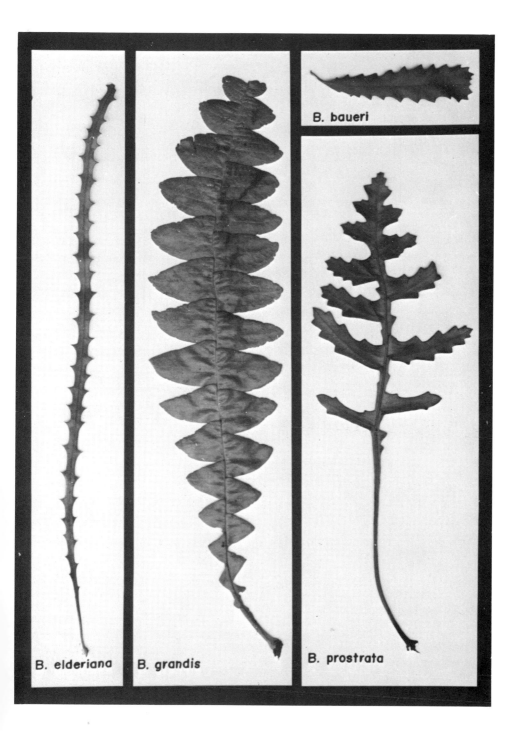

B. baueri

B. elderiana

B. grandis

B. prostrata

contemporary species. For example, one can offer correlations between ecology and leaf morphology in *Banksia* (fig. 8.13). But one cannot present precise, detailed correlations. *Banksia coccinea* has leaves different from those of *B. baxteri,* but the two can grow together, as at Hopetoun (however, one may note a similar area and thickness of leaf despite difference in form).

Banksia (fig. 8.13) and *Hakea* (fig. 8.14) are presented here as examples of the wide gamut to be found within particular genera—although even for these genera, the figures by no means include all the southwestern species. In other photographs stressing leaf morphology (figs. 8.12, 8.15–8.20), an attempt has been made to compare similar features shown by unrelated genera. We can note briefly the parallelisms in terete and hollylike leaves cited by Went (1971), but each of these categories itself contains great diversity and is not mutually exclusive but intercontinuous with other types, and can, contrary to Went's claim, easily be explained by ordinary selective factors. We do not need hypotheses of "floating genes" or "orthogenesis" at all. Such hypotheses tend to thrive best when examples are selected incompletely or in a preconceived manner.

Broad Leaves. Broad, lobate leaves are relatively infrequent in the southwestern flora as a whole. Such leaves, which often have stellate pubescence, are surprisingly characteristic of the southwesternmost forests, particularly the karri (*Eucalyptus diversicolor*) forests. *Dampiera hederacea* (fig. 8.12, top right) of the Goodeniaceae and *Chorilaena quercifolia* (fig. 8.12, top left) of the Rutaceae are typical of this mode. Other "oak-leaved" species of these forests include *Dampiera phlebopetala* and *D. striata;* in Sterculiaceae, *Lasiopetalum floribundum, Rulingia grandiflora, Thomasia quercifolia,* and *T. solanacea.* The endemic genus *Tremandra* (Tremandraceae) is a good example of this syndrome. Not surprisingly, the species of *Banksia* with the most oaklike leaves, *B. solandri* and *B. coccinea* (fig. 8.13), are characteristic of moist forests in and near the Stirling Range. *Banksia grandis* and *B. prostrata* (fig. 8.13), with the greatest leaf surface of any *Banksia* species, occur on moister coastal plain. The largest-leaved species of *Scaevola* in southwestern Australia, *S. crassifolia* (fig. 8.12, bottom right), *S. nitida,* and *S. porocarya,* are all coastal species. Coastal and moister sites are the habitats occupied by *Hakea* species with the broadest leaves: *H. conchifolia* (fig. 8.15, top left), *H. cucullata* (fig. 8.15, top right), and *H. victoriae* (fig. 8.15, bottom left), as well as *H. amplexicaulis, H. roei, H. smilacifolia, H. elliptica, H. undulata, H. auriculata, H. ferruginea, H. hookeriana, H. baxteri,* and *H. flabellifolia* (fig. 8.14). Some narrower-leaved species of *Hakea* can also be found in these habitats, but the broadest-leaved species are never in drier, inland localities.

Hakea trifurcata (fig. 8.14) provides an interesting problem because it produces not only trifurcate leaves with terete leaves, but also a limited number of broad elliptical leaves, with only a few intermediate types. The broader leaves seem to be formed during moister portions of the year, not during the drier portion of the growing season.

Isolateral Leaves. As Diels (1906) notes, isolateral leaf construction is extraordinarily common in southwestern Australia. *Acacia* and *Eucalyptus* contain many examples of this form, both in the southwest and in other parts of Australia. Of course, needle-shaped leaves, or leaves with terete segments, are by definition isolateral. Isolateral leaves occur scattered through genera in which bifacial leaves predominate; *Dampiera teres* (fig. 8.12, bottom right), for example, is an isolateral-leaved species. Examples of isolateral leaves (acicular and otherwise) have been cited in *Daviesia* and are obvious in the illustrations of *Hakea* (fig. 8.14). Broom shrubs are stem equivalents of isolateral leaves. Abundance of isolateral leaves in various genera of Australia is related to mediterranean climate: exposure of minimal leaf surface with maximal photosynthetic layers; isolateral leaves are, with few exceptions, displayed at various angles other than more-or-less horizontal.

With respect to isolateral-leaved species that occur in genera with other laminar types, I have repeatedly had the impression that some of these broader leaves have been derived phylogenetically from narrower-leaved ancestors. If we suppose that acicular or linear leaves are ancestral in certain southwestern Australian groups, broader leaves would represent evolution toward mesomorphy. I have gained this impression where leaf venation is markedly different from the venation typical for dicotyledons (a central midvein, with pinnate arrangement of lateral veins and reticulate areoles). This "typical" condition is found in *Hakea amplexicaulis, H. roei,* and *H. auriculata* (fig. 8.14). Yet how can we explain the longitudinally oriented veins characteristic of leaves in the well-named *H. multilineata* (fig. 8.14), or the broader-leaved species *H. elliptica, H. undulata,*

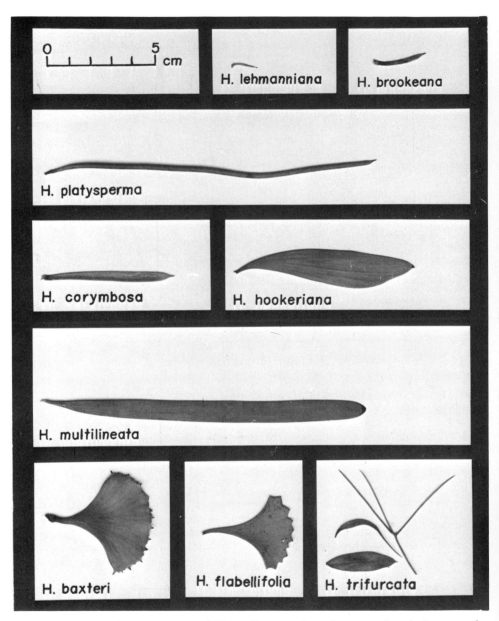

FIG. 8.14. Leaves of various species of *Hakea* (Proteaceae) to show several evolutionary tendencies in this genus in southwestern Australia. Comments on the ecological correlation and morphological significance of these various types are in the text.

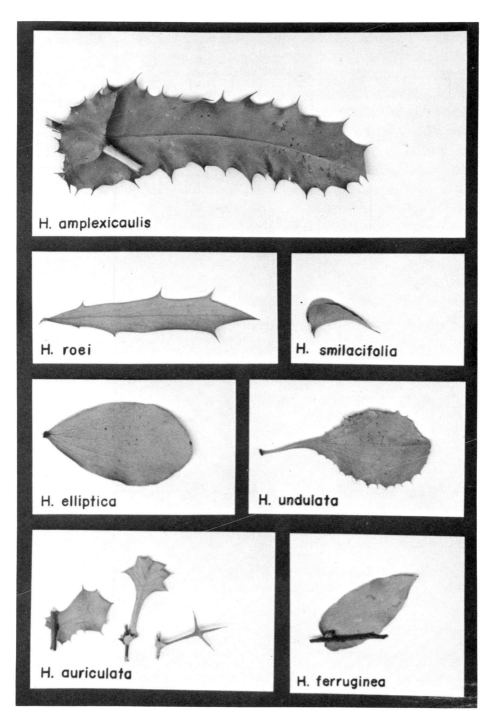

H. amplexicaulis

H. roei

H. smilacifolia

H. elliptica

H. undulata

H. auriculata

H. ferruginea

285

and *H. ferruginea* (fig. 8.14), in which transverse veins are frequent but several main "parallel" veins are predominant? Likewise, how can one explain leaves with flabellate venation, such as *H. baxteri* and *H. flabellifolia* (fig. 8.14)? Parallel-veined leaves of some *Hakea* species, including *H. hookeriana* (fig. 8.14), *H. laurina*, and *H. pandanicarpa*, are remarkably reminiscent of phyllodes of *Acacia*, both in form and in anatomy (isolateral structure, etc.). I feel there is a distinct possibility that certain broader leaves in *Hakea* may represent expansion from acicular or linear leaves, and may be an accompaniment of ecological shift into moister regions, which form a relatively small area in Western Australia. If so, such broader leaves are much like phyllodes and could perhaps be called "pseudophyllodes." If my interpretation is correct, they would not be true phyllodes, as in *Acacia*, in which the leaf surface results from phylogenetic expansion of petioles. Some Myrtaceae (e.g., broader-leaved species of *Callistemon* and *Melaleuca*: *M. globifera*, *M. megacephala*) may exemplify pseudophyllodes. In the parallel-veined and flabelliform leaves cited, expansion of a midrib of an acicular or linear leaf would contribute the majority of the flattened surface, not merely the petiole (which may not be involved at all). I suggested this interpretation earlier for broader-leaved species of *Stylidium* such as *S. maitlandianum*, *S. rigidifolium*, and *S. amoenum* (Carlquist, 1969), which have flabellate venation.

Another odd venation type that may be the result of expansion of linear leaves includes leaves which form perfect or nearly perfect dichotomous branching systems, each branch a linear segment of the leaf. The genera *Stirlingia* (fig. 8.17, bottom right) and especially *Franklandia* of the Proteaceae exhibit such dichotomous leaves in a striking fashion. This tendency, which seems virtually endemic to southwestern Australia, is also represented in *Corynotheca micrantha* and *Thysanotus dichotomus* of the Liliaceae, as well as in such Proteaceae as *Isopogon divergens*, *I. laticornis*, *I. villosus*, *Petrophila conifera*, *P. divaricata*, *P. semifurcata*, and *Adenanthos cunninghamii*. A broader scope is introduced by consideration of a family widespread in Australia, Epacridaceae. This family has an amazingly stereotyped parallel venation, and seems derived from, or very close to, Ericaceae. Ericaceae have unilacunar nodes, and it is believed (I. W. Bailey, personal communication, 1955) that Epacridaceae represent expansion from unilacunar ancestry to a multilacunar condition. The broader

FIG. 8.15. Leaves of other species of *Hakea* (Proteaceae) from southwestern Australia: because of their three-dimensional shapes, these species are shown photographically and supplement

(continued)

leaf form of Epacridaceae would represent an external manifestation of this expansion. At any rate, the question of pseudophyllodes and other possibly expanded leaf types in the floras of southwestern Australia and other parts of Australia is one that needs examination by developmental and comparative techniques.

There is an additional category of probable surface expansion. *Acacia urophylla*, an understory element of the wet karri forests in southwestern-most Australia, appears to have unusually broad phyllodes, probably derived from an ancestor with narrower phyllodes, and the nature of phyllode venation in this species suggests exceptional expansion of the phyllode as an accompaniment to ecological shift into unusually wet (for Western Australia) forests. The examples given show the factors of reversibility and independent origins of similar-appearing leaf types. More importantly, they illustrate the great plasticity of angiosperms (a plasticity which appears, in many cases, to exceed that of the conceptualizations of botanists who study them).

Smaller Leaves. That narrower leaves are correlated with xeromorphy is almost axiomatic. The instances of leaf restriction in the Western Australian flora are simply too numerous to cite adequately. Some of these, at least, appear to be secondary restrictions phylogenetically of once-broader leaf surfaces. One such phenomenon is inrolling of margins to the abaxial surface (ericoid leaves). *Tetratheca* species, particularly *T. conferti-folia* (fig. 8.16, top right) as compared to *T. setigera* (fig. 8.16, top left), show this. In *Banksia*, *B. occidentalis*, *B. sphaerocarpa* (fig. 8.13) and other species show these tendencies clearly. Many examples of ericoid leaves from such families as Lamiaceae and Verbenaceae can be cited in the southwest. Southwestern Rutaceae (*Phebalium*, *Eriostemon*, *Philotheca*, *Boronia ericifolia* and other species of *Boronia*) are excellent examples, as are all the species of *Frankenia* (Frankeniaceae) and a number of species of *Hibbertia* (Dilleniaceae). Casual perusal of the southwestern flora could add many species to the list, particularly from such families as Myrtaceae.

FIG. 8.15 (*continued*)
those of fig. 8.14. TOP LEFT, *H. conchifolia*, fruit can be seen within tapered, hoodlike leaf; leaf about 6 cm long; near Eneabba. TOP RIGHT, *H. cucullata*, cuplike leaves about 8 cm in diam., capitate inflorescence within each; between Porongorups and Stirlings. BOTTOM LEFT, *H. victoriae*, prickly leaves, about 12 cm long, which conceal axillary flowers; East Mt. Barren. BOTTOM RIGHT, *H. clavata*, tip of twig showing fruit and leaves, which are 2 cm wide and so succulent they are nearly terete; granite headlands of Cape Le Grand.

That acicular leaves have evolved in numerous groups in Western Australia seems very likely. This form is the ultimate in condensation, and ericoid leaves may be an intermediate step. The genus *Platytheca* (Tremandraceae) can hardly have any other explanation, considering the remainder of this family, its characteristics and distribution. Acicular leaves are common in *Hakea* (see fig. 8.14) *Calothamnus* (figs. 8.19, top left, right; 8.33, bottom right), *Petrophila* (fig. 8.18, bottom right), *Darwinia* (figs. 8.22, top right, bottom right; 8.23), *Acacia*, and many other genera. The hypothesis proposed earlier, that pseudophyllodes have resulted from expansion of acicular leaves, in no way contradicts evolution of acicular-leaved plants from broader-leaved ancestors. One would indeed expect the latter tendency to occur more often, in view of the broad dry areas of Western Australia, and conversion of narrower leaves into broader forms to be a relatively infrequent phenomenon characteristic of entry into the limited wet-forest and moist coastal areas of southwestern Australia.

Another way in which leaf surface is reduced is so obvious as to be perhaps overlooked: mere microphylly, without special change in form. *Comesperma drummondii* (fig. 8.16, bottom left, right), with small glaucous leaves appressed to stems, is an example. However, there are more numerous instances in such families as Myrtaceae, where *Lhotzkya, Wehlia, Micromyrtus, Thryptomene, Baeckia, Sholtzia,* and *Balaustion* serve as definitive examples.

Succulence. By contrast, succulence is a rather rare phenomenon in Western Australia, rarer than one would expect. It is not unusual in halophytes (*Calandrinia* spp., *Carprobrotus* spp., *Arthrocnema* spp., *Scaevola spinescens*), but few nonhalophytes have evolved succulence. One notable exception is *Hakea clavata* (fig. 8.15, bottom right), in which large, fibrous, obviously succulent leaves that dry with extreme slowness have evolved autochthonously in southwestern Australia. Although a few other examples of succulence could be cited, the interesting phenomenon is that succulence, where present in nonhalophytes, often occurs in underground structures, such as bulbs, tubers, or corms. These are discussed later under mechanisms that tend to represent resistance to fire as well as to desiccation. Minimal succulence in the southwestern flora may also be related to herbivore pressure, for succulent plants would tend to be vulnerable to

FIG. 8.16. Plants illustrating evolution of particular leaf types in southwestern Australia. TOP LEFT, *Tetratheca setigera* (Tremandraceae), leaves sparse, relatively narrow, about 2 cm long; near Pinjarra. TOP RIGHT, *Tetratheca confertifolia*, leaves narrow, "ericoid," ca. 12 mm long; near Mogumber. BOTTOM LEFT, RIGHT, *Comesperma drummondii* (Polygalaceae). BOTTOM LEFT, habit of plant, showing sparse branching; Ghooli. BOTTOM RIGHT, branch showing leaves, which are glaucous, about 15 mm long.

herbivores—which presumably might avoid the excessively salty leaves of halophytes.

THREE-DIMENSIONALIZATION

There seems no existing term to cover a number of angiosperm plant forms, several of which are unique to southwestern Australia. Only field experience can make the concept of "three-dimensionalization" real, for herbarium specimens and even photographs do not unequivocally illustrate the tendency of so many southwestern plants to arrange typically flat or terete structures—especially (but by no means exclusively) spiny, thorny, or prickly portions—in such a way as to deter intrusion into the center of a plant. Some of these phenomena are obvious, some subtle. They seem, however, to be best interpreted as herbivore-deterrents. We are all familiar with the way in which cactus spines radiate from glochids, so that an herbivore would suffer puncture no matter what the angle of approach. The same—plus other qualities—is true of three-dimensionalization of southwestern plants.

Radiating Armament. A simple type of three-dimensionalization is created by leaves with margins the spiny teeth of which point upward and downward with reference to the plane of the lamina. Leaves with such spiny teeth could be termed "hollylike" except that they exceed spiny-leaved holly forms in the degree to which teeth are divergent in their positioning. Even a single leaf may radiate spiny teeth at various angles. This is illustrated by *Synaphaea decorticans* (fig. 8.17, bottom left) of the Proteaceae. Most other species of *Synaphaea* have this habit, as do many other Proteaceae: *Hakea amplexicaulis, H. undulata, H. auriculata,* and, to a lesser degree, *H. baxteri* and *H. flabellifolia* (fig. 8.14) are examples. In an obvious although different way, *H. victoriae* (fig. 8.15, bottom left) and *H. conchifolia* (fig. 8.15, top left) show this phenomenon. The great toughness—almost like thin sheet metal—of proteaceous leaves tends to reinforce the effectiveness of the spines or prickles, giving them a stronger positioning than a flexible leaf would allow. Thus, the tough leaves of *Banksia* (fig. 8.13) are effective out of proportion to their seemingly moderate teeth. Other Proteaceae in which toothed leaf margins form excellent armor include *Dryandra horrida* (and, for that matter, virtually the entire genus *Dryandra*), *Grevillea acrobotrys, G. amplexicans, G. apiciloba, G.*

291

FIG. 8.17. Leaves of Proteaceae to show tendencies in "three-dimensionalization" in the flora of southwestern Australia. TOP LEFT, *Grevillea patentiloba*, leaves about 3 cm long, terete segments spreading divaricately. TOP RIGHT, *Hakea varia*, twig showing flattened leaves, about 2.5 cm long, which are prickly and project at various angles from twigs. BOTTOM LEFT, *Synaphaea decorticans*, prickly-lobed leaves project at various angles. BOTTOM RIGHT, *Stirlingia tenuifolia*, leaf (shown sideways) with dichotomous branching of the terete segments; leaf about 7 cm long.

astericosa, *G. bipinnatifida*, *G. cirsiifolia*, *G. flexuosa*, *G. glabrata*, *G. ma-crostylis*, *G. muelleri*, *G. phanerophlebia*, *G. platypoda*, *G. pulchella*, *G. rudis*, *G. synapheae*, *G. trifida*, *G. triloba*, *Hakea ceratophylla*, *H. cristata*, *H. dolichostyla*, *H. glabella*, *H. pritzelii*, *Isopogon alcicornis*, *I. baxteri*, *I. roseus*, *I. tridens*, *Lambertia echinata*, *Petrophila biternata*, *P. diversifolia*, *P. macrostachya*, *P. trifida*, and *Xylomelum occidentale*. Examples from other families are too numerous to cite; *Hovea chorizemifolia*, and various species of *Daviesia* and *Chorizema* are among many such Fabaceae.

A heightened form of this armor is achieved when leaf segments are linear and project at various angles. Examples shown here include *Grevillea patentiloba* (fig. 8.17, top left) and *Hakea varia* (fig. 8.17, top right). Other species of these genera with remarkably divaricating, linear, spine-tipped leaf segments include *Adenanthos meissneri*, *A. pungens*, *Grevillea annulifera*, *G. armigera*, *G. asparagoides*, *G. brevicuspis*, *G. intricata*, *G. leptobotrya*, *G. paniculata*, *G. paradoxa*, *G. stenostachya*, *G. tenuiloba*, *G. teretifolia*, *G. thelemanniana*, *G. tridentata*, *G. tripartita*, *G. wilsoni*, *Hakea erinacea*, *H. purpurea*, *Isopogon divergens*, *I. formosus*, *I. teretifolia*, *Petrophila drummondii*, and *Synaphaea petiolaris*, all of Proteaceae. Representatives of other families include *Gompholobium baxteri* and *Jacksonia furcellata* (Fabaceae).

The simplest and most obvious form of radiating armament is display of linear, terete, spine-tipped leaves in such a way that they, like cactus spines, radiate in all directions from a stem. Examples are too numerous to mention fully, but include many species of *Hakea*, such as *H. lehmanniana*, *H. brookeana*, *H. platysperma* (fig. 8.14), and *Grevillea*, *Acacia*, *Daviesia* (figs. 8.1, bottom left, right; 8.2, top left, right), *Melaleuca*, *Calythrix*, *Calothamnus*, *Bassia*, and *Stylidium*.

Spiralization. A remarkable feature, rarely encountered in other floras except as an anomaly, but of almost common occurrence in southwestern Australia, is the presence of spirally (helically) twisted leaves. *Hakea stenoptera* (fig. 8.18, top left) has decidedly curved lanceolate leaves. *Persoonia tortifolia* (fig. 8.18, top right) has corkscrewlike lanceolate leaves. And *Petrophila linearis* (fig. 8.18, bottom left) has curved lanceolate leaves. In *P. stricta* (fig. 8.18, bottom right), leaves are terete, curved, and spine-tipped. Another protead with this leaf habit is *Conospermum incurvum*. Similar leaves occur in *Acacia viscifolia*, *A. triptycha* var. *subflexuosa*, and *A. merinthifolia.* Helical leaves have been mentioned in the orchid *Thelymitra spiralis.* In Epacridaceae, curved and often markedly helical leaves occur in *Sphenotoma gracile* and many of the 22 currently recognized species of *Andersonia,* such as *A. grandiflora, A. involucrata,* and *A. echinocephala.*

Spiralized stems in broom shrubs have a similar net effect, and in this category one can cite *Dampiera curvula, Scaevola tortuosa,* and *Tetratheca efoliata* (fig. 8.7, bottom right). Among monocotyledons, one notes this habit in several restiads: *Restio megalotheca, Loxocarya flexuosa,* and *Caloraphus gracillima,* for example.

The tendency toward dichotomously branched leaves, mentioned earlier, is clearly a form of three-dimensionalization. *Stirlingia* and *Franklandia* are so marked in this respect that individual leaves resemble aerial axes of *Psilotum* (especially in *F. fucosa*).

The explanation for the various forms of three-dimensionalization is not clear. However, the most likely explanation consistent with tendencies in the remainder of the flora is that this phenomenon, like the tangled branches of thorn shrubs, forms a sort of deterrent to herbivores. The number of instances, in each of the categories, is too large to be explained by chance, and the phenomenon offers an interesting opportunity for further evolutionary speculation and investigation.

SHORT SHOOTS AND LONG SHOOTS

Presence of both long shoots and short shoots on a plant, known as heteroblasty, is not rare in dicotyledons at large, but it has been evolved autochthonously in several genera of the southwestern flora. It is strikingly represented by *Calothamnus pinifolius* (fig. 8.19, top left, right). The long shoots in this species are few and branched, but almost every axil on the long shoots bears a short shoot. Heteroblasty is strongly marked in *Plagianthus helmsii* (fig. 8.19, bottom left, right). This cactoid-appearing malvaceous plant has been segregated as a separate genus, *Selenothamnus.* Considering the wide divergences in habit within various Australian genera, *P. helmsii* is not completely incongruous when compared with other species of *Plagianthus,* although it is distinctive. In *P. helmsii,* long shoots are few and are densely covered with short shoots of almost determinate length. The explanation for heteroblasty in these plants probably does not

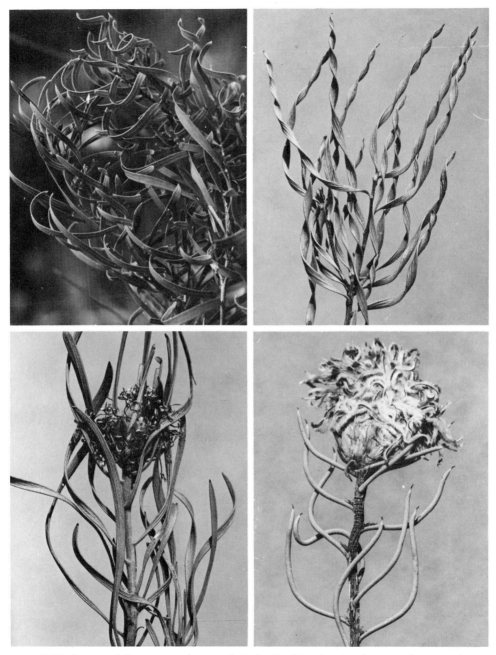

FIG. 8.18. Leaves of Proteaceae, showing "spiralization" tendencies, from southwestern Australia. TOP LEFT, *Hakea stenoptera*, leaves 7 cm long, curved into one or more spirals. TOP RIGHT, *Persoonia tortifolia*, leaves ca. 5 cm long, twisted into numerous gyres. BOTTOM LEFT, *Petrophila linearis*, showing flattened leaves curved into about one spiral each. BOTTOM RIGHT, *Petrophila stricta*, spiral-tending leaves, terete and tipped by a spine.

FIG. 8.19. Plants of Western Australia with marked dimorphism into long and short shoots. TOP LEFT, RIGHT, *Calothamnus pinifolius* (Myrtaceae). TOP LEFT, habit of plant, 2 m tall; south of Ravensthorpe. TOP RIGHT, branch showing short shoots bearing needlelike leaves (lower portion; flowers above), leaves about 4 cm long. BOTTOM LEFT, RIGHT, *Plagianthus* ("*Selenothamnus*") *helmsii* (Malvaceae). BOTTOM LEFT, habit of plant—this plant 0.5 m tall, mature plants reach 3 m. BOTTOM RIGHT, surfaces of two branches, showing flowers (one branch male, one female) at tips of short shoots that cover these branches.

have to do with herbivore deterrence as much as with climatic regime, since similar heteroblasty occurs in plants of southern California (e.g., *Artemisia californica, Eriogonum fasciculatum, Adenostoma fasciculatum*), in which growth of short shoots can take place when moderate rainfalls permit, but long shoots are formed after winter rains, with increased temperature. Condensation of form in plants with heteroblasty, such as *P. helmsii*, may bear some relationship to xeromorphy.

WOOLLY VESTURE

Conspicuous in many southwestern genera—including some where one would not expect it—is an exceptional degree of covering by dense, and usually white, nonglandular trichomes. Notably, not merely stems and leaves, but also inflorescences and flowers can be strongly hairy. *Ptilotus (Trichinium) rotundifolius* (fig. 8.20, top left) of the Amaranthaceae has wool on the inner side of the perianth segments, as do other species of this genus; leaves are closely and densely woolly. Likewise, *Dampiera luteiflora* (fig. 8.20, top right) of the Goodeniaceae has leaves and stems covered with a very dense tomentum, and even calyces are densely clad. Other species of *Dampiera* are also notably hairy, some with slate gray wool on leaves, corolla, and calyx. Other Goodeniaceae of the southwest, such as *Verreauxia reinwardtii*, share these characteristics. Verbenaceae as a whole are often densely hairy in southwestern Australia. Examples shown here include *Lachnostachys ferrugineus* (fig. 8.20, bottom left), *L. albicans* (fig. 8.24, top right), and *Pityrodia oldfieldii* (fig. 8.20, bottom right). Calyces as well as leaves and stems commonly are densely woolly in these genera. In *Hemiphora elderi*, a monotypic genus of the southwestern Verbenaceae, herbage is white-woolly, but calyces and corollas are densely red-woolly. Other genera in which hairiness of southwestern species seems exceptional include *Thomasia* and *Lasiopetalum* of the Sterculiaceae (see *Lasiopetalum drummondii*, fig. 8.24, top right), *Hemigenia* (Lamiaceae), *Kochia* (Amaranthaceae), *Bonamia* (Solanaceae), *Rulingia* (Malvaceae), *Actinotus* and *Xanthosia* (Apiaceae), *Conospermum* (Proteaceae), and *Diplolaena* (fig. 8.21, top left) of the Rutaceae. The hairiness of vegetative portions of all of these seems exceptional, but one notes much more hairiness on floral portions than one would expect. Flowers of *Anigozanthos, Macropidia, Conostylis,* and *Blancoa* (Liliaceae *sensu lato*, sometimes Haemodoraceae)

FIG. 8.20. Tendencies toward exceptionally woolly vesture in plants of southwestern Australia. TOP LEFT, *Ptilotus rotundifolius* (Amaranthaceae), leaves 3.5 cm long, covered with short dense wool. TOP RIGHT, *Dampiera luteiflora* (Goodeniaceae), leaves and calyces woolly; Ghooli. BOTTOM LEFT, *Lachnostachys ferrugineus* (Verbenaceae), inflorescence and adjacent extremely woolly, cuplike leaves 3 cm in diam.; north of Moora. BOTTOM RIGHT, *Pityrodia oldfieldii* (Verbenaceae), portion of stem showing hairy leaves, stem surface, and calyx; north of Moora.

are quite noteworthy in this respect, and must represent autochthonous developments in southwestern Australia, because three of these genera are endemic to the province.

Several possible explanations can be suggested for the exceptional woolliness of the taxa cited. There may be ecological correlations. Many of these genera and species tend to grow in drier, sunnier localities, in which case desiccation resistance or shading from insolation might be operative. Such genera as *Ptilotus* (*Trichinium*), *Kochia,* and *Lachnosta-chys* are more markedly inland in distribution than most larger angiosperm genera in the southwestern flora. Such inland locations, moreover, are more frequently subject to frost than are coastal locations. The inland area of southwestern Australia in which frost exceeds 5 days per year on the average includes the ranges of many of the taxa cited above. This area extends roughly from Wongan Hills south to Southern Cross and east to Coolgardie.

Excessive hairiness may prove a deterrent to herbivores. In some cases, such as *Lachnostachys,* purplish colors of corollas stand out clearly against white woolly vesture and may be related to pollination. In *Hemiphora,* contrast between red wool of flowers and white wool of herbage is marked, although this circumstance does not explain why the flowers would be hairy. This is also true in *Anigozanthos, Macropidia, Blancoa,* and *Cono-stylis,* where the distinctive colors of portions of these flowers are contained in the dense hairs that cover the perianths. Obviously, there is no single or simple explanation of woolliness in angiosperms of southwestern Australia, and experimental evidence on possibilities such as the above would be very desirable.

OILS, OLEORESINS, AND OTHER CHEMICAL CONTENTS

Many plant groups well represented in the southwest contain oil-rich secretory cavities (e.g., Rutaceae and Myrtaceae) or have external coverings of resinlike or varnishlike materials; *Anthocercis* (Solanaceae), for example. In *Anthocercis,* restriction of transpiration is to be suspected (from the degree of difficulty experienced in preparing dried specimens). Internal oil deposits and strong scents from essential oils contained in glandular hairs (Lamiaceae, Verbenaceae) may deter herbivores. As yet we know nothing certain about these possibilities, but the abundance of these characteristics in the flora suggests adaptive significance.

Pollination Mechanisms

Every flora has pollination mechanisms of interest, but southwestern Australia has several exceptional modalities. Among these are the highly colorful nature of the flora and the large number of plants apparently adapted to ornithophily. Although one could simply say that the southwestern flora is exceptional in its colorfulnes, particular examples are illustrative. For example, Amaranthaceae are often colorless in perianth parts, but *Ptilotus* (*Trichinium*) often has flowers with large magenta perianths, as in *P. rotundifolius* (fig. 8.20, top left). Blue flowers are exceptionally frequent, as in *Dampiera* and *Leschenaultia*. Adaptation to particular color-sensitive pollinators is to be suspected. This certainly is true in the ornithophilous groups. Obviously a large number of genera have entered the ornithophilous mode, including *Anigozanthos* and the closely related *Macropidia*, the colorful patterns of which can only be appreciated in the field or with good color photographs. In addition to heightened color and lengthened or enlarged flower form, there are other obvious ornithophilous devices. *Calothamnus* (figs. 8.19, top right; 8.33, bottom right) has fascicles of bright red stamens arranged in a curved pattern. Increased prominence of stamens related to ornithophily can be suspected in the gigantic flowers on *Eucalyptus macrocarpa*. I have seen both *Calothamnus* and *E. macrocarpa* visited by meliphagids. The congestion of flowers into colorful heads in proteads such as *Banksia*, *Dryandra*, and some species of *Grevillea* relates to ornithophily, and I have also observed honeyeaters visiting these genera.

Congestion of flowers, coupled with development of bracts around the inflorescence (the bracts thus taking over the display function), is a feature autochthonously developed in a number of southwestern groups. *Diplolaena* (fig. 8.21, top left) of the Rutaceae exemplifies this. Most species of *Pimelea* have congestion of flowers but with green, inconspicuous bracts, as in *P. floribunda* (fig. 8.21, top right). However, *P. physodes* (fig. 8.21, bottom left, right) has long bracts that are red purple outside, cream

FIG. 8.21. Tendencies toward capitate inflorescences and showy bracts in southwestern Australian plants. TOP LEFT, *Diplolaena dampieri* (Rutaceae), one head in flower, one in fruit; heads about 6 cm in diam.; Canal Rocks. TOP RIGHT, *Pimelea floribunda* (Thymeleaceae), head of flowers, bracts greenish, conspicuous; Moora–Jurien Bay road. BOTTOM LEFT, RIGHT, *P. physodes*, head nutant, surrounded by long purplish bracts; near Ongerup. BOTTOM LEFT, heads with bracts in natural position; bracts 4–5 cm long. BOTTOM RIGHT, head in which bracts have been folded back in order to show old flowers.

white within, an obvious adaptation to ornithophily. Other instances of this phenomenon are the three species of *Johnsonia* (Liliaceae) in which the papery bracts are pink or reddish and are longer than the flowers, which are white and inconspicuous. In *Andersonia echinocephala* (Epacridaceae), bracts surrounding the congested inflorescence are white or even pinkish. This is true also in *Grevillea bracteosa* (Proteaceae).

The most outstanding example of conversion of inflorescence bracts to an attractive device suitable for bird pollination is, however, *Darwinia* (Myrtaceae). The Stirling Range species of *Darwinia* (fig. 8.23), for example, all show this habit. If we examine a series of *Darwinia* species, we can see the development within a single genus. *Darwinia diosmoides* (fig. 8.22, top left) has few-flowered, capitate inflorescences, and flowers appear scattered over the branches. The papery white petals form the attractive display apparatus of these flowers, which are probably not ornithophilous. *Darwinia sanguinea* (fig. 8.22, top right) has larger, congested inflorescences that are borne in such a way that they sprawl on the soil surface at the periphery of the plant. Bright red perianth parts form the attractive portions of the flowers. In *D. citriodora* (fig. 8.22, bottom left) both bracts and flowers are colorful organs: flowers are orange, but the head of flowers is enclosed in spreading, open bracts that are greenish at their tips but reddish orange at their bases. Heads of *D. citriodora* are borne more or less upright, at random over a shrub. In *D. leiostyla* (figs. 8.22, bottom right; 8.23), the achievement of the campanulate head is complete. Heads terminate branches and are nodding—which means, presumably, that visiting birds will perch below the heads and face upward in search of nectar. The bracts are bright red, forming an obviously attractive pseudo-perianth for the head. To be sure, flowers are red to pink, but they are not visible unless one peers into the head. The other campanulate species and semi-campanulate species of *Darwinia* offer distinct bract patterns. For example, *D. helichrysoides* and *D. hypericifolia* (fig. 8.23) have reddish bracts. Bracts of *D. macrostegia* are creamy white, veined red; in *D. collina*, bracts are lemon yellow, whereas in *D. fimbriata* (*D. squarrosa*), bracts are deep pink. *Darwinia meeboldii* has white bracts, greenish at the base, tipped crimson.

Among the Stirling species of *Darwinia*, there is a habitat difference between the valley species, *D. leiostyla*, and the remainder, which grow

FIG. 8.22. Tendencies in inflorescence formation in *Darwinia* (Myrtaceae). TOP LEFT, *D. diosmoides*, flowers in heads, scattered over branches (from a color photograph by Fred W. Humphreys, courtesy of Mrs. Evelyn Hymphreys). TOP RIGHT, *D. sanguinea*, heads of flowers borne on branches that lie on ground; Cockleshell Gully. BOTTOM LEFT, *D. citriodora*, heads of orange flowers surrounded by bracts orange at bases; Darlington. BOTTOM RIGHT, *D. leiostyla*, heads of flowers nutant, surrounded by scarlet bracts to 6 cm long; Red Gum Springs.

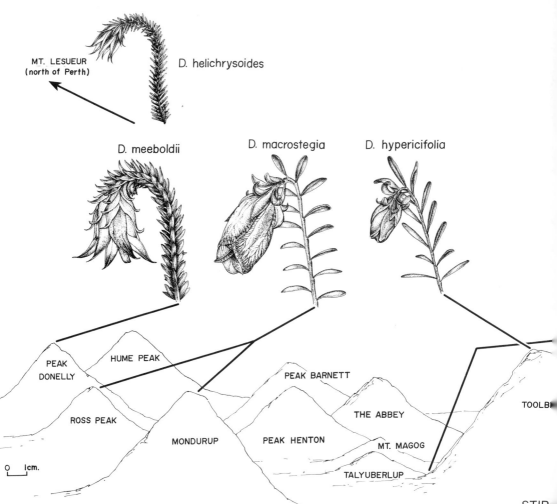

FIG. 8.23. Narrow endemism by species of *Darwinia* (Myrtaceae) on the Stirling Range of southwestern Australia. Each of these species, which have notably bracteate ornithophilous inflorescences, is endemic to the few hills and peaks indicated, and has not been found in any other areas. *Darwinia leiostyla* grows not on peak tops, but in valley areas between peaks. A

at the summits of the peaks. Distinctive size, color, pattern, shape, and texture of the heads may provide isolating mechanisms among the Stirling Darwinias. Peak-to-peak isolation may account for their narrow endemism, although the distances involved are so small that the situation of the Stirling Darwinias is notable and difficult to explain with certainty. Non-Stirling Darwinias, such as *D. helichrysoides*, may also represent such

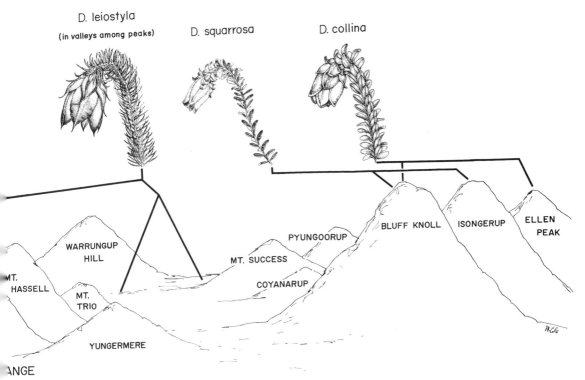

non-Stirling species, endemic to Mt. Lesueur, is also shown. The Stirling Range is shown as seen from the south, hills and peaks drawn at a single scale (the highest, Bluff Knoll, reaches 3640 ft).

isolating factors. The Stirling assemblage may well be not a single autochthonous radiation but more than one invasion of these shale peaks.

The evolution of congested inflorescences surrounded by bracts might represent another ornithophilous adaptation: landing platforms. The stout leaves of *Hakea cucullata* (fig. 8.24, bottom left), each surrounding a group of flowers, may well accommodate claws of visiting birds. This certainly

FIG. 8.24. Unusual flower types in the flora of southwestern Australia, showing probable evolution of new pollination mechanisms. TOP LEFT, *Lasiopetalum drummondii* (Sterculiaceae), flower parts excessively woolly with stellate hairs; Three Springs. TOP RIGHT, *Lachnostachys albicans* (Verbenaceae), inflorescence congested and hairy; leaves densely felty; leaves 4 cm

(*continued*)

would be true for *H. victoriae* (fig. 8.15, bottom left); every head of flowers is axillary to a large leaf, which—perhaps serving as the attractive organ as well as a potential landing platform—is whitish to orangeish at the base and could serve as a "guide" to bird visitors. The bracts of *Dryandra* of the Proteaceae (see *D. runcinata*, fig. 8.25, bottom right) are rarely colorful, usually only brown, but may contrast with flowers (white, yellow, orange) and possibly aid in perching of visiting birds.

Inflorescence bracts that lack attractive functions also occur. Diels (1906) has called attention to taxa in southwestern Australia in which bracts are papery. These include *Acacia squamata*, *A. restiacea*, *Conostephium pendulum*, and *Daviesia hakeoides*. Their bracts are sufficiently inconspicuous that one cannot cite a function in pollination; although to cite bracts as a protective device is facile, one cannot easily find other reasons for their existence in these taxa.

Conversion to ornithophily within particular genera can be cited. In *Verticordia* (Myrtaceae), flowers tend to be pastel-colored, broadly cuplike, and small—all features suggesting bee flowers. In *V. insignis* and *V. mitchelliana* of the southwest, petals are large, tend to form a tube, and are bright red. These species, moreover, tend to have branching suited for perching, whereas other Verticordias do not.

How are we to interpret the rather numerous instances in which clearly ornithophilous flowers are borne at ground level? Instances occur in *Brachysema aphyllum* (fig. 8.3, bottom right), *B. daviesioides* (fig. 8.5, top left, right), *B. tomentosum* (fig. 8.5, bottom left, right), *B. chambersii*, *Banksia prostrata* (fig. 8.6, bottom right), and perhaps *Banksia nutans* (fig. 8.6, bottom left); *Darwinia sanguinea* (fig. 8.22, top right) and *D. speciosa*; and several species of *Grevillea* with what could be called "ground-level flagelliflory." *Grevillea pectinata* (fig. 8.25, top left, right, bottom left) is a good example of these *Grevillea* species. Branches from a shrub tend to sprawl; they terminate in inflorescences borne on the ground at distances of up to 2 m from the plant base. Flowers in these plants are bright red and congested, and, as with the others cited above, they are evidently

FIG. 8.24 (*continued*)

long. BOTTOM LEFT, *Hakea cucullata* (Proteaceae), close view of cuplike leaves enclosing groups of flowers; Porongorups, Stirlings. BOTTOM RIGHT, *Rhizanthella gardneri* (Orchidaceae), photograph of pickled specimen (see text for explanation of underground-flowering habit). (From a color photograph by Alex George.)

FIG. 8.25. Tendencies to flowering at ground level in Proteaceae of southwestern Australia. TOP LEFT, RIGHT, BOTTOM LEFT, *Grevillea pectinata*. TOP LEFT, habit; leafy stems at center, flowering stems inconspicuous, trail up to 2 m away from plant; near Perenjori. TOP RIGHT, leaves; flowering stems bear reduced leaves, vegetative leaves like this only in center of plant. BOTTOM LEFT, inflorescence at tip of trailing shoot. BOTTOM RIGHT, *Dryandra runcinata*, flowers surrounded by cup of brown bracts, inflorescence is about 8 cm high; near Badgingarra.

ornithophilous (although actual observations seem lacking). Apparently the ground can serve as a perch for feeding from large bright flowers borne at that level. Although ground-level ornithophily seems fantastic compared to ornithophily in other regions (except South Africa), there is no reason to believe it is not operative.

Pollination relationships such as the preceding, which have probably evolved autochthonously in southwestern Australia in most cases, are quite unusual and are worth extensive study. Erickson's (1958) comments on pollination in Stylidiaceae and my own theories on evolution of pollination types in this family (Carlquist, 1969) have endeavored to show, on the basis of fieldwork, the almost unbelievably intricate patterns of evolution in these respects in Stylidiaceae. Many other groups would repay study. What is the function of the markedly fringed petals in *Thysanotus* (fig. 8.11, bottom right) and *Verticordia?* Do flowers with marked, hairy perianths, such as *Lasiopetalum drummondii* (fig. 8.23, top left), have distinctive pollination schemes? Few efforts have been made to study pollination in plants of the southwest. One can cite, however, the occurrence of pseudocopulation in the orchid *Cryptostylis ovata* (Morcombe, 1968). Pollination of *Banksia* by the marsupial *Tarsipes spenseri* (Morcombe, 1968) is unusual, but is probably a secondary phenomenon in the primarily ornithophilous *Banksia.* I will cite only one more example, one of the truly bizarre plants of southwestern Australia, *Rhizanthella gardneri* (fig. 8.24, bottom right). This "underground orchid" apparently completes its entire life cycle below the soil surface. If it emerges (and that has not been observed in the three collections now made of this elusive plant), it must do so briefly at best. I suspect pollination by burrowing beetles, or self-pollination. Likewise, the eastern Australian orchid *Cryptanthemis* with similar habits (but with emergence barely above ground surface) has not been observed with respect to pollination mechanism. These are some of the challenges to the botanist interested in evolution in southwestern Australia.

Evolution of Dispersal Types

Likewise, many unusual seed and fruit-dispersal types occur in southwestern Australia, and little is known about them. I am presenting a few examples only to show interesting evolutionary tendencies and to suggest the opportunities for further work. The flora of southwestern Australia can be explained easily enough as originating from long-distance dispersal, as well as shorter transport events across dry land. Prevailing winds during summer—when seeds are likely to be dispersed—are from east to west, so that transport of airborne seeds in that direction would be expected. Those who like to categorize seed-dispersal mechanisms would find analysis of the southwestern flora highly interesting. Whatever the original mode of transport to Western Australia, evolution has subsequently occurred in dispersal mechanisms of many groups.

One family that shows a diversity of dispersal mechanisms is Goodeniaceae. This family, centered in Australia, has undoubtedly evolved the various dispersal mechanisms described here within the Australian continent. Some of them have evolved autochthonously in southwestern Australia. *Anthotium* (fig. 8.26, top left) is endemic to the southwest. The calyx is adherent to the ovary. The capsule is quadrivalvate, and release of minute seeds that could be dispersed by any of various methods is to be expected. The sharp-tipped calyx lobes might be devices for lodging the fruit in fur, but this is very doubtful. On the other hand, dispersal of fruits with inferior ovaries and with numerous stout hairs is to be expected in *Verreauxia paniculata* (fig. 8.26, top right); this genus is endemic to Western Australia and the central desert. The fruits are one-seeded.

Pentaptilon (fig. 8.26, center left) is a monotypic genus of Western Australia. *Pentaptilon* fruits are the product of an inferior ovary, are one-seeded and indehiscent. The five wings (some of which remain underdeveloped) on *Pentaptilon* fruits, together with light weight of the fruits, make them excellent for wind dispersal, although presumably only in a tumbling fashion across relatively short distances. *Pentaptilon careyi* is a highly localized species. Wind dispersal would be expected for *Calogyne, Velleia* (fig. 8.26, bottom right), *Symphyobasis* (fig. 8.26, center right), and *Goodenia* (fig. 8.26, bottom left). These have capsular fruits (formed from superior or semisuperior ovaries) containing flat seeds of such a size that wind dispersal is conceivable. In *Velleia, Calogyne,* and some species of *Goodenia,* seeds are not only flat but winged, enhancing dispersibility. An additional feature, stressed by Carolin (1966), is the presence of mucilage cells in seed coats of these genera, with some excep-

FIG. 8.26. Fruits (and for some, seeds) of Goodeniaceae of southwestern Australia to show radiation in fruit type. TOP LEFT, *Anthotium rubriflorum.* TOP RIGHT, *Verreauxia paniculata.* CENTER LEFT, *Pentaptilon careyi.* CENTER RIGHT, *Symphyobasis macroplectra.* BOTTOM LEFT, *Goodenia incana.* BOTTOM RIGHT, *Velleia paradoxa.* All at same scale (*Pentaptilon* fruits 10 mm in diam.).

311

tions, such as *Velleia montana*. Presence of gelatinous cells in seed coats would promote adherence of seeds, when wet, to fur or feathers.

Two genera close to *Goodenia* show an interesting divergence in fruit and seed dispersal. *Neogoodenia* has a one-seeded, indehiscent fruit that is flat, however, and mimics seeds of *Goodenia* (Carolin, 1966). Another genus, once considered part of *Goodenia*, is *Coopernookia* (Carolin, 1968). In *Coopernookia*, seeds are ovoid and have no flattened margins or mucilage cells. Instead, as illustrated by Carolin (1968), they bear a strophiolate body that might serve as a myrmecochore. If dispersal by ants occurs in *Coopernookia*, this is indeed a marked departure from the *Goodenia* pattern.

Catosperma, a monotypic genus of Goodeniaceae from streams, has an indehiscent fruit derived from an inferior ovary (fig. 8.27, top left). These fruits have no obvious dispersal mechanism. I attempted to test them for floatability because of the habitat of this genus; those tested sank at the end of 24 hr. The dispersal mechanism of *Leschenaultia* is unclear. These fruits, derived from an inferior ovary, are linear, and although they appear as though they might be capsular, in fact they are indehiscent and break into loment-like segments (Carolin, 1966). Seeds of *Leschenaultia* are cuboidal (fig. 8.27, top right) and their outermost layers are derived from inner portions of the fruit wall. Although one can imagine various types of seed dispersal, there is no obvious adaptation; mere wind dispersal of seeds or loment-like segments, or even herbivore dispersal could be envisioned.

Scaevola is a very interesting genus of Goodeniaceae with respect to fruit dispersal. *Scaevola* has indehiscent fruits representing one or more ovules maturing into seeds. Some *Scaevola* species have relatively small dry seeds, such as *S. hookeri* (fig. 8.27, center left). These do not float and are presumably distributed by birds or (over short distances) by wind. Some species of *Scaevola* have a fleshy fruit exocarp, and these are either bird-dispersed or seawater-dispersed. The widely distributed *S. taccada* and *S. plumieri* are distributed by oceanic drift (see chapter 2). *Scaevola calendulacea* occurs on Australian (but not other Pacific) beaches, and although fresh fruits with fleshy exocarp can float, the endocarp (fig. 8.27, bottom right) does not float, whereas endocarps of *S. taccada* and *S. plumieri* can float (fig. 2.6, top right). Perhaps these latter, wider-ranging

FIG. 8.27. Fruits (and for some, seeds) of additional Goodeniaceae species of Western Australia to show radiation in fruit types. Scale same as in fig. 8.26. TOP LEFT, *Catosperma goodeniacearum*. TOP RIGHT, *Leschenaultia striatum*. CENTER LEFT, *Scaevola hookeri*. CENTER RIGHT, *S. collaris*. BOTTOM LEFT, *S. collaris* fruits float. BOTTOM RIGHT, fruits of *S. calendulacea* and *S. spinescens* do not float.

313

species evolved from ancestors such as *S. calendulacea* and by minor changes in fruit structure evolved floatability. Most Pacific insular Scaevolas have fruits that do not float and are instead bird-dispersed. This may be true of an Australian species (primarily Western Australian), *S. spinescens,* whose fruits have a fleshy exocarp but a nonbuoyant endocarp (fig. 8.27, bottom right).

A unique development in Western Australia is the evolution of water-dispersed inland halophytic species of *Scaevola. Scaevola collaris* (fig. 8.27, center right), which grows on the shores of Lake Austin, has relatively large fruits with a dry, papery exocarp. This exocarp, however, contains large air chambers, and the fruits float (fig. 8.27, bottom left). These fruits are ribbed or somewhat winged. Because of their morphology and lightness, a secondary dispersal mechanism of tumbling in wind gusts across stretches of inland desert can be hypothesized. In such a way, fruits of *S. collaris* could be transported from one inland salt lake to another.

Fruits of *Dampiera* are like those of small, dry-fruited species of *Scaevola,* and are presumably dispersed in the same manner. Although the above dispersal types (all genera of Goodeniaceae are cited) represent a broad spectrum of fruit form and therefore dispersal devices, some of which have evolved autochthonously in Western Australia, much more needs to be learned about dispersal mechanisms in this family. The vectors of those Goodeniaceae that appear to be bird-dispersed or ant-dispersed need to be discovered, and buoyancy in water is to be suspected in some species not named above. Indeed, we know virtually nothing about dispersal in most Australian angiosperms.

One interesting group with respect to dispersal is *Darwinia* of the Myrtaceae. Because some of the Darwinias are narrowly restricted to mountain peaks, especially those of the Stirling Range (fig. 8.23), I wanted to discover if any show loss of dispersibility. One might expect loss of dispersibility in narrowly restricted species. There does appear to be a clear range in dispersibility within *Darwinia* (fig. 8.28). Fruits of *D. pauciflora,* with prominent papery petals, are ribbed and relatively light in comparison to volume (fig. 8.28, top left). The petals serve as the display organ of flowers of *D. pauciflora,* which are borne in a noncapitate fashion, and may serve as wings that aid in dispersal of this nonmontane species.

FIG. 8.28. Tendencies in fruit morphology and potential dispersibility in species of *Darwinia* (Myrtaceae) from southwestern Australia. TOP LEFT, *D. pauciflora*. TOP RIGHT, *D. acerosa*. CENTER LEFT, *D. oederoides*. CENTER RIGHT, *D. hypericifolia*. BOTTOM LEFT, *D. macrostegia*. BOTTOM RIGHT, *D. meeboldii*. Seeds of *D. meeboldii* are 10 mm long; all photographed at the same scale.

In contrast, fruits of *D. acerosa*, a capitate species, are small and have small petals (fig. 8.25, top right). This species is not widely distributed (Mogumber, possibly also Mt. Gibson), perhaps because of edaphic preferences, but its fruits are typical of those of more widely distributed species of *Darwinia*. Small size of seeds in such species ought to aid dispersal. *Darwinia oederoides* is a subshrub with capitate bracteate inflorescences, distributed in boggy places of Denmark to Manjimup, a short range. Seeds look poorly dispersible (fig. 8.28, center left), but their small size would lead one to expect that they could be scattered over longer distances. The distinct ecological preferences of this species and its habit (very short stems; it grows as a "cryptic" understory element in bog scrub) may help explain why it is so restricted.

Darwinia hypericifolia is a Stirling Range endemic. Its fruits (fig. 8.28, center right, probably somewhat immature) are relatively large, suggesting lowered dispersibility. However, two other Stirling species of *Darwinia*, each restricted to a single peak, distinctly show sharply reduced dispersibility. *Darwinia macrostegia* (fig. 8.28, bottom left) has fruits with persistent perianth, but the body of the shiny fruits is large and relatively heavy. *Darwinia meeboldii* has fruits in which perianth is absent, and their large size and weight and shiny surface suggest no obvious dispersal mechanism (fig. 8.28, bottom right). Thus there is indeed reduced dispersibility in those species of *Darwinia* that are restricted to peaks in the Stirling Range. Many other examples of change in dispersibility in the southwestern flora could surely be uncovered. For example, *Stylidium* characteristically has minute, wind-borne seeds. However, *Stylidium galioides*, an endemic of East Mt. Barren, has notably large seeds. This change may be related to restriction of this peculiar species by its preference for quartz-block hills localized along the southwest coast. Loss of dispersibility in this case is entirely "insular" in that its strange habitat is just as much an island as is a true oceanic island.

Loss of dispersibility can be detected by casual perusal of certain other southwestern Australian genera. For example, the fruits of *Eucalyptus macrocarpa* are notably large for the genus. Seeds are correspondingly large, and one may suspect loss of dispersibility. This species is, in fact, fairly narrowly restricted to sand plains near Perth.

Insectivorous Plants

Discussion of insectivorous plants in southwestern Australia would be merely presentation of a botanical curiosity, except that they illustrate well the nature of evolution in the southwest. The number of species (especially in *Drosera*) is greater than in any comparable area. This may reflect capability of insectivorous plants to cope with nutrient-deficient soil conditions in southwestern Australia, together with opportunity in this area to radiate. Insectivorous plants in Western Australia have been the subject of a good, recent, semipopular book (Erickson, 1968).

Cephalotus (fig. 8.29, top left, right), a monotypic genus, is the sole representative of Cephalotaceae and is endemic to boggy areas of southwesternmost Australia. The pitchers of this plant, although somewhat reminiscent of those of Sarraceniaceae or Nepenthaceae, are a totally independent development. It is the only pitcher plant in temperate areas of the southern hemisphere, and is apparently a derivative of saxifragoid ancestors. *Drosera* (Droseraceae) has experienced explosive evolution—which has taken the form of adaptive radiation—in southwestern Australia. Of the 56 species endemic to Australia, 47 are restricted to southwestern Australia. (The total of *Drosera* species worldwide is 90.)

Some southwestern species of *Drosera* appear to be annuals, such as *D. pulchella* (fig. 8.29, bottom left). Other minute rosette Droseras may perennate; during dry periods, foliage leaves disappear, and the plant consists only of white, fimbriate scales covering the apical bud. At another extreme is a plant of seasonally wet sand flats, *D. gigantea* (fig. 8.29, bottom right), which grows to 1 m high or more, is prominently branched, and perennates from underground stems. Some, such as *D. stolonifera*, grow by means of underground stolons. *Drosera macrophylla* (fig. 8.34, top left, right) is a perennial species with semi-succulent leaves. The vining species, such as *D. heteromera* (fig. 8.11, bottom left), grow by means of succulent underground structures that have been termed bulbs (fig. 8.30, top left).

We are only beginning to understand the diversity of the many species of *Utricularia* endemic to Western Australia. Bladders of these differ markedly from one species to another, as do flowers (see Erickson, 1968).

FIG. 8.29. Tendencies in insectivorous plants of southwestern Australia. TOP LEFT, RIGHT, *Cephalotus follicularis* (Cephalotaceae). TOP LEFT, habit, showing leaves modified into pitchers. TOP RIGHT, detail of pitchers, one of which is shown in longisection. BOTTOM LEFT, *Drosera pulchella* (Droseraceae), an ephemeral species; leaf rosette 2 cm in diam.; Bornholm. BOTTOM RIGHT, *D. gigantea*, with stems to 0.7 m tall; Cannington.

We know virtually nothing about the significance of these varied expressions, and to what prey and pollinators (flowers range from pale violet to bright red orange) they may be related. *Utricularia* has speciated in the southwest probably because of the "insular" distribution of the winter-wet boggy areas, most of which dry completely in summer.

Adaptation to Fire

Adaptation to fire is clearly an aspect of adaptive radiation, but different mechanisms may occur within a single plant, and so fire-resistance is best discussed collectively. One would not exaggerate much by saying that all native plants in southwestern Australia are adapted to fire. I can show only a few of these to illustrate the range of adaptations, some of which are unexpected and doubtless autochthonously evolved within the province. Seeds of certain species are probably resistant to fire in various ways, and may even require fire for germination, but this aspect appears to have been examined little. Nonetheless, the variety of easily visible fire-resistance mechanisms is astonishing, and they definitely form phases of adaptive radiation. The importance of this feature is considerable, for not only have various groups adapted to fire in a variety of ways, but also resistance to fire must have been one of the obstacles for establishment of the original immigrants in the southwestern flora, an obstacle not readily perceptible when we think about disharmony of the province. If fire resistance has been a factor in producing disharmony, it is one of the factors that, added to peculiarities of climate and soils, have provided broad opportunities for radiation of those colonists able to establish.

UNDERGROUND RENEWAL ORGANS

Plants that can resist dry seasons by means of bulbs, tubers, or corms are not unusual in temperate climates. Such organs are undoubtedly correlated with the dry summers of the southwest. They can also, however, be considered as ideal preadaptations to surviving fires. Bulbs and bulblike structures are obvious mechanisms, and those of *Drosera* (fig. 8.30, top left) can be cited in this regard. Another group that typically does not bear bulbs but has evolved them autochthonously in southwestern Australia

FIG. 8.30. Underground renewal structures, also capable of fire resistance, in plants of south-western Australia. TOP LEFT, *Drosera macrantha* (Droseraceae), "bulb" at base of stem; near Perenjori. TOP RIGHT, *Phylloglossum drummondii* (Lycopodiaceae); unearthed plant shows old tuber, new tuber at base of leaf rosette; Cannington. BOTTOM LEFT, *Chamaescilla corymbosa* (Liliaceae), base of unearthed plant, showing tubers; Three Springs. BOTTOM RIGHT, *Dampiera wellsiana* (Goodeniaceae), plant showing basal rosette which perennates from buds below ground level; near Calingiri.

is *Stylidium.* Ephemeral vernal species, like S. *petiolare,* can survive both drought and fire by means of these structures (Erickson, 1958; Carlquist, 1969). *Stylidium bulbiferum* and other species of *Stylidium* with wiry stems do not have below-ground bulbs but have renewal buds at nodes on the wiry stems, and these can sprout after fire. *Phylloglossum drummondii* (fig. 8.30, top right), the curious monotypic genus of Lycopodiaceae, has an anomalous structure, often termed a tuber, that survives both drought and fire. This structure is evidently a sort of specialized leafless axis, one of which is produced annually by each plant, that bends downward into the soil, develops a protective epidermis, and can produce shoot, strobilus, and roots the following year.

The ordinary type of tuber, as in *Chamaescilla corymbosa* (fig. 8.30, bottom left) is obviously suited to drought and fire survival. There are many monocotyledons in the southwestern Australian flora, such as orchids, that have underground storage and perennating structures, tending to be succulent. Many angiosperms, however, merely have renewal buds at or slightly below the soil surface. Leaves can be burned (they would mostly be dried during the summer anyway), but the plant is not killed by fire. The rosette habit, as in many species of *Stylidium,* is an indication of this adaptation to fire as well as to a mediterranean climate. *Dampiera wellsiana* (fig. 8.30, bottom right) is a typical rosette perennial. Caespitose, clump-forming plants, such as *Lomandra* (fig. 8.31, top left), *Conostylis,* and restiads, have nonsucculent underground stems that can provide renewal buds. This is a very common type of fire survival that has even been evolved autochthonously in the southwest in *Banksia prostrata* (fig. 8.6, bottom right). *Actinostrobus acuminatus* (Cupressaceae) is unusual both within its genus and within cypresses at large; it branches below ground, sends up shoots, and bears cones at or near the surface of the ground— where fire temperatures would be expected to be minimal. This habit is perhaps also related to the fact that this (like the other species of *Actinostrobus*) is a native of sand areas where growth underground is easy, and where shifting of sand will be less harmful than to a species in which roots could be exposed or buried too deeply.

A number of shrubs in the southwestern flora characteristically branch from ground level. At ground level is a somewhat swollen stem that usually gives rise to new shoots each year. *Tetratheca* (Tremandraceae), *Dampiera*

FIG. 8.31. Mechanisms for fire-resistance in the southwestern Australian flora. TOP LEFT, *Lomandra* sp. (Liliaceae), clump with leaves burned but rhizomes sending up new leaves; Regan's Ford. TOP RIGHT, *Scaevola oxyclona* (Goodeniaceae), showing underground stolon; Spargoville. BOTTOM LEFT, *Xanthorrhoea* sp. (Liliaceae), plant burned but new leaves emerging; Regan's Ford. BOTTOM RIGHT, *Macrozamia riedlei* (Cycadaceae), old plants with new leaves after fire; note charred stem; Badgingarra.

(Goodeniaceae), and *Loudonia* (Haloragaceae) are typical examples of this growth form. Stems can die down to the basal "caudex" each year, and the caudex can yield renewal buds after fire. This habit has been evolved autochthonously in subshrubby species of *Stylidium* such as *S. falcatum*, which I have observed sprouting from a calluslike, swollen stem base after a fire in the Tutanning Reserve (Carlquist, 1969). Even species of *Acacia* have this habit.

Stolons are an excellent source of fire-surviving renewal buds. Among southwestern plants that have autochthonously evolved such structures are *Scaevola oxyclona* (fig. 8.31, top right) and *Drosera stolonifera*.

WOODY PLANTS

Obviously a true shrub cannot possess renewal buds of the same kind as a typical "chamaephyte" or "geophyte." Yet survival of at least some main stems after fire would seem to have a potential selective value for shrubs and trees. One mechanism for survival is the presence of a cork, fire-resistant cortex, or bark. Another requisite is the ability to form buds after fire not just by outgrowth of axillary buds but by formation of buds *de novo* on whatever branches were not killed. Eucalypts are capable of this, and tree eucalypts are surely a magnificent example of trees adapted to fire dispersal (also with regard to fruits, as mentioned later). Other Myrtaceae commonly have fire-resistant bark; the paperbark (*Melaleuca quinquenervia*) is an excellent example. Unusual, corky, excrescent bark has been developed in *Melaleuca exarata* (fig. 8.33, bottom left) and *Calothamnus gracilis* (fig. 8.33, bottom right). Sprouting of branches— protected by a thick, seemingly corky cortex and bark—after fire is shown here for *Banksia menziesii* (fig. 8.32, top left). Of course any bark so specialized with respect to fire resistance by means of cork development must also be effective in desiccation resistance, so that separation of the two phenomena is impossible. All of the shrubs that have fire-resistant bark do, in fact, contain appreciable amounts of cork cells.

Some rosette trees have succulent stems together with relatively noncombustible (or expendable) leaves. The only requirement of these plants is that the living tissues of the trunk and the apical meristem not be killed by fire. *Macrozamia* of the Cycadaceae (fig. 8.31, bottom right) and the various species of *Xanthorrhoea* (fig. 8.31, bottom left) and *Kingia*

FIG. 8.32. Examples of fire-resistance seen in Proteaceae at Regan's Ford, site of a fire the year preceding photographing. TOP LEFT, *Banksia menziesii*, partially burned trunk sending out new shoots. TOP RIGHT, *B. menziesii* tree, showing base, a swollen lignotuber from which new shoots are emerging. BOTTOM LEFT, *B. laricina*, shrub burned and killed, but all fruits opened by fire to release unharmed seeds. BOTTOM RIGHT, *B. laricina*, conelike aggregate fruits, showing one with opened woody follicles, and one with unopened follicles.

FIG. 8.33. Examples of fire-resistance relating to cork formation in plants of southwestern Australia. TOP LEFT, *Hakea obliqua* (Proteaceae), opened fruit, valves 4.5 cm long, showing prominent cork excresences. TOP RIGHT, *H. pandanicarpa*, unopened fruit (6 cm long) on plant, showing numerous small corky pyramids. BOTTOM LEFT, *Melaleuca exarata* (Myrtaceae), showing stems bearing prominent corky ridges; Cape Le Grand. BOTTOM RIGHT, *Calothamnus gracilis* (Myrtaceae), which bears ovaries and fruits embedded within stems that develop abundant cork; Wanneru.

of the Liliaceae (sometimes Xanthorrhoeaceae) are excellent examples. There are very few individuals of *Macrozamia* or *Xanthorrhoea* of any age in Western Australia that do not have blackened stems, indicating repeated burning. This is also true of the tree genus of Loranthaceae, *Nuytsia,* which survives fire much as eucalypts and tree Banksias do.

"LIGNOTUBERS"

Bases of many Western Australian trees are swollen and burllike. These are sources for renewal buds after burning. Because these trees have woody branches that survive the dry season intact (unless burned), lignotubers cannot be considered a desiccation-resistance mechanism. They are clearly an adaptation to fire. Regrowth after fire from a lignotuber is illustrated for *Banksia menziesii* (fig. 8.32, top left). The mallee eucalypts, such as *E. macrocarpa, E. tetraptera,* and *E. preissii,* all possess lignotubers. Lignotubers are not unlike the caudex-like base of subshrubs such as *Dampiera,* mentioned earlier. Lignotubers and caudex-bearing subshrubs are also common in the Californian flora, where again they can be regarded as mechanisms for fire resistance (*Arctostaphylos* spp., *Adenostoma* spp.).

FIRE-ADAPTED FRUITS

A fire-adapted fruit must be able to resist igniting, or at the most to char on the outside but be thick enough that damaging temperatures do not reach the seeds within. Superb examples of this adaptation are presented by Proteaceae. Several southwestern species of *Hakea* have fruits covered with corky excrescences. *Hakea obliqua* (fig. 8.33, top left), *H. pandanicarpa, H. brookeana,* and *H. roei* are good examples of this tendency.

Some *Hakea* fruits tend to open when mature and thoroughly dry—presumably at the end of the potential fire season. The pair of winged seeds in *Hakea* fruits is protected by fire up to this point, however. Even fruits of *Hakea* that do not bear cork tend to be so massive and fire-resistant that fire damage to seeds at any stage prior to dehiscence is forestalled. This mechanism may also be hypothesized for Myrtaceae—especially *Eucalyptus*—in which the thickness and nonflammability of capsules are noteworthy.

Another category of fire-adapted fruit is offered by *Banksia. Banksia* fruits are woody follicles, mostly clustered into conelike aggregate fruits. *Banksia* fruits tend to stay closed indefinitely, even when dry, until the high temperatures created by fire open them. Examples are shown here for B. *laricina* (fig. 8.32, bottom left, right). Even if entire individuals are destroyed by fire, as they are in B. *laricina*, fire temperatures trigger opening of the fruits, which react not during the fire but immediately afterward; thus the seeds are released intact. These seeds fall onto ground burned clear of underbrush, and their potential for successful growth is enhanced. One might say that because of the great frequency of fires in southwestern Australia, all plants that grow there are, in a sense, pioneer plants.

Fruits many years old yet still unopened can be seen on trunks of *Banksia* trees that have not experienced burning since production of those fruits. In this respect the fruits resemble closely—even in appearance—the cones of California's closed-cone pines (*Pinus radiata*, P. *attenuata*, P. *muricata*). Many other species in southwestern Australia also typically retain seeds in fruits until fire creates conditions suitable for opening of capsules. Especially prominent among them are the bottlebrushes *Calothamnus* and *Callistemon*, as well as other Myrtaceae, such as a number of species of *Melaleuca*. In *Melaleuca exarata* (fig. 8.33, bottom left) and *Calothamnus gracilis* (fig. 8.33, bottom right), C. *planifolius*, C. *lateralis*, C. *microcarpus*, and C. *schaueri*, capsules are immersed in the rapidly exfoliating corky bark. Thus capsules in these species are as effectively protected from fire damage as are the cork-covered follicles of *Hakea pandanicarpa*.

FIRE-INDUCED FLOWERING

A phenomenon repeatedly noticed by botanists in Western Australia is that some plants flower rarely or not at all until they have been burned. *Xanthorrhoea* (Liliaceae) is often cited in this regard. Although one can see individuals flowering without any apparent prior burning, a burned area containing Xanthorrhoeas almost always shows abundant flowering of this plant the following year. In this case, we have a condition one step removed from fruits that open only after fire. The fruits of plants induced to flower by fire *need not be fire resistant* for survival of seeds. In fact, the likelihood of fires in a given region in two successive years is small compared to that of fires at intervals of several years, during which time

FIG. 8.34. Examples of flowering after fire in the flora of southwestern Australia. TOP LEFT, RIGHT, *Drosera macrophylla* (Droseraceae), rosettes of plants. TOP LEFT, rosette of plant from a region not recently burned; near Toodyay. TOP RIGHT, rosette of plant that has flowered the year after its habitat had been burned; Perenjori. BOTTOM LEFT, RIGHT, *Lyperanthus nigricans* (Orchidaceae). BOTTOM LEFT, one-leaved but mature plant during potential flowering· season, but not flowering; Badgingarra. BOTTOM RIGHT, flowering plants in a region that had burned the preceding year; Cannington.

combustible matter has had a chance to accumulate. Seeds that are shed after fire have an enhanced opportunity of growth because, as in the *Banksia laricina* example cited earlier, they are shed into an area cleared the preceding year by fire.

Examples of induction of flowering by fire include an orchid, *Lyperanthus nigricans,* and *Drosera macrophylla.* One can often see these species in vegetative form, in which case *L. nigricans* appears as a single leaf (fig. 8.34, bottom left), *D. macrophylla* as a sterile rosette of leaves 4–6 in. in diameter (fig. 8.34, top left) at the season when flowering of such apparently mature plants would be expected. In a burned area, however, these species can be seen in flower abundantly (fig. 8.34, top right, bottom right). The contrast with angiosperms that release seeds after fire is interesting. Both *Drosera* and *Lyperanthus* have relatively delicate capsules containing seeds that are not at all resistant to fire. Thus, fire as a mechanism for inducing flowering is favorable, whereas fire would be destructive to these plants when in fruit.

Discussion

Obviously not all aspects of adaptive radiation in seed plants of southwestern Australia can be covered here. The annual habit—a growth form abundant in mediterranean climates—is present in the southwest but not mentioned here. My comments can be considered only an introduction to the many truly exciting phenomena yet to be discovered or explained. Because these plants are vanishing, owing to increasing pressure on land usage, work of a "natural history" nature is much needed. The reasons for detailed field studies of the phenomena mentioned in this chapter are just as compelling as the reasons for Darwin, Lack, and Bowman to have studied the Darwin's finches on the Galápagos Islands.

By discussing the flora of southwestern Australia in terms of phenomena primarily, I have, unfortunately, diffused the presentation of adaptive radiation in individual taxonomic groups. I hope that the reader interested in the Australian flora will synthesize for particular groups, such as *Acacia, Eucalyptus,* and *Scaevola,* a picture (all too often missing where taxonomy is the main, or sole, focus) of the remarkable adaptational aspects of speciation in this flora.

I also regret that I could not include a balancing account of adaptive radiation in animal groups. Plainly my own training biases my presentation in favor of plants. Elsewhere the reader can find pertinent data on frogs (Main, 1965), lizards (Glauert, 1962), spiders (McKeown, 1963), and birds (Keast, 1961). Further information on these groups from an evolutionary perspective would be desirable, and a survey of insects in Australia and particularly Western Australia from such a viewpoint would undoubtedly be remarkably revealing.

References

Atlas of Australian resources. 1952–1966. Canberra, Department of National Development. (The various maps and booklets that comprise this series were published and revised variously, with some contributions apparently not credited to particular authors.)

Beadle, N. C. W. 1966. Soil phosphate and its role in molding segments of the Australian flora and vegetation, with special reference to xeromorphy and sclerophylly. *Ecology* 47:992–1007.

Beard, J. S., ed. 1965. *Descriptive catalogue of West Australian plants.* Perth, W.A., King's Park Board.

Blackall, W. E., and B. J. Grieve. 1956, 1959, 1965. *How to know Western Australian wildflowers.* 3 vols. Nedlands, W.A., University of Western Australia Press.

Carlquist, S. 1969. Studies in Stylidiaceae: New taxa, field observations, evolutionary tendencies. *Aliso* 7:13–64.

Carolin, R. C. 1966. Seeds and fruit of the Goodeniaceae. *Proc. Linnaean Soc. New South Wales* 91:58–83.

Carolin, R. C. 1968. *Coopernookia:* A new genus of Goodeniaceae. *Proc. Linnaean Soc. New South Wales* 92:209–16.

Diels, L. 1906. *Die Pflanzenwelt von West-Australien sudlich des Wendkreises. Die Vegetation der Erde,* ed. A. Engler and O. Drude, vol. 7. Leipzig, Verlag Wilhelm Engelmann.

Erickson, R. 1958. *Triggerplants.* Perth, W.S., Paterson Brokensha.

Erickson, R. 1968. *Plants of prey in Australia.* Osborne Park, W.A., Lamb Publication.

Glauert, L. 1962. *A handbook of the lizards of Western Australia.* Perth, W.A., Western Australian Naturalists' Club.

Keast, A. 1961. Bird speciation on the Australian continent. *Bull. Mus. Comp. Zool. (Harvard)* 123:305–495.

Lewis, H. 1962. Catastrophic selection as a factor in speciation. *Evolution* 16:257–71.

Main, A. R. 1965. *Frogs of southern Western Australia.* Perth, W.A., Western Australian Naturalists' Club.

McKeown, K. C. 1963. *Australian spiders.* 2d ed. Sydney, Angus and Robertson.

Morcombe, M. K. 1968. *Australia's western wildflowers.* Perth, W.A., Landfall Press.

Noakes, L. C. 1966. Geology. In *Atlas of Australian resources,* 2d ser., pp. 1–27. Canberra, Department of National Development.

Raven, P. H. 1964. Catastrophic selection and edaphic endemism. *Evolution* 18:336–38.

Snaydon, R. W. 1970. Rapid population differentiation in a mosaic environment. I. The response of *Anthoxanthum odoratum* populations to soils. *Evolution* 24:257–69.

Went, F. W. 1971. Parallel evolution. *Taxon* 20:197–226.

CHAPTER NINE

ADAPTIVE RADIATION: CONTINENTAL ISLANDS, FRINGING ARCHIPELAGOS, CONTINENTAL ISLANDLIKE AREAS

This chapter, although intended to cover instances of adaptive radiation not included earlier, has been designed as a way of illustrating the various ways in which areas within continents or near continents show evolutionary characteristics of adaptive radiation much like those discussed earlier.

Madagascar

Madagascar may deserve more consideration in relation to adaptive radiation than some of the areas discussed in earlier chapters. However, I have hesitated to present an extensive synthesis of the Madagascan biota not only because it is so complex compared with those of other islands (and really deserves a book by itself), but also because of my own unfamiliarity with this island.*

Madagascar is generally considered an old continental island and, as such, might be expected to have relict groups. Chief among these relicts are the lemurs. Known from fossils from the Paleocene and Eocene of North America and Europe (Hill, 1953), lemurs have escaped extinction in Madagascar. How much of the diversity of lemurs is due to autochthonous evolution in Madagascar is therefore a difficult question. One could

---

* Such a book is now available: G. Richard and R. Battistini, eds., *Biogeography and ecology of Madagascar*, The Hague, Dr. W. Junk, Publishers, 1972.

argue that absence of monkeys from Madagascar has permitted radiation of lemurs there, but one could equally well argue that this absence merely has permitted survival of lemurs in Madagascar, and has no bearing on whether the Madagascan lemurs represent more than a single invasion of that island. Significant contributions on the lemurs which also cite and summarize earlier literature include the works of Hill (1953), Petter (1962, 1969) and Jolly (1966).

Although the tenrecs (Tenrecidae) have long been known as an endemic Madagascar family of insectivores notable for adaptive radiation, we have lacked a careful field study of this group. This has now been admirably supplied by Eisenberg and Gould (1970). Although they were unable to provide new observations on some of the scarcer genera, such as *Limnogale*, these authors have provided a wide variety of observations on most tenrecs, both in the field and in captivity, and have added many new aspects to knowledge of the adaptive radiation of the group; their book is deserving of study.

Unfortunately, there is no such recent, comprehensive account of the vanga shrikes (Vangidae), which form an example of adaptive radiation rivaling the Darwin's finches and the Hawaiian honeycreepers in many respects. Distributional and habit data may be found in the field studies of Rand (1936); some data and good illustrations are available in the work of Milne-Edwards and Grandidier (1878–1885).

The iguanid genera of Madagascar, *Hoplurus* (*Oplurus*) and *Chalarodon*, and the boid snakes and pelomedusid turtle are often considered relictual (Mertens, 1934). Uroplatidae, a family of lizards endemic to the island, has no close relatives. Geckos have diversified on mainland Madagascar, and distinctive species and subspecies may be found on offshore islands. For a nearly complete taxonomic account of the diverse skinks, geckos, and chameleons on Madagascar, the lizard fauna of Angel (1942) will provide a convenient summary.

With respect to plants, the striking cactoid forms of the endemic family Didiereaceae (perhaps a relative of Portulacaceae) are an obvious example of radiation within the drier regions of Madagascar. The older monograph of Choux (1934) has now been supplanted by the exhaustive studies of Rauh (1956, 1961, 1963, 1965). An endemic family of dubious affinities, Sarcolaenaceae (Chalenaceae), has radiated into various habitats and shows great diversity not only in size, leaf shape, flower details and anatomy (Gérard, 1919; Cavaco, 1952), but even to a remarkable extent in its pollen tetrads (Carlquist, 1964).

Fringing Archipelagos

Recent offshore islands—either those formerly connected to mainland areas, or those that have emerged as oceanic islands—often contain merely depauperate floristic and faunistic assemblages, differing little from comparable close mainland areas. However, evolutionarily active groups may well be able to show at least some phases of adaptive radiation on insular areas.

California Islands. Among the Pacific offshore islands of California and Baja California, only one group of plants, the genus *Hemizonia* (Asteraceae: Heliantheae, subtribe Madiinae), shows what could be called adaptive radiation. The insular populations of these shrubby Hemizonias may well be to some extent relictual. This group of species is represented on the mainland only by a small population of *H. greeneana* (otherwise on Guadalupe I.) at Punta Banda, near Ensenada, Baja California, and by *H. minthornii*, a xeromorphic species in the vicinity of Santa Susanna Pass, southern California. Even if the shrubby Hemizonias have survived more abundantly on the offshore islands than on mainland areas, there is every reason to believe that autochthonous diversification has occurred on the islands (Carlquist, 1965). Disregarding the markedly different species of the southern islands for the moment—*H. frutescens, H. greeneana, H. palmeri,* and *H. streetsii*—we find that *H. clementina* on the northern islands seems to be in the process of forming distinctive races. Although populations within any given island may be variable, differentiation among the islands does seem to be occurring. Such islands as Santa Barbara, San Clemente, and Anacapa have populations that appear to be differentiating with respect to hairiness, leaf shape, leaf size, leaf margins (toothed or not), and other characteristics. A careful, perhaps statistically oriented, study of insular populations of *H. clementina* would be of interest for showing modal differences, if any, and whether any of these differences are adaptive in nature. Species of the southern islands appear to differ in characteristics that could be called adaptive, keyed to their particular habitat preferences (Carlquist, 1965).

Gulf of California Islands. Differentiation of races of *Uta stansburiana* (*sensu lato;* segregate species have been recognized) has occurred on islands in the Gulf of California. These differences are chiefly in respect to body size and scale size. Although these are clear indications of differentiation, and can be called, as Soulé (1966) does, "radiation," some aspects are adaptive and some may not be. This group is reviewed in chapter 15 in relation to the phenomenon of insular gigantism of animals.

Philippines. Although they are offshore islands only in the wider and much more profound sense, mention should be made of certain apparent instances of adaptive radiation in the Philippines. This phenomenon is not characteristic of most plant and animal groups in the Philippines, presumably because this archipelago is relatively harmonic in many respects with the floras and faunas of the major islands of Malesia, which are themselves relatively harmonic. However, mention should be made of the murid rodents of Luzon (Dickerson, 1936). Presumably Luzon's inaccessibility to mammals has permitted radiation of rodents there, just as rodents have undergone radiation in Australia (albeit not spectacular in comparison to the marsupials there). Adaptive radiation has taken place in *Brachymeles* of the Scincidae (Brown and Rabor, 1967) and perhaps in some snakes (Brown and Alcala, 1970). However, one Philippine example of adaptive radiation is outstanding, the cyprinid fishes of Lake Lanao (see the next section).

Large Freshwater Lakes

Although other freshwater lakes demonstrate aspects of speciation very well, there are five in which adaptive radiation of fishes has been spectacular: the three great lakes of Africa—Lake Victoria, Lake Tanganyika, and Lake Malawi (= Lake Nyasa)—for the cichlids; Lake Lanao, Mindanao, Philippines, for the cyprinids; and Lake Baikal, eastern USSR, for the cottids. Because different groups of fishes are involved, each of these situations casts light upon the others.

Lake Lanao. From fairly conclusive evidence, we know that Mindanao, uplifted during Miocene time, formed a central plateau by means of basalt flows. Within this plateau, volcanoes formed a dam around streams, whereby Lake Lanao was created. The damming of Lake Lanao at the Camp Keithly outlet has been quite reliably dated (Bailey Willis, in Myers, 1960a) at the significantly recent time of approximately 10,000 years ago. The basis for this dating is the erosion of the Agus River canyon at the main outlet of Lake Lanao. Although this event does not completely preclude possible earlier instances of damming of the lake (Myers, 1960a), it is conceivable that virtually all of the remarkable evolution of cyprinid fishes in Lake Lanao has taken only 10,000 years. Herre (1933) confidently states that one cyprinid, *Barbodes binotatus*, still extant in the Philippines, or possibly *B. quinquemaculatus*, was the ancestor of the 5 genera (*Barbodes* and 4 endemic genera) and 18 species of cyprinids endemic to the lake. Even more species may yet be found (Myers, 1969a).

Herre (1933) considered that the *Barbodes* ancestor (presumptively *B. binotatus*; *B. quinquemaculatus* may be only a geographical race of *B. binotatus* on the Zamboanga Peninsula) developed into the extant Lanao species, *B. tumba*, which in turn invaded streams and lakes of the Lanao plateau as a whole. It has presumably replaced *B. binotatus*, which no longer occurs on the Lanao plateau. As Lake Lanao reached maturity, a *Barbodes* flock differentiated. *Barbodes tumba* has become an inhabitant of the Lanao streams and tributaries, and occurs in the turbulent outlet at the falls above the Agus River. However, it evidently once gave rise to a flock of species of the shallow, still margins of the lake. In these shallows, where *Potamogeton* is the common aquatic plant, occur *B. amara*, *B. lanaoensis*, *B. lindog*, and a derivative of *B. lindog*, *B. disa*. Another shallow-water derivative of *B. lindog* has been recognized as a monotypic genus, *Spratellicyparis palata*, because of its peculiar lower-jaw modifications. *Barbodes clemensi*, notable for its robustness and distinctive color (green above, yellow beneath, lustrous gold on its sides), occurs in the *Potamogeton* zone, as does *B. manalak*, the largest species of Cyprinidae in the entire Philippines.

A deep-water derivative of *B. tumba* is *B. baoulan*, which rises to surface depths only during storms or in midwinter. Other endemic species of *Barbodes* are restricted to shallow, muddy bays with a junglelike vegetation of reeds and similar plants. These species are blackish or dusty brown, a melanism evidently part of their adaptation to these darkish waters. Herre

(1933) cites as a parallel the strongly melanistic goby from other densely marshy Philippine lakes, *Glossogobius griseus*.

A very small Lanao endemic, *Barbodes sirang*, is also melanistic, but its habits are unknown. Large-headed species of *Barbodes*, the adaptational mode of which is not yet clear, include *B. flavifuscus* and *B. katolo*, both believed to be offshoots of *B. amara*. From *B. katolo*, in turn, two endemic genera are believed to have arisen. The monotypic *Cephalokompsus* (*C. pachycheilus*) is notable for a continual postlabial groove on the lower jaw (this grove is interrupted in *Barbodes* and most other cyprinids). *Ospatulus* (two species, *O. truncatulus* and *O. palaemophagus*) is distinctive by virtue of its truncate lower jaw, much shorter than the upper.

Mandibularca (monotypic, *M. resinus*) is, according to Herre (1933), "the most remarkable of the Lanao Cyprinidae." It occurs only in the excessive turbulence of the Agus River outlet of Lake Lanao. The lower jaw is exceptionally elongate, upwardly curved, shaped like a spatula, and "fleshless." Herre believed that it originated from *Barbodes clemensi*, some individuals of which have lower jaws that seem to foreshadow the condition in *Mandibularca*.

The various papers by Herre (1924, 1926, 1932, 1933; Herre, in Dickerson, 1928) have not, surprisingly, been followed by new field studies, but his material does suggest that the Lanao cyprinids are a virtually unparalleled situation (see Myers, 1960a).

Lake Malawi (Lake Nyasa). In dealing with adaptive radiation and speciation in Lake Malawi and the other African lakes, we are dealing with cichlid fishes: 78 percent of the Lake Malawi fishes, 62 percent of those in Lake Tanganyika, and 71 percent of those in Lake Victoria are cichlids. The number of these cichlid species in the three lakes is about 193, 134, and 127, respectively, and the percentage of endemic cichlids in the three lakes is 97, 98, and 98, respectively. Lake Malawi has 20 endemic genera of cichlids, Lake Tanganyika 30, and Lake Victoria 4 (Lowe-McConnell, 1969). Thus with respect to cichlids the great African lakes are as remarkable as Lake Lanao. The reasons for this situation are not entirely clear in the case of Lake Malawi. Fryer (1959a) presented an account of evolution of the Lake Malawi fishes, but Myers (1960b) felt that more data on possible ecological distinctions among the numerous cichlid species and genera were required to explain this remarkable autochthonous evolution.

Fryer (1960) replied that some ecological distinctions do exist. He cited, for example, adaptive radiation in mimicry of these fishes, as studied by Trewavas (1947), in nest-building and other habits (Lowe, 1953, 1959; Fryer, 1956, 1959b), and in such habits as burrowing in sand and feigning death. Fryer also cited morphological features: *Petrotilapia tridentiger* has mouth structures that facilitate scraping of algae from rocks; *Lathrinops furcifer* has a protractile mouth capable of sifting chironomid larvae from sand. However, Fryer (1960) still relied on factors he cited earlier: scattered habitats around the lake margins (rocky outcrops, for example), various types of precinctiveness, and predation. With respect to precinctiveness, he noted that the Lake Malawi cichlids typically are mouth-breeders; the young shoal together; the "*Tilapia* mark" on juvenile fins serves as a signal; and the young, while losing parental orientation as they adolesce, do not scatter. Fryer stressed that in Lake Malawi predation is heavy, and that crossing a sandy bottom to another rocky outcrop would render individuals visible and easier prey. Predation, as noted by Greenwood (1964), might help coexistence of prey species by keeping them below the level where they would compete excessively for food, presumably to the point where one species would replace another.

In addition, Lowe-McConnell (1969) cites temporal and ethological barriers for cichlids in Lake Malawi. *Tilapia saka* breeds in shallow water before the rainy season; *T. lidole* breeds at the same time but in much deeper water or off open sandy beaches; *T. squamipinnis* (a species very close to *T. saka*) breeds in deeper water during the rainy season (December to February). Also differences in breeding colors can be cited: *T. saka* and *T. lidole* have black males, whereas *T. squamipinnis* males are sky blue, and white at the face (Lowe, 1953).

It seems that we cannot compare evolution of the Lake Malawi cichlids to that of the Darwin's finches, where noncompetitive utilization of food sources and visible geographical barriers (channels between islands) provide obvious partitioning devices. In the cichlids, these factors do operate to some extent, but behavioral and other differences must also operate as partitioning devices. Admittedly, fish may be more difficult to study with respect to both behavior and ecological preferences than birds.

Lake Tanganyika. Lake Tanganyika is at least 1.5 million years old, and may be even older (Brooks, 1950). The characteristics of its fish fauna suggest a more mature stage in evolution if we compare its cichlids with those of Lake Malawi (Poll, 1946). Lowe-McConnell (1969) claims that most Lake Tanganyika cichlids tend to live around rocky outcrops at lake margins. Thus, these outcrops may function as centers, if not discrete subdivisions, for speciation, as Fryer suggests they do in Lake Malawi. In addition, Lake Tanganyika cichlids exhibit notable morphological specializations (Myers, 1960b). *Perissodus* has large, double-pointed, heavy-based teeth. *Asprotilapia* and *Enantiopus* have pelvic fins specialized for bottom-living. Myers (1960) draws comparisons—typical in illustrations of adaptive radiation—between Lake Tanganyika cichlid genera and non-cichlid families they resemble: *Telmatochromis* is comparable to Blenniidae, *Tropheus* to Girellidae, *Asprotilapia* to European Percidae.

Lake Victoria. In Lake Victoria, *Haplochromis* is a major genus, with about 120 species. Feeding habits vary. Twelve species feed on molluscs, but in two different ways. The least specialized (i.e., most like riverine ancestors), about 40 species, feed on insect larvae and detritus. Four species feed on algae and 1 on vascular plants. At least 50 species prey on other fish: 8 of these are known to feed on eggs and fry of other *Haplochromis* species, presumably by sucking them from the mouths of their parents. With such differences, in addition to some of the evolutionary factors cited for the other great African lakes, one can understand how adaptive radiation and speciation may have occurred in a lacustrine "island" where terrestrial concepts of adaptive radiation do not, at first, seem to apply—and where methods of study must be quite different.

Lowe-McConnell (1969) cites an interesting ecological mechanism in the Malagarazi waterlily swamps of Tanzania. Characoids feed on and partially digest leaves, buds, and fruits of the waterlilies. This semidigested material and its contained microorganisms form a carpet on the swamp bottom, which four cichlids (two *Tilapia* species, two *Haplochromis* species) feed upon. In turn, small fish of these four cichlids can be prey of piscivorous species of cichlids.

Lake Baikal. Lake Baikal presents a different picture, if only because of its age and the more markedly cold climatic regime. It is ancient compared to other freshwater lakes; its southern basic dates from the Paleocene. In Lake Baikal, the family Cottidae is represented (Taliyev, 1955) along with an endemic family, Comephoridae, derived from cottids. One subfamily of Cottidae is sometimes recognized as a distinct family, Cotto-comephoridae. Comephoridae are not found along the shore, but occupy open waters of Baikal, where they live from the surface to below 500 m. There are two species, *Comephorus dybowskii*, which mates from September to November, and *C. baicalensis*, which mates from April to June (Koryakov, 1955). Comephoridae give birth to living young.

In Cottidae, there are five endemic genera. *Cottocomephorus* (two species) inhabits the coastal belt and spawns at shallow places near the shore, on the rocky bottom. *Abyssocottus* (five species), as its name suggests, inhabits great depths; it has a slender form and an elongate jaw. The other endemic genera include *Metacottus* (monotypic), *Batrachocottus* (four species), *Paracottus* (four species) and *Procottus* (monotypic). Taliyev's (1955) illustrations (some reproduced by Kozhov, 1963) and data show these genera to be amply distinct.

As might be expected, a lake as ancient as Baikal demonstrates adaptive radiation in other groups as well. Fifty-six species of Mollusca are endemic to Lake Baikal. Most of these belong to six genera endemic to Lake Baikal and nearby Lake Kosogol (Kozhov, 1963). Two of these genera comprise an endemic family of prosobranchs, Baicaliidae. The range of shell forms in *Baicalia* is quite remarkable (Kozhov, 1951, 1963). It ranges from ovoid to turret-shaped, smooth or with various types of ridges (*B. costata*) or fine spines (*B. ciliata*). This radiation in form is not unlike that of the Hawaiian amastrids, and demonstrates that isolating mechanisms have been operative within Lake Baikal, which is, however, much older than the Hawaiian Islands.

Another Baikal group that shows considerable diversification is gammarid shrimps. These range from colorless, pale-eyed, slender types of deep waters (*Abyssogammarus*) to markedly spinescent genera (*Acanthogammarus*). The nature of ecological distinctions among these species does not seem clear; all gammarids have long breeding seasons (Kozhov, 1963).

Continental Areas

Lack (1971) has hypothesized, with good reason, that there are probably few or no open ecological niches for birds on islands at present, unless habitat alteration by man occurs. If this is true for land birds, which have moderately good dispersal to oceanic islands (most of which are recent), one can well imagine the situation, by comparison, on continents. Continents are undoubtedly "saturated" constantly, but shifts in geology and climate make them subject to floristic and faunistic readjustments as particular areas become temporarily disharmonic. For example, previously glaciated areas, volcanically devastated areas, and emerged embayments offer new territories. The process by which niches are filled is not the same, in general, as on islands. Because of the harmonic nature of continental biotas, invasion of new niches tends to be "buffered" since so many "entrants" compete for niches. Some radiative speciation can occur, as exemplified by Keast's (1971) summary of niche-occupation following glaciation on Tasmania. Because, in this case, dispersal across Bass Straits is involved, there is some simulation of dispersal to distant oceanic islands, but there is less disharmony, so each of the immigrants has been able to radiate only to a limited extent. A clear exception to buffered radiation on continents occurs when large freshwater lakes are created, because they usually offer a variety of habitats and must begin the process of population with a few occupants suited to fresh water (perhaps mostly from inflowing streams, or via long-distance dispersal from other lakes)—in other words, the situation is as disharmonic as that of an oceanic island.

Cataclysmic events leading to adaptive radiation do occur, however, in terrestrial continental areas. The California flora offers some examples. With the mid-Tertiary drying of the Southwest, a fertile field for more xerophytic plants arose. Although a few boreal groups (e.g., *Arctostaphylos* —perhaps not strictly a boreal example) have adapted to Californian xeromorphy, most of the entrants are from more southerly, chiefly Mexican, groups. For example, the invasion of California by various groups of Asteraceae (a family notably competent in dry situations) has led to adaptive radiation in such genera as *Eriophyllum, Haplopappus,* and the genera that comprise the tarweeds (Heliantheae, subtribe Madiinae). All of these are not only capable of success in a mediterranean climate but also show preferences for pioneer situations—and pioneer situations tend to be distributed in an insular fashion. The various papers of Axelrod can be consulted for a fuller account of occupancy of the southwestern United States during the Tertiary.

Southwestern Australia, cited in chapter 8 as a superb example of an insular area, is perhaps the most striking continental area for adaptive radiation, at least where angiosperms are concerned. However, Australia as a whole is insular not merely in being the smallest of the continents, but in being so far removed from areas of similar temperate climate and being separated from Indo-Malesia for very protracted periods. Consequently, one is not surprised that "heightened" examples of adaptive radiation occur there, such as the marsupials, proteads, and eucalypts.

Many other interesting examples of adaptive radiation on continents can be cited, such as the radiation into mimicry situations and other leaf types by the South African "living stones" of the Aizoaceae (*Conophytum, Lithops, Pleiospilos*). Radiation in plant form, floral form, and pollination mechanisms in the stapelioids and ceropegioids (Apocynaceae) of South Africa offer another series of examples. *Euphorbia* species in Africa have experienced a wide range in diversification of growth form, as have the cacti in the Americas—and the radiation in growth form is only one dimension of radiation in those groups. Interestingly, many of these examples are from drier regions, which suggests that only a limited number of invasive groups can thrive in such conditions, but if they do, they can radiate widely.

Thus, phases of insular adaptive radiation can illuminate continental situations and lend perspective to their interpretation. Various authors have speculated that if the "supralimital" products of adaptive radiation in insular situations (e.g., the Lanao fishes or the Hawaiian honeycreepers) had occurred on continents, we would, in fact, be seeing how larger taxonomic categories originated on continental areas. The interplay of continental and insular patterns, and their analysis separately, then synthesis, has of recent years been highly illuminating. We can achieve more comprehensive constructs of evolution if different types of evidence, from different areas and different taxonomic groups, are fed into the synthesis.

Oceanic Areas

Shelf Areas. Some areas of ocean tend to have insular qualities, but not in the sense of offering both definitive barriers from other ocean areas and, at the same time, a wide variety of habitats. The "East Pacific Barrier" (Briggs, 1961) and other restricted shelf areas (Briggs, 1970) are "isolated environments within the ocean," although they are not within themselves highly diversified so as to host spectacular examples of adaptive radiation, although endemism can be high.

Invertebrates on Reefs. Other marine organisms that are not widespread but have very localized requirements could be cited as examples of adaptive radiation. The mollusc *Conus* and other invertebrates notable for large numbers of "sympatric" species on reefs and evident resource-partitioning of reef areas of given islands (Kohn, 1968, 1971) should be cited. According to Kohn (1971), specialization to particular food sources is of prime importance, adaptation to particular habitat niches (microhabitats) of secondary importance, in permitting the numbers of "co-curring" species on given islands. Such resource-partitioning is one of the evidences for the occurrence of adaptive radiation.

Pediculate Fishes. The great deeps of the Pacific are topographically "islands," but they are also highly specialized habitats. The pediculate fishes that have entered these deeps are particularly interesting. They can be considered products of adaptive radiation not merely within those deeps, but as part of a larger scheme in which slower-moving predatory fishes (exactly which contemporary representatives gave rise to pediculate fishes is not certain) developed lures or "angles" and diversified into various habitats. These anglerfish may be divided into three groups, representing three adaptational modes:

Antennariidae (frogfishes), in depths of less than 50 fathoms, mostly shallower

Ogcocephalidae (batfishes), in depths of 50 to 150 fathoms

Ceratioidea (lantern fishes), comprising several families, in depths of 150 to 3600 fathoms (bathypelagic)

Assuming these groups—and their ancestors—to be products of adaptive radiation, we may find cycles of radiation within each of them. In the Antennariidae, radiation seems to be enhanced by the slowness in bodily movements during feeding activities. Pectoral fins are modified for walking. As voracious predators, they must lure prey and then suck it in rapidly, rather than pursue it. This behavior, in turn, is linked to camouflage: they must be virtually invisible to prey. In Pacific, Atlantic, and Indian Ocean species of *Antennarius*, speciation has been accompanied by mimicry to resemble backgrounds of the habitats which they frequent. For example, *A. sanguifluus* of the Pacific has red and brown splotches that comprise camouflage patterns closely resembling the coral and algal backgrounds of the reefs where it lives. Various features of *Antennarius* morphology contribute to radiation in background mimicry (Allen, 1970; Jordan, 1905; Schultz, 1957, 1964; Strasburg, 1966). Condensation of form and irregularities of outline are important in this regard; fins are squat, thick, and colored like the body; eyes are inconspicuous. Various flaps of tissue and ciliate appendages around the mouth, as well as elsewhere on the body, simulate algal lobes or filamentous algae or animal colonies. Scales would decrease mimicry ability; *Antennarius* lacks scales and has instead dermal papillae whose texture is capable of various resemblances.

Species of *Antennarius* within a given region may be assumed to have a low dispersal rate (for fish); their endemism to particular islands and atolls is high. Where several species occur together, we may assume the likelihood of monophylesis or development within at least close portions of an ocean—although this is not necessarily true. If *Antennarius* species in an archipelago are monophyletic, we have a definitive example of adaptive radiation. This does not alter the picture of *Antennarius* as a whole representing adaptive radiation for purposes of mimicry. Whichever explanation obtains in the Bermuda species of *Antennarius* (table 9.1), we have an illustrative example. Moreover, each of the Bermuda species of *Antennarius* has a distinctive lure, or angle (the illicium, tipped by the esca, or "bait"). In *A. multiocellatus*, the esca is bulbous, with lateral hairs. In *A. ocellatus*, the esca consists wholly of hairs. The other three species have lanceolate lobes on the esca: three in *A. tenebrosus*, several in *A. pauciradiatus*, two with a central bulb in *A. bermudensis*. Because the illicium is so rarely seen in action, we cannot be sure of the resemblances, created by these forms, to animals eaten by prey of the *Antennarius*, but evidently a radiation has occurred. In the Bermudan species of *Antennarius*, distinctive color patterns and depths assure lack of overlap in ecological niches. The predators of *Antennarius* are not known, but one may assume that such precise mimicry has been the product of intense selective forces, and

TABLE 9.1.

Bermudan species of *Antennarius*

	Depth and habitat	Color and pattern	Probable resemblances
A. *multiocellatus*	Less than 20 ft, sandy bottoms	Dark gray, with spots	Loggerhead sponges
A. *ocellatus*	Tidal pools	Brown (juveniles with pink spots); "ocelli"	Colonies of invertebrates on rocks
A. *tenebrosus*	Less than 8 ft, rocky outcrops	Brown, with yellow and black spots	Rocks, with flat algal and animal colonies
A. *pauciradiatus*	25–50 ft or more, coralline bottoms	Brownish yellow, mottled	Aging coral heads
A. *bermudensis*	Beds of coral and coralline red algae	Rust color, with reddish spots	Corals and red algae

predators would tend to enforce the excellence of mimicry, lack of intermediacy, and ecological separation.

Histrio histrio, the sargassum fish, forms a distinct subfamily in the Antennariidae. Unlike *Antennarius*, it floats freely among the tangles of *Sargassum* in the Sargasso Sea. Its fins are better suited to locomotion than are those of *Antennarius*, but its capture of prey is not achieved by pursuit, at which *Histrio* would be inadequate. Its coloration perfectly matches the various shades of *Sargassum*, and flaps and tubercles resembling *Sargassum* fronds occur not only on the upper surface and sides, but on the lower surfaces as well, for predators are, in fact, more likely to occur at levels below it. Unlike other Antennariidae, *Histrio* has a mouth whose inside is a tawny color matching *Sargassum* shades.

Ogcocephalidae are also widespread in Pacific and Atlantic areas, but, as indicated earlier, favor depths intermediate between those of the antennarioids and the ceratioids. They are, like Antennariidae, poor at swimming. Flattened laterally like the manta, these fish have pectoral and pelvic fins modified to act as forelegs and hindlegs. Although there are distinctive patterns and textures, batfish have radiated with respect to morphology of the esca as well (Bradbury, 1967).

Ceratioidea is the name generally given to an assemblage of rather tentative families and genera of lantern fishes, which inhabit great depths.

The uncertainty of taxonomy derives from the fact that known specimens often represent unique finds, occasionally taken during deep-sea dredging, rather than series of specimens of any one species. We know little or nothing of their habits. Bertelson's (1951) summary provides most of the information available on them, although additional illustrations may be found in Jordan (1905). They represent an entry into extreme abyssal conditions by the same general pediculate stocks from which Antennariidae and Ogcocephalidae have also been derived.

Modifications for life in abyssal conditions include lack of bones (except for the large and powerful jaw), condensed form, lack of a swimming bladder, probable capability of oxygen intake through capillaries near the skin surface, and marked sex dimorphism in at least four, perhaps six, families. In these families, at sexual maturity the small males attach themselves to various localities on females, which are relatively large in proportion, and become interconnected to the vascular system of the female and degenerate in several ways. The parasitic habit of males presumably assures fertilization of eggs under conditions of great sparsity of population and difficulty of pair-occurrence when swimming ability is so limited and perpetual dark is present.

The ceratioids have bioluminescent, stalked lures (except for *Neoceratias* and *Coelophryne*) and other portions of their bodies may be luminescent as well. Because our concepts of their phylogeny and taxonomy are tentative, we cannot construct anything but a fragmentary picture of adaptive radiation within ceratioids. Presumably the remarkable differences in morphology of illicium and esca among the known species (Bertelson, 1951) do, however, represent adaptation to distinctive predatory behavior and perhaps diet. The means whereby knowledge of their habits can be improved seems technologically almost unobtainable at present. Needless to say, ceratioids brought to the surface are dead, and their sparsity alone would make study difficult even if technical problems of observation at great depths could be overcome.

References

Allen, G. R. 1970. Two new species of frogfishes (Antennariidae) from Easter Island. *Pacific Sci.* 24:517–22.

Angel, F. 1942. Les lézards de Madagascar. *Mém. Acad. Malgâche* 36:1–193.

Bertelson, E. 1951. The ceratioid fishes. Ontogeny, taxonomy, distribution, and biology. *Dana Rep.* (Carlsburg Found.) 39:1–276.

Bradbury, H. G. 1967. The genera of batfishes (Ogcocephalidae). *Copeia* (1967): 399–422.

Briggs, J. C. 1961. The east Pacific barrier and the distribution of shore fishes. *Evolution* 15:545–54.

Briggs, J. C. 1970. Tropical shelf zoogeography. *Proc. Calif. Acad. Sci.,* 4th ser., 38(7):131–38.

Brooks, J. L. 1950. Speciation in ancient lakes. *Quart. Rev. Biol.* 25:30–60, 131–76.

Brown, W. C., and A. C. Alcala. 1970. The zoogeography of the herpetofauna of the Philippine Islands, a fringing archipelago. *Proc. Calif. Acad. Sci.,* 4th ser., 38(6):105–30.

Brown, W. C., and D. S. Rabor. 1967. Review of the genus *Brachymeles* (Scincidae) with description of new species and subspecies. *Proc. Calif. Acad. Sci.,* 4th ser., 34(15):525–48.

Carlquist, S. 1964. Pollen morphology and evolution of Sarcolaenaceae (Chlaenaceae). *Brittonia* 16:231–54.

Carlquist, S. 1965. *Island life.* New York, Natural History Press.

Cavaco, A. 1952. Chlaénacées. In *Flore de Madagascar et des Comores,* ed. H. Humbert, 126e:1–37. Paris, Musée National d'Histoire Naturelle.

Choux, P. 1934. Les didiéréacées, xérophytes de Madagascar. *Mém. Acad. Malgâche* 18:1–71.

Dickerson, R. E. 1936. *Distribution of life in the Philippines.* Manila, Bureau of Printing.

Eisenberg, J. F., and E. Gould. 1970. The tenrecs: A study in mammalian behavior and evolution. *Smithsonian Contrib. Zool.* 27:1–137.

Fryer, G. 1956. Biological notes on some cichlid fishes of Lake Nyasa. *Rev. Zool. Bot. Afr.* 54:1–7.

Fryer, G. 1959a. Some aspects of evolution in Lake Nyasa. *Evolution* 13:440–51.

Fryer, G. 1959b. The trophic interrelationships and ecology of some littoral communities of Lake Nyasa with especial reference to the fishes, and a discussion of the evolution of a group of rock-frequenting Cichlidae. *Proc. Zool. Soc. London* 132:153–281.

Fryer, G. 1960. Evolution of fishes in Lake Nyasa. *Evolution* 14:396–400.

Gérard, F. 1919. Étude systématique, morphologique et anatomique des Chlaénacées. Thesis, Faculté des Sciences de Paris (printed by J. Vin, Marseilles).

Greenwood, P. H. 1964. Explosive evolution in African lakes. *Proc. Roy. Inst. Gr. Brit.* 40:256–69.

Herre, A. W. 1924. The Philippine Cyprinidae. *Philippine Jour. Sci.* 24:249–307.

Herre, A. W. 1926. Two fishes from Lake Lanao. *Philippine Jour. Sci.* 29:499–502.

Herre, A. W. 1932. Five new Philippine fishes. *Copeia* (1932):139–42.

Herre, A. W. 1933. The fishes of Lake Lanao: A problem in evolution. *Amer. Natur.* 67:154–62.

Hill, W. C. O. 1953. *Primates: Comparative anatomy and taxonomy*, vol. I. *Strepsirhini: A monograph*. Edinburgh, Edinburgh University Press.

Jolly, A. 1966. *Lemur behavior*. Chicago, University of Chicago Press.

Jordan, D. S. 1905. *A guide to the study of fishes*. 2 vols. New York, Henry Holt and Co.

Keast, A. 1971. Adaptive evolution and shifts in niche occupation in island birds. In *Adaptive aspects of insular evolution*, ed. W. L. Stern, pp. 39–53. Pullman, Wash., Washington State University Press.

Kohn, A. J. 1968. Microhabitats, abundance and food of *Conus* on atoll reefs of the Maldive and Chagos Islands. *Ecology* 49:1046–62.

Kohn, A. J. 1971. Diversity, utilization of resources, and adaptive radiation in shallow-water marine invertebrates of tropical oceanic islands. *Limnol. Oceanog.* 16:332–48.

Koryakov, E. A. 1955. On the fertility and type of the spawning population of *Comephorus*. *Dokl. Akad. Nauk. S.S.S.R.* 101:965–67 (in Russian).

Kozhov, M. M. 1951. On the morphology and history of the Baikalian endemic molluscs of the family Baicaliidae. *Tr. Baik. Limnol. Stud. Akad. Nauk. S.S.S.R.* 13:93–119 (in Russian).

Kozhov, M. M. 1963. *Lake Baikal and its life*. The Hague, Dr. W. Junk, Publishers.

Lack, D. 1947. *Darwin's finches*. Cambridge, Cambridge University Press.

Lack, D. 1971. Island birds. In *Adaptive aspects of insular evolution*, ed. W. L. Stern, pp. 29–31. Pullman, Wash., Washington State University Press.

Lowe, R. H. 1953. Notes on the ecology and evolution of Nyasa fishes of the genus *Tilapia*, with a description of *T. saka* Lowe. *Bull. Brit. Mus. (Natur. Hist.) Zool.* 2:349–68.

Lowe, R. H. 1959. Breeding behavior patterns and ecological differences between *Tilapia* species and their significance for evolution in the genus *Tilapia* (Pisces: Cichlidae). *Proc. Zool. Soc. London* 132:1–30.

Lowe-McConnell, R. H. 1969. Speciation in tropical freshwater fishes. *Biol. Jour. Linnaean Soc.* 1:51–75. (Also as *Speciation in tropical environments*, ed. R. H. Lowe-McConnell. London, Academic Press.)

Mertens, R. 1934. Die Insel-Reptilien, ihre Ausbreitung, Variation, und Artbildung. *Zoologica* 32(6):1–209.

Milne-Edwards, A., and A. Grandidier. 1878–1885. Histoire naturelle des oiseaux. In *Histoire physique, politique, et naturelle de Madagascar* (1 vol. text: 1885; 3 vols. plates: 1878, 1879, 1881). Paris, Imprimerie National.

Myers, G. S. 1960a. The endemic fish fauna of Lake Lanao, and the evolution of higher taxonomic categories. *Evolution* 14:323–33.

Myers, G. S. 1960b. Fish evolution in Lake Nyasa. *Evolution* 14:394–96.

Petter, J. J. 1962. Recherches sur l'ecologie et l'ethologie des lémuriens malgâches. *Mem. Mus. Nat. Hist. Natur., n.s.*, ser. A, Zool. 27:1–146.

Petter, J. J. 1969. Speciation in Madagascan lemurs. *Biol. Jour. Linnaean Soc.* 1:77–84. (Also as *Speciation in tropical environments*, ed. R. H. Lowe-McConnell, pp. 77–84. London, Academic Press.)

Poll, M. 1946. Revision de la faune icthyologique du Lac Tanganyika. *Ann. Mus. Congo Belge, Zool.* (1), 4:145–364.

Rand, A. L. 1936. The distribution and habits of Madagascar birds. *Bull. Amer. Mus. Natur. Hist.* 72(5):143–499.

Rauh, W. 1956. Morphologische, entwicklungsgeschichtliche, histogenetische, und anatomische Untersuchungen an dem Sprossen der Didieraceen. *Arch. Akad. Wiss. Lit. (Mainz)* 1956(6):341–444.

Rauh, W. 1961. Weitere Untersuchungen an Didiereaceen. 1 Teil. *Sitzungsber. Heidelberg. Akad. Wiss. (Math.-naturwiss. Kl.)* (1960/61) no. 7:182–300.

Rauh, W. 1963. Didiéréacées. *Flore Madagascar Comores* 121e:1–36.

Rauh, W. 1965. Weitere Untersuchungen an Didiereaceen. 2 Teil. *Sitzungsber. Heidelberg. Akad. Wiss. (Math.-naturwiss. Kl.)* (1965) no. 3:217–434 (with supplement by H. Straka: Die Pollenmorphologie der Didiereaceen, pp. 435–43).

Schultz, L. P. 1957. The frogfishes of the family Antennariidae. *Proc. U.S. Nat. Mus.* 107 (no. 3383):47–105.

Schultz, L. P. 1964. Three new species of frogfishes from the Indian and Pacific Oceans with notes on other species (family Antennariidae). *Proc. U.S. Nat. Mus.* 116 (no. 3500):171–82.

Soulé, M. 1966. Trends in the insular radiation of a lizard. *Amer. Natur.* 100:47–64.

Strasburg, D. N. 1966. *Golem cooperae*, a new antennariid fish from Fiji. *Copeia* (1966):475–77.

Taliyev, D. N. 1955. The miller's thumbs (Cottoidei) of Lake Baikal. *Tr. Akad. Nauk. S.S.S.R.* 9:603 (in Russian).

Trewavas, E. 1947. An example of mimicry among fishes. *Nature* 160:120.

CHAPTER TEN

INSULAR WOODINESS

Darwin (1859, p. 392) claimed that representatives of predominantly herbaceous families (particularly dicotyledonous families) tend to be woodier
on islands than their mainland counterparts: "Again, islands often possess
trees or bushes belonging to orders which elsewhere include only herbaceous species." However, Hemsley (1885), in a review of insular botany
derived from observations during the *Challenger* voyage, says that Darwin's
statement is "incorrect, as may be seen from the following parallels in insular and continental floras." Despite the apparent contradiction, neither
Darwin nor Hemsley is wrong. If we examine certain insular floras, such
as those of the Hawaiian Islands, St. Helena, or Juan Fernandez, we see
remarkably woody representatives of "typically" herbaceous families—
notably Asteraceae in the islands mentioned. We can also see equivalent
arborescence in certain continental areas, as for Hemsley's (1885) admittedly incomplete listing of arboreal continental Asteraceae. However, what
one notes if one is familiar with geography, geology, and climate of certain
mainland areas is that they exhibit many of the same features strongly
represented on islands, so that similar growth forms may be expected.
The phenomenon of paramount importance, seemingly neglected by those
who have dealt with growth forms in dicotyledonous families, is that relatively few predominantly herbaceous families are incapable of evolutionary
increase in production of secondary xylem. Why are phylogenetic series
always read from woodiest to most herbaceous, with uniformitarian unidirectionality (e.g., Meusel, 1952)? There is considerable evidence, if we
wish to investigate more deeply, that angiosperms are supremely plastic in
evolving growth forms suited to situations, and that invasion of regions

350

suited to greater woodiness may be expected to result in evolution of that woodiness. It would be strange indeed if all groups of dicotyledons were doomed to progressive loss of cambial activity. To be sure, there are some families in which ability to produce secondary xylem has apparently been completely lost (Callitrichaceae, Podostemonaceae, Nymphaeaceae), but many families of dicotyledons seem still to be flexible where degree of cambial activity is involved.

The purpose of this chapter, then, is twofold: to examine insular representatives of increased woodiness as well as noninsular localities in which similar tendencies occur; and to attempt to find the common denominators and evidence for this phenomenon. To present only the insular picture would be unrealistic.

Some workers have regarded the woody insular representatives of predominantly herbaceous groups as relicts. For example, Meusel (1952) and Lems (1961) interpreted Macaronesian "woody herbs" in this way, although Lems modified his views in a subsequent paper (Lems and Holzapfel, 1968) and in conversations with me prior to his death. Skottsberg (1956) also held the relict hypothesis. This concept is also accepted by Werner (1966), who amazingly and erroneously claims all but universal acceptance for the relict hypothesis. The reverse hypothesis, that rosette trees, rosette shrubs, and other woody herbs have evolved autochthonously on islands, has been held by a number of workers, including Schenck (1907), Rikli (1912), Johnston (1953), and Carlquist (1965, 1970a). The reasons for this latter hypothesis are as follows:

1. The moderated climate of islands favors evolution of woodier forms there. This also holds for continental areas that are like islands in climate and other factors. The nature of these climatic regimes will be detailed later. There are exceptions in the cases of islands at high latitudes (which cannot be said to have moderated climates, however), and atolls and small islands where dryness, chiefly, deters increase in woodiness (and dry islands also cannot be said to have moderated climates).

2. Rosette trees and other woody forms are present on oceanic islands all over the world, suggesting independent evolution into this habit.

3. Quite different taxonomic groups represent woody herbs on different islands, and, like replications or control populations in experimental

work, serve to demonstrate the selective factors involved. Parallel evolution from herbaceous or less woody ancestors is indicated.

4. There are, to be sure, groups of woody herbs that occur both on islands and on narrow strips of continental coastal areas with similarly moderated climate (*Coreopsis gigantea* in California, for example). However, if the relict hypothesis were correct, there ought to be more numerous continental representatives, for volcanic islands are relatively recent and would be expected to bear few relicts. Meusel (1952) seems to think that relictualism is indicated because some "candelabrum shrubs" or "rosette shrubs" occur on islands and similar species (usually less woody!) occur in neighboring areas of similar climate (e.g., the Canary Islands and Mediterranean coastal areas). Meusel (1952) and Werner (1966) seem to imply that "woodier" is always "more primitive," that progressive placement of renewal buds closer to or below the ground in successively more northern European localities is the end product in such a series, and that the fact that one can construct such a series constitutes a form of evidence. There seems an obvious fallacy involved in choosing highly specialized island forms as a starting point. Why not, for instance, choose an intermediate mainland type as a starting point for both extremes, instead of maintaining unidirectionality? Moreover, Meusel and Werner simply analyze diagrams of growth forms (which can, of course, be arranged in any sequence one wishes) and geographical ranges; their work does not stress evolutionary depth in its approach.

5. If the relict hypothesis were correct, the rosette trees and shrubs on islands ought to represent groups with more numerous primitive features. However, this is not true: the insular woodier herbs all belong to families that are highly plastic and evolutionarily upgrade.

6. Insular woodier herbs belong to groups that basically have excellent dispersal mechanisms and would be expected to reach islands easily. There is also a strong link between good dispersibility, ability to establish in pioneer conditions, and ability to evolve a variety of forms because of capabilities for ecological polymorphism. Such a family as Asteraceae illustrates this link well.

7. Although only the most striking forms, such as rosette trees, are usually mentioned, the groups that have become woody on islands show various degrees of woodiness; larger plants are often characteristic of rain

forests. However, because various degrees of woodiness occur on islands, we would have to say that the most nearly herbaceous were reductions if woodiness were a relictual feature on islands. This seems awkward, because we would have to explain why herbaceous groups evolve into woody forms on continental areas, then the woody forms disperse to islands, and some of these undergo progressive evolution back to more herbaceous forms again. The easier hypothesis is that herbaceous types were the ones dispersed to islands, and that they have become progressively woodier as they undergo ecological shift (notably into wet forests). Groups that do show a gamut in woodiness on islands include *Echium* and *Sonchus* (Macaronesia), lobelioids, and various groups of Asteraceae. Even one example is illustrative: *Euphorbia piscatoria* is a low shrub in coastal localities on Madeira but is a tree (presumably a genetically different race) in laurel forests on that island. These gamuts seem best explained as aspects of adaptive radiation. The tendency for adaptive radiation to occur on islands such as the Hawaiian Islands has never been questioned—but proponents of the relictual hypothesis seem to overlook this.

8. Woody herbs on islands tend to retain some of the pioneering qualities we would expect of herbaceous, weedy groups. This observation was made by Skottsberg (1953) in the case of Juan Fernandez rosette trees, and is true elsewhere, as in Macaronesia, where wet-forest species of *Echium* and *Sonchus* invade openings in the forest. In the Hawaiian Islands, *Lobelia hypoleuca*, a shrubby species, appeared in abundance on the bare areas created by construction of the Mt. Kaala road. It is true that some wet-forest woodier herbs on islands lack this ability, but one would expect a gradual loss of weediness during evolution into the wet forest.

9. If the relict hypothesis were true, one would expect a higher proportion of woody herbs on old continental islands or old oceanic islands (e.g., New Guinea, New Caledonia). In fact, this is not true: the woody herbs occur chiefly on recent high islands with strongly disharmonic floras.

Why Does Secondary Woodiness Occur?

The reasons for secondary woodiness depend on the geographical location —otherwise we would expect woody representatives of predominantly herbaceous groups to be distributed uniformly throughout the world, as they clearly are not. The precise proportion of factors cited below whereby woodiness may occur cannot, unfortunately, be estimated. I doubt that only one of these factors is operative in any particular case, and I will attempt to elucidate, by means of a few examples that seem relatively explicable, which factors have operated to which extent.

DISHARMONY

In the case of oceanic islands remote from source areas, tree species are less likely to arrive by natural means than are herbaceous species. De Candolle and Darwin noted the precinctiveness to continental areas of many trees. "Now trees . . . generally have, whatever the cause may be, confined ranges. Hence trees would be little likely to reach distant oceanic islands" (Darwin, 1859). The "cause" which mystified Darwin involves poorer dispersibility of tree seeds as compared to those of herbs. Large seed size characterizes many continental forest trees, and immediately rules out many species (e.g., conifers are notably absent on oceanic islands). Many genera and families of large-seeded angiosperms have no representatives on oceanic islands. In addition, we must not underestimate the potent but imponderable factor of lessened viability of seeds of wet-forest trees. That many such species have short viability is well known, and is undoubtedly related to the weaker selective pressure for seed longevity in wet forest than in dry, open habitats. Large seeds with abundant food reserves are adapted to seedling development in shaded areas of a forest, and if the substrate is often wet, longevity to survive long dry periods is of no selective value. In these respects (as well as, perhaps, adaptation by forest trees to narrow ranges of tolerance), forest trees are specialized and would represent an evolutionary dead end except that the continental areas to which they are adapted are extensive; they suffer no disadvantage, but are poor for long-distance dispersal.

That seed size and viability are prime factors in absence of trees from oceanic islands is well illustrated by the exceptions: *Metrosideros* has reached virtually all the high islands of the Pacific because its seeds are small and resistant to cold, desiccation, and even seawater (see chapter 2). *Weinmannia*, the chief forest tree on Tahiti, has similar

and so freezing may be expected. Occurrence of temperatures below 0 C need not rule out occurrence of insular woodiness. One may cite genera of arborescent Asteraceae—for example, *Olearia* in New Zealand, Tasmania, Victoria, and the Chatham Islands, in areas where absolute minima below 0 C occur and where mean daily minima for the coldest months are about 4 C. Another climatic regime that fulfills low temperatures but on a uniform basis is found on equatorial mountains. Arborescence does occur in these regions, and is discussed in chapter 14. The equatorial climate of northeastern South America is represented by the diagram for Bogotá in figure 10.1. That of montane equatorial Africa is approximated by the diagram for Nanyuki (fig. 10.1). However, Nanyuki is on the plateau from which peaks such as Mt. Kenya rise, and Nanyuki represents the climatic uniformity of this region, but mean temperatures would be lower if there were reporting stations at higher elevations. Arborescent species are less frequent in uniformly cool areas than they are in areas with high mean temperatures, owing to problems of occasional frosts.

A mean temperature no lower than 10 C (Hawaii: Volcano Observatory, for example) might be expected to be the lower threshold · for arborescent species in most areas. In general, a mean annual temperature of 15–20 C would be expected to favor arborescence most. For example, the Hawaiian rain forests fall in this category, as do the Juan Fernandez Islands and St. Helena (fig. 10.1).

There undoubtedly is an upper temperature threshold for insular woodiness also. The reason for this limit would appear to be that herbaceous groups are, in general, those of temperate regions, and are limited

---

FIG. 10.1 (*continued*)

temperatures (in accordance with markings on left side of diagram; each mark = 10 C) and monthly means of rainfall (markings at right; mark = 20 mm rainfall). Where rainfall exceeds 100 mm, curve is drawn at truncated scale (1:10) and the portion above 100 mm is in black. Where rainfall curve is higher on diagram than temperature curve, space between the curves is filled by vertical lining (or black, if rainfall above 100 mm) whereas if rainfall curve drops below temperature curve, that space is filled by dotted pattern. At top left of each diagram is name of station and altitude. In brackets below name are numbers of years on which records are based—the first figure for temperature, the second for rainfall. At lower left are figures for temperature minima: the upper is mean daily minimum of the coldest month, the lower is absolute minimum recorded. Figures at upper left, if specified, are for maxima. At upper right are figures for mean annual temperature in degrees centigrade and for mean annual sum-total of precipitation in mm. These diagrams are selected from the *Klimadiagramm-Weltatlas*, by H. Walter, H. Lieth, and H. Rehder, 1967 (parts issued 1960–1967), © Verlag Fischer, Jena. Reproduced by permission of the publisher.

in ability to adapt to hot tropical areas. The upper threshold would appear to occur in areas with a mean annual temperature of about 23–25 C (sea level on Fiji, Hawaii, and New Caledonia). Arborescent lobelioids (near Hilo, Hawaii) or *Scaevola* of the Goodeniaceae (Fiji, New Caledonia) occur in such localities. The arborescent lobelioids and Scaevolas are most abundant and most arborescent in areas with mean annual temperatures of about 20 C (Tantalus, Oahu; Keanae Valley, Maui; see fig. 10.1).

There is no doubt that proximity to the temperature-insulating effect of the ocean moderates climate considerably, and absence of the extremes, in effect, produces a year-long growing season that seems desirable for arborescence in herbaceous groups. Proximity to the coast is, one must remember, a feature of all but the largest islands. The effect of coastal versus inland localities is shown by the following figures from California. Avalon, on offshore Santa Catalina Island, is at sea level; Claremont, about 50 mi. inland from the coast, has an elevation of approximately 1200 ft.

Locality	Mean Annual Temperature	Mean July Temperature	Mean January Temperature
Avalon	60.3 F	66.0 F	53.9 F
Claremont	62.1 F	74.2 F	50.7 F

These means are not as important as the extremes, even though differences are evident. There is an average of only 2 days per year with temperatures of 32 F (0 C) at San Diego, Calif., on the coast. At Claremont, there is an average of 28 days per year on which temperatures fall to 32 F, 8 days per year to 28 F, and 5 days per year with minima of 24 F. Such temperatures are unfavorable for many insular species (see below and chapter 5). There are several localities in coastal southern California where frost has never been reported.

Rainfall. With respect to total rainfall, one can say that precipitation of about 1000 mm (ca. 40 in.) per year or more favors arborescence. This figure is almost exactly that reported for sea-level stations on the Juan Fernandez Islands and St. Helena (fig. 10.1) and stations somewhat above sea level in the Hawaiian Islands (compare Honolulu, Tantalus, and Keanae in fig. 10.1). Rainfall below 1000 mm per year probably does not permit arborescence to any great extent, unless we take into account stem succulents. For example, there are arborescent plants, but all stem succulents, on the lowland Galápagos and Sokotra (Socotra); see figure 10.1.

There is perhaps no upper limit of rainfall above which arborescence is no longer favored (unless bog situations are formed). Many arborescent species occur in Hawaiian areas with rainfall above 2500 mm (100 in.) per year.

Uniformity of rainfall throughout the year is important. The occurrence of a strongly marked dry season vitiates the effect of high rainfall. Exceptions occur only where humidity is great, where cloud cover and moisture condensed on vegetation from clouds rather than by direct rainfall is available, or where deep, shady localities (valley bottoms) remain moist during dry seasons. Cooler temperatures during drier parts of the year would reduce evaporation and conserve available moisture. However, this condition is rare, and could be said to exist only on St. Helena (fig. 10.1), where rainfall is, however, not extremely low during any period of the year.

Unfortunately, rainfall recording stations on islands are most frequently near sea level. One can only guess at the increase in moisture with altitude, but obviously there is an appreciable effect. In the Hawaiian Islands, there are enough stations so that this effect can be seen. For example (fig. 10.1), Honolulu at sea level has an annual rainfall of 703 mm, a marked dry period during the summer, and an average temperature of 23.3 C. Tantalus, a station at 408 m only a few miles inland, has an annual rainfall of 2520 mm, no marked dry period during the summer, and an average temperature of 20.0 C. On Tantalus, arborescent species of *Clermontia* and *Cyanea* (Campanulaceae, Lobelioideae), *Scaevola* (Goodeniaceae) and *Dubautia* occur, whereas none of these (except for the semisucculent shrubby species of beach *Scaevola, S. taccada*) occurs at Honolulu or similar Hawaiian localities.

Similarly, upland sites in the Canary Islands must be considerably more mesic than lowland sites. We can suspect that the cloud forest on Tenerife has a climate like that of upland Madeira (Queimada, fig. 10.1), whereas lowland sites on both islands have a typical mediterranean climate, with warm, dry summers and cool, moist winters. At sea level, there is undoubtedly considerable moderation in temperature and humidity compared with inland continental localities in the same latitude. At altitudes

359

above the cloud forest on the Canary Islands, rainfall drops off, as it does at higher elevations in the Hawaiian Islands. The increase in rainfall in cloud forest in the Canary Islands and Madeira is not nearly so great as it is in the Hawaiian Islands, and the Macaronesian cloud forests are just within the range of tolerance for arborescence of herbaceous groups. However, shrubby representatives of herbaceous groups are favored in drier localities, both lowland and alpine, in the Canary Islands, Madeira, and the Hawaiian Islands, and stem succulents (*Euphorbia* in the Canary Is.; *Reynoldsia* in the Hawaiian Is.) are also suited to such regimes. The climate of Honolulu differs little from the oceanic mediterranean pattern: only the slightly higher mean temperature distinguishes it from, say, the climate of La Laguna (fig. 10.1) on Tenerife, or Santa Cruz (La Palma I.) in the Canary Islands. The rainfall in the Canaries is not nearly as heavy as in Hawaii, and so Macaronesia could be said to have at most a cloud forest, whereas the Hawaiian Islands have true rain forest.

The most striking example of how cloud forest has barely permitted evolution of arborescence is to be found in the Galápagos Islands. The only recording station is at sea level (Seymour I., fig. 10.1). The climatic profile of this station is very similar to that of Villa Cisneros, on the coastal Sahara south of the Canary Islands. The mean temperature at Seymour Island is somewhat greater than at Villa Cisneros, which is farther from the equator, but otherwise the two are comparable. However, *Scalesia pedunculata* and a few other species of *Scalesia* form trees in upland situations in the Galápagos. At such stations, there is a cloud-forest condition. The helianthoid Asteraceae as a whole seem to have a capability for woodiness in xeromorphic conditions (i.e., shrubby species of *Scalesia* occur at sea level in the Galápagos), so a moderate increase in moisture availability in the uplands has permitted arborescence. Woody lobelioids (which seem to require greater moisture availability) are common in Andean South America but are absent in the Galápagos. The climate of Sokotra (fig. 10.1) is roughly comparable to that of Galápagos sea-level localities.

Humidity. The relatively small diameter of most oceanic islands permits the higher humidity produced by ocean surface to affect the entire surface of the islands. On continental areas, the reverse is true; thermal patterns alter to a considerable extent the incoming weather patterns, and offshore winds created by land masses minimize humidity even at coasts. The effect of humidity on islands is twofold: it acts as a form of insulation, preventing wide fluctuations in temperature, and it attenuates considerably the effect of moisture availability to a plant, because transpiration is reduced and evaporation from soil is lessened. Of course, if an inversion layer is present, as it is in the Hawaiian Islands (Blumenstock, 1961), and suitable updrafts occur, humid air can condense into precipitation. Higher humidity, then, is a prime factor in moderating insular climates.

Unfortunately, data on relative humidity are gathered less frequently than are data on temperature, or in a fashion where one station's methods of reporting are not comparable to those of another. One can measure humidity at a specified hour, in which case the average humidity is not known. Or if humidity is measured five times a day, the average may well be quite different from when it is measured twice. That humidity is high on insular areas can be suggested by the fact that the average humidity (average for an entire year) at Hilo, Hawaii, is 81 percent. At Orotava, Canary Is., it is 75 percent; at Lihue, Kauai, Hawaiian Is., it is 74 percent. While coastal areas of continents are comparable, humidity drops off sharply inland. Los Angeles Airport, on the coast, has an average humidity of 71 percent (with probably, however, greater fluctuations during days and during the year than on Hawaiian coasts), but the Civic Center of Los Angeles registers an average of 61 percent. In Los Angeles, a low of 20 percent may occur commonly during the dry season, and lows of 5 percent occur occasionally. In contrast, humidity rarely falls below 40 percent even in dry lowland localities of the Hawaiian Islands.

ECOLOGICAL SHIFT

Many if not most instances of arborescence seem related to a change in ecological preference. As a generalization, many cases can be said to involve change from open habitats characteristic of weedy plants to forest habitats, particularly wet forest. In a few cases, the woody herbs even become emergents (e.g., *Brachylaena* in Madagascar, *Brachyglottis* in New Zealand). More commonly, however, the woodier herbs are understory elements (e.g., Hawaiian lobelioids), occupants of more open areas within a moist forest (Juan Fernandez Asteraceae), or shrubby elements in a scrub area (shrubby Macaronesian species of Brassicaceae, Boraginaceae). In a few cases, stem succulence has permitted formation of a shrubby habit in a group that otherwise would not tolerate dry lowland conditions (*Sonchus leptocephalus* on the Canary Islands).

What must be stressed strongly, however, is that species with increased woodiness are often part of a spectrum of adaptive radiation, and cannot be considered in isolation. Thus, in the listings later in this chapter, of genera "woodier on islands," some genera contain nonwoody as well as markedly woody species (e.g., *Sonchus*, *Cyrtandra*). For example, most species of *Argyroxiphium* (Asteraceae) are acaulescent, but some species of the related genus *Dubautia* are trees. Ecological shift is an integral component of adaptive radiation (chapter 3).

Basic to the process of ecological shift is that an island offers *some* sites comparable to those of mainland ancestors but also other habitats. If an island did not offer these differing zones, ecological shift would not occur, but if zones like those of continental areas did not exist as well, an immigrant species could not establish. The fact that weeds have established readily on oceanic islands illustrates that congruent zones do exist.

ABSENCE OF LARGE HERBIVORES

Another explanation for arborescence of woodier herbs on islands is the absence there of large vertebrate herbivores (herbivorous birds are not considered to play a significant role). The reverse might obtain where herbivore pressure is so heavy that only annual grasses and annual dicotyledons can complete their life cycle. This situation does exist on Guadalupe Island, Mexico, where herbivores were absent in prehuman times; now goats prevent reproduction of trees and shrubs except in sites inaccessible to them: steep cliffs and offshore islets (see Carlquist [1965] for a review of the Guadalupe situation). However, on the Canary Islands, where goats are plentiful and denude the islands to an appreciable extent, few species of woody herbs have been extinguished—although this may be expected with time. Introduced herbivores have had a serious effect on the Hawaiian Islands, and it is impossible to imagine evolution of the present species composition and growth forms had these herbivores been present as early, prehuman immigrants. Recording of future extinctions in areas invaded by pigs, goats, sheep, deer, and cattle in the Hawaiian Islands will give us a fairly precise estimate of how significant is the absence of large herbivores for evolution of woody herbs on oceanic islands.

"RELEASE" FROM SEASONALITY

Although climatic moderation is obviously instrumental to release from seasonality, the response of any herbaceous immigrant to an island in which moderation prevails will take the form of release from events in the growing pattern that, on continental areas, prevent arborescence. Release from winter cold would permit positioning of innovations (renewal buds) above the surface of the ground. It would also involve continual growth, rather than cessation during the winter (which, in herbaceous plants of cold regions, involves overwintering either in the form of seeds or as renewal buds at or below ground level). Moreover, if an insular climate is more mesic, not only can growth continue—instead of being interrupted by seasonal dryness—it can thereby form a tree. Percentages of trees in relationship to other growth forms (shrubs, annuals) are low in floras of areas with mediterranean climate. This can be simply correlated with the fact that summer drought prevents a root system from being able to support an appreciable leaf surface and growth throughout the summer; the plant must either die or cease growth until sufficient ground water becomes available again. Release from any of these events that limit or terminate growth of an herb will tend to favor arborescence. Presumably, adjustment to the new situation will involve genetically fixed adaptation to a less seasonal environment, with all that this connotes (increased production of wood, for example).

Does disappearance of thermoperiodic responses accompany increased woodiness or adaptation to insular climates where day-length differences and seasonal fluctuations in temperature are less marked? In the Hawaiian Islands, well-defined flowering seasons occur in some plants but not in others. The most marked retention of flowering seasonality may be in dry lowlands and dry alpine localities, but even in rain forests, seasonality in flowering can be observed (although to what degree and in what groups is a subject appropriate for further studies). Photoperiodicity has, likewise, not been studied in Hawaiian native plants to any appreciable degree. One relevant study, however, is that of Ray and Alexander (1966) on the widespread weed *Xanthium strumarium* (Asteraceae), a plant noted for photoperiodicity. They found clinal variation that was proportional to latitude within North American populations. Strains from Hawaii, however, showed notably tardy short-day response, with a critical night length of about 11 hr. This suggests that photoperiodicity might be in the process of disappearing there. Separating periodicity in response to rainfall, day length, temperature fluctuations, and light availability from each other in insular plants may not be easy, but these problems very much deserve study.

Some woody insular plants do survive frost. This is well known in the Afroalpine Senecios and Lobelias, and probably occurs in *Espeletia* of the paramos of Colombia as well (see chapter 14). However, the shrubby *Silene struthioloides* (Caryophyllaceae: alpine Maui) and *Plantago webbii* (Plantaginaceae: alpine Tenerife) seem to protect vegetative buds by means of the upwardly appressed leaf position at stem tips.

OTHER POSSIBLE FACTORS

Explanations for insular woodiness by Darwin and Wallace seem dubious. Darwin (1859), on the basis of the Galápagos genus *Scalesia*, suggested that competition among individuals within a species has favored taller individuals. This clearly could not be true for lowland Scalesias, in which individuals are shrubby and widely spaced. *Scalesia pedunculata* and *S. microcephala* are arborescent and can form dense stands in their native upland regions. However, these Scalesias provide one of the few examples of an insular woody representative of an herbaceous family that forms stands. None of the Hawaiian woody herbs do this—they are scattered throughout a forest community composed of woody species. Even in this latter case, one may doubt that competition for light is a selective factor. The more logical explanation of their degree of arborescence is that they grow in areas moist enough to support trees—admittedly, *Scalesia* can form a tree in moderately dry cloud forest whereas other genera (e.g., *Cyrtandra*) would not even survive there. However, the best explanation seems to be that degree of arborescence is directly proportional to available moisture. The only exceptions on islands would seem to be those species that can form arborescent stem succulents, *Opuntia* and

Euphorbia, for example. However, continental species of these genera are at least as arborescent as insular species and occur in open country in any case, not in closed stands.

Wallace (1878) claimed that woodiness of island plants connotes greater longevity, which permits repeated flowering and thereby a greater chance for cross-pollination in situations where paucity of pollinating insects would make cross-pollination of more ephemeral plant species less likely. He assumes that paucity of insular pollinating insects is a bottleneck. This assumption is dubious: plants may self-pollinate (see chapter 13), at least in a number of cases. Moreover, if conditions are suitable for an insect species with pollinating capabilities, population density of the insect should, if anything, be greater than in a mainland species (assuming the nature of insect faunas on islands is disharmonic), or else a suitable insect would be expected to be entirely absent—but rarely the intermediate condition Wallace predicates. If Wallace's assumption were true, more ephemeral species would be expected to evolve on islands as suitable insects became available, but ephemeral species are the exception on oceanic islands, as seen later in this chapter. Climatic factors, again, seem to be overriding in evolution of growth forms on islands. Less pronounced seasonality in flowering does occur in some insular plants, but this extension of flowering time appears to be the result of adjustment to less seasonal insular climates, not a factor for establishment of groups.

Measures of Selection and Adaptation

TRANSPLANT STATIONS

Thus far, no rigorously chosen and monitored transplant stations, such as those employed by the Carnegie Institute of Washington in the various studies by Clausen, Keck, and Hiesey, have been used for the study of insular plants and their tolerances. Cultivation of plants of *Echium* (Boraginaceae) from Macaronesia was described in chapter 5. Some insular species have been cultivated in the following California localities, however, and even though the results are crude, they may suggest the value of carefully performed studies:

1. San Francisco (Golden Gate Park, ca. 2 mi. inland from coast). Both *Wilkesia* (Asteraceae: from Kauai, 2000–3000 ft) and *Lobelia*

gibberoa (Campanulaceae: Mt. Kenya, ca. 9000 ft) have been cultivated to maturity. *Wilkesia gymnoxiphium* seems to have flowered prematurely (after only 3–4 years, as opposed to about 10 years or more in the wild), perhaps because of greater sunlight in open conditions or more continual availability of water. *Echium pininana* (Boraginaceae: Canary Is.) performed similarly in this respect; *Echium candicans* (Madeira) also grows successfully here. The climate of San Francisco is probably nearly equivalent to that of the Macaronesian laurel forest.

2. Santa Barbara (garden of my parents, Mr. and Mrs. R. M. Bauer, ca. 2 mi. inland). A wide variety of Hawaiian forest species has been grown successfully to maturity here, including *Tetraplasandra waimeae* (Araliaceae), *Wilkesia gymnoxiphium* (Asteraceae), *Bidens waianaeensis* (Asteraceae), *Scaevola gaudichaudiana* (Goodeniaceae), and *Pisonia umbellifera*. Species grown successfully but not yet to flowering include *Osmanthus sandwichensis* (Oleaceae) and *Mezoneurum kauaiense* (Fabaceae). *Scaevola floribunda* (Fiji) grows well but has not flowered after 10 years of cultivation, and the same is true of *Meryta lanceolata* (Araliaceae: Bora Bora). Plants from Guadalupe I., Mexico, grown to flowering include *Talinum guadalupense* (Portulacaceae), shown in figure 10.15, top left and right, and *Lavatera lindsayi* (Malvaceae). *Stephanomeria blairii* (Asteraceae) from San Clemente I., Calif., also succeeds well here. Macaronesian species that have been grown with total success include *Echium pininana* (Boraginaceae, fig. 5.2, bottom right), *E. simplex*, *E. candicans*, *Plantago arborescens*, *Laurus indica* (Lauraceae), and *Centaurea arbutoides* (Asteraceae). *Dendriopoterium menendezii* (Rosaceae: Gran Canaria) has not been able to reach maturity. One Juan Fernandez woody herb, *Dendroseris macrophylla*, has been cultivated successfully at the nearby University of California, Santa Barbara campus.

3. Claremont (my residence; also at Rancho Santa Ana Botanic Garden). Californian insular species do reasonably well here, some excellently. *Stephanomeria blairii* (fig. 10.3, top left, right) succeeds well, although it loses its leaves during the hottest summer days. Among the Guadalupe Island woody herbs, *Talinum guadalupense* and *Lavatera lindsayi* do not reach maturity. Hawaiian species are notably unsuccessful: *Wilkesia gymnoxiphium* readily succumbs to heat and low humidity. Macaronesian plants can be grown, but results are different from those at

Santa Barbara. *Dendriopoterium menendezii* has grown to be larger than plants I have seen on Gran Canaria; apparently its success in Claremont is related to the fact that it is from highlands of Gran Canaria, where the climate more closely resembles that of Claremont than that of Santa Barbara. *Echium pininana* has grown to maturity well and flowered. *Echium candicans* is successful, but for a much shorter period of time than in coastal localities, where its longevity is appreciably greater. *Plantago arborescens* has grown readily in my garden during the winter and even naturalized, but plants have died in the hot, dry summer; it is therefore a facultative annual in Claremont, but grows as a perennial in Santa Barbara, just as it does in Macaronesia. I have managed to keep alive a plant of *Dendroseris macrophylla* (fig. 10.2, bottom right) in Claremont, although each summer it loses all or nearly all its leaves for the hottest months; it is distinctly unhealthy compared with plants at Santa Barbara.

The preceding accounts do not include truly woody shrubs and trees. Many such insular species cultivate well in California, although even in these (with a few exceptions, such as *Pinus canariensis*, from relatively high elevations in the Canary Islands), insular plants from Macaronesia and New Zealand succeed better in coastal localities.

GROWTH-FORM SPECTRA AS CRITERIA OF NATURAL SELECTION

The plant species introduced by man to islands may or may not establish themselves and become weeds and escape into wild situations. If they do, one may assume that they simulate prehuman establishments in all respects except that they lack the mechanisms suited to natural dispersal to islands. One might claim that introduced species tend to be therophytes (annuals and biennials) mostly, since we tend to equate annuals with agricultural and horticultural weeds. However, large numbers of other growth forms have also been introduced by man to islands. In fact, the huge number of ornamentals other than annuals introduced to the Hawaiian Islands would suggest that shrubs and trees may, in some cases, have even been introduced preferentially.

However, we can compare human introductions to the "normal" spectrum of life forms (namely, angiosperms as a whole), and use this figure as a "control" for both the naturalized introductions and the native floras. Such comparisons were used by Skottsberg (1953), based on the

FIG. 10.2. Rosette herbs on islands, showing trunk formation owing to noncessation of growth. TOP LEFT, cabbage (*Brassica oleracea*); near Orotava, Tenerife, Canary Is. TOP RIGHT, *Tauschia* (*Melanoselinum*) *decipiens* (Apiaceae), with inflorescence; plant about 1.7 m tall; between Ribeiro Frio and Funchal, Madeira. BOTTOM LEFT, *Geranium maderense* (Geraniaceae), plant about 0.3 m tall; cultivated, Strybing Arboretum, Calif. BOTTOM RIGHT, *Dendroseris macrophylla* (Asteraceae), plant about 0.4 m tall, 4 yr. old; cultivated, Claremont, Calif.

FIG. 10.3. Plants from California and its insular areas. TOP LEFT, RIGHT, *Stephanomeria* (*Munzothamnus*) *blairii* (Asteraceae), an endemic of San Clemente I. TOP LEFT, plant flowering at end of first season of growth. TOP RIGHT, same plant 1 yr. 9 mo. later, just prior to its third flowering. BOTTOM LEFT, *Lotus scoparius* var. *scoparius* (Fabaceae), ca. 0.4 m tall, removed from ground to show branching from base, sparse and small leaves; Claremont. BOTTOM RIGHT, *Lotus scoparius* var. *dendroideus*, plant ca. 1.2 m tall; note trunk and density of crown; near Avalon, Santa Catalina I.

concepts of Raunkiaer (1934). I have modified the categories to follow Lems (1960). I have, however, recalculated Lems's data on the Canarian flora in order that native species and introduced, naturalized (adventive) species could be separated. I have similarly calculated data for the Hawaiian

TABLE 10.1.

Life-form spectra of angiosperms in floras

(expressed in percentages; actual species numbers in parentheses)

| | Life-form types [a] | | | | | | | | | | Total species |
---	M	N	C	H	G	HH	T	E	L	S	
"Normal spectrum" (world)	25	15	9	26	4	2	13	3	1	2	
Canary Is. native	6.5 (54)	26.2 (217)	26.7 (221)	14.9 (123)	6.0 (50)	1.5 (13)	14.1 (124)	—	1.8 (15)	1.1 (9)	(826)
adventive	1.3 (8)	2.8 (17)	3.3 (20)	17.7 (107)	2.9 (18)	0.7 (4)	69.4 (420)	—	0.5 (3)	1.3 (8)	(605)
Juan Fernandez Is. native	23.2 (34)	24.0 (35)	25.3 (37)	22.0 (32)	—	1.4 (2)	3.4 (5)	0.7 (1)	—	—	(146)
adventive	2.3 (2)	3.4 (3)	2.3 (2)	29.9 (26)	—	4.1 (4)	60.9 (53)	—	—	—	(87)
Hawaiian Is. native	17.7 (261)	41.6 (613)	1.1 (16)	34.1 (502)	1.7 (25)	0.3 (4)	1.1 (16)	?	2.3 (34)	0.1 (1)	(1472)
adventive	5.6 (9)	6.8 (11)	0.6 (1)	26.1 (42)	9.3 (15)	1.8 (3)	44.6 (72)	—	3.7 (6)	1.2 (2)	(161)

[a] The categories used are as follows: M = macrophanerophyte (tree over 2 m); N = nanophanerophyte (shrub, 0.3–2 m); C = chamaephyte (renewal buds between soil level and 0.3 m); H = hemicryptophyte (renewal buds at soil level); G = geophyte (renewal buds below soil level); HH = hydrophyte (renewal buds submersed); T = therophyte (annual or biennial); E = epiphyte; L = liana; S = stem succulent.

flora. For native species, I have used a modification of Fosberg's data in Zimmerman (1948). Figures for the adventive Hawaiian flora are derived from Hillebrand (1888) with a few additions; they are definitely incomplete, but no current listing of adventive Hawaiian species is available—and the number is continually increasing. The other data in table 10.1 are from Skottsberg (1953), and the "normal spectrum" is from Raunkiaer (1934).

Skottsberg (1953) believes that the life-form spectrum of the Juan Fernandez flora ought to resemble that of the Canary Islands (or Madeira, which has a spectrum very similar to that of the Canary Islands). When Skottsberg adds the adventive Juan Fernandez flora to the native, the combined figures, expressed in percentages, resemble the Macaronesian spectrum more closely than does the native flora alone, and he believes the spectrum based on native + adventive species is a more accurate reflection of the Juan Fernandez climate than the native flora presents. The higher percentages of trees, rosette trees, and shrubs in the native as opposed to the adventive flora Skottsberg attributes to the "anomaly" of persistence of relict elements.

Contrary to Skottsberg, I interpret the native floristic spectrum of the Juan Fernandez Islands as an accurate indication of the climate—or, if one prefers, the ecological niches provided by the areas of climatic zones in these islands. Surely time has been sufficient on these and the other islands of table 10.1 for evolution into growth forms precisely suited to localities of the native species. At sea level, the rainfall of the Juan Fernandez Islands is at least twice that of sea-level localities on the Canary Islands, and clearly the Fernandezian rain forest must be much wetter than the Canarian cloud forest.

If we calculate the percentage of phanerophytes (renewal buds above 0.3 m: trees and shrubs), the native Hawaiian flora is obviously highest, 61.7 percent; the native Fernandezian flora second (48.2 percent); and the Canarian native flora third (35.6 percent). This is precisely what one would expect on the basis of rainfall. I have estimated trees in the Hawaiian flora somewhat conservatively as compared with Skottsberg's estimate of what constitutes a tree (macrophanerophyte) in the Juan Fernandez Islands; a more liberal estimate in the Hawaiian flora might well make the figure for trees the same as or greater than the Juan Fernandez figure.

In any case, the 261 species of trees in the Hawaiian flora are many more than the 34 in the Juan Fernandez flora. The broad lowlands, the bogs, and the alpine zone of the Hawaiian Islands favor hemicryptophytes or cryptophytes; if Hawaiian topography matched that of the Juan Fernandez Islands in narrowness of lowlands and lack of alpine and bog localities, then these categories would be much lower in the Hawaiian flora, and percentages for phanerophytes relatively higher.

In any event, both the Hawaiian Islands and the Juan Fernandez Islands have a higher proportion of phanerophytes than the world flora taken as a whole (46 percent).

The most important feature to me, however, is that the spectra of growth forms in the Hawaiian, Fernandezian and Canarian native floras represent not relictual features but adaptive modes (and therefore, indirectly, optima of natural selection) precisely or nearly suited to the climatic regions of these respective archipelagos. To believe otherwise would be to believe that angiosperms can occur in localities to which they are not adapted.

The spectra of life forms for adventive floras in these archipelagos are much alike—but markedly different from those of the native floras. The adventive floras are rich primarily in therophytes, secondarily in hemicryptophytes. These, presumably, grow mostly in disturbed and lowland sites. However, even if the life-form spectra of the adventive floras are not precisely like those of the original prehuman plant immigrants to these archipelagos, they undoubtedly show some resemblance to the makeup of ancestral stocks. There is no reason to believe that the present native spectra are precisely the same as the immigrant spectra. For example, the adventive trees in the Canary Islands include *Castanea*, *Quercus* spp., and *Prunus* spp., and these are types very unlikely to have arrived via long-distance dispersal. We would not even expect the "normal" or world spectrum to simulate immigrants to these islands, because of the poor dispersibility of trees—yet trees have "exceeded expectations" based on the world flora as a whole.

At least some portion of the discrepancies between adventive floras and native floras on these islands can be considered expressions of selective pressures. Thus, in all three floras, there is selective pressure favoring trees and shrubs and (to a lesser extent) chamaephytes—at the expense chiefly of therophytes. In all three floras, the percentage of native shrubs is at least six times the percentage of adventive shrubs, the percentage of native trees at least three times the percentage of adventive trees.

Although the concepts suggested by table 10.1 must of necessity be somewhat vague, there does seem to be a selective pressure toward trees and shrubs, and an indication that these are not what establish most easily at first. Thus, we can expect evolutionary shift into greater woodiness—a shift that also corresponds to shift into wetter forest. Conversion from herbs into shrubs is relatively easy, and may help to explain why shrubs bulk large in the proportions of growth forms on these islands. In at least some cases, the native trees of these islands have evolved from ancestors that were woody shrubs, in all likelihood, at their time of original establishment. If genetic systems were a consideration, therophytes ought to bulk very large in insular floras, for they would represent maximum population size, which ought to be valuable where space is limited and inbreeding potentially a liability. However, outbreeding trees and shrubs are what we find, chiefly, and the ecology of the island seems of prime importance in governing what growth forms will establish—but more importantly, toward what modes evolution will take place. Increased woodiness seems the inevitable interpretation of these data, particularly if one takes into account factors of anatomy and systematics.

Ways in Which Woody Growth Forms Evolve

If one considers the various herbaceous groups that are woodier on islands, one soon concludes that there are a wide variety of ways in which this process can occur, as suggested below.

1. Rosette herbs, experiencing prolonged vegetative growth over a period of years, develop elongate stems and eventually flower. The monocarpic rosette tree is relatively infrequent on islands, but examples can be cited. Outstanding among these are *Wilkesia* (Asteraceae: Hawaii) *Trematolobelia* (Campanulaceae: Hawaii); *Lobelia* spp. (Campanulaceae: Hawaii); *Echium pininana* (Boraginaceae: Canary Is. [fig. 5.2, bottom left, right]); *Tauschia* (*Melanoselinum*) *decipiens* (Apiaceae) on Madeira (fig. 10.2, top right); *Dendroseris* (*Phoenicoseris*) *pinnata* and *D. regia* (Astera-

373

ceae, tribe Cichorieae: Juan Fernandez Is.); *Centaurodendron dracaenoides*, *C. palmiforme*, and the closely related, monotypic *Yunquea tenzii* (Asteraceae, tribe Cynareae: Juan Fernandez; for photographs of these Juan Fernandez taxa, see Skottsberg [1953] and Carlquist [1965]). Monocarpic species of *Lobelia* occur in Afroalpine areas (see chapter 14). The monocarpic species of *Aeonium* on the Canary Islands could be called miniature, monocarpic rosette trees.

In relation to rosette plants, one may note that the commonly cultivated cabbage (fig. 10.2, top left) takes this form when grown on subtropical islands. One might also cite *Geranium maderense* (fig. 10.2, bottom left), which is not monocarpic, but appears to be merely a rosette plant that forms a somewhat elongate stem by virtue of growth through a succession of seasons. Lowe (1868) states that *Tauschia (Melanoselinum) decipiens* does not always die upon flowering: rarely lateral branches form near the base of the main stem. This pattern suggests the origin of the transitional type discussed next.

2. Development of the ability to form lateral branches may convert a monocarpic rosette plant into a shrub. This seems plainly what has happened in the case of *Stephanomeria (Munzothamnus) blairii* (fig. 10.3, top left, right). I was able to observe this phenomenon by maintaining a plant in cultivation. Many species of *Stephanomeria* (e.g., *S. virgata*) are autumn-flowering annuals. During the first year, *S. blairii* forms a terminal inflorescence (fig. 10.3, top left), much as would an annual *Stephanomeria*, differing only in its paniculate inflorescence. At this point, the plant, instead of dying, produces innovations *from the base during the winter*, which is mild enough in its native habitat, San Clemente I., Calif., that such shoots are not killed by frosts. During the second year these innovations grow out, each ultimately tipped by an inflorescence. Some of these second-year shoots may die, but some of them produce lateral shoots distally during the third year; during the third year, additional basal shoots can form (fig. 10.3, top right). Thus a shrubby or suffrutescent form is achieved, although there is no trunk per se. Some of the lateral branches eventually become woodier than others, and the caudexlike base continues to increase in size. This shrublike habit can be seen as failure of the plant to die from winter frosts. Moisture is perhaps also a factor; the broad leaves (compared with other species) suggest lowered transpiration in the deep

canyons of San Clemente and in the greater humidity of insular conditions. Species of *Lobelia* in the Afroalpine flora may follow this pattern— *L. gibberoa*, for example, appears like a monocarpic, tall *Lobelia*, but I have observed innovations forming near the bases of plants in flower on Mt. Kenya. This is occasionally true of other Lobelias, such as *L. keniensis* (Hedberg, 1957).

3. Evolution in habitats free from frost can mean that innovations need not take place from below or at ground level, but can occur above ground level on one of the main stems of a plant. A good example of this tendency is found in *Lotus scoparius*. *Lotus scoparius* var. *scoparius* (fig. 10.3, bottom left) is a microphyllous broom shrub of mainland southern California, branched from ground level. On Santa Catalina I., southern California, *Lotus scoparius* var. *dendroideus* (fig. 10.3, bottom right) becomes a miniature tree, almost invariably from a single trunk. The crown is richly branched and bears a dense tangle of herbage with relatively large leaves.

4. Consistent growth of lateral branches from nodes just beneath an inflorescence can take place. The resultant growth form varies, but a distinction from the *Stephanomeria* example above is evident, in that *Stephanomeria* forms basal innovations at least as frequently as it does branches just below inflorescences.

The ability to form axillary inflorescences would appear a more direct pathway to prolonged growth of stems but is evidently a more difficult process to achieve evolutionarily in a number of taxonomic groups. For example, none of the Macaronesian species of *Sonchus* (figs. 10.4–10.8) has developed axillary inflorescences. During the first year of growth, these *Sonchus* species may flower, as shown for a young plant of *S. radicatus* (fig. 10.5, top right). At this stage, a Macaronesian *Sonchus* resembles an annual species, such as the widespread weed *S. oleraceus*. However, in most of the species a *single* innovation grows out after flowering, from just below the inflorescence. This, as it matures, pushes the dead inflorescence axis to one side so that a relatively straight continuation of the original branch is formed—a rather striking substitute for an axillary inflorescence position. In rosette-tree species such as *S. abbreviatus* (fig. 10.6, top left, right), which rarely branches, this condition has been perfected most clearly. Branching does occur in most of the Macaronesian *Sonchus* spe-

FIG. 10.4. Species of *Sonchus* (Asteraceae) endemic to the Canary Is. and Madeira. TOP LEFT, *S. ustulatus*, plant about 0.2 m tall, acaulescent, leaves 6–8 cm long; Machico, Madeira. TOP RIGHT, *S. brachylobus*, plant branching but small, ca. 0.3 m tall, leaves 6–8 mm long; northern coast of Gran Canaria. BOTTOM LEFT, *S. congestus*, plant acaulescent, with large leaves, to 1 m; middle elevations, Barranco de San Andres, Tenerife. BOTTOM RIGHT, *S. platylepis,* acaulescent plant with leaves ca. 15 cm long; summit region, Gran Canaria.

cies, least often perhaps in the acaulescent *S. congestus* (fig. 10.4, bottom left), occasionally in the short-stemmed species *S. ustulatus* (fig. 10.4, top left), *S. brachylobus* (fig. 10.4, top right), and *S. platylepis* (fig. 10.4, bottom right). Branching occurs most readily in *S. leptocephalus* (fig. 10.8), which is often branched freely from near the base, but elongate branches

376

FIG.10.5. *Sonchus radicatus* (Asteraceae), an endemic of the Canary Is. TOP LEFT, habit of older plant, ca. 0.5 m tall; cliffs of upper Barranco de San Andres, Tenerife. TOP RIGHT, younger (probably 1 yr. old) plant in flower, showing nature of leaves, ca. 12 cm long; lower Barranco de San Andres. BOTTOM LEFT, transection of secondary xylem. BOTTOM RIGHT, tangential section of secondary xylem. Scale of magnification of wood sections is shown at bottom of fig. 10.16.

FIG. 10.6. Rosette-tree species of *Sonchus* endemic to the Canary Is. TOP LEFT, RIGHT, BOTTOM LEFT, *S. abbreviatus*; Anaga Peninsula near Bailladero, Tenerife. TOP LEFT, habit of plant, ca. 3 m tall. TOP RIGHT, flowers from plant; open heads measure about 4 cm in diam. BOTTOM LEFT, transection of secondary xylem. BOTTOM RIGHT, *S. jacquinii*, tangential section of secondary xylem; between Icod de los Viños and Puerto de la Cruz, Tenerife. Scale of magnification of wood sections shown with fig. 10.16.

FIG. 10.7. Rosette-tree species of *Sonchus* from the Canary Is. and Madeira. TOP LEFT, RIGHT, *S. pinnatus*; near Machico, Madeira. TOP LEFT, habit of plant, ca. 1.5 m tall. TOP RIGHT, portion of plant in flower; leaves are 15–30 cm long. BOTTOM LEFT, CENTER RIGHT, BOTTOM RIGHT, *S. fruticosus*; near waterfall, Ribeiro Frio, Madeira. BOTTOM LEFT, habit, plant is 4.5 m tall. CENTER RIGHT, stem of same plant, showing formation of aerial roots. BOTTOM RIGHT, base of same plant, showing maximum diameter of this stem; hand indicates scale.

379

FIG. 10.8. *Sonchus leptocephalus*, an endemic of the Canary Is. TOP LEFT, habit of plant, ca. 1.2 m tall; between Santa Cruz de Tenerife and San Andres. TOP CENTER, view of stem tips in leafless condition during dry season, same plant. TOP RIGHT, plant with leafy stems; leaves are ca. 10 cm long, leaf segments terete; near Puerto de la Cruz, Tenerife. BOTTOM LEFT, transection of secondary xylem. BOTTOM RIGHT, tangential section of secondary xylem. Scale of magnification of wood sections shown with fig. 10.16.

can also be formed by the mechanism described above. In the species with little branching, the stems bear a succession of old and almost imperceptible weathered inflorescence bases, noticeable as irregularities along what seems at first glance to be an axis that has been built from continual growth of an unbranched axis.

The Macaronesian *Sonchus* species show a variety of growth forms, so that this mechanism of bearing exclusively lateral inflorescences obviously lends itself to a wide variety of growth forms from acaulescent rosette shrub, to broomlike shrub, small rosette shrub, and sparsely branched rosette tree.

Stephanomeria and *Sonchus* both belong to the tribe Cichorieae of Asteraceae. The Juan Fernandez Cichorieae conform to the same pattern (except for monocarpic species), as the diagrams of Skottsberg (1953, p. 851) show for *Dendroseris litoralis* (see also the habit of *D. litoralis* as illustrated by Skottsberg [1922, pl. 18] or Carlquist [1965]).

Insular Asteraceae other than Cichorieae also show this pattern, as diagrammed by Skottsberg (1953) for *Robinsonia*, *Rhetinodendron*, and *Symphyochaeta* (Senecioneae).

In Macaronesia, woody species of *Centaurea* (fig. 10.9, top left, right) and *Carlina*, of the tribe Cynareae of Asteraceae, agree with the pattern described. Meusel (1952) has diagrammed "candelabrum shrubs" in which this form is achieved by innovations from below inflorescence bases; he illustrates *Carlina*, *Echium*, and *Euphorbia*. Werner (1966) has shown this growth habit diagrammatically for Macaronesian species of *Isoplexis* (Scrophulariaceae). *Pterocephalus* of the Dipsacaceae forms shrubby species in Macaronesia (fig. 10.9, bottom left, right) conforming with this type.

Macaronesian Brassicaceae such as *Parolinia* (fig. 10.10, bottom right), *Cheiranthus*, *Crambe*, and *Sinapidendron* have this scheme. The Hawaiian *Lepidium serra* (Brassicaceae) is a small rosette shrub (see Carlquist, 1970a) resembling *Sonchus radicatus* in habit.

In the Hawaiian Islands, genera of Asteraceae such as *Dubautia* and *Argyroxiphium* (some species) follow this pattern. A series of growth forms including rosette herb (*A. caliginii*), sprawling matlike shrub (*D. scabra*), rosette shrub (*D. plantaginea*), scandent shrub (*D. latifolia*), and even trees (*D. paleata*, *D. reticulata*) has been formed on this basis. The sole

FIG. 10.9. "Rosette shrubs" of the Canary Is. TOP LEFT, RIGHT, *Centaurea arbutoides* (Asteraceae). TOP LEFT, habit of plant, 1.7 m tall; cliffs above Agaete, Gran Canaria. TOP RIGHT, flower heads, 4 cm in diam. BOTTOM LEFT, RIGHT, *Pterocephalus dumetorum* (Dipsacaceae). BOTTOM LEFT, habit of plant (Günther Kunkel shown standing by plant). BOTTOM RIGHT, heads of flowers, 3.5 cm in diam.

FIG. 10.10. Woody herbs from the Canary Is. TOP LEFT, RIGHT, *Plantago arborescens;* middle elevations, Barranco de San Andres, Tenerife. TOP LEFT, habit of plant, 0.4 m tall. TOP RIGHT, leaves and inflorescences; leaves are 3–4 cm long. BOTTOM LEFT, *P. webbii,* habit of plant, 0.3 m tall; Los Roques, El Teide, Tenerife. BOTTOM RIGHT, *Parolinia ornata* (Brassicaceae), showing habit of this sparsely branched species, 2 m tall; middle elevations, Barranco de Arguineguin, Gran Canaria.

exception appears to be *D. knudsenii,* a true tree with a single trunk, but in fact inflorescences are terminal. The various species of *Argyroxiphium* and *Dubautia* have been illustrated by Carlquist (1970a).

All of the Asteraceae native to St. Helena (see Carlquist, 1965, pp. 202–3 for illustrations) show the *Sonchus* type of innovations. These species vary from shrubs to sizable trees, and belong to the tribes Astereae, Senecioneae, and Heliantheae. The South Pacific helianthoid genera *Fitchia* and *Oparanthus* (Asteraceae) also show this type of innovation (Carlquist, 1957, 1965). The Galápagos helianthoid *Scalesia* also has exclusively terminal inflorescences, and varies from shrub to tree (Howell, 1941; Harling, 1962).

Dicotyledons with anomalous secondary thickening also show terminal inflorescences. *Chenopodium arborescens* (Juan Fernandez Is.) and *C. oahuense* (Hawaiian Is.) can be cited. *Nototrichium* (Amaranthaceae: Hawaiian Is.) can be added. Another amaranthaceous genus with considerable stature and terminal inflorescences is *Bosea* (fig. 10.12, top left, right), a Canarian endemic. *Bosea*, however, tends to be branched often near the base, thus forming a fountain-shaped shrub.

Although not arborescent, the relatively large (for its genus) stem succulent *Talinum guadalupense* (Portulacaceae) can be added to this mode of growth (fig. 10.15, top left). The Afroalpine species of *Senecio* have terminal inflorescences (see chapter 14).

5. Axillary inflorescences occur in some insular woodier herbs, and thus axes can continue growth directly. The Hawaiian lobelioids (other than *Lobelia* and *Trematolobelia*) exemplify this type. Illustrations of these can be found in Rock (1919) and Carlquist (1970a). Thus, evolution of the tall palmiform species of *Cyanea* is merely a matter of continued growth, as it is in the related genera *Delissea* and *Rollandia*. *Clermontia* species are mostly shrubby and much branched, usually with a single trunk; branching is not related to production of inflorescences. Flowers are axillary in the South Pacific lobelioid genus *Apetahia*.

Axillary inflorescences are characteristic of the genus *Plantago* (Plantaginaceae), on islands and elsewhere. Illustrative of this are the Macaronesian Plantagos (fig. 10.10, top left, right, bottom left). These are shrubs of dry localities. On the other hand, single-stemmed or little-branched, macrophyllous, rain-forest species on Hawaii (*P. princeps*) and Juan Fernandez (*P. fernandeziana*) still have the same plan with regard to inflorescences.

Other axillary-inflorescence shrubs and trees that can be cited include Pacific species of *Scaevola* (Goodeniaceae); *Nothocestrum* (Solanaceae: Hawaii); *Lysimachia* (Primulaceae: Hawaii); *Convolvulus* (Convolvu-

FIG. 10.11. Woody representatives of herbaceous families from the Canary Is. TOP LEFT, RIGHT, *Convolvulus scoparius* (Convolvulaceae). TOP LEFT, habit, plant 3.2 m tall; Barranco de Arguineguin, Gran Canaria. TOP RIGHT, flowers of this broom shrub; flowers 2 cm in diam. BOTTOM LEFT, *Limonium rumicifolium* (Plumbaginaceae), old plant 1 m tall; Era del Cardon, Gran Canaria. BOTTOM RIGHT, *L. arborescens*, habit of plant 1.4 m tall; cliffs of northwestern Tenerife.

FIG. 10.12. Insular plants with anomalous secondary thickening. TOP LEFT, RIGHT, *Bosea yervamora* (Amaranthaceae). TOP LEFT, habit of plant, 5 m tall; La Calzada, Gran Canaria, Canary Is. TOP RIGHT, fruits from same plant; leaves are 3.5–4 cm long. BOTTOM LEFT, RIGHT, *Charpentiera obovata* (Amaranthaceae), sections of stem; Kokee, Kauai, Hawaiian Is. BOTTOM LEFT, transection. BOTTOM RIGHT, tangential section. Wood sections at magnification shown with fig. 10.16.

386

laceae: Macaronesia, fig. 10.11, top left, right); *Charpentiera* (Amaranthaceae: Hawaii and Austral Is.); *Limonium* (Plumbaginaceae: Macaronesia, fig. 10.11, bottom left, right); and *Espeletia* (Asteraceae: Colombian paramos; see chapter 14).

6. *Viola* has axillary flowers. However, the Hawaiian species of *Viola* appear to have achieved woody stature by an unusual change in growth form. North temperate *Viola* species are typically prostrate and rhizomatous, as are the Hawaiian bog species. *Viola robusta*, a wet-forest Hawaiian species, begins with an unbranched prostrate stem, but then the stem turns upward, so that a mature plant looks entirely upright unless one studies the base. The most nearly arborescent species, V. *tracheliifolia* of the Hawaiian Islands, also shows vestiges of this change in orientation. For illustrations, see Carlquist (1970a).

7. The Hawaiian species of *Euphorbia* (with the exception of a single, recently described species, *E. haeleeleana* D. Herbst) belong to the section *Chamaesyce*, sometimes termed a genus (also called *Euphorbia* sect. *Anisophyllum*). Continental species of this section assume a matlike form because the terminal shoot aborts and the lateral shoots become prostrate stems. Lowland Hawaiian species (e.g., *E. degeneri*) also show this form. Other Hawaiian chamaesycoid Euphorbias are trees and shrubs. Study of early stages in these species shows that they all undergo abortion of the terminal shoot, but a lateral innovation in the seedling turns upward and forms a new main axis which can eventually become a woody trunk, as in the tree *E. rockii*. This process of upright shoots based on lateral innovations was described by Degener (1937). For illustrations of these Euphorbias, see Degener (1937) and Carlquist (1970a). These species all have axillary inflorescences.

8. The endemic genus of Cucurbitaceae on Socotra, *Dendrosicyos*, has a large erect trunk. Hypocotylary tissue may be involved, but a young plant in cultivation at the University of California, Berkeley, illustrates that thickening occurs in regions involving internodes above the cotyledons. This water-tank construction is unique among examples of insular woodiness and is remarkable for its occurrence in a family of vining plants (for illustration, see Carlquist, 1965). To be sure, there are other water-tank plants on the island of Socotra, but these are no different from water-tank plants on the African mainland.

9. Although ancestrally herblike groups of angiosperms are the primary concern of this chapter, in certain groups shrubby species have increased in stature during their evolution on insular areas. One clear example is *Sarcopygme*, a rubiaceous Samoan endemic rosette tree probably related to the genus *Morinda*. Other instances are more subtle: are Hawaiian Araliaceae, Rubiaceae, or Urticaceae more arborescent than their nearest noninsular relatives? In some cases this is almost certainly true. For example, *Platydesma cornuta* is a cauliflorous rosette tree with gigantic leaves. It almost surely represents an autochthonous alteration in size and shape, although its ancestors in Rutaceae (*Pelea* or *Melicope*, perhaps) were most likely woody shrubs, perhaps with smaller stature but surely with smaller leaves and narrower branches.

The Canarian species of *Bencomia* (Rosaceae) are probably woodier than their alchemilloid ancestors; *Hagenia*, in high African cloud forest (see chapter 14), has almost certainly increased in woodiness compared with other alchemilloids or with *Bencomia*. The subtlety of increase in woodiness on islands of a group of basically woody plants is a problem, for one must survey the world representatives of a genus to see if insular species are larger. Heights for each species are difficult to estimate (or unknown). There are, nevertheless, a number of examples of increase in size of shrubby species on islands. This is the simplest of all paths to increased woodiness, of course. Analysis is complicated by the fact that we would not expect any notable changes in wood anatomy between less woody noninsular species and more woody insular species in such groups.

10. A factor suggested earlier but not clearly enunciated is that ecological shift into wet forest may accompany increased woodiness in some groups, but others become woody under dry conditions. These latter instances appear to be plants adapted to growth under very dry conditions. In the Hawaiian flora, one can cite *Nototrichium* (Amaranthaceae), *Chenopodium* (Chenopodiaceae), *Kokia* and *Hibiscadelphus* (Malvaceae), and *Nothocestrum* (Solanaceae). Some shrubby species of *Lipochaeta* (Asteraceae, Heliantheae) occur in Hawaiian lowlands. This is true of *Scalesia* in the Galápagos (same family and tribe); very likely, few other genera could have formed trees under the relatively dry cloud-forest conditions of the Galápagos, but *Scalesia* (*S. pedunculata*) has. *Sida eggersii* (Malvaceae) is a true tree in dry regions of Jost van Duke, Culebra, and other

West Indian islands. Didiereaceae on Madagascar are a spectacular example of this pattern.

11. Expressions of insular woodiness will vary according to the climatic regime of any given island or archipelago. Although I cannot take space to discuss these modalities extensively, I can mention a few examples. In Macaronesia, arborescence or shrubbiness in herbaceous groups often takes the form of stem succulents (*Sonchus, Euphorbia*), broom shrubs (*Convolvulus*) or microphyllous shrubs (*Plantago*) in dry regions. In dry lowlands of the Hawaiian Islands, groups with increased woodiness are broad leaved and generally not very succulent. Only a few groups with increased woodiness have entered the Macaronesian laurel forest, whereas many good examples of woodier herbs may be found in wet Hawaiian forests. These distinctive modalities in different zones on islands in different climatic regimes illustrate not only the diversity of expression of insular woodiness, but also that there are probably various pathways in this evolution; in other words, palmiform species of *Cyanea* on the Hawaiian Islands have developed from herblike ancestors in ways and for reasons entirely different from those that have been basic to evolution of the Afroalpine Dendrosenecios.

Anatomical Correlations of Insular Woodiness

CAMBIAL ACTIVITY

Axiomatically, increased woodiness of insular representatives of herbaceous groups involves an increase in production of secondary xylem. This can occur in several ways.

1. A sluggish cambium gradually produces a wider ring of secondary xylem. This usually involves retention of a large pith and a large cortex. The Afroalpine Senecios (e.g., *S. keniodendron*) or monocarpic rosette trees (*Lobelia gaudichaudii* of Hawaii) exemplify this mode of construction.

2. During the life-span of an herb capable of secondary xylem activity, the amount of secondary xylem accumulated increases with the size of the plant. Except for lessened mechanical strength and the anatomical features discussed below, these plants can mimic truly woody species in growth form. Examples include *Sonchus fruticosus* and *Euphorbia rockii*.

3. An herb capable of secondary xylem activity becomes a stem suc-

culent, in which case the mechanical strength of xylem is often of less significance (cortical and pith parenchyma serve for support, and the presence of few or no leaves lessens wind resistance). Examples include *Euphorbia balsamifera, Sonchus leptocephalus, Coreopsis gigantea,* and *Talinum guadalupense.*

4. Anomalous secondary growth, characteristic of a particular family, produces successive cambia to an extent greater than would be characteristic of ancestors. Species of Centrospermae (Caryophyllales) would be included in this category, such as insular Amaranthaceae (*Nototrichium, Charpentiera*) and Chenopodiaceae (*Chenopodium* spp.).

FEATURES OF WOOD ANATOMY

The anatomical mode of secondary xylem construction will obviously not be the same for all the groups just listed. Some features are common to all types, some are not. In a series of studies on wood anatomy of various predominantly herbaceous groups of dicotyledons, I have attempted to discover principles of construction underlying woody members of these groups (Carlquist, 1962a; Carlquist, 1966, and the various preceding papers on wood anatomy of Asteraceae summarized therein; Carlquist, 1969a, 1969b, 1970b, 1970c, 1970d, 1971).

Vessel-element Length. Length of vessel elements is a simple and relatively accurate measure of length of fusiform cambial initials. Early in my studies of woody herbs, I found that they often have vessel elements longer than one would expect. However, the ontogenetic dimension of this phenomenon plainly became an important key, leading to the concept of paedomorphosis (Carlquist, 1962a). The ontogeny of only some of the species discussed here was investigated, although I feel a sufficiently large number of species have been investigated that I can state the following principles with regard to woodier herbs:

1. Greater length of fusiform cambial initials, characteristic of the opening stages of cambial activity, is continued with little change as production of secondary xylem continues.*

---

* NOTE: The significance of longer elements proves to be primarily in the greater mechanical strength of imperforate elements (libriform fibers); in the plants under consideration, longer elements therefore relate to greater plant size, which in turn tends to relate to mesomorphy (Carlquist, unpublished data).

2. The greater length (as compared with decreased length character-istic of early secondary-xylem production in "truly woody" plants) is either ontogenetically lessened, or more commonly changed very little (gradual ontogenetic increase characterizes most truly woody plants, on the con-trary). Although we have no clear way of knowing, there is the possibility that phylogenetic increase in length of fusiform cambial initials might occur within some herbaceous groups.

3. From earlier data on a broad sampling of Asteraceae (Carlquist, 1966), there is every reason to believe that mesomorphy is related to longer vessel elements (and therefore to fusiform cambial initials), and the reverse is true of xeromorphy. If a genus capable of paedomorphosis evolves into an insular habitat more mesic than that of ancestral types, longer vessel elements are to be expected. Two genera have been selected for presenta-tion here—*Euphorbia* and *Sonchus* (table 10.2). The Hawaiian species of *Euphorbia* sect. *Chamaesyce* show a wide range in habitat, whereas the Macaronesian species of *Sonchus* and of *Euphorbia* sect. *Tithymalus* do not have available to them the "more mesic" end of the spectrum that occurs in Hawaii.

Vessel-element Width. That vessel-element width is an indicator of degree of mesomorphy or xeromorphy in groups that show insular woodi-ness has emerged from a series of studies (Carlquist, 1966, 1969a, 1969b, 1970b, 1970c, 1970d, 1971). Vessel width is not under the control of length of fusiform cambial initials, and therefore serves as confirmation of meso-morphic or xeromorphic adaptation. Wider vessel elements seem clearly correlated with greater mesomorphy.

In table 10.2, figures for average vessel-element length and width are presented. If length and width are independent indicators of moisture availability, conceivably either might be significant. Consequently, a com-bined width + length figure is presented for each species. Sequences within genera (and sections, in *Euphorbia*) in table 10.2 have been ar-ranged according to this combined figure.

In insular Euphorbias, the correlation with rainfall is startlingly per-fect and needs no comment. I am reminded of a similar correlation with leaf area in *Dubautia* (fig. 4.4). The correlation in *Sonchus* (table 10.2) is nearly as perfect. The rainfall figures for the Hawaiian Islands are rela-tively accurate, because of the numerous recording stations. The Canarian

TABLE 10.2.

Ecological correlations of vessel dimensions in insular angiosperms

	Locality	Approximate rainfall mm	Average vessel-element length, μ	Average vessel width μ	Width + length
Euphorbia, sect. *Chamasyce*					
E. degeneri	Makapuu, Oahu	300[a]	206	32	238
E. celastroides var. lorifolia	Wainea Canyon, Kauai	750	248	44	292
E. celastroides var. amplectans	northeastern Lanai	420	282	42	324
E. celastroides var. mauiensis	Ulupalakua, Maui	1000	327	56	383
E. remyi var. pteropoda	Kokee, Kauai	2000	356	53	409
E. halemanui	Kokee, Kauai	2500	406	64	470
E. clusiifolia	lower Konahuanui, Oahu	2500	423	39	482
E. rockii	upper Punaluu, Oahu	5000	624	61	685
Euphorbia, sect. *Tithymalus*					
E. piscatoria	Ribeiro Brava, Madeira	550	321	60	381
E. piscatoria	Ribeiro Frio, Madeira	2500	452	62	514
Sonchus (Macaronesian)					
S. pinnatus	Machico, Madeira	340	153	73	226
S. leptocephalus	La Calzada, Gran Canaria	350	176	70	246
S. platylepis	above Agaete, Gran Canaria	450	207	46	253
S. ustulatus	Ribeiro Brava, Madeira	550	204	54	258
S. brachylobus	Cenobio de Calderon, Gran Canaria	400	207	59	263
S. congestus	Barranco de San Andres, Tenerife	450	176	103	278
S. jacquinii	San Juan de Rambla, Tenerife	680	225	89	314
S. fruticosus	Ribeiro Frio, Madeira	2500	251	78	329
S. pinnatus	Curral de Freiras, Madeira	2000	270	75	345
S. abbreviatus	Anaga, Tenerife	2500	277	85	362

[a] Data on Hawaiian Islands from Blumenstock (1961).

data are much less reliable, and I have made estimates, based on altitude, leeward versus windward exposure, aspect of vegetation at the various localities, and the few recording stations. One must remember in either case that at stations of low rainfall, high evaporation lowers the available soil moisture still further. At stations of high rainfall, cloud cover and shade from trees increase available soil moisture appreciably, so that the gamut in rainfall is a foreshortened expression of conditions experienced by the plants themselves.

Several other factors must be taken into account in relating tracheary element length with moisture availability. If, as seems frequent, there is a decrease in element length with age in woody herbs, a large wood sample might be expected to have elements shorter than the moisture correlation would dictate. A number of examples can be cited: in Lobelioideae (Carlquist, 1969a), *Cyanea pilosa*, which forms little wood, has notably long tracheary elements, but *Clermontia clermontioides*, which has the largest stems I have collected in Lobelioideae, has rather short tracheary elements. To test this correlation, measurements were taken from sections near the pith of a basal sample, from the periphery of a basal sample, and from an upper branch. Data (Carlquist, 1969a) on *Clermontia arborescens*, *C. hawaiiensis*, *C. kakeana*, *C. montis-loa*, *Cyanea leptostegia*, and others confirm this tendency: in lobelioids as in other woody herbs (Carlquist, 1962a; Carlquist, 1970b) there is a decrease in element length with age. Interestingly, upper branches often have longer elements than does the inside portion of the base. The explanation for this difference is possibly stress on strength in the branches.

At any rate, woodier species in a group are likely to occur in rain forests, less woody ones in lowlands. Therefore, sections from the former may exhibit shorter elements than expected on the basis of their mesomorphy. This probably accounts for the fact that vessel elements in *Sonchus fruticosus* and *S. abbreviatus* are not spectacularly longer than those of the lowland *Sonchus* species.

Even with these restrictions, the vessel-element dimensions, derived as they are from independent taxonomic groups and independent island groups, show clearly that evolution into situations of increased water availability is accompanied by increase in vessel-element length and width. Surely no one is going to propose the reverse hypothesis: for example,

Euphorbia degeneri resembles the wide-ranging *E. atoto* stock that is probably basic to this complex, whereas *E. rockii* is unique; beginning a series with *E. rockii* seems preposterous. In insular species that occupy rather xeric localities, rather short tracheary elements would be expected. This proved true in most Macaronesian taxa (Carlquist, 1970b, 1970c, 1971). Brassicaceae have evolved into the cloud forest to a negligible degree in Macaronesia, and *Echium* shows only a few forest species (which do, however, have slightly longer tracheary elements).

Length of libriform fibers in all cases parallels vessel-element length for a given species. Collection of data on this feature (see the various papers cited earlier) served little purpose except to reinforce the picture of vessel-element length and to demonstrate that length of fusiform cambial initials is basic in length considerations.

A photographic indication of vessel-element dimensions in *Sonchus* species is given in the bottom pictures of figures 10.5, 10.6, and 10.8.

Ray Histology. If vessel-element length reflects the condition of the vascular cambium, we might look to ray initials and the ray cells they produce to see if similar conditions apply. They do indeed, and transverse divisions of both ray initials and fusiform cambial initials lag in woods that show paedomorphosis. Where vessel elements are long for a particular group, a higher percentage of erect ray cells as opposed to procumbent cells was almost invariably observed. Predominance of erect ray cells, or presence of erect and square ray cells to the exclusion of procumbent cells, is unusual in truly woody dicotyledons; in fact, Kribs (1935) did not even include such ray types, common in woody herbs, in his survey of rays of dicotyledons. These ray types seem a protraction of a juvenile condition, in which case, as with vessel-element length, derivation from more herbaceous ancestors is indicated.

Raylessness. Raylessness characterizes woody herbs (Barghoorn, 1941; Carlquist, 1961, 1970c), many of which are insular. I advanced the hypothesis (Carlquist, 1970c) that in a species which is herbaceous and has specialized wood (very short fusiform cambial initials), increase in xylem production under appropriate conditions (involving paedomorphosis) may often lead to production of libriform fibers like ray cells in height, and thus so short as to be histologically equivalent to ray cells. As Barghoorn (1941) noted, continual production of xylem sometimes does lead to subdivision in ray initials, so that rays eventually appear in stems that begin with a rayless condition.

These considerations apply to two rayless woods, hitherto unreported. *Viola tracheliifolia* (fig. 10.14, top left, right) is probably the most woody species of its genus, and shows complete absence of rays. Although up to 10 ft tall, this species is not truly arborescent (taller individuals grow in a leaning posture among other shrubs); production of secondary xylem may be relatively finite, and eventual production of rays impossible. This may also be true of *Lysimachia kalalauensis* (fig. 10.14, bottom left, right), also a Hawaiian species, which possibly has greater accumulation of secondary xylem than other Primulaceae. *Lysimachia kalalauensis* is a rosette shrub, chiefly branched from the base, which grows in underbrush of semiexposed areas in upper Kauai.

Among insular species of *Plantago*, rays have developed only in the Macaronesian species, in which secondary xylem production is maximal for the genus. Even here, however, rays are relatively few and small (Carlquist, 1970c).

Raylessness in young stems, followed by eventual production of rays, characterizes Hawaiian species of *Geranium* (Barghoorn, 1941). Another group in which this occurs is the Hawaiian species of the gesneriaceous genus *Cyrtandra* (fig. 10.13, top left, right). The transection illustrated (fig. 10.13, top left) shows initiation of rays. Other species of *Cyrtandra* are similar. Ray production begins soon, so that in all samples of *Cyrtandra* studied (10 species), rays occurred in outer portions of the secondary xylem. In the species illustrated, rays are few and small, however (fig. 10.13, top right).

Ixanthus, a monotypic Canarian genus of Gentianaceae, shows an almost rayless condition (fig. 10.13, bottom left, right). The inner portions of secondary xylem are rayless, and the oldest stems available show only a few inconspicuous rays in their outermost portions.

Although the physiological significance of raylessness is difficult to assess, we might say that the value of rays as transport or storage tissues in woody species with larger secondary xylem cylinders is minimized in herbaceous species incapable of indefinite production of xylem. Thus the herbaceous species of relatively small and finite xylem production are most likely to be rayless, whereas others (*Geranium, Cyrtandra*) which

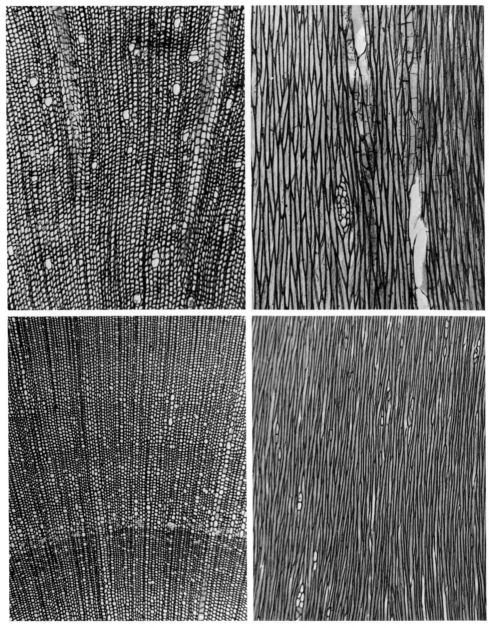

FIG. 10.13. Sections of woods of insular plants that are rayless at first, eventually develop rays. TOP LEFT, *Cyrtandra* sp. (sect. *Chaetocalyx*), transection of secondary xylem; Kahana Valley, Oahu, Hawaiian Is. TOP RIGHT, *Cyrtandra* cf. *propinqua* (Gesneriaceae), tangential section of secondary xylem; Waikane, Oahu, Hawaiian Is. BOTTOM LEFT, RIGHT, *Ixanthus viscosus* (Gentianaceae); laurel forest of Anaga Peninsula, Tenerife, Canary Is. BOTTOM LEFT, transection of secondary xylem. BOTTOM RIGHT, tangential section of secondary xylem. Magnification shown by scale with fig. 10.16.

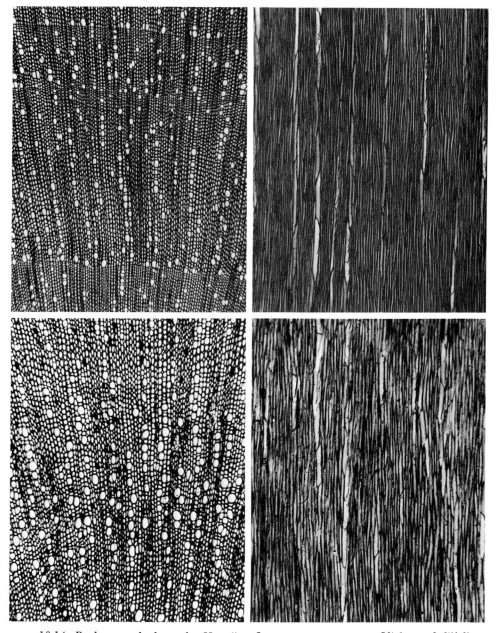

FIG. 10.14. Rayless woods from the Hawaiian flora. TOP LEFT, RIGHT, *Viola tracheliifolia* (Violaceae), sections; Waimea, Kauai. TOP LEFT, transection of secondary xylem. TOP RIGHT, tangential section of secondary xylem. BOTTOM LEFT, RIGHT, *Lysimachia kalalauensis* (Primulaceae), sections; Kalalau Lookout, Kauai. BOTTOM LEFT, transection of secondary xylem. BOTTOM RIGHT, tangential section of secondary xylem. Magnification shown by scale with fig. 10.16.

FIG. 10.15. *Talinum guadalupense* (Portulacaceae), an exceptionally large stem succulent for its genus; Outer Islet, Guadalupe I., Mexico. TOP LEFT, habit of plant, ca. 0.8 m in diam. (shown sideways). TOP RIGHT, flower, 4 cm in diam., and leaves. BOTTOM LEFT, transection of secondary xylem. BOTTOM RIGHT, tangential section of secondary xylem. Magnification for wood sections shown by scale with fig. 10.16.

eventually develop larger secondary xylem cylinders are likely to acquire rays ontogenetically. Raylessness is by no means an exclusively insular phenomenon. However, considerations implicit above (for a lengthier discussion, see Carlquist, 1970c) suggest that such indications of paedomorphosis as raylessness, rays composed wholly or predominantly of erect cells, and relatively long vessel elements are interpreted best as criteria for herbaceous or more nearly herbaceous ancestry. Woods with these phenomena would be difficult to interpret as products of a more woody ancestry.

Parenchymatization. Increased parenchymatization is a common phenomenon in insular woody herbs. This might, at first glance, appear to run counter to the trend of raylessness. However, stems rich in axial parenchyma are larger than those which exhibit raylessness; increased parenchymatization is particularly characteristic of stem succulents. *Talinum guadalupense* (fig. 10.15, bottom left, right) is a good example. In this species, rays are exceptionally wide and probably little altered from the conformation of pith rays in the primary stem. Ray cells are nonlignified. In the axial xylem, nonlignified parenchymal cells are present to the exclusion of libriform fibers; the axial xylem consists wholly of vessel elements and parenchyma. *Brighamia insignis* (Carlquist, 1969a) also contains these features except at the base of the plant and in roots, where the narrow bands of axial xylem do contain thin-walled fibers.

In another stem succulent, *Coreopsis gigantea* (fig. 10.16, bottom left), libriform fibers are present but axial parenchyma is abundant in patches and bands. Rays are wide. *Macropiper excelsum* (fig. 10.16, top left, right) could be described as a stem succulent. In this species, wide rays are present almost exclusively. As new rays are initiated in an enlarging stem, they are converted rapidly to wide rays resembling those already present. A number of stem succulents (e.g., the cactoid Euphorbias [Carlquist, 1970d]) do not have wide rays, and have parenchyma chiefly in the cortex.

Increase in axial parenchyma is characteristic of some other succulents or semisucculents—*Scaevola coriacea, S. crassifolia,* and *S. spinescens* of Goodeniaceae, for example (Carlquist, 1969b). There are rain-forest species of *Scaevola* (*S. glabra*) in which a marked increase in axial parenchyma does not seem related to succulence.

Bands of parenchyma ("marginal parenchyma") are characteristic of

FIG. 10.16. Anatomical details of woody herbs. TOP LEFT, RIGHT, *Macropiper excelsum* (Piperaceae), sections; between Westport and Greymouth, New Zealand. TOP LEFT, transection. TOP RIGHT, tangential section. BOTTOM LEFT, CENTER, *Coreopsis gigantea* (Asteraceae), a species from California islands and adjacent coast; Malibu, Calif. BOTTOM LEFT, transection of secondary

(*continued*)

certain insular species. They have been observed chiefly in Asteraceae. They are shown here in *Sonchus radicatus* (fig. 10.5, bottom left), whereas other species of *Sonchus* lack them (figs. 10.6, bottom left; 10.8, bottom left). Other examples include the insular California species of *Hemizonia* and species, chiefly alpine, of *Dubautia* (Carlquist, 1958). In these, bands of parenchyma are believed to have resulted from "fiber dimorphism" (Carlquist, 1961). Because, in Asteraceae, libriform fibers may not differ from axial parenchyma except in length and a little in wall thickness, a minor shortening and a persistence of a nucleus result in a cell, type that we must term axial parenchyma. The significance of parenchyma in these Asteraceae is not obvious, although it appears in insular species with growth forms that stress mechanical strength less and those that live in a climate with marked dry seasons.

Woods with anomalous secondary xylem, such as *Charpentiera* (fig. 10.12, bottom left, right), *Bosea* (fig. 10.12, top left, right), *Nototrichium*, *Chenopodium*, and *Convolvulus* (fig. 10.11, top left, right), obviously have a mode of parenchymatization related to successive cambium formation. Genera characterized by anomalous secondary thickening would seem good candidates for insular woodiness because the process of anomalous secondary thickening seen in annual representatives of Chenopodiaceae, Amaranthaceae, and others can be continued indefinitely in situations where climatic moderation permits.

Libriform-fiber Characteristics. Although one can select a few examples of woodier insular herbs in which libriform fibers are thick walled, thin-walled fibers characterize the great majority of them. The species of *Sonchus* illustrated here are notable in this regard (bottom left and right of figs. 10.5, 10.6, 10.8). Fibers are so thin walled in this genus that sectioning is extremely difficult. This is also true in insular species of *Echium* (Carlquist, 1970b), Lobelioideae (Carlquist, 1969a), Plantaginaceae (Carlquist, 1970c), most Brassicaceae (Carlquist, 1971), *Euphorbia* (Carlquist, 1970d), *Cyrtandra* (fig. 10.13, top left, right) and many Asteraceae (see papers cited

FIG. 10.16 (*continued*)

xylem. BOTTOM CENTER, vessel from tangential section of wood. BOTTOM RIGHT, *Dendroseris berteriana* (Asteraceae), section of secondary phloem and adjacent cortex to show lack of fibers in bark; specimen collected by Carl Skottsberg on Masatierra, Juan Fernandez Is. Scale of magnifications for all except bottom center is shown at bottom. Vessel in bottom center, $\times$ ca. 600.

in Carlquist, 1966). The exceptions to the rule are interesting. In Lobelioideae, thick-walled fibers could be said to characterize only upper portions of *Cyanea leptostegia*. Thick-walled fibers definitely seem correlated with mechanical strength in this tall, palmiform species (Carlquist, 1969a).

Among the exceptional insular species of herbaceous groups with hard wood (owing to thick-walled libriform fibers), one can cite *Parolinia ornata* (fig. 10.10, bottom right). However, predominance of thin-walled fibers suggests that selective pressure for mechanical strength is lessened. However, if insular woodier herbs have, in general, longer fusiform cambial initials and therefore longer libriform fibers, this length might offer greater mechanical strength.

Gelatinous fibers or fiber-tracheids characterize some insular groups. Most notable are species of *Euphorbia* (Carlquist, 1970d) and Goodeniaceae (Carlquist, 1969b).

Pitting. Occurrences of scalariform or near-scalariform pits on vessels in woods of herbaceous plants that are woodier on islands are too numerous to mention here. These instances have been discussed in virtually all of my recent papers dealing with woods (1962a, 1962b, 1969a, 1969b, 1970d, for example). Such pitting occurs in *Coreopsis gigantea* (fig. 10.16, bottom center). An almost perfect example is offered by *Macropiper excelsum* (Carlquist, 1962a). I have advanced two explanations, which can be regarded as complementary rather than mutually exclusive, for this phenomenon. First, this pitting pattern is a protraction into secondary xylem of metaxylem pitting patterns (Carlquist, 1962a). Second, it tends to occur in groups in which stem succulence or other factors place low stress on mechanical strength. "Release" from narrowness of pits is possible where vessel elements of greater mechanical strength are not of selective value (Carlquist, 1969a, 1970d). The role that stem succulence plays is obvious from the presence of wide, gaping, elongate pits, often with minimal wall area between pits, in such families as Crassulaceae and Cactaceae (notably cereoids) at large.

Growth Rings. Degree of growth-ring development in insular woody herbs is related, with few exceptions, to seasonality of the environment in temperature or rainfall. Insular woods also have fewer growth rings than do their continental counterparts. In general, Macaronesian woody herbs show relatively marked growth-ring development except for laurel-forest species, such as *Sonchus abbreviatus* (fig. 10.6, bottom left). Growth rings in Macaronesian woody herbs are a response to dry summers; stem succulents, however, do not show growth rings very much, as one would expect, for a stem succulent is not affected directly by soil moisture.

Growth rings are relatively mild in Hawaiian woods; they are usually expressed in the form of somewhat wider vessels in early woods. The Hawaiian lobelioids (Carlquist, 1969a) and Goodeniaceae (1969b) are relatively poor in growth rings. Interestingly, the least demarcation of growth rings was observed in Afroalpine *Lobelia* species (Carlquist, 1969a), Afroalpine *Senecio* species (Carlquist, 1962b), and the Espeletias of the equatorial Andes (Carlquist, 1958). The uniform temperature regime throughout the year in these regions evidently is responsible. In addition, there is an aspect of stem succulence in these groups. Equatorial alpine bog species have, of course, a constant source of water.

PHLOEM AND CORTEX

Herbs are often plants with minimal mechanical strength. To the extent that this generalization is true, it applies not only to xylem but to extraxylary fibers as well. Among families and genera that are woody on islands and in which I found little or no extraxylary fiber formation are Boraginaceae, Brassicaceae, Campanulaceae, Goodeniaceae, Solanaceae, and many groups of Asteraceae (e.g., *Dendroseris* [*Phoenicoseris*] *berteriana*, fig. 10.16, bottom right). Families with anomalous secondary thickening and succulence of stems can be added to this list. Extraxylary fibers are definitely present in some groups of woody herbs on islands, but even in these, they rarely reach the abundance or strength of fibers in families of truly woody dicotyledons, such as Fagaceae, Moraceae, and Sterculiaceae. Lack of extraxylary fibers may be one indication of an herbaceous ancestry for a particular group.

A Catalogue of Woody Herbs on Islands

The lists below have been compiled to demonstrate groups in which at least some taxa are generally greater in size than are their continental counterparts. This accounts for omission of some arborescent insular groups in which continental relatives often exceed insular species in size (cactoid Euphorbias and cacti, for example). Because oceanic islands are not the sole sites for evolution of woody herbs, a discussion of continental areas with insular characteristics follows. I believe these continental areas are important, because their woody herbs show some portions of the insular syndrome. Climatic regions on islands are not exclusively different from those on mainland areas, even if islands do offer more definitive examples. Our understanding of insular woodiness would be incomplete if we failed to take into account continental situations where woody herbs have evolved. Arrangement of the insular areas is geographical: Pacific, Atlantic, then Indian Ocean islands, followed by equatorial montane situations and subtropical continental climates with certain degrees of climatic moderation, disharmony, and other features that tend to promote insular woodiness. Estimates of size of plants and of numbers of species are approximate. Endemic genera are indicated by "e" within the parentheses listing species and their sizes.

HAWAIIAN ISLANDS

The list is based on F. R. Fosberg's data in Zimmerman (1948), on Hillebrand (1888), Rock (1913, 1919), Sherff (1935, 1937a), and Carlquist (1970a).

Amaranthaceae: *Charpentiera* (4 spp.; 2–6 m); *Nototrichium* (e, 3 spp. + vars.; 2–6 m). Asteraceae: *Argyroxiphium* (e, 4 spp. acaulescent, but *A. grayanum* a shrub to 2 m); *Bidens* (ca. 40 spp.; some to 3 m, others subshrubs or suffruticose); *Dubautia* s.l. (e, ca. 30 spp. + vars.; *D. knudsenii* and *D. arborea* to 8 m, others shrubby to decumbent); *Hesperomannia* (e, 3 spp. + subsp.; to 5 m); *Lipochaeta* (e, ca. 25 spp. + vars.; to 1.5 m, some species decumbent); *Remya* (e, 2 spp.; to 2 m); *Wilkesia* (e, 1 sp.; to 5 m). Brassicaceae: *Lepidium* (3 spp.; *L. arbuscula* and *L. serra* to 1.5 m). Campanulaceae, tribe Lobelioideae: *Brighamia* (e, 1 sp.; stem succulent to 1.5 m); *Clermontia* (e, ca. 40 spp.; all shrubs, some—*C. arborescens*—to 8 m); *Cyanea* (e, ca. 50 spp.; 2–14 m); *Delissea* (e, ca. 6 spp.; to 5 m in *D. undulata*); *Lobelia* (10 spp.; some to 5 m—*L. gaudichaudii*; some subherbaceous); *Rollandia* (e. ca. 8 spp.; to 6 m); *Trematolobelia* (e, 1 sp. + vars.; to 2 m). Caryophyllaceae: *Alsinodendron* (e, 2 spp.; to 2 m); *Schiedea* (e, ca. 30 spp. + vars.; to 1.5 m but mostly herbaceous); *Silene* (5 spp.;

S. struthioloides and *S. alexandri* shrubby, to 1 m, others herbaceous).
Chenopodiaceae: *Chenopodium* (1 sp.; *C. oahuense* to 6 m). Euphorbia-
ceae: *Euphorbia* (ca. 16 spp. + vars.; *E. haeleeleana* to 14 m, *E. rockii*
and several others to 7 m, others shrubby or decumbent). Geraniaceae:
Geranium (ca. 6 spp.; *G. arboreum* to 4 m, others shrubs, one decumbent).
Gesneriaceae: *Cyrtandra* (ca. 140 spp.; some to 7 m, some subherbaceous).
Goodeniaceae: *Scaevola* (ca. 7 spp.; several to 6 m, *S. coriacea* decumbent).
Malvaceae: *Hibiscadelphus* (e, 3 spp.; 2–8 m; one a shrub); *Kokia* (e, 3
spp.; trees to 8 m). Nyctaginaceae: see discussion below. Plantaginaceae:
Plantago (ca. 10 spp. + vars.; *P. princeps* to 2 m, others rosette herbs).
Primulaceae: *Lysimachia* (ca. 13 spp.; to 2 m in *L. kalalauensis*, others
shrubs or subshrubs). Polygonaceae: *Rumex* (2 spp.; *R. giganteus* to 2 m
as a shrub, to 12 m scandent). Solanaceae: *Nothocestrum* (e, ca. 6 spp.;
to 10 m in *N. breviflorum*, others at least 3 m); *Solanum* (ca. 7 spp.; *S.
kauaiense* to 5 m, others shrubby). Violaceae: *Viola* (7 spp.; *V. tracheliifolia* to 5 m, others smaller).

   Charpentiera is known only from the Hawaiian and Austral Islands;
its closest affinities appear to be with *Chamissoa* from Mexico. Among
Asteraceae, the *Argyroxiphium-Dubautia-Wilkesia* complex is discussed in
chapter 4. Hawaiian *Bidens* species appear close to such North American
species as *B. pilosa* but may have been derived via the southeastern
Polynesian species; *Bidens* is more arborescent on the Hawaiian Islands
than elsewhere. The affinities of *Hesperomannia* are imprecisely known,
but must lie with actinomorphic-flowered American mutisioids such as
Gochnatia, *Anastraphia*, *Stenopadus*, and *Stifftia*. *Lipochaeta* belongs to
Heliantheae, subtribe Verbesininae, and may be allied to *Zexmenia*,
Wedelia, and *Verbesina* from western North America. Reports of *Lipochaeta* elsewhere have been discredited (Harling, 1962). *Remya*, today
nearly extinct, has obscure affinities with *Haplopappus* or other asteroid
genera of North America. In Brassicaceae, the Hawaiian species of
Lepidium may have had various origins; the genus is pan-boreal. The
same can be said for Hawaiian species of *Lobelia* (Campanulaceae), and
therefore also *Trematolobelia*, a probable derivative of *Lobelia*. *Clermontia*,
Cyanea, *Delissea* and *Rollandia* (see also chapter 4) form a close grouping
and have their closest affinities with similarly baccate Andean genera such
as *Burmeistera* and *Centropogon*, which can become woody at their bases.

Brighamia, although not truly woody, is probably greater in stature than its ancestors; such genera as *Hippobroma* and *Isotoma* have been suggested, but there are possible resemblances to *Apetahia* of southeastern Polynesia. In Caryophyllaceae, *Alsinodendron* and *Schiedea* are almost intercontinuous, but their relationships are obscure and could lie with any of several boreal herbaceous genera, such as *Minuartia*. *Chenopodium oahuense* (Chenopodiaceae) is the most arborescent species of its genus; its origins may be boreal. The Hawaiian Geraniums are distinctive and have even been segregated as an endemic genus (*Neurophyllodes*), but are best regarded as sect. *Neurophyllodes* of *Geranium*. *Geranium jahnii* (sect. *Paramenses*) may be close. *Cyrtandra* (Gesneriaceae) is an Indo-Pacific genus, and only a few Hawaiian species are exceptionally woody. *Scaevola* (Goodeniaceae) is clearly Australian in origin, but the Hawaiian species, which include the tallest shrubs and trees, probably reached the Hawaiian Islands via South Pacific way stations. In Malvaceae, *Hibiscadelphus* is close to *Hibiscus*, from Indo-Malesia. *Kokia* is alleged to be related to *Gossypium*, in which case its affinities would lie with New World species such as *G. arboreum*. *Abortopetalum*, claimed to be an endemic Hawaiian genus, is perhaps only an exceptional species of *Abutilon*. *Lysimachia* (Primulaceae) is a boreal genus, but Hawaiian species are exceptional in woodiness. Shrubby species of *Rumex* (Polygonaceae) can be found in various parts of the world, but probably derive from boreal ancestors. *Nothocestrum* (Solanaceae) seems close to Andean species of *Cestrum*, which are shrubs; Hawaiian Solanums could have had various origins. The same can be said for Hawaiian species of *Viola*, which are related to boreal Violas.

One could add Nyctaginaceae to the list. *Pisonia umbellifera* and *P. sandwicensis* form sizable trees; however, they are related to *P. inermis*, an Indo-Malesian strand species that may have become arborescent on continental beaches rather than on islands. The problem of how much increase in size can be attributed to Hawaiian Rubiaceae, Rutaceae, and Araliaceae has been mentioned; *Gunnera*, although gigantic in the Hawaiian Islands, is not truly woody—it has little secondary xylem activity in its polystelic stem and is just a "giant herb."

The chief site for evolution of arborescence in the Hawaiian flora appears to be the wet (*Metrosideros*) forest, although an appreciable number of the species listed above occur in the somewhat drier *Acacia* forests. Arborescence in lowland Amaranthaceae, Chenopodiaceae, and Malvaceae has been discussed earlier in this chapter. Woodiness has increased in bogs only in *Argyroxiphium grayanum* and *Lobelia gaudi-chaudii*, and the opposite effect is seen in *Pelea waialealae* and the bog ecotypes of *Metrosideros*. The distribution of growth forms of *Dubautia* (chapter 4) in various ecological zones shows that maximal arborescence is related to wet forest. Even *Nothocestrum*, characteristically a lowland genus, has entered the rain forest (*N. peltatum*). Because much of the Hawaiian forest is scrubby (e.g., the Koolau Range *Metrosideros* forest), evolution toward shrubby species rather than tall trees is to be expected. In tall Hawaiian forest, or in gulches, woodier herbs tend to occur as understory elements rather than emergents.

SOUTHERN POLYNESIA

The lists are based on data from Brown (1935), Carlquist (1957, 1969b), Carlquist and Grant (1963), Christophersen (1928), Moore (1933), Sherff (1937a, 1937b), and Wimmer (1953, 1956).

Marquesas Islands. Asteraceae: *Bidens* (9 spp. [e]; mostly to 1 m); *Oparanthus* (*O. albus*, 1–3 m). Campanulaceae: *Apetahia* (*A. longistigmata* to 1 m). Gesneriaceae: *Cyrtandroidea* (e, *C. jonesii* to 8 m). Goodeniaceae: *Scaevola* (2 close spp.; to 2 m).

Society Islands. Asteraceae: *Bidens* (8 spp. [7 e]; *B. mooreensis* to 3.6 m, others somewhat smaller); *Fitchia* (5 spp. + 1 subsp.; *F. nutans* to 8 m, others at least to 2 m). Campanulaceae: *Apetahia* (*A. raiateensis* to 2 m); *Sclerotheca* (3 spp.; *S. arborea* to 8 m, others at least 2 m). Goodeniaceae: *Scaevola* (*S. tahitensis* to 2 m). Onagraceae: *Fuchsia* (*F. cyrtandroides* to 2 m).

Rapa. Asteraceae: *Fitchia* (*F. rapensis* to 8 m); *Oparanthus* (3 spp.; *O. rapensis* to 6 m, *O. intermedius* to 4 m). Campanulaceae: *Sclerotheca* (*S. margaretae* to 8 m).

Austral Islands. Amaranthaceae: *Charpentiera* (*C. australis* to 11 m).

Rarotonga, Cook Islands. Asteraceae: *Fitchia* (*F. speciosa* to 10 m). Campanulaceae: *Sclerotheca* (*S. viridiflora* to 2 m).

Henderson Island. Asteraceae: *Bidens* (*B. hendersonensis* + 1 var., to 7 m).

Oeno Island. Asteraceae: *Bidens* (B. *hendersonensis* var. *oenoensis* to 3 m).

Pitcairn Island. Asteraceae: *Bidens* (B. *mathewsii* to 1 m).

Mangareva, Gambier Islands. Asteraceae: *Fitchia* (F. *mangarevensis* to 5 m).

Samoa. Goodeniaceae: *Scaevola* (S. *nubigena* to 2 m). Rubiaceae: *Sarcopygme* (e, 5 spp.; at least two reach 7 m).

The total number of species showing insular woodiness in southern Polynesia is not very great. *Cyrtandra* has been omitted from the listings because none of the southern Polynesian species are exceptionally woody. *Cyrtandroidea* (originally placed in Campanulaceae, Lobelioideae by F. B. H. Brown) is included because it is exceptional in height. *Fitchia* and *Oparanthus* are interesting endemics of southern Polynesia (Carlquist, 1957; Carlquist and Grant, 1963); they are without any doubt related to *Bidens* and may be considered an early introduction of a *Bidens*-like stock into this region. *Apetahia* and *Sclerotheca*, also endemics of south-eastern Polynesia, are capsular lobelioids presumably derived from *Lobelia*-like ancestors. Some *Bidens* species in southern Polynesia are notably tall; *B. saintjohniana*, a species from Marotiri, near Rapa, was not included since it is a subshrub. *Fuchsia cyrtandroides* is included, although it is less woody than *F. excorticata* of New Zealand, to which it is related; it is, however, still woodier than many species of *Fuchsia*. *Sarcopygme* is derived from woody ancestors—perhaps *Morinda*—but because of its peculiar rosette-tree habit (see Carlquist, 1965), it is judged to be increased in height and altered in habit. The smaller number of examples of insular woodiness in southern Polynesia may be due to limited land area (especially limited area of wet forest), remoteness of the islands from one another, and remoteness from source areas. The ecological gamut of the southern Polynesian islands is not as great as that of the Hawaiian Islands.

MELANESIA

Data are from Guillaumin (1948), Krause (1912), and Leenhouts (1964).

If we consider islands from Fiji westward to the Asiatic mainland, except for Australia, New Zealand, and Taiwan, we find only one genus we can clearly cite as an example of insular woodiness: *Scaevola* (sect.

Scaevola, the fleshy-fruited species) of the Goodeniaceae. *Scaevola flori-bunda* is a shrub or tree to about 8 m on Viti Levu, Fiji. On New Caledonia there are also several species of comparable size—*S. montana* and *S. indigofera*; the lowland *S. beckii* never exceeds about 1 m in height. Additional *Scaevola* species, some of questionable taxonomic status, have been reported from New Caledonia: *S. racemigera, S. coccinea, S. cylindrica,* and *S. balansae*. On Mt. Doorman, New Guinea, there is the recently described *S. pauciflora* Leenhouts. There are also in this series *S. micrantha* (Palawan, Talaud Is., Mt. Kinabalu in Sabah) and the recently described (Leenhouts, 1964) Borneo species, *S. verticillata*. There is, to be sure, a variable species of *Scaevola, S. oppositifolia* (segregate species variously recognized), which ranges from Queensland into New Guinea, Indonesia, and the Philippines, but it belongs to sect. *Enantiophyllum* and is not very woody, in any case. It tends to be scandent, and woody only at its base. *Brachionostylum* (Asteraceae) is a monotypic genus reported from New Guinea; it is a shrub close to (perhaps even congeneric with) *Senecio*.

The lack of insular woodiness in Melanesia probably represents the harmonic nature of Melanesian floras compared to those of Polynesia. Suitably large and wet areas are certainly present, and have been for long periods of time. The reasons why Polynesia is so much more strongly disharmonic than Melanesia have been discussed elsewhere (Carlquist, 1965).

NEW ZEALAND

Data are from Allan (1961).

Asteraceae: *Brachyglottis* (e, 1 sp. + vars.; tree to 6 m or more); *Cassinia* (5 spp.; *C. retorta* to 5 m, others smaller); *Olearia* (32 spp.; shrubs or trees 2–6 m); *Senecio* (40 spp.; 23 are shrubs or trees; *S. stewartiae, S. huntii, S. reinoldii*—all from southernmost New Zealand—to 6 m or more); *Traversia* (e, 1 sp.; shrub to 1 m). Caprifoliaceae (?): *Alseuosmia* (e, 1 sp.; shrub to 2 m). Coriariaceae: *Coriaria* (7 spp.; *C. arborea* a shrub to 6 m, branched from base). Malvaceae: *Hoheria* (e, 5 spp.; all trees to ca. 6 m); *Plagianthus* (2 spp.; *P. betulinus* a tree to 15 m). Onagraceae: *Fuchsia* (4 spp.; *F. excorticata* a tree to 12 m). Piperaceae: *Macropiper* (1 sp.; *M. excelsum* to 6 m). Scrophulariaceae: *Hebe* (ca. 80 spp.; many are shrubs, some trees, *H. parviflora* var. *arborea* to 7.5 m).

A number of larger genera are only marginally includable in this listing. Some that might have been included are *Homalanthus polyandrus* (Euphorbiaceae), the only New Zealand species of this genus, a tree to 8 m; and *Carmichaelia*, a genus of Fabaceae endemic to New Zealand and Lord Howe Island—*C. arborea* is a shrub or tree 3–5 m tall. Although *Hebe* was included above, many species are diminutive shrubs, of course. The taxonomic position of *Alseuosmia* may not be in Caprifoliaceae; it has rayless wood, which suggests herbaceous ancestry.

The presence of an appreciable number of woodier herbs in New Zealand reflects greater disharmony and greater ecological opportunity than in Melanesia. Glaciation may have contributed to this disharmony. One should also note that herbaceous groups are typically temperate, so that New Zealand is a more likely site for their establishment than are the tropical islands of Melanesia. The woodier herbs listed occur in pioneer or more strongly disharmonic portions of New Zealand. Interesting in this regard is that the most arboreal species of *Senecio* are characteristic of the offshore islands. *Coriaria* appears on glaciated rubble, new lava, and road cuts. With a few exceptions (e.g., *Fuchsia*), Australia seems to be the source of most of the herbaceous groups that have become notably woody on New Zealand. Some basically woody groups, such as Araliaceae, may have increased in stature on New Zealand.

JUAN FERNANDEZ ISLANDS

Data are from Skottsberg (1922, 1953, 1956).

Apiaceae: *Eryngium* (4 spp.; *E. bupleuroides* with main stem to 1 m long, *E. fernandezianum* to 0.75 m, others to 0.5 m). Asteraceae: *Centaurodendron* (e, 2 spp.; to 4 m); *Dendroseris* (including *Phoenicoseris*, *Rea*, and *Hesperoseris*) (e, 9 spp.; *D. macrantha* to 5 m, others most typically 2 m tall); *Erigeron* (5 spp.; *E. fruticosus*, to 1 m, is tallest); *Rhetinodendron* (e; *R. berterii* to 5 m); *Robinsonia* (e, 7 spp, incl. *Symphyochaeta*; *R. thurifera* to 6 m, others mostly to 4 m); *Yunquea* (e; *Y. tenzii* to 3 m). Boraginaceae: *Selkirkia* (e; *S. berteroi* a "miniature tree" to 1 m). Campanulaceae: *Wahlenbergia* (5 spp.; shrubs or subshrubs 0.5–1 m). Chenopodiaceae: *Chenopodium* (3 spp.; shrubs, *C. nesodendron* to 2.8 m). Plantaginaceae: *Plantago* (*P. fernandezianum* to ca. 1 m).

Some questionable groups could have been added. *Cuminia* is an endemic genus of Lamiaceae, but its species are shrubs, and shrubby Lamiaceae are common on mainland areas. Likewise, shrubby species of *Erigeron* are certainly not lacking on continents. Fernandezian species of *Haloragis* are not notably woody; *Gunnera* is not included (see discussion earlier under Hawaiian flora). That Asteraceae bulk so large as examples of woodier herbs is interesting. Three distinct tribes (Lactuceae, Cynareae, and Senecioneae) are involved; four (Astereae) if *Erigeron* is included. The good representation of woody herbs derives from the fact that the Juan Fernandez Islands are temperate, suitable for establishment of temperate weedy groups; the climate in the cloud forest is uniformly moist, providing excellent growing conditions. Some lowland species (*Dendroseris litoralis, Chenopodium* spp.) have achieved woodiness, perhaps by virtue of succulence or drought resistance. The distance of the Juan Fernandez Islands from South America is great enough to insure disharmony of this flora, but close enough to permit arrival of Asteraceae and others. Despite the presence of the apparently relictual genera *Lactoris* and *Thyrsopteris*, there is every reason to believe that the groups listed above have achieved woodiness autochthonously.

DESVENTURADAS ISLANDS

Data are from Skottsberg (1937).

Thamnoseris, an endemic genus with probably only one species, *T. lacerata*, could be called an instance of insular woodiness, or a sort of "giant lettuce" (Asteraceae, tribe Cichorieae, probably related to the Fernandezian genus *Dendroseris*). However, *Thamnoseris* tends to be acaulescent or have aspects of a stem succulent rather than a true shrub. The only other Desventuradas plant worthy of mention is *Lycapsus tenuifolius* (Asteraceae), a monotypic endemic genus; plants reach 70 cm. The affinities of *Lycapsus* are uncertain; if a member of Heliantheae, it certainly is not a plant of exceptional size for that tribe.

GALÁPAGOS ISLANDS

Data are from Stewart (1911), Howell (1931, 1941), Harling (1962), Dawson (1962), Anderson (1967), and Eliasson (1968).

Asteraceae: *Darwiniothamnus* (e, 2 spp.; to 3.5 m); *Macraea* (e; *M. laricifolia* to 3.5 m); *Scalesia* (e; the tallest species, *S. pedunculata,* to

20 m, *S. cordata* to 8 m; larger shrubs—*S. atractyloides, S. darwinii,* and *S. stewartii,* to about 3 m). Cactaceae: *Jasminocereus* (3 spp.; to ca. 6 m); *Opuntia* (*O. echios, O. galapageia,* and *O. megasperma* qualify as trees). Portulacaceae: *Calandrinia* (*C. galapagosa* is an unusual succulent rosette shrub to at least 60 cm).

The Galápagos flora includes only a few striking instances of arborescence, of which the truly outstanding example is *Scalesia pedunculata.* The remaining species of *Scalesia* range downward to relatively small shrubs. Possible relatives of *Scalesia* include such genera of Heliantheae, subtribe Verbesininae, as *Wulffia, Wedelia, Perymenium,* and *Mirasolia.* Some of these are shrubby. *Macraea* is close to *Wedelia,* which can be a shrub, so autochthonous increase in woodiness is not marked. Similarly, *Darwiniothamnus,* although perhaps not as close to *Erigeron* as once thought (Harling, 1962), is not exceptionally woody for Astereae when one considers the arborescent species of *Olearia* in Australia and New Zealand. Likewise, the endemic genus *Lecocarpus* (Asteraceae, Heliantheae, subtribe Melampodiinae) is only a small shrub.

Visitors to the Galápagos Islands find the tree-Opuntias of lowland areas striking. Likewise, *Jasminocereus* (a *Cereus* segregate of questionable validity) can form candelabrum-shaped trees. However, the fact remains that arborescent species of *Opuntia* and *Cereus* (or *Cereus* segregates) are common in dry areas of Mexico, and Central and South America, and Galapageian populations (e.g., *O. echios* var. *zacana*) can be low and shrubby. The possibility remains that there has been some autochthonous increase in arborescence among Galápagos Opuntias. In any case, the Galápagos Islands are notable for the few instances in which woody herbs have increased in size. The obvious explanation is the dry climate; only a limited number of groups could achieve tree stature under these circumstances.

CALIFORNIA OFFSHORE ISLANDS

Data are from Thorne (1969).

Under the category of offshore islands are recognized islands that lie off of both California and Baja California (Pacific coast). Some, such as San Clemente and Guadalupe, are volcanic oceanic islands; others can be called continental islands but have been populated at least in recent geological time by overwater dispersal (for a discussion, see Thorne, 1969).

Asteraceae: *Coreopsis* (*C. gigantea* to 2 m, on mainland also); *Erio-phyllum* (1 insular sp., *E. nevinii*, to 1 m); *Haplopappus* (2 insular spp., *H. canus* and *H. detonsus*, to 1 m); *Hemizonia* (5 insular spp. [4 e], to about 1 m; *H. greeneana* also on mainland); *Perityle* (*P. incana* [e, Guada-lupe], to 1 m); *Senecio* (*S. palmeri* [e, Guadalupe], to 1 m; *S. lyoni* to 1 m, on both mainland and islands); *Stephanomeria* (*S. blairii* [e, San Clemente], to 2 m; *S. guadalupense* [e, Guadalupe], to 1 m). Brassicaceae: *Erysimum* (2 insular spp., *E. insulare* and *E. moranii*, to 1 m). Fabaceae: *Lotus* (*L. scoparius* var. *dendroideus* with single trunk, to 1.5 m). Papaveraceae: *Eschscholzia* (*E. palmeri* and *E. frutescens* e on Guadalupe, to 1 m). Portulacaceae: *Talinum* (*T. guadalupense*, to 1 m, e on Guadalupe). Polygonaceae: *Eriogonum* (*E. arborescens* to 2 m; *E. giganteum*, endemic to islands, to 4 m). Rubiaceae: *Galium* (e; *G. angulosum*, to 1 m, Guadalupe).

Climatic moderation obviously plays a strong role in permitting greater size of these insular species as compared with their mainland relatives. Larger leaves and shrub size can be seen in other genera, such as *Dendromecon*, *Cercocarpus*, and *Ceanothus*, on these islands. *Lavatera* of the Malvaceae should probably have been included in the list, although present ranges of *Lavatera* species may be more restricted now than formerly. This is certainly true of the rosaceous tree *Lyonothamnus*, now an insular endemic but formerly known (as fossils reveal) from mainland areas, and presumably surviving on islands only because of the maritime climate. In addition, lack of herbivore pressure may have permitted survival of some insular species. The degree of increase in size in the insular species listed as compared with mainland relatives is not great, probably reflecting that the moderated climate of the California offshore islands is only slightly more favorable than that of the mainland—certainly not at all spectacular.

CANARY ISLANDS

Data are from Lems (1960) and from original observations.

Amaranthaceae: *Bosea* (e; *B. yervamora* to 4 m). Asteraceae: *Allago-pappus* (e, 1 or 2 spp.; to 2 m); *Andryala* (3 spp.; *A. pinnatifida* to 1 m); *Carlina* (*C. canariensis* to 2 m, *C. salicifolia* to 3 m); *Centaurea* (11 spp.;

C. arbutifolia and some others to 4 m); *Chrysanthemum* (13 spp.; *C. broussenetii* and others forming shrubs, to 2 m); *Gonospermum* (e, 4 spp.; *G. canariense* to 4 m); *Kleinia* (*K. neriifolia* a succulent shrub to 2 m); *Schizogyne* (e; *S. sericea* to 2 m); *Sonchus* (20 spp.; *S. abbreviatus* to 5 m, others ranging downward in height); *Tolpis* (8 spp.; herbs to subshrubs 1 m); *Vierea* (e; *V. laevigata* a sprawling shrub to 1 m). Boraginaceae: *Echium* (18 spp.; mostly shrubs 1–2 m tall; *E. pininana* a monocarpic rosette tree to 4 m). Brassicaceae: *Cheiranthus* (3 spp.; shrubs to 1.5 m); *Crambe* (7 spp.; some to 1 m); *Descurainia* (6 spp.; subshrubs to 1 m); *Parolinia* (e, 1 sp.; to 4 m); *Sinapidendron* (2 spp.; shrubs to 1 m). Caryophyllaceae: *Dicheranthus* (e, monotypic; to 1 m). Convolvulaceae: *Convolvulus* (8 spp.; some shrubs or fountain-shaped trees to 4 m, as in *C. floridus, C. scoparius*). Crassulaceae: *Aeonium* (31 spp.; about 10 shrubby, to 1 m or more). Dipsacaceae: *Pterocephalus* (3 spp.; *P. dumetorum* a shrub to 4 m). Euphorbiaceae: *Euphorbia* (8 spp. of sect. *Tithymalus*; the common *E. balsamifera* to 2 m, *E. regis-jubae* to 3 m, *E. mellifera* to 5 m; cactoid spp. not listed because mainland species are equally woody). Gentianaceae: *Ixanthus* (e, monotypic; *I. viscosus* to 1.5 m). Hypericaceae: *Hypericum* (5 spp.; some are shrubs to 2 m). Lamiaceae: *Bystropogon* (3 spp.; shrubs to 3 m). Plantaginaceae: *Plantago* (15 spp.; mostly rosette herbs, but *P. arborescens* and *P. webbii* "miniature trees" to 1 m). Plumbaginaceae: *Limonium* (18 spp.; some are shrubs to 2 m— *L. arborescens, L. fruticans, L. preauxii*—others smaller). Polygonaceae: *Rumex* (2 spp.; *R. lunaria* a shrub to 2 m). Rosaceae: *Bencomia* (2 spp.; trees to 4 m); *Dendriopoterium* (e; close to *Bencomia*, a tree to 4 m); *Marcetella* (1 sp.; to 3 m). Scrophulariaceae: *Isoplexis* (2 spp.; to 1.5 m); *Lytanthus* (*L. salicinus*, a shrub to 2 m). Solanaceae: *Withania* (3 spp.; shrubs to 3 m). Urticaceae: *Gesnouinia* (e, 2 spp.; trees to 4 m).

In the Canarian flora, few typically herbaceous groups have achieved anything like true arborescence. As the sizes above indicate, evolution from herb to shrub is common, however. Interestingly, all the genera endemic to the Canary Islands or to the Canary Islands plus one or more other Macaronesian islands (*Marcetella, Bencomia, Lytanthus, Isoplexis,* and *Sinapidendron*) are in the list, with the exception of two herbaceous genera, *Greenovia* (Crassulaceae) and *Legendraea* (Convolvulaceae). Thus, those groups in which woodiness has increased and which are endemic have very likely evolved this characteristic autochthonously. If the endemic genera were relictual, one would expect at least some of them to be from typically woody families. Only Lauraceae could be called relictual elements in the Macaronesian flora, and even these must have arrived via long-distance dispersal. *Bencomia, Marcetella,* and *Dendriopoterium* have been included because they seem appreciably woodier than their closest relatives (*Poterium, Sanguisorba, Acaena*). The affinities of *Parolinia* (Brassicaceae) are not readily evident (*Diceratella* of Socotra, Somali Republic, and Southern Iran?), but it appears woodier than any possible relatives. Literally all zones of the Canarian flora contain expressions of increased woodiness—least perhaps in alpine zones and laurel forest. For example, Brassicaceae have not penetrated (as shrubs) into the laurel forest, and *Aeonium* is absent (presumably because of frost susceptibility) in the alpine zone. The degree of increased woodiness in the laurel forest (*Echium pininana, Sonchus abbreviatus, Ixanthus, Bencomia* spp., *Gesnouinia, Isoplexis*) is perhaps greater than one would expect, considering the limited area of this forest (see chapter 5).

MADEIRA

Data are from Lowe (1868) and original observations.

Apiaceae: *Tauschia* (*Melanoselinum*) (*M. decipiens,* monocarpic, to 2 m); *Tauschia* (*Monizia*) (*M. edulis,* large-leaved, short-stemmed succulent). Asteraceae: *Andryala* (2 spp.; *A. crithmifolia* a subshrub); *Centaurea* (*C. massoniana* a shrub to 2 m); *Sonchus* (3 spp., probably with introgressants: *S. fruticosus* a rosette tree to 5 m, *S. pinnatus* to 2 m, *S. ustulatus* to 0.6 m); *Tolpis* (4 spp.; *T. succulenta* a shrub to 1 m). Boraginaceae: *Echium* (*E. nervosum* a shrub to 1.5 m, *E. candicans* a broad shrub to 3 m). Brassicaceae: *Cheiranthus* (3 spp.; shrubs to 1 m); *Crambe* (*C. fruticosus* a shrub to 2 m); *Sinapidendron* (3 spp.; shrubs 1–2 m). Campanulaceae: *Musschia* (e, 2 spp.; *M. wollastonii* a rosette tree to 4 m, *M. aurea* an acaulescent cliff rosette herb). Convolvulaceae: *Convolvulus* (3 spp.; only *C. massonii* a woody shrub). Euphorbiaceae: *Euphorbia* (*E. piscatoria* a shrub at sea level, to 4 m in laurel forest). Rosaceae: *Bencomia* (*B. caudata,* also on Canaries, to 4 m).

The limited number of woody herbs on Madeira as compared with the Canaries simply reflects that Madeira is a single island and has offered relatively little "intramural" isolation for speciation to occur within the genera; at least some of the species listed may be natural immigrants from the Canarian flora (*Sonchus pinnatus, Bencomia caudata*). Introgression has occurred among species in several genera (*Sonchus, Cheiranthus, Sinapidendron*), and some of Lowe's species are probably only ecotypes. The laurel forest contains the most spectacularly woody species—*Sonchus fruticosus, Echium candicans, Melanoselinum decipiens,* and *Musschia wollastonii.* The climate of Madeira is much like that of the Juan Fernandez Islands (see fig. 10.1), and only the lack of land area and archipelagic effects has favored Madeira less.

CAPE VERDE ISLANDS

Data are from Chevalier (1935).

Apiaceae: *Tauschia* (*Melanoselinum*) (5 spp.; range from an annual to a short-stemmed herb, *M. insulare*). Asteraceae: *Sonchus* (*S. gorgadensis* to 1 m; *S. daltoni* to 2 m). Boraginaceae: *Echium* (3 spp.; *E. hypertropicum* a "small tree to 2 m" and *E. vulcanorum* a shrub to 2 m). Brassicaceae: *Sinapidendron* (5 spp.; less woody than the Madeiran species). Euphorbiaceae: *Euphorbia* (*E. tuckeyana* to 1.5 m). Scrophulariaceae: *Lytanthus* (*L. amygdalifolius* a decumbent shrub to 0.5 m).

AZORES

Data are from Palhinha (1966).

Apiaceae: *Tauschia* (*Melanoselinum*) (*M. decipiens*, also on Madeira). Asteraceae: *Tolpis* (*T. succulenta*, also on Madeira).

The depauperate woody-herb floras of both the Cape Verde Islands and the Azores are readily apparent, despite the fact that archipelagic status might be thought to favor the Azores, which have laurel-forest and heather belts. Remoteness, lack of high mountains, and lack of ecological diversity may militate against a greater representation of the Macaronesian woody herbs on the Azores. The Cape Verde Islands are relatively dry and far from Mediterranean source areas, but their proximity to the Canaries, and similarity in climate, may explain why there are more Canary-Madeira elements on the Cape Verde Islands than on the Azores.

ST. HELENA

Data are from Melliss (1875).

Asteraceae: *Aster* (3 spp.; all shrubs 1.5–3 m); *Commidendron* (e, monotypic; *C. robustum* a flat-topped tree to 7 m); *Melanodendron* (e,

monotypic; *M. integrifolium* a spreading tree to 5 m); *Petrobium* *
(e, monotypic; *P. arboreum* a tree to 4 m); *Psiadia* (1 sp.; *P. rotundifolia* a
tree to 7 m); *Senecio* (1 sp., also called *Pladaroxylon*; a tree to 5 m). Campanulaceae: *Wahlenbergia* (3 spp.; 2 shrubby to 1.25 m). Frankeniaceae:
Frankenia (1 sp.; subshrub to 0.75 m). Geraniaceae: *Pelargonium* (1 sp.;
P. cotyledonis an acaulescent cliff plant with large, gnarled base). Plantaginaceae: *Plantago* (*P. robusta* to 1 m). Rubiaceae: *Hedyotis* (1 sp.; *H.
arborea* to 7 m). Solanaceae: *Mellissia* (e, monotypic; *M. begoniaefolia* a
shrub to 3 m).

The preponderance of arboreal composites is evident. *Commidendron*
and *Melanodendron* are probably derived from *Conyza*-like ancestors. *Petrobium*, despite its resemblances to *Oparanthus* (Carlquist, 1957), is probably a derivative of *Bidens* (to which *Oparanthus* may be independently related). *Lobelia scaevolifolia*, a St. Helena endemic, may be woodier than
mainland relatives, but subshrubby Lobelias do occur in both Africa and
South America. Hemsley (1885) discounts the "insular woodiness" of
Frankenia portulacaefolia on St. Helena, since there are shrubby Frankenias in Australia. However, the Australian Frankenias are probably parallel instances of insular woodiness. The *Hedyotis* (like those in Hawaii)
seems likely to have increased in woodiness over its ancestors. The same
can be said for *Mellissia* if it is, in fact, a derivative of *Physalis*. The *Pelargonium* is included only because it forms a striking parallel to *Monizia*
(Apiaceae) on Madeira and *Brighamia* (Campanulaceae) on the Hawaiian
Islands. Possibly the St. Helena species of *Phylica*, including the segregate
genus *Nesiota* (Rhamnaceae), are larger than their ancestors. This also is
possible in *Melhania* (Sterculiaceae) on St. Helena. The abundance of
woody herbs there is amazing, considering the small area of the island.
Perhaps St. Helena is of relatively great age, as volcanic islands go.

WEST INDIES

Cuba. Data are from Alain (1953–1962).

Asteraceae: *Ekmania* (e, monotypic; to 3 m). Campanulaceae: *Lobelia* (7 spp.; only *L. cubana* is shrubby, to 3 m). Euphorbiaceae: *Euphorbia*,
sect. *Cubanthus* (sect. endemic: 3 spp.; shrubs or small trees to 4 m); *Eu-

* The correct name for this tree is *Laxmannia*, and conservation of *Petrobium*
has failed; however, *Laxmannia* continues in use for an Australian genus of Liliaceae.

phorbia sect. *Euphorbiodendron* (7 spp.; shrubs or small trees to 5 m). Gesneriaceae: *Rhytidophyllum* (12 spp.; shrubs or small trees to 4 m; an Antillean genus). Polygalaceae: *Polygala* (24 spp.; 1, also known as *Phlebotaenia cuneata*, a tree to 15 m). Solanaceae: *Espedaea* (e, 1 sp.; *E. amoena* a small tree); *Henoonia* (e, 2 spp.; shrubby).

Hispaniola.

Asteraceae: *Narvalina* (e, monotypic; shrub to 2 m); *Piptocoma* (e, monotypic; shrub). Euphorbiaceae: *Euphorbia* (of several spp., only *E. petiolaris* a tree, to 7 m). Solanaceae: *Coeloneurum* (e, 2 spp.; to 3.5 m).

Puerto Rico. Data are from Little and Wadsworth (1964).

Asteraceae: *Eupatorium* (of native spp., *E. portoricense* a tree, to 7 m). Euphorbiaceae: *Euphorbia* (of native spp., *E. petiolaris* a tree to 7 m). Malvaceae: *Montezuma* (e, monotypic; *M. speciosissima* a tree to 15 m). Polygalaceae: *Polygala* (1 of native spp., also known as *Phlebotaenia cowellii*, a tree to 10 m). Solanaceae: *Goetzia* (e; *C. elegans* a tree 8–10 m).

Virgin Islands. Data are from Little and Wadsworth (1964).

Euphorbiaceae: *Euphorbia* (of native spp., *E. petiolaris* a tree to 7 m; extends from Hispaniola to the Lesser Antilles and the Venezuelan island, Santa Margarita). Malvaceae: *Sida* (of native spp., *S. eggersii*, on Culebra, Tortola, and Jost van Dyke; a tree to 8 m).

The arborescent species of the West Indies are notable, when compared to those of other islands, for two reasons: the West Indian list is relatively small and has few mesic species. If the Antilles are oceanic islands with a relatively broad spread of ecological conditions, why should this be true? Apparently the wet forest of the Antilles is relatively harmonic. The Antillean wet forest contains many of the same species seen in mainland wet forests of comparable conditions. Thus, there is much less opportunity for herbs to become arborescent during shift into wet forest. Lowland forest, however, is relatively scrubby, and apparently genera of dry habitats have become arborescent in this zone, as has happened with *Kokia*, *Chenopodium*, *Nothocestrum*, and *Nototrichium* in dry lowland Hawaiian forest. The West Indian woody genera listed seem, in some cases, derivatives of littoral elements. *Montezuma* may be a relative of *Thespesia*, and *Sida* is generally a coastal element. The four genera of Solanaceae, *Goetzia*, *Espadaea*, *Coeloneurum*, and *Henoonia*, belong to the tribe Cestreae, as does the Hawaiian *Nothocestrum*.

The low number of Asteraceae on West Indian islands—especially arborescent species—is notable; herbaceous species are frequent on the Antilles. Apparently ecological shift into wet forest is required for woodiness, but the harmonic wet forest has not permitted this to occur.

MADAGASCAR AND COMORO ISLANDS

Data are from Choux (1934), Perrier de la Bâthie (1950a, 1950b, 1960, 1962, 1963), and Rauh (1963).

Asteraceae: *Apodocephala* (8 spp.; 3 are shrubs and the remainder trees 6–30 m tall); *Brachylaena* (5 spp. trees, to 40 m in *B. merana*); *Dicoma* (4 spp. shrubs to trees); *Oliganthes* (4 spp. small trees to 6 m); *Psiadia* (28 spp.; mostly shrubby; *P. altissima* a small tree to 5 m); *Senecio* (many native spp.; 4 spp. shrubs; *S. humblotii* and *S. myricaefolius* trees to 15 m); *Vernonia* (of native spp., at least 9 are shrubs or small trees, most to 5 m); *Vernoniopsis* (1 sp.; *V. caudata* to 8 m). Didiereaceae (e): *Alluaudia* (6 spp.; lowest, *A. dumosa*, to 5 m; tallest, *A. adscendens*, to 12 m); *Alluaudiopsis* (2 spp.; to 4 m); *Decaryia* (monotypic; shrub or small tree to 6 m); *Didierea* (2 spp.; the taller, *D. madagascariensis*, to 6 m). Hypericaceae (*s.s.*): *Eliaea* (e, monotypic; *E. articulata* a small tree); *Haronga* (e; *H. madagascariensis* a "small tree"); *Psorospermum* (25 native spp.; 10 spp. trees to 10 m or more). Malvaceae: *Hibiscus* (*H. mangindranensis* a tree to 30 m; 8 other spp. trees but shorter); *Humbertianthus* (e, monotypic; *H. cardiostegius* a tree); *Macrostelia* (e, 3 spp.; trees to 5 m or more); *Neohumbertiella* (e, 3 spp.; shrubs or small trees). Turneraceae: *Piriqueta* (3 spp. endemic to Madagascar; 2 are small trees).

This list cannot be considered exhaustive, because widespread genera like *Vernonia* and *Hibiscus* are represented by arboreal species in regions other than Madagascar, and we do not know the growth forms of the stock ancestral to the Madagascan species. This statement certainly applies also to the family Sarcolaenaceae (Chlaenaceae). However, there definitely is increased woodiness in several genera. *Brachylaena* (Asteraceae) is represented in South Africa and Madagascar, but the Madagascan species include the tallest for the genus; *B. merana* may even be the largest tree-composite in the world. Other genera of Asteraceae could have been added to the list; the preponderance of increased woodiness among Asteraceae is not surprising in view of similar tendencies by this family on other islands.

Didiereaceae are exceptionally interesting, because the family is endemic to Madagascar, and it is difficult to imagine that it did not evolve woodiness autochthonously there. Didiereaceae belongs to Caryophyllales (Centrospermae), and its closest affinities appear to lie with such herbaceous families as Portulacaceae. Didiereaceae also shows the less frequent phenomenon of increased woodiness in a dry area rather than in a rainforest area.

The fact that insular woodiness occurs in Madagascar is curious, because the flora seems so large that one would expect it to be relatively harmonic. Evidently it is not, or was not at times when rather invasive groups such as Asteraceae established there. The Madagascan wet forest, one must remember, is rather distant from moist forest areas on continents, so disharmony is not unexpected. Even if once connected to Africa, Madagascar has been isolated for such a long time that extinction of some elements and establishment of other new ones have undoubtedly taken place, and radiation among the new establishments has been inevitable.

SOCOTRA

Data are from Balfour (1888).

Apiaceae: *Nirarathamnos* (e, monotypic; *N. asarifolius* a small tree). Cucurbitaceae: *Dendrosicyos* (e, monotypic; *D. socotrana* to 4 m); Moraceae: *Dorstenia* (1 sp.; *D. gigas*, to 2 m).

The listing may be misleading, because some remarkable arborescent plants other than these occur on Socotra. For example, the bizarre stem succulent *Adenium sokotranum* (Apocynaceae) and the giant liliaceous tree *Dracaena cinnabari* deserve mention, but these genera have equally arborescent counterparts elsewhere. *Nirarathamnos* is probably only an unusual segregate of *Bupleurum*. *Dendrosicyos* does seem unique (except for *Acanthosicyos*) as a water-tank plant in a family of vines. Stem succulence, rather than simple arborescence, is the hallmark of Socotra's larger and more conspicuous plants. As we have seen, Socotra's climate (fig. 10.1) is not one that would permit arborescence except for stem succulents. The Didiereaceae of dry Madagascar offer a good parallel.

MASCARENE ISLANDS (MAURITIUS, RÉUNION, RODRIGUEZ)

Data are from Baker (1877).

Asteraceae: *Faujasia* (3 spp.; shrubs to 2 m); *Monarrhenus* (2 spp.; shrubs to 1.5 m). Campanulaceae: *Heterochaenia* (e, monotypic; *H. ensifolia* a shrub to 80 cm). Turneraceae: *Mathurina* (e, monotypic [Rodriguez]; *M. penduliflora* a small tree).

Additional woody herbs that could be cited include *Cylindrocline* (endemic, monotypic; Asteraceae, tribe Inuleae) and shrubby Helichrysums. *Faujasia* (endemic to Madagascar and the Mascarenes) is obviously close to *Senecio*, and *Monarrhenus* (endemic to Madagascar and the Mascarenes) perhaps is close to *Helichrysum*. *Heterochaenia* seems a derivative of *Campanula*, and *Mathurina* is apparently allied to the widespread genus *Piriqueta*. Thus, the list of plants woodier on the Mascarenes (excluding Madagascar) is not great, nor are these plants exceptionally woody or distinct from their closest relatives. The impoverishment of this list recalls that of southern Polynesia, and the reasons may be similar—the land areas may be too small to have fostered evolution and persistence of more numerous arborescent taxa, or the Mascarene flora may be relatively harmonic. I cannot claim any clear instances of insular woodiness for the Seychelles. Here, other elements such as palms seem to have preempted niches into which waif flora derivatives might have evolved.

By way of concluding the listings for insular areas, one may note that tree ferns and palms are, in fact, abundant on many of the islands, at least the wetter ones (see Holttum [1964] on *Cyathea* in the Pacific). In New Zealand, the pioneering qualities of tree ferns are clearly evident from their appearance in overgrown pastures and other disturbed sites. In New Zealand, and elsewhere, the waif flora that has evolved arborescence tends to be represented more often in semi-open areas of wet forest. This may not be typical for the Hawaiian flora, but it is true of some arborescent genera there, *Clermontia* and *Scaevola*, for example.

AUSTRALIA

Australia—or parts of it—can qualify as an island or islands in several respects. Many taxonomic groups have probably increased in woodiness in Australia. The most obvious is *Eucalyptus*. Because this genus contains the tallest tree species in angiosperms, one can readily conclude that eucalypts represent some autochthonous gigantism in Myrtaceae, despite the fact that this family is woody in any case. Eucalypt seeds at their smallest seem readily wind dispersed; ancestors of the eucalypts may have reached Australia in this fashion at a time when the flora was highly disharmonic and, by virtue of the amazing drought-tolerance of this genus, radiated widely throughout the continent.

Aside from major floristic elements such as the eucalypts, however, there are some genuine instances of insular woodiness in special areas of Australia. The Tasmania-Victoria region summarized below is one. Comparatively recent disharmony in this area may be related to glaciation, opening up large areas to temperate plants. The relatively moist climate of this region provided opportunity for ecological shift into the wet forest, but wet forest moderated by maritime climates. Thus the Tasmania-Victoria region provided opportunities for insular woodiness not unlike those in New Zealand or even the Juan Fernandez Islands, which are rather cool. Data on the Tasmania-Victoria plants listed here are from Curtis (1956–1967) and Ewart (1930).

Asteraceae: *Bedfordia* (2 spp.; *B. salicina* a tree to 10 m, *B. linearis* somewhat smaller); *Cassinia* (numerous spp.; most notably arborescent are *C. longifolia* and *C. trinervia*, to 7 m); *Helichrysum* (spp. formerly known under the generic name *Ozothamnus*, now a section, are notably shrubby; at least 7 spp. reach 3 m); *Olearia* (many spp. prominently woody; most notable is *O. argophylla*, 5–15 m tall, but others would qualify as trees); *Senecio* (*S. centropappus* a tree 2–4 m tall, on Tasmania). Goodeniaceae: *Goodenia* (*G. ovata*, an understory shrub to 2 m). Lamiaceae: *Prostanthera* (*P. lasianthos* a small tree to 6 m, *P. melissifolia* to 4 m, *P. rotundifolia* to 5 m, others large- to medium-sized shrubs); *Westringia* (*W. angustifolia* a shrub to 3 m, other species smaller). Solanaceae: *Solanum* (many shrubby species; *S. laciniata*, to 3 m, may be tallest).

One could add many other species from these and other families, and the listing may be considered a token one. Lamiaceae have been neglected in listings of insular areas because of the frequency of shrubs on mainland areas in this family; *Prostanthera* is clearly exceptional within the family in size, however. The entire family Gyrostemonaceae might be cited as an example, for some species of this family are trees; ancestors of Gyrostemonaceae appear likely to have been herbaceous or nearly so. Goodeniaceae, a basically herbaceous family, and strongly represented in Western Australia, might be cited in greater numbers: *Scaevola spinescens* and other species of *Scaevola*, *Leschenaultia*, and *Verreauxia* might be listed (see Krause, 1912). Stylidiaceae form an interesting example; the only woody species of this family (and these are only slightly woody by virtue of anomalous secondary thickening) are *Stylidium laricifolium* (New South Wales, to 2 m), *S. glandulosum* (known with certainty only from the Recherche Archipelago off southwestern Australia) and *S. imbricatum* (Stirling Range, W.A.)—all relatively mesic or maritime localities (Erickson, 1958). One could add some exceptionally woody species of basically woody groups: for example, *Richea pandanifolia* from Tasmania forms trees 2–12 m tall, and other Epacridaceae from this region could be cited. In Loranthaceae, the tree-mistletoe *Nuytsia floribunda* of Western Australia, which has anomalous secondary thickening, clearly deserves mention.

SOUTH AMERICA AND AFRICA

Chapter 14 is devoted to the vegetation of equatorial uplands in South America and Africa, which form a special case. In chapter 14, attention is paid not only to the alpine belts, which contain the famous rosette trees *Espeletia* and *Senecio* sect. *Dendrosenecio*, but also the subadjacent vegetational belts which exhibit part of the same program of insular woodiness.

However, medium elevations south of the equator—particularly in Peru—constitute an area much like the true insular areas cited above. The uplift of the Andes is relatively recent, so that it represents a pioneer area. Certain herbaceous groups have been able to establish by virtue of good dispersibility and become woodier under the equable, cool conditions. These represent temperate groups; apparently, tropical groups, as in the equatorial alpine and subalpine situations, are not able to adapt so readily. The roster of herbaceous groups with woody representatives is strikingly like that for oceanic islands, and is presented here to demonstrate that secondary woodiness is a very real phenomenon on particular continental areas as well. The listing below has been compiled largely from MacBride's (1937 et seq.) "Flora of Peru."

Apiaceae: *Eremocharis* (*E. piscoensis* and *E. triradiata* to 2 m). Asteraceae: many genera and species, including *Flotovia*, *Gynoxys*, *Senecio*.

Begoniaceae: *Begonia* (*B. peruviana* to 2.5 m). Campanulaceae: *Burmeistera* (several spp. shrubs to 2 m); *Centropogon* (several spp. 2–3 m; *C. densiflorus* "arborescent, 4–8 m"); *Siphocampylus* (several spp. shrubs to 4 m). Caricaceae: *Carica* (several spp., some are sparsely branched, small trees); *Jacaratia* (*J. digitata*, "tall tree"). Convolvulaceae: *Ipomoea* (*I. calodendron* a tree 4–10 m); *Maripa* (several spp., "lianas when unsupported becoming trees"). Euphorbiaceae: *Acalypha* (*A. macrostachya* a tree to 12 m; *A. samydaefolia* to 10 m; several others small trees); *Euphorbia* (*E. tessmannii* a tree to 3 m). Flacourtiaceae (*s.l.*): *Cochlospermum* (*C. orinocense* "a large tree"). Gentianaceae: *Lisianthus* (*L. revolutus* a small tree to 5 m, *L. corymbosus* to 4 m, *L. ovalis* 2–3 m); *Macrocarpaea* (*M. pachystyla* "arborescent," *M. guttifera* a shrub 2–3 m). Hydrophyllaceae: *Wigandia* (*W. crispa* to 6 m; *W. urens* to 4 m). Lythraceae: *Cuphea* (many shrubby spp., such as *C. cordata*, "most frequent shrub of the E. Andes between 1800–2500 m"). Malvaceae: *Abutilon* (*A. arboreum* to 6 m). Plantaginaceae: *Plantago* (*P. sericea* a subshrub). Polemoniaceae: *Cantua* (at least 6 spp. to 3 m or more); *Huthia* (2 spp.; to 1 m). Solanaceae: *Cestrum* (many shrubby spp., notably *C. longiflorum*, "known to attain 8 m," and *C. laevifolium*, a "tree about 4.5 m"); *Cyphomandra* (*C. endopogon* a tree to 7 m; *C. pendula* to 5 m; others small trees); *Nicotiana* (*N. tomentosa* to 7 m, *N. setchellii* to 5 m, others small trees); *Solanum* (many arboreal and arborescent spp., such as *S. verbascifolium*, 10 m or taller). Valerianaceae: *Valeriana* (several shrubby spp). Violaceae: *Hybanthus* (*H. sprucei* a small shrub); *Viola* (several shrubby spp.).

A number of additional examples could be cited: perhaps some species of *Heliotropium* (Boraginaceae), *Croton* (Euphorbiaceae), *Salvia* (Lamiaceae), or the giant *Puya*, *P. raimondii* (Bromeliaceae).

To lesser degrees, other continental areas show insular woodiness and serve to remind us that secondary increase in xylem production occurs in particular situations. *Ipomoea arborea* of the Mexican highlands would certainly qualify, as would the woody Asteraceae of that region.

References

Alain, H. 1953–1962. *Flora de Cuba*, vols. 3–5. Vol. 3, 1953; vol. 4, 1957; Havana, Imp. P. Fernandez y Cia. Vol. 5, 1962, Rio Piedras, Universidad de Puerto Rico.

Allan, H. G. 1961. *Flora of New Zealand*, vol. I. Wellington, R. E. Owen, Government Printer.

Anderson, E. F. 1967. An account of my cactus-collecting trip to the Galápagos Islands. *Cactus Succulent Jour.* 39:186–99.

Baker, J. G. 1877. *Flora of Mauritius and the Seychelles*. London, L. Reeve & Co.

Balfour, I. B. 1888. Botany of Socotra. *Trans. Roy. Soc. Edinburgh* 31:1–446.

Barghoorn, E. S. 1941. The ontogenetic and phylogenetic specialization of rays in the xylem of dicotyledons. III. The elimination of rays. *Bull. Torrey Bot. Club* 68:317–25.

Blumenstock, D. I. 1961. *Climates of the states. Hawaii.* U.S. Dept. of Commerce Weather Bureau. Washington, D.C., U.S. Government Printing Office. 20 p.

Brown, F. B. H. 1935. Flora of southeastern Polynesia. III. Dicotyledons. *Bishop Mus. Bull.* 130:1–386.

Carlquist, S. 1957. The genus *Fitchia* (Compositae). *Univ. Calif. Publ. Bot.* 29:1–144.

Carlquist, S. 1958. Wood anatomy of Heliantheae (Compositae). *Trop. Woods* 108:1–30.

Carlquist, S. 1961. *Comparative plant anatomy.* New York, Holt, Rinehart & Winston.

Carlquist, S. 1962a. A theory of paedomorphosis in dicotyledonous woods. *Phytomorphology* 12:30–45.

Carlquist, S. 1962b. Wood anatomy of Senecioneae (Compositae). *Aliso* 5:123–46.

Carlquist, S. 1965. *Island life.* New York, Natural History Press.

Carlquist, S. 1966. Wood anatomy of Compositae: a summary, with comments on factors controlling wood evolution. *Aliso* 6(2):25–44.

Carlquist, S. 1969a. Wood anatomy of Lobelioideae (Campanulaceae). *Biotropica* 1(2):47–72.

Carlquist, S. 1969b. Wood anatomy of Goodeniaceae and the problem of insular woodiness. *Ann. Missouri Bot. Gard.* 56:358–90.

Carlquist, S. 1970a. *Hawaii, a natural history.* New York, Natural History Press.

Carlquist, S. 1970b. Wood anatomy of *Echium* (Boraginaceae). *Aliso* 7(2):183–99.

Carlquist, S. 1970c. Wood anatomy of insular species of *Plantago* and the problem of raylessness. *Bull. Torrey Bot. Club* 97:353–61.

Carlquist, S. 1970d. Wood anatomy of Hawaiian, Macaronesian, and other species of *Euphorbia*. *Biol. Jour. Linnaean Soc.* 63 (suppl. 1):181–93.

Carlquist, S. 1971. Wood anatomy of Macaronesian and other Brassicaceae. *Aliso* 7(3):365–84.

Carlquist, S., and M. L. Grant. 1963. Studies in *Fitchia* (Compositae): novelties from the Society Islands; anatomical studies. *Pacific Sci.* 17:282–98.

Chevalier, A. 1935. Les îles du Cap Vert. Flore de l'archipel. *Rev. Bot. Appl.* 15:733–1090.

Choux, P. 1934. Les Didiéréacées, xérophytes de Madagascar. *Mém. Acad. Malgâche* 18:1–71.

Christophersen, E. 1938. Flowering plants of Samoa—II. *Bishop Mus. Bull.* 154:1–77.

Curtis, W. M. 1956, 1963, 1967. *The student's flora of Tasmania*, vols. 1–3. Hobart, Tasmania, Government Printer.

Dale, R. F. 1959. *Climates of the states: California*. U.S. Dept. of Commerce Weather Bureau. Washington, D.C., U.S. Government Printing Office. 37 p.

Darwin, C. 1859. *On the origin of species by means of natural selection*. Reprint of first edition, 1950. London, Watts & Co.

Dawson, E. Y. 1962. Cacti of the Galápagos Islands and of coastal Ecuador. *Cactus Succulent Jour.* 34:67–74, 99–105.

Degener, O. 1937. Euphorbiaceae. In O. Degener, *Flora Hawaiiensis* (parts published variously by the author).

Eliasson, U. 1968. Studies in Galápagos plants. VI. On the identity of *Calandrinia galapagosa* St. John. *Svensk Bot. Tidskr.* 62:365–68.

Erickson, R. 1958. *Triggerplants*. Perth, Paterson Brokensha.

Ewart, A. J. 1930. *Flora of Victoria*. Melbourne, Government Printer.

Guillaumin, A. 1948. *Flore analytique et synoptique de la Nouvelle-Calédonie: Phanérogames*. Paris, Office de la Recherche Scientifique Coloniale.

Harling, G. 1962. On some Compositae endemic to the Galápagos Islands. *Acta Horti Bergiani* 20(3):63–120.

Hedberg, O. 1957. Afroalpine vascular plants. A taxonomic revision. *Symb. Bot. Upsalienses* 15(1):1–411.

Hemsley, W. B. 1885. Report on present state of knowledge of various insular floras. *Rep. Sci. Results Voyage H.M.S. Challenger, Bot.* 1:1–75.

Hillebrand, W. 1888. *Flora of the Hawaiian Islands*. London, Williams & Norgate.

Holttum, R. E. 1964. The tree ferns of the genus *Cyathea* in Australasia and the Pacific. *Blumea* 12:241–74.

Howell, J. T. 1931. Cacti in the Galápagos Islands. *Cactus Succulent Jour.* 5:513.

Howell, J. T. 1941. The genus *Scalesia*. *Proc. Calif. Acad. Sci.*, 4th ser., 22(11):221–71.

Johnston, I. M. 1953. Studies in the Boraginaceae. XXV. A revaluation of some genera of the Lithospermeae. *Jour. Arnold Arboretum* 34:258–99.

Krause, K. 1912. Goodeniaceae. In *Das Pflanzenreich*, ed. A. Engler, 54:1–207. Berlin, Akademie Verlag.

Kribs, D. A. 1935. Salient lines of structural specialization in the wood rays of dicotyledons. *Bot. Gaz.* 96:547–57.

Leenhouts, P. W. 1964. A new montane *Scaevola* from Borneo: S. *verticillata* (Goodeniaceae). *Blumea* 12:317–18.

Lems, K. 1960. Floristic botany of the Canary Islands. *Sarracenia* 5:1–94.

Lems, K. 1961. Botanical notes on the Canary Islands. III. The life form spectrum and its interpretation. *Ecology* 42:569–72.

Lems, K., and C. M. Holzapfel. 1968. Evolution in the Canary Islands. I. Phylogenetic relations in the genus *Echium* (Boraginaceae) as shown by trichome development. *Bot. Gaz.* 129:95–107.

Little, E. L., Jr., and F. H. Wadsworth. 1964. *Common trees of Puerto Rico and the Virgin Islands*. U.S.D.A. Forest Service Agricultural Handbook no. 249. Washington, D.C.

Lowe, R. T. 1868. A *manual flora of Madeira*. London, John Van Voorst.

MacBride, J. F. (and collaborators). 1937 et seq. Flora of Peru. *Field Mus. Natur. Hist. Publ.*, bot. ser., vol. 13 (numerous parts, currently not complete).

Melliss, J. C. 1875. *St. Helena*. London, L. Reeve & Co.

Meusel, H. 1952. Über Wuchsformen, Verbreitung, und Phylogenie der einiger mediterran-mitteleuropaischen Angiospermen Gattungen. *Flora* 139:333–93.

Moore, J. W. 1933. New and critical plants from Raiatea. *Bishop Mus. Bull.* 102:1–53.

Palhinha, R. T. 1966. *Catálogo dos plantas vasculares dos Açores*. Lisbon, Sociedade de Estudos Açorianos, Alfonso Chaves.

Perrier de la Bâthie, H. 1950a. Turneraceae. In *Flore de Madagascar et des Comores*, ed. H. Humbert. Paris, Musée National d'Histoire Naturelle.

Perrier de la Bâthie, H. 1950b. Hypéricacées, Guttifères. In *Flore de Madagascar et des Comores*, ed. H. Humbert. Paris, Musée National d'Histoire Naturelle.

Perrier de la Bâthie, H. 1960. Composées, vol. I. In *Flore de Madagascar et des Comores*, ed. H. Humbert. Paris, Musée National d'Histoire Naturelle.

Perrier de la Bâthie, H. 1962. Composées, vol. II. In *Flore de Madagascar et des Comores*, ed. H. Humbert. Paris, Musée National d'Histoire Naturelle.

Perrier de la Bâthie, H. 1963. Composées, vol. III. In *Flore de Madagascar et des Comores*, ed. H. Humbert. Paris, Musée National d'Histoire Naturelle.

Rauh, W. 1963. Didiéréacées. In *Flore de Madagascar et des Comores*, ed. H. Humbert. Paris, Musée National d'Histoire Naturelle.

Raunkiaer, C. 1934. *The life forms of plants and statistical plant geography*. Oxford, Clarendon Press.

Ray, P. M., and W. E. Alexander. 1966. Photoperiodic adaptation to latitude in *Xanthium strumarium*. *Amer. Jour. Bot.* 53:806–16.

Rikli, M. 1912. *Lebensbedingungen und Vegetationsverhältnisse der Mittelmeerlände und der Atlantischen Inseln*. Jena, Verlag Kramer.

Rock, J. F. 1913. *The indigenous trees of the Hawaiian Islands*. Honolulu, privately published.

Rock, J. F. 1919. A monographic study of the Hawaiian species of the tribe Lobelioideae, family Campanulaceae. *Mem. Bishop Mus.* 7(2):1–394.

Schenck, H. 1907. Beitrage zur Kenntniss der Vegetation der Kanarischen Inseln. *Wiss. Ergebn. Deutsch. Tiefsee-Exped. Dampfer "Valdivia" 1898–1899* 2(1:2): 225–406.

Sherff, E. E. 1935. Revision of *Tetramolopium, Lipochaeta, Dubautia* and *Railliardia*. *Bishop Mus. Bull.* 135:1–136.

Sherff, E. E. 1937a. The genus *Bidens*. Part I. *Field Mus. Natur. Hist. Publ.*, bot. ser., 16:1–346.

Sherff, E. E. 1937b. Some Compositae of southeastern Polynesia (*Bidens, Coreopsis, Cosmos*, and *Oparanthus*). *Occas. Papers Bishop Mus.* 12(19):1–19.

Skottsberg, C. 1922. The phanerogams of the Juan Fernandez Islands. *Natur. Hist. Juan Fernandez Easter I.* 2:95–240.

Skottsberg, C. 1937. Die Flora der Desventuradas-Inseln. *Acta Horti Gotoburg.* 5(6):1–88.

Skottsberg, C. 1953. The vegetation of the Juan Fernandez Islands. *Natur. Hist. Juan Fernandez Easter I.* 2:793–960.

Skottsberg, C. 1956. Derivation of the flora and fauna of Juan Fernandez and Easter I. *Natur. Hist. Juan Fernandez Easter I.* 1:193–438.

Stewart, A. 1911. A botanical survey of the Galápagos Islands. *Proc. Calif. Acad. Sci.,* 4th ser., 1:7–288.

Thorne, R. F. 1969. The California Islands. *Ann. Missouri Bot. Gard.* 56:391–408.

Wallace, A. R. 1878. *Tropical nature and other essays.* London, MacMillan & Co.

Walter, H., H. Lieth, and H. Rehder. 1967. *Klimadiagramm-Weltatlas.* Jena, Verlag Fischer.

Werner, K. 1966. Die Wuchsformen der Gattungen *Isoplexis* (Lindl.) Benth. und *Digitalis* L. *Bot. Jahrb.* 85(1):88–149.

Wimmer, F. E. 1953. Campanulaceae-Lobelioideae. Teil II. *Das Pflanzenreich* IV, 276b (107 Heft). Berlin, Akademie Verlag.

Wimmer, F. E. 1956. Campanulaceae-Lobelioideae. Teil I. *Das Pflanzenreich* IV, 276b (106 Heft). Berlin, Akademie Verlag.

Zimmerman, E. C. 1948. *Insects of Hawaii,* vol. 1: *Introduction.* Honolulu, University of Hawaii Press.

CHAPTER ELEVEN

LOSS OF DISPERSIBILITY
IN ISLAND PLANTS

While working with evolutionary phenomena in the Hawaiian Islands and other Polynesian islands, I observed types of fruits and seeds that seemed incongruously poor at dispersal. The floras of these islands must have arrived by long-distance dispersal, yet during evolution on the island areas various groups of plants have lost dispersibility. My recognition of this fact stemmed not merely from observation of unexpected fruit and seed types and comparison of these with source-area relatives, but from cognizance of flightless insects and birds on islands. Although I did not deliberately attempt to find a counterpart in plants, my observations soon indicated that a parallel phenomenon did exist, and for much the same reasons.

At the outset, I wish to stress that loss of dispersibility is by no means limited to islands. More striking examples may, in fact, occur in certain mainland situations. If one takes the broadest possible view, large-seeded forest trees such as mangos (*Mangifera indica*), avocados (*Persea americana*), and a host of others are adaptations in which the large size of seeds represents a definite loss of dispersibility. Although botanists are familiar enough with the fact that in any given family a variety of dispersal types may exist, they sometimes do not express clearly that not only dispersal mechanisms but dispersal capability shows evolutionary change. Some

NOTE: This chapter is a revised version of two papers (Carlquist, 1966a, 1966b). For permission to present portions of these papers, acknowledgment is extended to *Evolution* and *Brittonia*. Preliminary description of these concepts may also be found in my book *Island life* (1965).

changes in dispersibility yield marked improvement in capability for crossing long distances of land, water, or both. Some show retrograde tendencies.

There is no reason to believe that only a single tendency occurs within a given group. In a particular genus, therefore, we may have difficulty in saying whether ease of dispersibility is primitive or specialized, and whether both trends may prevail. For example, Sauer (1964) includes data on permeability and buoyancy of seeds in his monograph of *Canavalia* (Fabaceae). The vast majority of species have seeds that are nonbuoyant and permeable by water. Are they all examples of loss of dispersibility? Probably not. One can envision that *Canavalia* might have evolved littoral species that, as part of their adaptation to growth near shores, developed increasingly buoyant and impermeable seeds. One or more such maritime species may have reached other beaches in the world, and lost capability for seawater dispersal after establishment.

The endemic Hawaiian species of *Canavalia* (sufficiently distinctive to constitute a subgenus, *Maunaloa*) offer no problem, however, in interpretation. All five of these species have large, nonbuoyant, permeable seeds (Sauer, 1964). Because 12 species of *Canavalia* have seeds that are buoyant and/or impermeable, arrival of *Canavalia* on the Hawaiian Islands by oceanic drift seems likely. One suspects, however, that the stock of *Canavalia* that gave rise to the endemic species did not arrive repeatedly by drift, but only on a single occasion, or at most a limited number of times. If this were true, the *Canavalia* stock could undergo evolutionary shift into inland sites and concomitantly lose buoyancy and permeability. If continually reintroduced, a maritime *Canavalia* would probably swamp out ecological shift and prevent the accompanying loss of dispersibility via oceanic drift. Thus, isolation is required for loss of dispersibility—not merely in *Canavalia*, but in all other instances cited as examples below.

Ecological shift does seem inextricably related to loss of dispersibility. For this reason, and because my field experience has been more extensive in the Hawaiian Islands than elsewhere, chiefly Hawaiian examples are cited below. The Hawaiian flora appears to have been derived primarily from moderately dry regions, and the wet Hawaiian forest seems composed chiefly (but certainly with exceptions) of plants that have evolutionarily adapted to more mesic habitats. This ecological shift, so pervasive in instances of loss of dispersibility on islands, is possible in a region with such abundant areas of rain forest (and relatively great duration of time—5 million years, perhaps more) as the Hawaiian Islands offer. If ecological shift is a prime accompaniment to loss of dispersibility, one can then understand why one would see this phenomenon on the Hawaiian and other Pacific islands, but not to any appreciable degree on the Galápagos or the Canary Islands (or other Macaronesian islands). These latter archipelagos have no true rain forest—only, at best, a cloud forest. Also, equatorial alpine plants would not be expected to show loss of dispersibility. These are plants of temperate (usually temperate alpine) climates, and their occurrence in an equatorial region represents a minimal change: adaptation to a climate that is still temperate alpine, but with a prolonged growing season (the entire year, provided a species has resistance to the nightly frost at higher altitudes on equatorial peaks).

I must emphasize that the observations offered here are limited in nature, and the student of island biology can uncover many interesting facts I have not investigated. For example, shortened viability is almost certainly involved in loss of dispersibility, and tests of viability of species of wet Hawaiian forest in comparison to their non-Hawaiian relatives would probably enlarge appreciably the number of examples cited here. In the case of species hypothesized as having been introduced to islands by oceanic drift, I tested only buoyancy. Whether these species also show loss of resistance to seawater (permeability) has not yet been determined except in a few obvious cases, such as the Seychellean "double coconut," *Lodoicea*, known from beaches all over the world yet never found in a viable condition. Another possible means of loss of dispersibility concerns the nature of seeds or the endocarp of fruits in bird-dispersed species. Typically, for successful transport by birds one would expect that the seed coat or fruit endocarp would be altered little, or only to the point of permitting more reliable germination by action of their digestive tract. In loss of dispersibility, possibly the seeds may be more vulnerable to destruction by action of the digestive tract of birds. Other factors not investigated here that would be criteria of loss of dispersibility would include loss of resistance to extremes of cold, heat, and desiccation. Fertility of a plant may be expected to alter under insular conditions. I suspect that in some insular species the fertility is lowered to whatever point maintains the species in the area of ecological conditions suitable to its adaptation. Because of the numerous variables, fertility is difficult to measure, but suitable measures probably would show a lessening in some insular groups. The results of Sohmer (1972) in *Charpentiera* on the Hawaiian Islands point clearly to lowered fertility. Also, if a species has fewer, larger fruits than its ancestors, and if seed number is proportionately lowered per plant, this could be said to constitute loss of dispersibility. The trend to fewer seeds per plant can be seen in Hawaiian species of *Zanthoxylum* (= *Fagara*), *Plantago* (*P. princeps*), *Breweria*, and *Stenogyne*.

One need not hypothesize complete loss of dispersibility, however, and perhaps I should have termed this phenomenon "lessened dispersibility" rather than "loss." Obviously, some species that have lost dispersibility on islands still can disperse within an island and within an archipelago. An example is *Bidens sandvicensis* (Asteraceae), which certainly shows diminished dispersibility (fig. 11.3), but which occurs nonetheless on most major islands in the chain—Kauai, Oahu, Maui, and Hawaii.

Hypotheses for Loss of Dispersibility

The operative factors that result in loss of dispersibility are several and may differ in various cases. They cannot, therefore, be rated as to which is more, which is less important in the instances as a whole. One factor of probable importance may be described as precinctiveness, a tendency noted by Beccari and Rock (1921) in the palm genus *Pritchardia*. Briefly defined, precinctiveness denotes reproduction in such a fashion that most propagules are shed within a limited zone of stable conditions, such as wet forest, to which a species has a definitive and narrow degree of adaptation. Potentially, this permits survival of more numerous propagules than would random, widespread dissemination into a variety of habitats. One can assume that species adjust their reproductive abundance to a rate suitable for occupation of favorable sites. In strand plants and weedy species, reproductive rates may be high because longevity of individuals may be shorter, and because favorable sites are widely scattered and change rapidly. In species of stable forest, a lower reproductive rate would be expected to suffice.

An extreme function of precinctiveness would be the tendency for lowered dispersibility to prevent the majority of propagules from being blown away from an island. Excessive loss of propagules seems unlikely in Hawaiian flowering plants, where most species with lowered dispersal ability occupy not windy sites, but relatively protected places in forests. Likewise, wind pressure seems insufficient to explain development of flightlessness in Hawaiian insects (Perkins, 1913). Wind pressure is, however, a very real factor for plants with minute propagules, such as ferns.

A second probable factor in loss of dispersibility is the tendency for immigrants to oceanic islands to be originally weedy plants, capable of establishing in pioneering conditions, and for these immigrants then to evolve characteristics of stable forest species. A continental type of forest can be characterized as having relatively poor dispersal ability in its species because forest trees tend to have large seeds (the abundant storage tissue suited to growth of seedlings in shady forest floors), shorter seed viability, and a high degree of ecological specialization. Plants of pioneer habitats, on the contrary, are suited to long-distance dispersal, corresponding with the scattered nature of disturbed or new habitats, and they typically live in sunny areas, have less seed storage and smaller fruits and seeds (smallness contributes to their dispersibility), and are mostly herbaceous, relatively short lived, and establish easily because of plasticity of ecological requirements. Shift from the pioneering-plant syndrome to the forest syndrome is a prime source of ecological change on islands. The evolution of Asteraceae from herbaceous, weedy types to shrubs and trees of forest regions is a prime example (chapter 10). This ecological shift is possible under insular conditions because wet forest is a relatively uncontested zone, a fact related to the few wet-forest-species propagules successfully established on islands after long-distance dispersal. Increase in fruit and seed size is an adjustment to this change in ecological preferences, and loss of dispersibility is a by-product. Ecological shift is invoked in explaining loss of dispersibility of insular insects by Darlington (1943) and Wilson (1959).

A third possible factor can be described as failure of a plant to maintain the link with the dispersal mechanism that brought an ancestral stock to an oceanic island. An outstanding example of this tendency is evident in *Bidens* (Asteraceae). The Pacific island species of *Bidens* (figs. 11.2, 11.3) that have the best dispersal mechanisms, and appear most similar to ancestors, live on cliffs where seabirds typically nest or once nested. This suggests that attachment of fruits to bird feathers was the vector for immigration of *Bidens,* and that ancestral species occupied areas near nests of seabirds. As a population of *Bidens* evolved into upland forest sites, where marine birds are absent, the contact with the dispersal vector would be lost, and either the old mechanism would be lost, a new one developed, or both would occur. Evolution into inland sites by plant groups brought to islands by oceanic drift would also involve loss of contact with a dispersal vector, as mentioned above for *Canavalia.* Thus, floatability has either a neutral or negative value in an inland site. The value of floatability could be said to be negative if this tended to reinforce the littoral preference and thus restrict a species permanently to a narrow coastal zone and deprive it of occupying broad zones of inland forest. Loss of contact with a dispersal vector is a by-product of evolutionary opportunity and ecological shift, which in turn are produced by the disharmonic nature of oceanic island floras.

The number of species occupying a given acre of forest on an oceanic island is likely to be limited for reasons of disharmony. In an island forest, such as those of the Hawaiian Islands, a relatively poor rate of reproduction and dispersal will suffice to maintain a species. In a comparable continental forest area, the number of species is much higher, the probable attrition of propagules of each species high, so despite adaptation to the forest habitat, a continental species might be expected to maintain a higher rate of reproduction and dispersal. This would explain why a number of genera represented both in the relatively unspecialized forests of continents (or continental islands) and also in forests on oceanic islands would tend to reach maximum fruit size in the island locality (e.g., *Alectryon, Fagara,* and *Tetraplasandra* in the Hawaiian Islands). It would also tend to explain why little gigantism or loss of dispersibility can be observed west of the andesite line in the Pacific, in floras such as that of Fiji, where many of the same genera present in the Hawaiian flora occur.

Other factors may involve pleiotropic genes. Assuming that there is a selective value for gigantism in flowers, as in the gigantic heads in *Argyroxiphium* (Asteraceae), enlargement of flower size may result in changes in proportions of the flower, and the dispersal mechanism (pappus in *Argyroxiphium*) might deteriorate accordingly. Or one can imagine that if a dispersal mechanism is discontinued (by loss of link with a vector, for example), and the associated structure has a neutral value, its loss may be an inevitable result of economy in the energy budget of a plant. One may hypothesize that continued selective pressure is required to maintain a particular dispersal mechanism, and once this pressure is reduced by altered dispersal modes, change or deterioration of structure or construction is inevitable. The grotesque fruits of *Dendroseris litoralis* (fig. 11.8G), *D. pinnata* (fig. 11.8F) and *Yunquea tenzii* (fig. 11.7C) probably represent forms "tolerated" by lack of selective pressure for typical fruit forms in Asteraceae. Odd-shaped seeds occur in Hawaiian species of *Dianella*, *Haplostachys* (fig. 11.11), *Stenogyne*, *Pittosporum* (fig. 11.12) and *Alsinodendron* (fig. 11.9). Improvement in dispersibility of island plants is also conceivable, and may have occurred in *Lecocarpus* (fig. 11.5E) and *Trematolobelia* (Carlquist, 1962). In any case, I would expect alteration to a new dispersal mechanism to occur rapidly once any of the various factors suggested has become operative.

Methods and Problems of Comparisons

In order to assess loss of dispersibility, one must be able to compare insular species with their closest continental relatives. In the case of the Hawaiian flora, the comments of Hillebrand (1888) on what the relationships of endemic Hawaiian genera might be, proved helpful. For other floras, affinities were determined on the basis of the closest morphological and phytogeographic affinities I could determine. Dispersal mechanisms seem clear for some species, but several possibilities must be conceded for others. Despite the wealth of information offered by Guppy (1906), Ridley (1930), and others, mechanisms of dispersal in most plants are suppositions based upon the morphology of fruits and seeds compared to those of species for which good observational data are available.

Phenomena of lessened dispersibility may not be subject to experimental proof in the ordinary sense, but the array of data given here does provide "controls." If a number of different taxonomic groups on a single archipelago, such as the Hawaiian Islands, show parallels, one can say that controls or replications in the experimental sense exist. Likewise, different island groups on which a particular group (e.g., *Bidens*) is represented and shows, on each, similar tendencies, serve as controls or independent "proofs."

Adaptations for dispersal in particular plant groups have been outlined earlier, as for the Hawaiian flora in chapter 2. One can hypothesize that the maximum size of fleshy fruits dispersed by frugivorous birds to the Hawaiian and other oceanic islands is about 1 cm, and that if the fruit is drupoid the contained seed is 8 mm long or less. Some groups have shiny black seeds not accompanied by fleshy pulp (seeds of Rutaceae, for example); these seeds are nevertheless attractive to seed-eating birds. Gigantism in fruits and seeds of bird-dispersed plants would be considered a loss of dispersibility.

Oceanic drift only accounts for a small proportion of the floras of most high islands, but it accounts for a higher proportion of the Hawaiian flora (fig. 2.7). Guppy emphasizes a "Fijian difficulty," whereby coastal strand plants fail to evolve into forest sites and forest plants do not evolve into coastal sites. For this reason, Guppy seems reluctant to acknowledge the existence of ecological shift from strand to forest in the Hawaiian flora. One should note that Fiji, although insular, retains an essentially continental (harmonic) flora, whereas the Hawaiian flora is strongly disharmonic. In Hawaii, immigrant groups were offered more numerous ecological opportunities that would have been preempted on Fiji by the many and varied genera native there. Hawaiian groups (other than those which are now exclusively strand plants) that may be suspected of having immigrated via seawater include all the native Fabaceae and Malvaceae, at least some Apocynaceae, and the native species of *Colubrina, Dodonaea, Gouania, Haplostachys, Myoporum,* and *Peucedanum* (see chapter 2). For these, absence of both buoyancy and impermeability by seawater constitutes an easily measurable loss of dispersibility.

For spores or seeds suspected of being dispersed by wind or in mud on feet of birds, evolutionary increase in size would curtail dispersibility. Adherent fruits are less likely to be dispersed if barbs or hooks are lost, sticky seed coatings disappear, or gigantism in fruits or seeds renders adherence mechanisms less effective than they would be for small seeds or fruits. A feature worthy of note for types of transport other than oceanic drift is that only a slight decrease in transportability would markedly increase the precinctiveness of a species. This is particularly true of wind-dispersed seeds or spores.

The instances selected for presentation represent, in my opinion, easily interpreted cases. More detailed statistical treatment of other groups might reveal additional valid examples. Data and observations were derived from material collected in the field and from specimens studied in the herbarium. Living materials were utilized wherever possible. Experiments to determine floatability of seeds and fruits were undertaken, following the methods of Guppy (1906). Such tests were considered valid only if seeds contained normal embryos, and if seeds or fruits either sank readily or floated for prolonged periods. In the illustrations, scales of magnification are consistent within families, although different from one family to another. Sources of non-Hawaiian species are indicated in parentheses. All species for which no source is cited in the drawings are endemic to the Hawaiian Islands.

Ferns

Warren H. Wagner, Jr., kindly contributed data on spore size, ecology, and nomenclature of Hawaiian ferns. A selection from these data is given in table 11.1. Data on spore size in non-Hawaiian Schizaeas is from Brown and Brown (1931) and from Selling (1944, 1946). Data on the fossil Schizaeas (*S. skottsbergii* and var. *mauiensis*) are from Selling (1946). Selling's measurements apparently are uniformly too large by about 10 percent and have been corrected in accordance with Wagner's guidance (personal communication, 1965). Spore sizes represent an average of the greatest dimension of spores from one or more collections. Exotic ferns have been added to the table where, in a given family, there are no Hawaiian representatives in low forest, and a general picture of typical spore sizes in a family is necessary for comparison with species of wet Hawaiian forest.

The examples given in table 11.1 indicate a clear correlation between ecology and spore size. Because average size in most fern spores centers around 30 μ, the dimensions of the spores in the wet-forest species are truly exceptional. This may be regarded as a specialization with reference to wet forest except in *Athyrium*, where the small-spored *A. molokaiense*

437

TABLE 11.1.

Comparison of spore size with ecology for Hawaiian native ferns,
with spore sizes given for selected non-Hawaiian species
for purposes of comparison

Family	*Species of low forest, or widespread species*
Schizaeaceae	*Schizaea dichotoma* (Old World Tropics), 60 μ
	Schizaea digitata (Old World Tropics), 42 μ
Gleicheniaceae	*Dicranopteris emarginata*, 32.4 μ
	Dicranopteris linearis, 28.7 μ
	Hicriopteris pinnata, 26.3 μ
Hymenophyllaceae	*Vandenboschia cyrtotheca*, 38.4 μ
	Vandenboschia davallioides, 41.4 μ
Adiantaceae	*Microlepia speluncae*, 26.1 μ
	Pellaea ternifolia, 41.1 μ
	Pityrogramma calomelanos (New World Tropics), 40.3 μ
	Pteris excelsa, 42.9 μ
	Pteris vittata, 34.8 μ
Blechnaceae	*Blechnum occidentale*, 42.2 μ
	Doodia kunthiana, 39.2 μ
	Doodia lyonii, 40.9 μ
Aspidiaceae	*Athyrium molokaiense*, 36.4 μ
	Rumohra adiantiforme (New Zealand), 32.2 μ
	Rumohra aristata (Michigan), 33.4 μ
	Rumohra hispida (New Zealand), 37.0 μ

may represent the reverse adaptation to dry lowland conditions. Hawaiian species of *Cibotium* (Cyatheaceae) are not included in the table. These species do have notably large spores (*C. chamissoi*, 54.6 μ; *C. glaucum*, 49.3 μ; *C. st.-johnii*, 46.5 μ; *C. splendens*, 52.2 μ). This large spore size characterizes not merely Hawaiian Cibotiums, however, but all Cibotiums. The genus is adapted to wet forest almost uniformly, and thus both Hawaiian and non-Hawaiian Cibotiums may be said to show correlation between wet-forest habitat and large spore size.

The explanation for the good correlation shown in table 11.1 seems

Species of intermediate forest	Species of high, wet forest
	Schizaea skottsbergii, 100 μ
	S. s. var. *mauiensis*, 90 μ
	Sticherus owyhensis, 36.9 μ
Vandenboschia draytoniana, 48.6 μ	*Callistopteris baldwinii*, 54.8 μ
Goniocormus minutus, 53.4 μ	*Mecodium recurvum*, 57.5 μ
	Sphaerocionium lanceolatum, 54.8 μ
	Pteris lidgatii, 74.1 μ
Sadleria cyatheoides, 49.6 μ	*Sadleria squarrosa*, 62.0 μ
Sadleria pallida, 48.9 μ	*Sadleria unisora*, 56.3 μ
Sadleria souleyetiana, 46.9 μ	
Athyrium kaalanum, 39.8 μ	
Athyrium marginale, 41.0 μ	
Athyrium meyenianum, 42.6 μ	
Athyrium microphyllum, 36.4 μ	
Athyrium sandwichianum, 40.3 μ	
	Rumohra curvifolia, 58.8 μ

Source: Carlquist, 1966b.

chiefly one of precinctiveness: the large spores of wet-forest species will fall nearer the parent plant and will be more likely to survive, for this specialized habitat is quite limited in geographical extent. Although the ferns listed represent a selection from the Hawaiian fern flora, no cases which definitely run counter to the trend of increasing spore size in wetter areas can be said to exist. There are large groups of native Hawaiian ferns which show in spore size neither a positive nor a negative correlation with forest ecology. These—mostly Aspleniaceae, Polypodiaceae, and Grammitidaceae—have spores that range mostly between 30 and 45 μ. Significantly, these ferns are almost all epiphytes, whereas the ferns listed in table 11.1 are terrestrial. The epiphytic habit represents occupancy of an "open habitat," one which is widely scattered. Small- or medium-sized spores seem better adapted by virtue of their vagility to reach the many, widely dispersed sites suitable for growth of epiphytes. Trees bearing epiphytes are limited in life-span, suggesting another reason for vagility of spores of epiphytic ferns.

Polyploidy and apogamy do influence spore size, of course. However, none of the ferns listed in table 11.1 is known to be apogamous, nor do chromosome numbers form a good correlation with the spore-size trends (Wagner, personal communication, 1965). Indeed, according to Wagner, the endemic Hawaiian ferns, among which the high-forest species may be cited, tend to be diploid, whereas wider-ranging native species in the Hawaiian fern flora contain the bulk of the species in which Wagner has now established the existence of polyploidy. The explanation for larger spore sizes in the Hawaiian fern flora seems clearly related to ecology.

Another noteworthy feature that Wagner has established for Hawaiian ferns is the exceptional degree to which they possess paraphyses in sori. Although the functions of paraphyses and the reasons for abundance of these structures in Hawaiian ferns cannot be elucidated at present, paraphyses might have the effect of hindering free discharge of spores, and might thereby increase precinctiveness of ferns which possess them.

The large size of *Sadleria* spores is related to the fact that only 16 are borne per sporangium (Robert Lloyd, personal communication, 1967); the genus does reproduce sexually, however. Precinctiveness in some ferns on islands as well as on mainland areas may be aided by the fact that chlorophyllous spores (such spores average only 48 days' viability, according to Lloyd) may be a form of lessened dispersibility. Nonchlorophyllous spores average 2.8 yr. in viability, according to Lloyd. Among the fern families in the Hawaiian flora with chlorophyllous spores, one can cite Hymenophyllaceae. For some hymenophylls, spores even germinate within a sporangium (Lloyd and Klekowski, 1970). Lloyd and Klekowski believe that for some groups of ferns at large, the green-spored condition may be primitive (Osmundaceae), but in others, relaxation of selective pressure for longevity (chiefly in wet-forest areas) has resulted in the attainment of chlorophyllous spores.

Gymnosperms

Because few gymnosperms are present on oceanic islands, this group could be expected to provide few examples of lessened dispersibility. However, one notes that *Podocarpus ferrugineus* on New Zealand and *P. minor* (= *P. palustris*) on New Caledonia have exceptionally large seeds. These examples may constitute instances of autochthonous evolution of seed gigantism on these islands.

Dicotyledons

Apiaceae. Dispersal mechanisms of most umbellifers appear obscure. Whereas the hooked fruits of *Sanicula* or the barbed fruits of *Drusa* or *Bowlesia* are obvious enough, the dry, corky mericarps of most Apiaceae, often without wings, do not appear readily dispersible at first glance. However, birds may consume these fruits. That some Apiaceae without "obvious" dispersal mechanisms have wide ranges, including many of the world's oceanic islands, speaks for itself. However, some insular Apiaceae may have an autochthonously lessened degree of dispersibility. Perhaps *Myodocarpus* on New Caledonia and *Peucedanum* on the Hawaiian Islands fall into this category.

Apocynaceae. Among Hawaiian Apocynaceae, only the endemic genus *Pteralyxia* suggests a fruit size possibly greater than that of ancestral types. Unfortunately, the relationships of *Pteralyxia* have not yet been clearly established. Hillebrand (1888) claimed affinity with the American genus *Vallesia*, whereas Schumann (1895) emphasized resemblances to the wide-ranging Pacific genus *Alyxia*. The single-seeded drupes of *Alyxia* do show a close resemblance to those of *Pteralyxia* in features such as the large locule, filled with ruminate endosperm. Fruits of *Alyxia* do not float and, because of fleshy exocarp and small size, are probably dispersed by frugivorous birds. Fruits of *Pteralyxia*, on the other hand, are fusiform and much larger—ranging from about $5 \times 2 \times 2$ cm in *P. kauaiensis* to about $6 \times 4 \times 3$ cm in *P. macrocarpa*. This large size would seem clearly to preclude bird dispersal, despite the fleshy exocarp. If *Pteralyxia* is, in fact,

441

related to *Alyxia*, this would constitute a remarkable case of loss of dispersal mechanism. However, dried fruits of *Pteralyxia* are capable of floating indefinitely, either with or without the fleshy exocarp. This feature is found in such Apocynaceae as *Ochrosia oppositifolia* (= *O. parviflora*), a widespread species of the Pacific which is, very likely, seawater dispersed. *Ochrosia sandwicensis*, a Hawaiian endemic, probably stems from seawater-dispersed ancestors like *O. parviflora*, a possibility conceded by Guppy (1906). If *Pteralyxia* is, indeed, related to seawater-dispersed ancestors like *Ochrosia*, there may be relatively little loss of dispersibility, although seeds of *Pteralyxia* might be rendered inviable by soaking in seawater. Indeed, the woody endocarp is relatively thin and fragile, especially at the peduncle end. The large size of fruits of *P. macrocarpa* suggests difficulty of transport on land, in any case. *Pteralyxia* remains an enigmatic genus with regard to ancestral dispersal type, and information about its relationships is very much needed.

Araliaceae. Among Hawaiian Araliaceae an almost classical case of loss of dispersibility is furnished by the genus *Tetraplasandra*. The remainder of Hawaiian araliads have dupes of relatively small size, suggesting ease in dispersal by frugivorous birds. Within the Hawaiian species of *Tetraplasandra*, however, a trend toward marked gigantism of fruits and seeds is evident (fig. 11.1). Of the species recognized by Rock (1913) or Sherff (1955), most have fruits which range from 7 to 10 mm in length, averaging 8 mm, and generally fusiform. Typical of these is *T. oahuensis*

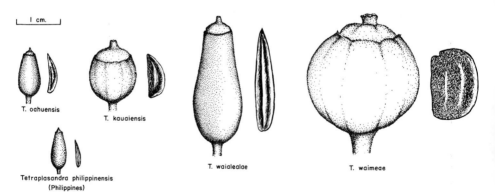

FIG. 11.1. Comparison of fruits and seeds of *Tetraplasandra* (Araliaceae). All species except *T. philippinensis* are endemic to the Hawaiian Is.

(fig. 11.1). This fruit size seems clearly ancestral among Hawaiian species, for it is shared by the non-Hawaiian species of *Tetraplasandra*: *T. philip-pinensis* (Palawan, Philippine Is. [fig. 11.1]), *T. paucidens* (New Guinea), and *T. koerdersii* (Celebes). Hawaiian species with slightly larger fruit include *T. hawaiiensis* (10 mm in diameter), *T. waianensis* (10–12 mm long, 3–4 mm thick), *T. meiandra* (13–14 mm long, 5–6 mm thick), and *T. kauaiensis* (ca. 14 mm in diameter [fig. 11.1]). More marked gigantism is shown by two Kauai species: *T. waialealae* and *T. waimeae* (fig. 11.1). Drupes of *T. waialealae* are fusiform, 25–32 mm long, whereas those of *T. waimeae* are spheroidal, ca. 30 mm in diameter. Pyrenes (seeds) in these species are in proportion to size of fruits, as shown in figure 11.1. There seems to have been a trend toward gigantism in Tetraplasandras with relation to upper wet rain forest. The two species with the largest fruits are native to wet forest on the oldest major island, Kauai.

Asteraceae. Of all families, the composites show tendencies in loss of dispersibility most clearly, and so they bulk largest in this account. My field work in Polynesia was useful in demonstrating relationships. Additional ecological data of a simple sort were gleaned from labels of specimens and from the works of Brown (1935), Harling (1962), Papy (1954–1955), Sherff (1937b), Skottsberg (1953, 1954), Stewart (1911), and Zimmerman (1948). Nomenclature for Pacific Asteraceae is according to the following authors: for *Bidens*, Sherff (1937b); for *Oparanthus*, Sherff (1937a); for *Fitchia*, Carlquist (1957) and Carlquist and Grant (1963); for *Scalesia*, Howell (1941); for *Macraea*, Harling (1962); for *Lipochaeta*, Sherff (1935b); for *Argyroxiphium* and *Wilkesia*, Carlquist (1959); for Juan Fernandez Asteraceae, Skottsberg (1922, 1951, 1958), although the segregate genera of *Dendroseris* are not used here.

The genus *Bidens* (tribe Heliantheae, subtribe Coreopsidinae) is well represented by endemic species in the Pacific (figs. 11.2, 11.3). *Bidens pilosa*, a widespread tropical weed, has been introduced by man to many Pacific islands and is included here only as representative of a mainland species. The Pacific species of *Bidens* may be regarded as close to the *B. pilosa* complex, and this species (fig. 11.2, top left) probably represents a reasonable approximation of the stock or stocks of *Bidens* that established on Pacific islands aboriginally. For each of the insular species shown in figures 11.2 and 11.3, a typical achene is shown (or, for a few, variables

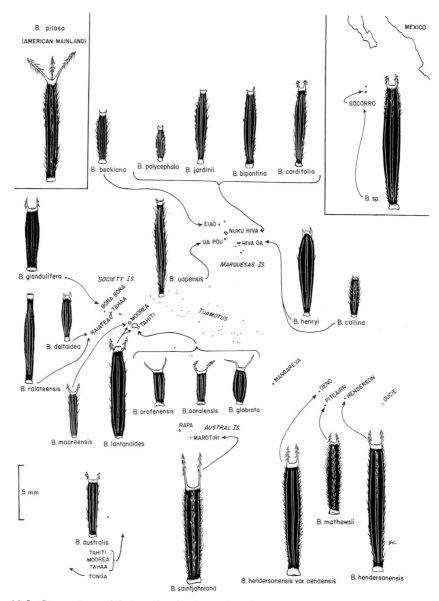

FIG. 11.2. Comparison of fruits of endemic species of *Bidens* (Asteraceae) from southeastern Polynesia, shown geographically. These species, together with those from the Hawaiian Is., represent the extent of this genus in the Pacific. Inset, top right, an unnamed species native to Socorro I., Revillagigedo Is., Mexico. Inset, top left, a typical achene of *B. pilosa*; this fruit probably approximates the achene type ancestral to the Pacific species of *Bidens*. Species omitted from this map include *B. ahnei*, which may be conspecific with *B. polycephala*, and *B. hivoana*, which is a synonym of *Oparanthus albus*.

in morphology are illustrated). Achene morphology does vary considerably within some species of *Bidens*.

The dispersal mechanism of *Bidens* is evidently quite efficient, for the genus has reached, by natural means, many of the smaller islands of Polynesia. However, the genus appears to have "bypassed" many seemingly suitable islands (Rapa, Mangareva, and the Austral Islands other than Marotiri); this suggests that chance has operated in dispersal of *Bidens*. On Tonga a single collection of *B. australis* has been made; although not unlikely, this record needs confirmation. If *B. australis* is present on Tonga, one would expect this or other *Bidens* species on Samoa and other islands.

None of the endemic Pacific species of *Bidens* seemingly has dispersal mechanisms quite as efficient as *B. pilosa*. Five features may be said to comprise the dispersal mechanism of *B. pilosa:* (1) awns long compared to the body of the achene; (2) awns spreading; (3) awns armed with stiff retrorse barbs (unicellular, thick-walled trichomes); (4) upward-pointing hairs on lateral margins of the achene; (5) upward-pointing hairs on the dorsiventral margins (flattened faces of the achene). The length of awns seems important because it controls the number of barbs and thus the likelihood of attachment to animal fur or bird feathers. Even without barbs, some degree of adhesion can be effected by long awns, especially if they are spreading. The presence of retrorse barbs on the awns in conjunction with upward-pointing hairs on the achene body seems important. Oriented counter to each other, these structures probably secure a firmer adhesion than either alone would achieve. Any depreciation in the five features listed may be said to constitute a lessening of dispersibility.

Among the South Pacific species of *Bidens*, only a few retain the specified features to a marked degree. Those best equipped seem to be the trio of species from the southeasternmost islands: *B. hendersonensis*, *B. mathewsii*, and *B. saintjohniana*. All three species have numerous hairs on the achene body (dorsiventral as well as lateral margins, except for some populations of *B. hendersonensis*). Similarly well equipped is the unnamed species from Socorro Island, Mexico (fig. 11.2, top right). Awns are short and not spreading in these species, however.

Second in potential dispersibility among South Pacific species are those with short, but still barbed, awns and with hairs on the achenes (lateral margins only): *B. australis*, *B. lantanoides*, *B. mooreensis*, and *B. cordifolia*. Efficiency of dispersal in these species is confirmed by the fact that two (*B. australis*, *B. lantanoides*) occur on more than one island, whereas all other South Pacific species are restricted to single islands.

A third category is represented by species with awns barbed but achene body glabrous: *B. glandulifera*, *B. aoraiensis*, and *B. glabrata* (*p.p.*). *Bidens orofenensis* and *B. glabrata* (*p.p.*) lack barbs on awns but have, like *B. aoraiensis*, markedly spreading awns.

Lack of awns (except as ineffective vestiges) is shown by the Marquesan species other than *B. cordifolia*. All the Marquesan *Bidens*, however, have hairy achenes (lateral margins only, except for *B. collina*). Similarities in achene morphology and other features suggest that the Marquesan species originated from a single introduction. The presence of achene hairs alone would probably suffice to secure transport via bird feathers throughout that archipelago.

The two species from Raiatea show the greatest loss of dispersibility among South Pacific *Bidens* species, for they lack any hairs or appendages (except for vestigial awns and a few hairs near the achene summit in *B. deltoidea*).

Within the Hawaiian species of *Bidens* (fig. 11.3), a wide gamut in achene morphology can be seen. For purposes of illustration, these have been grouped into categories based upon features of morphology related to potential dispersibility. The four species of A are equipped with all features. One (*B. hillebrandiana*) has spreading awns, another (*B. nematocera*) notably long awns. Diminution of awn length is shown by the species of B, whereas those of C have awns of varying length but lack achene-body hairs. Near-absence of awns and restriction of hairs to the base of the achene is shown in the species of D. A few hairs occur near the summit of the achene body in *B. cuneata* and *B. forbesii*. Lack of awn vestiges, combined with a hairy achene body, characterizes the species of E, which thus resemble the Marquesan species. In F are species that possess a glabrous achene body and only the most vestigial awns. Awn vestiges in *B. menziesii* and *B. mauiensis* are flat and toothlike, and are seemingly functionless. A few hairs crown the achenes of *B. cosmoides*, which are otherwise glabrous.

The species in the upper half of figure 11.3 have no peculiarities not

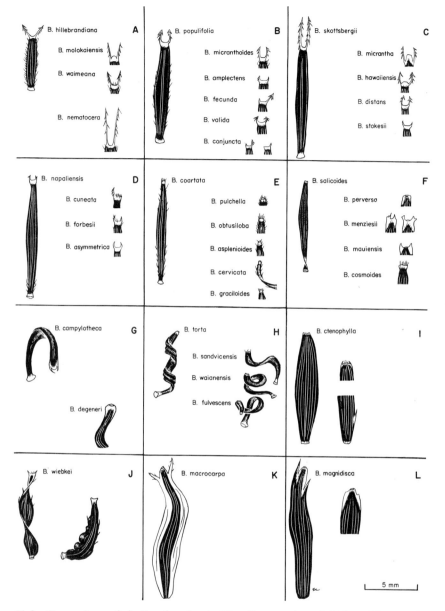

FIG. 11.3. Comparison of fruits of endemic Hawaiian species of *Bidens*. The species are arranged into groups according to achene morphology. The groupings shown are not intended to represent natural groups, although in some cases they apparently represent closely related species. In each grouping shown here, one achene is drawn in its entirety; achenes of the remainder within a grouping agree in details of achene body, but differ in details of awns, etc., at the achene apex. Achenes may differ in size within a grouping, however. Some species of *Bidens* are variable in achene morphology; a "typical" achene is shown for each. Scale (bottom right) applies to all figures.

447

also seen in the South Pacific species. In the lower half of figure 11.3, however, are features of achene morphology unique to the Hawaiian Islands. Achenes of *B. campylotheca* (G) are glabrous, have vestigial awns, and are bent into an arc. Achenes of *B. degeneri* have no awn vestiges (only callous margins at the achene summit) and may be straight or curved like those of *B. campylotheca*. More prominently curved are the species of H, which often exhibit achenes twisted into three or more helices. Although achenes in these species are narrow in diameter, the embryo is relatively large and occupies nearly the entire length of the achene. Because several species have curved or helical achenes, there may be a selective value for this form, but I am not willing to speculate as to the possible function of this shape. *Bidens campylotheca* and *B. sandvicensis* each occur on four of the major islands. Therefore this achene form can be effective over relatively short distances. Achenes of the species in H differ from each other only in minor respects.

The remaining Hawaiian species (I–L) have large, flat achenes that can sometimes be described as winged and that have awns vestigial, lacking, or highly modified. *Bidens ctenophylla* (I) has vestigial awns, if any, on broad black achenes that occasionally bear a tooth along the lateral margins. Achenes of *B. wiebkei* (J) are flat, have awns vestigial or lacking, and bear a few stiff hairs on lateral margins of achenes. These hairs have broad, multiseriate bases. Some achenes of *B. wiebkei* are distorted in shape and have wavy lateral margins. Achenes of *B. macrocarpa* (K) are the largest among Hawaiian species. They have broad yellowish wings and are glabrous. Flat awnlike appendages are modified in conjunction with the formation of wings, and are thus different from true awns. A few hairs are present on these appendages, but most hairs are not retrorse. Achenes of *B. magnidisca* (L) are like those of *B. ctenophylla* but have awns like those of *B. macrocarpa*, with yellowish winglike webbing between the awns and the body of the achene; or awns may be lacking, with narrow yellowish wings at the achene summit. The species of I through L may be flat enough to suggest transport by wind, but such transport would be effective over short distances at best.

Ecology correlates clearly with morphology of achenes for the insular *Bidens* species. Of the South Pacific species (fig. 11.2), those with the best dispersal mechanisms are all coastal species. *Bidens saintjohniana* occupies

Marotiri, which can be regarded as nothing more than a few rocky islets inhabited by seabirds. Oeno and Henderson, occupied by *B. hendersonensis*, are small low islands on which seabirds are abundant. *Bidens mathewsii* grows on exposed sea cliffs of Pitcairn Island. In other South Pacific *Bidens* species, greater diminution of dispersibility has occurred; these are species which grow in localities inland from the immediate coast. Those species with awns still barbed occupy relatively low elevations in open scrubby forest or on grassy ridges. The unnamed *Bidens* from Socorro Island grows in open dry forest at about 1000 ft. *Bidens australis* has been collected at low elevations on Tahaa recently; it has not been collected recently on the other islands of its range, perhaps because of destruction of low-elevation forests by burning and farming. This may be true of *B. lantanoides* also. *Bidens aoraiensis* and *B. orofenensis* are not low-elevation species, but they do grow on exposed rocky outcrops of ridges high on Tahiti and could not in any way be considered forest species. *Bidens glandulifera* occurs on exposed grassy ridges of montane Bora Bora.

The Marquesan species occupy grassy ridges and open forest of middle elevations, as do *B. deltoides* and *B. mooreensis* of the Society Islands. *Bidens raiateensis*, with the poorest dispersal means of any South Pacific *Bidens*, grows in wet upland forest. Thus, in the South Pacific species, the farthest penetrations into forest sites are accompanied by greatest diminution of dispersal mechanism.

Among the Hawaiian species, similar ecological correlations occur. The species of A in figure 11.3 are occupants of seacoast bluffs (*B. hillebrandiana, B. molokaiensis, B. nematocera*) or open, low-elevation slopes (*B. waimeana*). The species of B through F occupy low-elevation sites except for *B. micranthoides* (open places in mid-elevation dry koa forest, Kauai), *B. hawaiiensis* (open lava fields of Mauna Kea, Hawaii), *B. conjuncta* (wet but open grassy sites of higher Oahu and Maui) and *B. cosmoides* (rain forest of upper Kauai). The species in the bottom half of figure 11.3 mostly occupy relatively wet upland forests. These species, in general, have large embryos suited to germination in shady forest sites. A notable exception is *B. ctenophylla* (open lava slopes near Puuwaawaa, Hawaii). This might be a case of a species which has been derived from a forest-inhabiting ancestor rather than a coastal one. Another exception is *B. degeneri* (arid regions of lower Oahu, Molokai, and Maui).

Despite the exceptions noted, the progress of Hawaiian species of *Bidens* from seacoast to interior and the accompaniment of this adaptive shift by loss of dispersal mechanism are clear. One can hypothesize that *Bidens* originally established in coastal sites where seabirds nested. The fact that many coastal areas of the Hawaiian Islands are not now occupied by seabirds is probably a result of human interference. One should not expect perfect ecological correlation, and there seems to be a degree of flexibility within many species in expression of the dispersal mechanism —a flexibility that suggests weak selectivity for "good" dispersal mechanisms. Interestingly, George W. Gillett (personal communication, 1966) has demonstrated that features indicating good dispersibility (e.g., like *B. pilosa*) are genetically dominant, and that the various loss-of-dispersibility features are genetically recessive.

Pacific species of *Bidens* are well suited for entry into Polynesian forests because they are perennial and can become large shrubs up to about 3 m in height. They are not, however, strongly woody, and seem not to have advanced as far toward arborescence as, for example, *Fitchia*. There seems little question that the woodier species of *Bidens* do represent specialization—adaptation to forest situations.

Oparanthus (fig. 11.4) consists of four species native to the Marquesas and Rapa. This recently recognized genus (Sherff, 1937a) may be considered a derivative of an early immigrant stock belonging to Heliantheae, subtribe Coreopsidinae. The distribution of *Oparanthus* suggests relictualism of a recent order or poor dispersal capacity. Anatomical studies (Carlquist, 1957) show relationships to such Coreopsidinae as *Bidens* and *Coreopsis*, as well as to *Fitchia*. *Oparanthus* has fertile ray achenes (at right in each species, fig. 11.4) and sterile (male) disc achenes. The disc achenes— which have no function in reproduction—retain a single awn in *O. rapensis* and *O. coriaceus*. The ray achenes are flattened (curved in *O. rapensis*), although not broadly winged. Awns are modified into winglike structures in *O. albus*, reminiscent of *Bidens macrocarpa* or *B. magnidisca*. Achene body and awns in *Oparanthus* are completely glabrous. Thus, achenes have a low dispersibility. This correlates well with ecology and habit of *Oparanthus*. All species are shrubs or trees, markedly woody, and thus have a growth form frequent in Polynesian forests. *Oparanthus* seems to

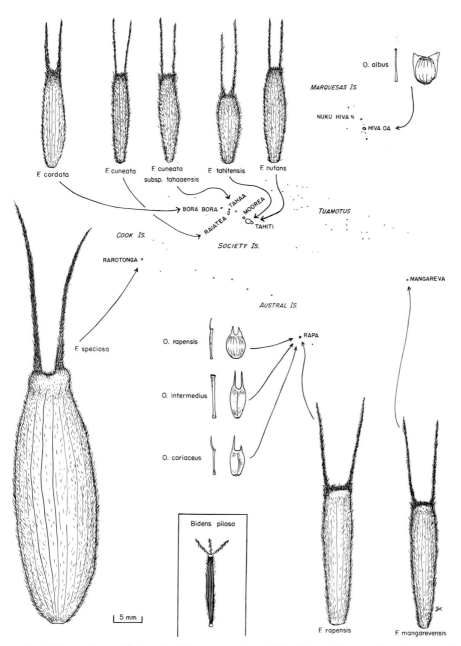

FIG. 11.4. Comparison of fruits of all known species of *Fitchia* and *Oparanthus* (Asteraceae), shown geographically. Note that the scale of magnification is half that of figs. 11.2 and 11.3. An achene of *Bidens pilosa* is shown, bottom center, for comparison of size and morphology.

451

represent a more complete adaptation to the rain forest than does *Bidens,* and probably signifies a longer history in Polynesia.

Fitchia (fig. 11.4) seems clearly related to Coreopsidinae, but by virtue of homogamous capitula and other features it seems worthy of recognition within a separate subtribe, Fitchiinae (Carlquist, 1957). *Fitchia* is a truly woody genus, ranging from small shrubs to true trees. I suspect that it represents a South American ancestor whose mainland relatives have now vanished. The achenes of *Fitchia* are relatively large; the smallest occur in the Society Islands species (particularly small ones, smaller than those figured, have been observed recently on Tahiti by Van Balgooy [personal communication, 1971]). *Fitchia mangarevensis* and *F. rapensis* have fruits of intermediate size, whereas *F. speciosa* has gigantic achenes—probably the largest in the family Asteraceae. All species are provided with long awns, but, except in *F. speciosa* and *F. cordata,* the awns seem thin and break easily from the achene body. Achenes in all species are densely covered with upwardly appressed hairs, as are the awns. Lack of retrorse barbs on the awns does not seem strongly disadvantageous in dispersal. Fruits with hairs oriented in a single direction disperse quite well (e.g., grasses). The ancestors of *Fitchia* probably were brought to Polynesia in feathers of birds, perhaps seabirds.

One might speculate that the ancestors of *Fitchia* had smaller fruits than do the current species. The relatively large size of achenes in the Society Islands species (except as noted above) seems no severe disadvantage, for this group has become distributed throughout the high islands of the archipelago. The southern pair of species, *F. rapensis* and *F. mangarevensis,* are very close and their intermediate fruit size may have originated in southeastern Polynesia. However, ancestors have evidently succeeded in dispersing across the distance between Mangareva and Rapa, for it is difficult to imagine that achenes of this size originated independently on the two islands when other features of the two species are so much alike. The large achene size of *F. speciosa* seems likely to have originated on Rarotonga autochthonously, perhaps from ancestors with achenes like those of *F. cordata.* Not only does *F. speciosa* represent the farthest penetration of the genus into the Pacific, it is also the most arborescent species in the genus.

Fruit size correlates well with size of plant in *Fitchia.* The Society

Islands species are chiefly shrubs which occur in scrubby forest on ridges. *Fitchia rapensis* and *F. mangarevensis* are small trees, whereas *F. speciosa* is a relatively tall tree of deep forest. The large fruit size of *F. speciosa* is reminiscent of the large fruits of other forest trees. It seems an ultimate point in adaptation to rain forest.

Fitchia seems a more primitive genus than *Bidens* or *Oparanthus* and may have, during a longer occupancy in Polynesia, perfected this forest adaptation (just as it has evidently evolved ornithophily, and the other genera have not). Even if ancestors of modern Fitchias had fruits as large as those of the Society Island species, subsequent increase in fruit size has undoubtedly occurred within Polynesia, and this increase is correlated with degree of entry into forest habitats—a farther penetration than that of *Bidens*. Although no direct evidence can be adduced, I suspect that ancestors of *Fitchia* did arrive in Polynesia by means of fruits smaller than those of modern species, and perhaps rather like those of *Bidens*. The absence of *Fitchia* from the Marquesas, Hawaiian, and Austral Islands (other than Rapa), all of which offer suitable ecological sites (*F. speciosa* has escaped from cultivation on Oahu), suggests its present dispersibility is effective only over rather short ranges. A feature not related to fruit size but probably deleterious to dispersibility is the nodding habit of the heads. Heads shatter at maturity, but instead of displaying fruits above foliage, tend to drop fruits beneath the parent plant.

Scalesia, endemic to the Galápagos Islands, belongs to Heliantheae, subtribe Verbesininae. It is probably closely related to several verbesininoid genera, of which *Viguiera* (fig. 11.5A) can be considered an example. Of the 18 species of *Scalesia*, only a few, like *S. microcephala* (fig. 11.5B), have one or two awns, usually rather short. *Scalesia cordata* has the longest awns (1–2 mm) but does not seem markedly more dispersible than the other species. The remainder of the species have only small, "callous" pappus rudiments, as in *S. aspera* (fig. 11.5C), or none at all. The achenes are not hairy. Hairs on achenes of Asteraceae serve not only for adhesion to dispersal agents, but for release from the head as well. At maturity, achene-body hairs flex outward when dry, forcing the fruits out of the head. Thus, lacking hairs, achenes of *Scalesia* have no device for release. There seems little question that *Scalesia* has a somewhat diminished dispersibility. Its dispersal throughout the Galápagos might be due to seed-eating birds.

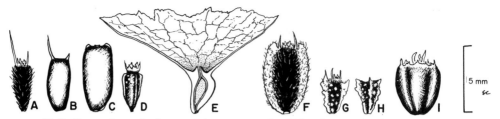

FIG. 11.5. Comparison of achenes of Asteraceae, tribe Heliantheae. Subtribe Melampodiinae is represented by E, all others from subtribe Verbesininae. All achenes are from disc flowers unless otherwise stated. Mainland species are included for comparison with the insular species. A, *Viguiera linearis;* Mexican mainland. B, *Scalesia microcephala;* Albemarle I., Galápagos Is. C, *S. aspera;* Indefatigable I., Galápagos Is. D, *Macraea laricifolia;* Charles I., Galápagos Is. E, *Lecocarpus pinnatifidus;* Charles I., Galápagos Is.; the ray achene and the bract with peltate wing that permanently enfolds the achene are shown in longitudinal section. F, *Zexmenia brevifolia;* Mexican mainland. G, *Lipochaeta rockii;* Molokai, Hawaiian Is. H, *L. remyi;* Oahu, Hawaiian Is. I, *L. lavarum;* Maui, Hawaiian Is.

Some of the species appear to have reached their present stations after loss of awns, because awnless species occur on many of the islands; perhaps awns are not as important in dispersal as they are in *Bidens.*

Adaptation to new ecological situations does not appear to have played a dominant role in loss of dispersibility in *Scalesia.* To the extent that dispersibility has been lost in this genus (and that is difficult to estimate, since the vector and mode of transport are not at all clear), it might be a by-product of other evolutionary changes.

Macraea, a monotypic genus from the Galápagos (fig. 11.5D), was formerly united with *Lipochaeta* but is worthy of recognition as a separate genus (Harling, 1962). Harling claims that *Macraea* is close to American species of *Wedelia* and *Aspilia,* whereas *Lipochaeta* has generally been conceded to have close affinities to *Zexmenia* (Sherff, 1935b). All of these genera belong to subtribe Verbesininae of Heliantheae, and are perhaps not distant from one another. *Macraea laricifolia* occurs at lower elevations of the Galápagos. Achenes are winged and crowned by a circle of short scales. Outer achenes in each head are broader and warty. The dispersal mechanism is unknown but apparently is effective over interisland distances in the archipelago. A few achenes in specimens of *Macraea* have short awns like those of *Viguiera* (fig. 11.5), so *Macraea* may be in the process of losing these awns.

Lecocarpus (fig. 11.5E), a genus endemic to the Galápagos, seems to be in the process of altering to a new mode of dispersal. As in other members

454

of Heliantheae, subtribe Melampodiinae, ray achenes are fertile; each is enclosed within a highly modified bract which bears a peltate wing. The wing is thin and leaflike. The two genera closest to *Lecocarpus* are *Melampodium*, in which fruit-enclosing bracts are like an additional seed coat and are not winged, and *Acanthospermum*, in which enclosing bracts bear hooks (Hoffmann, 1890–1893). The morphology and weight of bract-enclosed fruits of *Lecocarpus* suggest wind dispersal across relatively short distances. *Lecocarpus* occurs on two of the Galápagos Islands. Either the winged bract has been evolved since the arrival of the ancestral stock, or *Lecocarpus* has now vanished from the American mainland. Further studies might elucidate this point.

Lipochaeta (fig. 11.5G–I) contains 24 species endemic to the Hawaiian Islands. A species alleged to be native to New Caledonia proved to be *Wedelia uniflora* (Harling, 1962). *Lipochaeta* characteristically occupies lowland sites. Compared with relatives such as *Zexmenia* (fig. 11.5F) species of *Lipochaeta* have what appear to be relatively poor dispersal mechanisms (although one must concede that the precise mode of dispersal is not known). Some Lipochaetas, such as *L. rockii* (fig. 11.5G), retain both aristae and wings on achenes, but most have short wings and no aristae, as in *L. remyi* (fig. 11.5H), or large fruits with no wings and only vestigial aristae (*L. lavarum*, fig. 11.5I). Fruits of *Lipochaeta*, unlike those of *Zexmenia*, lack hairs.

The genera *Argyroxiphium*, *Wilkesia*, and *Dubautia* (including *Railliardia*) must be considered endemic Hawaiian representatives of Heliantheae, subtribe Madiinae. These "tarweeds" are otherwise restricted to western North America, with one species in Chile (Carlquist, 1959). Some mainland tarweeds, such as *Madia* and *Layia* (fig. 11.6A, B), have fertile ray achenes that have little pappus but that are enfolded within sticky bracts, and thus have the dispersal mechanism transferred from the achene to the bract. This seems true, to some extent, also of *Argyroxiphium* (fig. 11.6D, E), but few ray flowers are present in that genus, and fertile disc achenes have no such adherent bracts. All achenes of *Wilkesia* (fig. 11.6C) are disc achenes, without adherent bracts. The scales which crown the gigantic achenes of *Argyroxiphium* and *Wilkesia* seem relatively inefficient, but might become caught in birds' feathers. Hairs are few or absent on these achenes. When mature, heads in these genera shatter, and most

455

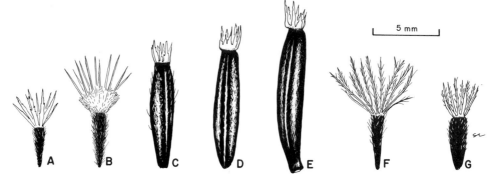

FIG. 11.6. Comparisons of achenes of Asteraceae, tribe Heliantheae, subtribe Madiinae. All achenes shown are disc achenes. A, *Madia nutans*; California mainland. B, *Layia platyglossa*; California mainland. C, *Wilkesia gymnoxiphium*; Kauai, Hawaiian Is. D, *Argyroxiphium virescens*; Maui, Hawaiian Is. E, *A. sandwichense*; Maui, Hawaiian Is. F, *Dubautia latifolia*; Kauai, Hawaiian Is. G, *D. knudsenii*; Kauai, Hawaiian Is.

fruits fall near the parent plant. *Wilkesia* is restricted to Kauai, but *Argyroxiphium* occurs on both Maui and Hawaii. Both *Wilkesia* and *Argyroxiphium* seem gigantic versions of mainland tarweeds. With such relatively large fruits, an exceptionally good dispersal mechanism would be required if long-distance dispersibility were to be retained. Thus, dispersibility of *Argyroxiphium* and *Wilkesia* appears to have fallen well behind that of ancestral forms.

Dubautia (fig. 11.6F, G) apparently has retained better dispersal mechanisms, owing to possession of the plumose-bristle type of pappus. This genus may be related closely to the preceding two, and a hybrid between *Argyroxiphium* and *Dubautia* has been reported. Some species, such as *D. knudsenii* (fig. 11.6G), however, do have pappus rather short in proportion to the achene; these bristles (or scales) do not spread well at maturity. Moreover, *D. knudsenii* has relatively few achene-body hairs, and bracts of the head do not reflex well to release the achenes. The heads are nodding and tend to drop achenes to the ground. Appropriately, *D. knudsenii* is a rain-forest tree, whereas species with longer bristles on achenes and heads that tend to open better, such as *D. latifolia* (fig. 11.6F), are characteristic of exposed situations. There does appear to be a dispersal diminution in relation to ecology in *Dubautia*, and the genus may be in a state of transition in this respect. Better dispersibility in *Dubautia* may account for the fact that the genus occurs the length of the chain of major Hawai-

ian Islands, and has more species (27) and has occupied more diverse ecological sites than *Argyroxiphium* or *Wilkesia*.

The sole entry of the tribe Cynareae into the Pacific is a pair of
closely related genera, *Centaurodendron* (two species) and *Yunquea*
(monotypic) endemic to the Juan Fernandez Islands. These genera are
probably close to *Centaurea* sect. *Plectocephalus*, which have fruits as
shown in figure 11.7A. In such Centaureas, pappus bristles are numerous
and strong, although somewhat caducous, and generally are retained in
large numbers at the achene summit. Pappus bristles spread outward well
when dry, forcing mature achenes out of the head. Bracts of the head reflex well at maturity, liberating the achenes. In *Centaurodendron* (fig.
11.7B), on the contrary, bracts of the involucre do not reflex appreciably,
so that fruits are well retained within the head. Furthermore, achenes
bear relatively short pappus bristles which "come off at the slightest touch,
and there can be little doubt that they are useless for the transport of the
achene" (Skottsberg, 1938). Moreover, the bristles break easily into tiny

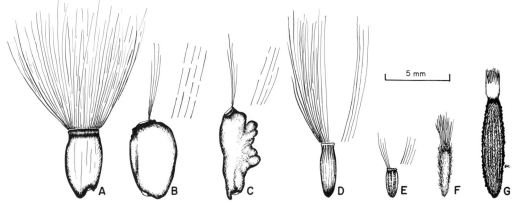

FIG. 11.7. Comparison of achenes of Asteraceae, tribes Cynareae (A–C) and Senecioneae
(D–G). Continental species are shown for comparison with insular ones; all achenes are disc
achenes. Where pappus bristles or setae are shown to the right and above the achene (A–E),
a portion of the setae is caducous. In B, C, and E, only a small number of setae remain
attached to the achene at maturity. In D, some setae may break from the fruit, but the
majority are persistent. Setae are shown as broken lines in B and C because they tend to
crumble easily and are rarely intact on mature achenes. A, *Centaurea tweediei*; Argentina. B,
Centaurodendron dracaenoides; Masatierra, Juan Fernandez Is. C, *Yunquea tenzii*; Masatierra,
Juan Fernandez Is. D, *Senecio macrantha*; Australia. E, *Robinsonia gayana*; Masatierra, Juan
Fernandez Is. F. *Rhetinodendron berterii*; Masatierra, Juan Fernandez Is. G, *Symphyochaeta
macrocephala*; Masatierra, Juan Fernandez Is.

fragments. Mature fruits are even larger than those of *Centaurea,* and would require an even more efficient pappus to equal its dispersal. On all accounts, *Centaurodendron* exhibits greatly lessened dispersibility. Fruits are released only with gradual weathering of the heads. Achenes of *Yunquea* (fig. 11.7C) are similar to those of *Centaurodendron* in all respects except that they have an oddly convolute surface and are irregular in shape —features which would certainly hinder dispersal. Such distortions of the achene may represent mutations which, although they would be unfavorable in a species where efficiency of dispersal is a requisite, are not deleterious in *Yunquea,* where dispersibility is already minimal. Both *Centaurodendron* and *Yunquea* are rosette trees of rain forest. This adaptation is an unusual one for Cynareae, and the adaptation of these genera appears to be "complete."

Three genera of Senecioneae, closely related to each other, are also endemic to the Juan Fernandez Islands: *Robinsonia* (fig. 11.7E), with five species, and *Rhetinodendron* and *Symphyochaeta* (fig. 11.7G), each monotypic. Typical mainland Senecioneae, such as the *Senecio macrantha* illustrated in figure 11.7D, have many fine pappus setae that are longer than the achene body, are persistent to somewhat caducous, and flex outward at maturity, liberating achenes as well as providing a parachutelike structure for flotation in wind. Release of achenes is aided by reflexing of involucral bracts. In *Robinsonia,* achenes are relatively small, but the pappus bristles are notably short and clearly caducous. Mature female heads of Robinsonias are cupules that do not open well and contain nearly bare fruits that disperse mainly by falling from the head.

Rhetinodendron (fig. 11.7F) has female heads with narrow involucres usually containing only three fruits each. The achenes are hairy, but these hairs do not spread outward appreciably upon drying, and achenes tend to remain within the involucres. The short pappus bristles, although persistent, do not reflex but are permanently upright. Involucres open only a little at maturity.

In *Symphyochaeta* (fig. 11.7G), female achenes are notably large. The achenes are not hairy, and ridges on the achene body are knobby. The pappus bristles are short and united into a tube, thus definitively canceling any possibility of wind dispersal. Involucral bracts do not reflex at maturity.

All three genera of Juan Fernandez Senecioneae show advanced stages

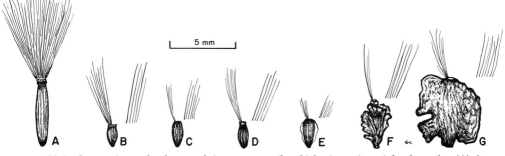

FIG. 11.8. Comparison of achenes of Asteraceae, tribe Cichorieae. A mainland species (A) is shown for comparison with insular species. A, *Lygodesmia juncea;* southwestern United States. B, *Stephanomeria (Munzothamnus) blairii;* San Clemente I., Calif. C, *Thamnoseris lacerata;* San Ambrosio I., Desventuradas Is. D, *Dendroseris (Hesperoseris) gigantea;* Masafuera, Juan Fernandez Is. E, *Dendroseris (Rea) micrantha;* Masatierra, Juan Fernandez Is. F, *Dendroseris (Phoenicoseris) pinnata;* Masatierra, Juan Fernandez Is. G, *Dendroseris (s.s.) litoralis;* Santa Clara, Juan Fernandez Is.

in dispersal loss. As in *Centaurodendron* and *Yunquea,* this alteration is accompanied by entry into the rain-forest habitat, an ecological preference of relatively few Senecioneae.

The tribe Cichorieae of Asteraceae is represented on a few Pacific islands. The achene of *Lygodesmia juncea* (fig. 11.8A) is typical of mainland forms. The achene is crowned by numerous pappus setae; these reflex at maturity, as do the involucral bracts. The setae in this species are persistent. In the same subtribe is an insular endemic, *Stephanomeria (Munzothamnus) blairii,* of San Clemente Island, off the coast of California. *Stephanomeria blairii* (fig. 11.8B) does not seem to show appreciable diminution of dispersibility. However, pappus setae are more caducous than in many of the tribe.

The remaining genera of Lactuceae (Cichorieae) shown in figure 11.8 belong to subtribe Dendroserinae, a subtribe claimed to be close to Stephanomeriinae (Stebbins, 1953). *Thamnoseris* (fig. 11.8C) is endemic to the Desventuradas Islands, Chile, where it grows on barren lava slopes (Skottsberg, 1963). Involucres of *Thamnoseris* are composed of bracts with large swollen bases; involucres apparently do open when mature and dry to release fruits (Skottsberg, 1947). Pappus setae are short and "fall very easily" from the achene body (Skottsberg, 1937). These pappus features suggest some diminution of dispersal capability.

459

The Juan Fernandez Cichorieae (fig. 11.8C–G) form an unusually rich assemblage which Skottsberg (1951) concluded were best regarded as four genera, although Stebbins (1953) has demurred. *Dendroseris (Hesperoseris) gigantea* (fig. 11.8D) has achenes with fairly good potential dispersal ability, although pappus setae are relatively caducous. In *Dendroseris (Rea) micrantha* (fig. 11.8E), pappus setae are very short and caducous. Involucral bracts are not caducous in *D. (R.) micrantha*, although they are in *D. (R.) pruinata*.

Dendroseris (Phoenicoseris) pinnata has achenes which are oddly angled, sometimes triquetrous, but which have strikingly convolute surfaces (fig. 11.8F). This is, in part, related to embryo volume, but the considerations cited above for *Yunquea* may also apply here. Pappus setae in *D. pinnata* are too short to offer appreciable lift to achenes released into the air. Setae do not reflex well in mature dry achenes and are quite caducous. Moreover, mature involucres open poorly when dry, and seeds are tardily and irregularly released.

All four species of *Dendroseris* sect. *Dendroseris* have achenes with fantastically sculptured, flattish achenes (fig. 11.8G). The shape and size of the achenes is related to the broad cotyledons of the embryos, as noted by Skottsberg (1922). In their large size, fruits of these *Dendroseris* species represent an evolutionary culmination in Lactuceae comparable to that of *Fitchia speciosa* in Heliantheae. Also contributing to minimized dispersibility in the sect. *Dendroseris* species is the tuft of short, caducous pappus setae, far too short and too few either to release achenes from the involucre or to aid in their aerial flotation. Achenes are, in fact, retained at maturity within the well-closed involucres composed of massive involucral bracts. The reasons for highly contorted achene shapes may, in part, be the same as those given for *Yunquea*, although the value of a larger embryo might relate to forest conditions.

Genera of Astereae in the Pacific show a few instances of apparently diminished dispersibility. Achenes of *Remya* (Hawaiian Is.) bear a few vestigial bristles. *Remya* is difficult to discuss in connection with dispersibility, however, for its affinities are unclear. Many species of the genus *Tetramolopium* on the Hawaiian Islands appear to have a pappus typical of the tribe Astereae, but at least one species (*T. remyi*) has few setae.

Campanulaceae. Attempts to germinate seeds of the baccate Hawaiian lobelioids tend to meet with poor success, probably because of very short viability (J. F. Rock, personal communication, 1960); this could be considered a phase of loss of dispersibility. Seeds of one of the baccate genera, *Delissea*, are relatively large. On the other hand, as mentioned earlier, *Trematolobelia*, a capsular Hawaiian genus of lobelioids, has probably evolved improved dispersibility autochthonously by virtue of its markedly winged seeds (Carlquist, 1962).

Caryophyllaceae. The Hawaiian endemic genus *Schiedea* would seem to retain in at least some species the same dispersibility of ancestral types that immigrated to the Hawaiian Islands. Seeds in this genus are most frequently very small and sculptured in various ways that would enhance their adhesion within mud or debris on birds' feet. Capsules open so that the valves spread widely, providing unimpeded release of seeds. *Schiedea globosa* (fig. 11.9) serves as an example of good retention of dispersibility, as do other lowland species. Exceptions in regard to seed sculpturing are found in species of somewhat higher altitudes, *S. amplexicaulis, S. kealiae,* and *S. diffusa,* which have smooth seeds. This trend is also shown in *S. viscosa* (fig. 11.9) and *S. lychnoides,* both from middle elevations on Kauai; these species not only have somewhat larger seeds than do the other Schiedeas, but they also have prominent sepals which enfold the capsule at maturity, hindering the release of seeds. This suggests a shaker type of dispersal, in which seeds are disseminated more gradually. Hillebrand (1888) claimed that *S. viscosa* and *S. lychnoides* are transitional to another endemic Hawaiian genus, *Alsinodendron*; possibly they may be included in the latter (Sherff, 1944). *Alsinodendron trinerve* (fig. 11.9) is notable not

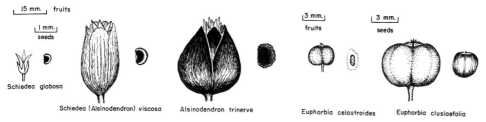

| 15 mm. | fruits | | 3 mm. | 3 mm. |
| 1 mm. | seeds | | fruits | seeds |

Schiedea globosa   Schiedea (Alsinodendron) viscosa   Alsinodendron trinerve   Euphorbia celastroides   Euphorbia clusiaefolia

FIG. 11.9. Comparison of fruits and seeds of the endemic Hawaiian genera *Schiedea* and *Alsinodendron* (Caryophyllaceae) and of species of *Euphorbia* (Euphorbiaceae) endemic to the Hawaiian Is. *Schiedea viscosa* has also been treated under *Alsinodendron* and may be intermediate between the two genera. Dotted line around seed of *E. celastroides* indicates presence of a gelatinous sheath when seeds are wet. Scales are shown for fruits and seeds of Caryophyllaceae and for fruits and seeds of Euphorbiaceae.

only for seeds which are markedly larger than those of *Schiedea*, but also for sepals which enclose the capsule and are fleshy, becoming dark blue at maturity. This suggests a drupelike structure that might well represent a shift to dispersal by frugivorous birds. Certainly A. *trinerve* represents the furthest penetration in this series into a forest habitat, for it grows in wet scrubby forest near the summit of Oahu's highest mountain, Mt. Kaala.

Convolvulaceae. The Hawaiian *Breweria menziesii* is notable for its large ovoid seeds, 8–9 mm long, which are often borne singly in capsules. The precise affinities of *B. menziesii* need to be established. Other species of *Breweria*, however, have smaller seeds. *Breweria media* of Australia has seeds 2 mm long, two or more per capsule. *Breweria cordata* (= *Bonamia semidigyna*) of Indonesia has four seeds per capsule, each 5–6 mm long. The fleshy outer testa of seeds of *B. menziesii* suggests attractiveness to birds, a feature that may or may not have been present in ancestral stocks. This testa is said to be mucilaginous, but is probably not sufficiently so to permit adhesion to bird feathers. Seeds of *Breweria* do not float.

Jacquemontia sandwicensis has nonbuoyant seeds. This characteristic was interpreted by Guppy (1906) as indicating that seeds arrived in crevices of logs that rafted to the Hawaiian Islands. Ridley (1930) reached what appeals to me as the more logical conclusion, that *J. sandwicensis* has been derived from a littoral species from America that had buoyant seeds.

Cucurbitaceae. Guppy (1906) noted that some Hawaiian species of *Sicyos* have hooked fruits, whereas others do not. Although the vector for *Sicyos* is not clear, hooked fruits would seem to aid in dispersibility by birds.

Ebenaceae. The two Hawaiian species of *Diospyros* differ appreciably in fruit and seed size. The smaller-fruited species, *D. ferrea*, has fruits ca. 18 mm long. These fruits are elongate, and thus much smaller in volume than those of the other Hawaiian species, *D. hillebrandii*. Fruits of *D. hille-brandii* are 20–25 mm long, and 15–18 mm wide. Size of seeds parallels that of fruits: a typical seed of *D. ferrea* is $13 \times 7 \times 4$ mm, whereas in *D. hillebrandii* a comparable seed is $17 \times 10 \times 6$ mm, approximately twice as great in volume. Appropriately, *D. hillebrandii* is much more re-stricted in distribution and ecology, occurring at about 2000 ft in certain valleys on Oahu, whereas *D. ferrea* grows at lower elevations, even down to near sea level, on all of the major islands. The fruit and seed sizes of other Pacific species of *Diospyros*, such as *"Maba elliptica"* and *"M. savaiensis"* of Samoa, are slightly smaller than those of *D. ferrea* (Christophersen, 1935). Evolutionary increase in size of fruits and seeds may be suspected in *D. samoensis* (non *Maba samoensis* Hieron.), the fruits of which are 45–50 mm long, with seeds about 30 × 9 × 5 mm.

Elaeocarpaceae. The Hawaiian species of *Elaeocarpus*, *E. bifidus*, has fruits which are ovoid, 22–30 mm long, 18–20 mm wide. This size seems best regarded, in view of the trends demonstrated in this chapter, as an increase over fruit size in ancestral species. Large-fruited species of *Elaeocarpus* also occur on Samoa: 4 cm long in *E. magnifolius*, 5 cm long in *E. ulianus* (Christophersen, 1935). Fruit gigantism may characterize a number of genera in the Samoan flora, however. Species with much smaller drupes are scattered throughout the Pacific. *Elaeocarpus rarotongensis* of Rarotonga has drupes 12 mm long (Brown, 1935). *Elaeocarpus hookerianus* of New Zealand has drupes 8 mm long, and several Australian species have fruits in this range. Smaller-fruited species such as these may be suspected of being ancestral to the Hawaiian *E. bifidus* and to the Samoan species. Frugivorous birds are probably the agent of dispersal. Fruits of *Elaeocarpus* do not float.

Euphorbiaceae. The native Hawaiian species of *Euphorbia* (except *E. haeleeleana*) belong to the subgenus *Chamaesyce* (*Anisophyllum* of some authors [see Sherff, 1937c]) and range from seacoast to wet rain forest. Seacoast species, e.g., *E. degeneri* and *E. skottsbergii*, suggest in morphology a relationship to species of southeastern Polynesia: *E. atoto, E. taitensis,* and *E. pitcairnensis.* Such coastal species as these may disperse by oceanic drift. Guppy (1906) lists seeds of *E. atoto* as floatable by virtue of air space within the seed coat. Mid-altitude Hawaiian species of *Euphorbia* may represent a different introduction; they are clearly different in their basic dispersal mechanism—which may be the same as that by which their ancestors arrived on the islands. Seeds of the low-altitude (but inland) species *E. celastroides* (fig. 11.9) are small (1.5 × 1 × 1 mm) and are ridged and covered, when wet, by a prominent gelatinous coating. This suggests adherence to birds' feathers as a means of dispersal. Species of high, wet forests, however, show marked fruit and seed gigantism. In *E. clusiaefolia* (fig. 11.9), capsules range from 6 to 9 mm in length, and seeds are 3 mm in diameter. Not only are these seeds smooth, rather than markedly pitted or ridged, but no appreciable gelatinous coating can be observed on them. This would seem clearly to indicate loss of dispersibility. Seeds of neither *E. celastroides* nor *E. clusiaefolia* float, and there is no reason to believe that their ancestors had floatable seeds. The Hawaiian species which possesses the largest capsules is *E. rockii*. Unfortunately, all capsules available for study contained nothing but markedly shrunken seeds that were clearly infertile. Because the capsules of *E. rockii* are so much larger (13–22 mm in length) than those of *E. clusiaefolia*, one would expect larger seeds as well. In any case, the large-seeded species of *Euphorbia*, which are restricted to upland wet-forest areas, have clearly diminished dispersibility.

Fabaceae. Because native Hawaiian legumes are chiefly found in lower dry forest—down to the seacoast in many cases—and because legume seeds are notably capable of seawater transport without loss of viability (Guppy, 1906; Ridley, 1930), one might suspect that the Hawaiian legumes as a whole stem from such a history of immigration and have to various degrees evolved into forest habitats. Moreover, almost all genera in the indigenous Hawaiian legume flora contain non-Hawaiian species that are widespread beach species, known to be capable of seawater flotation. Loss of floatability within the Hawaiian legumes would represent a discontinuation of this means of dispersal. Some genera within the Hawaiian legumes do have seeds which are black and shiny or colorful, suggesting attractiveness to seed-eating birds. Pods in most Hawaiian legumes open poorly, however. Moreover, the large size of seeds in these species—like that in related non-Hawaiian species—suggests that such seed-eating birds would have to be large. Such birds have not played any appreciable role, apparently, in long-distance dispersal, and so oceanic drift seems the best hypothesis.

Seeds of the endemic *Erythrina sandwichensis* (fig. 11.10) will not float, although seeds of other *Erythrina* species do float. Guppy (1906) reported buoyancy of seeds in *E. indica* and *E. ovalifolia*, but failure of flotation in *E. sandwichensis* (then regarded as conspecific with the Tahitian *E. monosperma*). I have found that seeds of *E. variegata* (fig. 11.10) also float. Moreover, the legumes of *E. variegata* remain closed and are themselves a flotation mechanism. Guppy attributed floatability of *Erythrina* seeds to a "light kernel," since the testa does not float and

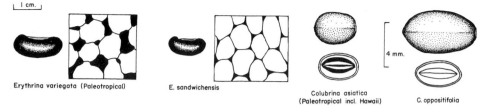

Erythrina variegata (Paleotropical)   E. sandwichensis

Colubrina asiatica
(Paleotropical incl. Hawaii)   C. oppositifolia

FIG. 11.10. Seeds of endemic Hawaiian Fabaceae (*Erythrina sandwichensis*) and Rhamnaceae (*Colubrina oppositifolia*) compared with wide-ranging species (*E. variegata, C. asiatica*) that are dispersed by seawater. Insets beside seeds of the Erythrinas are drawings of parenchymas of cotyledons. A prominent intercellular space system (black) is present in *E. variegata* but not in *E. sandwichensis*. Transections of seeds are shown beside the drawings of entire seeds in the *Colubrina* species. Prominent spaces between cotyledons and endosperm in *C. asiatica* are indicated in black. Scales are shown for seeds of Fabaceae and of Rhamnaceae.

mature seeds contain no air space. The difference in specific gravity between floatable *Erythrina* seeds and those of *E. sandwichensis* was investigated by means of hand sections of living seeds. My sections (fig. 11.10) show that a prominent air-space system in cotyledons of *E. variegata* is probably responsible for flotation; air spaces are much smaller in cotyledons of *E. sandwichensis*. Legumes of *E. sandwichensis* could serve for seawater dispersal if they remained closed but, in fact, they do not. The only probable agent for dispersal might be the seed-eating honey-creeper *Psittarostra* or some similar bird; if so, a shift in dispersal mechanism might be hypothesized. There seems little doubt that ancestors of *E. sandwichensis* arrived on the Hawaiian Islands by oceanic drift. The near-identity of *E. sandwichensis* with the Tahitian *E. monosperma* and the tendency of both to occupy coastal stations, stations so remote geographically from those of the nearest other *Erythrina* species, would tend to support this idea.*

A similar situation obtains with the Hawaiian koas (*Acacia koa* and *A. kauaiensis*). Seeds of these species will not float, and unopened mature pods float only for a day or two. Dried branches bearing unopened but mature pods might be washed down to sea during torrential storms, and such "rafting" might be envisioned as a means of dispersal for *A. koa*. *Acacia koa* is very similar to *A. heterophylla* of Mauritius (Indian Ocean); the distance between the stations for these species alone would suggest

* Study of the type specimen of *E. monosperma* shows that *E. sandwichensis* should be regarded as a synonym of *E. monosperma*.

the likelihood of seawater dispersal. A phyllodial *Acacia* similar to, but perhaps not immediately related to, *A. koa* occurs on Samoa and Tonga: *A. simplicifolia*. The legumes of this species, unlike those of *A. koa*, do not open readily at all, and because each seed is sealed into a loment-like segment which contains an air space adequate to float an enclosed seed, flotation would appear likely. Seeds of *A. simplicifolia* will not float when removed from the legume. The legumes, or segments thereof, will float for several days, but eventually become wetted and sink. *Acacia simplicifolia* is a beach species and, like the Hawaiian Acacias, doubtless owes its arrival in Polynesia to oceanic drift. Probably Polynesian Acacias came from a source in or near Australia, where phyllodial Acacias are abundant. Pods of *A. koa* seem to show vestiges of adhesion between the two halves of the legume in zones which separate adjacent seeds, suggesting the *A. simplicifolia* condition. The fact that most pods of *A. koa* open readily means that legumes of the species are now ill-suited for seawater dispersal. Koa seeds may have been distributed over short distances among the Hawaiian Islands by birds.

The endemic Hawaiian *Sophora*, *S. chrysophylla*, forms another parallel. Seeds of *S. chrysophylla* will not float, a fact noted by Guppy (1906) and confirmed by me. Legumes of this species, however, do not open readily. They are, moreover, formed with narrow constrictions between some of the seeds, so that either the entire legume or parts of it can float. Guppy claims that the legume in this species is too delicate to provide good flotation. Nevertheless, *Sophora* undoubtedly owes its original advent on the Hawaiian Islands to oceanic drift. Both legumes and individual seeds of *S. tomentosa* and *S. tetraptera* float well. Legumes in these species are more durable than those of *S. chrysophylla*. At least some species of *Sophora* are still littoral, such as *S. tomentosa*. Loss of dispersibility in *S. chrysophylla* is shown not only in fragility of legumes and failure of seeds to float, but also in its adaptation to inland dry forest primarily; to the extent that it has left the coastal areas, it could not disperse by seawater regardless of floatability (except for rafting of branches washed down in streams). Sykes and Godley (1968) find that *S. prostrata* has nonbuoyant seeds, which would constitute a loss of dispersibility in this New Zealand species. *Sophora microphylla* (New Zealand, Gough I., southern Chile) has various degrees of floatability in seeds (Sykes and

Godley, 1968)—perhaps this species is in the process of losing dispersibility. *Sophora chrysophylla* in the Hawaiian Islands may represent a change to a new mode of dispersal if, as Guppy (1906) claimed, seeds are eaten by birds and successfully transported short distances within the archipelago.

The example of *Canavalia* was discussed in the introductory portion of this chapter. Sauer (1964) reports nonbuoyant seeds in the endemic Hawaiian species *C. galeata*, *C. molokaiensis*, *C. hawaiiensis*, *C. kauaiensis*, and *C. pubescens*. I confirmed nonbuoyancy for the latter three species. Sauer seems to believe that species such as these were derived from a wide-ranging ancestor with buoyant seeds, an interpretation my studies would endorse. Other Pacific species that are restricted to one island or several nearby islands and that have nonbuoyant seeds (thereby suggesting loss of dispersibility) include *C. vitiensis* (Fiji), *C. raiateensis* (Raiatea) and *C. megalantha* (Marianas Is.). Wide-ranging species of the Pacific with buoyant seeds include *C. sericea* and *C. maritima* (Sauer, 1964).

Seeds of the Hawaiian endemic *Mezoneurum kauaiensis* showed no floatability in my experiments. Mixed results were obtained with seeds of *Strongylodon lucidus*: of five seeds tested, only one floated. Seeds of *Mucuna gigantea* (a coastal element in the Hawaiian flora) did float.

These results suggest that loss of buoyancy—and thereby dispersibility—has occurred quite conspicuously in endemic legumes of Pacific islands. Loss of dispersibility in these seems to have occurred almost in direct proportion to the extent to which the species have adapted to upland forest conditions.

Goodeniaceae. The Hawaiian species of *Scaevola* represent three main groups: *S. taccada* (= *S. sericea*), which is widespread on beaches throughout the Pacific; species such as *S. gaudichaudiana* and *S. mollis* with small, ovoid, purple drupes, which are representatives of a montane group of species that extends from Australia to the Hawaiian Islands; and *S. glabra* (including *S. kauaiensis*), a curious and isolated species of high wet forest on Oahu and Kauai, which has sometimes been treated under a segregate genus, *Camphusia*. Among the second group of species, some variation in size of drupe and endocarp does occur, but drupes mostly range from 4 to 10 mm in length, with the woody endocarp 3–7 mm long. These species seem easily dispersible by frugivorous birds. Well outside that range of size is the fruit of *S. glabra*, which is spheroidal or pyriform,

467

15–20 mm long. The endocarp is typically ovoid, ca. 13 × 8 mm. The fruit dimensions of *S. glabra* clearly exceed those of any other Scaevolas of montane Pacific islands. *Scaevola glabra* probably represents an early immigrant to the islands, a hypothesis suggested both by its curious morphology and its restriction to relatively older mountains. If so, the greater time available for its evolutionary change on the Hawaiian Islands may have permitted it to approximate more nearly the large-fruited habit characteristic of trees of wet forest.

Scaevola coriacea, although a species from coastal and near-coastal areas in the Hawaiian Islands, has fruits incapable of flotation (chapter 2). It is probably a derivative of the montane species and never had buoyancy, despite a superficial resemblance to the widespread *S. plumieri*, a purple-fruited species with buoyant seeds. *Scaevola coriacea* is probably dispersed by birds. Likewise, *S. spinescens*, an Australian species with nonbuoyant seeds (chapter 8), may never have had seed buoyancy, despite its occurrence near salt lakes. For further comments on dispersibility of Goodeniaceae, see chapter 8.

Occasionally I have been asked whether the purple-fruited montane Scaevolas of the Pacific are derivatives of *S. taccada*, the beach species with buoyant, white-fruited seeds. There seems little doubt on this point: *S. taccada* is a relatively uniform species, and although it is like the montane, purple-fruited species in some respects, the montane species are closely related to each other, and each is endemic to an island or an archipelago. There seems no likelihood that *S. taccada* could have given rise to each of the montane species independently, yet left no trace of any intermediates.

Haloragidaceae. The Hawaiian species of *Gunnera* cannot be said to be large-fruited in comparison with forest trees, but they do represent a marked increase in fruit size over species of other Pacific islands. Dried fruits of *G. mauiensis* (Hawaiian Is.) are 3 mm in diameter, whereas those of *G. macrophylla* (New Guinea) are ca. 1.5 mm in diameter and those of *G. prorepens* (New Zealand) ca. 1.2 mm in diameter.

Lamiaceae. Phyllostegia is endemic to the main Hawaiian Islands except for *P. variabilis* on Laysan Island and *P. tahitensis* on Tahiti. *Phyllostegia* and an endemic Hawaiian genus, *Stenogyne*, have been placed together in the tribe Prasieae. This tribe is distinctive in possessing genera with fleshy drupelets rather than dry nutlets. *Phyllostegia* and *Stenogyne* may have evolved from such ancestors as the Indo-Malesian *Gomphostemma*, which also possesses drupelets. Because of fruit morphology, dispersal by frugivorous birds may be suspected. Among the 24 species of *Phyllostegia* recognized by Sherff (1935a), there is variation in size of the drupelets, but data are difficult to obtain because mature drupelets are unknown in some species, and although the size of dry endocarp is known for the remainder, dimensions of fresh fruits are rarely recorded. The average length of dried drupelets in *Phyllostegia* appears to be about 2 mm, with fresh drupelets 4 mm long. The related genus *Stenogyne* (fig. 11.11) shows a more dramatic series in increase of drupelet size. Species belonging to the section *Microphyllae* of Sherff (1935a), such as *S. diffusa*, have small drupelets. Dried drupelets of these species are ca. 2–4 mm long. These species inhabit dry, grassy areas on recent volcanic craters, such as Haleakala, Mauna Kea, and Mauna Loa. Most species, such as *S. calaminthoides* (fig. 11.11), have drupelets which are 3–5 mm long when dried. A few species (usually those of very wet forest areas) have drupelets 6–8 mm long. These species grow in patches of forest adjacent to the high wet bogs of the Hawaiian Islands: *S. kaalae* (Mt. Kaala, Oahu), *S. kamehamehae* (Puu Kolekole, Molokai), and *S. purpurea* (Alakai Swamp, Kauai). The large-fruited *Stenogyne* shown in figure 11.11 is presumably referable to *S. purpurea*, although it differs in leaf shape and in the size of drupelets, which are appreciably larger than indicated for that species by Sherff (1935a). The series in fruit sizes within *Stenogyne* appears closely correlated with ecology and perhaps indicates tendencies toward precinctiveness. Increase in fruit size is accompanied in some species by a tendency

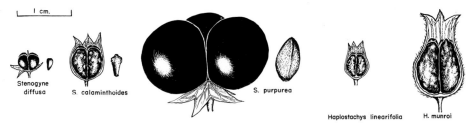

FIG. 11.11. Fruits of the Hawaiian genera *Stenogyne* and *Haplostachys* (Lamiaceae). Seeds with fleshy exocarp removed are shown to the right in each *Stenogyne* species. Fruits are shown with the facing portion of the enclosing calyx removed, except for *Stenogyne purpurea*.

to bear fewer drupelets per flower. Another indication of lowered dispersibility might be the habit of some species of *Stenogyne* (e.g., *S. rotundifolia*) of enveloping drupelets within a persistent tubular calyx which may hinder shedding of fruits.

The Hawaiian genus *Haplostachys* differs from *Stenogyne* and *Phyllostegia* in its dry nutlets. Fosberg (1948) suggests a common origin of this genus with the other two. Most species of *Haplostachys*, such as *H. linearifolia* (fig. 11.11), occupy dry grassy areas only a few feet above sea level. *Haplostachys munroi* (fig. 11.11), with larger fruits, grows in dry forest areas on Lanai. Fruiting calyces and also individual nutlets of all species of *Haplostachys* tested are capable of flotation in water, a result inferable from the coastal habitat of the species, but also suggesting possible derivation of the genus independently of *Phyllostegia* and *Stenogyne*. The corky nature of the nutlet exocarp is responsible for floatability of the fruits. The larger seed size in *H. munroi* seems related to the entry of that species into the forest habitat. Occasional fruits of *H. munroi* are composed not of four triquetrous nutlets but of two larger hemispherical ones. Nutlets of *H. munroi* are often somewhat misshapen, with irregular margins.

Lauraceae. Cryptocarya in the Hawaiian Islands is represented by two close species, *C. oahuensis* and *C. mannii*. Both are unusual in the genus in their large fruit size. Drupes in these species are spheroidal, 30–35 mm in diameter when dry; the figure of 16 mm given by Rock (1913) is probably in error, perhaps based on immature material. These fruits are covered by a thin, fleshy exocarp which overlies a thick (2–4 mm) woody endocarp. These features are in contrast with those of other *Cryptocarya* species, in which fruits are much smaller and have a thin, almost papery endocarp which can be broken easily. In the Australian species *C. angulata* and *C. hyposporlia*, fruits are ovoid, 11–12 × 8 mm when dry. Dried fruits of the Fijian *C. hornei* are somewhat larger, 16 × 14 mm. The presence of a fleshy, though thin, blackish exocarp suggests that frugivorous birds would be responsible for dispersal of these fruits. If so, the large size of fruits in the Hawaiian Cryptocaryas would seem to have foreclosed this avenue of dissemination. Large-fruited Cryptocaryas are also present in Samoa: *C. samoensis* has drupes 40 × 17 mm, and *C. glaucescens* has similarly large fruits (Christophersen, 1935). Dried fruits of *Cryptocarya* containing well-developed embryos are capable of flotation, but the fragile nature of endocarp in some species—as well as the probability that they will not be viable when thoroughly dried and washed out to sea—suggests that oceanic drift is a relatively unlikely means of dispersal. Cryptocaryas are not lowland forest trees, which one would expect if they were, in fact, seawater dispersed. In the Hawaiian Islands, *Cryptocarya* occurs only in the geologically oldest areas (Kauai; Waianae Mts., Oahu), a fact which suggests that time has been available for evolution of the gigantic fruit size.

Malvaceae. The problem of whether the Hawaiian and Tahitian cottons are native has been discussed by Stephens (1963, 1964), who concludes that they are probably native and that a hypothesis of prehuman natural arrival by means of oceanic drift seems most acceptable. Guppy (1906), Stephens (1958), and I (1966b) have indicated relatively poor floatability for seeds of the Hawaiian cotton, *Gossypium sandvicense.* However, the matter of seed floatablity and resistance to salt water in cottons has been more recently and exhaustively investigated by Stephens (1966). Seeds of *G. sandvicense* (Hawaiian Is.) and *G. hirsutum* (various Pacific islands; Puerto Rico) show sufficiently long buoyancy to explain their arrival on these various islands. Saltwater tolerance is retained in *G. sandvicense* and in *G. hirsutum* from Wake Island. Stephens (1966) seems mystified by loss of saltwater tolerance in *G. hirsutum* from Samoa and the Marquesas. The explanation is clearly a loss of dispersibility for reasons such as suggested in the opening pages of this chapter. Seeds of most cottons retain great viability after soaking in seawater (Stephens, 1958), and this fact, together with their typical preference for habitats along coasts, strongly suggests oceanic drift as the means of dispersal basic to the genus. In addition to lack of subspecific variation, the presence of *G. sandvicense* on all major islands of the Hawaiian chain shows that it can utilize oceanic drift for interisland dispersal.

The peculiar endemic Hawaiian genus of tree-cottons, *Kokia*, may have been derived from a *Gossypium*-like ancestor. With *Kokia*, the problem is much like that of *Gossypium. Kokia* species occupy low arid sites, characteristic of species introduced by oceanic drift. Seeds of *K. cookii* and *K. rockii* float for several days, but sink as soon as the fibers become thoroughly wetted. This degree of floatability might suffice for dispersal of the genus throughout the major Hawaiian islands. Capsules in *Kokia* float

471

only for a few hours. The capsules ordinarily flare widely, releasing seeds. Seed flotation, as with *Gossypium*, seems possible for *Kokia*, but one must hypothesize a loss of dispersibility if ancestors did arrive by means of oceanic drift.

Precisely the same results as with *Kokia* were obtained with another Hawaiian genus, *Hibiscadelphus*. Tests were made on seeds and capsules of *H. giffardianus*, *H. hualalaiensis*, and *H. wilderianus*.

Of the endemic species of *Hibiscus* tested (*H. arnottianus*, *H. brack-enridgei*, *H. immaculatus*, and *H. waimeae*), none had flotation ability in either seeds or capsules. If these species did stem from seawater-dispersed ancestors, this ability has been entirely lost. Seeds of the widespread littoral *Hibiscus* of the Pacific, *H. tiliaceus*, do float and have undoubtedly dispersed in this fashion. In addition, tests on seeds of the non-insular *H. mutabilis* showed that seeds, even when deprived of their covering of hairs, float indefinitely. Dispersal of *Hibiscus* species throughout the Pacific, with loss of dispersibility following establishment, might still be postulated. Dispersal of hispid seeds in bird feathers is another possibility that cannot be ignored. Seeds of a few native Hawaiian *Hibiscus* species still possess some stiff hairs. In either case, autochthonous loss of dispersal capability seems to have occurred in Hawaiian species, a loss correlated with evolution into moist upland sites.

Formation of endemic species in *Gossypium* and other Malvaceae, as in insular legumes, especially those of Hawaii, may be explained by infrequency in events of oceanic drift. This concept and reasons why oceanic drift may operate on rare occasions to particular islands are discussed in chapter 2.

Myrtaceae. An excellent series in loss of dispersibility related to mountaintop endemism is demonstrated by species of *Darwinia* from southwestern Australia (chapter 8). Attention is also called to other instances of loss of dispersibility cited there, as in *Eucalyptus macrocarpa* and *Stylidium galioides*.

Nyctaginaceae. The native Hawaiian Nyctaginaceae probably show little loss of dispersibility, if any, with respect to fruit morphology. The fact that *Pisonia (Ceodes) umbellifera* is absent from some suitable islands in the Pacific might be due to the large size of the fruiting perigones, although the perigones are certainly markedly viscid. The same may apply to *Pisonia (Rockia) sandwicensis,* which is endemic to the Hawaiian Islands. I have cited this species as an example of loss of dispersibility (Carlquist, 1965). The sticky perigones suggest retention of ability for dissemination by birds, but the ecological preference of the species—forests between 2000 and 4000 ft altitude—would place it well out of the range of seabirds, its best means for long-distance dispersal. The loss of dispersibility in *P. sandwicensis* may consist not of morphological change but of ecological shift and attendant cessation of contact with long-range vectors. Its endemism is suggestive of loss of the link with vectors.

Pittosporaceae. Fruiting structures that are exceptionally viscid can be quite large and still presumably retain good dispersibility. Increase in size of seeds in the Hawaiian species of *Pittosporum* may not, therefore, actually cancel their ability to be transported, although it would seem to diminish the probabilities. Species of *Pittosporum* with very large seeds have evolved in the Hawaiian Islands, a gigantism that may be primarily related to ecological adaptation to shady forests. Also, adaptation to high forests puts *Pittosporum* out of the range of seabirds. According to Rock (1913), the Hawaiian crow seeks *Pittosporum* seeds; the very localized distribution of the Hawaiian crow rules it out as a vector of *Pittosporum* seeds, but other birds might carry them. Seeds of most of the Hawaiian species of *Pittosporum* recognized by Sherff (1942) are somewhat discoid and 5–7 mm in diameter. Species with larger seeds (7–9.5 mm) include *P. sulcatum, P. dolosum, P. cauliflorum, P. hawaiiense* and *P. hosmeri* (fig. 11.12). Notably long seeds occur in a few, such as *P. confertiflorum* (fig. 11.12). The gigantism is evident when one compares other Pacific Pittosporums: *P. niueana* (4–5 mm); *P. taitense* (ca. 4 mm [fig. 11.12]); *P. raro-*

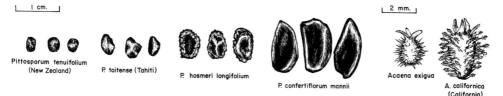

FIG. 11.12. Comparison of seeds of Hawaiian and non-Hawaiian species of *Pittosporum* (Pittosporaceae) and of *Acaena* (Rosaceae). Viscid coating is not shown on *Pittosporum* seeds. Fruiting calyces of *A. exigua* have prickles and hairs, but lack retrorse barbs on prickles that are characteristic of *A. californica* and other species of *Acaena*. Scales are shown for seeds of *Pittosporum* and for fruits of *Acaena*.

tongense (4.5–5 mm), and *P. rapense* (5.5–6 mm). Seeds of Australian and New Zealand Pittosporums are much smaller by comparison: many of them have seeds no more than 3 mm long, as in *P. tenuifolium* (fig. 11.12). Species in the western Pacific also have relatively small seeds: *P. megacarpum* of the Philippines (4–6 mm), *P. resiniferum* of the Philippines (3–4 mm), and *P. moluccanum* of the Philippines and Indonesia (3 mm).

Plantaginaceae. Of the two Hawaiian species of *Plantago* with the widest distribution in the archipelago, *P. grayana* has lost the mucilaginous quality of the seed coat whereas *P. augusta* has retained it. Of the four *Plantago* species sympatric on Mt. Waialeale, Kauai, two have a non-mucilaginous seed coat (Melvern Tessene, unpublished data).

Primulaceae. Although some Hawaiian species of *Lysimachia* have large woody capsules (such as *L. forbesii*) that seem to open poorly, seeds are no longer than 2 mm, a size which suggests ease in dispersal. Gigantism in fruits without corresponding increase in seed size also characterizes other Hawaiian genera: *Labordia*, of Loganiaceae, compared with the closely related South Pacific genus *Geniostoma*; *Cyanea* and *Clermontia* of the Campanulaceae, compared among themselves.

Rancunculaceae. The two endemic species of *Ranunculus*, *R. mauiensis* and *R. hawaiiensis*, differ in the degree to which achenes are beaked. Neither species has a stigmatic beak that is hooked. A *Ranunculus* with a hooked achene may not, however, have been ancestral to these species, and travel by means other than mechanical attachment is conceivable. Species with the same achene size (2–4 mm) and similar morphology include *R. fibrosus*, *R. plebius*, and *R. sieboldii* (Java).

Rhamnaceae. As was noted by Hillebrand (1888), the Hawaiian *Alphitonia ponderosa* has larger fruits (ca. 13 mm in diameter) than *A. zizyphoides* of Tahiti and Tonga (ca. 10 mm in diameter) or *A. franguloides* of Fiji. These distinctions in fruit size do not appear great. However, one should note that in *A. zizyphoides* and other species the fleshy exocarp and the woody cocci which the exocarp encloses fall from the mature fruit, leaving a pair of brownish seeds, surrounded by contrasting red arils, exposed upon the pedicel. This presentation would seemingly offer an excellent display for seed-eating birds. However, Hillebrand (1888) notes that in the Hawaiian *A. ponderosa* the exocarp does not fall away, so that seeds

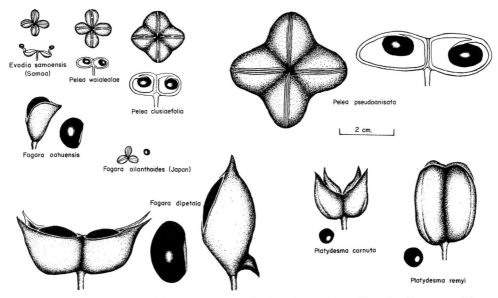

FIG. 11.13. Comparison of fruits and seeds of Hawaiian and non-Hawaiian Rutaceae. The genus *Pelea*, endemic to the Hawaiian Is. and the Marquesas, is closely related to *Evodia* (*Euodia*), one species of which is shown for comparison. For each species of *Evodia* and *Pelea*, a view toward the summit of the fruit and a view of a longitudinal section of a fruit are shown. There are most often two seeds per follicle in *Pelea*; because follicles are shown sectioned, only a single seed is visible. Habits of fruits and seeds are shown for two Hawaiian and one non-Hawaiian species of *Fagara* (perhaps better termed *Zanthoxylum* now). One or two follicles may develop in the Hawaiian species. Two species of the endemic Hawaiian genus *Platydesma*, which may be closely related to *Pelea*, are shown. Scale applies to all drawings.

size for the genus. *Pelea waialealae*, with very small seeds, might at first sight, if the principles suggested here were to apply, seem as though it should be a lowland species instead of a native of high bogs, as it is. Actually, the correlation of small seed size with the open bog habitat is understandable, because smaller seeds seemingly characterize the bog plants of the Hawaiian Islands, whereas seeds of forest plants are much larger. This suggests that one factor operative in increase in fruit and seed size in *Pelea* has been adaptation to the large-seeded forest-tree habit; precinctiveness may also play a role. A feature that appears to accompany increase in fruit size in *Pelea* is the tendency for seeds not to be exserted, as they are in *Evodia samoensis* (fig. 11.13). The funiculus that in *Evodia* aids in display of seeds is present in *Pelea* but does not have that function. Mature fruits in *Pelea* exhibit loculicidal dehiscence of follicles, followed by shattering of the valves and fall of seeds. Increase in seed size can be seen progressively by the species of *Pelea* illustrated in figure 11.13, terminating with *P. pseudoanisata.*

In the genus *Fagara*, a wide range of fruit and seed sizes is visible, as suggested in figure 11.13. The seed size shown for *F. oahuensis* represents a minimal size for Hawaiian Fagaras, as well as one that characterizes all Hawaiian species except *F. dipetala*. The same as for *F. oahuensis* can be seen in seeds of *F. pinnata* (Tonga), *F. megistophylla* (Fiji), and *F. gillespieana* (Fiji). The seed size in the Hawaiian *F. dipetala* ($20 \times 14 \times 12$ mm) is remarkable, and represents a definitive lessening of dispersibility. Contrasingly minute fruits and seeds are shown for the Japanese species *F. ailanthoides* (fig. 11.13).

Within *Platydesma*, a marked increase in fruit and seed size may be seen by comparing *P. cornuta* and *P. remyi* (fig. 11.13). A feature in *Platydesma* which is of interest in connection with loss of dispersibility was observed by Rock (1913) for *P. campanulatum* (= *P. spathulatum*): "The capsule often rots away but the seeds remain attached to the placenta for some time."

Santalaceae. The Hawaiian species of *Santalum* form a good series with respect to size of drupes. At maturity, drupes in *Santalum* are reddish or purplish. The majority of the Hawaiian sandalwoods have drupes 8–12 mm in diameter, a size which, together with the nature of the fruit, makes dispersal by frugivorous birds likely. Species of *Santalum* elsewhere, such as *S. album*, also have drupes in this size range. Rather small drupes occur in *S. ellipticum* var. *littorale* (6–7 mm long) and *S. cuneatum* (8 mm in diameter); both of these are lowland Hawaiian plants, growing on the coastal plain. Notably large-fruited is *S. pyrularium*—characteristic of dry but upland forests of Kauai. In *S. pyrularium*, drupes attain 23 mm in length, and ca. 15 mm in width. The endocarp measures about $15 \times 10 \times 10$ mm. This large size suggests that dispersal by birds might be more difficult.

Sapindaceae. Of all examples of gigantism in fruits in the Hawaiian flora, perhaps none is so dramatic as *Alectryon*. This genus of about 30 species ranges from Australia, New Zealand, New Guinea and the Philippines through Melanesia; in Polynesia, it is represented in Samoa and the Hawaiian Islands. Most species have relatively small fruits, as repre-

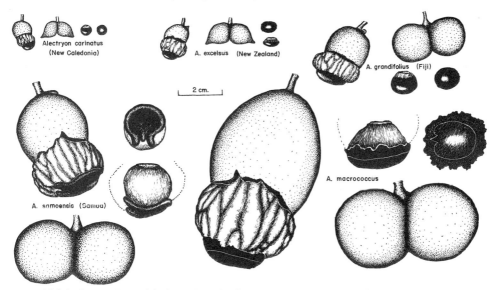

FIG. 11.14. Comparison of fruits and seeds of non-Hawaiian species of *Alectryon* (Sapindaceae) with those of the Hawaiian A. *macrococcus*. One or both cocci of the fruits may develop in all species. At maturity cocci are broken open by the expanding red aril, at the tip of which the seed is borne. For each species, an opened monococcate and an unopened bicoccate fruit are shown; also two views of each seed: one lateral view (chalazal end of seed above) and one polar view (surface opposite chalazal end). Dotted lines around lateral views of seeds of A. *samoensis* and A. *macrococcus* indicate outline of aril. Scale applies to all drawings.

sented in figure 11.14 by A. *carinatus* and A. *excelsus*. Cocci of A. *carinatus* measure 10 mm in diameter if borne singly; if borne in pairs, each coccus is ca. 8 mm long, 6 mm wide. In A. *excelsus* single cocci are 12 mm in diameter, paired cocci 10 mm each. As the drawings of various species of *Alectryon* show, mature cocci open so as to expose the fleshy red aril surrounding the black seed (see photograph of the Australian species A. *subcinereum*, fig. 2.4, top left). The relatively small seed size of these smaller-seeded Alectryons, together with the contrast with the red aril, suggests ease in distribution by frugivorous birds. The seeds in the two species mentioned are only 5–6 in diameter, and would be easily swallowed by a bird seeking the arils. If so, the remainder of the species shown in figure 11–14 may be said to form a series in loss of dispersibility. *Alectryon grandifolius* of Fiji has single cocci 22 mm in diameter, paired cocci 18 mm each. The seed measures about $12 \times 10 \times 8$ mm, and thus by itself would be as large as the smallest drupe (including fleshy exocarp) that one would expect birds ordinarily to have carried over long distances. *Alectryon samo-*

479

ensis is well beyond this size range. Single cocci measure ca. 35 mm in diameter, and paired cocci about 30 × 28 mm each. The seeds are about 22 × 20 × 20 mm. The Hawaiian species of *Alectryon* represent the logical conclusion of this trend toward gigantism. *Alectryon macrococcus* and a closely related segregate species, A. *mahoe*, have fruits somewhat variable in size but of enormous proportions. In these species, cocci borne singly may reach 60 mm in diameter. When borne in pairs, each coccus is ca. 34 × 40 mm. Seeds in these species can easily be 32 × 30 × 20 mm. Dispersal of such seeds by frugivorous birds—especially those of the Hawaiian Islands—is unthinkable. Seeds of this size would tend to drop within a short range of the parent plant, so that a high degree of precinctiveness is likely. Tendency to reproduce within the moderately dry mid-altitude forests where this tree is native may explain the gigantism. The value of a large amount of storage tissue within seeds does not seem preeminent in the relatively open forests where the Hawaiian Alectryons live, although it may be a factor. One can postulate that the immigrant ancestors of the Hawaiian Alectryons had fruit and seed sizes comparable to those of A. *excelsus*. Gigantism in the Fijian and Samoan Alectryons has probably been achieved parallel to that of the Hawaiian species.

Sapindus oahuensis is also notable for relatively large fruits and seeds. In this species, only one of the two potential drupelets per flower ordinarily matures. Each drupelet when fresh measures ca. 33 × 24 × 20 mm. The seed measures ca. 21 × 12 × 10 mm. The fleshy exocarp, which has a datelike odor and texture when drying, suggests that the ancestors of S. *oahuensis* were sought by frugivorous birds. There are also species with large fruits elsewhere in the Pacific, such as S. *mukorossi*, which occurs in the Bonin Islands. The wide-ranging S. *saponaria*, however, has fruits 15–18 mm in diameter, with most seeds less than 10 mm in length. Such a species—or one with even smaller fruits—likely was ancestral to S. *oahuensis*. Neither fruits nor seeds of *Sapindus* are known to be capable of flotation.

According to Guppy (1906), Hawaiian species of *Dodonaea* vary in the ability of their seeds to float. This suggests ecological shift toward inland sites by a typically lowland or littoral genus.

Sapotaceae. The genus *Planchonella* (*Sideroxylon* of earlier authors) is represented in the Hawaiian Islands by a single highly polymorphic species, *P. sandwicensis*. Segregate species were recognized by Rock (1913). There are distinctive populations within *P. sandwicensis*, some notable for distinctive fruit shapes and sizes. Some fruits of *P. sandwicensis* are only 2 cm in diameter at maturity, with seeds about $17 \times 6 \times 3$ mm. Others, as in the population recognized by Rock as *Sideroxylon rhynchospermum*, are 5.5 cm in length, 3.5 cm or more in width, and contain seeds $35 \times 14 \times 3$ mm. Thus, within the Hawaiian Planchonellas there may be tendencies toward fruit and seed gigantism. The smaller fruit and seed sizes mentioned are about the same as those of species of *Planchonella* on other Pacific islands, such as *P. costata* ($=$ *P. vitiensis*) of Fiji, *P. garberi* of Samoa, and *P. novozelandica* of New Zealand. The sizes of fruits in these species seem excessive for overwater dispersal by frugivorous birds. Although fruits can be viscid, the seeds are exceptionally smooth and would not adhere easily to birds. However, tests on flotation prove that dried fruits of *Planchonella* float almost indefinitely, perhaps because the papery endocarp with which each seed is surrounded contains a generous air space. Individual seeds also will float, at least for several days. Because *Planchonella* is a component of lowland forests, one might suspect that at least some species are distributed by oceanic drift. Also, the occurrence of the same subspecies (according to Lam's determination) on Fiji and on Rurutu in the Austral Islands is suggestive of oceanic drift.

There are a number of Sapotaceae in the New Caledonian flora with notably large fruits and seeds. One can suspect autochthonous gigantism in at least some of these.

Strasburgeriaceae. The affinities of the monotypic genus *Strasburgeria*, sole genus of the family and a New Caledonia endemic, are not clear. However, these massive fleshy fruits, which contain fibrous endocarps (for illustrations, see Carlquist, 1965), have no evident dispersal mechanism and in all likelihood constitute an instance of loss of dispersibility.

Winteraceae. I earlier cited *Zygogynum*, a New Caledonia endemic, as an example of loss of dispersibility and illustrated the fruit (1965). *Zygogynum* seems an outstanding example of this phenomenon. I suspect that further analysis of the New Caledonian flora would reveal a number of other instances of loss of dispersibility.

Monocotyledons

Arecaceae (Palmae). *Pritchardia* is a palm that ranges from Fiji to the Hawaiian Islands and that may be regarded as an extension of *Livistona* of Asia and Indo-Malesia. The westernmost species, *P. pacifica* and *P. thurstonii* of Fiji, have the smallest fruits, 12 and 7 mm in diameter, respectively. The Hawaiian Pritchardias were split into a large number of species by Beccari and Rock (1921); only a fraction of these are likely to be recognized by most workers. The polymorphic nature of *Pritchardia* in the Hawaiian Islands is evident, however. Most of the Hawaiian species recognized by Beccari and Rock have fruits that vary from 20 to 30 cm in diameter. Ten of the species they recognize have fruits that exceed 40 cm in diameter. Of these, some have quite gigantic seeds (6×4 cm in *P. lowreyana*; 5×3 cm in *P. rockii*; 5.5×4 cm in *P. montis-kea*). Beccari and Rock (1921) note the irony in the fact that large-fruited species such as these tend to occur in pockets high in wet rain forest, situations to which access by such cumbersome fruits seems unlikely. Dried fruits, however, have a relatively low specific gravity and might be transported short distances by violent winds. To explain the development of such large fruits in Hawaiian Pritchardias, Beccari and Rock invoke the concept of precinctiveness, which seems quite acceptable. Regarding the possible mode of introduction of *Pritchardia* to the Hawaiian Islands, one could say that the relatively small size of fruits in the Fijian *P. thurstonii* would suggest edibility and therefore transport by frugivorous birds. However, there is also a distinct possibility of oceanic drift. My tests of fruits of *P. martii* (summit of Castle Trail, Oahu) showed that fresh fruits sink immediately when placed in water. However, these same fruits, if allowed to dry for several days and then placed in water, are capable of floating indefinitely (in my tests, 2 weeks, at which time the experiment was terminated). The occurrence of *Pritchardia* on such a low and dry island as Nihoa, in the Hawaiian Leeward chain, as well as on low small islands in southeastern Polynesia, suggests the possibility of seawater dispersal, at least on rare occasions. The Nihoa species, *P. remota* (also once apparently on Laysan Island), is relatively small fruited ($18–20 \times 17–19$ mm). The large-fruited species from the major Hawaiian islands are all characteristic of rain forest. Thus, a correlation between fruit size and ecology can be said to exist in *Pritchardia*.

Liliaceae. Exact systematic affinities are difficult to establish for the Hawaiian Dracaenas, of which two species, *Pleomele aurea* and *P. fernaldii*, have been recognized. *Pleomele*, an endemic genus, is a segregate of *Dracaena*, and some authors prefer to retain the Hawaiian species under *Dracaena*. With regard to species of *Dracaena* elsewhere in the world, in most species the fruits are 5–9 mm in diameter and contain several seeds, each 3–5 mm long. Such fruits might have been ancestral to the Hawaiian Dracaenas. Such fruits would be edible by birds; most *Dracaena* fruits have a reddish fleshy exocarp. Fruits of Dracaenas are not known to float. *Pleomele fernaldii* has fruits 10–12 mm long, 5–10 mm in diameter if one carpel develops, 10–17 mm in diameter if two or three carpels develop. Seeds are about 4–8 mm in diameter. In *P. aurea*, fruit and seed size vary somewhat, but fruits are usually 14–25 mm in diameter, with seeds 9–18 mm in diameter when fresh. *Pleomele aurea* is a tree that ranges from dry lowland lava areas to well into higher portions of dry (*Acacia-Metrosideros*) forest. Relatively large fruits can be seen on trees in the latter region. *Pleomele* exhibits probable gigantism of fruits and seeds.

Geography of Loss of Dispersibility

The Hawaiian Islands have predominated in the examples cited, for reasons outlined in the introductory section of this chapter: all of the probable reasons for loss of dispersibility are fulfilled in Hawaiian conditions. A number of examples from the Juan Fernandez Islands (independent instances in Asteraceae) and Samoa (*Diospyros*, *Elaeocarpus*, *Alectryon*) suggest that these islands, with wet forest and moderate area, may show loss of dispersibility chiefly because of ecological shift into the wet forest. There is a scattering of examples throughout southeastern Polynesia, all of which could be said to involve ecological shift into wetter areas from dry coastal forest. A few examples can be cited from Fiji, several prominent instances occur on New Caledonia, and a very few on New Zealand. These islands are more nearly harmonic than the Hawaiian

Islands, so there has been less opportunity for ecological shift into forest areas, which are more nearly "saturated."

Again, attention should be called to the role of loss of dispersibility on continental areas. Although large-seeded trees of wet forests, especially in the tropics, represent this phenomenon, one can find it elsewhere as well. In particular, I would like to mention the work of Wilson (1970), who showed some examples of degrees and types of dispersibility, as well as drastic loss of dispersibility (*Abronia alpina*) in Nyctaginaceae of western North America.

References

Beccari, O., and J. F. Rock. 1921. A monographic study of the genus *Pritchardia*. *Mem. Bishop Mus.* 7(1):1–77.

Brown, E. D. W., and F. B. H. Brown. 1931. Flora of southeastern Polynesia. II. Pteridophytes. *Bishop Mus. Bull.* 89:1–123.

Brown, F. B. H. 1935. Flora of southeastern Polynesia. III. Dicotyledons. *Bishop Mus. Bull.* 130:1–386.

Carlquist, S. 1957. The genus *Fitchia* (Compositae). *Univ. Calif. Publ. Bot.* 29:1–144.

Carlquist, S. 1959. Studies on Madiinae: Anatomy, cytology, and evolutionary relationships. *Aliso* 4:171–236.

Carlquist, S. 1962. *Trematolobelia*: Seed dispersal; anatomy of fruits and seeds. *Pacific Sci.* 16:126–34.

Carlquist, S. 1965. *Island life.* New York, Natural History Press.

Carlquist, S. 1966a. The biota of long-distance dispersal. II. Loss of dispersibility in Pacific Compositae. *Evolution* 20:433–55.

Carlquist, S. 1966b. The biota of long-distance dispersal. III. Loss of dispersibility in the Hawaiian flora. *Brittonia* 18:310–35.

Carlquist, S., and M. L. Grant. 1963. Studies in *Fitchia* (Compositae): Novelties from the Society Islands; anatomical studies. *Pacific Sci.* 17:282–98.

Christophersen, E. 1935. Flowering plants of Samoa. *Bishop Mus. Bull.* 128:1–221.

Darlington, P. J., Jr. 1943. Carabidae of mountains and islands: Data on the evolution of isolated faunas, and on atrophy of wings. *Ecol. Monogr.* 13:37–61.

Fosberg, F. R. 1948. Derivation of the flora of the Hawaiian Islands. In *Insects of Hawaii*, vol. 1: *Introduction*, E. C. Zimmerman, pp. 107–19. Honolulu, University of Hawaii Press.

Guppy, H. B. 1906. *Observations of a naturalist in the Pacific 1896–1899*, vol. 2: *Plant dispersal.* London, Macmillan & Co.

Harling, G. 1962. On some Compositae endemic to the Galápagos Islands. *Acta Horti Bergiani* 20:63–120.

Hillebrand, W. 1888. *Flora of the Hawaiian Islands.* London, Williams & Norgate.

Hoffmann, O. 1890–1893. Compositae. In *Die natürlichen Pflanzenfamilien*, ed. A. Engler and K. Prantl, 4(5):87–402. Leipzig, Verlag Wilhelm Engelmann.

Howell, J. T. 1941. The genus *Scalesia*. *Proc. Calif. Acad. Sci.*, 4th ser. 22:221–71.

Lloyd, R. M., and E. J. Klekowski, Jr. 1970. Spore germination and viability in Pteridophyta: Evolutionary significance of chlorophyllous spores. *Biotropica* 2(2):129–37.

Papy, H. R. 1954–1955. Tahiti et les îles voisines. La végétation des îles de la Société et de Makatea. *Trav. Lab. Forest. Toulouse* 5(2:1):1–386.

Perkins, R. C. L. 1913. *Fauna Hawaiiensis: Introduction.* Cambridge, Cambridge University Press.

Ridley, H. N. 1930. *The dispersal of plants throughout the world.* London, L. Reeve & Co.

Rock, J. F. 1913. *The indigenous trees of the Hawaiian Islands.* Honolulu, privately published.

Sauer, J. 1964. Revision of *Canavalia*. *Brittonia* 16:106–81.

Schumann, K. 1895. Apocynaceae. In *Die natürlichen Pflanzenfamilien*, ed. A. Engler and K. Prantl, 4(2):109–306. Leipzig, Verlag Wilhelm Engelmann.

Selling, O. 1944. A new species of *Schizaea* from Melanesia and some connected problems. *Svensk Bot. Tidskr.* 38:207–21.

Selling, O. 1946. Studies in Hawaiian pollen statistics. Part I. The spores of the Hawaiian pteridophytes. *Bishop Mus. Spec. Publ.* 37:1–87.

Sherff, E. E. 1935a. Revision of *Haplostachys, Phyllostegia* and *Stenogyne. Bishop Mus. Bull.* 136:1–101.

Sherff, E. E. 1935b. Revision of *Tetramolopium, Lipochaeta, Dubautia* and *Railliardia. Bishop Mus. Bull.* 135:1–136.

Sherff, E. E. 1937a. Some Compositae of southeastern Polynesia (*Bidens, Coreopsis, Cosmos,* and *Oparanthus*). *Occas. Papers Bishop Mus.* 12(19):1–19.

Sherff, E. E. 1937b. The genus *Bidens*. Part I. *Field Mus. Natur. Hist. Publ.*, Bot. ser. 16:1–346.

Sherff, E. E. 1937c. Revision of the Hawaiian species of *Euphorbia* L. *Ann. Missouri Bot. Gard.* 25:1–75.

Sherff, E. E. 1942. Revision of the Hawaiian members of the genus *Pittosporum* Banks. *Field Mus. Nat. Hist. Publ.*, Bot. ser. 22:467–566.

Sherff, E. E. 1944. Some additions to our knowledge of the flora of the Hawaiian Islands. *Amer. Jour. Bot.* 31:151–61.

Sherff, E. E. 1955. Revision of the Hawaiian members of the genus *Tetraplasandra* A. Gray. *Fieldiana, Bot.* 29:47–142.

Skottsberg, C. 1922. The phanerogams of the Juan Fernandez Islands. *Natur. Hist. Juan Fernandez Easter I.* 2:95–240.

Skottsberg, C. 1937. Die Flora der Desventuradas-Inseln. *Acta Horti Gotoburg.* 5(6):1–88.

Skottsberg, C. 1938. On Mr. C. Bock's collection of plants from Masatierra (Juan Fernandez), with remarks on the flowers of *Centaurodendron. Acta Horti Gotoburg.* 12:361–73.

Skottsberg, C. 1947. Eine kleine Pflanzensammlung von San Ambrosio (Islas Desventuradas, Chile). *Acta Horti Gotoburg.* 17:49–57.

Skottsberg, C. 1951. A supplement to the pteridophytes and phanerogams of Juan Fernandez and Easter I. *Natur. Hist. Juan Fernandez Easter I.* 2:763–92.

Skottsberg, C. 1953. The vegetation of the Juan Fernandez Islands. *Natur. Hist. Juan Fernandez Easter I.* 2:793–960.

Skottsberg, C. 1954. A geographical sketch of the Juan Fernandez Islands. *Natur. Hist. Juan Fernandez Easter I.* 1:89–192.

Skottsberg, C. 1958. Über *Yunquea tenzii* Skottsb. *Ber. Deutsch. Bot. Ges.* 71:45–52.

Skottsberg, C. 1963. Zur Naturgeschichte der Insel San Ambrosio (Islas Desventuradas, Chile). 2. Blütenpflanzen. *Ark. Bot.*, ser. 2, 4:465–88.

Sohmer, S. H. 1972. Evolutionary trends in the genus *Charpentiera* (Amaranthaceae). *Brittonia* 24:283–312.

Stebbins, G. L., Jr. 1953. A new classification of the tribe Cichorieae, family Compositae. *Madroño* 12:33–64.

Stephens, S. G. 1958. Salt water tolerance of seeds of *Gossypium* species as a possible factor in seed dispersal. *Amer. Natur.* 92:83–92.

Stephens, S. G. 1963. Polynesian cottons. *Ann. Missouri Bot. Gard.* 50:1–22.

Stephens, S. G. 1964. Native Hawaiian cotton (*Gossypium tomentosum* Nutt.). *Pacific Sci.* 18:385–98.

Stephens, S. G. 1966. The potentiality for long range oceanic dispersal of cotton seeds. *Amer. Natur.* 100:199–210.

Stewart, A. 1911. A botanical survey of the Galápagos Islands. *Proc. Calif. Acad. Sci.*, 4th ser., 1:7–288.

Sykes, W. R., and E. J. Godley. 1968. Transoceanic dispersal in *Sophora* and other genera. *Nature* 218:495–96.

Wilson, E. O. 1959. Adaptive shift and dispersal in a tropical ant fauna. *Evolution* 13:122–44.

Wilson, R. C. 1970. Anthocarp dispersal in *Abronia* and its ecological implications. Ph.D. thesis, Claremont Graduate School, Claremont, Calif.

Zimmerman, E. C. 1948. *Insects of Hawaii.* vol. 1: *Introduction.* Honolulu, University of Hawaii Press.

CHAPTER TWELVE

LOSS OF DISPERSIBILITY
IN ISLAND ANIMALS

The most obvious loss of dispersibility in insular animals is the loss of flying ability in insects and birds whose ancestors were capable of flight when they immigrated to islands. Before proceeding with that conspicuous phenomenon, I would like to discuss some more subtle ways in which dispersibility can be lost in insular animals.

As an example of a "nonflying" animal that is nonetheless definitely capable of aerial dispersal, one may cite a remarkable range of dispersal abilities among spiders. In the genus *Pardosa*, Richter (1970) has rated populations of the species according to the percentages of individuals which, on the basis of their behavioral characteristics, are "potential aeronauts." These percentages range from a low of 0.05 percent in *P. lugubris* to a high of 65.00 percent in *P. palustris*. Richter finds a close correlation between low dispersal ability and preference for stable habitats. However, when he rated habitats as to their abundance or rarity, he found high dispersibility correlated with "rare" habitats. These findings are eminently acceptable on the basis that species of far-flung habitats of limited extent—like beach plants among angiosperms—have high dispersal capacity, and that these same habitats also tend to be unstable. Thereby, a selective advantage for high dispersibility is characteristic for species inhabiting unstable, dispersed habitats of limited extent. Such species would make good immigrants to islands—indeed they can be regarded as living on a series of ecological islands within continents. If such a species should migrate to an oceanic island and adapt to stable conditions (as are characteristic of most islands in prehuman times), one would expect a loss of dispersibility. Available habitat is then "abundant" in a sense—the new island population is a solitary population, not one of many populations among which interchange can take place. This principle applies to high islands—atoll plants and animals remain vagile and form populations among which interchange occurs.

In carabid beetles, both Lindroth (1945–1949) and Boer (1970) believe that "species living in unstable habitats invest extensively in dispersal" (quoted from Richter, 1970), a concept in effect advanced somewhat earlier by Southwood (1962). The inverse seems obvious: the more stable the habitat, the less the pressure for dispersibility. Darlington (1943) stated this, in essence, when he said, "The principal function of flight is found to be to maintain sparse, unstable populations in large, unstable areas. In small, stable areas, where populations are dense and stable, flight presumably loses this function, permitting existence of flightless . . . Carabidae, especially geophiles."

These considerations also apply to various other animal groups. On the Hawaiian Islands, Perkins (1913) noted the remarkable tendency of *Achatinella* (Gastropoda) colonies to reside in a single tree over a period of months. Clarke and Murray (1969), noting that the *Partula* species of Moorea tend to remain isolated (although hybridization does occur), cited geographical barriers within the island but believed that other factors must be responsible for maintaining integrity of the species of these land shells. If *Partula* resembles *Achatinella* in its precinctiveness, lack of mobility may well provide the mechanism that could explain maintenance of species. Indeed, in *Achatinella* the numerous species, each restricted to a very few valleys, must have been produced and maintained by both geographical isolation and precinctiveness.

Dispersibility of plants and animals is subject to evolutionary modification. Once a population (other than that of a repetitively introduced beach species or the like) has been established on an oceanic island, the factors that favor precinctiveness are many, the factors that favor increased dispersibility are few and exceptional. Different groups and different islands will not provide identical pressures for precinctiveness. In extremely windy and cold subantarctic islands, precinctiveness will be favored for reasons different from those operative in deep forest of tropical islands. As Darlington stated (1943), "Whether or not flight is useful, and whether or not wings atrophy, depends on a balance of factors very much more complex than Darwin guessed." I will attempt to assess which factors may be favored in which situations. Nevertheless, it appears to me that precinctiveness does operate in insular plants and animals and that we must consider flightlessness only one manifestation of it. It is entirely possible for an insect species capable of flight to be highly precinctive also, but there are only a few observations at present that note this (see, however, some examples below from subantarctic islands).

In the discussion that follows, continental areas are considered peripherally, and flightlessness is also briefly considered in chapter 14 in a discussion of the equatorial alpine biota. As Darlington (1943) compellingly showed for carabid beetles, flightlessness can be definitely characteristic of certain continental areas. Likewise, loss of dispersibility in plants is far from an exclusively insular phenomenon, as suggested in the preceding chapter. The majority of instances, in fact, occur on continents.

Flightless Birds

In my account of flightless birds on islands (1965, pp. 224–41), a listing of flightless birds and references to them (pp. 416–18) are given, together with illustrations and brief descriptions. Because most of these (other than the large continental ratites and the penguins) are endangered or extinct, the account of Greenway (1958), the I.U.C.N. Red Data Book (vol. 2, Aves), and the literature they cite are the most complete sources of material. Attention is called to De Beer's (1956) account on the evolution of the ratites. To my 1965 listing I can add that the Ascension Island rail (listed as "*Crecopsis* sp." in the I.U.C.N. Red Data Book) is now known from complete skeletal material (Olson, 1971), and can be added to the list of now-vanished insular Rallidae of the world. My mention of the flightless duck or teal might be amended to indicate that two subspecies are now recognized, *Anas aucklandica aucklandica* on the Auckland Islands and *A. a. nesiotis* on Campbell Island. Personal observations during my 1966 visit to Laysan Island show that the Laysan teal can, in fact, be frightened into flight rather easily, but the birds merely fly to another portion of the lagoon. Geographically, they can still be said to be quite sedentary.

In reviewing my (1965) account of flightless birds, I find that several features become apparent. First, no truly arboreal birds or bird groups are in the list, with the exception of the flightless parrot (*Strigops habroptilus*) and the flightless wren (*Xenicus lyallii*), both of New Zealand—and these flightless representatives are, of course, terrestrial in their habits. The relatively abundant time available in New Zealand, as well as the absence of mammals, is undoubtedly a factor in the evolution of so many flightless birds there. The Mascarene dodos and solitaires are of obscure ancestry, but may well stem from nonarboreal birds.

To find that flightless birds are derived from groups that are ground-feeders is no surprise. We must make an exception, at first glance, for flightless waterbirds: the penguins, the giant auk (*Pinguinus impennis*), the Galápagos flightless cormorant (*Phalacrorax harrisii*), and the flightless grebe of Lake Titicaca, *Rollandia micropterum* (= *Centropelma micropterum*). These are all analogous to ground-feeding birds, however, in that swimming (together with underwater diving) is all that is required, not flight. With these exceptions, flightless birds are descended from terrestrial-feeding bird groups, and these habits are merely maintained and heightened on islands. Another feature common to the flightless insular birds (other than the waterbirds mentioned) is their virtually omnivorous feeding habit. This is particularly true of rails. In view of the limited size of the islands on which many of the rails exist or once existed, broad food tolerances are necessary for survival of viable populations. Another feature Rallidae exemplifies is the tendency to fly not so much in long migratory patterns, but merely from one suitable feeding area to another. On islands, this would predispose them not to use flight as a tactic to any appreciable degree. During feeding per se in such terrestrial birds as rails, flight does not play a role, as it would for a frugivorous bird or nectarivorous bird. Flight does occur in Rallidae as an evasive mechanism where predation occurs.

The preadaptation of Rallidae to dispersal to islands, survival on islands, and evolution into flightlessness there becomes obvious from the preceding. Because they are somewhat migratory in their feeding habits and not territory-bound as passerine birds typically are, Rallidae are likely to occur as stragglers to islands, more so, one would expect, than passerine birds. On islands, they will survive because of their broad food tolerances. Their feeding at ground level or in shallow water continues. Flight to new feeding grounds is impossible because of oceanic distance. If an island can support a rail population at all (and evidently small islands can), the food supply can be exploited without resort to flight. The only further requisite for evolution into flightlessness is then the absence of predators. Even flight for evasive purposes may not be necessary. The flightless Tasmanian native hen (*Tribonyx mortieri*, of Rallidae) can run at speeds up to 30 mph, faster than can the Rallidae of Tasmania that are still capable of flight (Sharland, 1958). One cannot stress too strongly that of all natural methods of locomotion, flight is the most highly expensive of energy; therefore, in any condition under which flight is not a necessity for a volant organism, there will be a positive selective pressure for flightlessness.

The continental ratites (emus, ostriches) substitute rapidity of running for flight as an evasive mechanism. They are also able to use feet, legs, and beak defensively; the cassowary, in addition, can use its horned crest. Penguins, subject to predation by porpoises, use "underwater flight" as a means of escape. Survival of flightless birds has either depended on lack of predation or, where predation occurs, has involved compensatory evolution of evasive mechanisms other than flight. Although one tends to think of flightlessness as a retrogressive tendency, it can also be considered a new and even efficient adaptive mode that is possible under certain circumstances. One can cite exploitation of habitats in the fashion of large herbivores (dodos, moas, ratites) as features of efficient ground locomotion made possible by "release" from wing formation and maintenance.

Flightless Insects

Darlington (1943) views flightlessness in carabid beetles as an inevitable trend wherever flight is not of high selective value in order to maintain large, sparse, unstable populations over large, unstable areas. The smallness of occupiable area and the stability of the environment are, in his considerations, of prime importance. Going farther, Darlington cites an instance in weevils where flightless individuals may, in fact, show better viability than winged individuals within a single species (Jackson, 1928), and tends to regard flightless insects as having "inherent superiority" due to "simplicity and vitality." One might wish for some physiological measures to demonstrate actual types of advantage in reduced-wing insects, other than the obvious one that an economy is involved if wings and even hapteres are lost. Spencer (1932) did show that vestigial-winged *Drosophila* mutants survived better under conditions of food and water deprivation than normal-winged populations. However, Lindroth (1945–1949), with the aid of some experimental work, contradicts the idea that flightlessness improves viability. Brinck (1948) would seem to agree with Darlington, for he states that "on oceanic islands, where the conditions occasionally become very unfavorable, a vestigial [flightless] type might even oust the normal." However, Brinck's discussion obviously favors the selective effect of wind pressure as operative in producing a high proportion of flightless insects on Tristan da Cunha. Darlington does not believe wind pressure is a factor in evolution of flightless insects, but the subantarctic insects may be an exception (see below). Tristan da Cunha has some of the aspects of a subantarctic island.

Perkins (1913) subscribed to the "disuse" theory to explain flightlessness in Hawaiian insects. Interestingly, a high proportion of *arboreal* Coleoptera are flightless in the Hawaiian Islands. Among instances Darlington cites where flight *is* useful in carabids are hydrophiles or arboreal species; species in areas likely to be flooded; species on low tropical islands; and species on dry lowlands of tropical islands. Small, low, tropical islands (e.g., coral platforms like the Cayman Islands) are, as Darlington notes, often recent, with no endemism. However, applying the considerations of MacArthur and Wilson (1963), one can say that extinction rate is high on a small, low island, so that influx of new stocks by a constant stream of immigrants is required to maintain a given number of species. In the case of carabids, fully winged, widespread, tropical species would presumably be the immigrants to such islands. If repetitive and continual immigration to a small low island occurs, even without extinction, new immigrants with wings would doubtless swamp out any winglessness, assuming (as seems likely) that brachyptery and aptery are the results of recessive genes.

492

Darlington (1943) would explain lack of flightless carabids in tropical lowlands (insular and otherwise) by the fact that these dry areas, poorer in food resources, fall under the category of the "large and unstable areas" he designates as correlated with selective advantage for flying forms.

Darlington discounts altogether the possibility that wind pressure may exercise a selective force leading to flightlessness. His data on montane carabids demonstrate, in his opinion, no appreciable difference in flying versus flightless in exposed or protected situations, respectively. Wind pressure was claimed by Darwin to make flightlessness advantageous in insular insects, in that excessive numbers would be blown out to sea (on mountains, wind pressure would presumably blow insects to ecologically unsuitable locations according to the Darwinian reasoning, although Darwin did not comment on flightlessness in montane situations). An alternative explanation would be that where wind pressure is excessive, wings are disadvantageous because wind would tend to hinder flight during feeding. Darlington (1943) analyzed data for carabids of the Presidential Range, New Hampshire. His results show that when hydrophiles, non-resident, and arboreal species are excluded, 70 percent of the forest geophiles and 64 percent of the exposed-area geophiles above 3000-ft elevation are flightless. This he attributes to the geophilous habit and the concentrated area of suitable habitat—the latter related to the concept of precinctiveness that I have cited earlier. Flightless Carabidae for New Hampshire as a whole amount to 13 percent, so there is, without doubt, a much higher percentage in montane carabids in Darlington's data. Greenslade (1968) finds similar data in Argyll, Scotland, although the percentages are much less striking than in Darlington's data—and the number of species of carabids involved is relatively small also.

Whether wind pressure is a factor in winglessness has not been resolved, to judge from the literature. Downes (1962) noted reduction of mating flight in insects of far northern Canada. The experiments of L'Heritier, Neefs, and Teissier (1937) with brachypterous and normal-winged *Drosophila* races in culture dishes open to wind showed that normal-winged flies tended to be blown away, while the flightless flies had a low rate of attrition. This experiment, however, may well not be definitive in demonstrating the effect of wind.

SUBANTARCTIC ISLAND INSECTS

Either insects of subantarctic islands add data to illuminate the question of wind pressure in relation to flightlessness, or else they form a special case. Gressitt (1970) says that Darlington's hypotheses "do not apply" to the subantarctic islands, and he also finds the models of MacArthur and Wilson (1963) inapplicable. Cold makes flying much more difficult for insects, and the subantarctic islands are exceptionally cold— cool even during the summer. This, together with the added "burden" of wind pressure, may prove a definitive selective pressure for flightlessness and eventually aptery (see the last portion of chapter 14 for a discussion of these points).

In any case, subantarctic and Antarctic insects have been the subject of intense study during the past decade. For references to biological work of all kinds on the "true" subantarctic islands, Gressitt's (1970) summary is invaluable. Somewhat more northern islands of the far south are summarized by Gressitt (1962, 1964), and Gressitt, Leech, and Wise (1963) have provided a summary for Antarctic entomology. Attention should be called to monographic papers, not cited here, which accompany Gressitt's papers (1962, 1964, 1970).

The comments of Gressitt (1962, 1964) and the rich base of data on which he operates are of especial significance to Antarctic entomology. In particular, the effect of climate—presumably strong winds and cold—is examined. Gressitt's data (1964, 1970) show the following degrees of flightlessness for insect faunas of subantarctic islands:

	Total number of species	Percentage flightless		Total number of species	Percentage flightless
Campbell I.	183	40	Kerguélen	26	85
Crozet Is.	36	89	South Georgia	16	75
Marion I.	18	89	Heard I.	9	100
Macquarie I.	20	55			

On Antarctica itself, only a single insect capable of flight is known (out of 20 land arthropods, mostly insects): a chironomid midge, *Parochlus steineni* (Gressitt, 1970). Gressitt's data are subdivided further than my table shows; he indicates various degrees of wing reduction from moderate to complete. The strong degree of flightlessness is evident. In addition, the degree of nonflying behavior in insects capable of flight is manifest in his observations. He cites, on Campbell I. (Gressitt, 1964), many species known to fly but never taken in trapping experiments. These include pyralid moths, geometrid moths, and an ichneumon wasp. The smaller wasp *Campoplex disjunctus* was, however, taken in nets. Gressitt states, "These species which were not trapped are weaker fliers than some of the types commonly caught in the nets, like calliphorid flies, muscids, and others, yet are stronger fliers than some which were taken abundantly in the nets, like the aphids, psychodids, sciarids, and others." According to Gressitt and Weber (1959), wingless or partially winged subantarctic insects as a whole may be termed "active," whereas winged species are "sluggish." The highly sedentary aspect of the far-southern insect fauna is strongly evident.

Lepidoptera are particularly interesting in respect to flightlessness. Lepidoptera, with few exceptions, have evolved flightlessness only on the subantarctic islands (Enderlein, 1909; Viette, 1948, 1952a, 1952b, 1954, 1959). This, together with the tendency for strong-flying insects not to fly during periods of high wind, suggests that extreme wind pressure may indeed be a factor in the evolution of the subantarctic fauna. The most important feature may not even be that an excessive number would be carried out to sea (although lack of flightless forms in nets would seem to offer support for this), but that there might be interference with locomotion by wind pressure on wings or that there would be loss of heat through wings during conditions of low temperatures.

Three Campbell Island flightless moths are shown here: *Tinearupa sorenseni* of the Hyponomeutidae (fig. 12.1); *Campbellana attenuata*, also of Hyponomeutidae (fig. 12.2); and *Exsilaracha graminea* of the Pyralidae (fig. 12.3). *Exsilaracha* is nearly twice as large as the others, and has a pronounced jumping habit that substitutes for flying (Munroe, 1964). *Exsilaracha* lives exclusively in grass tussocks, and its hopping habits resemble those of grasshoppers, according to Salmon and Bradley (1956). *Tinearupa* (fig. 12.1) is found on coastal rocks, where its coloring and markings form a perfect camouflage, according to these authors. Sorensen (quoted in Salmon and Bradley [1956]) finds that *Campbellana* is a tussock insect, also with grasshopperlike habits. Strong development of legs is

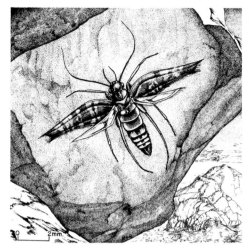

FIG. 12.1. *Tinearupa sorenseni,* a flightless moth from Campbell I.

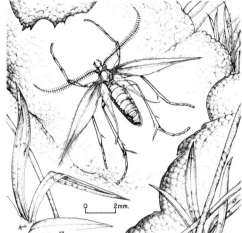

FIG. 12.2. *Campbellana attenuata,* a flightless moth from Campbell I.

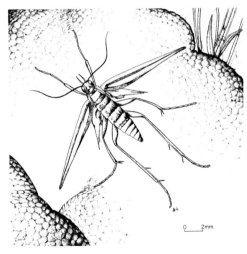

FIG. 12.3. *Exsilaracha graminea,* a flightless moth from Campbell I.

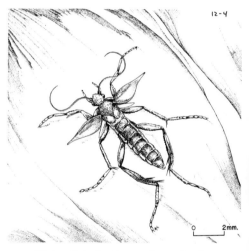

FIG. 12.4. *Pringleophaga kerguelensis,* a flightless moth from Kerguélen I. It is shown on a leaf of *Pringlea antiscorbutica,* the "Kerguélen cabbage."

evident in both *Exsilaracha* (fig. 12.3) and *Campbellana* (fig. 12.2). The abundance of flightless moths on Campbell Island may be related to the closeness to New Zealand, which could have served as an efficient source area for entry of moths into these southerly islands. Relative absence of moths from remote Macquarie Island is cited by Gressitt (1970) as a reason why the proportion of flightless insects is lower there than one might expect on the basis of the extreme climate.

A curious feature of the Campbell Island moths is their tendency to sham death or seek refuge in tussocks or crevices despite the seeming lack of predatory birds—the pipit is the only insectivorous bird on Campbell Island (Gressitt, 1964).

One notable flightless moth on a remote subantarctic island is *Pringleophaga kerguelensis* on Kerguélen (fig. 12.4). As its generic name suggests, this insect's host plant is the curious Kerguélen "cabbage," *Pringlea antiscorbutica*. Comparison of many flightless moths of sub-antarctic islands shows remarkable similarity in that the wings are reduced by narrowing, although shortening is obviously involved as well. Extreme wing reduction is shown in the moth *Dimorphinoctua cunhaensis* of Tristan da Cunha (Viette, 1952a) and *Brachyapteragrotis patricei* of Amsterdam Island (for illustrations, see Carlquist, 1965).

A tendency noted by various authors is that in subantarctic moths the males have somewhat less wing reduction than females. For comparisons, see Viette (1948), Salmon and Bradley (1956) and Carlquist (1965, p. 222). This is also true in the one Hawaiian moth with flightless tendencies, *Hodegia apatela*. One is tempted to speculate that the males are more "expendable" than the females. Wind pressure alone might be a selective agent, but predation on males that are more conspicuous by virtue of longer wings might also be evoked. Field investigation of this dimorphism would, of course, be difficult yet very valuable.

In subantarctic Diptera, there is great variation in wing development, even within a single species. On Macquarie Island, the entire endemic species *Schoenophilus pedestris* (fig. 12.5) is flightless, yet some individuals have longer wings than others; there is no evident correlation with habits or habitats (Gressitt, 1964). *Schoenophilus pedestris* moves by hopping and tends to occur in tussock plants, such as *Colobanthus* (Kohn, 1962). Kohn compares *Schoenophilus* to a Hawaiian member of the same family, Dolichopodidae, in its wing reduction. A dolichopodid of Campbell Island, *Acropsilus borboroides*, has the ultimate in wing reduction: lack of wings and even halteres (Oldroyd, 1955).

Apataenus watsoni (Coelopidae) is another dipteran from Macquarie Island (fig. 12.6). It tends to be found under stones, particularly those

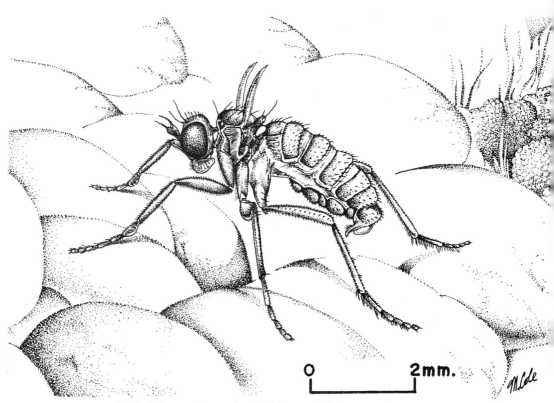

FIG. 12.5. *Schoenophilus pedestris* (Diptera: Dolichopodidae), from Macquarie I.

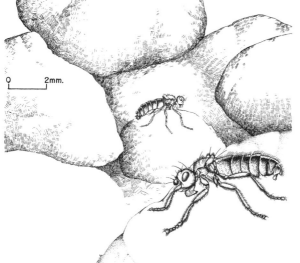

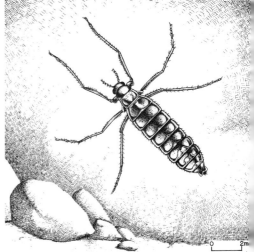

FIG. 12.6. *Apataenus watsoni* (Diptera: Coelopidae), from Macquarie I.

FIG. 12.7. *Belgica antarctica* (Diptera: Chironomidae), a flightless midge from the Antarctic mainland.

498

of bird rookeries (Hardy, 1962). Its wings may be up to half as long as the thorax. Extreme wing reduction is found in a midge from the Antarctic continent, *Belgica antarctica* of the Chironomidae (fig. 12.7). It occurs in penguin rookeries and can even be found on the penguins themselves (Gressitt, Leech, and Wise, 1963).

With respect to flightless Diptera of subantarctic islands, Seguy (1940) claimed several structural trends: robust pharynx, long malpighian tubules, reduced gastric coeca, short hind intestine, abundant adipose tissue; tough pupaia; adults with heavily sclerotized mouthparts, atrophied notopleural callus, small thorax, and reduced wing and leg muscles. However, Gressitt (1964) found that on Campbell Island an increase in leg size and musculature occurred with reduction in wing size. This is certainly obvious in his figures of the dipteran *Baeopterus robustus* and *Icaridion nasutum* (both of Coelopidae). The latter has no wings or halteres.

Kleidotoma subantarctica of the Encoilidae (fig. 12.8) is the first record of a cynipid wasp from any subantarctic island (Yoshimoto, 1964). It shows an interesting series in wing reduction, and one individual with fully developed wings has even been collected. *Kleidotoma subantarctica* is an endemic of Campbell Island. It lives on algae-covered rocks, to judge from collection data, but its feeding habits are as yet unknown (Yoshimoto, 1964).

Hymenoptera are not abundant in flightless species in areas other than the subantarctic islands, but they clearly occur with frequency on the far-southern islands. Various hymenopteran families are represented. *Antipodencyrtus procellosus* of Campbell Island (fig. 12.9) is a representative of Encyrtidae. It is evidently a parasite on a soft-bodied coccid of tussock grass (Kerrich, 1964). Occurrence of a parasite under the difficult conditions for establishment on subantarctic islands is interesting. Another curious feature of *Antipodencyrtus* is the presence of very long antenna branches.

Aucklandella flavomaculata (fig. 12.10) is an ichneumonid wasp discovered during an early survey of the subantarctic islands of New Zealand (Chilton, 1909). It occurs in Carnley Harbor of Auckland Island and may have a habitat similar to that of *Kleidotoma subantarctica*. There is another flightless ichneumonid on Campbell Island, *Gelis campbellensis*. Other flightless subantarctic Hymenoptera include two diapriids, *Antarc-*

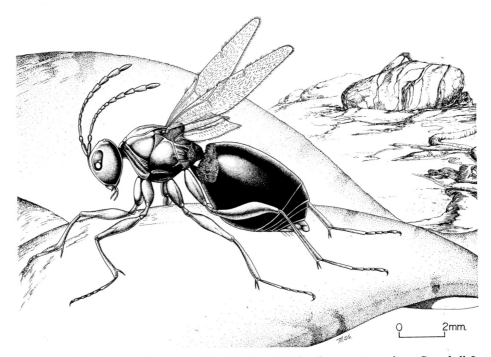

FIG. 12.8. *Kleidotoma subantarctica* (Eucolidae), a flightless hymenopteran from Campbell I.

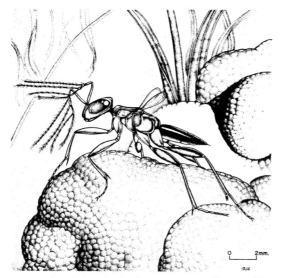

FIG. 12.9. *Antipodencyrtus procellosus* (Encyrtidae), a flightless hymenopteran of Campbell I.

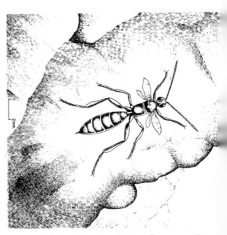

FIG. 12.10. *Aucklandella flavomaculata* (Ichneumonidae), a flightless hymenopteran from the Auckland Is.

500

topria latigaster of Macquarie Island, and a subspecies, A. *l. campbellana,* on Campbell Island (Gressitt, 1964).

Judging from insect groups that have flightless representatives in insular situations elsewhere in the world, one would not expect, a priori, that subantarctic islands would bear numerous flightless Lepidoptera, Hymenoptera, and Diptera, yet only a scattering of Coleoptera. Coleoptera are probably underrepresented because larger-bodied insects travel poorly over long distances and in cold wind currents—which also would account for the absence of Orthoptera and Neuroptera, and the paucity of Homoptera other than widespread aphids on the subantarctic islands. Interestingly, according to Beardsley (1964) the family Pseudococcidae of Homoptera is represented on subantarctic islands by several genera and species in which males are flightless and completely apterous (female wingless-ness would be expected in this family in any case).

An interesting feature of Coleoptera discussed by Brinck (1948) is the tendency for the ratio of carnivorous to phytophagous species to vary with habitat. Although the ratio is high in northern Europe, including some insular areas (7.53 in the Faeroe Is., 6.08 in the Shetland Is., 4.5 in Greenland, 3.05 in Norway), the proportion is lower farther south (1.17 on Corsica, 1.33 on Madeira, 2.14 on the Cape Verde Is.). However, subantarctic islands have an extraordinarily high number of phytophagous insects, so that the ratios are 0.17 on Tristan da Cunha and 0.12 on Kerguélen. The explanations for this are not at all clear, although Brinck (1948) offers a number of possibilities.

MADEIRAN AND OTHER ATLANTIC ISLAND INSECTS

Darwin, upon reading Wollaston's *Insecta Maderensia* (1854), was struck by the high proportion of flightless forms. As we have seen earlier, Darwin's explanation has seemingly been supplanted by Darlington's (1943) detailed and compelling considerations. However, assuming that precinctive populations and geophily are, as Darlington suggests, the most important factors in evolution of flightlessness of Coleoptera, it is interesting to review Wollaston's data to see how these factors operate on Madeira. Wollaston's work is of particular interest because he studied these species extensively in the field and dealt with their habits in great detail. Although Wollaston's monograph is outdated by subsequent faunistic

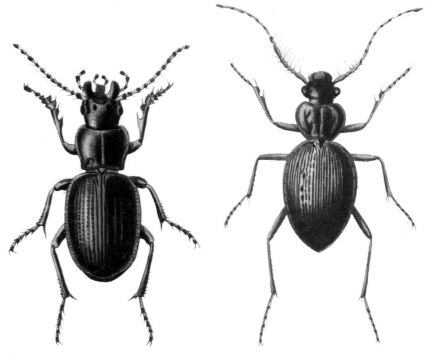

FIG. 12.11. *Eurygnathus latreillei,* male, a flightless carabid (Coleoptera) from Madeira (from Wollaston, 1854).

FIG. 12.12. *Loricera wollastoni,* a flightless carabid (Coleoptera) from Madeira (from Wollaston, 1854).

work, it can still be admired for its care to ecological detail. Indeed, such information would be perhaps impossible to secure today. For purposes of precise reference to Wollaston's volume, I am retaining his nomenclature.

Eurygnathus latreillei (fig. 12.11) is interesting to us for several reasons. Not only is this carabid beetle apterous, but its elytra are connate— or "soldered" as some have said—definitely canceling the power of flight. Its ancestors were, with little doubt, carabids capable of flight. In addition to this striking expression of flightlessness, *E. latreillei* exhibits different size tendencies in different localities. Although found beneath stones on the small islands of Porto Santo and on the Desertas (both offshore islet groups of Madeira), specimens on Deserta Grande are much larger than those on Porto Santo, according to Wollaston. This is also true of another carabid, *Olisthopus maderensis,* much larger on Deserta Grande than on Madeira itself. Wollaston erects a new genus, *Thalassophilus,* for a flight-

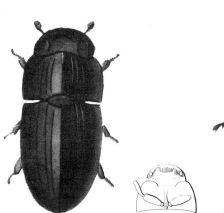

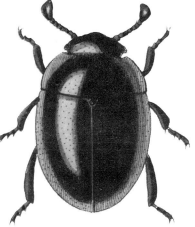

FIG. 12.13. *Cossyphodes wollastoni* (Colydia-dae), a flightless and eyeless coleopteran from Madeira (from Wollaston, 1854).

FIG. 12.14. *Cholovocera madaerae* (Coleoptera: Lathridiadae), a flightless beetle from Madeira (from Wollaston, 1854).

less reduced-wing carabid of gigantic size compared with its closest relative, *Aëpus*. *Bembidium obtusum*, a widespread species, attains a much greater size on Madeira than in Europe. Comments on gigantism on islands, which may be relevant to the preceding instances, will be found in chapter 15.

The carabid *Loricera wollastoni* (fig. 12.12) has vestigial wings but normal elytra. It lives chiefly under logs and leaves. Wollaston suggests that its peculiar antennae and long legs are virtually "supralimital" characteristics within the genus *Loricera*.

Another Madeiran carabid, *Harpalus vividus*, is wingless, with elytra connate to various degrees. Lowland and high-elevation populations have soldered elytra and are dull in color, whereas elytra are separate and body colors are brighter in mid-elevation populations.

Other families of Coleoptera on Madeira show flightlessness independently. *Tarphius* (Colydiadae) is an example, with reduced wings. Wollaston notes that *Tarphius* species are strictly nocturnal. Interestingly, Greenslade (1968) notes that nocturnalism and dark colors are much more common in Coleoptera with reduced wings, whereas diurnalism and brighter colors are commoner in normal-winged species. Another genus of Colydiadae, *Cossyphodes* (fig. 12.13), a Madeiran endemic, is interesting not merely in its winglessness and exceptional shape, but in its loss of eyes. It feeds in nests of an ant, *Oecopthora pusilla*. Although the legs of *Cossyphodes wollastoni* are apparently small in relation to body size and it is blind, it runs with exceptional velocity. Another endemic colydiad genus, *Pleiosoma*, is also wingless and occurs "in the very center of moist decaying wood."

In the family Lathridiadae, *Cholovocera maderae* (fig. 12.14) is notable in its vestigial wings. Although not blind, its eyes are much reduced, with many fewer facets than are characteristic for beetles. It is not surprising, therefore, that it, like *Cossyphodes*, is predatory in nests of ants. Reduced eyes of this type occur in an endemic Madeiran species of another ant-predaceous genus, *Metophthalmus*, which has European species as well.

In Ciidae, the Madeiran endemic species *Cis wollastoni* is exceptional for its genus by virtue of its large and elongated body. Among flightless curculionids, numerous Madeiran species could be cited, such as *Atlantis vespertinus* (fig. 12.15). Wollaston created this endemic genus for flightless species in which wings are absent and elytra firmly united. These features are also shared by another endemic curculionid genus that Wollaston named *Echinosoma*. *Echinosoma porcellus* (fig. 12.16) is exceptionally setose and has an unusual "robust" rounded form, yet it has delicate antennae. *Atlantis* lives beneath moss on trees and is strictly nocturnal. *Echinosoma* occurs beneath stones and logs.

LAKE BAIKAL INSECTS

Lake Baikal exhibits many insular features, as do other freshwater lakes (see chapter 9), so it is not surprising to find certain situations of flightlessness there among a family of aquatic caddis flies, Limnophilidae. In Lake Baikal, there are two endemic genera, *Baicalina* and *Thamastes*, while the only other genus of the tribe Baicalinini, *Radema*, lives in the Lena and other creeks that flow into Lake Baikal. Larvae of *Baicalina* and *Thamastes* live on the rocky bottom of the littoral of Lake Baikal, *Radema* larvae occur underwater in streams. As the water rises in spring and summer in Lake Baikal, adults formed from larvae occur at a distance from the newly expanded shoreline, toward which they swim in droves. Wings and legs of the three endemic caddis-fly genera are modified for swimming (Martynov, 1929, 1935). The wings are not capable of flight but are used

FIG. 12.15. *Atlantis vespertinus* (Coleoptera: Curculionidae), a flightless weevil from Madeira (from Wollaston, 1854).

FIG. 12.16. *Echinosoma porcellus* (Coleoptera: Curculionidae), a flightless weevil from Madeira (from Wollaston, 1854).

as "paddles." Kozhov (1963) attributes the wingless habit to the limited habitat available. He states that fully winged insects with a typical caddisfly life cycle would be bound to be driven far from the shore and could not have offspring. This is reminiscent of the Darwinian interpretation of the effect of wind pressure on insular insects. Certainly, at least precinctiveness and a limited stable habitat are involved. Lake Baikal is unusual in its low temperature, and larvae of the endemic limnophilid genera are adapted to this and might not survive under other temperature regimes.

NEW ZEALAND INSECTS

Among the many interesting flightless insects of the mainland islands of New Zealand, the wetas (Orthoptera) have received abundant comment because of their flightlessness, hopping habits, and adaptive radiation in wet recesses in caverns and forest situations (see chapter 7). Among hopping Orthoptera, the wetas are also unusual in their capability to regenerate appendages of near-normal size (Ramsay, 1964). Is this ability related to their total reliance on legs for locomotion, or does the relative longevity of the wetas (two years or longer) play a role? This is one of the many intriguing questions possibly related to loss of flight on insular areas.

References

Beardley, J. W. 1964. Insects of Campbell Island. Homoptera: Coccoidea. *Pacific Insects Monogr.* 7:238–52.

Boer, P. J. den. 1970. On the significance of dispersal power for populations of carabid-beetles (Coleoptera, Carabidae). *Oecologia* 4:1–28.

Brinck, P. 1948. Coleoptera of Tristan da Cunha. *Results Norwegian Sci. Exped. Tristan da Cunha 1937–1938* 17:1–120.

Carlquist, S. 1965. *Island life.* New York, Natural History Press.

Chilton, C., ed. 1909. *The subantarctic islands of New Zealand.* 2 vols. Wellington, John Mackay, Government Printer.

Clarke, B., and J. Murray. 1969. Ecological genetics and speciation in land snails of the genus *Partula. Biol. Jour. Linnaean Soc.* 1:31–42. (Also as *Speciation in Tropical Environments,* ed. R. H. Lowe-McConnell. London, Academic Press.)

Darlington, P. J., Jr. 1943. Carabidae of mountains and islands: Data on the evolution of isolated faunas, and on atrophy of wings. *Ecol. Monogr.* 13:37–61.

De Beer, G. R. 1956. The evolution of the ratites. *Bull. Brit. Mus. (Natur. Hist.) Zool.* 4(2):1–63.

Downes, J. A. 1962. What is an Arctic insect? *Can. Entomol.* 94(2):143–62.

Enderlein, G. 1909. Die Insektfauna der Insel St. Paul. Die Insektfauna der Insel Neu Amsterdam. *Deutsch. Südpolar-Exped., Zool.* 2(4):481–92.

Greenslade, P. J. M. 1968. Habitat and altitude distribution of Carabidae (Coleoptera) in Argyll, Scotland. *Trans. Roy. Entomol. Soc. London* 120(2):39–54.

Greenway, J. C., Jr. 1958. *Extinct and vanishing birds of the world.* New York, American Committee for International Wild Life Protection.

Gressitt, J. L. 1962. Insects of Macquarie Island. Introduction. *Pacific Insects* 4:905–15.

Gressitt, J. L. 1964. Insects of Campbell Island. Summary. *Pacific Insects Monogr.* 7:531–600.

Gressitt, J. L. 1970. Subantarctic entomology and biogeography. *Pacific Insects Monogr.* 23:295–374.

Gressitt, J. L., R. E. Leech, and K. A. J. Wise. 1963. Entomological investigations in Antarctica. *Pacific Insects* 5:287–304.

Gressitt, J. L., and N. A. Weber. 1959. Bibliographic introduction to Antarctic-subantarctic entomology. *Pacific Insects* 1:441–80.

Hardy, D. E. 1962. Insects of Macquarie Island. Diptera: Coelopidae. *Pacific Insects* 4:963–71.

L'Héritier, P., Y. Neefs, and G. Teissier. 1937. Aptérisme des insectes et sélection naturelle. *Compt. Rend. Acad. Sci. Paris* 204:907–9.

Jackson, D. J. 1928. The inheritance of long and short wings in the weevil, *Sitonia hispidula*, with a discussion of wing reduction among beetles. *Trans. Roy. Soc. Edinburgh* 55:665–735.

Kerrich, G. J. 1964. Insects of Macquarie Island. Hymenoptera: Encyrtidae. *Pacific Insects Monogr.* 7:504–6.

Kohn, M. A. 1962. Insects of Macquarie Island. Diptera: Dolichopodidae. *Pacific Insects* 4:959–62.

Kozhov, M. 1963. *Lake Baikal and its life.* The Hague, Dr. W. Junk, Publishers.

Lindroth, C. H. 1945, 1946, 1949. Die Fennoskandischen Carabidae, eine tiergeographische Studie. *Medd. Göteborgs Mus. Zool. Avd.* 109:1–707, 110:1–277, 122:1–911.

MacArthur, R. H., and E. O. Wilson. 1963. An equilibrium theory of insular biogeography. *Evolution* 17:373–87.

Martynov, A. 1929. Ecological prerequisites for the zoogeography of freshwater benthonic animals. *Russk. Zool. Zh.* 9(3):3–38.

Martynov, A. 1935. The caddis-flies of the Amur region. *Tr. Zool. Inst. Akad. Nauk. S.S.S.R.* 2(2–3):205–395 (in Russian).

Munroe, E. 1964. Insects of Campbell Island. Lepidoptera: Pyralidae. *Pacific Insects Monogr.* 7:260–71.

Oldroyd, H. 1955. A wingless dolichopodid (Diptera) from Campbell Island. *Rec. Dominion Mus. Wellington* 2(4):243–46.

Olson, S. L. 1971. A flightless bird, lost and found. *Smithsonian* 2(3):63–65.

Perkins, R. C. L. 1913. *Fauna Hawaiiensis: Introduction.* Cambridge, Cambridge University Press.

Ramsay, G. W. 1964. Regeneration of appendages in some New Zealand wetas (Insecta: Orthoptera). *Trans. Roy. Soc. New Zealand, Zool.* 4(6):139–44.

Richter, C. J. J. 1970. Aerial dispersal in relation to habitat in eight wolf spider species (*Pardosa*, Araneae, Lycosidae). *Oecologia* 5:200–214.

Salmon, J. T., and J. D. Bradley. 1956. Lepidoptera from the Cape Expedition and Antipodes Islands. *Rec. Dominion Mus. Wellington* 3(1):61–81.

Seguy, E. 1940. Diptères. *Mém. Mus. Nat. Hist. Natur. Paris, ser. A., Zool.* 14:203–67.

Sharland, M. 1958. *Tasmanian birds,* 3d ed. Sydney, Angus and Robertson.

Southwood, T. R. E. 1962. Migration of terrestrial arthropods in relation to habitat. *Biol. Rev.* 37:171–214.

Spencer, W. P. 1932. The vermillion mutant of *Drosophila hydei* breeding in nature. *Amer. Natur.* 66:474–79.

Viette, P. 1948. Croisière du Bougainville aux îles australes Françaises. 20. Lepidoptera. *Mém. Mus. Nat. Hist. Natur. Paris, ser. A., Zool.* 27:1–28.

Viette, P. 1952a. Lepidoptera. *Results Norwegian Sci. Exped. Tristan da Cunha 1937–1938* 23:1–19.

Viette, P. 1952b. Lepidoptera. *Sci. Results Norwegian Antarctic Exped.* 33:1–4.

Viette, P. 1954. Une nouvelle espèce de Lépidoptère de l'île Campbell. *Entomol. Medd.* 27:19–22.

Viette, P. 1959. Lépidoptères de l'île d'Amsterdam (récoltés de Patrice Paulian, 1955–1956). *Bull. Entomol. Soc. France* 64:22–29.

Wollaston, T. V. 1854. *Insecta Maderensia.* London, John Van Voorst.

Yoshimoto, C. M. 1964. Insects of Campbell Island. Hymenoptera: Cynipoidea: Eucolinae. *Pacific Insects Monogr.* 7:509–12.

CHAPTER THIRTEEN

REPRODUCTIVE BIOLOGY

ON ISLANDS

As yet we know little about modes of reproductive biology on islands. One can cite the fact that field observations are required to establish data in this general topic, and that prolonged stays on many insular areas are, unfortunately, difficult. In other instances, no such reasons exist, and one can only note the absence of qualified investigators who are willing to study these very important "natural history" aspects on insular areas where research institutions are present. Characteristic modes of speciation, hybridization, floral biology, pollination relationships, shift in seasonal phenomena of reproduction, and changes in fertility and longevity of individuals are among the neglected phenomena. I take pleasure in citing results obtained thus far, but concede that these studies are as yet inadequate in number and scope, and invite other workers to enter this interesting field.

The data and commentary that follow are presented to suggest the significance of such phenomena as the high degree of dioecism in insular plants, polymorphism in insular species, and seemingly low rates of reproduction in island plants and animals. These suggestions have been organized so as to place them into the context of what may be called the "insular syndrome" of interrelated evolutionary phenomena. Analysis of single phenomena on islands has not always led to sound or thoroughgoing interpretations. Floral morphology, breeding systems, ecological preferences, growth forms, dispersal mechanisms, fertility, and other features of insular

NOTE: Portions of this chapter are revised segments of a paper (Carlquist, 1966). I wish to express appreciation to *Evolution* for permission to use this material.

groups are closely linked together. When considered conjunctively, these features appear more comprehensible.

Reproductive Biology in Plants

The emphasis in this chapter is the presentation of data from the Hawaiian Islands (modified from Carlquist, 1966) and citation of information on other insular areas where data are available—particularly New Zealand and the Galápagos Islands. The New Zealand flora is a waif flora in post-Mesozoic time, and probably earlier as well (Darlington, 1965). Thus, the New Zealand flora may be considered almost entirely a waif flora, differing from that of the Hawaiian Islands in its greater age and the climatic conditions to which plants have adapted.

Long-distance dispersal to an island is a drastic event in the history of a species. In virtually all groups that establish by means other than oceanic drift, genetic contact with the parent population is irretrievably broken. The subsequent evolution of such a stock may be regarded as involving compensation for this broken contact. To the extent to which the species has evolutionary plasticity, is endowed with favorable characteristics for maintenance on a relatively small land area, and manages to maximize outcrossing, it may be able to perpetuate a lineage of descendents into a relatively long career. With the variability of mainland relatives no longer accessible, the variability that remains or can be developed within an island population must, for best success, be circulated throughout the entire population. Dioecism, monoecism, and various other diclinous floral conditions tend to ensure the occurrence of this process. Self-sterility is of prime importance, and wind pollination can be regarded as a mechanism broadening the degree of, and geographical extent of, outcrossing. To a lesser extent, dichogamy (protandry and protogyny) and even showiness of flowers may aid in increasing the level of outcrossing. These various phenomena may be expected to reach a high pitch on oceanic islands. Such conditions do not exist independently of other factors, however. As suggested by Grant (1958), for example, poor seed dispersal would limit the amount of recombination which would occur. The topographical diversity within an island, the effectiveness of interisland isolation, and the size of land areas suitable for a particular species are other dimensions that would influence the genetic diversity likely to be contained within a species.

The floral condition and the genetic nature of each immigrant species will dictate which species are best suited for long-term success in an island situation, and what changes will maximize this occupancy. Dioecious species may seem disadvantaged by the requirement that two propagules rather than one establish when a species colonizes. In the Hawaiian flora, some arrivals seem clearly to have been dioecious prior to arrival, whereas others very likely evolved the dioecious condition on the Islands. In addition to diclinous conditions, other pathways for maintenance of genetic interchange within a phylad are open. Genetic barriers among island species, especially those which have resulted from adaptive radiation of a single immigrant, will be expected to be virtually absent. Reasons for this absence include the tendency of oceanic island floras to emphasize perennials, especially woody species. Such growth forms are favored in the moderate climate of many islands, and woody species characteristically develop few interspecific sterility barriers (Baker, 1959). Also, geographic isolation seems to predominate over sterility barriers as the main mechanism of isolation among species in genera on islands (observation and experimental evidence are cited below). Moreover, genetic barriers would be deleterious, for they would subdivide a stock into portions having less heterozygosity (and thus less genetic momentum for long-term survival in isolation) than the whole. Other factors that tend to maintain integrity of insular species include distinctive ecological adaptations, lessened dispersibility (precinctiveness), flower constancy of pollinators, and a tendency toward a high level of autogamy. Where one factor predominates, another may be lacking. Loss of dispersibility occurs prominently on oceanic islands (chapter 11). A dioecious species will harbor a high level of outcrossing. An alternative scheme, however, would be a group of interfertile species, capable of outcrossing, which reproduce mostly by autogamy. Hybrid swarms will form occasionally in such species. Lack of genetic barriers and other factors will tend to produce varied and fertile recombinants. Hybrid types can stabilize and persist. With good dispersibility in such a species group, hybrids may be disseminated to form new colonies—as may the parental types. The unit within which genetic interchange occurs in such a case is not the species, but the entirety of a genus as represented on an archipelago. The vehicle for genetic interchange is not mere outcrossing, but successive events of hybridization. In addition to the two examples given—dioecious specics and hybrid complexes—innumerable compromises in genetic and floral systems may be imagined, but all systems that succeed over long periods of time will contain means for effective outcrossing.

Rattenbury (1962) has stressed the value of hybridization as a means of retaining genetic vigor in the restrictive environments of the Pleistocene in New Zealand. The small land areas available during that period may have been significant in raising the selective value of hybridization and outcrossing. However, either a very large portion or all of the New Zealand flora was established via long-distance dispersal (Davis, 1950; Darlington, 1965). Therefore, New Zealand plants may, in fact, be compensating for loss of genetic contact with mainland relatives by a high degree of outcrossing (of which hybridization is a heightened form) within the island populations. If continental populations are larger than insular ones, only a small proportion of individuals need to participate in outcrossing to maintain a relatively high level of heterozygosity. If, on the other hand, island populations are smaller, a greater proportion of individuals must be involved in outcrossing if a similar level of heterozygosity is to be maintained. The mechanisms described in this chapter may be considered ways of ensuring interbreeding among as many individuals as possible within a population.

Hawaiian ferns form hybrids, but with relative infrequency (W. H. Wagner, Jr., personal communication, 1965). Although morphological change has been great in Hawaiian ferns, genetic systems may have changed little. Interspecific barriers characteristic of continental ferns may have been retained. This situation would be expected because relatively little autochthonous speciation has taken place among the native Hawaiian ferns. According to Wagner (in Fosberg, 1948), the number of probable immigrants (135) is only slightly smaller than the number of contemporary species plus varieties (168). This contrasts with angiosperms, where about 250 immigrants have given rise to between 1400 and 2000 species plus varieties native to the Hawaiian Islands (data from Fosberg, 1948). Ferns established easily in the Hawaiian flora, and the comparatively large number of immigrant groups may have inhibited the adaptive radiation of each stock. In the Hawaiian angiosperm flora, the relative paucity of successful immigrants coupled with great ecological opportunity has resulted in abundant radiation. The products of such radiation are interfertile species that are "ripe" for events of hybridization. As Ratten-bury (1962) claims for the New Zealand flora, these "species" could be regarded as subspecies. Taxonomy should take into account the fact that insular species may differ modally in genetic nature from continental species.

Hybridization may be expected to contribute to the high degree of polymorphism among the waif floras. This tendency has been noted not only for the Hawaiian flora, but also for those of the Galápagos Islands and New Zealand. Polymorphism may be a product of diversification within a species, but many cases seem derived from events of hybridization. Polymorphic species may be hybrid complexes in which segregation into distinctive populations has not taken place.

Most oceanic islands capable of supporting rich floras (Hawaiian Islands, Canary Islands) enjoy a relatively uniform maritime climate. That tends to prolong flowering times over a large portion of the year (see Skottsberg, 1928). Thus, outcrossing within species and hybridization among species are encouraged.

Autogamous species are definitely not barred from establishment on islands. Baker (1955) has justifiably claimed that such species may be favored for establishment in insular situations. The evolutionary careers of autogamous species may be expected to be short on islands, however, unless occasional outcrossing can occur, as mentioned earlier, or occasional reintroduction of the species from source areas can occur, bringing in new genetic material. The second possibility would be satisfied by species which arrive via oceanic drift. Littoral species in the Hawaiian flora and other insular floras are, in fact, mostly suited for autogamy. Autogamy is a condition characteristic of species of pioneer habitats, which open up and alter rapidly. Occasional reintroduction of a species would compensate for the genetic depauperation that would inevitably occur in the island situation. Reintroduction would also tend to swamp any ecological shift of a beach species and would inhibit radiation in the original population. These factors would tend to keep a beach species confined to the shore zone. Species brought by oceanic drift could change if reintroduction did not occur, or occurred only after ecological change to the forest had been accomplished; this curriculum can be expected in only a few groups. In the Hawaiian flora, endemic Fabaceae and Malvaceae seem to be good examples (see chapters 2 and 11 for explanation and description of inland shift of the drift flora).

Many species may retain flexibility in ability for exogamy and autogamy. Species that are autogamous or nearly so may establish; they may then maximize exogamy under appropriate circumstances. The partly or wholly exogamous flora will be semipermanent, provided that land area is sufficient to foster genetic variability over long periods. Special cases may be presented on particular island groups. The Faeroes suggest one such case; there autogamy permits reproduction in species that otherwise might be deprived of pollinators on account of extreme climatic conditions (Hagerup, 1951). In this case, repopulation of islands by subsequent immigrants of a native species could retain a species in the flora.

Because floral morphology is an essential part of the framework within which genetic recombination occurs, it becomes a significant matter in the preceding considerations. Anemophilous species have no pollination problem that would deter their establishment on islands. For this reason, they might be expected to bulk large in the floras of oceanic islands. Entomophilous species can establish most easily if their floral structure lends itself to access by a variety of pollinating agents. Absence of long-tongued bees on islands disfavors many angiosperms with larger and more colorful flowers (other than ornithophilous species). Simultaneous establishment of an ornithophilous flowering plant and its accustomed bird pollinator is unlikely, so most ornithophilous plants on islands would be expected to have very versatile floral forms (e.g., *Metrosideros*) or else to have evolved autochthonously on islands. Interestingly, Williams (1927) has shown that *Metrosideros* is often visited by the bee *Nesoprosopis*, showing that an ornithophilous flower can indeed be versatile. Linsey (1966), citing the work of Perkins (1906, 1913) and Williams (1927), also suggests another important pollination factor: any given pollinating insect may visit only a few species of flowering plants (oligolecty) on a mainland area, but broadens its range of angiosperm species visited on insular areas.

Basic to an understanding of genetic systems on islands is a sound knowledge of floral conditions and floral biology in an insular flora. The definitive flora for this purpose is that of the Hawaiian Islands. The Galápagos flora, where self-sterility was not encountered during tests (Rick, 1966), may be more recent and not show insular tendencies as well, or may be inhibited from speciation and radiation because of the dryness of the archipelago.

The listing of families and their floral characteristics given below is offered as a basis for discussion. For this purpose, the listing of genera and species given by Fosberg (1948) has basically been followed. The numbers of species and varieties given here are somewhat more conservative than Fosberg's figures. Information on sexual conditions is not entirely reliable, and field and herbarium studies were required to reassess their interpretations. Both Hillebrand (1888) and Skottsberg (1936a, 1936b, 1944a, 1944b, 1945) were keen observers of floral conditions in Hawaiian angiosperms, and their descriptions proved good starting points for this survey.

Recent information has been incorporated, making changes from my (1966) paper necessary. Sohmer's (1972) work on *Charpentiera* (Amaranthaceae) has shown that that genus is functionally dioecious and is therefore not truly gynodioecious. George W. Gillett (personal communication, 1971) has called my attention to the fact that ray flowers in Hawaiian species of *Bidens* (Asteraceae) are sterile, not female, so my earlier listing of this genus as gynomonoecious has been changed. However, Gillett has shown in his experimental work that at least three Hawaiian species of *Bidens* (e.g., *B. skottsbergii*) are, in fact, dioecious.

In the list that follows, data are given within parentheses after each genus name. The first figure is the estimated number of species plus varieties. This figure is, of course, an entirely tentative estimate. However, the percentages in table 13.1 would probably not be altered very much by different estimates of species numbers. Introduced species were not included in the list. Sexual conditions and other information are given within the parentheses according to the scheme of abbreviations below. Capital letters indicate that the condition designated characterizes the entire genus, lower case is used where only a portion of the genus has the condition. Designations are tentative and oversimplified in some cases (e.g., not all

Poaceae may be fully anemophilous). Additional instances of protandry and protogyny doubtless occur. More significant, many genera and species have not been tested with respect to self-sterility.

The last figure within the parentheses is a rating for degree of potential outcrossing ability according to the scale of values listed. Because knowledge is incomplete, the ratings must be considered minimal in some cases. Some combinations of characters tend to reinforce each other to promote outcrossing. However, the characters have not been treated additively in designation of the ratings; the feature with the highest numerical value is the one expressed as a rating for each genus.

Rating   Characteristics and abbreviations

5   Dioecism (D); functional dioecism: sterile pollen on some plants, sterile ovules on others (FD); self-sterility (SS)

4   Anemophily (W); water-pollination (WA)

3   Monoecism (M); polygamodioecism (PD); gynodioecism (GD); andromonoecism: male + bisexual flowers (AM); gynomonoecism: female + bisexual flowers (GM); polygamomonoecism: male + female + bisexual flowers (PM)

2   Dichogamy: protogyny (PG) or protandry (PA); spatial separation of anthers and style so that flower tends to be nonselfing (NS)

1   Flowers showy (S)

0   Tendency to occupy pioneer habitats (P)

MONOCOTYLEDONS: Arecaceae: *Pritchardia* (2, S, 1). Cyperaceae: *Baumea* (1, W, 4); *Carex* (9, W, PA, 4); *Cladium* (1, W, 4); *Cyperus* (23, W, 4); *Eleocharis* (1, W, 4); *Fimbristylis* (2, W, 4); *Gahnia* (6, W, 4); *Oreobolus* (1, W, 4); *Rhynchospora* (3, W, 4); *Scirpus* (5, W, 4); *Scleria* (1, W, M, PA, 4); *Uncinia* (1, W, M, PA, 4); *Vincentia* (1, W, 4). Flagellariaceae: *Joinvillea* (1, W, 4). Hydrocharitaceae: *Halophila* (1, WA, P, 4). Iridaceae: *Sisyrinchium* (1, S, 1). Juncaceae: *Luzula* (3, W, 4). Liliaceae: *Astelia* (12, D, 5); *Dianella* (3, S, 1); *Pleomele* (2, S, 1); *Smilax* (2, D, 5). Naiadaceae: *Naias* (1, WA, M, 4). Orchidaceae: *Anoectochilus* (2, NS, S, 2); *Habenaria* (1, NS, 2); *Liparis* (1, NS, S, 2). Pandanaceae: *Freycinetia* (1, D, S, 5); *Pandanus* (1, D, S, P, 5). Poaceae: *Agrostis* (3, W, 4); *Andropogon* (1, W,

AM, 4); *Calamagrostis* (2, W, 4); *Cenchrus* (1, W, 4); *Deschampsia* (3, W, 4); *Digitaria* (1, W, 4); *Dissochondrus* (1, W, 4); *Eragrostis* (12, W, 4); *Festuca* (1, W, 4); *Garnotia* (1, W, 4); *Heteropogon* (1, W, AM, 4); *Isachne* (2, W, 4); *Ischaemum* (1, W, AM, 4); *Lepturus* (1, W, 4); *Microlaena* (1, W, 4); *Oplismenus* (1, W, 4); *Panicum* (23, W, AM, 4); *Paspalum* (2, W, 4); *Poa* (4, W, 4); *Sporobolus* (1, W, 2); *Trisetum* (2, W, 4). Potamogetonaceae: *Potamogeton* (2, PG, 2).

DICOTYLEDONS: Aizoaceae: *Sesuvium* (1, P, 0). Amaranthaceae: *Achyranthes* (2, W, P, 4); *Aerva* (1, W, P, 4); *Charpentiera* (7, W, FD, 5); *Nototrichium* (5, W, P, 4). Anacardiaceae: *Rhus* (1, PM, 3). Apiaceae: *Daucus* (1, AM, P, 3); *Hydrocotyle* (1, P, 0); *"Peucedanum"* (2, AM, P, 3); *Sanicula* (4, AM, 3); *Spermolepis* (1, P, 0). Apocynaceae: *Alyxia* (1, NS, 2); *Ochrosia* (1, NS, P, 2); *Pteralyxia* (2, NS, 2); *Rauwolfia* (7, NS, S, 2). Aquifoliaceae: *Ilex* (1, D, S, 5). Araliaceae: *Cheirodendron* (5, S, 1); *Reynoldsia* (1, S, 1); *Tetraplasandra* (10, S, 1). Asteraceae: *Adenostemma* (1, PA, 3); *Argyroxiphium* (6, PA, GM, S, 3); *Artemisia* (5, W, GM, p, 3); *Aster* (1, PA, GM, S, 3); *Bidens* (30, PA, d, S, p, 2); *Dubautia* (40, PA, S, 3); *Gnaphalium* (1, PA, GM, P, 3); *Hesperomannia* (6, PA, SS, S, 5); *Lagenophora* (3, PA, GM, 3); *Lipochaeta* (30, PA, GM, S, p, 3); *Remya* (2, PA, GM, 3); *Tetramolopium* (10, PA, GM, S, P, 3); *Wilkesia* (1, PS, S, 2). Begoniaceae: *Hillebrandia* (1, M, S, 3). Boraginaceae: *Heliotropium* (2, P, 0). Brassicaceae: *Lepidium* (4, P, 0). Campanulaceae: *Brighamia* (1, PA, S, P, 2); *Clermontia* (45, PA, S, 2); *Cyanea* (60, PA, S, 2); *Delissea* (10, PA, S, 2); *Lobelia* (8, PA, S, 2); *Rollandia* (10, PA, S, 2); *Trematolobelia* (5, PA, S, 2). Capparaceae: *Capparis* (1, S, P, 1). Caryophyllaceae: *Alsinodendron* (3, PA, 2); *Schiedea* (30, PA, gd, p, 2–4); *Silene* (4, P, 0). Celastraceae: *Perrottetia* (1, W? PD, 3). Chenopodiaceae: *Chenopodium* (1, W, P, 4). Convolvulaceae: *Breweria* (2, S, P, 1); *Cressa* (1, P, 0); *Cuscuta* (2, P, 0); *Ipomoea* (9, S, P, 1); *Jacquemontia* (1, P, 0). Cucurbitaceae: *Sicyos* (8, M, P, 3). Droseraceae: *Drosera* (1, S, 1). Ebenaceae: *Maba* (2, D, 5). Elaeocarpaceae: *Elaeocarpus* (1, SS? 5?). Epacridaceae: *Styphelia* (2, GD, 3). Ericaceae: *Vaccinium* (8, S, 1). Euphorbiaceae: *Antidesma* (6, W, D, 5); *Claoxylon* (2, W, m, d, 4–5); *Drypetes* (1, W, D, 5); *Euphorbia* (31, M, p, 3); *Phyllanthus* (2, W? M, 4?). Fabaceae: *Acacia* (3, AM, S, 3); *Caesalpinia* (1, S, P, 1); *Cassia* (1, P, 0); *Entada* (1, S, P, 1); *Erythrina* (1, S, P, 1); *Mezoneurum* (1, S, 1); *Mucuna* (2, S, P, 1); *Sesbania* (1, S, 1); *Sophora* (1,

S, P, 1); *Strongylodon* (2, S, 1); *Tephrosia* (1, P, 0); *Vicia* (1, S, 1); *Vigna* (3, S, P, 1). Flacourtiaceae: *Xylosma* (2, W? D, 5). Gentianaceae: *Centaurium* (1, S, P, 1). Geraniaceae: *Geranium* (6, S, 1). Gesneriaceae: *Cyrtandra* (130, PA, gd, s, 2–3). Goodeniaceae: *Scaevola* (5, NS, S, P, 2). Haloragaceae: *Gunnera* (9, W, FD? PA, 5?). Hydrophyllaceae: *Nama* (1, P, 1). Lamiaceae: *Haplostachys* (5, PA, S, P, 2); *Lepechinia* (1, PA, S, P, 2); *Phyllostegia* (55, PA, S, 2); *Plectranthus* (1, PA, S, P, 2); *Stenogyne* (30, PA, S, 2). Lauraceae: *Cassytha* (1, PG, 2); *Cryptocarya* (2, PG, 2). Loganiaceae: *Labordia* (40, D, S, 5). Loranthaceae (see Viscaceae). Malvaceae: *Abutilon* (3, PA, S, P, 2); *Gossypium* (1, PA, S, P, 2); *Hibiscadelphus* (4, PA, S, P, 2); *Hibiscus* (10, PA, S, p, 2); *Kokia* (4, PA, S, P, 2); *Sida* (2, PA, S, P, 2). Menispermaceae: *Cocculus* (2, D, 5). Moraceae: *Pseudomorus* (1, M, P, 3). Myrsinaceae: *Embelia* (2, PD, 3); *Myrsine* (25, D, 5). Myrtaceae: *Metrosideros* (12, S, 1); *Syzygium* (4, S, 1). Nyctaginaceae: *Boerhaavia* (1, P, 0); *Pisonia* (3, d, 5). Oleaceae: *Osmanthus* (1, NS, 2). Papaveraceae: *Argemone* (1, S, P, 1). Pittosporaceae: *Pittosporum* (50, D, 5). Plantaginaceae: *Plantago* (10, W, ss, PG, 4–5). Plumbaginaceae: *Plumbago* (1, S, P, 1). Polygonaceae: *Polygonum* (1, PA, 2); *Rumex* (2, PA, 2). Portulacaceae: *Portulaca* (6, P, 0). Primulaceae: *Lysimachia* (13, ns, S, 1–2). Ranunculaceae: *Ranunculus* (2, S, 1). Rhamnaceae: *Alphitonia* (1, AM, 3); *Colubrina* (2, P, 0); *Gouania* (4, PM? P, 3?). Rosaceae: *Acaena* (1, W, 4); *Fragaria* (1, PG, s, P, 2); *Osteomeles* (1, S, P, 1); *Rubus* (2, S, 1). Rubiaceae: *Bobea* (4, D, 5); *Canthium* (1, FD, 5); *Coprosma* (30, W, D, 5); *Gardenia* (2, S, 1); *Gouldia* (25, GD, 3); *Hedyotis* (*Kadua*) (50, D, 5); *Psychotria* (3, PA, 2); *Straussia* (8, D, 5). Rutaceae: *Pelea* (80, D, 5); *Platydesma* (6, ss, S, 5); *Zanthoxylum* (*Fagara*) (14, d, m, 3–5). Santalaceae: *Exocarpus* (3, W, PM, P, 4); *Santalum* (6, PG, FD, p, 5). Sapindaceae: *Alectryon* (2, FD, 5); *Dodonaea* (8, d, pd, P, 3–5); *Sapindus* (1, P, 0). Sapotaceae: *Nesoluma* (1, GD, P, 3); *Planchonella* (*Pouteria, Sideroxylon*) (1, PG, 2). Saxifragaceae: *Broussaisia* (2, GD or D, S, 5). Scrophulariaceae: *Bacopa* (1, P, 0). Solanaceae: *Lycium* (1, PG, P, 2); *Nothocestrum* (6, PG, 2); *Solanum* (7, PG, S, 2). Sterculiaceae: *Waltheria* (1, P, 0). Theaceae: *Eurya* (2, D, 5). Thymeleaceae: *Wikstroemia* (18, D or pd, 4–5). Ulmaceae: *Trema* (1, W, M, 4). Urticaceae: *Boehmeria* (1, W, M, 4); *Hesperocnide* (1, W, M, 4); *Neraudia* (9, W, D, 5); *Pilea* (1, W, M, 4); *Pipturus* (13, W, m or d, 4–5); *Touchardia* (5, W, D, 5); *Urera* (3, W, D, 5). Verbenaceae: *Vitex* (1, S,

P, 1). Violaceae: *Isodendrion* (4, s, p, 0–1); *Viola* (7, s, 0–1). Viscaceae: *Korthalsella* (8, W, M, 4). Zygophyllaceae: *Tribulus* (1, S, P, 1).

TABLE 13.1.

Floral conditions and pollination types in the native Hawaiian flora

Sexual condition	Genera no.	Genera %	Species no.	Species %
Dioecious	34	15.3	412	27.7
Monoecious	16	7.2	75	5.0
Andromonoecious	9	4.1	36	2.5
Gynomonoecious	8	3.6	61	4.4
Gynodioecious	6	2.7	45	2.6
Polygamodioecious	2	0.9	6	0.4
Polygamomonoecious	4	1.8	7	0.5
Total, diclinous	79	34.8	639	44.1
Flowers monoclinous but dichogamous	31	14.7	445	29.8
Diclinous + dichogamous	110	49.5	1084	73.9
Wind-pollinated	72	32.4	295	19.8

A feature which emerges clearly from the tabulation is that species which show few features designed for exogamy are often pioneer species. Many of these, if studied, would doubtless prove to be self-fertile. This is true for the Hawaiian cotton, *Gossypium sandvicense* (= *G. tomentosum*), according to Stephens (1964). The beach *Scaevola*, *S. taccada* (= *S. sericea*) is cleistogamous according to George W. Gillett (personal communication, 1965). Baker (1967) speculates that the Hawaiian *Pandanus* may be apomictic. Flowers of Convolvulaceae are notably suited for self-pollination. Of the species termed pioneer-habitat species, the vast majority are rated 0 or 1 in potential outcrossing ability. Only a scattering are rated 4 (mostly owing to wind pollination). Because Asteraceae are typically plants of pioneer habitats, they may be expected in such sites regardless of ability to outcross. Of the beach species native to the Hawaiian Islands, most fall in rating 0 or 1. In the Galápagos flora, autogamy has been demonstrated in *Lycopersicon* (Rick, 1963) and many other genera (Rick, 1966). The Galápagos flora may be considered a pioneer flora almost entirely; true wet forest is absent there.

Unexpectedly low ratings characterize a few genera from the forest flora (*Cheirodendron*, *Cryptocarya*, *Elaeocarpus*, *Syzygium*, *Gardenia*,

Lysimachia, Metrosideros, Osmanthus, Tetraplasandra). Study of these genera may demonstrate features that would tend to prevent inbreeding. A combination of showy inflorescences, fragrance, and abundance of nectar (e.g., *Cheirodendron*) may be effective in securing some degree of outcrossing even if plants are self-fertile. Low ratings for some plants of the high bogs (*Drosera, Viola, Vaccinium*) suggest that bogs may be, in a sense, pioneer habitats and thus show a lack of exogamy, as in beach species. Hawaiian bog plants appear relatively close to bog plants elsewhere, and with few exceptions seem not to have evolved or radiated greatly in the Hawaiian Islands; instances of loss of dispersibility (chapter 11) are few in the bog flora.

DIOECISM

Grant (1958) states that evolution of dioecism requires a high selective pressure. The high percentage of dioecism in the New Zealand flora has been noted by various workers. Millener (1961) states that 25 percent of New Zealand plants show unisexuality, but Thomson (1880) claims 46 percent; "unisexuality" in Thomson's sense is probably equivalent to "Diclinous" in table 13.1, where the 44.1 percent would correspond closely to his estimate for New Zealand. Cockayne (1921) claims 49 percent diclinous in the lowland forest of New Zealand. The percentage of dioecious species in New Zealand is claimed to be 14.5 percent (Godley, quoted by Rattenbury, 1962). This figure is well below the Hawaiian flora's 27.7 percent. These insular floras have high dioecism compared with other floras, however: 4.4 percent of species are dioecious in southwestern Australia (McComb, 1966); the figure is 3.1 percent in the British Isles (McComb, 1966) and 2.6 percent in California (Baker, 1967). At any rate, the Hawaiian flora has a dioecism rate well above those previously reported.

Other oceanic islands also are notable for dioecism. In the Juan Fernandez Islands, the frequency of dioecism is perhaps less striking than the groups in which it occurs. Two endemic genera of Asteraceae, tribe Senecioneae, are dioecious: *Robinsonia* (*Symphyochaeta* is sometimes recognized as a segregate of this) and *Rhetinodendron*; the latter even suggests an approach toward wind pollination (Skottsberg, 1928). The endemic genus *Cuminia* (Lamiaceae) may have evolved dioecism autochthonously on the Juan Fernandez Islands. The presence of a dioecious palm there, *Juania*, parallels the dioecious *Lodoicea* of the Seychelles.

On St. Helena Island, an endemic genus of Asteraceae, tribe Heliantheae, *Petrobium* (*Laxmannia*) is dioecious or nearly so (Carlquist, 1957). *Senecio rapae* of Rapa appears to be functionally dioecious (Brown, 1935). The only other dioecious Senecios known are *S. antennaria* and *S. diclinous* of the high Andes—an area that might be regarded as insular in nature (chapter 14). Examples of groups that are monoclinous on continental areas but dioecious in the New Zealand flora could be mentioned, as in the Apiaceae (Dawson, 1964).

Pittosporum is dioecious in the Hawaiian Islands but represented by monoclinous species, *P. taitensis* and *P. orofenensis*, in southeastern Polynesia. Most New Zealand Pittosporums are monoclinous, but a few are dioecious. The Hawaiian species of *Pittosporum* (fig. 13.1) are all, as far as is known, dioecious.

A similar situation obtains in the Polynesian species of *Ilex* (Aquifoliaceae). The Hawaiian *Ilex sandwichensis* is entirely dioecious but *I. marquesensis* (Marquesas Is.) is "polygamous" (polygamodioecious) according to Brown (1935), as is, apparently, the Tahitian *I. tahitensis*.

The genus *Myrsine* (*Rapanea*) in the Hawaiian Islands forms another interesting case. Hawaiian species of *Myrsine* are described as having "flowers mostly polygamous" by Hillebrand (1888), although unisexuality of flowers was not observed by Skottsberg, who was ordinarily acute in these matters, nor is it discussed by the monographer Hosaka (1940). Sexual conditions are not easy to establish in Hawaiian Myrsines, because flowering occurs in winter, when few collections are made, and most species are collected in fruit. I was able to demonstrate dioecism for *M. knudsenii* (fig. 13.1) and *M. lanaiensis*. Anthers contained no pollen grains at all in the individuals which could be designated as female. In the individuals with functional anthers, ovaries appeared appreciably smaller.

In Santalaceae, there is the possibility of cryptic dioecism: microtome sections I prepared from flowers of one individual of *Santalum haleakalae* uniformly showed sterile anthers but well-formed embryo sacs, suggesting functional dioecism.

The genus *Charpentiera* (Amaranthaceae) provides an interesting case.

521

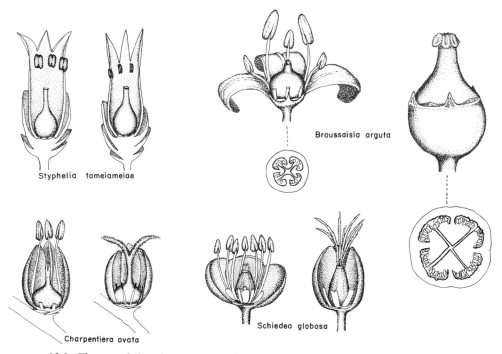

FIG. 13.1. Flowers of dioecious species endemic to the Hawaiian Is. Male flowers shown at left, female flowers at right in each pair. Some sepals, petals, and stamens are removed (cut surfaces indicated) on the facing side of flowers to show nature of ovaries. *Pittosporum acuminatum* (Pittosporaceae), × 3.8; *Myrsine knudsenii* (Myrsinaceae), × 8.4; *Pelea clusiaefolia* (Rutaceae), × 2.7; *Eurya sandwicensis* (Theaceae), × 4.2.

Flowers in this genus were reported by Hillebrand (1888) as bisexual; Skottsberg termed them gynodioecious. Morphologically, they are gynodioecious (fig. 13.2), and I reported them as such (1966). This characteristic would be expected, because the genus to which Hillebrand (1888) claims *Charpentiera* is allied, *Chamissoa*, has gynodioecious flowers (Müller, 1870). However, recent studies by Sohmer (1972) show that plants with morphologically bisexual flowers in fact act as staminate plants and set few or no seeds. Consequently, Sohmer (1972) concludes that "functionally, the members of the genus are often dioecious." Here, then, we have an instance of transition between gynodioecism and dioecism.

According to my observations, the genus *Eurya* (fig. 13.1) is entirely dioecious in the Hawaiian Islands.

The excellent observations of Skottsberg (1936a, 1936b, 1944, 1945) on sexual conditions of the native Hawaiian flora do not need repetition here. They show to what an amazing degree dioecism is present. A notable example is *Wikstroemia* (Thymeleaceae). Exploring the hint given by Hillebrand that the genus is effectively dioecious in the Hawaiian Islands although monoclinous elsewhere, Skottsberg (1936a, 1944a, 1964) located a few individuals with bisexual flowers in some Hawaiian species, but even in those species dioecism was also present, and the remaining species were found to be exclusively dioecious. A parallel to this behavior, also in Thymeleaceae, occurs in New Zealand. There the genus *Pimelea* is dioecious in at least some species, although the total picture is not entirely clear.

The Hawaiian Rubiaceae (Skottsberg, 1944b, 1945) present a nearly uniform picture of dioecism, almost as though dioecious species had been selected out from Rubiaceae at large. The few native species of *Gardenia*, *Nertera*, and *Psychotria* lack dioecism. *Nertera* is wind pollinated, *Psychotria* is protandrous. Fosberg (1956) finds that *Gouldia* is not truly dioecious, for flowers with connivent stigmas are still capable of setting fruit. In this case, *Gouldia* is to be regarded as gynodioecious. Paralleling the dioecism of Hawaiian species of *Hedyotis* (formerly recognized as a segregate genus, *Kadua*), the single species on St. Helena Island, *H. arborea*, is dioecious. The remarkable success indicated by speciation of *Coprosma* on both New Zealand and the Hawaiian Islands may, in part, be due to the efficient outcrossing mechanism provided by dioecism coupled with wind pollination.

The endemic Hawaiian genus of Loganiaceae, *Labordia*, is a uniformly dioecious extension of the South Pacific genus *Geniostoma*. Likewise, *Pelea* (fig. 13.1) of the Rutaceae is entirely dioecious in the Hawaiian Islands, although its South Pacific relatives (*Melicope*, *Acronychia*) have not attained true dioecism.

Astelia (Liliaceae), a widespread genus which is chiefly insular, was reported to be dioecious by Skottsberg (1934a, 1934b). However, exceptions do exist. Fruit set can occur (although never abundantly) on male plants of a few New Zealand species of *Astelia* (Moore, 1966; Moore and Edgar, 1970). Baker (1967) seems to feel for this reason that *Astelia* might have arrived in the Hawaiian Islands in a condition other than dioecious. However, no exceptions to dioecism have been found in Hawaiian species of *Astelia,* or in those of other islands, such as Tahiti, Mauritius, and New Guinea, where this genus occurs. If *Astelia* has not reached these islands in a dioecious condition, we have to hypothesize that dioecism has been *independently* evolved in all of these (presumably recent) insular species. The probability seems to me much less than the probability that *Astelia* reached these various islands in a dioecious condition, and I feel we must count the Hawaiian establishment of *Astelia* as having taken place in the dioecious condition.

Similar considerations apply to *Coprosma* (Rubiaceae). If Oliver (1935) is correct in implying that the Hawaiian *C. ernodeoides* (dioecious) is related to the Australian *C. moorei* (hermaphroditic), a hermaphroditic ancestry for that one Hawaiian species could be assumed. However, the remaining Hawaiian species of *Coprosma* form a natural group which seems not at all closely related to *C. ernodeoides,* and thus probably was derived from a second ancestor. These Hawaiian species all are dioecious, and are apparently related to dioecious non-Hawaiian species. The fact that there are monoecious plants of several species of *Coprosma* in New Zealand (see Allan, 1961) still faces us with the same situation as in *Astelia.* It is much easier to envision that *Coprosma* has arrived on the many islands where there are only endemic dioecious species (see Oliver, 1935) in a dioecious condition than to imagine that dioecism has been independently evolved from monoecism in all of these. A notable exception is *C. pumila,* which is dioecious in its broad range in the South Pacific except for Macquarie Island, where it is monoecious (Taylor, 1954).

All of the Hawaiian Peleas are, as noted, dioecious (fig. 13.1). The Marquesan Peleas are alleged to be monoecious by Brown (1935), although my studies on his material in the Bishop Museum could not confirm this. The species of *Pelea* claimed for New Caledonia are probably referable to *Melicope. Maba* (Ebenaceae) is apparently dioecious in the Hawaiian Islands, but data on species elsewhere in the Pacific are not available.

Genera that are native in the Hawaiian Islands and are entirely dioecious on a worldwide basis as far as is known include *Pandanus* and *Freycinetia* (Pandanaceae), *Smilax* (Liliaceae), *Antidesma* and *Drypetes* (Euphorbiaceae), and *Cocculus* (Menispermaceae). In addition, the Hawaiian species of *Eurya* (Theaceae) belong to the section *Proteurya,* which is entirely dioecious. The Hawaiian species of *Xylosma* (Flacourtiaceae), like the related Tahitian, Marquesan, Samoan, and Fijian species, are dioecious, providing good circumstantial evidence for immigration of dioecious stocks rather than independent dioecism in all these cases. *Pisonia* (*Ceodes*) *umbellifera* is dioecious (Skottsberg, 1936b) not only in the Hawaiian Islands but on all other Pacific islands where it is native.

In other genera, however, where non-Hawaiian relatives are non-dioecious, we can propose the possibility or probability that dioecism evolved autochthonously in the Hawaiian Islands. This can be suspected or is conceivable in Hawaiian species of the following genera: *Charpentiera* (Amaranthaceae), *Ilex* (Aquifoliaceae), *Claoxylon* (Euphorbiaceae), *Gunnera* (Haloragaceae), *Labordia* (Loganiaceae), *Myrsine* (Myrsinaceae), *Pittosporum* (Pittosporaceae), *Bobea* (Rubiaceae), *Canthium* (Rubiaceae), *Hedyotis* (Rubiaceae), *Straussia* (Rubiaceae), *Zanthoxylum* (Rutaceae), *Santalum* (Santalaceae), *Dodonaea* (Sapindaceae), *Broussaisia* (Saxifragaceae), *Wikstroemia* (Thymeleaceae), *Touchardia* (Urticaceae), and *Urera* (Urticaceae). *Pisonia* (*Rockia*) *sandwichensis* (Nyctaginaceae) is a dioecious species that may have evolved this condition autochthonously. We do not know for sure whether the Hawaiian *Fragaria chiloensis* is dioecious; this species is dioecious on coastal America (Baker, 1967).

The fact that Hawaiian species of at least 10 genera must be interpreted as dioecious prior to immigration (other interpretations are much less likely) is very interesting. It suggests that the value of dioecism in insular circumstances is so great that these genera have established and survived despite the requirement for more than a single propagule. As suggested in chapter 1, this requirement is probably no strong disadvantage, for occasional colonization by a group of propagules seems more likely than the hypothesis (implicit although never expressed) that *all* plant colonizations on islands begin with one and only one seed. Animals face a similar problem, unless we hypothesize that 100 percent of animal colonizations occur in the form of one and only one gravid female. Baker (1967) finds the 10 genera of plants that with little doubt reached the Hawaiian Islands in a dioecious condition to be a minor exception. Although even more than 10 may have, I felt justified in stating these as exceptions to "Baker's law" (1955) in my 1966 paper. Baker's "law," which he has graciously downgraded to a "rule" (1967), is an acceptable statement of the potential advantage of autogamous stocks in establishment on islands. By stressing the advantage of outcrossing in long-term survival (1966), I did not intend to exclude the potential advantage of autogamy for establishment.

The great value of dioecism for long-term survival on islands, where land area and population size are limited and outcrossing is therefore of presumptive value, is suggested by a fact which emerges from the figures in table 13.1. The number of species per genus in dioecious Hawaiian genera (12.8) is nearly twice the number of species per genus in the flora at large (6.7). The number of species per genus is also very high (13.6), however, in the Hawaiian genera that are monoclinous but dichogamous. These advantages are on an insular area; in contrast, on large continental areas such as Western Australia or the British Isles the number of species per genus is about the same, or higher, in hermaphrodite plants (McComb, 1966). In the Hawaiian Islands, the number of species per genus in diclinous genera is 8.0, versus 5.9 for hermaphrodite genera. In southwestern Australia, exclusively diclinous groups have 4.6 species per genus, exclusively hermaphrodite groups 9.0 species per genus (Mc-Comb, 1966). In the British Isles, exclusively diclinous groups have 3.2 species per genus, exclusively hermaphrodite groups 2.8 species per genus (McComb, 1966), which suggests little if any advantage there for non-hermaphrodite plants.

GYNODIOECISM

The occurrence of female flowers on some plants of a species, and bisexual flowers on other individuals, is a characteristic which seems prominent on islands. In the Hawaiian flora, seven genera contain species which are partly or wholly gynodioecious. *Styphelia tameiameiae* (fig. 13.2) and its varieties have some flowers with sterile anthers and others with fertile anthers. Ovaries appear identical in the two types of flowers. I have observed fruits on both types of plants. Herbarium specimens (e.g., *Sleumer 4559*, RSA) have flowers with well-formed pollen grains, with fruits formed on the same branches; such specimens have been annotated as bisexual by the monographer M. O. Sleumer. The species cannot, therefore, be regarded as dioecious, as claimed by Godley (1957). Godley's figures for other Epacridaceae—*Cyathodes acerosa* and *C. colen-*

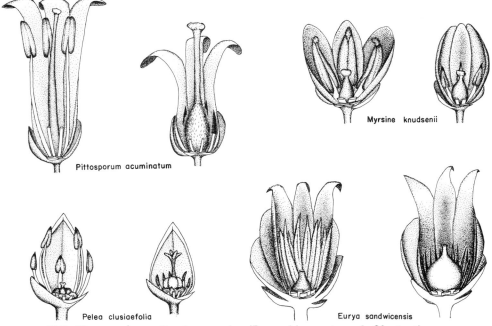

FIG. 13.2. Flowers of gynodioecious species (*Broussaisia arguta* and *Charpentiera* spp. are functionally dioecious, however), from the Hawaiian Is. Bisexual (or functionally male) flowers at left, female flowers at right in each pair. On facing side of flower, perianth, sepals, corolla portion, and anthers have been removed to show nature of ovaries. Ovaries in male flowers of *Broussaisia arguta* (in section, near center) contain normal ovules, although few of them; only ovaries of female flowers (in section, bottom right) appear to mature into fruits. Flowers of *Schiedea globosa* contain structures considered staminodes by some authors, although they may also serve as nectaries. *Styphelia tameiameiae* (Epacridaceae), × 7.6; *Broussaisia arguta* (Saxifragaceae), × 3.0; *Charpentiera ovata* (Amaranthaceae), × 9.5; *Schiedea globosa* (Caryophyllaceae), × 4.0.

soi—do suggest dioecism. Gynodioecism has been reported in *Leucopogon melaleucoides* of the Epacridaceae (McCusker, 1962). Godley reports functional dioecism for the New Zealand species *Leucopogon fasciculatus*. In the related family Ericaceae, either dioecism or gynodioecism may occur in New Zealand species of *Gaultheria* and *Pernettya* (Godley, 1957; Franklin, 1962).

The Hawaiian monotypic genus *Broussaisia* of the Saxifragaceae (a second species, *B. pellucida*, is sometimes recognized) has traditionally been regarded as dioecious, and functionally does appear to be so (fig. 13.2). No fruits like those of female plants are, in fact, formed on male plants, the flowers of which apparently wither without fruiting. Female flowers lack anthers and petals. Only the smallest vestiges of petals are present; minute staminodes may or may not be present. Female flowers have inferior ovaries, whereas ovaries are superior on male flowers. Male flowers appear hermaphroditic at first glance; petals and stamens are well formed, and the ovary appears normal, although smaller than that on a female plant. Sections of ovaries from male flowers reveal that normal ovules are present, although they are fewer in number than those of female flowers (fig. 13.2). Thus, there is a possibility a few seeds might be formed in "male" flowers, even though the fruits do not seem to mature normally. *Broussaisia* appears to have arrived at dioecism or near-dioecism via gynodioecism. The fact that anthers are virtually absent in female flowers, whereas well-formed ovules are present in male flowers, suggests this conclusion.

Charpentiera (Amaranthaceae) of the Hawaiian Islands and the Austral Islands is a genus that looks gynodioecious (fig. 13.2), and has been cited as an example of this. However, as a result of Sohmer's (1972) work we must, as stated earlier, regard this genus as well along in its progress from gynodioecism to dioecism, and it is now probably better cited as an example of dioecism.

Nesoluma polynesicum (Sapotaceae), confined to the Hawaiian Islands and Austral Islands, is gynodioecious according to the data of Lam (1938). Gynodioecism characterizes another species of *Nesoluma, N. saintjohnianum* (Henderson I.), although apparently *N. nadeaudi* (Society Is.) is hermaphroditic. Unisexual flowers have been reported in *Planchonella* and *Pouteria* (Lam, 1938) but are not definitely known in Hawaiian representatives of those genera.

Skottsberg (1944a) reported and illustrated in *Cyrtandra* (Gesneriaceae), a genus with bisexual flowers, two Hawaiian species in which individuals bearing female flowers were observed. I have reexamined Skottsberg's specimens in the Bishop Museum. The specimen of *C. platyphylla* var. *brevipes* (*Skottsberg 3178B*) alleged to have only staminodes proved to have reduced anthers, but one fertile anther bearing apparently good pollen was seen. In *Cyrtandra gayana*, the specimen *Skottsberg 3018* which was alleged to be female did, in fact, have only sterile staminodes in flowers. Thus, at least *C. gayana* may be said to be gynodioecious. Although more material must be studied to confirm that these are not merely chance occurrences of malformed flowers, the Hawaiian Cyrtandras may actually show the beginnings of gynodioecism; unisexual flowers do occur in non-Hawaiian species of *Cyrtandra.*

Because Fosberg (1956) has found that flowers of *Gouldia* (Rubiaceae) which Skottsberg (1944b) termed male can actually set some fruit, *Gouldia* must be regarded as an instance of gynodioecism, transitional to dioecism.

The genus *Schiedea* (Caryophyllaceae) is endemic to the Hawaiian Islands. Although no mention of sexual conditions other than hermaphroditic occurs in Hillebrand (1888), Sherff (1945), or Degener's *Flora Hawaiiensis*, my observations show that at least several species deviate from the bisexual condition. When I examined a flowering population of *S. globosa* (fig. 13.2) on the slopes between Hanauma Bay and Koko Head, Oahu, two kinds of flowers, bisexual and female, were apparent. As far as could be determined, each plant had only one type of flower, and thus the condition was gynodioecious. As can be seen from figure 13.2, the female flowers lack stamens; the small petaloid structures which are present in both female and bisexual flowers have been designated as staminodes by Sherff (1945). Liquid-preserved specimens of *S. globosa* revealed that fertile seeds are formed in both kinds of flowers, even though the ovaries are somewhat smaller in bisexual flowers. Study of herbarium specimens also revealed the presence of both female and bisexual flowers in *S. menziesii* and in *S. ligustrina*. Specimens of most species of *Schiedea* are not numerous, and field studies are much needed to determine if gynodioecism prevails in other species as well. At least some species of *Schiedea* are probably monoclinous.

A peculiar condition that is functionally near gynodioecism occurs in another genus of Caryophyllaceae, *Sanctambrosia*, which is endemic to San Ambrosio in the Desventuradas Islands (Skottsberg, 1963). In this genus, some plants bear female flowers, other plants bear both male and bisexual flowers. *Nesocaryum*, a genus of Boraginaceae also endemic to San Ambrosio, has a truly gynodioecious condition (Skottsberg, 1963). The occurrence, in a very small oceanic-island flora, of two genera that are in effect gynodioecious is most remarkable. On the Juan Fernandez

Islands is the notable annonalean relict *Lactoris*, a monotypic genus which is gynodioecious or nearly so (Skottsberg, 1928; Carlquist, 1964).

In the New Zealand flora, gynodioecism has been carefully studied in three endemic species of the grass *Cortaderia* (Connor, 1963, 1965), and four endemic species of *Pimelea* of the Thymeleaceae (Burrows, 1960). *Fuchsia excorticata* and *F. perscandens* prove to be gynodioecious (Godley, 1955); Godley describes *F. procumbens* of New Zealand as "trioecious" and the Tahitian species, *F. cyrtandroides*, as either gynodioecious or trioecious. *Gingidium* (Apiaceae) in New Zealand has been reported to be gynodioecious (Dawson, 1964).

The number of gynodioecious species in these insular floras is not dramatically high, but the presence of these, combined with the high proportion of dioecism, does call for some explanations. Baker (1963) finds no obvious selective force that would induce gynodioecism. Possible explanations which can be given are that (1), gynodioecism represents a transitional stage from bisexuality to dioecism, and may be the pathway through which dioecism must be achieved in some groups; and (2), gynodioecism promotes a high degree of outcrossing, while seed fertility is retained on all plants, thus providing a potentially high rate of reproduction. The two explanations may be interconnected, for if a plant were evolving from monoclinous to diclinous, retention of seed fertility on both female and bisexual plants would seemingly be more valuable than retention of pollen fertility on both male and bisexual plants (androdioecism is the alternative transitional condition). A study of the gynodioecious *Leucopogon melaleucoides* (McCusker, 1962) showed that female plants had a fruit set of 62 percent, whereas hermaphroditic plants had 43 percent. Androdioecism is extremely rare in flowering plants at large, so probably gynodioecism is the most successful pathway to dioecism. Gynodioecism is probably an unstable condition over long periods of time. Of the seven genera in the Hawaiian flora cited above, none appears well stabilized in this condition. *Broussaisia, Charpentiera, Styphelia,* and *Gouldia* tend toward dioecism, while gynodioecism is only incipient in *Schiedea, Nesoluma,* and *Cyrtandra*. Among these seven genera, the gynodioecious condition was almost certainly present in the stocks that arrived in the Hawaiian Islands in the cases of *Charpentiera* and *Nesoluma,* and possibly also in *Styphelia*.

MONOECISM AND ALLIED CONDITIONS

The occurrence in the Hawaiian flora of monoecism in Euphorbiaceae and Urticaceae, gynomonoecism (heterogamy) in Asteraceae, and andromonoecism in Apiaceae is not surprising since these conditions occur in those groups on mainland areas as well. Those groups, however, have succeeded well in the Hawaiian flora. With regard to Asteraceae, note should be taken that although many species in the family at large have a pollen-presentation mechanism which permits self-pollination to occur if cross-pollination has not already occurred, other features of the family are suited to outcrossing—such as gynomonoecism and protandry.

Among interesting floral conditions that deserve comment are those in *Acacia*, *Alectryon*, and *Alphitonia*. Skottsberg (1944a) has demonstrated andromonoecism in the Hawaiian Acacias, *A. koa* and *A. kauaiensis*. According to St. John and Frederick (1949), the two Hawaiian species of *Alectryon* (Sapindaceae), *A. macrococcus* and *A. mahoe*, must be regarded as polygamodioecious, because apparently bisexual flowers have been found in addition to ones that are functionally male or female. However, in his description of the genus *Alectryon*, Radlkofer (1931–1933) discounts the validity of hermaphrodite flowers, so the genus would have to be monoecious or dioecious. In *Alphitonia ponderosa*, Hillebrand (1888) reported short-styled flowers mingled with normal long-styled flowers, a report I have confirmed. Anthers are functional in both kinds of flowers. If the short-styled flowers are functionally male, *A. ponderosa* is andromonoecious.

In *Hillebrandia* (Begoniaceae), plants are monoecious, but as inflorescences open, female flowers only are receptive at first; male flowers (and additional female flowers) open later; thus, in order to be fertilized, the first female flowers must outcross.

HETEROSTYLY

Heterostyly is not, apparently, present in the Hawaiian flora (some Hawaiian genera were erroneously reported as heterostyled, on the basis of Hillebrand's vague terminology, in the first printing of my 1965 book, but that error was corrected in the second printing). The genetic basis for heterostyly appears more complicated than that for dioecism, and consequently the former has rarely evolved autochthonously on islands. Dioecism, on the contrary, is apparently evolved easily and rapidly in particular groups (Lewis, 1942). An example of a genus with both monomorphic and heteromorphic flowers, represented on continental and insular areas, is *Limonium* of the Plumbaginaceae (Baker, 1953). Baker's data reveal that, of the species confined to relatively small oceanic islands, 94.5 percent have dimorphic flowers; on islands of all kinds, the percentage is 87.0; in the genus as a whole, 79.6 percent have dimorphic flowers (my calculations). Baker (1967) seems to object to my (1966) citing of these percentages, but his objections are not specified, and I think that these percentages can still be cited as exemplifying the greater value that outcrossing has on limited land areas. During my 1967 visit to the Canary Islands, I studied populations of *Limonium* and was struck by the fact that the endemic *Limonium* species all seem confined to small population sizes, where outcrossing would be an advantage. *Limonium tuberculatum*, for example, occurs only in a small marshy part of the sand dunes near Maspalomas, Gran Canaria (it is probably extinct now because of construction). *Limonium rumicifolium* occurs in a few very small barrancos near Era del Cardon, Gran Canaria.

DICHOGAMY

The tabulation for the Hawaiian flora (table 13.1) shows an appreciable percentage of species that are either protogynous or protandrous; this percentage could doubtless be increased as a result of further studies. Whether the total figure would be greater or the same on a mainland area remains to be determined. Skottsberg (1928) noted dichogamy in the Juan Fernandez flora for *Eryngium* and *Colletia*, and implied it for *Gunnera*. Lauraceae tend to be protogynous, and the flowers of *Cryptocarya* in the Hawaiian Islands, as well as those of the various laurels in Macaronesia, may prove to have this condition. There can be little doubt that dichogamy appreciably increases the possibility of outcrossing. In an inflorescence of a protogynous species, such as *Plantago*, the flowers that open first can only form seed by outcrossing (or, of course, possibly by pollen from an older inflorescence on the same plant).

WIND POLLINATION

Anemophily will tend not only to promote outcrossing, but also to promote it over a relatively wide area. Anemophily characterizes 19.8

percent of the Hawaiian angiosperm species (32.4 percent of the genera), 34 percent of Juan Fernandez angiosperms (Skottsberg, 1928), and 29 percent of the New Zealand flora (Thomson, 1880). Although these percentages are not strongly different, one could say that they support Skottsberg's (1928) claim that the high percentage on the Juan Fernandez Islands is related to windy subantarctic weather. Interestingly, calculation of pollination mechanisms in the Florida Keys, using Small's (1913) flora, reveals that 19.7 percent of species are anemophilous—the same as in the Hawaiian Islands. The value of wind pollination in promoting outcrossing is obvious, but furthermore, because no animal vector is required in pollination, establishment of anemophilous groups should be facilitated on islands. The Hawaiian figures are interesting, because about a third of the hypothetical immigrants (roughly equating genera in the Hawaiian flora with the number of original establishments) are anemophilous, although these have not speciated as well as have the entomophilous and ornithophilous establishments, so that the percentage of anemophilous species is much lower than the percentage for genera. The number of species per genus in the anemophilous portion of the Hawaiian flora is 4.1; if two large genera (which might not be entirely wind pollinated), *Coprosma* and *Peperomia*, are deducted, the figure becomes only 2.8 species per genus. These figures are well below the average number of species per genus in the Hawaiian angiosperm flora as a whole (6.7 percent, a percentage identical to the ratio in the California flora as a whole). Perhaps wind pollination lowers isolation and thereby speciation. Dioecious, entomophilous flowers would be ideal for securing outcrossing yet would allow isolation that would tend to promote speciation: in the Hawaiian flora, dioecious plants have a species-per-genus ratio of 12.8.

Interestingly, *Plantago grayana*, a native of the very wet Alakai Swamp of Kauai successfully dehisces its anthers under experimental conditions of 100 percent humidity, whereas *P. lanceolata* (a boreal weed) does not under these conditions (Melvern Tessene, unpublished data).

PATHWAYS TO OUTCROSSING

There seems little doubt that, as Baker (1967) suggests, dioecism is easy to achieve genetically in comparison to self-incompatibility and heterostyly. Gynodioecism, monoecism, andromonoecism, and gynomonoecism are presumably also easy to achieve. In Hawaiian species of *Plantago,* a normally protogynous genus, Tessene (unpublished data) has discovered occasional gynomonoecious spikes. It will be interesting to see if any appreciable number of hermaphroditic angiosperms do occur on oceanic islands. Tessene (unpublished data) has shown that *Plantago grayana* of the Hawaiian Islands is, in fact, self-incompatible. I would guess that this condition may have evolved autochthonously on the Hawaiian Islands. As Baker (1967) suggests, however, the high proportion of dioecism in the Hawaiian flora (and presumably other insular floras) may well compensate for the lack of genetic self-sterility in hermaphroditic plants, a compensation representing the difficulty of evolving self-sterility but also illustrating the high value that outcrossing has on insular areas.

Although gynodioecism probably arises from hermaphroditism and does not, in most situations, continue on to dioecism (Lewis, 1942), Ross (1970) credits my contention (1966) that gynodioecism has continued on to dioecism in the Hawaiian Islands. Evidently the value of ensured outcrossing there (and apparently in New Zealand, where male plants outnumber females in the majority of dioecious species [Godley, 1964]) overrides the retention of a high level of fertility.

Hybridization

Reports of hybridization in insular floras depend on the tendency of systematists to recognize the presence of hybrids or to neglect them. There seems no question that with the recent interest by systematists in natural hybridization, and with an increasing number of botanists trained to discern hybrids, we may expect the roster of known and probable hybrids on islands to lengthen greatly. Emphasis here on insular hybrids should not be interpreted as a denial of the importance of hybrids on continental areas.

New Zealand botanists appear to have been very alert in reporting instances of hybridization and species polymorphism. The list of Cockayne and Allan (1934) has been supplemented by the accounts, under various dicotyledonous genera, of Allan (1961). Recent or well-documented studies include those of Oliver (1935), Dawson (1960), and Franklin (1962).

Rattenbury (1962) has offered a hypothesis concerning the survival value of groups with hybridization and polymorphism during New Zealand's Pleistocene.

On the Juan Fernandez Islands, Skottsberg (1922) reports an intergeneric hybrid, *Margyracaena* (*Margyricarpus setosus* × *Acaena argentea*) and interspecific hybrids in *Gunnera* (*G. peltata* × *G. bracteata*) and *Wahlenbergia* (*W. grahamae* × *W. larraini*). On the Canary Islands, hybridization probably occurs in *Aeonium* and *Sonchus*, and has been reported in *Adenocarpus* by Lems (1958). During my fieldwork in the Canary Islands in 1967, I discovered a hybrid swarm involving three species of *Micromeria* (Lamiaceae) at Tamadaba, Gran Canaria.

In the Hawaiian Islands, hybrids have been reported in Rubiaceae for *Gouldia* (Fosberg, 1937, 1956), and *Hedyotis* and *Coprosma* (Fosberg, 1943). In Asteraceae, hybrids have been noted in *Bidens* (Sherff, 1937; see, however, a more definitive list in Gillett and Lim, 1970); *Dubautia*, including *Railliardia* (Sherff, 1935); *Lipochaeta* (Sherff, 1935); *Argyroxiphium* (Keck, 1936); and there is even a report of a hybrid between two very distinctive genera, *Dubautia* and *Argyroxiphium* (Sherff, 1944). Hybrids between *Plantago pachyphylla* and *P. hillebrandii* occur on Puu Kukui, Maui (M. Tessene, unpublished data). In Campanulaceae, Rock (1919) reported hybrids between *Clermontia montis-loa* and *C. parviflora*. I have examined this colony (Kulani Camp Road, Hawaii) and found it to be a clear instance of hybridization, in which all degrees of recombination between the two parental species were represented and abundant. In the same region, *C. montis-loa* hybridizes with *C. hawaiiensis* (Carlquist, 1970, p. 113). The genus *Metrosideros* (Myrtaceae), notorious for polymorphism in the Hawaiian Islands, may have radiated to a certain extent by forming distinctive ecotypes, but hybridization of some sort must be occurring (Fosberg, 1943), because the variability and types found within a given population suggest active segregation and recombination. Additional instances will probably be revealed in such "difficult" and "polymorphic" groups as *Pittosporum* and *Euphorbia*. Potentially very important in this regard is that many Hawaiian genera contain not merely recent hybrids, but the products of ancient hybridizations as well. Older events of hybridization are not easily amenable to analysis, however.

The first example that has been carefully analyzed in the Hawaiian flora is *Scaevola mollis* × *S. gaudichaudiana* (Gillett, 1966). Aside from the pantropical beach *Scaevola, S. taccada,* and a distinctive (and probably old) high-mountain species, *S. glabra,* most populations of the commoner native species of *Scaevola* seem to involve some degrees of hybridization, recent or old. Gillett's analysis of the *S. gaudichaudiana* hybrids is interesting because apparently no sterility barriers exist in this group; chromosome studies indicate perfect pairing in obviously hybrid individuals. Hybrid populations do not seem to segregate markedly toward parental types, as would be expected in "typical" introgressive behavior where a partial sterility barrier often occurs. These findings suggest lack of generic barriers, and free exchange of genes is potentially possible among the vast majority of montane Hawaiian Scaevolas.

A population of *Scaevola* on Kauai, termed *S. procera* by certain authors, is particularly interesting. This population is nearly uniform, at least in the area studied by Gillett. It must be regarded as being hybrid, however. *Scaevola "procera"* seems probably the result of natural introduction to Kauai of a hybrid from one of the other islands. However, the intermediate quality of this hybrid has been retained within rather narrow limits, without marked segregation toward "typical" *S. gaudichaudiana* or *S. mollis.* A population such as *S. "procera"* could, now that it is isolated from its parents, develop distinctive characteristics not found in parental populations. This example shows some ways in which species may have arisen in various Hawaiian genera.

A recent study of the Hawaiian species of *Pipturus* (Urticaceae) by Nicharat and Gillett (1970) shows extensive hybridization, no apparent genetic barriers, and a combination of a few "source" species to form many more or less distinctive and "specieslike" hybrids. Skottsberg (1934a) does concede two hybrids in *Pipturus,* but some of the species he recognizes are probably "stable hybrids." Nicharat and Gillett find that the 13 species recognized by earlier authors can be considered races derived from hybrids between two valid species.

Gillett and Lim (1970) have experimentally analyzed Hawaiian species of *Bidens.* Their summary of experimentally produced F_1 and F_2 hybrids shows a notable absence of generic barriers among the species, except for the highly distinctive Kauai species *B. cosmoides.* Fully fertile hybrids between species endemic to different islands were easily obtained in many cases. This shows clearly that geographical isolation is the only major factor that prevents the numerous species (or "species") of *Bidens* from occurring as a single variable species (except for *B. cosmoides*). In the Hawaiian species of *Charpentiera*, Sohmer (1972) finds no sterility barriers; he believes that differing ecological requirements may be responsible for maintaining the integrity of the several species.

Although hybrids have not yet been produced in a controlled experimental manner for other insular genera, one can cite the garden hybrids of *Aeonium* (Praeger, 1932). These are so numerous and interbreed so freely that accurate naming of many *Aeonium* plants in culture is impossible.

Self-pollination would tend to maintain hybrid characteristics. If Hawaiian species of *Cyanea* and *Clermontia* (Campanulaceae), *Cyrtandra* (Gesneriaceae), or *Bidens* (Asteraceae) are frequently autogamous but occasionally outcross, a hybrid, once produced, might tend to maintain itself. Such a hybrid, if disseminated to a new locality, could found a distinctive population. Rick's (1963) analysis of Galápagos tomatoes and his subsequent studies on the flora of the Galápagos show a lack of genetic barriers, a high degree of autogamy, and the possibility that these features, combined with occasional hybridization events, have produced distinctive populations.

The genetic significance of a moderate to high degree of hybridism in insular groups is like that of outcrossing within a single species: both tend to maintain a high level of heterozygosity, which permits evolutionary flexibility despite loss of genetic contact with mainland relatives, and small land area. Hybridization probably does, as Rattenbury (1962) suggests, help a group survive a "bottleneck" of dwindling land area and climatic stress. Volcanic eruptions on oceanic islands could both temporarily diminish available land area and create new barriers. New land open to hybrid individuals is also thereby created.

Land area is limited on islands, especially when one considers that only a portion of an island is ecologically suitable for a particular species. Where land area is small, the total genetic variability of a species or a species-complex may be insufficient to maintain the species over a long period of time. MacArthur and Wilson (1963) have postulated a high rate of extinction for small and remote islands. This would seem to have a sound genetic basis. If so, the Hawaiian Islands probably lie above the minimal area necessary to foster radiation and long-term maintenance of the products of that radiation. The relatively poor (compared to Hawaii) floras of the Society Islands, the Marquesas, and other islands nearer important Indo-Malesian source areas than the Hawaiian Islands probably derive not so much from youth or ecology of southeastern Polynesia but from inability of species on these smaller land areas to maintain requisite genetic variability. Whereas the Hawaiian flora and fauna contain truly distinctive products of adaptive radiation (chapter 4), the oceanic islands of southeastern Polynesia with few exceptions merely contain species that are endemic but not exceptional within their genera or families. Lowered adaptive radiation can be shown in the smaller number of species per genus in the floras of southeastern Polynesia than is the case in the Hawaiian Islands.

Lack (1971) appears to wonder why plant species seem to withstand the "small island" effect better than, say, birds. Birds, of course, depend directly or indirectly on plant species. Land birds, with territorial requirements, require much larger land areas than do plants, which have the additional advantage of being autotrophic and thus are dependent directly on suitable area, not food supplies. A population of 50 plants of a species can occur on a small island, like *Portulaca lutea* on Gardner Pinnacles. If excessively inbred, this population might eventually die out and be replaced by a new stock brought by oceanic drift. However, vegetative reproduction of a genetically "healthy" *Portulaca lutea* (and this species can reproduce by rooting of fragmented stems) could keep such a population continuing almost indefinitely by apomixis.

With a plant-eating animal, like the reindeer introduced to St. Matthew Island that died by overeating their food supply (Klein, 1968), we see that not only must an animal have an appropriate ecological niche and a breeding population above a minimal size, it must also have a sufficient food supply to keep that population in equilibrium. Thus, two species of a given genus of passerine birds cannot be tolerated on some small islands (Lack, 1971; Lack and Southern, 1949).

Floral Biology

The species native to waif forest floras of islands have flowers that are notable for their inconspicuousness. These species are adapted mostly to cross-pollination, however. The inconspicuousness of insular flowers (with the exception of ornithophilous genera and species) is correlated with the paucity of large Lepidoptera, long-tongued bees, and various other pollinators on islands. Studies are much needed on pollinator relationships of insular species; since the pioneering work of Thomson (1880) and the observations offered and summarized by Cockayne (1921) on the New Zealand flora, there have been only a few major contributions. These include Heine's (1937) work on the New Zealand flora, Skottsberg's (1928) study of pollination in the Juan Fernandez Islands, and surveys by Linsey (1966), Rick (1966), and Linsey, Rick, and Stephens (1966) on the Galápagos Islands. In the Hawaiian Islands, we can admire the field-biologist approach of Perkins (1913), whose observations on floral biology and other aspects of the Hawaiian biota have, unfortunately, few sequels. A paper by Williams (1927) is worthy of note, however.

With respect to conspicuousness of flowers, a factor related primarily to size, Thomson finds that nearly 49 percent of the New Zealand angiosperm flora falls in the third, or least conspicuous, of three flower classes. On Masatierra in the Juan Fernandez Islands, 49 percent of angiosperms fall in the latter two, or less conspicuous, of three categories. In the Hawaiian flora, flowers are notably inconspicuous, with a few prominent exceptions. Smallness of flowers in these floras is due not only to anemophily, but also to smallness of the pollinators of entomophilous flowers. This, in turn, is related to the fact that small size classes of insects have been dispersed to islands, in the main. With small insular insects, angiosperms with suitably small flowers might be supposed to be most successful at establishment. An alternative possibility, that smallness of flowers has evolved autochthonously on islands, seems less likely. In either case, insect size appears a better explanation for inconspicuousness of entomophilous insular flowers than does the idea favored by Thomson and by Wallace (1891), that paucity of insects on islands influences floral characteristics.

With respect to color classes, the following data have been gathered:

New Zealand (data from Thomson, 1880): white, 33 percent; yellow, 11; red (of all shades), 5; blue or purple, 2.5; green, 48.5. (Ornithophilous and anemophilous flowers included.)

New Zealand (data from Cockayne, 1921): white, 36 percent; yellow, 18; reds, 11; blue or purple, 22; green, 11; brown, 2. ("Lowland forest, attractive" flowers only, anemophilous species apparently excluded.)

Juan Fernandez Islands (data from Skottsberg, 1928): white, 46 percent; yellow, 24; red, 5; blue, 10; green, 10; brown, 5. (Ornithophilous and anemophilous flowers excluded.)

Hawaiian Islands (data original): white, 33 percent; yellow, 24; red (including purple, rose, scarlet), 11; blue, 2; green, 29; brown, 1. (Anemophilous and ornithophilous flowers excluded.)

Saint Helena Island (data from Hemsley, 1885): white, 50 percent; whitish, tinged pink or bluish, 13; white and yellow (composites with white rays, yellow disc flowers), 17; yellow, 10; red, 7; green, 3. (Entirely native angiosperm flora.)

The similarity among these island groups is evident. The predominance of white, followed by green, then yellow and red, is clear. White and yellow are heavily predominant in the Galápagos flora (my observations).

Fragrance is claimed by Thomson to characterize only 22 percent of New Zealand flowers. A similar lack of fragrance may be found in the Hawaiian flora as well. Families in which one would expect to find strong scents—Rubiaceae, Loganiaccac, Lamiaceae—are virtually devoid of them. Fragrance and nectar are prominent in some Hawaiian plants, however, perhaps compensating for lack of conspicuousness (*Cheirodendron, Tetraplasandra, Schiedea*).

Many of the entomophilous flowers in the Hawaiian flora have a simple cuplike, bell-like or tubelike shape that would be suited to a wide variety of insects. This suggests that easy access by insect pollinators may have been a major factor in successful establishment of entomophilous species. The Hawaiian Islands are notably poor in orchids. Although this lack may derive from short seed viability, it probably is due in part to the specialized pollination requirements of most orchid flowers. Lack of specialized pollination requirements in the Hawaiian flora might tend to increase outcrossing and hybridization. Lack of flower-constancy among pollinating birds and insects would also have this effect.

Other factors that might tend to secure pollination include massing of flowers into large inflorescences, an insular tendency noted by Wallace (1891). Wallace's explanation that this secures pollination where the insular insect fauna is very poor seems possible. However, there is an alternative explanation, that congestion of flowers makes a plant in flower more conspicuous, and therefore induces pollination where individuals of a particular plant species may be scattered throughout a forest. Congestion of flowers would compensate for the small flower size that is, as noted earlier, typical of many insular species. Moreover, conspicuousness by virtue of clustering would aid in securing pollination where outcrossing is mandatory—as in dioecious species.

A long flowering season, a tendency noted by Skottsberg (1928) in the Juan Fernandez Islands and also quite apparent in the Hawaiian Islands, seems related to the mild maritime climate of many islands. A long flowering season may tend to promote outcrossing and hybridization; phenological barriers seem unlikely to develop under such conditions.

Difficulties of pollination might account for preponderance of male over female plants in dioecious species. Precisely this situation was found in a survey of the New Zealand flora (Godley, 1964), where results were analyzed for statistical significance. Studies of this sort should be done in the Hawaiian Islands.

Fertility in Insular Plants

The observations by Godley (1964), as well as the fact that in New Zealand and Hawaiian genera, gynodioecism has given rise to dioecism, and that dioecism (whatever its origin) is so extraordinarily common, all suggest that a high degree of seed fertility is not of prime selective advantage on those islands. Another subsidiary indication is that in so many Hawaiian genera, such as *Alectryon* (Sapindaceae), *Pritchardia* (Arecaceae), and many others, gigantic seeds are produced, but relatively few to a plant (see chapter 11).

In addition, attempts to grow wild-collected seeds of certain Hawaiian genera have shown remarkably low germination percentages in a number of cases. Among those in which I and others have found consistently low germinability, regardless of culture method, are *Argyroxiphium sand-wichense, Wilkesia gymnoxiphium,* and *Hesperomannia arbuscula oahu-ensis* (Asteraceae). "Weedier" natives, such as many of the Hawaiian species of *Bidens,* appear to have higher germinability. One might well guess that in many genera, fertility has decreased to an appreciable extent. Reliable measures of fertility are, of course, difficult to define and obtain. One might speculate that in the disharmonic Hawaiian situation, where so many genera compete only to a moderate extent compared with their mainland equivalents, a lower rate of reproduction suffices. Another possible explanation could lie in the high percentage of woody species. A relatively low set of seed each year would still, over a period of years, succeed in reproducing any plant quite adequately.

Reproductive Biology in Animals

FERTILITY IN ISLAND VERTEBRATES

Small clutch size in insular birds as compared to their mainland relatives has been observed repeatedly (Lack, 1946, 1948, 1954; Hagen, 1952). The data on this phenomenon are graphic. The average clutch size of robins in Europe and North Africa provides an example (Lack, 1954, p. 38). The extreme low among areas studied is reached in the Canary Islands (3.5 eggs per clutch). The Azores have a lower figure (4.7) than anywhere in mainland Europe (for example, 5.1 in England, 5.5 in Scotland, 5.9 in Germany, 6.3 in Sweden, 6.3 in Finland). Although the exact manner of physiological control of clutch size is not known, there seems little doubt from Lack's massive evidence that lower clutch size on islands is governed primarily by availability of food for the young. Although food availability on islands might, at first guess, appear favorable, food supplies are lower than on comparable continental areas. Lack (1971) has extended his interpretation of lower clutch size of birds on islands to include the uniform climatic conditions typical of many tropical and subtropical islands. Whereas in areas with marked seasonality, birds will raise large families at the flush of the growing season, on islands with uniform climates there is no seasonal abundance of food, and so because birds must live throughout the year at the limits of a moderate food supply, clutch size would be indirectly related to climate.

Interestingly, the wall lizards (*Lacerta sicula*) on offshore islands of Italy show similar tendencies. The clutch contains 2–4 eggs in insular populations, 4–7 on nearby mainland areas (Kramer, 1946). Kramer even demonstrated clutches of intermediate size by hybridizing mainland and insular individuals; thus, the feature is a heritable one. The island populations have larger as well as fewer eggs. Lack (1954) interprets this as a compensation for poorer food supplies on the small islands, and perhaps also as a mechanism that enables the young to escape cannibalism—a tendency of island lizards but not mainland ones. Smaller egg size in mainland lizards, according to Lack, may be related to the relatively abundant food supplies available to newly hatched lizards on mainland areas, whereas the young of insular lizards are faced with sparser food sources, and therefore provision of greater food supply in the egg enables them to survive better the difficult juvenile period. Also, there is more predation upon lizards of mainland areas, so that each individual that escapes predation can be said to have available the food supply that individuals removed by predation would have consumed. This makes the correlations of clutch size and egg size quite comprehensible. Island populations of at least some bird species are denser than on comparable continental areas (Grant, 1971); this would seem to support Lack's idea that island bird species live at the limit of their food supplies. The Bahaman hutia, endemic to small East Plana Cay, is notable for its small litter size: only a single young per litter is typical (Clough, 1969). The hutia has a high population density.

LONGEVITY OF ANIMALS

In plants, greater longevity on islands occurs in the case of arborescent representatives of typically herbaceous groups. Lack of seasonal extremes that would terminate the life of an herbaceous plant may have "released" some plants into longer life-spans, as suggested in chapter 10. In animals, we deal with somewhat different principles where longevity is concerned. Lack (1954) cites an inverse correlation between size of clutch and longevity. In other words, the more young produced each year, the higher the mortality rate has to be. He cites figures for the blue tit: in England, the average clutch is 11, and the annual adult mortality is 73 percent; in Spain and Portugal, the average clutch is 6, adult mortality 41 percent; in the Canary Islands, the average clutch is 4.25, adult mortality is 36 percent.

The same correlation occurs in the *Lacerta* lizards mentioned earlier, as we might expect (Kramer, 1946). Multiplying clutch size by brood number, we find that mainland lizards lay 24 eggs each year on the average, and individuals have an average life-span of 1.9 years. On the offshore islands, an average of 11 eggs are laid per year, and life-span averages 4.4 years. The factors discussed above (food supply, predation) may be called into play in explaining these aspects of mainland versus insular differences.

References

Allan, H. H. 1961. *Flora of New Zealand*, vol. I. Wellington, R. E. Owen, Government Printer.

Baker, H. G. 1953. Dimorphism and monomorphism in the Plumbaginaceae. II. Pollen and stigmata in the genus *Limonium*. *Ann. Bot.*, n.s., 17:433–45.

Baker, H. G. 1955. Self-compatibility and establishment after "long-distance" dispersal. *Evolution* 9:347–49.

Baker, H. G. 1959. Reproductive methods as factors in speciation in flowering plants. *Quant. Biol.* 24:177–91.

Baker, H. G. 1963. Evolutionary mechanisms in pollination biology. *Science* 139:877–83.

Baker, H. G. 1967. Support for Baker's Law—as a rule. *Evolution* 21:853–56.

Brown, F. B. H. 1935. Flora of southeastern Polynesia. III. Dicotyledons. *Bishop Mus. Bull.* 130:1–386.

Burrows, C. J. 1960. Studies in *Pimelea*. I. The breeding system. *Trans. Roy. Soc. New Zealand* 88:29–45.

Carlquist, S. 1957. The genus *Fitchia* (Compositae). *Univ. Calif. Publ. Bot.* 29:1–144.

Carlquist, S. 1964. Morphology and relationships of Lactoridaceae. *Aliso* 5:421–35.

Carlquist, S. 1965. *Island life*. New York, Natural History Press.

Carlquist, S. 1966. The biota of long-distance dispersal. IV. Genetic systems in the floras of oceanic islands. *Evolution* 20:433–55.

Carlquist, S. 1970. *Hawaii, a natural history*. New York, Natural History Press.

Clough, G. C. 1969. The Bahaman hutia: A rodent refound. *Oryx* 10:106–8.

Cockayne, L. 1921. *The vegetation of New Zealand. Die Vegetation der Erde*, ed. A. Engler and O. Drude, vol. 14. Leipzig, Verlag Wilhelm Engelmann.

Cockayne, L., and H. H. Allan. 1934. An annotated list of groups of wild hybrids in the New Zealand flora. *Ann. Bot.* 48:1–55.

Connor, H. E. 1963. Breeding systems in New Zealand grasses. IV. Gynodioecism in *Cortaderia*. *New Zealand Jour. Bot.* 1:258–64.

Connor, H. E. 1965. Breeding systems in New Zealand grasses. VI. Control of gynodioecism in *Cortaderia richardii* (Endl.) Zotov. *New Zealand Jour. Bot.* 3:233–42.

Darlington, P. J., Jr. 1965. *Biogeography of the southern end of the world.* Cambridge, Mass., Harvard University Press.

Davis, J. H. 1950. Evidences of trans-oceanic dispersal of plants to New Zealand. *Tuatara* 3:87–97.

Dawson, J. W. 1960. Natural *Acaena* hybrids from the vicinity of Wellington. *Trans. Roy. Soc. New Zealand* 88:13–27.

Dawson, J. W. 1964. Unisexuality in the New Zealand Umbelliferae. *Tuatara* 12:67–68.

Fosberg, F. R. 1937. The genus *Gouldia* (Rubiaceae). *Bishop Mus. Bull.* 147:1–82.

Fosberg, F. R. 1943. The Polynesian species of *Hedyotis* (Rubiaceae). *Bishop Mus. Bull.* 174:1–102.

Fosberg, F. R. 1948. Derivation of the flora of the Hawaiian Islands. In *Insects of Hawaii*, vol. 1: *Introduction*, E. C. Zimmerman, pp. 107–19. Honolulu, University of Hawaii Press.

Fosberg, F. R. 1956. Studies in Pacific Rubiaceae. I–IV. *Brittonia* 8:165–78.

Franklin, D. A. 1962. The Ericaceae in New Zealand (*Gaultheria* and *Pernettya*). *Trans. Roy. Soc. New Zealand, Bot.*, 1:155–73.

Gillett, G. W. 1966. Hybridization and its taxonomic implications in the *Scaevola gaudichaudiana* complex of the Hawaiian Islands. *Evolution* 20:506–16.

Gillett, G. W., and E. K. S. Lim. 1970. An experimental study of the genus *Bidens* (Asteraceae) in the Hawaiian Islands. *Univ. Calif. Publ. Bot.* 56:1–63.

Godley, E. J. 1955. Breeding systems in New Zealand plants. I. *Fuchsia*. *Ann. Bot.*, n.s., 19:549–59.

Godley, E. J. 1957. Unisexual flowers in the Ericales. *Nature* 180:284–85.

Godley, E. J. 1964. Breeding systems in New Zealand plants. 3. Sex ratios in some natural populations. *New Zealand Jour. Bot.* 2:205–12.

Grant, P. R. 1971. Comment on Simberloff's letter. *Amer. Natur.* 105:194–97.

Grant, V. 1958. The regulation of recombination in plants. *Cold Spring Harbor Symp. Quant. Biol.* 23:337–63.

Hagen, Y. 1952. Birds of Tristan da Cunha. *Results Norwegian Sci. Exped. Tristan da Cunha 1937–1938* 20:1–248.

Hagerup, O. 1951. Pollination in the Faeroes—in spite of rain and poverty in insects. *Kongl. Danske Vidensk. Biol. Selsk. Medd.* 18(15):1–47.

Heine, E. M. 1937. Observation on the pollination of New Zealand flowering plants. *Trans. Roy. Soc. New Zealand Bot.* 67:133–48.

Hemsley, W. B. 1885. Report on the present state of knowledge of various insular floras. *Rep. Sci. Results Voyage H. M. S. Challenger, Vol. 1, Bot.*, pp. 1–75. London and Edinburgh, Her Majesty's Stationery Office.

Hillebrand, W. 1888. *Flora of the Hawaiian Islands.* London, Williams & Norgate.

Hosaka, E. Y. 1940. A revision of the Hawaiian species of *Myrsine* (*Suttonia, Rapanea*), (Myrsinaceae). *Occas. Papers Bishop Mus.* 16:25–76.

Keck, D. D. 1936. The Hawaiian silverswords: Systematics, affinities and phytogeographical problems in the genus *Argyroxiphium*. *Occas. Papers Bishop Mus.* 11(10):1–38.

Klein, D. R. 1968. The introduction, increase and crash of reindeer on St. Matthew Island. *Jour. Wildlife Manage.* 32:350–67.

Kramer, G. 1946. Veränderungen von Nachkommenziffer und Nachkommengrösse sowie der Altersverteilung von Inseleidechsen. *Z. Naturforsch.* 1:700–10.

Lack, D. 1946. Clutch and brood size in the robin. *Brit. Birds* 39:98–109, 130–35.

Lack, D. 1948. Further notes on clutch and brood size in the robin. *Brit. Birds* 41:98–104, 130–37.

Lack, D. 1954. *The natural regulation of animal numbers*. London, Oxford University Press, Clarendon Press.

Lack, D. 1971. Island birds. In *Adaptive aspects of insular evolution*, ed. W. L. Stern, pp. 29–31. Pullman, Wash., Washington State University Press.

Lack, D., and H. N. Southern. 1949. Birds on Tenerife. *Ibis* 91:607–26.

Lam, H. J. 1938. Monograph of the genus *Nesoluma* (Sapotaceae). *Occas. Papers Bishop Mus.* 14:127–65.

Lems, K. 1958. Botanical notes on the Canary Islands. I. Introgression among the species of *Adenocarpus*, and their role in the vegetation of the islands. *Bot. Inst. Nac. Invest. Agron. (Madrid)* 39:351–70.

Lewis, D. 1942. The evolution of sex in flowering plants. *Biol. Rev.* 17:46–67.

Linsey, E. G. 1966. Pollinating insects of the Galápagos Islands. In *The Galápagos,* ed. R. I. Bowman, pp. 225–32. Berkeley and Los Angeles, University of California Press.

Linsey, E. G., C. M. Rick, and S. G. Stephens. 1966. Observations on the floral relations of the Galápagos carpenter bee (Hymenoptera: Apidae). *Pan-Pacif. Entomol.* 42:1–18.

MacArthur, R. H., and E. O. Wilson. 1963. An equilibrium theory of insular zoogeography. *Evolution* 17:373–87.

McComb, J. A. 1966. The sex forms of species in the flora of the south-west of Western Australia. *Austral. Jour. Bot.* 14:303–16.

McCusker, A. 1962. Gynodioecism in *Leucopogon melaleucoides* A. Cunn. *Proc. Linnaean Soc. New South Wales* 87:286–89.

Millener, L. H. 1961. Our plant world. In *New Zealand junior encyclopedia*, pp. 310–36. Melbourne.

Moore, L. B. 1966. Australasian asteliads (Liliaceae) with special reference to New Zealand species of *Astelia* subgenus *Iricella*. *New Zealand Jour. Bot.* 4:201–40.

Moore, L. B., and E. Edgar. 1970. *Flora of New Zealand*, vol. II. Wellington, A. R. Shearer, Government Printer.

Müller, F. 1870. Umwandlung von Staubgefässen in Stempel bei *Begonia*. Uebergang von Zwitterblüthigkeit in Getrenntblüthigkeit bei *Chamissoa*. Triadrisch Varietät eines monadrischen *Epidendrum*. *Bot. Z.* 28:149–53.

Nicharat, S., and G. W. Gillett. 1970. A review of the taxonomy of Hawaiian *Pipturus* (Urticaceae) by anatomical and cytological evidence. *Brittonia* 22:191–206.

Oliver, W. R. B. 1935. The genus *Coprosma*. *Bishop Mus. Bull.* 132:1–207.

CHAPTER FOURTEEN

EQUATORIAL HIGHLAND BIOTA

At first glance, plants and animals of equatorial peaks and highlands would appear not to merit consideration in an insular context. Temperate mountains, or even continental islands would seem to merit more consideration. Equatorial highlands do tend to offer rather predictable climatic conditions. These conditions can be considered too uniform for comparison with the varied ecology of oceanic islands only if we select a single zone on an equatorial peak. However, if we consider the equatorial highlands as isolated areas of temperate flora and fauna from, say, 1000 m to the uppermost limits of vegetation, they form a gamut in ecological conditions very much like those of oceanic islands. Although this gamut is not as wide as, for example, that of the Hawaiian Islands, an appreciable amplitude is presented, and some genera, like *Espeletia*, are able to show within that amplitude a surprising range of growth forms and adaptations. The lower limits of the equatorial upland flora tend to be uneven, merging into the uppermost tropical elements, whereas on oceanic islands the shoreline provides a very discrete limit. If we take this into account, however, we are dealing with a decidedly insular situation.

To be sure, species within the larger or more important genera of equatorial highlands often represent vicarious species that show only minor differences from one peak to another, differences that do not appear to be adaptive in nature. However, adaptive ranges do occur within the area described above, and the nature of these adaptational modes forms the primary concern of this chapter.

Obviously, I am defining "equatorial highland flora" more broadly than most botanists, who focus on the higher vegetational belts. For example, Hedberg's Afroalpine flora (1957) and Coe's (1967) monograph

549

cover the levels from about 3500 to 4500 m. Such elevations correspond to the "typical" paramos in Colombia and Venezuela. However, my own observations in the African highlands suggest that temperate elements dominate vegetation much lower than that, and if we omit these subalpine zones, we hinder our understanding of the temperate equatorial flora and fauna in all its insular aspects. The alpine zone represents a series of extreme adaptations which, although very interesting in themselves, are only one phase of the temperate equatorial biota.

That tropical highlands tend to have temperate elements, rather than cool-tolerant representatives from groups in nearby tropical lowlands, is well known. An analysis of the Afroalpine flora (Hedberg, 1965) shows this clearly. Thus, the equatorial highland flora is the product of long-distance dispersal and, if we define broadly the zones occupied by these elements, shows all the aspects of oceanic islands. In this chapter, I am considering three areas:

(1) The high equatorial mountains of Africa (Mt. Kenya, Mt. Elgon, Mt. Kilimanjaro, Mt. Meru, Arberdare, Ruwenzori, and to a lesser extent other eastern African highlands).

(2) Highlands of Malesia (the New Guinean highlands; Mt. Kinabalu; mountains of Java—Gedeh, for example).

(3) Highlands of Colombia and Venezuela (paramos and subadjacent regions.

Despite the fact that these areas are widely separated from each other as well as from the temperate zone, they have an astonishing similarity in temperate genera: *Gentiana, Ranunculus, Viola,* and *Geranium,* for example, are typically temperate genera found in two or all three of these regions.

In regarding these areas as insular, two additional features need to be stressed: that they have cool but relatively uniform climates throughout the year (see diagrams for Nanyuki and Bogotá in fig. 10.1), and that the flora and fauna of these highlands have been derived by means of long-distance dispersal. In both of these statements, however, there is need for qualification, because the situation presented by equatorial highlands is distinct from that of the typical oceanic island.

The equatorial alpine climate is indeed "cool," but in a unique manner. The best way to summarize the equatorial alpine (or even subalpine)

regime is to say, "Summer every day, winter every night." The consequences of this climate are highly important. First, plants of tropical lowlands are adapted to a regime in which night temperatures are only
slightly lower than day temperatures. Conversely, temperate regions, especially montane ones (during the growing season) not only can experience
marked difference between maximum and nightly minimum on a given
day and fluctuation from week to week in this regard, but also their plants
and animals are all equipped with physiological preadaptations to the extremes of cold. Thus, temperate species might be predicted to be much
better adapted to equatorial highlands than even the most versatile tropical species. For climatic information on the alpine zone of Mt. Kenya,
see Coe (1967, pp. 51–65) or Hedberg (1964). Climatography of lower
elevations in African highlands is fairly well known, and the diagram of
Nanyuki in figure 10.1 suggests such a regime. In the alpine zones of equatorial mountains, temperatures drop below 0 C every night or almost every
night, providing an extreme to which temperate plants and animals have
special adaptive mechanisms.

Even if temperature is relatively uniform month by month in the
equatorial highlands, precipitation is not (see Coe, 1967, and Hedberg,
1964). This variation causes special problems, for not only is there physiological dryness due to freezing, there can also be dry seasons, which make
the climate additionally xerophytic. The opposite problem characterizes
some equatorial highland areas: excessive moisture, resulting in boggy
conditions, often with continuous mistiness, causes difficulties in pollination of angiosperms, for example.

Also with regard to dispersal, equatorial highlands are exceptional
when compared to islands. The spectra of dispersal types on particular
islands are discussed in chapter 2. Hedberg (1971) has extended this type
of analysis to the Afroalpine flora. His results for dispersal spectra in the
highest alpine zone contrast markedly with the island situation; presumptive dispersal by air flotation bulks very large (27–31 percent) compared
to that on oceanic islands, as does dispersal in mud or on feet of mammals
or birds (55–56 percent). Although transport in feathers or fur is of medium
importance, comparable to oceanic islands (12–14 percent), internal transport of seeds and fruits in birds is almost negligible (1–2 percent). Lower
zones, according to Hedberg's data, show little change in proportions of

551

these dispersal types, but in the lowest alpine zone (2400–3000 m), transport internally by birds begins to increase. Presumably it increases with decrease in altitude, for tropical lowlands and rain forest would be expected to show a high proportion of seeds carried internally in birds. It is also interesting that the two modes of transport most effective in the African highlands are relatively ineffective in the colonization of oceanic islands. To be sure, other authors cited by Hedberg (1971) have postulated increase in anemochory with increased altitude. In this connection, one can note that for air flotation to be effective across oceanic distances, the distance must be relatively short, the seed very small and capable of withstanding the low temperatures of the rapid, high-altitude air streams that carry seeds for prolonged distances. Where equatorial highlands are concerned, however, there is much less problem of seeds carried by air flotation terminating fatally by falling into a zone of ocean. Should such a seed fall to the ground, it could ultimately reach a destination in a series of short hops, a circumstance that vastly increases chances of success over a dispersal event that *must* transport a seed totally without contact with ocean for thousands of miles. Moreover, since alpine plants and especially their seeds are adapted to cold, transport by cold, high-altitude jet streams and other extreme air systems is much more feasible than for airborne seeds of tropical plants, such as orchids.

The possibility of transport in "hops" rather than as "nonstop" dispersal events also favors transport of seeds in mud, for a bird or mammal involved in dispersal to an equatorial highland zone is not required, for successful transport, to make a nonstop journey in which contact of the adherent seeds with seawater would prove fatal.

Again, one must stress that events of dispersal do not need to be frequent to account for the equatorial alpine flora. If they were frequent, genera and species would be identical with those of temperate sources, and within each of the three areas discussed below, species would not be endemic to particular mountains or plateaus, as they often are. That generic endemism is very low in the three highland areas may suggest that dispersal from temperate areas has been rather good, but it may also reflect the fact that the East African mountains, the mountains of Indo-Malesia, and the Andes are all relatively recent geologically. The Guayana Highlands (discussed at the end of this chapter) have a much higher endemism rate, which probably reflects greater geological age.

East African Highlands

The various well-known mountain peaks of East Africa, volcanic in origin and relatively recent (see Coe, 1967), rise from a plateau. The plateau has a climate that can be closely compared with that of an oceanic island. At Nairobi (1675 m), for example, the mean temperature is 19.5 C and the coldest temperature ever recorded is 6.7 C, figures almost identical with those for Lord Howe Island, which, however, receives more rainfall, distributed more evenly through the year. Las Palmas (Canary Is.) has similar temperature figures, but with more marked dry seasons than Nairobi. The even temperature throughout the year is notable at Nairobi and other localities on the Kenya plateau, but one must remember that diurnal-nocturnal fluctuation does occur and is a temperate aspect.

Submontane Plateau. The temperate—but uniform—conditions of the East African plateau should make the vegetation of this region much like that of an oceanic island. In fact, if we examine a flora that includes this region, such as that of Dale and Greenway (1961), and subtract species of the lowland Kenya region, we find virtually the same phenomena—even some of the same groups—as on oceanic islands. To be sure, the *Acacia* savannah does not look insular, but it is evergreen and resembles the lowland savannah of introduced *Prosopis* in the Hawaiian Islands. More importantly, the genera are temperate with few exceptions. One sees large, lichen-festooned trees of *Podocarpus gracilior*. On distribution maps, *Podocarpus* may look like a tropical genus, but it grows typically in cool tropical uplands. *Dodonaea viscosa*, an abundant element in certain dry oceanic islands, occurs frequently here. More significantly, one sees examples of "insular woodiness." For example, the giant cactoid *Euphorbia* trees (fig. 14.1, top left) betoken a frost-free environment in which an essentially herbaceous genus has responded to uniform, frost-free, temperate conditions. Other typically herbaceous families with woody representatives abound on the Kenya Plateau at about 1800 m, as at Naro Moru and somewhat higher. For example, *Heteromorpha* (Apiaceae) is exceptional in its family in becoming arboreal, a truly woody small tree (fig. 14.1, top right). This is also true of the apiad *Steganotaenia* (a tree 10–15 ft). A number of arborescent and arboreal Asteraceae occur in this region: shrubby and tree species (some to 20 ft) of *Vernonia*; two woody species of *Psiadia*; *Brachylaena merana* (a tree to 80 ft); and *Tarchonanthus* (a shrub or tree to 20 ft). The absence of herbaceous Asteraceae in the plateau zone is quite notable. Other interesting arborescent and arboreal representatives of herbaceous groups here include *Cylicomorpha parviflora*, a tree to 80 ft, of Caricaceae; in Solanaceae, three species of *Solanum* and one of *Withania*; and several genera of Lamiaceae.

An interesting and central feature is that if one omits the plateau flora and considers only the Afroalpine flora, one omits a number of species in genera that occur also in the alpine zone, and thus one obtains a false picture of adaptive radiation in these genera. These temperate genera may well have immigrated not to the high alpine zone but to the plateau lands, and evolved up into the alpine zone by means of adaptive radiation—or at least established in intermediate altitudes and radiated both upward and downward in altitude (the high alpine species appear to be specialized end products of a radiation). For example, there are woody understory species of *Lobelia* in this zone that look like some of the nearly herbaceous, much-branched Lobelias depicted by Hauman (1933): *L. petiolata, L. squarrosa,* and *L. intermedia.* The genus *Crassocephalum* (fig. 14.1, bottom left, right) is only a segregate of *Senecio,* and can be considered a *Senecio* with fewer-flowered heads. Is *Crassocephalum* not merely a plateau tree (to 25 ft) representing the same lines—or something like them—that have produced the alpine tree-Senecios? If Hauman (1935) had not restricted his account of *Senecio* in Africa merely to sect. *Dendrosenecio* (the alpine species), we would have seen some of the lower-elevation species of *Senecio* that are very likely related to the Dendrosenecios.

Lower Montane Forest. When we consider lower elevational belts on Mt. Kenya and the other mountains, the phenomena just stressed become clearer yet. Hedberg (1957) does not include *Lobelia gibberoa* (fig. 14.2, bottom left, right) in his flora, but this species is clearly part of the radiation that has produced the alpine species of *Lobelia. Lobelia gibberoa* tends to occur in a wet-forest zone, at approximately 2000–3000 m (Hedberg, 1951), in the bamboo–*Podocarpus milanjianus* forest (a forest that

FIG. 14.1. Plants with probably increased woodiness from the plateau region of Kenya. TOP LEFT, *Euphorbia candelabrum* (Euphorbiaceae), tree 8 m tall; near Lake Nakuru, 1700 m. TOP RIGHT, *Heteromorpha trifoliata* (Apiaceae), branch from tree; Naro Moru, 1800 m. BOTTOM LEFT, RIGHT, *Crassocephalum mannii* (Asteraceae); Rift Valley near Nairobi, 1400 m. BOTTOM LEFT, habit, small tree 4 m tall. BOTTOM RIGHT, inflorescence and associated leaves; heads are about 8 mm long.

FIG. 14.2. Plants showing increased woodiness from lower elevations of Mt. Kenya. TOP LEFT, RIGHT, *Hypericum keniense* (Hypericaceae). TOP LEFT, habit of tree, ca. 8 m tall; at about 3000 m. TOP RIGHT, flower, 4 cm in diam., and foliage. BOTTOM LEFT, RIGHT, *Lobelia gibberoa* (Campanulaceae). BOTTOM LEFT, habit, ca. 5 m tall, including inflorescence; at about 2800 m. BOTTOM RIGHT, flowers on inflorescence; corolla pale green, staminal column purple.

also contains relatively "primitive" woody plants, in contrast, such as *Ocotea kenyensis* of the Lauraceae). In viewing evolution of *Lobelia* in Africa, we cannot neglect *L. gibberoa* merely because it is not in the alpine zone. It is a giant herb (taller than the alpine Lobelias) that has stems dying when they flower, but producing basal offshoots (as do the alpine Lobelias). Its leaves show no frost-resistance mechanisms. *Lobelia gibberoa* is, however, just as much a product of insular woodiness as is *Lobelia gaudichaudii* on the Hawaiian Islands.

At the upper borders of the podocarp-bamboo zone, one finds two other tree species that can hardly be interpreted as anything but examples of insular woodiness. They are in a uniformly cool, but presumably frost-free, cloud forest (Hedberg, 1951): *Hagenia abyssinica* (see shrubby plants, not yet trees, in foreground of figure 14.2, bottom left) and *Hypericum keniense* (fig. 14.2, top left, right).

Upper Forest. *Hagenia* is a genus, related to *Bencomia* and *Dendriopoterium* of the Canary Islands, which shows marked arborescence within the potentilloid line (broadly construed) of Rosaceae. Trees of *Hagenia* attain 50 ft. Trees of *Hypericum keniense* attain 40 ft. This size is truly exceptional within the shrub or subshrub genus *Hypericum* (Hypericaceae). Thus, the *Hypericum-Hagenia* zone is quite comparable to the wet cloud forest on the Canary Islands, although in their insular woodiness these two genera exceed what occurs on the Canaries. The more constant availability of moisture, along with the cool, uniform climate, has presumably permitted the amazing arborescence in *Hagenia* and *Hypericum* in the upper forest zone of Mt. Kenya.

Moorlands. Above the *Hypericum-Hagenia* forest is a bog area; here we see the effects of high-elevation bog, where wet, cold conditions (evidently with occasional frosts) permit less arborescence. There are, however, a number of woody species, some from temperate woody groups (*Erica* and *Philippia* of Ericaceae, for example), and some arborescent or shrubby forms from typically herbaceous groups. On rocky outcrops in the bog region we can find these ericads as well as shrubby species of *Helichrysum* (Asteraceae, tribe Inuleae) and *Nidorella* (a tree to 20 ft: Asteraceae, Inuleae). The open bog areas are notable for their species of *Lobelia*. On Mt. Kenya, *L. keniensis* (fig. 14.3, top left, right, bottom left) is a good example. Although these plants have elongate stems, the stems tend to be prostrate and to root in the bog (fig. 14.3, bottom left) and bend up-ward into leafy shoots (fig. 14.3, top left) which flower, then die (as in-dividual shoots); basal innovations may form other shoots from a given plant. *Lobelia keniensis* has prominent bracts concealing the purple flowers. These bracts are landing platforms for the pollinating sunbird, *Nectarinia johnstonii*. Photographs of a visit by the sunbird have been presented by Hedberg (1964, p. 40). The claw marks left in the bracts of inflorescences are universally present (fig. 14.3, top right) in plants with opened flowers, or toward the end of flowering, because repeated visits are made to each flower in an inflorescence. Nectarinids also visit, according to my observations in 1967, Lobelias of the lower regions, and I have seen them on inflorescences of *L. gibberoa*, in which the numerous dense flowers provide footholds during visits. *Lobelia keniensis* extends from the bogs into the alpine zone, and its ability to close leaves at night (see below) shows ability to withstand frost (Hedberg, 1964, pp. 57, 61).

The other main component of the bog region on Mt. Kenya is *Senecio brassica* (fig. 14.5, bottom left, right). Its growth habits are remarkably similar to those of *L. keniensis*. Like *L. keniensis*, it is frost resistant, the leaf rosettes can close at night (Hedberg, 1964), and the woolly indumen-tum on the lower leaf surfaces provides an excellent insulation, retaining a temperature above freezing in the apical bud (see Hedberg, 1964) even if the temperature on the outside of the rosette goes below freezing.

The bog species of *Lobelia* and *Senecio* are interesting in that they form such an extensive series of vicarious species on the African volcanoes. *Lobelia keniensis* on Mt. Kenya has close counterparts in *L. deckenii* on Mt. Kilimanjaro (fig. 14.3, bottom right), *L. elgonensis* on Mt. Elgon (Hedberg, 1964, p. 60), *L. sattimae* on the Aberdares (Dale and Green-way, 1961), and *L. bequaertii* on Ruwenzori (Hauman, 1933, p. 21). The differences among these species are relatively minor, and form a definitive example of vicarious species. It is interesting that *L. gibberoa* is found on various mountains in the form of subspecific (varietal) variants (Hauman, 1933). These may be considered vicarious subspecies, and perhaps are not distinct species because *L. gibberoa* occupies lower, broader zones less iso-lated from one another on different volcanoes than are the bog habitats of *Lobelia keniensis* and its vicariants.

FIG. 14.3. High-elevation species of *Lobelia* (Campanulaceae) from African mountains. TOP LEFT, RIGHT, BOTTOM LEFT, *L. keniensis*. TOP LEFT, habit of flowering plant in bog; ca. 3300 m, Mt. Kenya. TOP RIGHT, bracts of inflorescence, showing claw marks made by the bird *Nectarinia*. BOTTOM LEFT, portion of prostrate stem from bog, showing formation of large lateral roots. BOTTOM RIGHT, *L. deckenii*; from about 3400 m on Mt. Kilimanjaro.

FIG. 14.4. Species of *Lobelia* from high elevations on Mt. Kenya. TOP LEFT, *L. keniensis*, to show open habit of rosettes during day; rosettes are about 0.7 m in diam. TOP RIGHT, BOTTOM LEFT, RIGHT, *L. telekii*; from Teleki Valley, ca. 4100 m elevation. TOP RIGHT, leaf rosette in early morning, to show "closed position" of rosette during nighttime cold. BOTTOM LEFT, habit of plant in flower, 1.5 m tall. BOTTOM RIGHT, portion of inflorescence (pith hollow), showing flowers, very short, ca. 2–2.5 cm long, and hairy bracts, some of which have been cropped by an herbivore.

FIG. 14.5. Subalpine species of *Senecio* (Asteraceae) from African mountains. TOP LEFT, RIGHT, *S. meruensis*; Mt. Meru. TOP LEFT, habit of plant, to show relatively slender stem, broad thin leaves, and lack of accumulation of old, dead leaves on stem. TOP RIGHT, rosette and massive inflorescence. BOTTOM LEFT, RIGHT, *S. brassica*; from about 3500 m in bog on Naro Moru track, Mt. Kenya. BOTTOM LEFT, rosettes among grass in bog, showing woolly undersurface of leaf. BOTTOM RIGHT, plant in flower, about 2 m tall.

561

Senecio brassica is also notable for relationship to vicarious species. Among these are *S. brassicaeformis* on the Aberdares. There appears to have been much more specific differentiation among the *Dendrosenecio* species of *Senecio*, so that vicariads are harder to identify in the tree-Senecios of the higher alpine regions. For example, young individuals of *S. friesiorum* on Mt. Stanley look like *S. brassica* but grow into tall trees of the *S. keniodendron* type (Hauman, 1935). Hedberg (1969b) has shown that species of *Senecio* from a given climatic belt on one mountain are not clear-cut vicariants of species from the same belt on other East African mountains. There is the possibility that vicarious species occur upon a single mountain, he feels (e.g., a bog species may be most closely related to a high-altitude species on the same mountain), and thus there would be vicarious species *by zone*. There is no question that adaptation (probably toward higher elevations) has occurred. The question Hedberg (1969b) raises, in essence, is How many times? In other words, high-elevation species like *S. keniodendron* may have originated from lower-elevation ancestors more than once. Dispersal of Afroalpine *Senecio* species to comparable belts on other peaks has undoubtedly occurred, but does this account for only part of the speciation? As Hedberg indicates, the situation is not entirely clear, and deserves close further study.

Other bog elements include abundant *Festuca* tussocks (fig. 14.3, top left), and, as understory plants, *Alchemilla* spp., *Anagallis serpens*, *Viola* spp., *Swertia* spp., and *Eriocaulon* spp., panboreal genera that form prostrate stems (in the case of the first three) or dense rosettes (*Eriocaulon*) and are presumably frost resistant because of their growth near the ground in conjunction with other vegetation that would insulate them from frost. In the wet ground of the bogs, tussock formation and prostrate stems represent the chief adaptational modes.

Alpine Zone. The alpine zone is the region (mostly 3500–4200 m [Hedberg, 1968]) noted for giant *Senecio* species, and indeed their adaptations suggest that they and all other elements of this zone must exist under the highly taxing conditions of nightly frost. Hedberg (1964) has adequately summarized these, and I shall draw on his account only by way of showing how temperate genera, mostly those that also occur at lower elevations, have narrowly restricted adaptations that permit survival in this extreme environment.

Arborescence is possible only if terminal buds can be protected from frost, if stems can be protected from freezing, and if leaves can be resistant to both desiccation and frost. *Senecio keniodendron* illustrates all of these features clearly (fig. 14.6, top left, right, bottom left). Stems are heavily clothed with leaves (fig. 14.6, top left). Absence of old leaves on particular plants is apparently the result of burning. These old leaves form an insulation that keeps the tree trunks slightly above freezing at night (Hedberg, 1964). Even without leaves, the thick corky bark (fig. 14.6, top right) provides an appreciable degree of insulation. The massive leaves of S. *keniodendron* are thick, and when they form a closed bud at night (figure 14.6, bottom left), they protect the apical bud. Hedberg (1964) has shown that when temperatures on the outside of the leaf rosette are below freezing (−4 C), they are above freezing (+1.5 C) within the rosette. This is important for flowering, because the massive inflorescence, which is terminal, completes much of its growth within the rosette before emerging. What is not clear is how the inflorescence, once emerged, is able to flower and set fruit under conditions of nightly frost. It may be that, as with the leaves of the rosette, higher osmotic pressures within mature tissues are less subject to freezing than are primordia. Also, more freezing would be expected at ground level than at the height of an inflorescence on S. *keniodendron*. The massive rosette of durable leaves and extremely short internodes suggests a slow growth rate, and in fact Hedberg (1969a) has shown an annual increase in height of only 2.5 cm.

Resistance to Freezing in the Alpine Zone. Senecio keniodendron illustrates how the entire morphology of a plant can be adapted to frost resistance. The other large rosette plants show some of the same features. All of the alpine Senecios and Lobelias (see fig. 14.4, top right, *Lobelia telekii*) are able to close leaf rosettes at night and open them (fig. 14.4, top left) during the day. Hedberg (1964) believes that the very hairy bracts of the inflorescence in *L. telekii* (fig. 14.4, bottom left, right) may serve as an insulation. Some of the Senecios have leaves that are notably hairy, as in S. *cottonii* (fig. 14.6, bottom right)—undoubtedly an insulation, as such leaves may be for species of *Espeletia* in the Colombian paramos, discussed later in this chapter. Hauman (1935) presents drawings of *Senecio* leaves that show the hairy vesture. Where leaves are relatively thin and hairless in Senecios of African volcanoes, and where their old leaves

FIG. 14.6. Alpine species of *Senecio* (Asteraceae) from African mountains. TOP LEFT, RIGHT, BOTTOM LEFT, *S. keniodendron*; at 4100 m in Teleki Valley, Mt. Kenya. TOP LEFT, habit of old, branched tree about 6 m tall, showing accumulation of old leaves. TOP RIGHT, surface of bark, to show thick, furrowed accumulation of corky tissue. BOTTOM LEFT, rosette of young tree, showing leaves in "closed" position typical of nighttime; photograph taken in early morning. BOTTOM RIGHT, *S. cottonii*; trees about 5 m tall; at 4200 m on Mt. Kilimanjaro.

do not accumulate and stems are relatively slender, as in *Senecio meruensis* (fig. 14.5, top left, right) and *S. erici-rosenii* (Hedberg, 1964), I suspect frost-free growing conditions. These species grow not in the high alpine zone but in the ericaceous belt (Hedberg, 1965). The mechanisms for frost resistance by *Lobelia wollastonii* and *L. lanuriensis* are not readily apparent. These two Lobelias grow in company of Senecios much like *S. keniodendron* in morphology (Hauman, 1933), yet they look like *Lobelia gibberoa*, which probably grows in frost-free localities.

Aside from the giant rosette plants, the flora of the high alpine zone consists of plants that could be called cryptophytes—with renewal buds located at or near ground level (fig. 14.7, top left, right, bottom left), and with very short internodes. The flowers or inflorescences of these plants are virtually sessile. Many conflicting explanations have been advanced for the "nanism" of these plants (see Hedberg, 1964); this habit seems at first glance illogical, because night temperatures would be expected to be lowest near ground level. Hedberg (1964) advances a new explanation, that viscosity of water and consequent difficulty of transport of water within the plant are characteristic where temperatures fall to 0 C. Therefore, difficulty in translocation would dictate shorter internodes, pedicels, and peduncles. However, other explanations may be operative. If the buds of the giant Senecios are protected from freezing by a rosette of leaves, a rosette plant at ground level may share this ability. More significant, however, is the probability—since these low rosette herbs or cushion plants often grow in wet places—that ground water, during freezing, gives off considerable heat which prevents freezing of plants that grow on moist surfaces or near water. This physical phenomenon is well known and is used by horticulturists and agriculturists, who use watering as a means of preventing freezing of plants. If operative, the heat given off by freezing water extends to a localized area, so that plants with elongate internodes would not benefit from it. One would also expect that osmotic pressures in these plants are high, for they are covered by hoarfrost during the night (fig. 14.7, top right) yet are not, apparently, damaged. Young flowers and inflorescences develop within the protection of vegetative rosettes (fig. 14.7, bottom left) and emerge only as they mature, often becoming elongate only in fruit. Fruits and seeds are, of course, much more resistant to subfreezing temperatures than are flowers, so their emergence above

FIG. 14.7. Herbaceous plants in the flora of Mt. Kenya, to illustrate adaptations and characteristics of alpine flora. TOP LEFT, clumps of grass through which stream runs; flat-topped nature may be due to herbivores; narrowing of clumps below is probably due to freezing of

(*continued*)

the rosette plant at this stage is understandable. Further morphological features of small rosette plants, cushion plants, or trailing plants suggest frost resistance. Renewal buds are often located below ground level or within rosettes. In the case of cushion plants, new roots often grow not into open soil likely to be frozen, but down through the cushion itself, which does not freeze, and ultimately reach soil below the cushion, which is likewise protected by the cushion from freezing. Further comments on cushion plants are offered later in this chapter.

Xerophytism. Adaptations of Afroalpine plants to xeromorphy include the narrow, inrolled leaves of various grasses—*Festuca, Agrostis*—to expose minimal surface (fig. 14.7, top left). The microphylly of the Afroalpine species of Ericaceae could be cited in this regard. Microphylly characterizes the shrub *Alchemilla argophylla* (fig. 14.7, bottom right) as compared with the broad, cordate leaves of the prostrate Afroalpine species of *Alchemilla*. This tendency is true in *Helichrysum* as well. Hairy or woolly leaf coverings or thick cuticle—both distinctive in many Afroalpine plants—may also deter transpiration where water availability is low. If permafrost occurs, relatively shallow root systems would be expected. High osmotic pressure of leaf tissues, hypothesized above, would counter not only freezing but low humidity as well.

Protection Against Radiation. Intense sunlight in the alpine zone provides special problems. Although mist and clouds are frequent, sunlight is extremely brilliant during the hours when it does occur. The same hairiness that provides insulation in some alpine species may also function in filtering sunlight. This seems true in the Afroalpine species of *Helichrysum* (Hedberg, 1964), and would certainly explain the silvery leaves of *Alchemilla argophylla* (fig. 14.7, bottom right). Many plants have characteristic leaf positions other than horizontal, and can be shiny and therefore highly reflective, or glaucous. The grasses demonstrate some of these characteristics. Even the giant rosette plants do not display leaves in a

FIG. 14.7 (*continued*)

water between clumps at night. TOP RIGHT, *Ranunculus* sp., hoarfrost on plant early in morning; leaves are not damaged by it, however. BOTTOM LEFT, *Haplocarpha rueppellii* (Asteraceae), formation of heads sessile within rosettes; stem is below ground level, rosette is actually sunken beneath ground level. BOTTOM RIGHT, *Alchemilla argophylla* (Rosaceae), showing leaves 2–2.5 cm long, covered with shiny felt of hairs that probably resists solar radiation and possibly serves as insulation and a desiccation-resistance mechanism. All photographs taken in Teleki Valley, 4100 m, Mt. Kenya.

horizontal position; most leaves are more nearly vertical than horizontal. Restricted leaf surfaces (Ericaceae) or growth in shady places (*Alchemilla* spp. shaded by clumps of grasses) are other mechanisms that would lower the effects of intense insolation.

Fire and Herbivore Pressure in the Afroalpine Zone. Because of drought in these mountains, the Afroalpine belt is subject to burning, often by man. Succulent plants are not affected: the giant Senecios lose their sheaths of dead leaves but survive. Cryptophytic plants are unaffected, because fire is not generally a problem for ground-level rosette plants. The Ericaceae do appear to suffer from fire, but grasses seem, on the contrary, to be benefited (Hedberg, 1964). Often in alpine regions in various parts of the world, extensive grasslands may be the result of burning by man rather than a wholly natural phenomenon (this is almost certainly true in New Guinea).

Herbivore pressure in the Afroalpine flora is noticeable chiefly in grasses, which can have "trimmed-off" rosettes. Rodents and the *Hyrax* are the chief herbivores of this zone. Although some larger mammals (elephants) occasionally penetrate the alpine zone, the plateau herbivores do not. The typical plateau herbivores, such as impalas and various species of gazelles, are very specific in their preferences for particular grass species, and this fact may restrict them to lower zones.

Pollination in the Afroalpine Flora. In respect to pollination, we have an interesting parallel with oceanic islands. As perusal of Hedberg's (1957) Afroalpine flora shows, colorful flowers are rare. Exceptions occur in the lobelioids, with purplish flowers almost hidden (except for *L. gibberoa*, a subalpine species with greenish flowers); these species are ornithophilous, however. A fairly high degree of anemophily is present in this zone because of predominance of grasses and sedges. The remainder of plants have white or yellow flowers, some greenish and inconspicuous (*Alchemilla, Haplosciadium*). Reds, oranges, and blues are notably absent. Even *Arabis* (Brassicaceae) has pale flowers. The reasons for lack of colorful flowers may be the same as on oceanic islands (see chapter 13): absence of long-tongued bees, relative scarcity of butterflies. Insects are also remarkably sedentary in this zone (see later section, Insects of Equatorial Highlands). This situation contrasts with that of temperate mountains, where alpine flowers are notably colorful. The difference would seem to lie in the fact that temperate mountains have a relatively warm, frost-free growing season (albeit rather short) during which pollinators adapted to colorful flowers can become active. In the Afroalpine climate the nightly frosts would provide a different regime altogether. We would benefit greatly from a study of pollination in the Afroalpine region (or other equatorial highlands). Such studies have perhaps not been undertaken to date because of the discomfort and logistic difficulty involved in living in these regions, for extended stays are required to secure data on pollination.

Sources of the Afroalpine Flora. Hedberg (1965) has summarized the affinities of various plants in the African alpine and subalpine flora. The vast majority, of course, are either north-temperate or "pantemperate." The fact that the temperate lands of the northern hemisphere represent an enormous source area compared to land areas of the south temperate zone leads almost inevitably to high representation of boreal elements in the Afroalpine flora. Hedberg lists only 10 species with affinities to the Cape region of South Africa, 17 to South Africa other than the cape (most of these are subalpine and not alpine plants in any case). There are even five species Hedberg regards as having Himalayan affinities. Hedberg (1965) recognizes an "Afroalpine endemic element" and an "Afromontane element." I find these interesting and perhaps necessary categories, but regrettable, because even if species in these categories are endemic, their sources inevitably lie elsewhere than on the high volcanoes themselves. The Dendrosenecios, for example, are endemic to the high African mountains, but their ancestors must ultimately have been Senecios of some temperate region. Admittedly, we cannot easily unravel the affinities of the Afroalpine and Afromontane endemics, so it is easy to see why Hedberg is not more explicit about affinities of these elements (many are endemic species, not genera, as in the case of *Helichrysum*). The chief lesson is that size of temperate source area and distance from the African volcanoes are the factors that have governed immigration to the volcanoes. This reminds one a great deal of such Pacific islands as Rapa, where floristic affinities are governed by distance from source areas and ecological similarity to source areas (see chapter 2).

In my earlier book (Carlquist, 1965), I selected *Thlaspi alliaceum* as an example of a plant species that shows affinity to European montane areas. This appears to be an unfortunate example if Hedberg (1971) is correct in claiming that *Thlaspi* may be man-introduced. I might better have selected an example from Hedberg's "Boreal element," such as *Cerastium, Arabis, Astragalus, Cardamine, Sedum, Heracleum, Galium,* or *Carduus.*

Malesian Highlands

Alpine regions occur on several of the Malesian islands. Most notable, perhaps, are the central highlands of New Guinea, which reach 5029 m. The photographs of New Guinean highland plants presented here (figs. 14.8; 14.9, top left, right, bottom left) are from Mt. Piora, 3719 m, about 7° south of the equator. Other notable Malesian island peaks include Kinabalu (Sabah), 4101 m; Kerintji (Sumatra), 3805 m; and Smeroe (Java), 3670 m. There are numerous peaks above 3000 m on Java and several on Sulawesi (Celebes), but the greatest area above 3000 m occurs on New Guinea, and the Malesian highland and alpine flora is most richly represented on that island. Unfortunately, there is at present no single monograph on the Malesian alpine flora. Stapf (1894) and Meijer (1965) have offered accounts of the flora of Kinabalu. There are a number of monographs (notably Royen, 1964a, 1964b) and reports of collections in the journal *Nova Guinea*. The *Flora Malesiana* will ultimately contain accounts of all families represented in the Malesian alpine and subalpine flora. There are several studies that deal chiefly with Mt. Gedeh on Java (Rock, 1920; Faber, 1927). These, as well as my personal observations on Mt. Piora and Mt. Salawaket, New Guinea, are the sources of the commentary below.*

Malesian highlands below the alpine zone consist of forests rich in Podocarpaceae: *Podocarpus brassii, P. brevifolia, P. cupressina, P. imbricatus, Dacrydium falciforme, D. gibbsiae,* and *Phyllocladus hypophyllus,* for example. The presence of podocarp forest below an alpine zone is reminiscent of the vegetation belts on the African volcanoes. Intermixed with the podocarps are temperate genera such as *Drimys* (Winteraceae; chiefly *D. piperita*), *Olearia* spp. (Asteraceae), *Haloragis* spp. (Haloraga-

---

* A well-illustrated book, *The mountain flora of Java,* by A. Hamzah, M. Toha, and C. G. G. J. van Steenis (Leiden, E. J. Brill, Publisher, 1972) is now available.

ceae), *Eurya* (Theaceae), *Elaeocarpus* (Elaeocarpaceae), *Metrosideros* (Myrtaceae), and numerous species of *Rhododendron* (Ericaceae). In New Guinea, scraggly trees of *Podocarpus imbricatus,* often bearing *Dendrobium psychrophyllum* epiphytically, surround the open, grassy alpine swales. This grassland is at least partly the result of burning by man. Within the grassland, there are various shrubby species of such genera as *Vaccinium, Rhododendron, Styphelia,* and *Coprosma.* Tree ferns, such as *Cyathea hymenophylloides,* may be abundant (Carlquist, 1965). Within the grass tussocks, various temperate herbaceous plants may be found. Among those are cushions of *Centrolepis philippinensis* (fig. 14.8, top left, right), *Eriocaulon montanum* (fig. 14.8, bottom left), *Plantago aundensis* (fig. 14.8, bottom right), *Potentilla papuana* (fig. 14.9, top left), *Astelia papuana* (fig. 14.9, top right), and *Gentiana piundensis* (fig. 14.9, bottom left). I must emphasize that although these genera occur on various mountains of Malesia, the species vary from one mountain to another, and some may be endemic to a single massif. For example, Royen (1964a) lists 21 species of *Gentiana* from alpine New Guinea. On Kinabalu, there is yet another, *G. lycopodioides.* Among these herbaceous genera, vicarious species are as numerous as they are in the Afroalpine flora. Among other genera common in Malesian alpine areas are *Carex* (Cyperaceae), *Drapetes* (Thymeleaceae), *Epilobium* (Onagraceae), *Euphrasia* (Scrophulariaceae), *Gahnia* (Cyperaceae), *Gleichenia* (Gleicheniaceae), *Hypericum* (Hypericaceae), *Lagenophora* (Asteraceae), *Lycopodium* (Lycopodiaceae), *Myosotis* (Boraginaceae), *Ranunculus* (Ranunculaceae), *Rubus* (Rosaceae), and *Tetramolopium* (Asteraceae). Many characteristic alpine plants of Malesia could be added to this list.

However, the features of interest with respect to the Malesian alpine flora are the various characteristics these plants show that are related to alpine existence. In the Malesian alpine areas, as on Afroalpine peaks, temperatures can drop below 0 C at night. Thus, one should expect some of the same adaptations. That is precisely what occurs—although mostly in genera different from those of Africa. Tree ferns of *Cyathea* remind one somewhat of the *Dendrosenecio* habit—there are no rosette-tree composites on the Malesian peaks. Perhaps the drooping old leaves and the numerous leaves covering the apical bud in *Cyathea* offer frost protection in much the same way as they do in the Dendrosenecios, although prob-

FIG. 14.8. Alpine plants from Mt. Piora, New Guinea. TOP LEFT, RIGHT, *Centrolepis philip-pinensis* (Centrolepidaceae). TOP LEFT, habit of cushions, seed from surface. TOP RIGHT, side view of cushion broken open, showing inflorescences at surface level of cushion, and roots, be-low, that grow down through cushion. BOTTOM LEFT, *Eriocaulon montanum* (Eriocaulaceae), rosette showing short inflorescence; leaves about 3 cm long. BOTTOM RIGHT, *Plantago aunden-sis* (Plantaginaceae), rosettes flattened at ground level; leaves 3 cm long.

FIG. 14.9. Alpine plants from New Guinea (top left and right, bottom left) and Costa Rica (bottom right). TOP LEFT, *Potentilla papuana* (Rosaceae); leaves silvery, flowers on short pedicels; Mt. Piora. TOP RIGHT, *Astelia papuana* (Liliaceae), rosettes showing fruits among leaves; leaves 8–10 cm long; Mt. Piora. BOTTOM LEFT, *Gentiana piundensis* (Gentianaceae), stems ca. 4 cm tall; Mt. Piora. BOTTOM RIGHT, *Blechnum werckleanum* (Blechnaceae), tree fern dominating Páramo Ojo de Agua; Macizo de Buena Vista, Cordillera de Talamanca, Costa Rica. (Photograph by José Cuatrecasas.)

573

ably Cyatheas are not subject to such extreme frost as are the Dendro-senecios (the same may be said of tree ferns in the genus *Blechnum*, as in the highlands of Costa Rica [fig. 14.9, bottom right] and Colombia). The cushion-plant habit is represented by *Centrolepis philippinensis* (fig. 14.8, top left, right), and undoubtedly has the same ecological adaptation as mentioned for cushion plants in Afroalpine and paramo regions.

As in the Afroalpine flora, one notes many rosette plants that else-where would have elongate inflorescences, but in Malesian alpine areas have inflorescences that project little, if at all, above the leaves until fruit-ing. Among the examples shown here are *Eriocaulon montanum* (fig. 14.8, bottom left) and *Plantago aundensis* (fig. 14.8, bottom right), *Potentilla papuana* (fig. 14.9, top left) and *Astelia papuana* (fig. 14.9, top right). In *Plantago aundensis*, flowering occurs within the woolly rosettes. The in-florescences at anthesis are nearly sessile. During fruiting, the succulent, nonfibrous peduncle elongates rapidly, exposing fruits and seeds for dis-persal. This habit, unusual for *Plantago*, suggests the high selective value of flowering where protection is afforded by wool and leaves of the rosettes. The wool may insulate, the leaves may give off heat during the coldest portion of the night. Because the ground is usually quite moist in Malesian alpine localities, heat generated by freezing might well prevent freezing in low herbs. Also, the shelter of grass tussocks, as in Afroalpine areas, may deter freezing. *Potentilla papuana* (fig. 14.9, top left) is a prostrate plant among grass tussocks.

Microphylly is characteristic of numerous genera. In addition to the tree that occurs around grasslands, *Podocarpus imbricatus*, one can cite such examples as *Gentiana piundensis* (fig. 14.9, bottom left), *Coprosma*, *Rhododendron*, *Vaccinium*, *Styphelia*, *Drapetes*, and *Tetramolopium*. The hairiness of *Potentilla papuana* (fig. 14.9, top left) and *Astelia papuana* (fig. 14.9, top right) may serve to reflect bright sunshine. Hairiness might reduce transpiration somewhat in the dry alpine air, but low humidity certainly seems related to the microphyllous habit. Microphylly might also be related to lack of seasonality. Conditions are relatively uniform through-out the year, so that rapid expansion of large leaves, followed by their death at the end of a season (as in temperate-zone montane plants) is not to be expected. Instead, leaves suited to relatively harsh but uniform con-ditions must be formed, leaves suited to indefinite duration. Flowering in the Malesian alpine region takes place over an extended season, perhaps even throughout the entire year (see, for example, Royen, 1964a).

With respect to the geographical affinities of the alpine plants of Malesia, one can again cite distance from source and similarity in ecological preference as predetermining factors for floristic composition, just as they are on islands such as the Hawaiian Islands. There is, as one might expect, distinct affinity with temperate southern-hemisphere floras: *Astelia, Coprosma, Styphelia, Centrolepis, Brachycome,* and *Drapetes,* for example. Those without clear southerly relatives appear to belong mostly to what would be called pantemperate genera like *Ranunculus, Gentiana, Swertia, Eriocaulon, Veronica, Myosotis, Cardamine, Vaccinium, Hypericum, Adenostemma, Erigeron,* and *Plantago.* There are few, if any, genera characteristic only of boreal temperate regions. For example, although *Epilobium* is most highly developed in the northern hemisphere, it is a large genus in New Zealand, and one might guess that the New Guinean species have been derived from the south rather than from the north. There are resemblances to the New Zealand alpine flora, or even floras of subantarctic islands, but there are numerous differences, too. The subantarctic flora is indeed a flora of cool regions, but not uniformly cool as in alpine Malesia. One genus of remarkable distribution is *Tetramolopium* (Asteraceae) with 33 species: 22 occur in upland New Guinea, 11 in the Hawaiian Islands (Koster, 1966). Endemism in Malesian uplands is mostly at the species level, but one can cite the genus *Piora* of the Asteraceae (Koster, 1966). *Scyphostegia,* a monotypic genus and sole species of its family, is a Kinabalu endemic but occurs at lower elevations, about 700 m (Stapf, 1894).

There is considerable irony in the fact that the cool upland forest of Malesia contains many genera from woody families often regarded as rich in primitive features: *Podocarpus, Dacrydium,* and *Phyllocladus* of the Podocarpaceae; *Papuacedrus* of the Cupressaceae; *Drimys* and *Bubbia* of the Winteraceae; and several genera of Monimiaceae. Even though the Malesian uplands are geologically rather recent, these "primitive" genera are found there. However, the alpine flora, at a somewhat higher altitude than the cool-forest elements mentioned above, is composed of "specialized" genera—most of which are widespread herbs of temperate regions. The Asteraceae bulk large, as one might expect in a region of climatic extremes, somewhat xeric regime, and in general a pioneer nature. The same contrast between composition of upland woody forest and alpines occurs on the African volcanoes (*Podocarpus* forest containing *Ocotea*), and similar considerations apply in the subparamo versus the paramo regions of Colombia described next.

The Paramos of South America, and Subadjacent Vegetation Types

The paramos are high cool regions, with bogs and humid ground, in the central parts of the Andes. The lower limits of the paramos are around 3200 m in Colombia, and they extend upward to regions of permanent snow (4700–5000 m is the usual upper limit of vegetation in Colombia). Maximum registered temperatures approximate 12 C, and minima are about −2 C (Cuatrecasas, 1957). The "subparamo" regions (2500–3500 m) contain, like the subalpine forests of Africa and Malesia, many families and genera of woody plants considered to be rich in primitive features: *Podocarpus* (Podocarpaceae), *Drimys* (Winteraceae), *Ternstroemia* (Theaceae), *Weinmannia* (Cunoniaceae), *Nectandra* and *Ocotea* (Lauraceae), *Brunellia* (Brunelliaceae), *Clusia* (Clusiaceae), *Saurauia* (Saurauiaceae), *Escallonia* (Saxifragaceae, Escallonioideae), and *Ilex* (Aquifoliaceae). To be sure, these forests do not exclude representatives of specialized families such as Asteraceae, Rubiaceae, and Myrtaceae (Cuatrecasas, 1934, 1957, 1968).

The paramo proper is a relatively treeless region almost defined by the genus *Espeletia*, the "frailejon" (figs. 14.10–14.13). The paramos are comparable to the two equatorial highland regions just considered, but (although comparable weather data are not really available) are somewhat moister and more perpetually fogbound; because of the cloud cover, daytime temperatures are more depressed, and frosts much less frequent, evidently. Among the few trees (unless one considers the taller, rosette-tree species of *Espeletia* to be trees) are *Senecio vaccinioides*, *S. pulchellus*, and *S. carolii-tercii* (Asteraceae); *Hesperomeles ferruginea* (Rosaceae); *Oreopanax tolimanus* (Araliaceae); and *Vaccinium floribundum* of the Ericaceae (Cuatrecasas, 1934). The presence of a large *Vaccinium* reminds me

FIG. 14.10. Species of *Espeletia* (Asteraceae) with varied habits, in Colombia. TOP LEFT, *E. neriifolia* var. *columbica*; below Páramo de Tamá in Andean forest, 2800 m, easternmost Colombia. TOP RIGHT, *E. caldasii*; Páramo de Santurbán, 3400 m, Eastern Cordillera. BOTTOM LEFT, *E. phaneractis boyacensis*; Páramo de Canutos, 3300 m, Boyacá, Eastern Cordillera. BOTTOM RIGHT, *E. santanderensis*; Páramo de Santurbán, 3800 m, Santander, Eastern Cordillera. (All photographs by José Cuatrecasas.)

577

FIG. 14.11. Acaulescent species of *Espeletia* from paramos of Venezuela and Colombia. TOP LEFT, *E. conglomerata*; Páramo de Santurbán, 3800 m, Santander, Eastern Cordillera, Colombia. TOP RIGHT, *E. incana*; Páramo de la Rusia, 3550 m, Boyacá, Eastern Cordillera, Colombia. BOTTOM LEFT, *E. schultzii*, Páramo de Mucuchíes, 4100 m, Mérida, Venezuela. BOTTOM RIGHT, *E. rositae*; Páramo de Hüina, Boyacá, Eastern Cordillera, Colombia. (All photographs by José Cuatrecasas.)

578

FIG. 14.12. Rosette-tree species of *Espeletia* from paramos of Venezuela and Colombia. TOP LEFT, *E. timotensis*; between Páramo de Mucuchíes and Llano Grande de Mifafi, 4300 m, Mérida, Venezuela. TOP RIGHT, *E. uribei*; Macizo de Bogotá, 3350 m, Eastern Cordillera, Colombia. BOTTOM LEFT, RIGHT, *E. pleiochasia*; Páramo de la Rusia, ca. 3000 m, Boyacá, Eastern Cordillera, Colombia. BOTTOM LEFT, habit, showing broad leaves of this subparamo endemic. BOTTOM RIGHT, inflorescences; ray flowers are yellow. (All photographs by José Cuatrecasas.)

579

FIG. 14.13. Rosette-tree species of *Espeletia* from paramos of Colombia. TOP LEFT, RIGHT, *E. discoidea*; Páramo de Canutos, Boyacá, Eastern Cordillera. TOP LEFT, *E. discoidea* plants in landscape that features *Weinmannia fagaroides* (Cunoniaceae) trees, and shrubs such as *Senecio vaccinoides* and *Hypericum laricifolium*. TOP RIGHT, habit of a plant in flower. BOTTOM LEFT, RIGHT, *E. hartwegiana*. BOTTOM LEFT, tall trees in landscape; Páramo de Barragán, 3580 m, Valle, Central Cordillera. BOTTOM RIGHT, *E. hartwegiana* in flower; western slope of Nevado del Huilo, Cauca, Central Cordillera. (All photographs by José Cuatrecasas.)

of *Vaccinium varingiifolium* of alpine Java (Faber, 1927), and woody species of *Gaultheria* (Ericaceae) likewise suggest a similarity between uplands in equatorial South America and Malesia.

Espeletia. Although a common denominator of the paramos of Venezuela and Colombia, *Espeletia* is by no means always the rosette tree that one often associates with that generic name. To be sure, there are several such species in the genus (figs. 14.12, 14.13), but *Espeletia* ranges in form from a branched tree at least 4–5 m high, as in *E. neriifolia* (fig. 14.10, top left), to a virtual cushion plant, forming sessile rosettes, such as *E. caldasii* (fig. 14.10, top right). Interestingly, *E. neriifolia* occupies lower-forest altitudes (1500–3300 m) in the Andes of Venezuela, from Miranda westward to Mérida and easternmost Colombia. Other branched species, shrubs or small trees, include *E. glossophylla* (Colombia: Sierra Nevada de Santa Marta, 3200–4000 m) and *E. occulta* (Venezuela: paramos of Mérida, 3000–3500 m). *Espeletia neriifolia* is believed to have more numerous primitive characters for the genus (Smith and Koch, 1935). If so, one might suspect a woodier shrub or tree of forest subadjacent to paramos to be ancestral for the genus as whole. A few specializations, however, would be expected to occur in *E. neriifolia*. The shrubby species tend to be at the northeastern portion of the range of *Espeletia*, *E. neriifolia* especially so. If *E. neriifolia* represents origin of the genus in regions subadjacent to paramos, it may be like *Crassocephalum* (Asteraceae) and *Lobelia parvibracteata* and *L. gibberoa*, mentioned earlier as lowland relatives of African upland Senecios and Lobelias. In any case, *Espeletia* does show adaptive radiation. There seems no reason to look for origins of any of these genera in the high-alpine representatives. Cuatrecasas (1954c) states that in *Espeletia* there are "15 related species, each of which occupies a restricted area" within the "original pre-historic area of *E. neriifolia*."

Unlike the situation in the Afroalpine Senecios, neither the large rosette-tree species of *Espeletia* nor those with large rosettes and short trunks tend to branch. The difference between *Espeletia* and the Dendrosenecios in this respect seems to be largely a matter of inflorescence position. In *Espeletia*, inflorescences are lateral (see figs. 14.10 to 14.13), whereas in the Dendrosenecios they are terminal, and branching, when it occurs, results from production of more than one innovation below the terminal inflorescence.

Cuatrecasas (1954c) makes a distinction between the Venezuelan paramo species of *Espeletia*, which have a corymbose or racemose type of inflorescence, and those of the Colombian paramos. Species of the eastern Colombian Andes have a corymbose dichasial inflorescence; species of the central Colombian cordillera are strictly dichasial. Venezuelan species shown here are *E. schultzii* (fig. 14.11, bottom left), a widespread paramo and subparamo species of the states of Mérida and Trujillo; and *E. timotensis* (fig. 14.12, top left), a high-paramo species from Mérida. Species from the Eastern Cordillera of Colombia shown here include, in addition to *E. neriifolia*, *E. caldasii* (fig. 14.10, top right), *E. phaneractis boyacensis* (fig. 14.10, bottom left), *E. santanderensis* (fig. 14.10, bottom right), *E. conglomerata* (fig. 14.11, top left), *E. rositae* (fig. 14.11, bottom right), *E. uribei* (fig. 14.12, top right), *E. pleiochasia* (fig. 14.12, bottom left, right), and *E. discoidea* (fig. 14.13, top left, right). *Espeletia hartwegiana* (fig. 14.13, bottom left, right) is from the Central Cordillera of Colombia. Cuatrecasas (1954c) envisions origins of *Espeletia* in subparamos of Venezuela, followed by adaptation to paramo. When climatic belts were lowered in the Pleistocene, migration of *Espeletia* across depressions between the high ranges was facilitated, he feels. One such migration, according to his speculations, included a crossing of ancestors of *E. hartwegiana* to the south, continuing onwards "with prodigious vitality" as far south as the Páramo del Angel (Ecuador). *Espeletia* certainly seems capable of reasonably good dispersal, yet there is no doubt that strong barriers in the form of deep valleys between paramos have resulted in a high degree of differentiation and endemism among its species. That this speciation is largely induced by geographic isolation is suggested by the fact that hybrids form in disturbed areas, with consequent polymorphism (Cuatrecasas, 1954c). This situation is reminiscent of the situation in Hawaiian species of *Dubautia* and *Bidens*, also members of Asteraceae (chapter 4). Hybrids are also known to occur among the Afroalpine Dendrosenecios (Hedberg, 1957). Thus, an insular type of speciation is very much at work in the Asteraceae of equatorial highlands. Narrow endemics in *Espeletia* shown here include *E. discoidea* (fig. 14.13, top left, right), *E. pleiochasia* (fig. 14.12, bottom left, right), *E. uribei* (fig. 14.12, top left), *E. rositae* (fig. 14.11, bottom right), *E. incana* (fig. 14.11, top right) and *E. caldasii* (fig. 14.10, top right). These species are all endemic to the respective paramos given in the figure legends. In some cases, similar-appearing pairs (e.g., *E. conglomerata* and *E. incana*; *E. uribei* and *E. pleiochasia*) are produced by the islandlike geographic distribution of paramos within a single cordilleran range, and can be cited as examples of vicarious species.

There seem to be diversified aspects of adaptive radiation within *Espeletia*. In addition to the branched trees or large shrubs of the scrubby subparamo forest, such as *E. neriifolia*, there are small rosette species such as *E. caldasii* (fig. 14.10, top right) with one-flowered inflorescences, and sessile rosette species with very narrow leaves, such as *E. phaneractis* subsp. *boyacensis* (fig. 14.10, bottom left) and *E. santanderensis* (fig. 14.10, bottom right). Broader, woolly leaves occur in *E. conglomerata* (fig. 14.11, top left), *E. incana* (fig. 14.11, top right), *E. schultzii* (fig. 14.11, bottom left) and *E. rositae* (fig. 14.11, bottom right). *Espeletia rositae* has short stems, as does *E. timotensis* (fig. 14.12, top left), a species with notably broad, succulent stems. Taller rosette-tree species shown here include *E. uribei* (fig. 14.12, top right), *E. pleiochasia* (fig. 14.12, bottom left, right), *E. discoidea* (fig. 14.13, top left, right), and *E. hartwegiana* (fig. 14.13, bottom left, right). The taller rosette-tree species seem characterized by broader leaves—an obvious correlation, for a large plant with few leaves will be likely to have large leaves, as in the tall unbranched Hawaiian lobelioids (*Cyanea leptostegia*, chapter 4). As in the Dendrosenecios, woolliness might serve as insulation against freezing, but (because the paramos tend to freeze less at night than the high Afroalpine zones) there are probably better interpretations—or a combination of them. Protection against excessive radiation is one possibility. It is also possible that woolliness might resist wetting (and therefore rotting) in the excessively misty conditions. As a parallel, one can cite the exceptional woolliness of *Plantago krajinai*, endemic to the excessively wet and misty summit bog of Waialeale, Kauai, Hawaiian Is. (see Carlquist, 1970). It is interesting to note that the species of *Espeletia* with the least woolliness, for whatever reason, tend to occur at lower elevations: *E. neriifolia* (fig. 14.10, top left) and *E. pleiochasia* (fig. 14.12, bottom left, right), for example. Many species of *Espeletia* seem characterized by nutant heads: for example, *E. caldasii* (fig. 14.10, top right), *E. conglomerata* (fig. 14.11, top left), *E. incana* (fig. 14.11, top right), *E. rositae* (fig. 14.11, bottom right), *E.*

uribei (fig. 14.12, top right), *E. discoidea* (fig. 14.13, top left, right), and *E. hartwegiana* (fig. 14.13, bottom left, right). There is a striking parallel in another paramo plant, *Senecio canescens* subsp. *boyacensis* (fig. 14.14, top left, right). The phenomenon of nutant heads may well be a response of flowering under conditions of excessive mistiness. Interestingly, nutant heads characterize, and have probably been evolved autochthonously in, the two bog species of *Argyroxiphium* in the Hawaiian Islands, *A. caliginii* and *A. grayanum* (Carlquist, 1970). Nutant heads are readily accessible to pollinators yet are not likely to fill with water, which would hinder insect visits and other aspects of pollination—water in upright heads would tend to wash pollen grains away.

There obviously can be different adaptations within the genus *Espeletia* to what do not seem, at least at first glance, markedly different conditions. The tall rosette-tree *Espeletia* species occupy much the same altitudinal area as the species with sessile rosettes.

Herbaceous Components of the Paramos. Just as the open grasslands of alpine New Guinea contain numerous herbaceous elements such as Asteraceae and *Gentiana*, so do the paramos. Interestingly, the herbaceous equatorial flora of South America even contains some of the same genera. On the paramos, for example, one sees *Gentiana sedifolia*; a rosette *Eryngium* that reminds me of apiads in alpine Africa and New Guinea; *Erigeron ecuadoriensis*, a parallel to *Tetramolopium* in alpine New Guinea; and *Calamagrostis*, a tussock grass very characteristic of the paramos (fig. 14.15, top left). In the same locality shown in figure 14.15, top left, one can also find *Lycopodium* and *Espeletia hartwegiana*. *Calamagrostis effusa* and *Geranium multiceps* are shown in figure 14.15, top right. The Afroalpine flora is rich in species of *Alchemilla*; *Alchemilla orbiculata* of the Colombia paramos is shown in figure 14.15, bottom left. *Hypochaeris sessiliflora* with its short peduncles (fig. 14.15, bottom left) is a parallel to the similarly sessile heads of many other alpine Asteraceae, such as *Haplocarpha* (fig. 14.7, bottom left) in alpine Africa. *Gunnera magellanica* (fig. 14.15, bottom right) reminds us that the low, prostrate herbaceous elements characteristic of low elevations in subantarctic latitudes occur in moist localities at high elevations in the equatorial Andes.

Strikingly woolly herbaceous plants in the paramo include the justly

Errata: pages 585, 586, and 589

The photographs above the legends to figures 14.14, 14.15, and 14.17 have inadvertently been transposed. The photographs shown above 14.14 should be above 14.15; the photographs shown above 14.15 should be above 14.17; the photographs shown above 14.17 should be above 14.14.

FIG. 14.14. Species of *Senecio* (Asteraceae) from paramos. TOP LEFT, RIGHT, *Senecio canescens* subsp. *boyacensis*; Páramo de Chisicá, 3430 m, Cundinamarca, Eastern Cordillera, Colombia. TOP LEFT, acaulescent habit of plant. TOP RIGHT, inflorescence, showing nutant head. BOTTOM LEFT, *Senecio niveo-aureus*, leaves and inflorescence; paramo at 3700 m, Sierra Nevada del Cocuy, Eastern Cordillera, Colombia. BOTTOM RIGHT, *Senecio rigidifolius*, branches of shrub, an endemic of Páramo del Jabón, 3300 m, Trujillo, Venezuela. (All photographs by José Cuatrecasas.)

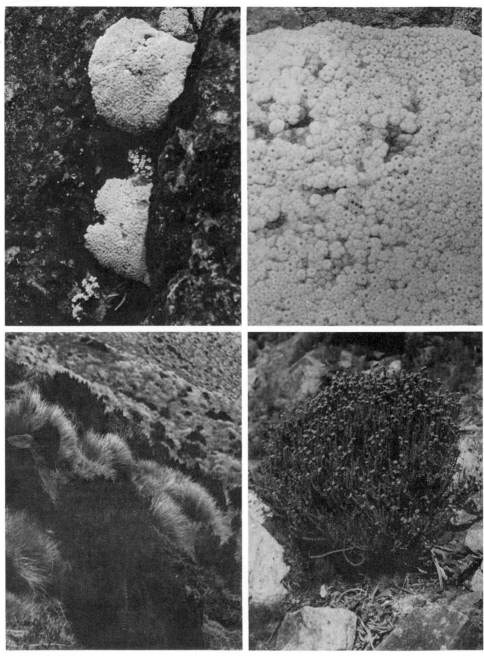

FIG. 14.15. Herbaceous components of the paramos of Colombia. TOP LEFT, *Eryngium humile* (Apiaceae), *Gentiana sedifolia* (Gentianaceae), and *Erigeron ecuadoriensis* in *Calamagrostis* grassland; Páramo de Barragán, 2450 m, Valle, Central Cordillera. TOP RIGHT, *Geranium*

(*continued*)

famous *Lupinus alopecuroides* (fig. 14.16, top left), a species of the super-paramo (above 4400 m, usually). Other superparamo elements shown here include *Senecio canescens* subsp. *boyacensis* (fig. 14.14, top left, right) and *Senecio niveo-aureus* (fig. 14.14, bottom left). The woolliness in these species can be interpreted as insulation, because superparamo regions are subject to frost. Woolliness also characterizes some cushion plants.

Cushion Plants. For reasons cited earlier in connection with the Afroalpine flora, cushion plants can be expected in the equatorial Andes (see also the discussion of cushion plants in New Zealand, chapter 7). A magnificent example is *Raouliopsis* (fig. 14.17, top left, right). This is such a superb mimic of *Raoulia eximia* of New Zealand (see Carlquist, 1965) that it is an outstanding example of parallel evolution; it belongs to the same tribe of Asteraceae as does *Raoulia* (Inuleae). Other cushion-forming plants in the paramo flora include some species of *Arabis* (Brassicaceae), as shown in figure 14.17, top left; *Azorella* (Apiaceae), notable for its "woody" cushions; *Paepalanthus* (Eriocaulaceae); *Plantago rigida* (Plantaginaceae), which forms dense cushions (Cuatrecasas, 1968); *Distichia tolimensis* (Juncaceae); *Oreobolus* (Cyperaceae); and various species of *Mniodes* (Asteraceae, tribe Inuleae), a cushion-plant genus that strikingly parallels *Haastia* of New Zealand (see monograph of *Mniodes* by Cuatrecasas, 1954a). Cushion plants in the equatorial Andes tend to be limited to higher elevations, the superparamo. An interesting footnote is provided by the cushion plants that have been developed in high elevations of Bolivia by the family *Isoëtes*: *I. andicola* and *I. gemmifera*, formerly segregated as a separate genus, *Stylites* (Kubitzki and Borchert, 1964; Rauh and Falk, 1959). The usually unbranched genus *Isoëtes* has, in the "*Stylites*" species, developed special rhizomorph modifications related to branching and the cushion-plant habit.

Shrubby Components of the Paramo. In the paramo proper, some shrubs tend to have narrow leaves and thus exemplify microphylly; this is shown well by *Hypericum laricifolium* of the Hypericaceae (fig. 14.18, top

---

FIG. 14.15 *(continued)*

multiceps (Geraniaceae) with *Calamagrostis effusa*; Páramo de Cruz Verde, 3450 m, Eastern Cordillera. BOTTOM LEFT, *Hypochoeris sessiliflora* (Asteraceae) heads in a mat of *Alchemilla orbiculata* (Rosaceae); Macizo de Bogotá, 3000 m. BOTTOM RIGHT, *Gunnera magellanica* (Haloragaceae) in flower; Páramo de Las Vegas, 3700 m, Central Cordillera. (All photographs by José Cuatrecasas.)

FIG. 14.16. Various high-elevation plants of Colombia. TOP LEFT, *Lupinus alopecuroides* (Fabaceae); paramo at 4300 m, Nevado de Santa Isabel, Central Cordillera. TOP RIGHT, *Masdevallia coriacea* (Orchidaceae); Macizo de Bogotá, 3400 m, Eastern Cordillera. BOTTOM LEFT, *Diplostephium phylicoides* (Asteraceae), shrub; paramos near Bogotá, Eastern Cordillera. BOTTOM RIGHT, *Chuquiraga jussieui* (Asteraceae), heads of flowers and leaves; Páramo de Las Vegas, 3700 m, Valle, Central Cordillera. (All photographs by José Cuatrecasas.)

FIG. 14.17. Plants of the superparamo of Colombia. TOP LEFT, RIGHT, *Raouliopsis seifrizii* (Asteraceae), a high-elevation cushion plant. TOP LEFT, habit of cushions, with flowering plants of *Draba sancta-martae* (Brassicaceae); slopes around Laguna Naboba, 4400 m, Sierra Nevada

(continued)

589

left), a common element in the *Espeletia* "woodland," and by *Aragoa abietina* of the Scrophulariaceae (fig. 14.18, bottom left). Relatively small, condensed leaves of *Chuquiraga jussieui* (fig. 14.16, bottom right) of Asteraceae, tribe Mutisieae. Foliar narrowness due to recurved leaf margins is shown by *Diplostephium phylicoides* (fig. 14.16, bottom left) of Asteraceae and *Arcytophyllum caracasana* (fig. 14.18, bottom right) of the Rubiaceae. Leaves not notably narrow, but restricted in size and exceptionally thick, are shown by *Senecio rigidifolius* (fig. 14.14, bottom right), which illustrates leaf condensation that could be termed sclerophylly as well as microphylly.

Extreme microphylly is shown by superparamo shrubs. *Loricaria thuyoides* of the Asteraceae, tribe Inuleae, is an outstanding example (fig. 14.17, bottom left). This genus (Cuatrecasas, 1954b) can only be described as cupressoid or juniperlike. The small size of the evergreen leaves is a perfect mimic of those of Cupressaceae, a family lacking in these high Andean regions. The "cupressoid" habit is suited to frost resistance and minimization of transpiration and the effects of alpine light conditions. While the gymnosperm family Podocarpaceae in alpine New Zealand illustrates cupressoid stature, so do species of *Hebe* of the Scrophulariaceae (see chapter 7). Not only does *Loricaria* suggest Cupressaceae in habit, but its ultraspecialized wood (by abundance of vascular tracheids) mimics, in a way, primitive conifer woods (Carlquist, 1961). It would be interesting to know if this mimicry occurs in another microphyllous shrub of the superparamo, *Valeriana karstenii* (fig. 14.17, bottom right). For other examples of paramo microphyllous shrubs, chiefly Asteraceae, see Cuatrecasas (1968).

Monocotyledons of the Paramo. Tussock species of grass (*Calamagrostis*) and the cushion plants *Distichia* (Juncaceae) and *Paepalanthus* (Eriocaulaceae) have been mentioned. One may cite the presence in paramos of Cyperaceae (*Oreobolus* spp., *Rhynchospora ruiziana*, *Carex pinetorum* [Cuatrecasas, 1934]). The presence in paramos of an orchid

FIG. 14.17 (*continued*)
de Santa Marta, Magdalena. TOP RIGHT, surface of cushion of *Raouliopsis*, same locality. BOTTOM LEFT, *Loricaria thuyoides* (Asteraceae) shrubs, in *Festuca tolucensis* grassland; slopes of Volcán Puracé, 4300 m, Central Cordillera. BOTTOM RIGHT, *Valeriana karstenii* (Valerianaceae); Laguna Naboba, 4400 m, Sierra Nevada de Santa Marta, Central Cordillera. (All photographs by José Cuatrecasas.)

FIG. 14.18. Paramo shrubs from Colombia, showing tendencies in reduction of leaf surface. TOP LEFT, *Hypericum laricifolium* (Hypericaceae); 3900 m, Nevado de Tolima, Central Cordillera. TOP RIGHT, *Hypericum magniflorum*; Páramo de Tamá, 3200 m, Eastern Cordillera. BOTTOM LEFT, *Aragoa abietina* (Scrophulariaceae); Macizo de Bogotá, 3400 m, Eastern Cordillera. BOTTOM RIGHT, *Arcytophyllum caracasana* (Rubiaceae); 3800 m, western slopes of Nevado del Nuilo, Central Cordillera. (All photographs by José Cuatrecasas.)

591

genus usually epiphytic in moderately cool, neotropical uplands, *Masdevallia*, is interesting. *Masdevallia coriacea* (fig. 14.16, top right) shows adaptation to the paramos in its thick, leathery leaves. The rosette habit of monocotyledons preadapts them to the paramos, where the rosette habit plainly has a selective advantage. In a moist paramo swale, one almost has the equivalent of an epiphytic community at ground level. This may be operative in the manner in which *Puya* of the Bromeliaceae (fig. 14.19) has been able to enter the paramo habitat. Species of *Puya* range from 2450 m for *P. hamata* (fig. 14.19, bottom right); 3100 m for *P. nitida* (fig. 14.19, top left), inhabitant of areas where the rosette tree *Espeletia grandiflora* grows; 3700 m for *P. trianae* (fig. 14.19, bottom left); to 3800 m for *P. cuatrecasasii* (fig. 14.19, top right). Bromeliaceae can be called a typically tropical family, and its entrance into paramo situations is an exception to the predominance of temperate families and genera. The elevations cited show that it does not enter superparamo, however. Evidently ornithophily is possible at the paramo altitudes, for *Puya* is characteristically a bird-pollinated plant. Of course, ornithophily occurs in the Afroalpine flora in the case of *Lobelia*, as mentioned earlier. The presence of conspicuous bracts in some paramo species of *Puya* (fig. 14.19, bottom left, right) suggests a resemblance to the bracts that serve as landing platforms for *Nectarinia* in its visits to *Lobelia keniensis* and the vicarious species related to it (fig. 14.3). However, the function of bracts in the paramo Puyas may not be precisely parallel; until pollination modes in the paramos are studied, little but speculation can be offered. There is a possibility that overarching bracts of *P. trianae* (fig. 14.19, bottom left) and the very woolly bracts of *P. hamata* (fig. 14.19, bottom right) could be mechanisms whereby the flowers—seemingly borne nearly horizontally in at least some paramo species of *Puya*—could serve to prevent entry of rainwater into flowers. The relatively low elevations at which *P. hamata* grows do not seem to imply the value of woolliness in insulation, although this possibility does exist.

Further Studies in the Paramos. Although much work of a taxonomic nature has been done in the paramos, the need for work of a "natural history" or ecological nature has been stressed in this section. Anatomical studies on the various groups of plants are desirable. Analyses of other

FIG. 14.19. Species of *Puya* (Bromeliaceae) from paramos of Colombia. TOP LEFT, *P. nitida*, habit in swale with *Calamagrostis*; paramos above Bogotá, 3100 m, Eastern Cordillera. TOP RIGHT, *P. cuatrecasasii*; paramo at 3800 m, western slope of Nevado del Huila, Cauca, Central Cordillera. BOTTOM LEFT, *P. trianae*, inflorescence; Páramo de Chisacá, 3430 m, Eastern Cordillera. BOTTOM RIGHT, *P. hamata*, upper part of inflorescence, showing notable woolliness; Páramo de Barragán, 2450 m, Valle, Central Cordillera. (All photographs by José Cuatrecasas.)

593

types are possible, too. For a view of birds of North Andean highlands as an insular model, see Vuilleumier (1970).

The Guayana Highlands

The Guayana Highlands, older than the paramos, are also much lower: 1000 to 3000 m (Maguire, 1971). These flat-topped mountains, or "tepuis," can be said to have insular qualities because of their distinctive geology and their almost insular distribution. Not surprisingly, they have a high endemism. Maguire (1971) seems to regard them as a relict area, but his case is poor: the tablelands of Guayana are, in fact, much like islands and seem clearly to have acquired their flora by dispersal over distance, perhaps by truly long-distance dispersal. To be sure, some relatively primitive features are to be seen in certain Asteraceae there (Carlquist, 1957). However, many of the Guayana Asteraceae are highly specialized. The occurrence of high endemism and distinctive adaptive features not in "primitive" families but in very specialized, "weedy," upgrade families such as Asteraceae (Maguire, 1956) is indicative. That the tepuis are older than volcanic islands seems clear, but their floras are only moderately relictual in nature. The primitive families Maguire (1971) cites as characteristic of the "Highland Area" of Guayana are, in fact, not really in the highlands to an appreciable extent: they are chiefly on the low and middle elevations below the steep cliffs, not on the summit areas of the tepuis. Maguire cites *Ocotea* and *Persea* as examples of how such a primitive family as Lauraceae has survived in the Guayana Highlands, but these two genera have reached Madeira and the Canary Islands by long-distance dispersal. To be sure, these Lauraceae on Madeira and the Canaries represent an element that has now vanished in the Mediterranean mainland with drying climates, but, as on all volcanic islands, their relictualism there is only "recent relictualism."

I note with interest the lack of conifers on the Guayana Highlands. If these tepuis were truly *the* relict area of South America, one would expect Araucariaceae to persist there. Instead, South American Araucarias are restricted to the southern Brazilian highlands and to the southern

Andes. Likewise, the "primitive" taxa of Podocarpaceae, such as *Saxe-gothaea,* persist in Chile despite recentness of the Andes. Among the highly specialized families of angiosperms other than Asteraceae that show high speciation and endemism on the Guayana Highlands are Cyperaceae, Rapateaceae, Bromeliaceae, Myrtaceae, Melastomaceae, and Rubiaceae. Interestingly, the families well represented on the Guayana Highlands are well adapted for long-distance dispersal, as the listing above may suggest. Even where a moderate degree of loss of dispersal can be hypothesized, the tepuis have a flora reminiscent of oceanic island floras in dispersibility of seeds and fruits. Of course, this dispersibility does not imply high levels of vagility—if it did, one would not expect the high endemism which occurs on the tepuis. The very unusual climatic and edaphic features of the tepuis contribute to a high degree of endemism (probably preventing easy establishment even if long-distance dispersal occurs frequently); these tablelands can be considered a natural biotic province.

In effect, I am saying that the Guayana Highlands are much like an archipelago of oceanic islands, and with many of the same features. That their flora is somewhat older than that of most volcanic islands may be hypothesized, but to a moderate degree only. In fact, the Guayana Highlands would very much repay study as an example of an archipelago, and I hope that biogeographers familiar with both continental and insular patterns will devote analysis to this region, which is indubitably highly interesting. For references to the Guayana flora, see Maguire (1971) and Steyermark (1966, 1967).

Equatorial Highland Insects

Because a recent book (Mani, 1968) on the subject of high-altitude insects has two chapters devoted to insects of equatorial highlands, there is no need for an extensive review of this topic here. The flightlessness of high-altitude insects is reviewed in his book (pp. 54–61). The question I wish to discuss is whether flightlessness in equatorial highland insects is compa-rable in evolutionary significance with that on tropical islands or temperate mountains, as indicated by Darlington (1943), or whether equatorial high-land insects are a special case. In chapter 12, the concepts of Darlington were discussed, as was the possibility (see Gressitt's conclusions cited there) that flightlessness in subantarctic insects may form a special case.

One distinctive feature of the subantarctic environment is that not merely the winter is extremely cold there, but midsummer temperatures are quite cool also. On equatorial highlands, generally low temperatures prevail, often below 0 C in some areas. Thus, exceptional cold, with no prolonged periods of moderate warmth, occurs in both areas, albeit in different modes. Rehn (1945) notes that in tropical and subtropical climates, cockroaches of both sexes fly easily, but females cannot fly in north temperate climates despite normal wing formation. Kramer (1958) found that most cockroaches cannot fly at temperatures below 21 C. Some of the work of Dewitz (1902, 1920) shows a correlation between cold and loss of ability to fly in insects. Flightlessness and aptery may be expected to occur in exceptionally cold localities, on the basis of such results.

The effect of low atmospheric pressure and more particularly low oxygen availability would seem to play an important role. The results of Dewitz (1902, 1920) seem to show loss of flying ability under such circumstances. Although Darlington (1943) discounts the effect of wind pressure on reduction of flight, the results of Digby (1958) would seem to indicate that wind pressure cannot be wholly discounted. However, one can say that if low temperature, low atmospheric pressure, and low oxygen availability all tend to decrease flying ability markedly in equatorial highland situations, the effect of increased winds might form a selective pressure in insects for either unusually strong flight or loss of flight with consequent wing reduction. The obstacles to any marked increase of flight efficiency in such conditions seem overwhelming when one considers the combined effect of these factors. The factors stressed by Darlington (geophily, advantage of flightlessness in stable communities of small extent) apply also to equatorial highlands, to be sure. The treelessness characteristic of these highlands makes geophily a necessity, and of course mountains provide areas of limited extent, more limited in area at each higher belt.

Winglessness is evident in Afroalpine insects, as Salt (1954) noted. *Parasphenus pulchripes* (fig. 14.20) is a completely wingless orthopteran from above 4500 m on Mt. Kilimanjaro. Orders other than Coleoptera (which are usually sensitive indicators of flightlessness, and demonstrate

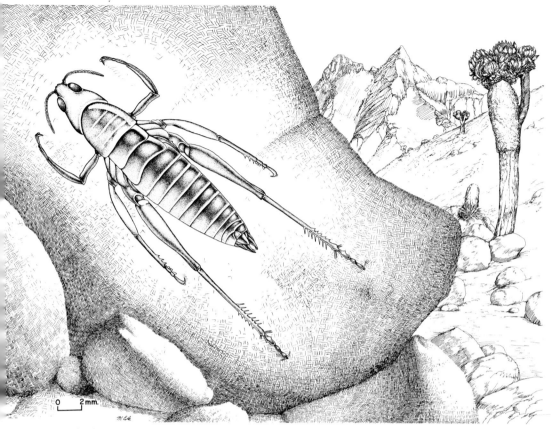

FIG. 14.20. *Parasphenus pulchripes,* a flightless orthopteran from the higher alpine zone of Mt. Kilimanjaro, Tanzania.

the tendency more easily than other insect groups) seem unusually subject to loss of flight on African peaks. In the northwest Himalayas, for example, 70 percent of Orthopera are apterous, and an additional 25 percent are flightless (Mani, 1968). Also from above 4000 m on Kilimanjaro, one finds a flightless tipulid, *Tipula subaptera* (fig. 14.21). As noted, if any insects become flightless, we would expect them to be Coleoptera. Above 4000 m on Kilimanjaro, one finds the apterous beetle *Plocamotrechus kilimanus* (fig. 14.22). Other flightless Coleoptera from these elevations on Kilimanjaro include *Peryphus sjoestedti* (micropterous) and *Parasystatiella agrestis* (elytra fused). Interestingly, flightless Lepidoptera also occur high on Kilimanjaro: *Saltia acrophylax* is brachypterous. Occurrence of flightless

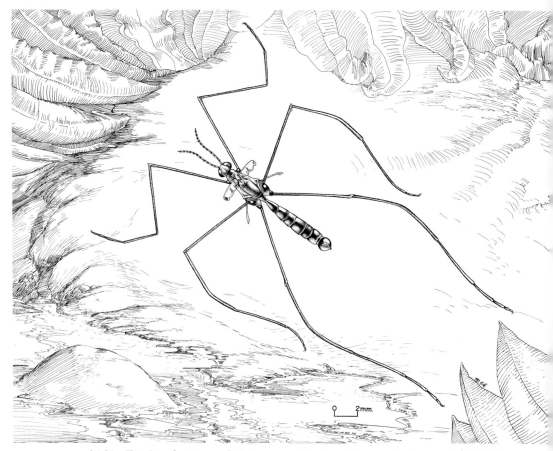

FIG. 14.21. *Tipula subaptera,* a flightless crane fly from the moorland zone of Mt. Kilimanjaro, Tanzania.

lepidopterans on equatorial highlands recalls the presence of numerous
flightless moths on subantarctic islands (chapter 12). We can say, in
conclusion, that the aggravations of severe climatic conditions both on
equatorial highlands and on subantarctic islands seem overriding considerations; at the very least, they are additive to the reasons cited by Darlington
(1943) for flightlessness in carabids.

   With the prominence of vicarious plant species on mountains within
East Africa, Malesia, and the Andean paramos, one might expect similar
occurrence of vicarious species among insects. This is certainly true in the
Afroalpine region, as Mani (1968, pp. 170–71) clearly indicates.

Other phenomena in equatorial highland insects seem related to cold. Mani (1968) relates melanism to increased receptivity to solar radiation, thus minimizing the effect of cold. This phenomenon, however, is typical of high-altitude insects in general, not just those of equatorial highlands. Hedberg (1964) reports that insects tend to seek the shelter of the thick accumulation of leaves on trunks of the Dendrosenecios, and attributes this to the same insulation effect that, as his experiments show, keeps temperatures above the freezing level within this leafy mass.

Although many facts about evolution on equatorial highlands can be obtained from short visits and study, special efforts to study them will undoubtedly reveal much of an ecological, physiological, and behavioral nature, and perhaps some of the speculative comments and vague inferences that one is forced to use in speaking of the curious characteristics of these plants and animals can be superseded by informative studies.

FIG. 14.22. *Plocamotrechus kilimanus*, a flightless micropterous beetle from the high alpine zone of Mt. Kilimanjaro, Tanzania.

References

Carlquist, S. 1957. Anatomy of Guayana Mutisieae. *Mem. N.Y. Bot. Gard.* 9:441–76.

Carlquist, S. 1961. Wood anatomy of Inuleae (Compositae). *Aliso* 5:21–37.

Carlquist, S. 1965. *Island life.* New York, Natural History Press.

Carlquist, S. 1970. *Hawaii, a natural history.* New York, Natural History Press.

Coe, M. J. 1967. *The ecology of the alpine zone of Mount Kenya.* The Hague, Dr. W. Junk, Publishers.

Cuatrecasas, J. 1934. Observaciones geobotánicas en Colombia. *Trab. Mus. Nac. Cienc. Natur. (Madrid),* ser. Bot., 27:1–144.

Cuatrecasas, J. 1954a. El género *Mniodes. Folia Biol. Andina* 1:1–7.

Cuatrecasas, J. 1954b. Synopsis der Gattung *Loricaria* Wedd. *Feddes Repert.* 56:150–72.

Cuatrecasas, J. 1954c. Distribution of the genus *Espeletia. Proc. Eighth Int. Bot. Congr. (Paris),* sect. 4:121–32.

Cuatrecasas, J. 1957. A sketch of the vegetation of the north-Andean province. *Proc. Eighth Pacific Sci. Congr.* 4:167–73.

Cuatrecasas, J. 1968. Geo-ecology of the mountainous regions of the tropical Americas. *Colloq. Geogr.* 9:163–86.

Dale, I. R., and P. J. Greenway. 1961. *Kenya trees and shrubs.* Nairobi, Buchanan's Kenya Estates.

Darlington, P. J., Jr. 1943. Carabidae of mountains and islands: Data on the evolution of isolated faunas and on atrophy of wings. *Ecol. Monogr.* 13:37–61.

Dewitz, J. 1902. Der Apterismus bei Insekten, seine künstlichen Erzeugung und seine physiologische Erklärung. *Arch. Anat. Physiol. (Abt. Physiol.)* (1902): 61–67.

Dewitz, J. 1920. Über die Enstehung rudimentärer Organe bei den Tieren. 4. Die Beeinflussung der Flügelbildung bei Insekten durch Kälte und Blausäuregase. *Zool. Jahrb., Allg. Zool.* 37:305–12.

Digby, P. S. B. 1958. Flight activity in the blowfly *Calliphora erythrocephala* in relation to wind speed, with special reference to adaptation. *Jour. Exp. Biol.* 35:776–95.

Faber, C. F. von. 1927. Die Kraterpflanzen Javas. *'s-Lands Plantentuin (Buitenzorg, Java: Arb. Treub Lab.)* 1:1–119.

Hauman, L. 1933. Les "Lobelia" géants des montagnes du Congo belge. *Mém. Inst. Colon. Belge* 2:1–52.

Hauman, L. 1935. Les "Senecio" arborescents du Congo. *Rev. Zool. Bot. Afr.* 38(1): 1–76.

Hedberg, O. 1951. Vegetation belts of the East African mountains. *Svensk Bot. Tidskr.* 45:140–202.

Hedberg, O. 1957. Afroalpine vascular plants. A taxonomic revision. *Symb. Bot. Upsal.* 15(1):1–411.

Hedberg, O. 1964. Features of Afroalpine plant ecology. *Acta Phytogeogr. Suec.* 49:1–144.

Hedberg, O. 1965. Afroalpine flora elements. *Webbia* 19:519–29.

Hedberg, O. 1968. Taxonomic and ecological studies on the Afroalpine flora of Mt. Kenya. *Hochgebirgforsch.* 1:171–94.

Hedberg, O. 1969a. Growth rate of the East African giant Senecios. *Nature* 222: 163–64.

Hedberg, O. 1969b. Evolution and speciation in a tropical high mountain flora. *Biol. Jour. Linnaean Soc.* 1:135–48. (Also as *Speciation in tropical environments*, ed. R. H. Lowe-McConnell. London, Academic Press.)

Hedberg, O. 1971. Evolution of the Afroalpine flora. In *Adaptive aspects of insular evolution*, ed. W. L. Stern, pp. 16–23. Pullman, Wash., Washington State University Press.

Koster, J. T. 1966. The Compositae of New Guinea. I. *Nova Guinea, Bot.* 24:497–614.

Kramer, S. 1958. Pigmentation in the thoracic musculature of cockroaches and related Orthoptera and the analysis of flight and stridulation. *Proc. Tenth Int. Congr. Entomol.* 1:569–79.

Kubitzki, K., and R. Borchert. 1964. Morphologische Studien an *Isoetes triquetra* A. Braun und Bemerkungen über das Verhältnis der Gattung *Stylites* E. Amstutz zur Gattung *Isoetes* L. *Ber. Deutsch. Bot. Ges.* 77:227–233.

Maguire, B. 1956. Distribution, endemicity, and evolution patterns among Compositae of the Guayana Highland of Venezuela. *Proc. Amer. Phil. Soc.* 100:467–75.

Maguire, B. 1971. On the flora of the Guayana Highland. In *Adaptive aspects of insular evolution*, ed. W. L. Stern, pp. 63–78. Pullman, Wash., Washington State University Press.

Mani, M. S. 1968. *Ecology and biogeography of high altitude insects.* The Hague, Dr. W. Junk, Publishers.

Meijer, W. 1965. A botanical guide to the flora of Mt. Kinabalu. In *Symposium on ecological research in humid tropics vegetation*, pp. 325–64. Kuching, Sarawak, Government of Sarawak and UNESCO Science Cooperation Office for Southeast Asia.

Rauh, W., and H. Falk. 1959. *Stylites* E. Amstutz, eine neue Isoetacee aus den Hochanden Perus. *Sitzungsber. Heidelberg. Akad. Wiss.* (1959):1–160.

Rehn, J. A. 1945. Man's uninvited fellow-traveller—the cockroach. *Sci. Monthly* 61:265–76.

Rock, J. F. 1920. The forest of Mt. Gedeh, west Java. *Hawaiian Planter's Rec.* 22:67–104.

Royen, P. van. 1964a. Sertulum Papuanum 10. Gentianaceae. *Nova Guinea, Bot.* 17:369–416.

Royen, P. van. 1964b. Sertulum Papuanum 11. Plantaginaceae. *Nova Guinea, Bot.* 18:417–26.

Salt, G. 1954. A contribution to the ecology of upper Kilimanjaro. *Jour. Ecol.* 42: 265–423.

Smith, A. C., and M. F. Koch. 1935. The genus *Espeletia*: A study in phylogenetic taxonomy. *Brittonia* 1:479–530.

Stapf, O. 1894. On the flora of Mount Kinabalu in North Borneo. *Trans. Linnaean Soc. London*, ser. 2, Bot. 4:69–263.

Steyermark, J. A. 1966. Contribuciones a la flora de Venezuela. Parte 5. *Acta Bot. Venez.* 1:9–256.

Steyermark, J. A. 1967. Flora del Auyan-Tepui. *Acta Bot. Venez.* 2:5–368.

Vuilleumier, F. 1970. Insular biogeography in continental regions. I. The northern Andes of South America. *Amer. Natur.* 104:373–88.

CHAPTER FIFTEEN

SELECTED ISLAND TOPICS

Gigantism in Animals

The phenomenon of gigantism has been noted repeatedly for birds, reptiles, and insects of islands. In birds, increase in size is most conspicuous in those that are flightless. Adoption of an irreversible ground-feeding habit by flightless birds seems an entry into a relatively unlimited ecological situation. The limits may well lie in problems of egg size as well as other limits of a physical and physiological nature that tend to preclude progress beyond a certain point in body size (see De Beer, 1956). Among normally winged birds, smaller body size is typical on low-latitude islands, whereas large body size characterizes birds of higher latitudes (Grant, 1968). This variation is interpreted by Grant as "physiological adjustments to energy sources and losses."

Large body size is characteristic of rodents living on islands and mountaintops in Europe (Zimmermann, 1950). Grant (1965a) considers this a pathway to "facilitate a greater exploitation of environmental resources." Grant also thinks that such gigantism is possible on islands (and islandlike areas) because of absence of predators.

In reptiles, gigantism has long been noted, especially in island lizards, but in other insular reptiles as well. The summary of Mertens (1934), upon which I drew (1965) for my account of this phenomenon, contains the widest variety of examples. One could also cite the work of Schuster (1950) and of Bole, Brelih, and Zei (1961). Since the review of Mertens, many contributions have compared mainland lizards with those on offshore islands or islets. Notable among these are the studies of Kramer and Mertens (1938), Kramer (1946, 1951), and Mertens (1961). Kramer (1961) describes situations on offshore islands of Italy. Radovanović (1956) studied lizards on offshore islands of Yugoslavia. His results show larger body size for insular populations of *Lacerta melisellensis,* but for *Lacerta sicula* (in which Kramer found gigantism in the Italian islands), Radovanović generally finds smaller body sizes in the island populations compared with the mainland populations. However, Radovanović notes exceptions to these trends in both species. This result is not surprising, because he studied lizards of such a large number of islets. More recently, we have the study of Soulé (1966) on lizards of islands off Baja California (almost exclusively those in the Gulf of California).

Soulé's study (1966) is of particular interest because he has compared, for insular and mainland populations of lizards, such dimensions as body size, island size, population density, and size of scales. Because his data were broadly based and because correlations were sought, he could present some meaningful conclusions. Soulé found an inverse relationship between island size and lizard size: larger lizards on smaller islands. The reason for this correlation is not fully evident. There is, to be sure, also a relationship between island size and number of resident species, according to Soulé's data. Soulé (1966) cites greater longevity for the island lizards; this agrees with the data of Kramer (1946) (see also chapter 13). Is absence of predation the reason for greater size and longevity of the insular populations? We do not have predation data on the Gulf of California islands, but lowered predation does seem to have been demonstrated sufficiently in the case of the offshore Italian islands. Lack of competitors on smaller islands may not be a factor. If a given food supply is available on an island and only a single species can take advantage of it, presumably population size will increase to the limits of that food supply. Would there be a concomitant increase in body size? Soulé (1966) tends to believe that an "ecological release" by lack of competitors may well lead to an "evolutionary release" into larger body size. There is a possibility that increased size might be of advantage in mating battles, but this should be true on any area. Although correlations seem fairly clear, the actual pathways in evolution of larger body size in insular lizards have not been demonstrated. Such further investigations should take into account those exceptional instances in which insular lizards are smaller than mainland counterparts; instances have been reported by Mertens (1934) and Radovanović (1956).

There seems to be a relationship between body size and scale size in the Gulf of California insular lizards (Soulé, 1966). The smaller the island, the smaller and more numerous the scales per unit area. Soulé finds that larger scales tend to be strongly keeled and markedly overlapping; these features, he claims, radiate excess heat and decrease tendencies toward overheating. The smaller scales of lizards from small islands are smooth and less overlapping, as opposed to those of mainland lizards. This contrast assumes that climates of small islands are cooler and overheating would be less likely to occur. The widespread phenomenon of melanism in insular lizards (Mertens, 1934, 1961; Radovanović, 1956) seems to be correlated with this. Darker colors would seem to promote heat absorption where island conditions are cooler and foggier than on the mainland. Larger body size would also make more efficient heat absorption advantageous. However, sunny tropical islands can heat to relatively high levels during the afternoon. The lizards' response seems to be a mid-day retreat (Soulé, 1968, and the literature cited therein).

An interesting although not easily explained change in body characteristics on the Gulf of California islands is the tendency for lizards to develop greater degrees of asymmetry on small islands than on large islands or mainland areas (Soulé, 1967).

Gigantism in insects often seems to occur on islands. A number of examples could be cited, including the carabid *Scarites* in Puerto Rico (Darlington, 1971), drosophilids in Hawaii (Spieth, 1968), the fossil giant earwig of St. Helena Island, *Labidura loveridgei*, the wetas of New Zealand (see Tillyard, 1926), and the various examples from Madeiran Coleoptera given by Wollaston (mentioned in chapter 12). Many more could be cited, especially the gigantic representatives of various groups in Australia: *Petalura gigantea* (Odonata: Petaluridae); *Macropanesthia rhinoceros* and other Blattidae; *Palophus titan, Acrophylla tessellata, Podacanthus wilkinsoni* and other phasmids; various giant moths (Hepialidae), and many others (Tillyard, 1926; Department of Entomology, 1970).

The reasons for insect gigantism may be several. Schoener and Janzen (1968) cite larger body size as better adapted to coping with predators; however, one would expect predator pressure to be less on at least some insular areas. Another factor cited by Schoener and Janzen seems to apply more generally: slower development. The equable climatic conditions of islands would appear to permit longer periods of development compared with sharply seasonal continental conditions. New Zealand wetas are notable for their longevity (see chapter 13). In the case of the giant flightless *Scarites* on Puerto Rico, which also have more poorly developed eyes, Darlington (1971) cites ecological shift into wet forest as a leading factor. Hawaiian drosophilids have notably large size; Spieth (1968) has cited mating battles as a possible factor whereby larger size would be advantageous.

Obviously, causes of insect gigantism on islands may be many. Any particular case may be explained on the basis of factors, or a syndrome of factors, that may not apply in other instances. This would seem to underline the need for fieldwork.

Many interesting changes in body shape occur in insular insects. Darlington (1971) has cited the *Colpodes bromeliarum* group of carabids on Jamaica, adapted to living in the sheathing leaf bases of bromeliad rosettes by virtue of their flattened form. A precisely analogous development has occurred in the delphacid leafhoppers of the Hawaiian Islands. Of 139 native species, only one, *Nesodryas freycinetiae*, has a flattened nymph. This is an adaptation to living in the closely fitting leaf bases of leaf rosettes of *Freycinetia* (Zimmerman, 1948).

Changes in form, color, and habits make the Australian Cerambycidae (Coleoptera) remarkable mimics of such diverse insects as creid bugs, thynnid wasps, and even ants (Tillyard, 1926). Other examples of so-called Batesian mimicry occur in the Australian insect fauna (Department of Entomology, 1970). In addition, insects that mimic habitat are common in Australia: many Hemiptera, larvae of the butterflies *Papilio aegeus* and *Eucyclodes* spp., the grasshopper *Acripeza reticulata*, and the "leaf-insects" (Phyliidae of Phasmatodea) (Department of Entomology, 1970).

One possible reason for gigantism of insects on oceanic islands is that it "reestablishes" a more normal distribution of sizes, comparable to those on mainland areas. The work of Gressitt and his co-workers on insect dispersal in the Pacific (chapter 1) shows that immigrants to islands tend to be relatively small in body size, because small size is a requisite for dispersal. During evolution of the immigrants that do establish, one might expect that larger-sized descendants might evolve, forming a size range more nearly like that on continents as they occupy the niches that are available.

This reasoning might also apply to land molluscs. "Gigantism"—but also "dwarfism"—has been noted for insular gastropods by Bole, Brelih, and Zei (1961). One can point to numerous examples. The amastrid and achatinellid snails of the Hawaiian Islands provide clear instances. Amastrinae is an endemic subfamily of Cochlicopidae; Achatinellinae is an endemic subfamily of Tornatellinidae. The widespread members of both of these families have very small shell size compared with these two endemic Hawaiian subfamilies (Zimmerman, 1948). Within amastrids, trends toward gigantism can be seen in the case of the genus *Carelia*, as well as within the genus *Amastra* itself (e.g., *Amastra knudseni*; for illustrations, see Carlquist [1970]). Among New Caledonian land molluscs, similar cases can be mentioned. Solem's (1961) data suggest gigantism in Paryphantidae (*Ougapia raynali* vs. *O. apoana*), and within *Microphyura* (Paryphantidae) and *Andrefrancia* (Endodontidae). The famous *Placostylus* (Bulimulidae) almost certainly represents gigantism both as a genus and within the New Caledonian species.

Changes in Appendages of Animals

Although the birds of the Tres Marías Islands (Mexico) are relatively small in body size, they have larger bills and tarsi than do their equivalents on the mainland (Grant, 1965a, 1971). According to Grant, the Tres Marías Islands lack mainland species with requirements similar to those of species resident on the Islands. Therefore, the species on the Tres Marías may be said to have extended their adaptations into new niches or even habits. The larger bill sizes enable these birds to take food of a greater variety of sizes, and the larger tarsus would enable a greater variety of perches to be utilized. This phenomenon is found on other islands as well. Larger bills (compared with mainland relatives) have been reported for insular birds of North America by Murphy (1938), for the Canary Islands by Volsøe (1955), for the Gulf of Guinea islands by Amadon (1953) and for the Philippines by Rand and Rabor (1960).

In instances of adaptive radiation on islands, bill size tends to show marked differences, as in the Darwin's finches (chapter 6) or the Hawaiian honeycreepers (chapter 4). Figure 4.5 shows divergence between congeneric species of *Loxops* on the islands of Hawaii and Kauai. These pairs "avoid" competition by having strongly marked divergences in food preferences. In the case of *Loxops*, one can consider this as a secondary (or tertiary) cycle of adaptive radiation—a sort of module of how adaptive radiation operates.

However, many islands have congeneric species that do not represent parts of programs of adaptive radiation. Grant (1968) gives examples of such pairs on various islands. These represent double invasions, as hypothesized for *Loxops*. Grant's (1968) figures show that the two sympatric species of particular genera on various islands differ markedly in bill length and wing length. Such differences are undoubtedly enforced strongly where a finite food supply is partitioned by two species. This is precisely what we would expect, and various factors contribute to this "enforcement." For example, population densities of animals tend to be greater on islands than on continental areas (Lack and Southern, 1949; Crowell, 1962; Grant, 1965a). That in most cases both wing and bill sizes are affected is interesting. The percentile difference in wing size between the congeneric pairs is, however, much smaller than the difference in bill size in virtually all instances. This suggests that bill-morphology differences are more critical in preventing ecological overlap than are wing sizes—as one might expect.

Differences in bill length between species of particular bird genera on islands are much greater, in general, than differences in bill length between species of the same bird genera on mainland areas (Schoener, 1965; Grant, 1968). The nature and abundance of specific food items appears to govern the nature of divergence of bills between congeneric species.

An example of how an unusually large bill may develop as an adaptation to a new food source is shown by the finch *Fringilla teydea* of Gran Canaria and Tenerife, Canary Islands. This bird has apparently evolved a larger beak in relation to feeding upon the rather large seeds of the Canary pine (*Pinus canariensis*), endemic to the Canary Islands (Volsøe, 1951).

Although differences in bills seem related primarily to differences in articles of diet, they may also serve a subsidiary function. Lack (1947) showed in the Darwin's finches that an individual can recognize a member of his own species (in the form of a stuffed specimen) by bill characteristics; plumage differences in this group are probably too minor to serve for recognition purposes.

In lizards, the genus *Brachymeles* (Scincidae) of the Philippines is notable for presenting a series in limb reduction (illustrated in Carlquist, 1965). This has been documented in detail by Brown and Rabor (1967). The more highly evolved species, in which reduction of limbs is great and some digits are lost, have a more limited distribution within the Philippines. They occupy only one or two, or a close group, of islands within the larger group. Differences in habits among the species have not been documented well, so the significance of degrees of loss of limbs is difficult to establish with any certainty. Clearly *Brachymeles* is limited to forest habitats and is secretive within them. A sort of precinctiveness, reinforced by loss of limbs, may be contributing to further speciation within the genus.

Changes in body proportions in the lizard *Lacerta* on Italian offshore islands have a different explanation (Kramer, 1951). The island races have shorter, fatter appendages and shorter tails. Evidently these represent reductions in agility that have developed in the absence of predators. Also, there is the possibility that with small islet size, efficiency in locomotion is no longer advantageous. If gigantism occurs in insular reptiles as compared with mainland ones, changes in proportions of limbs are often involved (Mertens, 1934).

Sexual dimorphism in structural characteristics is not unusual among animals at large, but there are some instances known in which sexual dimorphism occurs only in insular representatives of the group. The huia (*Heterolocha acutirostris*) of New Zealand, now extinct, had dimorphism in bills related to cooperative feeding of a pair; several published reports (see Oliver, 1955) suggest the validity of this interpretation. Phillipps (1963) claims that this cooperative feeding tended to insure greater intake by females, a fact he correlates with greater need for nutrition by females because of egg-production. Sexual dimorphism has also been noted in the proterhinid beetles of the Hawaiian Islands. In this group, males have heads that are weakly beaklike, but a pronounced beaklike extension is present in females. The ecological significance of this difference is obscure. Sexual dimorphism might, in theory, have the advantage of broadening the range of food articles taken (for a discussion, see Soulé and Stewart [1970]), but sexual dimorphism in feeding apparatus is so widespread geographically that it cannot be said to be an insular phenomenon at all.

Changes in Coloration Patterns

The most obvious example of island-related color patterns is the Paradisaeidae, which are too well known and thoroughly explored to be resurveyed here. There are several much more subtle examples that deserve mention. Notable among avian examples described recently is the account of Grant (1965b), which deals with the phenomenon of notably dull plumage in birds of the Tres Marías Islands. Grant describes this as "a byproduct of genetic reorganization." He envisions "simplified" plumage patterns, a sort of retrograde tendency permitted by *absence* of particular species from the Tres Marías Islands. Reinforcement of bright and distinctive color patterns is characteristic of continental areas, where sympatry of congeneric species makes recognition patterns of higher selective value. If only one species of a genus is present on the Tres Marías, such distinctiveness no longer is of high selective value, and may be expected to be lost incidentally.

The Darwin's finches do show distinctions in color patterns (see fig. 6.2). These are, as described, proportionate to time spent feeding on black lava surfaces versus time spent feeding in brownish trees. This suggests coloration of a protective sort, and indeed predators, such as the Galápagos hawk, are present.

The variety of color in plumage in the Hawaiian honeycreepers is difficult to explain. Why should the subfamily Drepanidinae exhibit blacks, reds, and various mottled patterns of such distinction? Why, conversely, does the subfamily Psittarostrinae have yellow green colors virtually identical throughout the highly distinctive genera that compose it? The great variety in color patterns in the Hawaiian land shell *Achatinella* also is not easily explained.

In contrast, there is a wealth of color patterns, evolved autochthonously, in many different Hawaiian insect groups that can only be explained as protective colorings that match host plants or substrates in a remarkable way. Some of these are reviewed in chapter 4, for wide divergences in substrate or host-plant mimicry are aspects of adaptive radiation. I refer the reader to the resumé of Zimmerman (1948, pp. 142–43) where the various insect groups that show protective coloration are described engagingly.

Mertens (1934) and other European herpetologists have noted increased melanism in insular reptiles. This melanism may provide screening from a component of solar radiation or may be related to sea salts in the diet, but is probably not directly related to thermoregulation. In any case, melanism is characteristic not just of insular reptiles, but of those in supratidal situations as well. For a review of this phenomenon, see Neill (1958).

Changes in Habits and Habitats

Hawaiian insects tend to show "supralimital" evolution in some respects. Usinger (1942) indicated this for the *Nysius* species, and Zimmerman (1948) cited a number of interesting examples. One of these that particularly arouses Zimmerman's enthusiasm is an odonatan, *Megalagrion oahuense.* Unlike all other members of this order, it has nymphs adapted not to aquatic existence but to foraging for prey on land. Likewise, bugs of the genus *Saldula* are characteristically riverine and lacustrine throughout the world. The Hawaiian Saldulas, however, are strictly arboreal. I can imagine an explanation for such shifts from aquatic to terrestrial or arboreal. Even though rainfall on the Hawaiian Islands is heavy, high porosity of soils and rocks results in a notable absence of permanent streams or lakes. Although enough aquatic habitats exist for establishment of a typically aquatic group, radiation from this niche would almost have to be terrestrial or arboreal, and there would be considerable selective pressure in that direction. We must not make the mistake of considering the floor of a Hawaiian rain forest as "dry land," however. It consists of almost perpetually wet litter or bryophytes. The same is true of tree trunks in certain localities, on which the thick coverings of epiphytes are related to frequent baths of mist, cloud, or rain, and which are constantly moist (the occurrence of Hymenophyllaceae, a family of ferns intolerant to desiccation, is a good indicator of moisture where these ferns are epiphytic on tree trunks). Such habitats would provide suitable zones for ecological shift of an aquatic organism.

Likewise, the shift from terrestrial to arboreal habitats occurs in Hawaiian insects. An exceptional number of Hawaiian Coleoptera are arboreal rather than terrestrial (Darlington, 1943). Larvae of the family of crane flies, Tipulidae, typically live in soil, decaying vegetation, or even water. However, one Hawaiian species, *Limonia foliocuniculator*, is a leaf miner and inhabits *Cyrtandra* of the Gesneriaceae (Swezey, 1915). At least three Hawaiian species of the weevil genus *Proterhinus* have shifted from boring in dead wood (the typical habit of the genus) to leaf-mining. Of these, one can be found in leaves of *Astelia* (Liliaceae), one in leaves of *Broussaisia* (Saxifragaceae), and one in living stems of *Broussaisia* (Zimmerman, 1948). How ecological shift of this sort might occur is evident on the basis of my field experience in the Hawaiian Islands. *Astelia* is often an epiphyte on rotting bark; *Broussaisia* grows in very wet forest, and, as in many shrubs and trees of the Hawaiian forest, both rotten and living portions may be found on a single shrub. Thus the ecotone that must be crossed is not as drastic as one might imagine, although the end product is rather remarkable.

The *Odynerus* wasps typically build mud nests in crevices or beetle burrows, or tunnel into wood or soil. One Hawaiian species, *O. oahuensis*, constructs entire independent mud cells (Williams, 1927).

Shifts in feeding habits of Hawaiian insects are seen in the drosophilids cited in chapter 4; many of these utilize food sources entirely alien to the typical slime-flux feeding habits of mainland drosophilids. One genus, *Titanochaeta*, is parasitic on spider eggs. Shifts in feeding habits are seen in Hawaiian hylaeid bees of the genus *Nesoprosopis*, some species of which have developed commensal and semiparasitic modes of existence (Zimmerman, 1948).

The Galápagos iguanas have become famous, although they do not represent remarkable features except in a few ways. There is nothing particularly noteworthy in the herbivorous habits of the land iguana, *Conolophus*, except that it is capable of consuming spiny fruits and stems of the cactus *Opuntia*. The marine iguana, *Amblyrhynchus*, is much more remarkable because of its various adaptations to life as a marine herbivore

(Carpenter, 1966). In feeding upon algal beds, it is able to dive to approximately 11 m. The laterally compressed tail enables it to swim efficiently, and it is capable of adjusting its buoyancy to different depths. The short snout and flat, triseriate teeth enable it to graze algae efficiently from rocks. Intake of saltwater during its feeding is inevitable, but it has compensated for this by increased efficiency of its salt-extracting gland.

Behavioral features of *Amblyrhynchus* also show alteration (Carpenter, 1966). Since it is a littoral animal of large size, congregating at feeding sites is an efficient use of resources, but this runs counter to the territoriality typical of lizards. Consequently, territoriality in male marine iguanas occurs only at mating time, and vanishes after the mating season has waned. For females, territorial antagonism occurs during competition for nesting sites in beaches, and disappears as soon as egg-laying has been completed. An insular rodent, the Bahaman hutia (known only from East Plana Cay), shows a notably low level of aggressiveness (Clough, 1969). Clough regards this placidity as an adaptation related to high population density.

Soulé (1966) mentions that the lizard *Uta* on San Pedro Martír Island feeds on marine invertebrates to a large degree, so that flies are not the sole article of subsistence, as in other *Uta* populations. Population density is greater in the Utas of San Pedro Martír Island than on any other island Soulé examined. Thus we can see how a shift to a marine food source might take place, with concomitant abandonment of territoriality except during reproduction, as in *Amblyrhynchus*.

New Zealand skinks and geckos are notable for their habit of vivipary. Only one New Zealand skink, *Leiolopisma suteri*, has been found to be oviparous (Whitaker, 1968). New Zealand is not exceptional in this high proportion of vivipary, however. It occurs at northern and southern limits of lizard distribution elsewhere in the world. This adaptation, related to intolerance of cool temperatures during egg incubation, permits extension of lizards farther south in the southern hemisphere and farther north in the northern hemisphere (Darlington, 1948). The single oviparous New Zealand skink, *Leiolopisma suteri*, is not an exception to the rule, because it is restricted to six islets off the Auckland-area coast of New Zealand; all the islets are north of the 37th parallel. The viviparous habit has permitted skinks to penetrate to 47°S. The two viviparous skinks there, *Leiolopisma zelandica* and *L. lineo-ocellatum,* may represent the southernmost lizard populations in the world.

Analyses of Islandlike Situations

That areas or conditions other than true islands present insular aspects does not need emphasis at this point. A number of biologists have endeavored to apply the considerations of MacArthur and Wilson (1967) to these situations. We have, for example, the comparison by Janzen (1968) of plant hosts and their insect parasites as an insular situation. Potentially informative as this analogy is, analysis of host-parasite relationships is forestalled, as Janzen notes, by lack of suitable data. Thus, although the analogy is a compelling one, collection of data that would build toward comparison with mathematical modes is a complicated and difficult task yet to be performed. Brown (1971) has found that mammals of continental mountaintops in the southwestern United States do not conform to an insular situation. The species-area curve is much steeper than the Mac-Arthur-Wilson curve for insular biotas. Brown finds that the rate of immigration for mammals to these areas is "effectively zero." He explains the situation by hypothesizing that these mountains were colonized during the Pleistocene, when intermountain areas did not present the climatic barriers they do today. After post-Pleistocene isolation, diversity of faunas was reduced. Because extinction-probability is inversely related to population size, body size, diet, and habitat, extinction has been low. The present residents of these mountaintops (which Brown literally terms "islands") are considered to be true relicts, beyond the MacArthur-Wilson equilibria between colonization and extinction.

On the other hand, Vuilleumier's (1970) analysis of northern Andean regions (considered as island regions) does bear out the MacArthur-Wilson equilibria. This is also true of cave arthropods, according to Culver (1970), who uses Simberloff's (1969) noninteractive model of island biogeography as the basis for his analysis. Those interested in caves as insular situations will want to consult the extensive reviews of Vandel (1965) and Barr (1968). Although cave animals are well known for such tendencies as depigmentation, loss of eyes, and endemism, there are other less well known tendencies with insular overtones in some cave animals. The tendencies toward flightlessness and aptery are strong. Gigantism characterizes many cave animals, especially Coleoptera. However, a tendency toward dwarfism occurs in a few others. Biotic tendencies of equatorial highlands have been presented in extended treatment in this book because, if construed broadly (i.e., as more than as a single alpine zone), equatorial highlands simulate many features of insular biotas. Caves, in comparison, present rather restricted habitats, although obviously there are certain ecological niches within them and caves do differ ecologically one from another.

Extinction

If we look at the geography of extinct or endangered species (e.g., Greenway, 1958; or the I.U.C.N. Red Data Books), we quickly see that insular species figure with exceptional prominence in the listings. In seeking the reasons for this, small land area will appeal as a prime cause of extinction. However, before we apply the MacArthur-Wilson curve to confirm that, as expected, smaller land areas suffer higher rates of extinction, we must remember that the roster of endangered and extinct species is not the product of the factors MacArthur and Wilson cite, because these are man-induced extinctions and near-extinctions, not "naturally occurring" ones over indefinite periods of time. Small land area is clearly involved, for a number of reasons. To be sure, population size is, in general, smaller, and there are no scattered pockets, as there might be on a continent, where survival might be possible. Adaptation to insular conditions seems irreversible, for various reasons, and the organisms must survive within the limited habitat or habitats available to them or suffer extinction. Encroaching influences—weeds, introduced pests, parasites, and predators—have an effect geometrically greater on a small land area than a large one. Smaller populations, in other words, are "easier prey." One can cite the presumptive genetic depauperation of a small endemic insular population, and it cannot be denied. One may express this as "loss of competitiveness" or say that insular organisms have "limited evolutionary potential" (Simpson, 1953; Darlington, 1948; W. L. Brown, 1957). Unfortunately we have no exact way of predicting vulnerability of any given species, or its ability to recover if land usage is discontinued and an area is allowed to return to its "natural" state. However, McDowall (1969) has shown that the higher the level of endemism of an organism's group (e.g., endemic family versus endemic subspecies), the more prone an insular organism is to extinction. The corollary seems evident, that the older the autochthone is, the more prone it is to extinction. This, of course, applies most clearly on islands, whereas more numerous exceptions can be cited on continental areas. The subject of extinction on insular areas and the factors that contribute to it has been formulated in detail by MacArthur (1972).

In "saving" insular species from extinction, we must discriminate between short-term sanctuary and long-term survival. Breeding in zoos and maintenance in botanic gardens so far give no indications of long-term success on their own terms. Long-term success is possible only if sufficient areas of the original habitat can be preserved, or if an area can be allowed to "renaturalize" and an endangered organism can then be re-released into it. These principles seem obvious, but practical demonstrations appear necessary. For example, the Hawaiian nene (*Branta sandvicensis*) was rescued from extinction and successfully bred in pens, but release into a known former habitat (Haleakala, Maui) failed because that habitat was no longer sufficiently intact. Those interested in prevention of extinction on insular areas will have to make decisions as to whether their actions are likely to lead to long-term survival, or only to short-term maintenance.

In the latter case, or in the case of organisms for which no protective measures at all are being taken, biologists have only a single choice: obtain as much data, preferably by field studies, as soon as possible. Studies such as that of Tomich (1971) on the Hawaiian crow—apparently now extinct— are to be congratulated. Because increasingly rapid extinctions are probable, the failure of biologists to study endangered insular organisms may justifiably be more criticized in the future than their failure to take part in well-meaning but ill-fated efforts to save species.

References

Amadon, D. 1953. Avian systematics and evolution in the Gulf of Guinea. *Bull. Amer. Mus. Natur. Hist.* 100:397–431.

Barr, T. C., Jr. 1968. Cave ecology and the evolution of troglobites. In *Evolutionary biology*, ed. T. Dobzhansky, M. K. Hecht, and W. C. Steere, vol. 2, pp. 35–102. New York, Appleton-Century-Crofts.

Bole, J., S. Brelih, and M. Zei. 1961. Les pulmonés et les lézards insulaires et le problème de leur speciation dans l'archipel de Rovinj (Rovigno). In *Le peuplement des îles méditeranéenes et le problème de l'insularité*. Paris, Colloques Internationaux du Centre National de la Recherche Scientifique.

Brown, J. H. 1971. Mammals on mountaintops: Nonequilibrium insular biogeography. *Amer. Natur.* 105:467–78.

Brown, W. C., and D. S. Rabor. 1967. Review of the genus *Brachymeles* (Scincidae) with descriptions of new species and subspecies. *Proc. Calif. Acad. Sci.*, 4th ser., 34(15):525–47.

Brown, W. L. 1957. Centrifugal speciation. *Quart. Rev. Biol.* 32:247–77.

Carlquist, S. 1965. *Island life.* New York, Natural History Press.

Carlquist, S. 1970. *Hawaii, a natural history.* New York, Natural History Press.

Carpenter, C. C. 1966. The marine iguana of the Galápagos Islands, its behavior and ecology. *Proc. Calif. Acad. Sci.*, 4th ser., 24(6):329–76.

Clough, G. C. 1969. The Bahaman hutia: A rodent refound. *Oryx* 10:106–8.

Crowell, K. L. 1962. Reduced interspecific competition among the birds of Bermuda. *Ecology* 43:75–88.

Culver, D. C. 1970. Analysis of simple cave communities. I. Caves as islands. *Evolution* 24:463–74.

Darlington, P. J., Jr. 1943. Carabidae of mountains and islands: Data on the evolution of isolated faunas and on atrophy of wings. *Ecol. Monogr.* 13:37–61.

Darlington, P. J., Jr. 1948. The geographical distribution of the cold-blooded vertebrates. *Quart. Rev. Biol.* 23:1–26, 106–23.

Darlington, P. J., Jr. 1971. Carabidae on tropical islands, especially the West Indies. In *Adaptive aspects of insular evolution*, ed. W. L. Stern, pp. 7–15. Pullman, Wash., Washington State University Press.

De Beer, F. R. 1956. The evolution of the ratites. *Bull. Brit. Mus. (Natur. Hist.) Zool.*, 4(2):1–63.

Department of Entomology, Commonwealth Scientific and Industrial Research Organization. 1970. *The insects of Australia.* Melbourne, Melbourne University Press.

Grant, P. R. 1965a. The adaptive significance of some size trends in island birds. *Evolution* 19:255–67.

Grant, P. R. 1965b. Plumage and the evolution of birds on islands. *Syst. Zool.* 14:47–52.

Grant, P. R. 1968. Bill size, body size, and the ecological adaptations of bird species to competitive situations on islands. *Syst. Zool.* 17:319–33.

Grant, P. R. 1971. Variation in the tarsus length of birds in island and mainland regions. *Evolution* 25:599–614.

Greenway, J. C., Jr. 1958. *Extinct and vanishing birds of the world.* New York, American Committee for International Wild Life Protection.

Janzen, D. H. 1968. Host plants as islands in evolutionary and contemporary time. *Amer. Natur.* 102:592–95.

Kramer, G. 1946. Veränderung von Nachkommenziffer und Nachkommengrösse sowie der Altersverteilung von Inseleidechsen. *Z. Naturforsch.* 1:700–10.

Kramer, G. 1951. Body proportions of mainland and island lizards. *Evolution* 5:193–206.

Kramer, G., and R. Mertens. 1938. Rassenbildung bei westistrianischen Inseleidechsen in Abhängigkeit von Isolierungsalter und Arealgrösse. *Arch. Naturgesch.* (N.F.) 7:189–234.

Lack, D. 1947. *Darwin's finches.* Cambridge, Cambridge University Press.

Lack, D., and H. N. Southern. 1949. Birds of Tenerife. *Ibis* 91:607–26.

MacArthur, R. H. 1972. *Geographical ecology.* New York, Harper and Row, Publishers.

MacArthur, R. H., and E. O. Wilson. 1967. *The theory of island biogeography.* Princeton, N.J., Princeton University Press.

McDowall, R. M. 1969. Extinction and endemism in New Zealand land birds. *Tuatara* 17:1–12.

Mertens, R. 1934. Die Insel-Reptilien, ihre Ausbreitung, Variation, und Artbildung. *Zoologica* 32(6):1–209.

Mertens, R. 1961. Die Inseleidechsen des Golfes von Salerno. *Senckenbergiana Biol.* 42:31–40.

Murphy, R. C. 1938. The need of insular exploration as illustrated by birds. *Science* 88:533–39.

Neill, W. T. 1958. The occurrence of amphibians and reptiles in saltwater areas, and a bibliography. *Bull. Mar. Sci. Gulf Caribbean* 8:1–97.

Oliver, W. R. B. 1955. *New Zealand birds.* 2d ed. Wellington, A. H. & A. W. Reed.

Phillipps, W. J. 1963. *The book of the huia.* Christchurch, Whitcombe and Tombs.

Radovanović, M. 1956. Rassenbildung bei den Eidechsen auf adriatischen Inseln. *Österr. Akad. Wiss. (Math.-Naturwiss. Kl.) Denkschr.* 110(2):1–82.

Rand, A. L., and D. S. Rabor. 1960. Birds of the Philippine Islands: Siquijor, Mount Malindang, Bohol and Samar. *Fieldiana, Zool.* 35:223–441.

Schoener, T. W. 1965. The evolution of bill size differences among sympatric congeneric species of birds. *Evolution* 19:189–213.

Schoener, T. W., and D. H. Janzen. 1968. Notes on environmental determinants of tropical versus temperate insect size patterns. *Amer. Natur.* 102:207–24.

Schuster, O. 1950. Die klimaparallele Ausbildung der Körperproportionen bei Poikilothermen. *Abhandl. Senckenberg. Naturforsch. Ges.* 482:1–89.

Simberloff, D. S. 1969. Experimental zoogeography of islands. A mode of insular colonization. *Ecology* 50:296–314.

Simpson, G. G. 1953. *The major features of evolution.* New York, Columbia University Press.

Solem, A. 1961. New Caledonian land and fresh-water snails. An annotated check list. *Fieldiana, Zool.* 41:413–501.

Soulé, M. 1966. Trends in the insular radiation of a lizard. *Amer. Natur.* 100:47–64.

Soulé, M. 1967. Phenetics of natural populations. II. Asymmetry and evolution in a lizard. *Amer. Natur.* 101:141–60.

Soulé, M. 1968. Body temperatures of quiescent *Sator grandaevus* in nature. *Copeia* (1969):622–23.

Soulé, M., and B. R. Stewart. 1970. The "niche-variation" hypothesis: A test and alternatives. *Amer. Natur.* 104:85–97.

Spieth, H. T. 1968. Evolutionary implications of sexual behavior in *Drosophila*. In *Evolutionary biology*, ed. T. Dobzhansky, M. K. Hecht, and W. C. Steere, vol. 2, pp. 157–99. New York, Appleton-Century-Crofts.

Swezey, O. H. 1915. A leaf-mining cranefly in Hawaii. *Proc. Hawaiian Entomol. Soc.* 3(2):87–89.

Tillyard, R. J. 1926. *The insects of Australia and New Zealand.* Sydney, Angus and Robertson.

Tomich, P. Q. 1971. Notes on nest and behavior of the Hawaiian crow. *Pacific Sci.* 25:465–74.

Usinger, R. L. 1942. The genus *Nysius* and its allies in the Hawaiian Islands. *Bishop Mus. Bull.* 173:1–165.

Vandel, A. 1965. *Biospeleology. The biology of cavernicolous animals.* Transl. B. E. Freeman. London, Pergamon Press.

Volsøe, H. 1951. The breeding birds of the Canary Islands. I. Introduction and synopsis of the species. *Vidensk. Medd. Naturhist. Foren. Kjobenhavn* 113:1–153.

Volsøe, H. 1955. The breeding birds of the Canary Islands. II. Origin and history of the Canarian avifauna. *Vidensk. Medd. Naturhist. Foren. Kjobenhavn* 117:117–78.

Vuilleumier, F. 1970. Insular biogeography in continental regions. 1. The northern Andes of South America. *Amer. Natur.* 104:373–88.

Whitaker, A. H. 1968. *Leiolopisma suteri* (Boulenger), an oviparous skink in New Zealand. *New Zealand Jour. Sci.* 11:425–32.

Williams, F. X. 1927. Notes on the habits of bees and wasps of the Hawaiian Islands. *Proc. Hawaiian Entomol. Soc.* 6(3):425–64.

Zimmerman, E. C. 1948. *Insects of Hawaii*, vol. 1: *Introduction.* Honolulu, University of Hawaii Press.

Zimmermann, K. 1950. Die Randformen der Mitteleuropaischen Wühlmäuse. In *Syllegomena Biologica Festschrift*, ed. A. Jordans and F. Peus, pp. 454–71. Leipzig, Kleinschmidt Verlag.

INDEX OF BIOLOGICAL NAMES

Numbers in italics refer to photographs.

SUBJECT INDEX

Numbers in italics refer to photographs. Certain geographical localities which are referred to repeatedly have been abbreviated: C.Is. Canary Islands; G.Is. Galapagos Islands; H.Is. Hawaiian Islands; J.F.Is. Juan Fernandez Islands; N.C. New Caledonia; N.G. New Guinea; N.Z. New Zealand; S.H. Saint Helena island; S.W.A. Southwestern Australia; W.A. Western Australia.

Abyssal depths, 343–46; fish life adaptations, 346; luminescent specialization in, 346; type of habitat, 343–44
Acacia: diversity of growth forms, Australia, 269; morphological aspects, 465–66
Acaulescent habit, 148, 381, *578, 579* (*see also* Cushion-plant habit)
Achatinellids (*Achatinella*) (*see also* Land snails); adaptive radiation, H.Is., 127; genetic drift, 176; gigantism, 607; host-plant fidelity, 176, 488
Achenes, of some Asteraceae, compared, *454, 456, 457, 459*
Acicular leaves, 283, 286, 289 (*see also* Leaf types)
Adaptation, conceptual aspects, 20–25, 97–98, 170, 603–16
Adaptive radiation, process of, 97–116; allopatry of plants, 114; of angiosperms and land snails, H.Is., compared, 127; in archipelagos, 108–9, 114–15; autochthonous development, 102; behavioral aspects, in fishes, 343, 346; of birds on islands, 103, 108, 128–29, 607–8; cataclysmic events, 341; competition, 220; in continental biotas, 108, 332–42; ecological factors, 21, 26–27, 100–101, 202, 204;

endemism and, 102, 114–15; of fishes (*see* Cichlid fishes; Cottid fishes; Cyprinid fishes; Pediculate fishes); of flowering plants (*see* Angiosperms; *also specific genera and species in* "Index of Biological Names"); of gekkonid lizards, N.C., 231–32; of geospizids, G.Is., 198–220; harmonic biota factors, 193–94, 227; in honeycreepers, H.Is. (*see* Drepanids); in insect behavior, 174–76 in insect groups: in H.Is., 169–76; in Macaronesia, 194–95; in N.Z., 249 insular biota factors, 21–22, 353 (*see also* Insular biota patterns); isolation a factor, 103, 171–72, 340, 511; land area requirements, 103, 538; in late arrivals on islands, 108; of lizards on islands (*see* Lizards); long-distance dispersal as stimulus, 510; low in some Polynesian islands, 4, 7, 211–12 (*see also* Continental island biotas); maximal differentiation, 100–101; secondary cycles 100; "small island" effect, 206, 538; "supralimital" speciation, 106–7; time requirements, 103–4
Aeonium species, adaptive radiation, Madeira Is., 191–92

Aerial dispersal, 9, 18, 32, 50–52, 59–62, 77–79, 552; in Afroalpine flora, 568; of algae and fungi, 52; as arrival mode, comparison, 53–55; as dispersal mechanism, assessed, 77–78; distance from source areas, 15, 51, 78; in equatorial highlands, 552; of fern spores to H.Is., 60–61; of flora to H.Is., 18, 59–63, 78; insect distribution by, 9, 46, 51; to Rapa I., 79; to Revillagigedo Is., 77, 79; to San Clemente I., 77, 79; of spiders, 46, 51, 487; of spores, 46, 51
Aeroplankton, studies of, 51
Aestivation (air-breathing), of galaxiad fishes, N.Z., 250
Africa (*see also* Afroalpine flora; East African highlands): amphitropical distributions with, 86–89; conifers not shared with, 88; equatorial highland zones, 550; Macaronesian ties with, 191–93
Afroalpine flora (*see also* East African highlands; Equatorial highlands): adaptations and characteristics, Mt. Kenya, *566;* affinities and sources, 569–70; bird pollination, 569; color factors, 568; dispersal, 551–52; endemic elements, 568–69; fire

634

Subject Index

Dioecious species (*Cont.*) 21; in N.Z. flora, high, 520; outcrossing and, 30, 511, 533–34; in S.H. flora, 522; strategic value on islands, 510–11, 525

Diptera (flies): flight loss, on subantarctic islands, *498,* 499, 501; wet-forest adaptation, H.Is., 126; wing-size variation, 497

Disharmony, in biota composition, 6–8; adaptation in, 101–3, 256, 319, 434; in continental (mainland) biotas, 7, 101, 340–42; in continental island, 7, 101; in equatorial highlands, 101–2 of fauna: in N.C., 233; in N.Z., 233, 249 of flora: in G.Is., 205; in H.Is., 146, 436, 541–42; in S.W.A., 253–59, 319; in Tasmania, 101 in Malesian area, 101; in oceanic islands, 7, 18, 101, 341, 434; reproduction and, 434, 542; woodiness on islands and, 354–55

Disjunctions, intercontinental (*see* Intercontinental disjunctions; Continental drift)

Dispersibility, 6–8, 45–95, 109 (*see also* specific types, families, and genera); adaptive radiation, at the limits of, 103; by air and wind (*see* Aerial dispersal; Wind dispersal); of birds to islands (*see* Land birds); by bird vectors (*see* Seed dispersal by birds); conditions affecting, 6–8, 14–15, 609–10; in displacement by competitors, 28; ecology and distance in, 77–82; evidence of, 14–16, 50–54; of ferns, 439–40, 512; of forest trees, 353–54; of fruit (*see* Fruit dispersal); group limitations, 103; of insects (*see* Insect dispersal); insular factors affecting, 5, 7, 18, 509–10; insular woodiness, 352; loss (*see* Plant dispersibility loss); operational factors, 429–32; pioneer factors, 6, 17, 107, 352, 433; plant adaptation for, 5, 6–18, 50–54; probability factor in, 14

Dissemination, of seed and fruit (*see* Plant dispersal)

Distance factor: in plant dispersal, 77–82; in adaptive radiation, 104

"Disuse" theory of insect flight loss, 492

Divaricating shrubs (*see also* Radiating armament; Thorn-shrub habit): California instances, 242; characteristics,

242–43; New Zealand instances, 242–43, *247*

Dodo, Mascarene, affinities, 490

Dolichopodid flies, color variation, 174

Downes, J. A., on insect flight loss in Canada, 483

Dracaena (Pleomele) (Liliaceae), Hawaiian species, 483

Drepanids (Drepanididae), (Hawaiian honeycreepers): adaptation and variation, 22–23, 128–29, 158–69, 608–9; antecedent affinities, 159 bill form, diet, and feeding habits, 158–69; of *Hemignathus lucidus, 164;* of *H. procerus, 165;* of *H. Wilsoni, 166;* of *Loxops coccinea, 162;* of *L. parva, 161;* of *L. sagittirostris, 162;* of *L. virens, 160;* of *L. virens stejnegeri, 163;* of *Pseudonestor xanthophrys, 167;* of *Psittarostra kona, 169;* of *P. psittacea, 168* character displacement and release, 128, 159; *Ciridops,* earlier distribution, 128; coloration in plumage, 159, 610; competition, avoidance of, 166, 608; diet (*see* bill form *above*); evolutionary development, 163, 169; extinction, 129, 158; flower-pollinator constancy, 144–45; *Himatione,* primitive genus, 128; illustrated studies, references, 158; lobelioid pollination, 144; *Loxops* as primitive genus, 128; nonadaptive factors in changes, 146; nonadaptive genetic drift, 159; *Psittarostra,* adaptive radiation, 128; sympatry among, 166; wet-forest adaptation, 158

Drift flora (*see* Oceanic drift)

Drosera (Droseraceae): adaptive radiation, 317; endemism, S.W.A., 317

Drosophilas in H.Is., summary of inter-island founders in the picture-winged, *122*

Drosophilid flies, H.Is.: adaptive radiation in behavior, 174–75; breeding environment, 172; gigantism, 605–6; host-plant specificity, 172; lek behavior, 174; specialization excessive, 29; wind role in survival, 403

Drought survival mechanisms, in flora, S.W.A., 320

Dry climate (*see* Xeric habitat; Xeromorphy)

Dry-forest elements, in plant dispersal, 78

Dubautia (Asteraceae), "tarweeds," 119–53, passim

Dubautia (sensu lato), 119, 120 (*see also Railliardia*)

Dubautia (senso stricto): adaptive radiation, H.Is., 149–52; alpine adaptation, 151–52; differentiation from related genera, 119, 120, 123, 149, 150, 151 (*see also Argyroxiphium, Dubautia-Argyroxiphium-Wilkesia* complex, *Railliardia,* and *Wilkesia*); distribution, by islands, tabulated, 120; leaves in silhouette, and vessel elements, *153;* loss of dispersibility, 456–57; primitive inflorescences, 123

Dubautia-Argyroxiphium-Wilkesia complex ("tarweeds"), 102, 108, 114, 405; adaptive radiation, H.Is., 147–53; insular adaptive radiation exemplified, 106; provenance, 59; relations among genera, 119, 123, 149–51

Dwarfism, on islands, 23–24, 607

East African highlands, 550, 553–70 (*see also* Equatorial highlands *and specific habitat zones indicated*); alpine habitat and flora, 23, 553–54, 562–69, *564, 566* (*see also* Afroalpine flora); bog habitat and flora, 557–58, 562; dispersal patterns, 551–53; endemic and vicarious flora, 552–53, 558, 562, 569; frost survival of flora, 563, 565, *566,* 567; lower montane habitat and flora, 554, *556,* 557; and Malesian highlands compared, 571; moorland habitat and flora, 557–62, *559;* protection against radiation, 567–68; submontane habitat and flora, 553–54, *555;* upper forest habitat and flora, 557; woodiness in herbaceous species, 423–24, 553, 562–63; xerophytism, 567

Easter Island: endemism in marine fauna, 34–35; flora dispersed to, 76, 80

Ebenaceae, morphology and dispersibility, 462–63

Echium (Boraginaceae): adaptive radiation, Macaronesian is., 182–91; effects of frost, tabulated, 190; species and adaptations, *183, 185, 187, 188;* woodiness increased on islands, 353

Ecological correlations, of vessel dimensions in insular angiosperms, tabulated, 392

640